120 —
AF677399

THE LAW OF RIGHTS OF LIGHT

The book provides the authoritative statement on the current law on rights of light in England and Wales. The protection of the access of natural light to properties has been a part of our property law for centuries but in recent years has come into particular prominence. This is due to a number of reasons including the existence of easements of light being regarded as an inhibition on new development and the unsatisfactory nature of parts of the law on this subject. This has given rise to two reports in recent years by the Law Commission (one on easements generally in 2011 and one on rights of light specifically in 2014), both containing major proposals for law reform.

The purpose of this legal textbook is to explain the law as clearly as possible. In practice rights of light issues and disputes involve technical subjects and inevitably answers to these questions require the expertise of technical experts such as light surveyors. An attempt is made in the book to explain from a non-technical point of view the way in which measurements and calculations are carried out in this area. It is therefore hoped that the book will be of use to lawyers as well as to landowners who may not always understand these technical subjects and to surveyors who may not always be familiar with the legal concepts and difficulties involved in the area of the law of rights of light.

The Law of Rights of Light

Michael Barnes, QC

·HART·
PUBLISHING
OXFORD AND PORTLAND, OREGON
2016

Published in the United Kingdom by Hart Publishing Ltd
16C Worcester Place, Oxford, OX1 2JW
Telephone: +44 (0)1865 517530
Fax: +44 (0)1865 510710
E-mail: mail@hartpub.co.uk
Website: http://www.hartpub.co.uk

Published in North America (US and Canada) by
Hart Publishing
c/o International Specialized Book Services
920 NE 58th Avenue, Suite 300
Portland, OR 97213-3786
USA
Tel: +1 503 287 3093 or toll-free: (1) 800 944 6190
Fax: +1 503 280 8832
E-mail: orders@isbs.com
Website: http://www.isbs.com

© Michael Barnes, QC 2016
Michael Barnes, QC has asserted his right under the Copyright, Designs and Patents Act 1988, to be identified as the author of this work.

Hart Publishing is an imprint of Bloomsbury Publishing plc.

All rights reserved. No part of this publication may be reproduced, stored in a retrieval system, or transmitted, in any form or by any means, without the prior permission of Hart Publishing, or as expressly permitted by law or under the terms agreed with the appropriate reprographic rights organisation. Enquiries concerning reproduction which may not be covered by the above should be addressed to Hart Publishing Ltd at the address above.

British Library Cataloguing in Publication Data
Data Available

Library of Congress Cataloging-in-Publication Data

Names: Barnes, Michael, 1943–

Title: The law of rights of light / Michael Barnes, QC.

Description: Oxford ; Portland, Oregon : Hart Publishing Ltd, 2015. | Includes bibliographical references and index. | Description based on print version record and CIP data provided by publisher; resource not viewed.

Identifiers: LCCN 2015044927 (print) | LCCN 2015043607 (ebook) | ISBN 9781509905522 (Epub) | ISBN 9781849468817 (hardback : alk. paper)

Subjects: LCSH: Solar access rights—England.

Classification: LCC KD940 (print) | LCC KD940 .B37 2015 (ebook) | DDC 346.4204/35—dc23

LC record available at http://lccn.loc.gov/2015044927

ISBN: 978-1-84946-881-7

Typeset by Compuscript Ltd, Shannon
Printed and bound in Great Britain by
CPI Group (UK) Ltd, Croydon CR0 4YY

This book is for Rachel, who is so very far away.

FOREWORD

Rights of light, sometimes called ancient lights, are one of the oddities of the law. They are interests in land, classified together with easements, some of whose characteristics they share. But in some respects they are very different.

Most easements subsist for the benefit of land, and remain unaffected by its development. Rights of light, on the other hand, exist only for the benefit of buildings, and even then only for the benefit of defined apertures in buildings. If the apertures are moved, the right may be lost, even though the building remains.

Most easements consist of the right to do something on someone else's land. A right of light is essentially a passive right to receive light passing over someone else's land.

Although all easements can be acquired by prescription, the landowner over whose land the right is being acquired will usually be aware that someone is exceeding their legal rights in the course of the acquisition. In the case of a right of light, the land owner will be unaware that the right is being acquired, unless he keeps a very close eye on all new construction going on around him. In the case of most easements, use will not give rise to a prescriptive easement unless the use is without force, without stealth and without permission. In the case of a right to light it is very difficult to see how the first two of these control mechanisms could ever apply.

In the case of most easements the land owner can take action on the ground to prevent the offending activity before it ripens into a prescriptive easement. In the case of a right to light, the land owner can erect a notional screen of infinite height which has the same effect as a real screen would have had.

Most easements exist only for the benefit of freehold land, with the consequence that a tenant cannot acquire an easement over his landlord's land. A right of light is different; and a tenant may acquire a prescriptive right over his landlord's land.

Unlike most easements, rights of light may also be affected by local custom. The Recorder of London was required to certify the custom of the City of London in 1757. One of the matters under debate was which robes he should wear to make his pronouncement (the answer was: his purple cloth robe, faced with black velvet; rather than his scarlet gown, his black silk gown or his common barrister's gown). No wonder rights of light are sometimes called ancient lights.

Although they are ancient, rights of light are also powerful modern weapons. In our increasingly crowded island they are often serious obstacles to redevelopment, which have to be bought out with large ransom payments.

Michael Barnes' scholarly and comprehensive treatise places rights of light within the legal and practical framework that they occupy, while explaining with clarity where they are different from other rights. Refreshingly, he also discusses the scientific and social importance of light in daily life. There can be few legal textbooks citing Newton, Einstein and Maxwell Clark, as well as the Book of Genesis: all of which makes for fascinating reading.

'More light' were said to have been Johann Wolfgang von Goethe's last words. This work sheds all the light one needs on rights of light.

Kim Lewison
Royal Courts of Justice
London WC2A 2LL

PREFACE

The right of a property to the receipt of natural light has long been protected by English law, probably since the late Middle Ages. *Necessitas luminatis*, the need for natural illumination, was described as one of the four essential characteristics of property to be protected by the law, in *Aldred's* case in 1610. After centuries of development the subject has come into some legal prominence in recent times.

There are a number of reasons for the current interest in the subject. With ever higher and denser urban development, the existence of rights of light is seen by some as an impediment to development, and against the general public and economic interest. There are obscurities and complexities in more than one area of the subject, and a notable subject of dissatisfaction is the complicated and unsatisfactory law of prescription as that now stands. The Prescription Act 1832 is an ill-drafted piece of legislation which has nonetheless endured for nearly two centuries, together with even older methods of prescription which may still be used. Of course prescription is a subject which applies to easements generally, although rights of light, as a species of easement, have in some respects their own rules regarding prescription.

The need for reform and clarification has engendered four publications relevant to rights of light by the Law Commission between 2008 and 2014. The last document, the 2014 report of the Commission on Rights of Light (Law Com No 356), contains comprehensive proposals for the alteration of the law and includes a draft Bill. The report includes radical recommendations for reform of areas of the law of rights of light, including prescription, remedies for breach, and the termination of easements of light. There has as yet been no response from the Government to these recommendations, or to the more general recommendations on easements made in the 2011 report of the Commission. It seems, therefore, that the existing law, with its difficulties and imperfections, may be with us for some time.

The aim of this book is to state as clearly and comprehensively as possible the present law of rights of light. On occasions the only way in which this can be done in a satisfactory fashion is to accept that the law is to a degree uncertain, and to suggest the most satisfactory answer to unanswered points. Two examples may be mentioned. The relevance of the use or potential use of artificial light to buildings in rights of light disputes is still far from wholly certain. The question of whether a leasehold easement terminates with the termination by various means of the lease of the property with the benefit or with the burden of the easement is still uncertain. It would not be difficult to find further instances of doubt on the exact content of rules of law relating to rights of light. However, especially when an aspect of the law is less than certain, it is not satisfactory simply to state the law or the probable law. A full understanding of rules of law is impossible without some examination of the background to and the reasons for the rules or, when it occurs, the present uncertainty in the content of some rules. This book attempts to provide a description of the law with this principle in mind.

Rights of light, and particularly disputes over rights of light, involve at least two professional disciplines: the legal profession and the surveying profession. In any specific case, landowners and developers are likely to depend upon the advice of specialists within both professions. This book has been written with this observation very much in mind. Lawyers may find that there are some general explanations of legal principles already familiar to them, but surveyors may be assisted by a description of legal concepts and niceties not always understood by them. Conversely, surveyors expert in rights of light will understand very well the details of such techniques as the Waldram methodology and the measurement of light received by parts of a room, but it is hoped that lawyers will benefit from a non-technical description of what is being done. Accordingly, Chapter 6 is devoted to the techniques used for the measurement of light, and the criticisms of those techniques. A glossary is also provided of legal and technical terms used in the context of rights of light.

The structure of the book is to describe first the nature and content of rights of light, and how such rights exist usually, but not exclusively, as easements. This is followed by the means of acquisition of rights of light by deed and by prescription or long use and enjoyment. As just mentioned, an explanation is given of the technical methods by which the illuminance to a room by natural light through a window or other aperture is measured. The next subject is the crucial subject of remedies, mainly an injunction or damages, where elements of uncertainty on the principles still remain. This is followed by a series of chapters on the extinguishment of rights of light, on the Rights of Light Act 1959 (which provides a method of preventing rights of light being acquired by prescription), on the impact of town planning, and on the registration and transfer of rights of light. Since reform of the law is such an important current topic, with detailed recommendations having been put forward, the last chapter examines the present proposals for reform.

Rights of light are plainly a specialist subject, both as regards their legal aspects and as regards their technical and surveying aspects. The latter aspects are dominated by a fairly small group of specialist expert surveyors, and it is to these to whom property owners concerned about rights of light in favour of or against their property understandably often first turn for advice. There are few areas of the law which are more permeated by various conventions and traditions than this area. Examples of this process explained in detail in the book are the Waldram methodology and its '0.2% sky factor' and its '50-50 test' for a sufficiency of light in a room. These are technical subjects (although in recent years the subject of cogent technical criticism), but other received notions of legal matters have grown up such as that where the infringement of a right of light will not be large, an injunction to prevent it will necessarily be refused, or that damages will be calculated on some arbitrary multiple (usually 2–3) of the reduction in value to a building caused by the infringement. Legal notions of the last-mentioned type are often bandied about, but there is no substantial legal justification for them. Landowners and their legal advisers would be ill-advised to apply so-called legal principles such as those mentioned without a careful examination of what the law and the decided authorities actually say. If this book can assist this process, it will have fulfilled one of its purposes.

It is desirable to keep a book on a specialist subject within a reasonable size. Rights of light are one aspect of the disputes which can arise between neighbours. Other aspects are boundary disputes, disputes about party walls, Part 8 of the Anti-social Behaviour Act 2008 which deals with high hedges, and the Access to Neighbouring Land Act 1992. None of these matters or areas of legislation are covered in this book.

The law of rights of light has of course its own particular principles and rules, and is heavily dependent on the more general principles of such subjects as the law of easements and the principle of non-derogation from grant. It is inevitable that these further areas of law are examined in some detail. That having been said, the subject of rights of light, and rights of light disputes, impact on other areas of law, such as the detailed procedure to be used in proceedings in the courts when rights of light are sought to be enforced, and aspects of town and country planning law. Reference is made where appropriate to these other areas of law, but it would make this book of an inordinate length if any attempt was made to examine such further subjects in detail. The further subjects naturally have their own specialist textbooks.

As with the previous book I have written, it gives me great pleasure to use this opportunity to thank the publishers, Hart Publishing, for their assistance and support, to thank colleagues at the Bar who have been willing to discuss matters with me, to thank Wilberforce Chambers of which I am a member for the use of their facilities in writing this book, and last, but certainly not least, to thank Janet Steel who has typed the text and without whose skill and patience this book would not have been possible.

Michael Barnes QC
Wilberforce Chambers

CONTENTS

1

Introduction

(A) THE NATURE OF LIGHT

The Book of Genesis tells us that in the beginning, God created the heavens and the earth. Darkness lay on the surface of the deep until God said: 'Let there be light, and there was light. God saw the light was good. . .'[1] From the earliest days of mankind on earth, light has been synonymous with good and beauty. Tennyson, in *Idylls of the King*, referred to 'that pure severity of perfect light'.[2] Darkness has the opposite connotation. 1.1

Apart from its religious and poetical aspects, and on a more practical level, natural light is essential to life. Without it, photosynthesis could not take place in plants. Our only significant source of natural light is from the sun, either as direct radiation or as radiation reflected from the moon and other planets in the solar system which are visible. Other stars provide a beautiful but not normally significant source of light. The natural recurring system of day and night, as the earth rotates, dictates the pattern of life for all persons. The fluctuating amounts of light which fall on a particular area of land as the earth, with its slightly tilted axis, orbits the sun, create the differences between summer and winter in both the northern and southern hemispheres. Natural light is therefore a prize, and it is not surprising that rules for protecting its access to one property over another property have developed in systems of law. In England and Wales the protection is provided mainly as an aspect of the more general law of easements. 1.2

Early mankind, though dependent on natural light, of course knew nothing of its nature. In early Greek philosophy, light was not one of the four essential elements of air, water, earth and fire, of which it was thought reality was composed.[3] It is only through modern science that the nature of light has come to be understood. Isaac Newton considered light as a stream of separate corpuscles, a description which in a sense accords with modern scientific ideas. However, subsequent experiments showed that light behaved in many ways as a wave, such as a water wave; for example, light could 'bend' around objects in its path, and two waves of light could interfere with each other, creating positive or negative interference rather as 1.3

[1] Genesis, chapter 1, verse 3. King James version.

[2] Tennyson, *Idylls of the King*, I, 640.

[3] Empedocles, a Greek philosopher who lived in Sicily in the fifth century before Christ.

water waves could.[4] James Clerk Maxwell in the nineteenth century produced his equations which state the nature of electricity and magnetism, and concluded that light was a part of the spectrum of electromagnetic waves or radiation.[5] Radiation with a longer wavelength than that within the visible spectrum, such as some radio waves, cannot be seen by the human eye; radiation with a shorter wavelength, such as X-rays and gamma radiation, is also invisible to our eyes. The first category was called infra-red radiation and the second category was called ultra-violet radiation. The radiation itself of all types travels at about 300,000 kilometres per second (186,000 miles per second) in a vacuum. Light of different colours is produced by radiation of different wavelengths within the total visible band of the electromagnetic spectrum. Light within particular small bands of wavelengths, and thus of a particular colour, is called monochromatic light. The light from the sun is white light, which is an amalgam of light of different wavelengths. It can be separated into its different wavelengths and colours by passing it through a prism. The light we receive from the sun is created mainly by the fusion of hydrogen atoms into helium atoms in the sun. Because of its speed of travel and the distance involved, it takes about eight minutes to reach us after its creation.[6]

1.4 These matters remain a good general description of light, but the development of quantum physics in the last century by persons such as Planck and Einstein showed that light (and other electromagnetic radiation) exists and travels as discrete 'particles' of energy, called photons. Einstein was awarded a Nobel prize for demonstrating this, by way of the photoelectric effect, rather than for his better-known theory of relativity.[7]

1.5 Humans have long sought to supplement natural light from the sun by light artificially created. Earlier use of candles gave way to the creation of light by oil and gas lamps. In the 1960s, street lighting in the Temple in London was by gas lamps, with a lamp-lighter who turned each lamp on each evening. Today, of course, artificial light is almost wholly created by electricity. One of the issues in the law of the rights of light is how far the effect of artificial lighting is relevant to the need to protect properties against the loss of natural light.[8]

[4] See eg the 'double slit' experiment of Thomas Young (1773–1829).

[5] Maxwell published *Electricity and Magnetism* in 1873.

[6] A fuller description of the nature of light and its measurement is given in ch 6.

[7] The best layman's account of photons and their interaction with matter is found in Richard Freyman, *QED* (London, Penguin Books, 1990). Feynman, who won a Nobel prize for his work on quantum electrodynamics, is sometimes considered the greatest theoretical physicist since Einstein. There is some suggestion in the decided cases that light received directly from the sun is 'a different kind of light' from that received after it has been reflected from some object: see eg *Price v Hilditch* [1930] 1 Ch 500, 506 (Maugham J). In fact all light, whatever its immediate source, is radiation within those wavelengths which form the visible band of the electromagnetic spectrum. Of course the fact that individual photons or units of light are received after being reflected from some object such as a wall may be relevant to the question of whether there has been an actionable infringement to a right to the access of light: see ch 3, section (B)1.

[8] See ch 3, section (B)4.

(B) LEGAL PROTECTION OF THE ACCESS OF LIGHT

The legal protection of the access of light to a property is the protection of light coming to buildings on properties. Primitive communities of hunter-gatherers or those who came to depend on the husbandry of animals and the harvesting of crops had little concern over any obstruction of daylight to their land. The advent of the construction of buildings in which to live and work brought about a radical change. Buildings protect people from the elements, but in doing so they inevitably limit the natural light which can pass into the building. The answer was obviously the placing of windows or similar apertures in the building with a form of glazing so that the building remains watertight but natural light can pass through the glazing in the windows. The modern tendency has been to increase the size of windows. Houses built in the seventeenth century often have small windows, whereas large modern offices give the impression of being constructed largely of glass. 1.6

The upshot of all this is that rooms in buildings may receive only a limited amount of light through a window or windows. If some other structure is built nearby, plainly it may reduce the amount of light which enters a building. Light from the sun is generally perceived as travelling in a straight line,[9] and much of the light which travels to one property is likely to pass across neighbouring properties. This is, of course, especially so for windows set in a vertical wall. In rural locations or in low-density urban developments the problem may not be acute, since the further away an obstruction is from the property whose light is affected, the less the effect is likely to be. In urban areas of high-density development and tall buildings, the problem can be more acute. A new building constructed up to a common boundary between two properties may substantially reduce, or even largely remove, the access of light over the property built upon to its neighbouring property. The law relating to rights of light has been developed to answer the questions of whether and to what extent this can lawfully be done. The purpose of this book is to explain the law on this subject. It should be noted that this aspect of the law is concerned wholly with the access of natural light to one property laterally over or across a neighbouring property. Natural light is, of course, also received by a property vertically from above it. The owner of a property generally owns the air space above the property, so that any obstruction of that air space without his consent will be a trespass against the owner and can be prevented.[10] 1.7

[9] Quantum electrodynamics, however, tells us that photons which pass from A to B may take many different paths, as is explained in Feynman's book mentioned in n 7.

[10] The general principle is that, subject to certain statutory interventions, the owner of an area of land owns property 'usque ad coelum et usque ad inferos', that is, out to the heavens and down to the centre of the earth: see *Bocardo SA v Star Energy Onshore Ltd* (2010) UKSC 35, [2011] 1 AC 380; *Commissioner of Railways v Valuer General* [1974] AC 328. This principle is said to be to some extent derived from Roman law. A right of light may be acquired in favour of a skylight, since a part of the light which reaches such an aperture may pass across neighbouring properties. See ch 2, para 2.46.

1.8 A major aspect of the law and protection of rights of light today is the difficulties which are caused to commercial developments in densely packed urban areas such as Central London and the central areas of other large cities. On occasions, landowners try to reduce the impact of this difficulty on further redevelopment by making rights of light agreements with adjoining landowners. The aim is often to prevent the acquisition of rights of light to each other's property, and to permit any future redevelopment irrespective of its effect on the access of light. Leases, particularly of commercial property in urban areas, often contain provisions permitting the landlord to develop land owned and retained by him irrespective of any reduction caused to the access of light to the property demised. Such provisions are effective in preventing the tenant from acquiring a right of light by long enjoyment of the access of light against that retained land.[11] Very often these precautions have not been taken, and a landowner wishing to redevelop his property, and with planning permission to do so, may find that the redevelopment is frustrated by rights of light owned over his property in favour of other property arising from the long and uninterrupted past access of light over his property to that other property. There are ways in which such situations might be prevented, perhaps by mutual rights of light agreements as just mentioned, or by the service of notices in good time under the Rights of Light Act 1959.[12] In these circumstances, and if these precautions have not been taken, the developer may be faced with the threat of an injunction to prevent the proposed development. His only recourse may then be to abandon the development or modify it, or to pay what may often be a substantial sum of money to buy off the exercise of rights of light by an adjoining owner.

1.9 The law fulfils the function of protecting the access of light to a building mainly, though not exclusively, by the operation of the law of easements. Other areas of law may be important, such as restrictive covenants which bind land and the operation of the law of town and country planning, but the core of the subject is the law of easements. A right of light is a particular type of easement and is subject to general rules which govern easements as well as to its own particular rules. Statutes have in part brought about these particular rules. For example, the acquisition of a right of light over a property by the enjoyment of the access of light over that property for a period is regulated by a different and looser form of required use than that applicable to the acquisition of other types of easement.[13] A statute, the Rights of Light Act 1959, was enacted in order to give property owners an efficient way of preventing an easement of light over their property being acquired by long enjoyment of that access in favour of other properties.

[11] See ch 5, section (D)6.

[12] See ch 9.

[13] Prescription Act 1832, ss 2 (general easements) and 3 (rights of light). See ch 5.

(C) OUTLINE OF THE LAW

The law on rights of light has various complexities, and is still obscure in some of its aspects. Nonetheless, the main underlying principles are well established. In order to set the detailed rules within their context it may be useful at the outset to summarise the main principles which underlie the detailed rules. There are six such principles. 1.10

First, there is no 'natural' right of light. A right of light can come into existence only by a recognised mode of creation, such as by a deed or by reason of long and uninterrupted access of light to one property over another property. Natural rights in this context mean rights which are protected by the law without having to be created in some particular way, for example, the right that others shall not trespass on a person's property, or that others shall not issue libels of him. By contrast to the access of light, some other rights affecting property may exist as natural rights in the above sense, such as the right of support which an owner of land has for his land (though not for buildings on his land) from the land of his neighbour, and the right to the flow of water across the land of a person where the water flows naturally in a defined channel.[14] 1.11

Secondly, an easement of light can protect only man-made structures, and is a right for the access of light through defined apertures in the structure. There is no right to the access of light to open ground.[15] The right when it exists as an easement can be enjoyed only in respect of buildings, as opposed to other structures.[16] 1.12

Thirdly, a right of light normally exists as a form of easement and so must in general conform to the rules which constitute the law of easements.[17] The obvious illustration of this principle is that there must be a dominant building which is benefited by the right and servient land over which the right is exercisable and which is burdened by the right. 1.13

Fourthly, as with other easements, an easement of light must be brought into existence by some recognised method of creation. These methods are: 1.14

(a) by an express grant;
(b) by a provision implied into a grant and arising from the circumstances of the grant (including the operation of section 62 of the Law of Property Act 1925); and

[14] See eg *Backhouse v Bonomi* (1861) 9 HL Cas 503 (right of support); *Chasemore v Richards* (1859) 7 HL Cas 349 (right to water through a defined channel). See para 1.7 for circumstances in which an obstruction to light could amount to a trespass.

[15] *Roberts v Macord* (1832) 1 Mood & R 230; *Daiton v Angus* (1881) 6 App Cas 740, 759.

[16] See ch 2, section (D). One consequence of this principle is that there cannot be an easement which protects the general receipt of light or other radiation to a property, such as television signals or light passing to solar panels on a roof. Such radiation does not enter a building through a defined aperture. See ch 3, section (B)1.

[17] What amounts to a right of light may also come into existence as a restrictive covenant, that is a covenant by the owner of a piece of land that he will not build on it, or will only build on it up to a certain height or bulk. The covenant must be for the benefit of other defined land if it is to be a proprietary interest. That which is akin to a right of light may sometimes be asserted in reliance on the doctrine which prevents derogation from grant: see ch 2, section (C)2.

(c) by prescription, ie by long and uninterrupted enjoyment of the access of light over a particular property.

1.15 Fifthly, a right of light as a type of easement is not a right that the person against whom the right is exercisable shall not in any way obstruct or reduce the access of light to the building which has the benefit of the right. The right is to sufficient light for the comfortable use and enjoyment or beneficial use and occupation of the building which has the right, judged according to the ordinary notions of mankind.[18] The corollary of this principle is that the person asserting the right of light will only be able to prevent building on the land subject to the right if:

(a) there is a part of his building which has a sufficiency of natural light through an aperture, and the building on the other land will reduce the access of light to a level below that which is sufficient; or
(b) there is a part of his building which has insufficient access of natural light through an aperture, and the building on the other land will increase that insufficiency by reducing the access of light still further.

A right of light once established gives a right to sufficient illumination by natural light. It does not give a right to a view or prospect, which may only be protected, if at all, by a restrictive covenant or sometimes as a result of restrictions on development under planning controls.

1.16 Sixthly, the person whose building has the benefit of the right of light may prevent building or other activities on the land burdened by the right by seeking an injunction to prevent the offending building, or by seeking damages for his loss, or by both remedies. A primary difference between the two remedies is that an injunction is a discretionary remedy, in the sense that the court may or may not grant the remedy at its discretion. In certain circumstances an injunction may be refused even though an existing or proposed future infringement of the right is proved, for example where the person claiming the right has unreasonably delayed in bringing his proceedings, or where the infringement is or will be slight. By contrast, an award of damages is not discretionary, and damages must be awarded if an infringement is shown. The recent tendency in the law has been to assess damages on the basis of the sum which would have been agreed in a reasonable negotiation between the parties for the voluntary release of the right of light so as to permit the erection of the offending building. The result is that awards of damages are likely to be higher than was formerly the case.[19]

1.17 These principles can be shortly stated and together they form the background to the law of rights of light. Even so they conceal a substantial number off complexities and uncertainties within the law. For example, a decision on whether there is a sufficiency of natural light to a room through a window involves a degree

[18] *Colls v Home & Colonial Stores Ltd* [1904] AC 179, 208 (Lord Lindley).
[19] The law on remedies is stated in ch 7.

of judgment and uncertainty, something which was recognised by Lord Lindley when he stated the principle in *Colls v Home & Colonial Stores Ltd.*[20] Attempts have been made by rights of light surveyors to introduce greater precision by suggesting that a room is sufficiently well lit if at least a half of the floor area receives at least a specified minimum amount of light, which they calculate by a particular means, the assumption being that any particular point in the room is sufficiently lit if it receives a certain minimum amount of natural light calculated by this method.[21] Questions such as the relevance of artificial lighting, or the exact circumstances in which a right of light acquired for a window in a building can be transferred to a new window in an altered or redeveloped building, in some ways await clarification. Light, being a form of energy transferred as electromagnetic radiation, can provide heat as well as illumination to a property, and it is not clear to what extent the law protects the former function of light.[22]

Certain expressions are used in this area of law. The expressions 'rights of light' and 'rights to light' are used interchangeably with no difference of meaning. The former expression is used in this book. The right may be called a right of light or an easement of light, again without any difference in meaning (save where the right has been created by a restrictive covenant or by the operation of the principle of non-derogation from grant). A further expression used is 'ancient lights'. This has no precise legal meaning but usually signifies that some windows, which are said to be ancient lights, or to have acquired ancient lights, have acquired a right of light against other property by long enjoyment of the access of light over that property and so by prescription.[23] The prescription period is twenty years, so that ancient lights may not in all instances be very ancient.[24] 1.18

The terminology in this area of the law often involves the concept of dominancy and serviency. The property with the benefit of an easement of light is called the dominant tenement or building (the word 'building' is used because the easement can only be appurtenant to a man-made structure which is a building). The property subject to or burdened by the easement is called the servient tenement or land. The servient land may or may not contain a building. The concept of dominant and servient land is common to all types of easements. 1.19

[20] *Colls v Home & Colonial Stores* [1904] AC 179, 208.

[21] The method of calculation depends on what proportion of the whole dome of the sky which would be visible if there was no form of obstruction is actually visible through an aperture at any point in a room. This is called the Waldram methodology, and is described in ch 6.

[22] See ch 3, section (B)1.

[23] In *Dalton v Angus* (1881) 6 App Cas 740, 794 Lord Coleridge said that the term 'ancient' light implied that a right to light might be acquired by prescription.

[24] Tindal CJ in *Penwarden v Ching* (1829) Moo & M 400, 401 observed: 'The question is, not whether the window is what is strictly called ancient, but whether it is such as the law, in indulgence to rights, has in modern times so called, and to which the defendant has a right.'

(D) STRUCTURE OF THE BOOK

1.20 The structure of this book proceeds in the following way.

(i) Following this introduction a description is given of the legal nature of the right of light in favour of a building mainly as a species of the wider category of proprietary rights known as easements.
(ii) This is followed by a description of the content of the right of light and in particular of the standard of light which is protected by an easement.
(iii) The next matter is the means of acquisition of rights of light by the express or implied provisions of a deed, or by prescription.
(iv) There is then an account of how the amount of light received through a window in a building may be measured so as to determine whether a sufficiency of light remains after an obstruction. By this means it can be determined whether there has been or will be an infringement of a right of light.
(v) There is then a description of the remedies available to protect a landowner against an infringement of his right of light, notably an injunction or an award of damages.
(vi) Following this there is an account of how an existing right of light may be terminated.
(vii) A chapter is devoted to the Rights of Light Act 1959, which provides a means of preventing a right of light arising by long enjoyment or prescription.
(viii) The impact of town and country planning on rights of light is then outlined.
(ix) A chapter is devoted to the protection of easements of light under the system of land registration or the system of land charges, and the effect on such easements of the transfer of the dominant or the servient property.
(x) Finally there is a brief account of proposals for reform of this area of the law.

2

The Legal Nature of the Right of Light

(A) BASIC CONCEPTS

Rights of light are a type of right embedded in English property law. They are proprietary rights. It is not possible to understand their nature and status without some reference to the general law of real property in this country. 2.1

The critical matter on which to be clear is what is meant in law by proprietary rights. A right in law is generally a right that a person has that some other person or persons shall do or abstain from doing some act.[1] Where the subject matter of the right is the land of some other person, the immediate question which arises is whether the right, initially owned by A and enforceable against B, is only enforceable against B as the owner of the land or interest in land at the time when the right was created, or is also enforceable against any successor in title to the land or interest in land of B. The question arises because land and interests in land have the character of permanency, or may have a long period of existence. The land or interest in land owned by B may be passed by him to some other person and may in turn be passed on by that person to other persons. It follows that if a right affecting a piece of land is not a proprietary right or interest, it may not be of great practical value since the land affected may be transferred so that the right becomes unenforceable at any rate as regards the land. 2.2

Not every right with land as its subject matter is enforceable against successors in title of the person by whom the right was first created or against whom the right first arose. The development of the land law has been to a considerable extent the categorisation of those rights affecting land which are, in law and in principle, capable of binding such successors in title. For example, it became established in late medieval and Tudor times that the rights and obligations of parties to a lease of land were enforceable against successors in title of the persons who were the landlord and the tenant at the time of the grant of the lease.[2] In the nineteenth 2.3

[1] More elaborate classifications are possible, such as in the teaching of the American jurist, Wesley Newcomb Hohfeld (1879–1918). The main explanation of his ideas is found in articles that appeared in the *Yale Law Journal* in 1913 and 1917. He taught that what are generally described as rights may be divided into rights, privileges, powers and immunities, with their juridical correlatives of duties, no-rights, liabilities and disabilities.

[2] See the Grantees of Reversion Act 1540 and *Spencer's Case* (1583) 5 Co Rep 16a, and see today the Landlord and Tenant (Covenants) Act 1995.

century the right to enforce a restrictive covenant over the land of another person, that is a covenant which restricted the use of that land, became enforceable against successors in title of the land of that other person, and so entered the category of proprietary interests in land.[3] The admission of a particular form of right into the category of rights so enforceable meant that further rules had to be worked out on the exact requirements which had to be satisfied for the right to be so enforceable. For example, it became established that when B created a restrictive covenant on the use of his land in favour of A, the covenant could only be enforced by A against successors in title of B if the covenant benefited the land of A.

2.4 This preamble leads to the major classification of rights which have land as their subject matter. Those rights which are, in principle and as a matter of law, enforceable against successors in title of the person who first created the rights or against whom those rights first arose are properly described as proprietary rights. A further piece of nomenclature sometimes used is to describe proprietary rights as rights *in rem*, or rights enforceable in principle against the land, as compared to rights *in personam*, or rights enforceable only against the other party to the contract or other instrument which has created the rights. A right of light is a proprietary right in the above sense, since it is enforceable against successors in title of the land over which it is exercisable. It is a proprietary right because it generally exists by reason of being a type of easement, and easements are proprietary rights.[4] Where a right of light is created expressly by a deed, it is of course possible that the deed will state that the right is enforceable only as long as the person who created it remains the owner of the land over which it was created. Equally the deed might state that the right is only enforceable by the person for whose benefit it was created, so that the benefit would not pass to his successors in title. Limitations on the enforceability of rights of light of this sort are unusual.

2.5 The concept of proprietary interests in land can be simply illustrated. If A as a freeholder grants to B a lease for 25 years, or grants a right of way over his land to C in perpetuity, and A then sells his freehold to X, both B and C are in principle entitled to exercise and enforce their rights under the lease and the easement of way against X. However, if A grants to D a licence to use his land, for example a right to deposit materials on some parts of his land at certain times, D is not able to enforce that right against X. This is so whether or not X knows of the licence and the rights of D when he acquires the land from A.[5] The reason is that licences

[3] *Tulk v Moxhay* (1848) 2 Ph 774.

[4] As explained elsewhere, what amount to rights of light can exist as a result of restrictive covenants and by reason of the existence in leases or transfers of land of the obligation of a landlord or transferor not to derogate from his grant. See section (C) of this chapter. Rights of light created in this way are also proprietary rights in the sense here explained. Implied easements of light often arise as a result of what are fundamentally rights derived from the general duty not to derogate from grant: see *Wheeldon v Burrows* (1879) 12 Ch D 31, 49 (Thesiger LJ), and see ch 4.

[5] *Ashburn Anstalt v Arnold* [1989] Ch 1; *IDC v Clark* [1992] 2 EGLR 184. In certain circumstances the grant of a licence can create a constructive trust in favour of the licensee, in which case the trust, and thus the licence, may become enforceable against successors in title of the licensor who are bound by the equitable interest created by the trust.

relating to land have not been allowed into the category of proprietary rights. The qualification 'in principle' is used in this description of the law since even when rights are proprietary rights, they may not in practice and in particular cases be enforceable against successors in title of the land or interest in land burdened by them, for instance because under the system of land registration they have not been properly protected on the registered title of the land against which they are enforceable.[6]

The fact that a right over land is not enforceable against a successor in title to the land does not necessarily deprive the owner of the right of all remedies. In the above example of the non-proprietary right of a contractual licence, if the licence had been granted so as to last for a period of three years and X had bought the land after two years and had refused to allow D to continue storage on the land, D would have had no remedy against X, but would have had a remedy in damages against A who had broken his contractual obligation to allow A to use the land for three years. This example illustrates the essential difference between contractual rights *in personam* enforceable only against a party to the contract and proprietary rights *in rem* enforceable against the land and against anyone with an interest in the land. 2.6

An easement is a right of the owner of property A which entitles him to exercise limited use or enjoyment over property B or which entitles him to prevent property B being used in some way. The words 'limited use or enjoyment' are used because the rights are unlikely to be an easement if the owner of property A has the right of exclusive possession over property B. Exclusive possession will normally give rise to a lease.[7] Easements have been recognised within the categories of proprietary rights since at least the seventeenth century.[8] 2.7

A distinction relevant to the law of easements is that which is sometimes drawn in law between corporeal and incorporeal interests, often called corporeal or incorporeal hereditaments, in land.[9] A corporeal interest means an interest in land, which gives a right to possession of the land either currently or in the future. Consequently the freehold and leasehold owners of land both have corporeal interests in land: the leaseholder because he currently has the right to possession of the land, and the freeholder because he will become entitled to possession of the land when the lease ends. An incorporeal interest is a proprietary right over land which does not give the right, currently or in the future, to possession of the land. The meaning of 'incorporeal' is not admitting of physical possession.[10] An example 2.8

[6] See the Land Registration Act 2002 and see ch 11.

[7] *Street v Mountford* [1985] AC 809.

[8] *Hughes v Keymish* (1609) 1 Bulstrode 115; *Aldred's Case* (1610) 9 Co Rep 57.

[9] A hereditament is an inheritable right in property.

[10] *Great Western Rly Co v Swindon and Cheltenham Rly Co* (1884) 9 App Cas 787, 807–08 (Lord Bramwell). In *Blackstone's Commentaries* (published 1765–70) an incorporeal hereditament was described as follows: 'It is a right issued out of a thing corporate (whether real or personal) or concerning, or annexed to, or exercisable within the same. It is not the thing corporate itself, which may consists in lands, houses, jewels, or the like; but something collateral thereto, as a rent issuing out of those lands or houses.' Incorporeal interests are sometimes described as *iura in re aliena*—rights in the property of another person.

of an incorporeal interest is an easement, which does not give the right to possession of the land over which it is exercisable. A further example is the benefit of a restrictive covenant, that is the right that some other person shall not use his land in a particular way. A right of light as an easement is therefore an incorporeal interest in land. It is sometimes said, incorrectly, that only corporeal interests are proprietary interests. This is clearly not correct, since incorporeal interests in land, including easements, are proprietary interests in the sense explained above, which is that they are, in law and in principle, capable of binding the land over which the right is exercisable, whoever owns that land at any particular time.

(B) EASEMENTS

1. General Nature and Characteristics

2.9 Because a right of light is one of that form of incorporeal interests known as easements, it is necessary to outline the essential characteristics of easements, since a right of light must conform with these characteristics. Easements are to be distinguished from profits a prendre, a similar type of incorporeal proprietary right, and the two are often treated together. A profit a prendre (often just called a profit) is a right to take some element of the natural components or produce of a piece of land owned by some other person, for example a right to take natural products such as crops or wood from trees, or to take minerals. The details of the law of profits are not of importance to the law of rights of light. As explained in the next paragraph, easements may exist as permanent (freehold) interests or as leasehold interests, and in either case may exist as legal or equitable interests.

2.10 An easement, including an easement of light, may be legal or equitable.[11] Most easements are legal. There are three main circumstances in which an easement may be equitable:

(a) It is provided by section 1(2)(a) of the Law of Property Act 1925 that, among the only interests which are capable of subsisting at law, are easements equivalent to an estate in fee simple absolute in possession (ie, a permanent interest or an interest equivalent to a freehold estate) or a term of years absolute (ie, a leasehold interest). Freehold or leasehold easements may therefore exist at law.[12] Consequently, since a term of years absolute, ie a lease, has to be for

[11] The difference between legal and equitable interests in land, and its historical basis, is explained in ch 11, para 11.2.

[12] An easement may therefore be a freehold or a leasehold easement. The two types of easement are by analogy with the two estates in land which may exist in law, a freehold and a leasehold estate, as described in section 1(1) of the Law of Property Act 1925.

a fixed term of years,[13] an easement granted for some other period, such as for the life of the grantee, must be equitable.

(b) An easement created may be appurtenant to a corporeal interest, which is itself equitable so that the easement is itself necessarily equitable. For example, an equitable lease may arise from a specifically enforceable agreement for a lease, and an easement to be granted as part of the lease will then also be equitable.[14]

(c) Where the title to land is registered and an express easement is created on or after 13 October 2003 in favour of dominant land against servient land, the easement cannot have effect as a legal easement, and so can be equitable only, until the registration requirements are satisfied. The requirements are that the proprietor of the title to the dominant land must be entered in the register of that title as the proprietor of the easement and a notice of the easement must be entered in the register of the title of the servient land.[15] This requirement does not apply to easements created by prescription or by implication, or by the operation of section 62 of the Law of Property Act 1925. The main disadvantage of an equitable easement as compared to a legal easement is that it may have less protection against a purchaser of the servient land.

It is usually said that there are four essential characteristics which must exist if a right over land is to constitute an easement. The characteristics are generally stated as being: 2.11

(a) that there must be a dominant and a servient tenement;
(b) that the easement must accommodate the dominant tenement;
(c) that the two tenements must not be both owned and occupied by the same person; and
(d) that the right must be capable of forming the subject matter of a grant.

A right of light as an easement must conform with these characteristics if it is to be enforceable as an easement. It is not necessary in this book to discuss extensively the ramifications and details of the four characteristics, and it is sufficient to explain how a right of light must conform with the characteristics.[16]

[13] A periodic tenancy, for example a weekly or annual tenancy which is capable of being determined by either party at the end of any week or year from its creation, may exist as a term of years absolute. Therefore an easement may be granted which is appurtenant to that lease, and that easement may be a legal easement. An obvious example would be an annual tenancy of a flat with an easement of way for the benefit of the tenant over other parts of the building within which the flat is situated.

[14] *Celsteel Ltd v Alton House Ltd* [1985] 1 WLR 204. See ch 11, para 11.47.

[15] Land Registration Act 2002, sch 2, para 7(2). See ch 11, section (B)2.

[16] A full account of the general law of easements will be found in *Gale on Easements*, 19th edn (London, Sweet & Maxwell, 2012).

2. The First Characteristic

2.12 The first two characteristics go largely together. The law of easements (and in effect the law of restrictive covenants) is centred on the concept of one defined area of land which has the benefit of the particular easement and another defined area of land which has the burden of that easement. They are traditionally called the dominant and the servient tenements.[17] The word 'tenement' means no more than that the land is held in tenure from the owner of a superior interest, and reflects the theory of the land law of England and Wales that ultimately the Crown owns all land and that all other persons with an interest in it own their interest as something held directly from the Crown, or from someone else who himself holds that interest from the Crown.[18] Therefore for the purposes of a right of light as an easement, there must be a definite area of land which enjoys the right (the dominant land or tenement) and a definite area of different land over which the right is exercisable (the servient land or tenement). This requirement is to be contrasted with certain rights over the land of another person which can be held 'in gross'. Profits a prendre can be held in gross in the above sense. All that this means is that the right so held is not of necessity annexed to a particular piece of land, but may be exercised by anybody in whom it is vested. An easement cannot be held in gross in this sense.[19] This rule of law relating to dominant and servient tenements is particularly applicable to rights of light. A right of light which is annexed to a particular building can of its nature only protect the benefit of the access of light over adjoining properties. It cannot protect the access of light to that building over properties some considerable distance away, since any access of light over those properties will not have any significant benefit to the particular dominant land. A particular characteristic of easements of light is that they can exist only for the benefit of windows or other apertures in buildings.[20] In legal usage, land usually includes buildings on land but it may technically be clearer to refer to the dominant property as the dominant building. The servient property may comprise land with or without any buildings or structures on it, and so may be called the servient land. This distinction in phraseology is used in the Rights of Light Act 1959.[21] An easement of light may be held for the benefit of more than

[17] 'An easement, however, is constituted over a servient tenement in favour of a dominant tenement': *Attorney General of Southern Nigeria v John Holt and Company (Liverpool) Ltd* [1915] AC 599, 618 (Lord Shaw).

[18] The theory of the land law is that all land vested in William the Conqueror in or after 1066 and that thereafter all interests are derived from the Crown. An excellent account of this theory for those interested is found in *Megarry & Wade on the Law of Real Property*, 8th edn (London, Sweet & Maxwell, 2012) chs 1–3. All landowners are technically and ultimately tenants of the Crown, and 'tenement' means property held by a tenant.

[19] *London and Blenheim Estates Ltd v Ladbroke Retail Parks Ltd* [1994] 1 WLR 31.

[20] See section (D) of this chapter.

[21] See ch 9.

one person who has an interest in the dominant building, for example a landlord and a tenant of that building.[22]

Where an easement of light is created by a deed, the dominant land will normally be readily identifiable from the language of the deed. Easements, including rights of light, are sometimes created as a part of the sale of land. It will usually be apparent from the deed that the dominant land is either the land sold or the land retained by the vendor. If this is not apparent, it may be necessary to look at all relevant circumstances as at the date of the deed in order to identify the dominant land.[23] Implied easements are usually created when the owner of an area of land transfers a part of the land and retains the remainder of it. An implied easement of light may in some circumstances arise for the benefit of the land transferred, which becomes the dominant tenement, against the land retained, which becomes the servient tenement. In such circumstances, although less readily, an implied easement of light may arise for the benefit of the land retained over the land transferred, in which case the designations of the dominant and the servient tenements will be reversed.[24] Where the easement is created by prescription, the building which contains the aperture or apertures through which light has passed during the prescription period, and which is therefore the dominant tenement, will be obvious. In the same way, any land over which light has passed to the dominant building will be the servient land. 2.13

3. The Second Characteristic

The second characteristic of an easement, namely that the exercise of the right created must accommodate the dominant tenement, is apparent from the nature of the first requirement or characteristic. In all cases where a right of light exists, whether created expressly by deed or by implication or by prescription, the dominant building or tenement must to some significant degree benefit from the light which passes to it across the servient land or tenement. Consequently if the alleged dominant building is some distance from the servient land, so that it does not rely to any significant extent on the access of light over the servient land, there cannot be an easement of light. The operation of these basic principles as regards easements is particularly stark and obvious in relation to that category of easements known as a right of light. 2.14

[22] Law of Property Act 1925, s 187(2). A frequent example of where this may occur is where an owner of a building has acquired an easement of light appurtenant to the building and then grants a lease or leases of it or of parts of it. The benefit of the landlord's easement will pass to the tenants, either automatically or by virtue of s 62 of the Law of Property Act 1925, unless there is an express provision in the lease excluding the transfer of easements.

[23] *The Shannon Ltd v Venner Ltd* [1965] Ch 682 in which a right of way created in favour of the purchaser of an area of land bought was held to be appurtenant not only to that land but also to land previously acquired by the purchaser.

[24] See ch 4, section (B) for the creation of easements of light by implication.

2.15 An easement is said to be appurtenant to or annexed to or appended to or attached as an incident of the dominant land. There seems no significance in which description is used.[25] The result is that on a disposal of the dominant land, including the grant of a lease of that land, the benefit of the easement automatically passes to the purchaser or lessee without the need for any express reference in the transfer or the lease.[26] It is possible that the easement is made personal to the initial grantee when the easement is created expressly by a deed, but this is unusual, particularly with easements of light, since the nature of the easement is that it protects the utility and value of the dominant building, rather than benefiting just the immediate owner of that building. It is also possible that on a disposal of the dominant building the benefit of the easement is expressly excluded from the disposal. Such a course would be most unusual on a sale of property as the seller will no longer be able to enforce the easement, since he will no longer have any interest in the dominant building.

2.16 To exclude the transfer of an easement of light might have more purpose on the grant of a lease since the landlord will remain entitled to enforce the easement by virtue of his reversion in the dominant building. One reason for a landlord wishing to exclude the passing of the easement to a tenant might be that the landlord could then come to an arrangement with the owner of the servient land as to future rights of light or as to permitting an obstruction to light, something which he could not do without the cooperation of the tenant if the tenant also had the benefit of the easement. Even so, specific exclusions of easements are unusual in leases. Leases contain a bewildering variety of phraseologies which purport to indicate what ancillary rights affecting the land are passed to the tenant or what ancillary rights are excepted from the demise. The truth is that many leases are granted with a use of language deriving from precedents of leases, with little thought given to the implication of the language on rights of light. An underlying

[25] S 187(1) of the Law of Property Act 1925 states as follows: 'Where an easement, right or privilege for a legal estate is created, it shall enure for the benefit of the land to which it is intended to be annexed.'

[26] The transfer of the easement on a sale of the dominant land will either be automatic (see *Godwin v Schweppes* [1902] 1 Ch 926) or will take place under s 62 of the Law of Property Act 1925. See ch 4, section (C) for an explanation of s 62. In the same way, the grant of a lease will transfer the benefit of an existing easement of light held by the landlord to the tenant without the need to refer expressly in the lease to light or rights of light. The point was said to admit of some doubt, by Mellish LJ in *Leech v Schweder* (1874) 9 LR Ch App 463, 473, but any doubt is now resolved by s 62 of the Law of Property Act 1925 which applies to the grant of leases. In much the same way when dominant land is compulsorily acquired, any easement then existing over servient land will pass under the compulsory purchase to the acquiring authority: *Sovmots Ltd v Secretary of State for the Environment* [1979] AC 144. In such a case the easement will pass either under an express transfer required by the acquiring authority following the service of a notice to treat or by a vesting declaration made under the Compulsory Purchase (Vesting Declarations) Act 1981. The transfer of the easement will occur whether or not the dominant land has registered title, unless of course there is an express exclusion of the easement. If the dominant land does not have a registered title, the transfer will normally be a triggering event which will bring into effect the duty of compulsory first registration under the Land Registration Act 2002. See generally ch 11.

principle is that rights of light appurtenant to the interest of the landlord will pass to the tenant on the grant of the lease, either automatically or by virtue of section 62 of the Law of Property Act 1925, unless there is some wording in the lease to the contrary effect.

The automatic annexation of the benefit of an easement to the dominant land is to be contrasted to the benefit of a restrictive covenant which only passes to a purchaser of the land of the original covenantee if: 2.17

(a) it is expressly or impliedly annexed to that land at the time of the creation of the covenant; or
(b) it is statutorily annexed to that land by the operation of section 78 of the Law of Property Act 1925; or
(c) it is expressly assigned in the transfer of that land.[27]

The burden of an easement also attaches to the servient land. It is in principle enforceable against the owner of the servient land at the time of its creation and against all persons who subsequently acquire an interest in the servient land. In practice, under the system of land registration now contained in the Land Registration Act 2002 the owner of the easement may protect it by notice or other means on the registered title of the servient land, lest the easement should become unenforceable against a person to whom the servient land is transferred.[28] 2.18

4. The Third Characteristic

The third characteristic, that the two tenements must not be owned and occupied by the same person, is perhaps obvious. Where a person owns and occupies a piece of land, that which he does on any part of it is done by virtue of his corporeal interest in the land as a whole. The right of a person to walk over any part of his property, or to enjoy the access of light over one part of his property to another part, arises by virtue of his ownership of the whole property, and does not require any separate origin such as a deed of grant or prescription. The enjoyment by a person of the access of natural light to windows in a building on his property over other land within his property is therefore a consequence of his ownership of the whole of his property. The point, which is really one of common sense, was 2.19

[27] See *Federated Homes Ltd v Mill Lodge Properties Ltd* [1980] 1 WLR 594.

[28] See ch 11 for a fuller explanation of when the burden of an easement of light passes to a purchaser of the servient land and the need of the dominant owner to protect his interest under the Land Registration Act 2002 (where the title to the servient land is registered) or under the Land Charges Act 1972 (where the title to the servient land is not registered).

explained in the following way by Lord Wilberforce in *Sovmots Ltd v Secretary of State for the Environment*:[29]

> The reason is that when land is under one ownership one cannot speak in any intelligible sense of rights, or privileges, or easements being exercised over one part for the benefit of another. Whatever the owner does, he does as owner and, until a separation occurs, of ownership or at least of occupation, the condition for the existence of rights, etc., does not exist …

2.20 It is unity of ownership and of occupation in the same person which prevents the existence of an easement over any part of the land in question. If a landlord of a property lets that property, he can grant an easement in favour of the tenant over other property of his or over other property of his let to another tenant (subject, of course, in the latter case to the terms of any existing lease held by the other tenant). Thus an easement, including an easement of light, created by express words in a deed may be exercisable by a tenant against his own landlord and against another tenant of his own landlord.[30] A tenant of land may expressly and by deed create an easement over his leasehold interest in the servient land. Of course the easement does not bind the landlord of the servient land and so will normally end when the lease of the servient land ends.[31] Covenants in leases sometimes prohibit the tenant from creating interests of this nature. There is a complication when an easement is acquired by long use or prescription, since the general theory of prescription is that it is by a fee simple owner of one area of land against a fee simple owner of another area of land, but this rule is to some extent relaxed in respect of rights of light acquired by prescription because of the wording of section 3 of the Prescription Act 1832, as is explained later. Where the prescription period is running and there is a time during which there is unity of ownership or of possession, the running of the period may be terminated or interrupted.[32]

[29] *Sovmots Ltd v Secretary of State for the Environment* [1979] AC 144, 169. See also *Bolton v Bolton* (1879) 11 Ch D 968, 970 (Fry J); *Long v Gowlett* [1923] 2 Ch 177. This statement was made in the context of the creation of rights under s 62 of the Law of Property Act 1925 for the benefit of land transferred over land retained when a transferor disposes of a part of his land and retains the remainder of his land. See ch 4 for the operation and effect of s 62 on the creation or transfer of easements of light. An easement is constituted over a servient tenement in favour of a dominant tenement and, as pointed out by Lord Shaw in *Attorney General of Southern Nigeria v John Holt & Co (Liverpool) Ltd* [1915] AC 599, 617, this is quite different from what a person does on his own land.

[30] See, eg, *Borman v Griffiths* [1930] 1 Ch 493, in which a right of way was implied in favour of one tenant against and over the land of another tenant of the same landlord. The creation of easements by implication is explained in ch 4.

[31] There is a possible exception to this rule where the lease of the servient land ends by surrender or merger: see ch 8, section (B).

[32] See ch 5, sections (B) and (C) and ch 8, section (B) for a fuller explanation of the effect of unity of ownership and unity of possession on (a) the running of the prescription period and (b) the bringing to an end of an easement. There is a possible relaxation of these principles in the case of easements of light, since it is possible that such an easement may come into existence by reason of s 62 of the Law of Property Act 1925 on a sale of the part of the land which receives natural light over the remainder of the land even though prior to the sale both areas of land were in the same ownership and occupation: see *Broomfield v Williams* [1897] 1 Ch 602, and see the observation of Lord Edmund-Davies in

An expression which has come into legal usage is 'quasi-easements'. Where a person carries out some activity on his own land, such as walking across a track on a part of it, and that activity could constitute the exercise of an easement if the track had been in the ownership of someone else, the enjoyment of the activity may be called a quasi-easement. The existence of such quasi-easements is not of importance while one person remains the owner and occupier of the whole of the land, but they may become of considerable importance when that owner disposes of part of his land by an outright sale or the grant of a lease. The reason is that in such circumstances there may be implied in favour of the purchaser or tenant of the part of the land disposed of a true easement equivalent in nature and extent to what was prior to the disposal a quasi-easement.[33] A right of light may exist as a quasi-easement within the meaning of this expression. An analysis of the type of situation will be of importance when an explanation is given of the creation of easements as an implication on the transfer by an owner of a part of his land.[34] 2.21

5. The Fourth Characteristic

The fourth characteristic means that the activity on the land of some other person must be capable of constituting an easement or, as it is sometimes put, must be capable of forming the subject matter of a grant. One principle is that a grant of rights which confer exclusive use and occupation of an area of land is unlikely to be considered an easement over that land and more likely to amount to the creation of a lease or a licence.[35] It is also said that the categories of possible easements are not closed, since changing conditions of life may involve the need for new types of rights attached to one piece of land over another piece of land to be recognised as easements. It is unnecessary to explore this matter in more detail, since it has been long established that a right of light may be an easement.[36] 2.22

Sovmots Ltd v Secretary of State for the Environment [1979] AC 144, 176. There is little consistency or logic in this particular area of the law.

[33] The main principle which governs the implication of an easement in such cases is called the rule in *Wheeldon v Burrows* (1879) 12 Ch D 31. In stating the principle, Thesiger LJ referred at p 49 to 'Easements which were obvious and apparent when enjoyed by an owner of land' as quasi-easements.

[34] See ch 4. The situation is also important when easements are created out of quasi-easements under s 62 of the Law of Property Act 1925, a matter also considered in ch 4.

[35] Recent decisions have involved the question of whether a right to park vehicles on a defined area of land can be considered an easement: see *Moncrieff v Jamieson* [2007] UKHL 42, [2007] 1 WLR 2620, a decision of the House of Lords in a Scottish case.

[36] In *Aldred's Case* (1610) 9 Co Rep 57 it was said that for a house, four things are desired and one of these was '*necessitas luminatis*', or the need for light, and that for hindrances of this light 'the ancient form of an action on the case was significant'. The protection by the law of 'ancient lights' certainly existed by the seventeenth century; see *Hughes v Keymish* (1609) 1 Bulstrode 115 (on the custom of London: see ch 5). It appears that the right against new buildings of protection of light to existing buildings was recognised as far back as the time of Henry VI (1422–71). The existence of an action for damages for a loss of light was referred to by Holt CJ in *Fitter v Veal* (1701) 12 Mod Rep 542, 544.

6. Ecclesiastical Land

2.23 Special considerations apply to rights over land held by the Anglican Church for ecclesiastical purposes.[37] The details of the subject can be found in books on ecclesiastical law. Where property is the property of a benefice, which includes a church and churchyard, the incumbent of the benefice may grant an easement over the property and may acquire an easement for the benefit of the property. If there is no incumbent of the benefice, the power may be exercised by the Bishop.[38] The exercise of the power requires the consent of the parsonage board or the diocesan board of finance of the benefice.[39] If the power is exercised by the incumbent, the consent of the Bishop must also be obtained.[40] Instead of an easement, a faculty may be granted which operates as a licence for a fixed period of time.[41]

2.24 The further question which arises is whether an easement can be acquired by prescription over ecclesiastical property. Prescription generally depends on the presumed existence of a grant in the past which is not now available. There appears to be no reason in principle why a prescriptive easement of light should not in appropriate circumstances be acquired against ecclesiastical property. However, a difficulty will arise where reliance is placed on common law prescription or the doctrine of lost modern grant. These doctrines depend on the existence of a presumed grant at some stage in the past. If there is no evidence that the appropriate consent, as set out in the last paragraph, has been obtained, as is very likely in most instances, a prescriptive easement of any sort based on these two doctrines is unlikely to be established against the property.[42] However, prescription under section 3 of the Prescription Act 1832 does not depend on a presumed grant; it is said to depend on *ius positivi*, which in this case means a statutory enactment.[43] Consequently there seems to be no reason in principle, subject to any other rules of ecclesiastical law, why an easement of light should not be acquired over the ecclesiastical property of the Anglican Church by prescription under section 3 of the Prescription Act 1832.[44] A church is in principle a building, for the benefit of which through its apertures an easement of light can exist.[45]

[37] Property is also of course owned by church authorities for investment purposes, and the ordinary principles of the law of easements apply to such property.

[38] Church Property (Miscellaneous Provisions) Measure 1960, s 9(1).

[39] ibid.

[40] ibid.

[41] *Re St Martin le Grand, York* [1990] Fam 63, 70.

[42] *Oakley v Boston* [1976] QB 270.

[43] *Tapling v Jones* (1865) 11 HLC 290, 304 (Lord Westbury).

[44] Prescription generally is considered in ch 5. In *Oakley v Boston* the claim to a prescriptive right of way was rejected so far as based on the Prescription Act 1832 because of an insufficiency of evidence of use of the way at the relevant time.

[45] See para 2.42.

7. Rights to Air

A right to receive the flow of air through a defined channel into a building may be acquired as an easement.[46] The principle is that the right can only be acquired through a definite aperture in the nature of a window in the property or through a definite channel over adjoining property.[47] An example is the passage of air through a disused well on the servient land and through a shaft cut through the rock into a cellar of the dominant building.[48] Such an easement can be created by deed or by prescription. It is said that having regard to this principle, there is little or no distinction between a right of light and a right to air.[49] Where there is an agreement between parties that development may take place on land notwithstanding any interference with an adjoining property, the language is often expressed in terms of interference with light or air. Such an agreement will usually be construed as the giving of consent by the servient owner to the passage of light and air over his property so as to prevent the running of the prescription period.[50] The acquisition of a right to air by prescription will be under section 2 of the Prescription Act 1832[51] or under the doctrine of lost modern grant.[52] An obstruction to the passage of air through the defined channel or defined aperture where an easement exists will be an infringement of that easement. The amount of air to which the dominant property is entitled is probably that for the reasonable use of that property, for example the cellar of a public house.[53] It follows that a general right of the passage of air to land or to structures cannot exist as an easement.[54] It appears that for this reason an easement of air required to turn a windmill cannot be obtained.[55] Today, wind turbines used to generate electricity are a modern equivalent of windmills, and no easement can be obtained to protect the flow of wind and air to such machines. 2.25

Most buildings have windows or other apertures designed and used for the access of light. Apertures designed and used for the passage of air are more rare, so that the existence of an easement to receive air through a defined passage over servient land is more unusual than a right of light. Where there is a general right to 2.26

[46] *Aldin v Latimer Clark, Muirhead & Co* [1894] 2 Ch 439.

[47] *Aldin v Latimer Clark, Muirhead & Co* [1894] 2 Ch 437, 446 (Sterling J); *Cable v Bryant* [1908] 1 Ch 259; *Harris v De Pinna* (1886) 33 Ch D 238; *Bass v Gregory* (1890) 25 QBD 481; *Hall v Lichfield Brewery Co* (1880) 49 LJ Ch 655; *Newham v Lawson* (1971) 22 P & CR 852.

[48] *Bass v Gregory* (1890) 25 QBD 481.

[49] *Cable v Bryant* [1908] 1 Ch 259, 263–64.

[50] See ch 5, section (D)6. An express grant of a right of light through a window may include a right of air: see *Aldred's Case* (1610) 9 Co Rep 57, 58b where it was said that where there was a grant of windows then 'for stopping up as well of the wholesome air as of light, an action lies, and damages shall be recovered for them, for both are necessary.'

[51] *Cable v Bryant* [1908] 1 Ch 259, 263 (Neville J).

[52] *Bass v Gregory* (1890) 25 QBD 481, 484 (Pollock B).

[53] ibid.

[54] *Webb v Bird* (1863) 13 CBNS 841; *Harris v De Pinna* (1886) 33 Ch D 238.

[55] *Webb v Bird* (1863) 13 CBNS 841.

receive air to land over adjoining property, there is likely to be a different legal source of that right. Such a right may be created by a restrictive covenant on the servient land, ie that nothing will be done on that land which impedes the passing of a sufficiency of light to the dominant land or a building on the dominant land for its use for a certain purpose.[56] A further and important source of a right to the general passage of air to land or a building is the operation of the doctrine of derogation from grant, the principle that when a person sells or lets a piece of land there is an implied obligation on him and his successors in title that he will not use or carry out works on land retained by him in such a way as to impede the use of the land sold or let for a purpose understood by the parties at the time of the transaction as that to which the land sold or let would be put.[57] An example is a case in which land was let to be used for the business of a timber merchant. It was held that there was a derogation from grant when successors in title of the landlord used adjoining land so as to impede the passage of air needed to dry timber as part of the business.[58] It is essential to the operation of this doctrine that:

(a) the grantor as owner of the retained land knew at the time of the grant the purpose for which the land sold or let was to be put;[59] and
(b) it was not understood between the parties that a purpose for which the retained land was to be used would or might be one which would impede the access of air to the land sold or let.[60]

2.27 There is no natural right for the passage of air to a property such as the right to support for land from adjoining land.[61]

(C) OTHER SOURCES OF A RIGHT OF LIGHT

2.28 A right of the owner or occupier of one piece of land that the light which passes to his land over other land shall not be unduly obstructed normally exists as a type of easement. It is characterised as a negative easement, in that it prevents the owner of the servient land from acting in a particular way to the detriment of the dominant land as opposed to permitting the owner of the dominant land to act in a certain way on or over the servient land. The easement must arise by a deed (or as an implication from the circumstances of a deed) or by prescription. A deed is of course the result of the voluntary acts of the parties to the deed. It is

[56] *Harris v De Pinna* (1886) 36 Ch D 238, 263 (Cotton LJ); *Bryant v Lefever* (1879) 4 CPD 172, 177 (Bramwell LJ).

[57] *Lyttelton Times Co Ltd v Warners Ltd* [1907] AC 476. See para 2.32 et seq.

[58] *Aldin v Latimer Clark, Muirhead and Co* [1894] 2 Ch 437.

[59] *Robinson v Kilvert* (1889) 41 Ch D 88.

[60] *Lyttelton Times Co Ltd v Warners Ltd* [1907] AC 476.

[61] *Aldred's Case* (1610) 9 Co Rep 57, 58a, citing *Bland v Moseley* (1587). A natural right in this context means a right to which land is inherently entitled and which does not depend upon some specific method of creation such as a deed or the rules of prescription.

conceivable that a court would order the grant of an easement of light as a means of giving effect to the existence of a proprietary estoppel, and this possibility is briefly explained in paragraph 4.2 of chapter 4. There are two other principles of the law of real property which may give rise to what amounts in a general sense to a right of light although no easement is created.

1. Restrictive Covenants

2.29 A person may undertake by way of a covenant that he will carry out or will refrain from carrying out some activity on his land; for example, he may undertake to maintain the fences on the boundary of his land in good repair, or he may undertake not to use his land for any purpose other than a residential purpose. The rule of the common law was that if the person making the covenant transferred his land, the covenant was not enforceable against the transferee. The reason is said to derive from the common law principle that a person cannot be made liable under a contract unless he was himself a party to the contract: the burden of a contract is not transferable.[62] Equity relaxed the rigour of this principle following the decision in *Tulk v Moxhay*[63] in 1848 to the extent that, subject to certain conditions, a covenant restrictive of the use of land could be enforced against successors in title of the original covenantor.[64] One of the conditions is that the covenant operates for the protection of, or benefits, land of the covenantee.[65]

2.30 One of the obligations which a covenantor may agree to impose on his land is that the land shall not be built upon so as to obstruct, or unreasonably obstruct, the access of light to the land of the covenantee. The covenant may be in general language of the above nature or may be more specific, in that it specifies the exact height or bulk or position to which building may be carried out on the land to which the restriction applies. Such a covenant is negative or restrictive in nature, and so may operate as a restrictive covenant and can in principle bind successors in title of the original covenantor. The similarities between the right to the access of light over other land by virtue of an easement and the same right by virtue of a restrictive covenant are obvious. In each case there has to be a definite piece of land which has the benefit of the covenant (the dominant land) and a definite piece of land over which the right is exercisable (the servient land). Indeed the development of the law of restrictive covenants has been described as 'the extension in equity of the doctrine of negative easements; such, for instance, as a right to the access of light, which prevents the owner of the servient tenement from

[62] *Rhone v Stevens* [1994] 2 AC 310 (Lord Templeman).

[63] *Tulk v Moxhay* (1848) 2 Ph 774.

[64] In other words the right of the covenantee to enforce the covenant became a proprietary interest in land in the sense explained in paras 2.2–2.7.

[65] *LCC v Allen* [1914] 3 KB 642.

building so as to obstruct the light'.[66] The content of a restrictive covenant is not constrained by limitations on the nature and content of an easement of light. For example, an easement of light is not available where the dominant land is open land with no buildings on it but a restrictive covenant which binds servient land may have the effect of preventing the overshadowing of dominant open land.

2.31 There are significant differences between a right of light which exists as an easement, and a right of light which is created by virtue of a restrictive covenant.

(a) The right of light protected by an easement is generally the right to a sufficiency of light as required for the reasonable enjoyment of the dominant building. A restrictive covenant will usually specify exactly what may or may not be done on the servient land, such as a restriction on building above a certain specified height. The owner of the dominant land can then prevent building above the specified height, even though there is little or no effect on the access of light to his property caused by it.

(b) Easements may be created expressly by deed or as an implication from the circumstances of a deed or by prescription. A restrictive covenant must be created expressly by a deed and cannot be created by implication or by prescription.

(c) A restrictive covenant may protect an interest of the dominant owner which cannot be protected by an easement, such as preventing the erection of a building which obstructs the view (as opposed to the access of light) available to the dominant land. The access of light to open land may be protected by a covenant, whereas an easement must be for the benefit of an aperture in a building.

(d) A restrictive covenant may be modified or discharged in certain circumstances by an order of the Lands Chamber of the Upper Tribunal under section 84 of the Law of Property Act 1925. An easement is not subject to this jurisdiction or risk.

(e) Once created, the benefit of an easement of light becomes automatically appurtenant to the dominant land and passes automatically to a transferee of that land. The benefit of a restrictive covenant only passes to a transferee if either it is annexed to the land benefited (by an express or implied annexation or a statutory annexation under section 78(1) of the Law of Property Act 1925) or is expressly assigned to the transferee. Annexation of the benefit of restrictive covenants is a subject on which there is a volume of legal learning which is not relevant to the benefit of easements. However, easements and restrictive covenants share the characteristic that there must be a defined area of land which can enjoy the benefit of the easement or the covenant.

(f) Restrictive covenants are enforceable only in equity. With the same general availability of remedies in chancery and common law courts today, this distinction may be of more historical than practical significance.

[66] *London & South Western Rly v Gomm* (1882) 20 Ch D 562, 583 (Jessel MR). See also *Pell Frischmann Engineering Ltd v Bow Valley Iron Ltd* [2009] UKPC 45, [2011] 1 WLR 2370, para 48(3) (Lord Walker).

2. Derogation from Grant

When a person sells or lets land there is generally an implied term in the document which effects the transaction that he will not act in such a way as to impede the use of the land for a purpose understood by both parties at the time of the transaction as that to which the land sold or let was to be put.[67] 2.32

A joint understanding of the purpose for which the property sold or let is to be used is essential for the operation of this doctrine. An understanding of the proposed use of property retained by the seller or lessor may also prevent a use of that property being a derogation from grant. For example, in *Lyttelton Times Co Ltd v Warners Ltd*[68] the owners of a building in Christchurch in New Zealand let the upper floors of it as additional bedrooms for an adjoining hotel, and themselves used the lower floors for operating printing machinery. The tenants of the upper floors claimed that the use of the printing machinery created noise and vibration which hindered the use of their property as hotel bedrooms. It was understood at the date of the grant that the lower premises would be used for printing machinery and it was believed that this would not unduly affect the use of the upper premises, so that in these circumstances there was held to be no derogation from grant. 2.33

It therefore appears that if an area of land is sold or let and the vendor and purchaser or the landlord and tenant both contemplate that the land shall be used or developed for a certain purpose which needs a sufficiency of light for its reasonable enjoyment, the doctrine of derogation from grant may prevent the vendor or landlord or his successors in title from constructing property on their land in a way which reduces the light which passes to the property sold or let to a level below that which is acceptable according to the ordinary notions of mankind for that purpose. In one case a maisonette was let which received natural light through skylights. It was held that the landlord would be derogating from his grant if he carried out development on his retained land which would substantially reduce the light received through the skylights.[69] A right which arises under this doctrine can be categorised as a proprietary right, since it is not only the vendor or lessor of the land who is bound by it but also any successors in title of that person.[70] 2.34

[67] The doctrine is of ancient origin but there is a modern expression of it by Lord Denning in *Molton Builders v Westminster City Council* (1975) 30 P & CR 182, 186. There is a full analysis of the doctrine by Nicholls LJ in *Johnston & Sons Ltd v Holland* [1988] 1 EGLR 264. The doctrine is said to embody in a legal maxim a rule of common honesty: see *Harmer v Jumbil (Nigeria) Tin Areas Ltd* [1921] 1 Ch 200, 225-26 (Younger LJ).

[68] *Lyttelton Times Co Ltd v Warners Ltd* [1907] AC 476.

[69] *Dorrington Belgravia Ltd v McGlashan* [2009] 1 EGLR 27.

[70] An example of the enforcement of a right which arose from the obligation by a vendor not to derogate from his grant is *Cable v Bryant* [1908] 1 Ch 259, in which a right to the access of air to a defined aperture was held to be binding on a purchaser of the freehold retained land of the vendor. A successor in title of the vendor is bound whether or not he had notice of the circumstances which gave rise to the implied obligation.

The creation of what amounts to a right of light by reason of the doctrine of derogation from grant is little different from the creation of a formal easement by implication, under the rule in *Wheeldon v Burrows,*[71] or as an intended easement.[72] Indeed the formulation of the rules governing implied easements is derived from the principle of non-derogation from grant.[73]

2.35 Despite the similarity between the obligation not to obstruct the access of light to neighbouring land which arises under the doctrine of non-derogation from grant, and the same obligation to the same effect which arises from an express or implied easement, there is an important difference between the ambit of the two obligations. An easement must bind a defined area of servient land. The obligation under the easement not to erect an obstruction to the passage of light to the dominant building adheres to what is done on that servient land. If the servient owner owns or acquires other land, the obligation under the easement does not apply to what he does on that other land. The obligation under the non-derogation from grant doctrine can in certain circumstances apply to land other than that which was owned by the vendor or lessor when he sold or granted a lease of a part of his land.

2.36 What has just been stated can best be illustrated by an example. Suppose that A owns a piece of land and sells a part of it to B, retaining the remaining part. Suppose that C owns land adjoining A's land. The effect of the sale will be to impose an obligation on A not to develop his remaining land in a way which obstructs the access of light to the part sold to B for the purposes for which that land was to be used. This is the effect of the rule against derogation from grant. As already mentioned, the same obligation will pass to a successor in title from A of the remaining land which is impressed with the non-derogation obligation. C is of course not concerned with the obligation, as he was not a party to the sale transaction which created the obligation under the non-derogation doctrine. Suppose, however, that A (or a successor in title of A to the retained land) subsequently acquires the land of C. The law is that in such a case the obligation not to obstruct the passage of light to the land sold to B then enures to the land of C which A has acquired.[74] In this way the 'servient land' in the case of an implied obligation not to derogate from grant can increase in a way not possible with an easement.

[71] *Wheeldon v Burrows* (1879) 12 Ch D 31.
[72] See ch 4, section (B).
[73] *Wheeldon v Burrows* (1879) 12 Ch D 31, 49 (Thesiger LJ).
[74] *Johnston & Sons Ltd v Holland* [1988] 1 EGLR 264.

(D) BUILDINGS AND APERTURES

1. Introduction

2.37 It has been pointed out that a right of light cannot exist in favour of open land with no building or structure on that land.[75] The existence of an easement of light depends on two physical factors:

(a) the existence on the dominant land of a building; and
(b) a defined aperture or apertures in that building through which light enters the building having passed across the servient land.[76]

2.38 Section 3 of the Prescription Act 1832 refers to the access of light to and for 'any dwellinghouse, workshop, or other building'. Section 2 of the Rights of Light Act 1959 refers to light passing to 'a dwelling-house, workshop or other building' which it calls 'the dominant building'. The language of the 1959 Act clearly follows that of the 1832 Act, save that modern practice introduces a hyphen and omits a comma. These statutes are concerned with the acquisition of a right of light by long use or prescription, or the prevention of such an acquisition. The requirement of a building and an aperture or apertures in the building which receive natural light is an essential element for the existence of an easement of light, however created, so that no easement of light could be created even by an express or implied grant in favour of open land or in favour of that which was not a building with an aperture or apertures. As regards open land it might not be easy to apply the test for the infringement of an easement, namely that the access of light was reduced to a level below that reasonably necessary for the enjoyment of the dominant land. Of course open land can be used for purposes which are not practical or usual in a building.[77] That which is very similar to an easement of light could be created in favour of open land or any other property by a restrictive covenant, for example a covenant that no development shall take place, or that no development shall take place beyond certain specified dimensions, on the servient land.[78]

[75] See ch 1, para 1.12.

[76] In *Dalton v Angus* (1881) 6 App Cas 740, 794 Lord Coleridge said: 'Although the general access of light from the heavens to the earth is indefinite, the light which enters a building by particular apertures does and must pass over the adjoining land in a course which, though not visibly defined, is really certain and, in that sense, definite.'

[77] The loss of natural light due to the erection of large buildings may in principle significantly affect the enjoyment of open spaces such as a cricket pitch where bad light can stop play or open-air swimming pools or areas used for sunbathing.

[78] See section (C)1 of this chapter.

2. Buildings

2.39 It is necessary to consider just what is a building for present purposes. It is not necessary to examine the meaning of a dwellinghouse or workshop for the purposes of the Prescription Act 1832, since obviously any dwellinghouse or workshop will be a building as is contemplated by the reference in the Act to 'other building'. A specific reference to additional types of building such as a dwellinghouse is a characteristic of Parliamentary drafting in the mid-nineteenth century.[79] The meaning of a building varies according to its context. There is little to be gained from an extended consideration. As a matter of usage, in the present context it may be useful to distinguish between structures and buildings. Structures are man-made objects attached to the ground, and buildings are a type of structure. What is generally understood by a building is a structure having walls and a roof, and buildings can of course be designed or used for a wide variety of purposes. For example, an open bridge over a railway line, or a permanently fixed statue, or a wall, would all be structures, but would not in ordinary parlance be a building. It may in some contexts be appropriate to refer to underground buildings or parts of buildings such as basements or vaults, but such areas may receive no, or only limited, natural light.

2.40 It may be useful to mention a few references to attempts by the courts to conclude whether some particular man-made artefact is a building. Often the expression used in statutes is 'structure or building', and a court may sensibly confine itself to deciding whether the object in question is a structure without deciding whether or not it is also a building. On occasions, a wide statutory definition is given to the word 'building'. In section 336(1) of the Town and Country Planning Act 1990 a building is defined to include 'any structure or erection', and so has a meaning which is considerably wider than that appropriate to the law of rights of light. It has been said that a covered reservoir was a building or structure within the meaning of the London Building Act 1884, although the Court declined to say within which description the reservoir fell.[80] It is difficult to find any consistency in the descriptions of buildings in different contexts. In one decision on the land tax legislation introduced by Mr Lloyd George's budget of 1909 it was said that a structure did not need to have a roof or cover for it to constitute a building, but sea defence embankments were held not to be a building.[81] In another case on the same legislation it was held that six feet high stone walls on a farm, used to divide up the land and to provide shelter for animals, were neither structures nor

[79] See, eg s 92 of the Lands Clauses Consolidation Act 1845 which provides that no party shall be required to sell to a body exercising powers of compulsory purchase a part only of any 'house or other building or manufactory'. This language is repeated today in s 8 of the Compulsory Purchase Act 1965.

[80] *Moran & Son Ltd v Marsland* [1909] 1 KB 744.

[81] *Waite's Executors v Inland Revenue Commissioners* [1914] 3 KB 196, 201 (Cozens-Hardy MR). The language being construed was that of s 25(2) of the Finance (1909–1910) Act 1910.

buildings.[82] The context may be different when the word 'building' is used in a contractual document such as a restrictive covenant, and in one case it was said that nobody in ordinary language would call a railway embankment a building, but that in the context of a particular covenant an embankment was a building.[83]

On occasions, the law of fixtures is referred to in the context of what is or is not a building, but to do so may introduce confusion and complexity into a matter of common-sense linguistic usage. A fixture is an object which starts its life as a chattel and is affixed to a building or land to such a degree and for such a purpose that it becomes in law a part of the building or the land. An example would be machinery permanently fixed to the floor of a factory, or components of an air-conditioning system introduced into a building. Whether or not an object has become a fixture, and so a part of the land, may be important to areas of the law of property, such as what passes on a sale or mortgage of a property, or the right of a tenant to remove objects which he has introduced, when his tenancy comes to an end.[84] The fact that an object has become a fixture cannot by itself make it a building; nobody would describe an air-conditioning compressor as a building. Of course in some cases the degree of annexation of objects to the land may be of relevance in deciding whether that object is a building for the purposes of rights of light. 2.41

A good deal of time can be taken up in academic discussions of what physical objects fall within one description or another, while the matter may be not of frequent or practical import. In the law of rights of light there may be borderline cases on what is or is not a building, such as a covered walkway or a covered bridge where the access of light to the windows of the structure may be important for the safety and convenience of users of it, and in such cases the tendency may be to include such structures within the meaning of a building. The practical applications of the question of what is a building in the context of rights of light seem to be sparse. Four categories of objects may be briefly considered. 2.42

(i) Caravans may receive light through their windows from adjoining property. However, it would be difficult to describe a caravan, whether a towed and mobile caravan or a static caravan left on a site for visits by holidaymakers, as a building. Even a caravan which is used as a permanent residence would not normally be considered to be a building. Consequently it is doubtful whether rights of light can attach to such an object. Mobile homes are an indefinite concept, and can encompass a number of types of artefact. If a mobile home is truly mobile, in the sense that it can be loaded onto a lorry and moved around, then it would not seem sensible to describe it as a building. On the other hand, if the so-called mobile home is permanently affixed

[82] *Morrison v Commissioners of Inland Revenue* [1915] 1 KB 716.

[83] *Long Eaton Recreation Grounds Co v Midland Rly Co* [1902] 2 KB 574.

[84] The House of Lords explained the general principles of the law of fixtures in *Elitestone v Morris* [1997] 1 WLR 687.

to some concrete structure and is intended to remain there permanently, then it may be reasonable to describe it as a building in the present context, since its need for light through its apertures will be as great as that of a bungalow. There are some structures which are prefabricated but intended to form permanent homes for persons when put in place. These 'prefabs' are sometimes a hangover from the need for housing after the destruction of property in the last war and few, if any, remain today. So far as they may exist, they do appear to be buildings. Clearly tents and similar structures are not buildings, even though they may be lived in for a period of time.

(ii) Houseboats may also offer permanent living or other accommodation to persons. However, their nature is that they float on water even though they may be more or less permanently affixed to the adjoining land. Again as a matter of common sense it would seem difficult to describe a houseboat as a building, so that it is unlikely that such objects can acquire an easement of light to portholes or other apertures which may exist in them.

(iii) A church or other place of worship may constitute a building for present purposes.[85] It is difficult to see why this should ever have been doubted.[86]

(iv) Carports, mainly outside residential buildings, are a feature of modern life. Such a structure may be a part of a building, but its open nature, at least on most sides, makes it unlikely that there will be windows or apertures through which light is received. Of course a separate or integral garage may be a building or a part of a building with windows through which rights of light may be acquired.

2.43 As with many questions of the present sort, there is a hazy boundary between structures which are and are not buildings. In one case a structure was erected with vertical columns on stone bases and with crossbeams at various levels which supported planks, so making a form of floor. There was also a covering at the top which served as a roof. The use of the building was to store timber. Three sides of the building were entirely open. A right of light was claimed for the structure. At first instance Chitty J held that the structure was not a building. In the Court of Appeal this question was left open, but it was held that no right of light could have been acquired, because there were no defined apertures.[87]

[85] *Newham v Lawson* (1971) 22 P & CR 852; *Attorney-General v Queen Anne Garden and Mansions Company* (1889) 60 LT 759 (The Guards' Memorial Chapel in London); *Ecclesiastical Commissioners v Kino* (1880) 14 Ch D 213. This last decision is also of significance for the proposition that rights of light acquired for the windows of a building can be transferred to the windows of a new building which are in the same or substantially the same position: see ch 3, section (C)5.

[86] In *Duke of Norfolk v Arbuthnot* (1880) 5 CPD 390, 392 Bramwell LJ said that he doubted whether an easement of light could exist through an arch between a parish church and a chapel, which he considered were two buildings. He also expressed doubt whether a church could be a building for the purposes of s 3 of the Prescription Act 1832. Taken as a whole, this decision does not support the view that an easement of light cannot be acquired for the benefit of a church. A church may need light for the activities within it as much as may any other building.

[87] *Harris v De Pinna* (1886) 33 Ch D 238. The matter of apertures is explained in para 2.45 et seq.

It seems that in principle the express grant of an easement of light in favour of a building not in existence at the date of the grant but to be erected in the future may be valid. Until 2009 such a grant might have been void for non-compliance with the rule against perpetuities, but that rule does not affect easements created by a deed executed on or after 6 April 2010.[88] 2.44

3. Apertures

Given that the dominant land is a building, the next question is whether there is an aperture or apertures through which an easement of light may be acquired. In this context an aperture means a gap in the opaque surfaces impermeable to light with which the building is constructed. This is an easy concept to understand when considering ordinary windows in buildings. It is necessary to mention a number of possible questions which can arise. 2.45

A window will usually be made largely of glass. It is said to be glazed.[89] The detailed configuration of the aperture should not affect its status as something able to acquire an easement of light. Windows may be rectangular or round, or of any other shape. A window may be in the roof (a skylight) or may be in the vertical or horizontal plane, or may slope.[90] Windows in mansard roofs are often of a sloping configuration. A right of light may be acquired for a skylight in the horizontal plane. Natural light which reaches such an aperture may come in part vertically from the sky and be unaffected by building on neighbouring land, but may also come in part horizontally across neighbouring property. Modern buildings such as large office buildings often have curtain walling, that is a structure in which the whole of a facade is glazed save for small structural elements. It may seem unusual to describe this continuous glazing as an aperture, but it can scarcely be doubted that the sides of such structures are capable of acquiring an easement of light. A right of light may be acquired in respect of a greenhouse which is constructed 2.46

[88] Perpetuities and Accumulations Act 2009, ss 1, 15(1). See *Newham v Lawson* (1971) 22 P & CR 852 (right of light); *McGrath v Parkside Hotels Ltd* [2011] EWHC 143 (Ch), [2011] 1 P & CR DG 23 (use of fire escape).

[89] Glass is sometimes considered as a super-cooled liquid with a non-crystalline, ie atomically disordered, structure. It is usually based on silicon dioxide. Glass does not generally permit the transfer through it of the whole of the light which reaches its surface, but only some proportion, varying from 84% up to 100% of the whole of the light, depending on the thickness of the glass and the wavelength of the light. See, eg Feynman, *QED*, referred to in ch 1, n 7.

[90] For example, in *Easton v Isted* [1903] 1 Ch 405, 408 it was held that a right of light could be acquired in favour of an aperture which sloped at an angle between the roof and the side of a conservatory. As Joyce J observed, and as was upheld in the Court of Appeal, 'The sloping top receives rays of light across, and in that sense overlooked the defendant's property in the same manner as, though to a less degree than, the fixed portions of the side'.

mainly of glass.[91] The fact that a window may often be covered by curtains or venetian blinds or movable shutters does not preclude an easement of light being acquired in respect of the window.

2.47 Some modern buildings have an atrium, which is an area within the building not built upon but having a glazed roof. Light is enjoyed at the floor of the atrium through the glazed roof and is also enjoyed by windows in the parts of the structure which face on to the internal atrium. There seems no reason in principle why these windows should not be able to acquire a right of light. In such a case any relevant obstruction of light caused by building on other land will of course be of light passing to the top of the atrium.

2.48 In *Harris v De Pinna*[92] the floors of the structure with mainly open sides were stacked at different times and in different places with piles of timber which prevented or hindered the access of light through the open sides. It was held, assuming that the structure was a building,[93] that there had not been the necessary definite apertures through which light had passed throughout the relevant prescription period. The decision might have been different if there had been no such obstruction of the access of light through the open sides. It does at least seem plain that an aperture may acquire an easement of light for present purposes even if it is open and not glazed.

2.49 An ordinary door without glazing is not an aperture even though it may be opened from time to time or even left open for some time so that light enters a building through it.[94] The reason is that the purpose of a door is to allow access to and egress from a building, rather than to let in light and, given that a door may be open for only limited periods of time, it is difficult to estimate the quantum of light which is lost if natural light passing to that door is obstructed. On the other hand, a door comprised mainly or partly of glass may obviously allow the access of light to a building at any time, and may be designed to do so. There seems no reason in principle why an easement of light should not be acquired in respect of such a door.

2.50 A question which sometimes arises is whether the prescription period for the acquisition of a right of light can start to run during the time when a building is under construction. It is not necessary that a building is actually used and occupied for the prescription period to start to run or continue to run, so that

[91] *Allen v Greenwood* [1980] Ch 119; *Clifford v Holt* [1899] 1 Ch 698. These decisions also establish that a greenhouse is a building. See ch 3, section (B)2, for a consideration of the question whether a particular type of building such as a greenhouse may acquire a right to a particularly high standard of natural light.

[92] *Harris v De Pinna* (1886) 33 Ch D 238. The facts of this decision are further set out in para 2.43.

[93] See para 2.43.

[94] *Levet v Gas Light and Coke Co* [1919] 1 Ch 24. Peterson J said that the authorities showed that the access of light referred to in s 3 of the Prescription Act 1832 was 'access to a window, or an aperture in the nature of a window'.

the fact that occupation of a new building has not commenced does not in itself prevent the period running. For example, a house may be complete and ready for occupation but not actually occupied for, say, three years from the date of completion of the works. The prescription period may run during those three years (as it may run if the building is unoccupied for a time during some later part of the prescription period). The principle as regards buildings under construction appears to be that the prescription period may start to run as soon as the building has apertures which are capable of allowing in the access of light for the purposes of persons such as builders or gas fitters who are completing the construction. The building need not be ready for ordinary occupation at that time. For example, in one case[95] it was held that the prescription period started to run when all external work was done in the construction of a house, the walls were finished, the window apertures were placed in position, the joists for the landings were in, and the roof was completely tiled. It did not matter that items such as frames or sashes for windows or glazing within the windows had not been completed.

An easement of light may be acquired in respect of an aperture even if the room or other area in the building lit by the aperture is unoccupied or unused.[96] 2.51

Other questions may arise relating to apertures, for example whether an easement of light is abandoned if an aperture is blocked up, or whether an aperture created in a redeveloped building but in the same position as the aperture in the old building can have transferred to it an easement of light which was appurtenant to the previous window. These questions are considered elsewhere in this book.[97] 2.52

It is a frequent practice to refer to a right of light as appurtenant to a particular window, and such phraseology is sometimes used in this book. A reason is that the exercise of rights of light may be generally dependent on the characteristics of a particular window, involving such questions as what occurs if the window is altered or there is more than one window providing light to a room, or a window is blocked up. However, an easement of light is strictly appurtenant to a dominant building or a part of a building which is lit through an aperture or apertures. For example, a right of light will remain enforceable, and the burden on the servient land may increase, if the layout or interior of rooms in the dominant building is changed.[98] 2.53

[95] *Collis v Laugher* [1894] 3 Ch 659, following *Courtauld v Legh* (1869) LR 4 Ex 126.

[96] ibid.

[97] For abandonment of an easement see ch 8, section (B), and for the transfer of rights to a new building see ch 3, section (C).

[98] *Carr-Saunders v Dick McNeill Associates* [1986] 1 WLR 922.

3

Content of the Right of Light

(A) THE BASIC PRINCIPLE

1. The General Principle

3.1 The basic principle of law today on the content of a right of light was established by the decision of the House of Lords in *Colls v Home and Colonial Stores Ltd* in 1904.[1] Prior to that decision there were two schools of thought on what was the test for deciding whether an obstruction did or did not infringe an established right of light. One school was that there was no particular standard of light which was protected by an easement of light, and that all that the owner of the dominant building had to show in order to establish an infringement of his easement was that an obstruction had substantially diminished the access of light through the windows in respect of which the easement existed.[2] It is a corollary of this rule that if there was a substantial reduction in the light which passed to an aperture in a well lit room, there would be an infringement of the easement even if after the reduction the room continued to enjoy good light.[3] This approach may owe its origin to the direction given to the jury by Tindal CJ in *Parker v Smith* in 1832,[4] which indicated that once an easement of light was shown to exist, any reduction in the access of light through a relevant aperture created an actionable wrong.

3.2 It was difficult to justify a rule in this extreme form. Such a rule would mean that a small reduction of the amount of light received through a window to a room which enjoyed excellent light would be an actionable wrong even though the room would still receive good light after the reduction. Strong authority existed for a different school of thought. As long ago as 1826 Best CJ had directed the jury in *Back v Stacey*[5] to a quite different effect, saying that there was no actionable

[1] *Colls v Home and Colonial Stores Ltd* [1904] AC 179.

[2] The high water mark of this approach was the decision of the Court of Appeal in *Warren v Brown* [1902] 1 KB 15. Other passages in the authorities can be found to lend support to this view of the law. For example, in *Scott v Pape* (1886) 31 Ch D 554, 572 Bowen LJ said: 'What the person who has acquired the right is entitled to is not the window but the free access of such an amount of light as has passed through that window'. See also *Yates v Jack* (1866) LR 10 Ch App 295.

[3] This was expressly stated to be the case by Romer LJ in *Warren v Brown* [1902] 1 KB 15, 21.

[4] *Parker v Smith* (1832) 5 C & P 438.

[5] *Back v Stacey* (1826) 2 C & P 465.

wrong unless the reduction in light was substantial and such as to render a house uncomfortable to occupy, or to prevent a business on a property being carried on as beneficially as it was before the reduction. Other expressions of high judicial authority supported a similar rule. In *Clarke v Clarke*[6] Lord Cranworth said that what had to be shown to establish a right of action was that the building erected or extended on the servient land 'caused such an obstruction of light as to interfere with the ordinary occupations of life'. The clearest expression of this approach was that of James LJ in *Kelk v Pearson*,[7] who said:

> The nature and extent of the right before that statute [the Prescription Act 1832] was to have that amount of light through the windows of a house which was sufficient, according to the ordinary notions of mankind, for the comfortable use and enjoyment of that house as a dwelling-house, if it were a dwelling-house, or for the beneficial use and occupation of the house if it were a warehouse, a shop, or other place of business. That was the extent of the easement—a right to prevent your neighbour from building upon his land so as to obstruct the access of sufficient light and air, to such an extent as to render the house substantially less comfortable and enjoyable.

This statement presages the established modern law.

It seems apparent that the second school of thought offered a more satisfactory rule on the standard of light. In *Colls v Home and Colonial Stores Ltd*[8] the House of Lords approved what James LJ had stated and itself stated the rule in much the same words and in the following way: 3.3

> That doctrine … is that generally speaking an owner of ancient lights is entitled to sufficient light according to the ordinary notions of mankind for the comfortable use and enjoyment of his house as a dwelling-house, if it is a dwelling-house, or for the beneficial use and occupation of the house if it is a warehouse, a shop, or other place of business.

This statement has become the established law on the subject ever since and it is now not necessary to explore in any detail the various nuances of expression which emerge from earlier cases. The principle as so stated has been uniformly applied in subsequent decisions, including recent cases.[9]

The test or standard as explained by Lord Lindley contains with it an inevitable element of uncertainty. Since a rigid rule that any substantial reduction in light 3.4

[6] *Clarke v Clarke* (1865) LR 1 Ch App 16, 20, 21 (Lord Cranworth).

[7] *Kelk v Pearson* (1871) LR 6 Ch App 809, 811 (James LJ). James LJ repeated this explanation of the law in *City of London Brewery Co v Tennant* (1873) LR 9 Ch App 212

[8] *Colls v Home and Colonial Stores Ltd* [1904] AC 179, 208 (Lord Lindley). Lord Lindley took his expression of principle from what had been said by James LJ in *City of London Brewery Co v Tennant* (1873) 9 Ch App 212, 216-17.

[9] See, eg *Higgins v Betts* [1905] 2 Ch 210; *Regan v Paul Properties Ltd* [2007] Ch 135 [55] (Mummery LJ); *Tamares (Vincent Square) Ltd v Fairpoint Properties (Vincent Square) Ltd* [2006] EWHC 3589 (Ch), [2007] 1 WLR 2148. In *Allen v Greenwood* [1980] Ch 119, 135 Buckley LJ re-stated the principle in the following way: 'The amount of light to which a dominant owner is entitled under a prescriptive claim is sufficient light, according to ordinary notions, for the comfortable or beneficial use of the building in question, again according to ordinary notions, for such purposes as would constitute normal uses of a building of its particular character.' This decision concerned a greenhouse and is discussed further at para 3.16 et seq.

through an aperture will necessarily constitute an actionable injury was rejected it was recognised that the application of the correct and more flexible test might involve some subjective judgment in each case and that the application of the test might depend on the character and layout of the property which enjoyed the benefit of the easement. Lord Lindley recognised this element of uncertainty but pointed out that a similar uncertainty exists in all cases of nuisance (for example, interference with the use of property by unreasonable noise from a neighbouring property).[10]

2. Other Matters

3.5 A suggestion is sometimes made that there should be different tests for residential and commercial buildings. The formulation by Lord Lindley and James LJ does distinguish linguistically between residential buildings, where convenient use and enjoyment is the test, and commercial buildings, where beneficial use and enjoyment is the test.[11] This is itself a recognition that a different amount of natural light may be needed for a property such as a house or flat, as a place of rest and recreation, as compared to a commercial property where the efficiency and utility of the business may be a more important consideration. Reference is made to this point again when the measurement of a sufficiency of light is considered.[12]

3.6 Prior to the decision in *Colls v Home and Colonial Stores Ltd* there were suggestions that some certainty could be introduced into the subject by a rule that the owner of the dominant building retained sufficient light to his property provided that any obstruction was built within the '45° angle'. What this meant is that a notional diagonal line at an angle of 45° from the vertical was drawn outwards from the street level of the dominant building, and that an obstruction could not constitute an actionable injury if light could still pass freely to the dominant building above this line. The origin of this test appears to have been section 85 of the Metropolitan Management Amendment Act 1862, which aimed to regulate the distance between buildings, and the height of the buildings, on new streets.[13]

[10] *Colls v Home and Colonial Stores Ltd* [1904] AC 179, 208.

[11] See para 3.3 and n 8. A century or more ago the word 'house' was sometimes used with a wider meaning than today, to include buildings used for commercial purposes.

[12] See ch 6.

[13] S 85 (now repealed) read: 'No building, except a church or chapel, shall be erected, on the side of any new street of a less width than 50 feet, which shall exceed in height the distance from the external wall or front of such building to the opposite side of such street, without the consent in writing of the Metropolitan Board of Works; nor shall the height of any building so erected be at any time subsequently increased so as to exceed such distance without such consent; and in determining the height of such building the measurement shall be taken from the level of the centre of the street immediately opposite the building up to the parapet or eaves of such building.' See *Hackett v Baiss* (1875) LR 20 Eq 494, 498 (Jessel MR) for the reliance on this statutory provision. The language of s 85 leads to a 45° angle calculation. The 45° angle test is usually described in relation to the erection of a new building on the opposite side of the street from an existing building, but it could of course be applied to a new building on any side of an existing building

A purpose of this legislation may have been to impose on new streets minimum standards of daylight and air, in contrast to the conditions in some Victorian slum areas in London, with a view to promoting health and hygiene, so that any effect of protecting the access of natural light to buildings fronting the new street may have been incidental. One version of the test seems to have been that an obstruction which went above the 45° angle necessarily amounted to an actionable injury to an easement of light, whereas an obstruction which stopped below the 45° angle might or might not be an actionable injury, depending upon the facts of the particular case.[14] A more flexible version of the test was to say that the 45° angle criterion was not a positive rule of law, but merely one element to be taken into account in deciding the question of fact of whether there is an undue interference with an access of light.[15] Once again, the House of Lords in *Colls v Home and Colonial Stores Ltd* preferred a more flexible approach, Lord Lindley observing that there was no rule of law that if a person had 45° of unobstructed light left to him through a particular window he could not maintain an action for a nuisance caused by diminishing the light which previously came through that window. However Lord Lindley added that experience showed that it was, generally speaking, a fair working rule to consider that no substantial injury is done to a plaintiff where an angle of 45° is left to him, especially if there is good light from other directions as well.[16] Today, any use of the 45° test has been largely superseded as a means of determining whether a sufficiency of light exists in a room by the use of the Waldram diagram method used by rights of light surveyors.[17] Assessments not wholly dissimilar to the 45° test are suggested in the BRE Guide, a document designed to assist planning authorities and others in the design of new buildings.[18]

Inevitably the application of the now established test requires a comparison between the room as lit through a window which enjoys the easement of light prior to the obstruction on the servient land and the same room as lit through the same window after the erection of the obstruction on the servient land. Three types of case may be considered: 3.7

(a) The first is where the room lit by the aperture in the dominant building is sufficiently lit prior to the obstruction on the servient land and after the effect of the obstruction is taken into account the room in the dominant building remains sufficiently lit. In such a case there is no actionable injury.

(b) The second case is where the room lit by the aperture in the dominant building is sufficiently lit prior to the obstruction but after the obstruction becomes insufficiently lit. In this case there will be an actionable injury.

[14] This was the approach adopted by Jessel MR in *Hackett v Bates*.

[15] *City of London Brewery Co v Tennant* (1873) LR 9 Ch App 212, 220 (James LJ). See also *Ecclesiastical Commissioners v Kino* (1880) 14 Ch D 213, 228 (Cotton LJ).

[16] *Colls v Home and Colonial Stores Ltd* [1904] AC 179, 210.

[17] See ch 6.

[18] Paul Littlefair, *Site Layout and Planning for Daylight and Sunlight—A Guide to Good Practice*, 2nd edn (Watford, BRE Trust, 2011) ('the BRE Guide'). See ch 10, section (C).

(c) The third case is where the room lit by the aperture in the dominant building is insufficiently lit prior to the erection of the obstruction and becomes more insufficiently or badly lit after the erection of the obstruction. In this case also there will be an actionable injury.

3.8 The test for determining whether there has been an actionable injury applies in whatever way the easement of light has come into being. As far as prescriptive easements are concerned, the Prescription Act 1832 introduced for easements of light, and for easements generally, a new method of acquiring an easement by prescription, but it did not alter the content of the easement of light as discussed in this chapter. Thus what the 1832 Act did was to create a fresh origin for an easement of light; not to affect the test for deciding whether there was in any particular case an infringement of that easement, given that it has been brought into existence.[19] The same test applies to an easement of light created by implication and normally to an easement of light created by express language in a deed. The express language of a deed may indicate some different standard[20] and, of course, a different degree of protection to the dominant land can be obtained by the express language of a restrictive covenant.[21]

3.9 It must be emphasised that an easement of light protects a building against the reduction to an unacceptable extent of the access of natural light to that building across other property. It does not offer protection against a loss of an attractive view or prospect, or against a loss of privacy.[22] As long ago as 1670 a plaintiff obtained a remedy in an action on the case when his neighbour had erected a brick wall, but the judgment was held to be an error and was reversed in the Court of King's Bench, since the wall had not caused any loss of light to the plaintiff's shop premises but had merely adversely affected their prospect.[23] In another old case, Lord Hardwicke LC in Chancery said that the reduction in light caused to a property by the building of a wall near to it did not sufficiently affect the access of light so as to create an actionable injury, and added: 'It is true that the value of the plaintiff's house may be reduced by rendering the prospect less pleasant, but that is no reason to hinder a man from building on his own ground.'[24] Equally, the

[19] *Colls v Home and Colonial Stores Ltd* [1904] AC 179, 210 (Lord Lindley).

[20] *Scott v Pape* (1886) 31 Ch D 554, 571 (Bowen LJ); *Allen v Greenwood* [1980] Ch 119, 132 (Goff LJ).

[21] See ch 2, section (C)1 for restrictive covenants.

[22] *Bland v Moseley* (1587), cited by Lord Coke in *Aldred's case* (1610) 9 Co Rep 57b; *Phipps v Pears* [1965] QB 76; *Browne v Flower* [1911] 1 Ch 219.

[23] *Knowles v Richardson* (1670) 1 Mod Rep 55.

[24] *Fishmongers Company v East India Company* (1752) 1 Dick 163; *Dalton v Angus* (1881) 6 App Cas 740, 824 (Lord Blackburn). In *Tapling v Jones* (1865) 11 HLC 290, 305 Lord Westbury said: 'If A is the owner of beautiful gardens and pleasure grounds, and B is the owner of an adjoining piece of land, B may build on it a manufactory with a hundred windows overlooking the pleasure grounds, and A has neither more nor less than the right which he previously had, of erecting on his land a building of such height and extent as will shut out the windows of the newly erected manufactory'. Nor is there known to the law an easement to be protected from the weather: *Phipps v Pears* [1965] QB 76, 83 (Lord Denning MR).

erection of a building will not be prevented because it would obstruct the view towards commercial premises and reduce customers.[25] It should also be stressed that what is protected by an easement of light is the illumination of a room or other area within a building by the access of natural daylight from the sky. Daylight or natural light from the sky is sometimes divided into direct sunlight (light which appears to emanate directly from the sun) and other light. Direct sunlight is valued by some owners and occupiers of buildings. An easement of light gives no separate and specific right to direct sunlight. The way in which the amount of light which illuminates a room through a particular aperture, the sky factor and the Waldram diagram methodology, concentrate on direct sunlight from a proportion of the total notionally available sky.[26]

It may be noted that when reference is made in the authorities to an infringement of an easement of light, or to an anticipated injury, the language used is that a nuisance has been or may be committed.[27] A nuisance is a condition or activity which interferes with the use or enjoyment of land.[28] It is usually an activity carried out on one person's land, such as the creation of noise or fumes, which interferes with the enjoyment of neighbouring land. Such activities may be a private nuisance. Other activities, notably the obstruction of a highway, may be a public nuisance. A private nuisance is a form of tort, that is a civil wrong independent of contract. Easements are created out of contractual or consensual arrangements. This is certainly true of easements created expressly or impliedly by a deed. Even where an easement is created by long use or prescription, the general legal theory is that the easement has its origin in a presumed grant.[29] It may therefore seem curious that a breach of the terms of the grant is considered to be a tort. Matters such as this may be mainly of historical interest and not have much practical importance today when all remedies are normally available in all courts. There may still be some practical consequence of the classification of the wrong. For example, the principles of remoteness of damage, and thus the amount of damages that may be recovered, are not the same in contract and in tort, and there are occasions, albeit today very limited, on which an activity which constitutes a nuisance may be abated by the private actions of the person who is wronged, as opposed to the commencement of legal proceedings.[30] 3.10

[25] *Butt v Imperial Gas Company* (1866) LR 2 Ch App 158.

[26] The measurement of light and the Waldram diagram methodology are explained in ch 6. Guidance on light from the sky and sunlighting are given in separate parts of the BRE Guide. See ch 10. When assessing whether a new building on the servient land will be an infringement of an easement of light, reflected light, for example from a wall in that building, is generally said to be ignored: see para 3.31.

[27] See eg *Lane v Capsey* [1891] 3 Ch 411, 415 (Chitty J) where the judge discussed the availability of old procedures for preventing a nuisance caused by the obstruction of a right of way.

[28] See Buckley, *The Law of Nuisance*, 5th edn (London, Lexis/Nexis, 2011).

[29] *Gardner v Hodgsons Kingston Brewery Co* [1903] AC 229, 239 in which Lord Lindley said: 'The common law doctrine is that all prescription presumes a grant.' One form of prescription, the acquisition of an easement of light under s 3 of the Prescription Act 1832, does not depend on the presumption of a grant. See ch 5, para 5.34(f).

[30] See ch 7, section (D) for the abatement of a nuisance.

3.11 Now that the general principle governing the content of an easement of light has been discussed it is necessary to go on to examine particular instances and problems which may arise in the application of that principle to particular situations.

(B) PARTICULAR SITUATIONS

1. Purposes of the Reception of Light

3.12 Light is received in a building through apertures so as to provide that illumination during the hours of daylight which, in the absence of artificial lighting, is necessary for the reasonable use and enjoyment of the building by carrying out ordinary activities such as reading. A question which arises is whether an easement of light can be obtained where the light is needed for, or is to be used for, purposes other than illumination to facilitate normal activities. There are three situations to consider:

(a) reception of television and similar signals;
(b) the use of solar panels; and
(c) light used as a source of heat as well as illumination.

3.13 Signals received for television viewing, whether from a terrestrial or satellite source, and other than through transmission by cables, are a form of electromagnetic radiation akin to light save that they are not within the visible spectrum.[31] No easement protecting the receipt of such signals can exist, whether created by grant or by prescription. A reason is that the purpose of light is to provide illumination and to enable visual perception through the human eye. Television signals, and similar signals such as radio signals and signals to mobile telephones and similar devices, are not visible and do not fulfil this purpose. A further reason is that rights of light are strictly a matter between immediate neighbours. In addition a right to light is a right to receive light to a building through a defined aperture. Television and similar signals do not reach buildings by a particular aperture but are able to pass through solid objects such as walls or are received by an aerial and then transmitted to a television set or similar receiver.[32]

3.14 Solar panels are coming increasingly into use as a means of generating electricity without the burning of fossil fuels and thus the emission of carbon dioxide into the atmosphere. The usual type of photovoltaic panel generates electricity through the photo-electric effect. Photons, the constituents of light, play on metal panels such that the energy of the photons dislodges electrons in the metal, and

[31] See ch 6, section (B)1.
[32] *Hunter v Canary Wharf Ltd* [1997] AC 655, 709 (Lord Hoffmann).

an electric current can be produced in this way.[33] Different metals are more apt to release electrons when they receive light and other radiation at different wavelengths or energy levels. Where overshadowing occurs it can have a serious effect on the electrical output of an array of photovoltaic cells. It is extremely unlikely that an easement can exist for the uninterrupted passage of light to solar panels. The same considerations apply as to television reception. Solar panels are of course placed on the exterior or outside of buildings, and the passage of light to them is not through an aperture in the building so as to illuminate the interior of that building. In its recent report on rights of light the Law Commission did not recommend that the access of light to photovoltaic panels should be protected.[34] Legislation in other countries permits the creation of what are in effect easements to protect sunlight to solar panels. Solar panels are popular in California, and section 801.5 of the California Civil Code permits agreements for 'the right of receiving sunlight across real property of anyone for a solar energy system'.

The radiation which is light, as well as radiation in other wavelengths, can heat objects which absorb the radiation. The use of microwave ovens is a good example of this process. The question which arises is whether there can be an easement of light where the purpose of its passage is to heat areas. It does appear that in limited circumstances this may be possible. As is explained later in this chapter, an easement for a higher standard of light than that generally required for the reasonable illumination of a building may be acquired by an express grant or by prescription.[35] The amount of light necessary for a greenhouse has been held to be the subject of an easement in accordance with this principle.[36] One of the purposes of the access of light to a greenhouse is to maintain it at a sufficiently high temperature to encourage the growth of plants.[37] Given that in principle there can 3.15

[33] See ch 6. It was for his work in 1905 explaining the photo-electric effect that Einstein was awarded a Nobel prize.

[34] Law Commission, *Rights to Light* (Law Com No 356, 2014) para 2.83. This report is considered more generally in ch 12. It is possible that overshadowing of photovoltaic cells on other buildings is something which will be taken into account by local planning authorities in deciding whether to grant planning permission for a new development. See BRE Guide, ch 4. The BRE Guide is considered generally in ch 10. In *Allen v Greenwood* [1980] Ch 119, 134, [1979] 2 WLR 187, Goff LJ left it open for further decision whether there could be some form of protection for solar heating. He said that it might be possible and right to separate the heat, or some other property of the sun, from its light. It is not easy to know what to make of this. The electromagnetic radiation emitted by the sun is the transfer of energy across space. It performs three separate functions: (a) it stimulates electrical activity in the eyes of living creatures, including humans, which is perceived by their brains as vision; (b) it is absorbed by atoms and molecules of matter and the imparted kinetic energy is heat; (c) the energy of photons of the radiation may dislodge electrons from their orbitals around the nuclei of atoms in matter and this, the photovoltaic effect, can be gathered to create an electrical current. It appears as a general proposition of law (and subject to what is said in the next paragraph) that it is only the first of these effects which is relevant to rights of light.

[35] See para 3.16 et seq.

[36] *Allen v Greenwood* [1980] Ch 119.

[37] In *Allen v Greenwood* Goff LJ at p 134 said that he accepted that warmth was an inseparable process of daylight, which led him to the conclusion that a higher than normal standard of light could be acquired by prescription for the benefit of properties on the possibility that the owner of the servient land was entitled to all of the benefits of the light including its warming effect. The correct analysis is

be such an easement of light the purpose of which is in part to maintain the heat within a structure, it is likely that only in limited circumstances will this be of any relevance. Apart from a greenhouse or conservatory attached to a property, an indoor or covered swimming pool might be a further example.[38] The receipt of light to outdoor or open areas such as an outdoor swimming pool cannot be the subject of an easement of light, since that easement is in law confined to the receipt of natural light to buildings through defined apertures.[39]

2. A Higher Standard

3.16 A question which sometimes arises is whether a property may acquire a right of light which is of a higher standard than that which would be applicable under the general principle. A number of reasons may explain why a particular property requires an exceptional amount of light: for example, the use of the property (the most usual reason), or its layout or its locality. Undoubtedly the language of a deed by which an easement of light is expressly created may specify some particular standard, which may be higher or lower than the standard enjoined by the application of the general principle.[40] A higher standard may be specified in some general way, such as an amount of light needed for a particular use of the dominant building where that building needs a particularly high amount of natural light, or may be specified by some more precise formula such as that particular rooms are to enjoy a sufficiency of light determined by some criterion or method of measurement such as a 0.2 per cent 'sky factor'[41] over at least 75 per cent of their area. Such a specification would be in contrast to the application of the general principle today, which is often that a room may be taken to be sufficiently lit if at least 50 per cent of its area at a given height above the floor receives a particular standard of light.[42] However, clear words will usually be needed if the right to an exceptionally high standard of light is to be created, and the same requirement applies to the express creation of a standard of light lower than the normal

that electromagnetic radiation in the visible spectrum (which we call light) stimulates electrical activity in the eyes of living persons (which we call vision) and imparts kinetic energy to the atoms and molecules which constituent matter (so producing what we call heat). It also has other effects, such as photosynthesis in plants. Any principled discussion of the permitted content of an easement of light should pay close regard to these distinctions.

[38] In *Allen v Greenwood* Goff LJ at p 133 suggested that where light entered a window of an indoor swimming pool and an obstruction on the servient land left enough light passable through the window for ordinary illumination, there would not be an infringement of the easement simply because the remaining light did not produce as much warmth as was previously produced.

[39] See ch 2, section (D)3.

[40] *Allen v Greenwood* [1980] Ch 119, 132 (Goff LJ).

[41] This method of measuring a sufficiency of light is explained in ch 6.

[42] See ch 6 for the details of the application of this test as carried out by rights of light surveyors.

standard or otherwise limited in some way.[43] There are well-known forms of words, used by conveyancers and found in books of precedents, for the creation of easements of light, for example: 'the right to the free and unobstructed passage of light and air to the premises at all times', and such language will nearly always create a right of light to the usual standard. It is suggested in the next paragraph that there could be exceptional circumstances in which a requirement for an unusual standard of light could be derived from the factual circumstances known to the parties at the time of the grant. The present discussion is concerned with buildings with a particular specialised use, such as a greenhouse or conservatory. The more general question of whether a different standard should apply to residential as opposed to commercial buildings is mentioned elsewhere.[44]

The question stated at the beginning of the last paragraph is usually asked in respect of a right of light acquired by prescription. An answer usually given to the question in the context of a prescriptive easement, as will be explained, is that an unusually high standard of light may be acquired by the use of the dominant building for a particular purpose having endured during the prescription period when that purpose required and received a particularly high standard of light. However, where the right of light is created by an express or implied grant (and assuming in the case of an express grant that the deed of grant does not itself specify a particular standard of light), there seems to be no reason in principle why in an exceptional case a particular use to which the dominant building is put at the date of the deed should not indicate that it needs and is to have a particularly high standard of light. Such a possible result would accord with the well-known principle of construction that the meaning of a document is to be elucidated by reference to all relevant facts and matters known to the parties at the time of the execution of the document—what is sometimes called the 'matrix of fact'.[45] 3.17

Where a right of light comes into being as a result of a restrictive covenant or by reason of the implied term in a sale or lease not to derogate from the grant, the standard of light protected in the property which is benefited by the right may be greater than that enjoined by the application of the general principle applicable to an easement of light. A restrictive covenant may specify that no obstruction on the land burdened by the covenant shall be erected which reduces the access of light to the land of the covenantee below some specified level. The covenant would then be akin to an expressly created easement which specified a particular 3.18

[43] *Frogmore Developments Ltd v Shirayama Shokusan Co Ltd* [2000] 1 EGLR 121. What may be of importance in addition to the language of a deed is the surrounding circumstances, which may indicate that a right to some particular standard of light was intended, applying the general rule that the matrix of fact surrounding a contractual document may be of assistance in interpreting the meaning of the document: see, eg *Rainy Sky SA v Kookmin Bank* [2011] UKSC 50, [2011] 1 WLR 2900; *Chartbrook Ltd v Persimmon Homes Ltd* [2009] 1 AC 1101.

[44] See ch 6, para 6.39(vi).

[45] *Prenn v Simmonds* [1971] 1 WLR 1381; *Investors Compensation Scheme Ltd v West Bromwich Building Society* [1998] 1 WLR 896; *Rainy Sky SA v Kookmin Bank* [2011] UKSC 50, [2011] 1 WLR 2900. See also n 43.

standard of light.[46] The extent of the obligation of a seller or landlord under the implied covenant not to derogate from the grant may depend on the use to which it is contemplated at the time of the grant that the property sold or let will be put. Thus if the grant or demise is made for a particular purpose, the grantor or lessor comes under an obligation not to use the land retained by him in such a way as to render the land granted or demised unfit or materially less fit for the purpose for which the grant or demise was made.[47] A particular use contemplated at the date of the grant may require a higher standard of light than the general standard, so that the erection of an obstruction by the seller or the landlord which impeded the access of light to the property transferred as needed for that particular use might be a breach of the implied obligation as to derogation from grant.

3.19 An infringement of a right of light is a nuisance. In the case of many nuisances the locality of the premises adversely affected may be relevant to the question of whether particular activities constitute a nuisance. A dwelling in a town cannot be expected to have as pure air or to be as free from smoke or noise as would a dwelling in the country some distance away from other dwellings.[48] The test is said in these instances to be elastic. The authorities are unclear on whether the locality of the property is a significant factor to be taken into account when deciding whether there is an actionable injury to a property by reason of a reduction in light passing to it. One view suggests that the standard of light remaining after an obstruction, so as to prevent the existence of a nuisance, is of necessity an absolute standard. As it was put in one decision, 'The human eye requires as much light for comfortable reading or sewing in Darlington Street, Wolverhampton, as in Mayfair.'[49] On the other hand, other decisions suggest that locality may have a place to play in the decision on whether an obstruction to light is an actionable injury,[50] so that a decision on what according to the ordinary notions of mankind is sufficient light for the comfortable use and enjoyment of a house can vary according to the location of the house.[51] In practice, the general amenities expected from a property do vary according to its position and the nature of the locality in which the property is situated. This is particularly the case for dwellings. A person living in an urban area may be less disturbed by some loss of natural light than would a person who lived in a rural village. The assessment of nuisances caused by noise or impurities

[46] For the differences between an easement and a restrictive covenant see ch 2, para 2.31.

[47] *Browne v Flower* [1911] 1 Ch 219, 225 (Parker J). In *Aldin v Latimer Clark, Muirhead & Co* [1894] 2 Ch 457 the obstruction of the passage of air to premises let as sheds in which to dry timber and which needed a flow of air for that purpose was held to be a derogation from grant. See also *Lyttelton Times Co Ltd v Warners Ltd* [1907] AC 476.

[48] *Colls v Home and Colonial Stores Ltd* [1904] AC 179, 185 (Lord Halsbury); *Polsue & Alfieri Ltd v Rushmer* [1907] AC 121: see this decision in the Court of Appeal at [1906] 1 Ch 234, 249 (Lord Cozens-Hardy LJ) who said that it was not reasonable to expect the same quiet and freedom from noise caused by printing machines in an area devoted to the printing trade as might be expected in a purely residential neighbourhood.

[49] *Hortons Estate Ltd v James Beattie Ltd* [1927] 1 Ch 75, 78 (Russell J).

[50] See *Ough v King* [1967] 1 WLR 1547, 1552 (Lord Denning MR); *Fishenden v Higgs & Hill Ltd* (1935) 153 LT 128, 140 (Romer J).

[51] *Kine v Jolly* [1905] 1 Ch 480, 497 (Romer LJ); see on appeal at [1907] AC 1.

in the air is elastic, depending upon the character of the locality of the property, and it is difficult to see why the same is not the case in deciding whether there is a nuisance or an actionable injury constituted by a reduction in the access of natural light to a property. Of course if a rigid test for measuring a sufficiency of light, such as a minimum sky factor of at least 0.2 per cent being available over at least 50 per cent of a room, as described in detail in Chapter 6 is used, then there is no opportunity to differentiate between properties in different localities, and this may be one argument against the adoption of such a test, at any rate as a rigid rule.

There was some older authority for saying that even 20 years of access of light greater than that required for general purposes, to a property which required that greater light, would not create an easement by prescription giving an entitlement to the greater amount of light.[52] However, other authority suggested that an easement of light obtained by prescription could give an entitlement to a higher standard of light than that provided by the general principle.[53] The issue was resolved in *Allen v Greenwood*,[54] in which it was held by the Court of Appeal that an unusually large amount of light could be acquired by prescription for the purposes of providing light to a domestic greenhouse. If this principle can be applied to a domestic greenhouse then it can equally be applied to a commercial greenhouse or any similar premises needing a large amount of light. Other premises which might require a particularly high standard of light could be picture galleries or the terraces of cafes, or properties used for processes needing particular precision, such as watch repairing or gem cutting. It is of interest that the primary conclusion of Buckley LJ in this case was that, given the use of the dominant land as a greenhouse, and the need for an exceptional amount of light for that use, an easement of light could be acquired by prescription so as to provide that unusual amount of light by reference to the general principle laid down in the *Colls* case.[55] 3.20

There is a possible analogy in this area of the law with the acquisition by prescription of an easement of way. Rights of way can exist for passage by foot, or passage by foot and with animals, or passage by foot and with animals and vehicles. The nature of the enjoyment of the right of way over the prescription period dictates which category of easement is acquired under section 2 of the Prescription Act 1832. The more intense the use has been, for example by vehicles as well as on foot, the more likely it is that the easement in question will be an easement for use of 3.21

[52] *Ambler v Gordon* [1905] 1 KB 417, 424 (Bray J). In *Colls v Home and Colonial Stores* [1904] AC 179, 204 Lord Davey reserved his position on the question.

[53] In *Lanfranchi v Mackenzie* (1867) LR 4 Eq 421 Malins V-C held that in principle such an easement for an extraordinarily amount of light could be acquired for premises used for displaying samples of raw silk to customers. In *Lazarus v Artistic Photographic Co* [1897] 2 Ch 214 Kekewich J reached a similar conclusion in respect of premises used for photography, which depended on an unusual amount of light to effect the necessary chemical processes. This again raises the question of whether an easement of light is for the protection of the access of light for purposes of illumination, or whether the easement can protect other effects of light such as creating heat by the transfer of energy or the carrying out of chemical processes. This last matter is discussed in paras 3.12–3.15.

[54] *Allen v Greenwood* [1980] Ch 119.

[55] ibid, 136.

the way by vehicles as well as by foot. The analogy is that if the access of light has been intense, in the sense that an unusually high amount of light has been received such as is required for a particular use, then that suggests that an easement may be acquired by prescription for that unusually high amount of light.[56]

3.22 A question which can arise is whether a building with stained glass windows (often a building used for religious services) can acquire by prescription a right to an unusually high amount of light, since the stained glass may prevent the transfer of light which would pass through ordinary glass. It is likely that in accordance with the principles here described the right to an unusually high amount of light can be acquired by prescription through stained glass windows.[57] It should be noted that in such a case what would be sought to be established would not be that an unusually high amount of illumination should reach the interior of the building, but rather that an unusually high amount of light should reach the exterior surfaces of the stained glass windows, since only a limited amount of that light would pass through the windows and so reach the interior of the building.

3.23 In order that an easement can be acquired by prescription for the access of an unusually high amount of light to the dominant building, it appears to be necessary that three conditions have to be fulfilled:

(a) The use of the dominant building during the prescription period has to have been a use which requires an unusually high amount of light.
(b) An unusually high amount of light must actually have been received to the premises in order to accommodate that use during the prescription period.
(c) The servient owner must have known during the prescription period that an unusually high amount of light was needed in order to serve a particular use within the dominant building.

The third of the conditions is perhaps unusual in that in general it is irrelevant to the acquisition of an easement of light by prescription that the owner of the servient land did or did not know what use was actually being carried on in the dominant building. It seems probable that the requisite knowledge on the part of the owner of the servient land is both knowledge of the use of the dominant building, and knowledge that that use requires an unusually high standard of light. The three factors must probably have been present throughout the whole of the prescription period, if the claim to an unusually high standard of light is to be sustainable. It may be useful in this type of case to distinguish between two situations. One situation is where the dominant building is by its nature and form

[56] See *Allen v Greenwood* [1980] Ch 119, 137 (Buckley LJ).

[57] *Attorney-General v Queen Ann Garden and Mansions Co* (1889) 60 LT 759. See however *Newham v Lawson* (1971) 22 P & CR 852, 859 where Plowman J said: 'I very much doubt, as a matter of law, whether the plaintiffs who have a prescriptive right of light through church windows are entitled to claim any greater degree of protection if those windows are stained glass windows than if they were clear glass windows.' The reasoning of the judge was that by introducing stained glass into an aperture, so making the aperture opaque or semi-opaque, the dominant owner was by his own acts increasing the burden on the servient land.

of construction likely to require unusually good light for its use, examples being a greenhouse or a conservatory or an artist's studio. In such a case the requisite knowledge of the owner of the servient land may readily be proved, even if the precise use is not known to that owner. The other situation is where the dominant building may of its nature be put to a number of purposes of which one, the actual use, requires unusually good light. In such a case it will be necessary to show that the owner of the servient land knew of the particular actual use to which the dominant building was being put.

In summary therefore, an easement of light entitling the dominant owner to the access of a greater amount of light than would be available by the application of the general principle may be acquired: 3.24

(a) by an express provision in a deed creating the easement which specifies the greater amount of light or specifies that light is to be received suitable for a particular use which requires that greater amount of light; and
(b) in the case of an implied grant of an easement arising from the circumstances of a deed where the need for the greater amount of light was known to the parties at the time of the deed;
(c) where an easement is acquired by prescription, and during the prescription period the dominant building has been used for a purpose requiring a greater amount of light than would be required for the generality of premises and that amount of light has been received during the prescription period and during that period the servient owner has known of the need in the dominant building for the greater amount of light because of the particular use of the dominant building.

In addition, a right to an unusual high standard of light may be acquired by virtue of a restrictive covenant or by the operation of the doctrine of derogation from grant.

It is possible that due to some activity on neighbouring land a property may receive an excess of light, or light in an unacceptable form. An illustration of this situation is a New Zealand case in which light from the sun was reflected by the glass roof of a veranda, so that a dazzling glare was thrown on neighbouring properties. It was held that this constituted a nuisance in accordance with the general law of nuisance, rather than the breach of an easement.[58] 3.25

3. Different Sources of Light and Reflected Light

(a) The General Rules

The law as so far described has been founded on the assumption that the room or other area which receives light from an aperture receives its light from that 3.26

[58] *Bank of New Zealand v Greenwood* [1984] 1 NZLR 525.

aperture alone. In fact many rooms receive light from more than one window or aperture. The question of principle which then arises is whether, if one window is obstructed, the light which is received from one or more other windows is to be taken into account in deciding whether after the obstruction to the first window the room retains a sufficiency of natural light by reason of the light received from the other window or windows. The answer given by the authorities is that (a) if the other window itself enjoys a right to the access of light through it, then account is to be taken of that light, but (b) if the other window has no such right, then any light received through that window is to be ignored.[59]

3.27 The first limb of the rule, that natural light from other sources themselves enjoying rights of light[60] may be taken into account in deciding whether a room remains adequately lit after an obstruction to the light from one source, is readily understandable. If a room is well lit from windows A and B, and the light received through window A is reduced, but leaving an overall sufficiency of light in the room when account is taken of light received through window B, the owner of the dominant building will be able, if in the future it becomes necessary, to prevent a further reduction of light from window B by asserting his right to receive light through window B. In effect the owner of servient land who obstructs window A increases the burden on the owner of the same or other servient land as regards window B. It may be that the simplicity of the first limb of the rule has to give way to a more pragmatic approach in certain circumstances.[61]

3.28 The second limb of the rule, that no account is to be taken of light received from a different source of light if there is no enforceable right to the receipt of light from that different source, seems more problematical. There are competing considerations. On the one hand it is correct to say that the dominant owner is put in a precarious position if the other source may be obstructed at any time, so that he may be faced with a poorly lit room and have no remedy against anyone. On the other hand there could occur a situation in which window A is obstructed such that an actionable injury is created if light from window B is ignored, when in fact good light is received through window B so that the room remains well lit. The dominant owner will then obtain remedies appropriate to a room which is notionally poorly lit but which is in fact well lit. The prospect that there will in the future be an obstruction of window B may in fact be remote, for instance because planning policies and restrictions may make it unlikely that any building would be erected so as to obstruct the light to window B, or because other persons such as the owners of an estate may have the benefit of a restrictive covenant which would prevent development which would obstruct window B. In such a case the dominant owner

[59] *Colls v Home and Colonial Stores Ltd* [1904] AC 179, 210–11 (Lord Lindley); *Jolly v Kine* [1907] AC 1, 7–8 (Lord Atkinson).

[60] Any other source of natural light may be sufficient, for example light from a skylight: *Smith v Evangelisation Society (Incorporated) Trust* [1933] Ch 515.

[61] See section (C)8 of this chapter for the tension between principles which can arise in this area of the law.

may obtain damages on the footing that a room is insufficiently well lit when in fact it is well lit and is likely to remain so, at any rate for some considerable time. Despite these difficulties the rule of law has been laid down twice by decisions of the House of Lords, and so must be applied with both its limbs. One possible solution to the difficulty described in this paragraph is that in the circumstances postulated, a court might refuse an injunction to the dominant owner and award him only limited damages.[62] The rule as stated in this paragraph applies when a room contains two or more windows and there is an obstruction of the access of light to one window without any alteration to any window. The considerations may not be wholly the same when existing windows are altered in some way or are incorporated with alterations in their horizontal or vertical plane in a redeveloped building. The effect of such an alteration is mentioned in the next paragraph and is discussed more fully later in this chapter in connection with alterations to windows and the replacement of windows in redeveloped buildings.[63]

The potential injustice in the second limb of the rule established by the House of Lords has led to some degree of tempering of the consequences of the rule. In one case[64] a building with windows having rights of light was demolished and replaced by a new building in which the windows were to some extent co-incident in area with those of the previous building. There is a principle that when windows in a new building wholly or partly replicate those in a previous building which had rights of light the rights may sometimes be transferred to the new windows.[65] In such a case the second limb of the rule, if applied literally, suggests that in deciding whether there is an actionable obstruction to the new windows the light which enters the new windows through the area which is coincident with the old windows (to which rights of light are transferred) must be taken into account, but that the light which enters through the remainder of the new windows (to which no rights of light are transferred) must be ignored. It would be as if the greater part of the new windows had to be regarded as notionally blocked off. The Court refused to accept that this unsatisfactory conclusion was the result of what had been said in the House of Lords in the *Colls* case, and held that all light entering through the whole of the new windows had to be taken into account in deciding whether there was any actionable obstruction. The reason given for this decision was that the rule stated in the *Colls* decision must give way to the wider principle that a person cannot by his own acts increase the burden on the servient land.[66] 3.29

The rules established in the *Colls* decision were applied in unusual circumstances in a subsequent case.[67] A window in a room had acquired a right of light by prescription. The servient owner obstructed that window. At the beginning of 3.30

[62] Remedies are discussed in ch 7.
[63] See section (C) of this chapter.
[64] *News of the World Ltd v Allen Fairhead & Sons Ltd* [1931] 2 Ch 402.
[65] See section (C)5 of this chapter.
[66] *News of the World Ltd v Allen Fairhead & Sons Ltd* [1931] 2 Ch 402, 406–07 (Farwell J).
[67] *Smith v Evangelisation Society (Incorporated) Trust* [1933] Ch 515.

the prescription period the room in the dominant building was also lighted by skylights which had been removed during that period. It was held that in deciding whether the obstruction reduced the light of the room to an unacceptable level, it had to be assumed that the skylights had been reinstated and received light. The reasoning was that the dominant owner had increased the burden on the servient land by removing the skylights and that such an increase in the burden was to be disregarded. If the skylights had not been removed they would have enjoyed a right of light acquired by prescription, so that to take account of any light which passed through them into the room was in accord with the first limb of the rules stated in *Colls*. Again, therefore, the Court in order to arrive at a fair result had recourse to the very wide and general principle that a dominant owner cannot by his own voluntary actions increase the burden on the servient land.

(b) Reflected Light

3.31 It is useful in the present context to state the law on reflected light. Natural light may enter into an aperture in a building either directly from the sun, or having been reflected back from some object or material such as a wall. In locations where there is little direct sunlight because of high neighbouring buildings, white glazed tiling is sometimes found on walls, since that tiling is a good reflector of direct light. It has been argued that in deciding whether an obstruction creates an actionable injury, reflected light should be taken into account as something which provides illumination to the dominant building. This argument has been rejected and such reflected light is ignored, since it is precarious in the sense that the person owning the surface which reflects the light may at any time alter that surface so as to reduce or remove the amount of light reflected. This reasoning accords with the second limb of the rule established in the *Colls* decision.[68] The same reasoning supports the rule that where the servient owner erects an obstruction which reduces the access of light to the dominant building to the extent that an actionable injury is caused, the servient owner cannot escape liability by offering to install white glazed tiling or some other reflecting surface on the wall of his property. The dominant owner has no way of ensuring that the reflecting surface will be maintained.[69] Even a covenant offered by the servient owner to maintain the reflecting surface or material would be of no assistance since, not being a restrictive covenant, the covenant would not be enforceable against successors in title of

[68] *Price v Hilditch* [1930] 1 Ch 500. In this case a wall on the servient land was increased in height so as to form the side of a building. The court, in deciding whether there was an actionable injury, refused to take account of light reflected from the wall since the reflection could have been removed or reduced at any time by the servient owner erecting trellis on the wall or putting a creeper on it, or some similar action. See also *Smith v Evangelisation Society (Incorporated) Trust* [1933] Ch 515.

[69] *Dent v Auction Mart Co* (1866) LR 2 Eq 238, 251–52 (Page Wood V-C). It was said by Giffard LJ in *Staight v Burn* (1869–70) LR 5 Ch App 163, 166 that a dominant owner is entitled to light of the same nature as he had before an obstruction was erected on the servient land, and was not obliged to put up with reflected light.

the servient owner. When calculations are carried out of whether a room receives a sufficiency of natural light through a window using the 'Waldram' or '0.2 per cent sky factor' methodology, no account is taken of reflected light, whether from external surfaces or from internal surfaces and objects in the room in question.[70]

(c) A Qualification

A possible qualification to the first limb of the rule in *Colls* has emerged. The essence of that limb of the rule is that if a room has two windows, A and B in different walls, and both have rights of light, if the servient owner in respect of window A obstructs the access of light to window A, the question of whether after the obstruction sufficient light remains available to the dominant building is decided taking account of the light which enters the room through window B. The reason is that following the obstruction of window A the dominant owner can prevent any further loss of light through an obstruction to window B. Yet it has been held in such a case that the servient owner as regards window A can only build to such a height as, assuming a similar building by the servient owner as regards window B, would still leave a sufficiency of light in the dominant building.[71] This result can be described as a triumph of 'share and share alike' over 'first come, first served'. It is not easy to reconcile this approach with the stark simplicity of the two limbs of the rule in the *Colls* decision.[72] 3.32

4. Artificial Light

There have been major changes in the design of commercial properties since the basic rule on the sufficiency of light was formulated in the early years of the last century. One of these changes is the widespread use of artificial electric lighting.[73] Another change is the provision in many modern office buildings of floor-to-ceiling glazing; the walls have in effect become windows, so allowing the access of more natural light. The third change is that larger shops such as supermarkets or department stores may rely very little on natural light. A question which has received modern attention is whether, when the dominant building relies on artificial light or could be provided with much greater artificial light, the servient owner can contend that there is no infringement of a right of light, since any reduction in natural light could be made up by the use or the increased use of artificial light. 3.33

[70] See ch 6, para 6.39(iii).

[71] *Sheffield Masonic Hall Co Ltd v Sheffield Corporation* [1932] 2 Ch 17.

[72] See para 3.30 for a further modification of the effect of the *Colls* decision in the context of different sources of light to a building.

[73] For example, the third Marquis of Salisbury, the future Prime Minister, installed a form of electric light in his property, Hatfield House, in 1874. See Andrew Roberts, *Salisbury Victorian Titan* (London, Weidenfeld & Nicholson, 1999) 111.

3.34 This question was considered in *Midtown Ltd v City of London Real Property Co Ltd*.[74] The dominant building was an older office building in Fetter Lane in London. The servient land was to be developed as high, modern offices. The dominant building was normally lit by artificial lighting. It was held by Peter Smith J that no account was to be taken of the use of artificial lighting in deciding whether there would be an actionable injury to the dominant building. However, the reliance on artificial light to illuminate the dominant building was to be taken into account in deciding whether an injunction rather than damages was the appropriate remedy, and this was one of the factors which led to an injunction being refused.

3.35 The judge justified his first conclusion, that artificial light was not to be taken into account in deciding whether a right of light had been infringed, by a number of reasons which have considerable cogency.[75] Taken to its ultimate conclusion, the assertion that the dominant building could always be adequately lit by artificial light would mean that there could never be a breach of a right of light, since a diminution in natural light, or even the complete removal of natural light, could always be remedied by electric lighting. This happens for some buildings which have no windows, and happens for all buildings at night. Although the current use of a dominant building might be carried on satisfactorily with artificial light, there might be a reasonably anticipatable future use which would have a greater need of natural light.[76] Even though a dominant building may rely on artificial light, the occupiers may value the amount, possibly small, of natural light which the building does receive. The running costs of the dominant building might be increased by a reliance on electric lighting. It was also said that persons should not be required to bargain away their rights if they do not wish to do so, even though in practice many people are willing to do this. In fact in the *Midtown* case the dominant owners were in practice forced to bargain away their right of light, since they were refused an injunction to prevent the construction of a building which would infringe their right of light and were confined to damages, which were likely to be assessed as the amount which would have been paid as part of a bargain for the voluntary release of their rights.[77]

3.36 It is difficult to fault the second conclusion of the judge, that the availability of existing or increased artificial lighting is relevant to the question of whether an injunction or damages is the appropriate remedy for a breach of a right of natural light, although the weight to be allowed for this factor in the overall exercise of the discretion on the grant of an injunction will vary according to the particular

[74] *Midtown Ltd v City of London Real Property Co* [2008] EWHC 33 (Ch), [2005] 1 EGLR 65.

[75] There is a critique of these reasons in paras 3.67–3.70 of the report of the Law Commission on *Rights of Light*, (Law Com No 356, 2014). In its recommendations for the making of a decision on whether an injunction is an appropriate remedy where there is an infringement of a right of light, the report recommends that the availability of artificial light to a room in the dominant building should be a relevant consideration. This is just what Peter Smith J did in the *Midtown* case.

[76] See para 3.40 et seq.

[77] See ch 7 for remedies and methods of assessing damages.

circumstances of individual cases.[78] The more fundamental and logically anterior question is whether the use or availability of artificial light should be relevant to the decision on whether a right of light has been or would be infringed by building on the servient land.

The *Midtown* decision should not be taken to create an absolute rule of law that artificial light is never to be relevant to the question of whether a right of light is infringed. It will be explained in Chapter 6 that the question of whether a right of light is or will be infringed by development on the servient land is often answered by considering whether the development will leave less than a half of a room in the dominant building in receipt of an amount of natural light of at least 1 lumen per square foot (1 foot candle). The calculations which establish whether this standard is met are unaffected by any artificial light which the room has or could receive. If actual or potential artificial light is to be taken into account in deciding whether there is an actionable injury, then this factor is something which will have to be considered as an additional matter after the more precise test as just described has been applied. 3.37

The correct resolution of the question here under discussion is surely that there is no absolute answer to the question of whether or not artificial light is relevant to the decision on whether a reduction in natural light is an actionable injury. Everything depends on the particular characteristics of each individual case. Nobody would suggest that a well-lit drawing room or living room in a house could have most of its natural light removed by a nearby development without any remedy available to the owner of the room, on the plea that the lights could be left on permanently. On the other hand, a poorly lit storeroom within a commercial building where the light always had to be turned on for its use might suffer little by a further reduction in its natural light, because of its reliance on artificial light. 3.38

A sensible and practical way forward may be to apply a threefold and sequential approach. First, the reduction in natural light caused or to be caused by a development on the servient land could be assessed and a decision taken on whether it would cause an actionable injury to the dominant building, ignoring at this stage the use or potential use of artificial light in that building. If there is or would be no actionable injury on this basis, then *cadit quaestio*. Secondly, if on the initial approach there is or would be an actionable injury, then normally that should settle the question. Thirdly, however, there may be unusual cases in which despite the answer given at the second stage, no actual injury occurs. An example of this situation might be the type of badly lit storeroom just mentioned, a room unsuitable for use for any other purpose, where only 15 per cent of its floor area was adequately lit by natural light and where electric light was always necessary and used, and where the development on the servient land would reduce the floor area adequately lit by natural light from 15 per cent to 10 per cent. It seems reasonable 3.39

[78] In *Price v Hilditch* [1930] 1 Ch 500 Maugham J refused to grant a mandatory injunction to remove an obstruction to light to a scullery, giving as one of his reasons that the scullery could continue to be used for that purpose 'by a moderate increase in the use of electric light'.

to conclude that in such an exceptional case there would be no infringement of the right of light by the reduction in light. It does not seem reasonable in such a case to confer on the owner of the storeroom a right to damages such that, on the usual modern method of assessing damages, he might obtain some significant share in a large development value which attached to the servient land.[79] The adoption of an overall approach as just suggested seems to be in conformity with the general test of the sufficiency of light stated in *Colls v Home and Colonial Stores Ltd* in 1904.[80]

5. Changes of Use and Layout

3.40 In considering the content or the possible infringement of an easement of light, a matter to be considered is how the easement is affected by changes which have been made in the past or might be made in the future to the use of the dominant building. An associated question is how the easement is affected by actual or anticipated changes in the physical layout of the dominant building. These are two logically separate questions, although it is usual to treat them together as regards rights of light. It is useful for the purposes of an orderly explanation of the law to divide alterations to the dominant building into four categories, namely

(a) changes of use of that building;
(b) changes in the internal layout of that building;
(c) alterations to the windows of that building; and
(d) the replacement of windows in that building by windows in a redeveloped building.

The first two categories of alteration are considered here, and the second two categories are considered in section (C) of this chapter. The first two alterations, changes in use and changes in internal layout, appear to be governed by the same principles.[81]

3.41 The authorities state that when deciding whether an obstruction to the access of light to an aperture constitutes an actionable injury because there will be insufficient light left after the obstruction, account should be taken not only of the actual use of the dominant building at the time of the obstruction but also of any change in that use which at that time can reasonably be anticipated.[82] Thus if a

[79] See ch 7 as to the assessment of damages.

[80] *Colls v Home and Colonial Stores Ltd* [1904] AC 179. See para 3.3 for the general principle.

[81] The leading decision on the subject, *Carr-Saunders v Dick McNeil Associates* [1986] 1 WLR 922 considered in the next paragraph, involved both types of change. A change in internal layout must be distinguished from more substantial external and structural alterations to the dominant building which reduce the access of light through its windows and which may result in an implied abandonment of a right of light appurtenant to that building: see *Ankerson v Connolly* [1967] 1 Ch 678, as explained in para 3.58.

[82] *Moore v Hall* (1878) 3 QBD 178; *Colls v Home and Colonial Stores Ltd* [1904] AC 179, 202–04 (Lord Davey) and ibid 211 (Lord Lindley); *Midtown v City of London Real Property Co Ltd* [2005] EWHC 33 (Ch), [2005] 1 EGLR 65.

room is used as a lumber or storage room which requires little light, the dominant owner can resist an obstruction to light passing to that room on the basis that he might reasonably change its use in the future to a use which requires more light.[83] Where a room had been used as a scullery which needed little light, the effect of an obstruction had to be judged by reference to some other residential use to which in the future that scullery might reasonably have been put.[84] In principle, possible future changes from open plan space to single rooms, or from single rooms to open plan space, may increase the burden on the servient land in the circumstances of any particular building. Equally changes of use in the past before the obstruction to light is erected do not prevent the loss of light being assessed by reference to the use of the building at the date of the obstruction. Where a floor of the dominant building had been used as an open plan office that had been converted into six small consulting rooms, it was held that the question of whether an obstruction created an actionable injury had to be decided on the basis of the use of the floor as separate consulting rooms.[85] A further point which supports the law as stated in this paragraph is the statement sometimes made that an easement of light in favour of an aperture in a building is for the benefit of the building as a whole, and not necessarily for one particular room which happens to be lit by light through that aperture at any particular time.[86] In practice, calculations of whether there will remain a sufficiency of light through an aperture in the dominant building after the erection of a structure on the servient land are nearly always made by considering the loss of light to a particular room (or other area, such as a staircase) which receives light through the aperture.[87] Of course if the owner of the dominant building alters its layout or internal structure so as to create an area or areas of poorly lit floorspace, that will not of itself mean that an actionable injury to light is created. There can only be an actionable injury if there is some obstruction to light created on the servient land. On the other hand, by reason of the principles just stated the alteration in the dominant building may reduce the capacity of the servient owner to erect or extend a building on his land.

An obvious question is how it is to be determined whether some future use of the dominant building likely to require more light than the use at the time of the obstruction can reasonably be anticipated. No precise boundaries can be given as to what is relevant to a question of this sort. The main relevant considerations are likely to be whether an owner or future owner of the dominant building is likely to change its use, having regard to the attractions to him of doing so and whether external circumstances may prevent him doing so. For example, some future use 3.42

[83] *Colls v Home and Colonial Stores Ltd* [1904] AC 179, 211 (Lord Lindley).

[84] *Price v Hilditch* [1930] 1 Ch 500.

[85] *Carr-Saunders v Dick McNeil Associates* [1986] 1 WLR 922. One of the principles stated in this case by Millett J was that, whatever had been the use of the dominant building in the past, the dominant owner was entitled to such access of light as would leave the building adequately lit for all ordinary purposes for which it might reasonably be expected to be used.

[86] *Carr-Saunders v Dick McNeil Associates* [1986] 1 WLR 922.

[87] See ch 6. A further practice has developed whereby it is only light to the 6 m of the room measured back from the aperture which is generally taken into account in the assessment of damages: see ch 7, para 7.86.

may be likely to be prevented by planning policies which make it unlikely that a planning permission would be granted, or a consent might be needed from a landlord which was unlikely to be given, or the changed use might be contrary to the terms of a restrictive covenant the benefit of which was vested in some third party. There appear to be two limitations on future uses being taken into account. One limitation is that a future use for some special or extraordinary purpose is not to be taken into account.[88] The second limitation is that the changed use, although not special or extraordinary, is not a use which is reasonably foreseeable, perhaps for one or more of the reasons just mentioned. It may be that in practice the two limitations merge into each other.

3.43 The principles stated in the last few paragraphs are not difficult to describe or to apply. Nonetheless the law on the exact content and extent of a right to light is largely if not entirely dependent on decisions of the courts as opposed to a statutory provision, and different principles emerge from different judicial statements in different contexts. This causes difficulty in any coherent exposition of the law. An example arises from the statement of Lord Davey in the *Colls* decision, mentioned in the last paragraph, that no account is to be taken of a future use of the dominant building which is for 'some special or extraordinary purpose'. In itself this statement may be unexceptionable, but examples given by Lord Davey create doubts. He considered that the burden on the servient owner could not be increased by converting a part of a house into a photographic studio or combining two or more rooms of a house into one without making provision for adequate lighting. Yet such changes of use may be within the realm of that which is reasonably foreseeable. Indeed in one subsequent decision the burden on the servient owner was increased by the conversion of a single room used as an open plan office into a number of smaller units used as consulting rooms.[89]

3.44 A further difficulty is perhaps more fundamental. In cases of easements created by prescription or by implication from a deed, there had been a series of sometimes conflicting decisions on the extent to which the dominant owner could change the use of the dominant land so as to increase the burden on the servient land but still retain the benefit of his easement. The decisions had mainly concerned rights of way where a changed or intensified use of the dominant land could mean an increased intensity of vehicular use of the easement. Certainty was introduced into this subject by the judgment of Neuberger LJ in the Court of Appeal in *McAdams Homes Ltd v Robinson*.[90] It was held that a change in the use of the dominant land did not prevent the easement being exercised unless both of two conditions were fulfilled, the conditions being:

(a) the change represented a radical change in the character or the identity of the dominant land; and

[88] See *Colls v Home and Colonial Stores Ltd* [1904] AC 179, 202–03 (Lord Davey).
[89] *Carr-Saunders v Dick McNeil Associates* [1986] 1 WLR 922.
[90] *McAdams Homes Ltd v Robinson* [2004] EWCA Civ 214, [2004] 3 EGLR 93.

(b) the change in the use would result in a substantial increase or alteration in the burden on the servient land.

It may be that the second condition explained by Neuberger LJ should refer only to an increase, not an alteration in the burden on the servient land, since an alteration in the burden on the servient land which decreased that burden could scarcely be a justification for the easement no longer being exercisable. However this is a minor and technical point of language. These are coherent and comprehensive principles of law which bring together the disparate expressions of principle in earlier cases. The issue before the Court of Appeal in the *McAdams* case concerned a right to the passage of water, but Neuberger LJ ruled out any difference between such an easement and an easement of way. In the same way no difference of principle should exist between an easement of light and other easements. The *McAdams* principles were also concerned with proposed changes to the dominant land, which could include physical changes, but it seems clear that they should apply also to changes which are purely a change of use.

The difficulty is how to reconcile what Neuberger LJ said with the principles relating to rights of light derived from the authorities mentioned.[91] A part of the difficulty may be caused by the underlying tension between the particular rules stated in some of the authorities and the more general underlying principle that a dominant owner should not be permitted to act so as unduly to increase the burden on the servient land.[92] One line of authority indicates that a change in the use of the dominant land does not generally prevent an easement of light being exercised, and that any future change in the use must be taken into account if that change was reasonably foreseeable at the time of the obstruction. The other line of authority indicates that a change in the use may prevent the continued exercise of the easement if the two conditions stated by Neuberger LJ are satisfied. It is not easy for legal or other practitioners to advise their clients on the law in this situation. It may be that the various decisions and lines of authority may be reconciled by saying that: 3.45

(a) in deciding whether an obstruction constitutes an actionable injury, a future use of the dominant land may in principle be taken into account;
(b) a future use will not be taken into account if it is 'special or extraordinary';
(c) a future use will not be taken into account if it is one which is not reasonably foreseeable as a future use at the time of the obstruction; and
(d) a future use will not be taken into account if it would represent a radical change in the character or the identity of the dominant building and would result in a substantial increase in the burden on the servient land.

[91] See in particular *Price v Hilditch* [1930] 1 Ch 500 and *Carr-Saunders v Dick McNeil Associates* [1986] 1 WLR 922.

[92] See *Ankerson v Connolly* [1967] 1 Ch 678 and *News of the World Ltd v Allen Fairhead & Sons Ltd* [1931] 2 Ch 402 for applications of the more underlying principle. See para 3.78 for the tension between principles.

The law as sometimes stated, that in deciding whether an obstruction to the access of light to a window through which there is an easement of light must be judged by reference not only to existing uses of the dominant building but also to possible future uses, is therefore a proposition which needs to be suitably qualified.

6. Overall Effect on a Building

3.46 It is said that an easement of light enures to a building as a whole and not to a particular window or windows, or even to a particular room within the dominant building.[93] This principle raises the question of what is the position if a development on the servient land reduces the light to some rooms in the dominant building but increases the light to other rooms in that building. This could occur if a building on the servient land is demolished and is replaced by a new building which is taller and bulkier at some points but is smaller at other points, so creating a different effect on different parts of an adjoining dominant building. One possible answer to the question is that each room in the dominant building has to be considered separately, such that if the obstruction reduces the light to that room to what is below an acceptable standard, there is an actionable injury even though the light to a different room in the building is increased from being below to being above an acceptable standard. A different possible answer is that the gain in terms of light to one room has to be set off against the loss to a different room, in order to determine whether there is an overall actionable injury to the dominant building.

3.47 The answer usually given on the authority of *Davis v Marrable*[94] is that the matter must be judged on an overall basis, so that if the value of the dominant building has increased in overall terms there is no actual injury, despite the fact that the light to a particular room may be reduced to an unacceptable level. This decision is a slender thread on which to hang the principle of an overall approach. There was in the decision no exact analysis of the effect of the new building on the servient land on the dominant building, and it was merely observed that, upon the whole and in the opinion of the judge, access of light to a window was improved. It was also said that the window in question received sufficient light.

3.48 There are serious objections to the principle of law said to be derived from this decision.

(a) It seems more attractive to reason that one room in a building receiving light through a window or windows is entitled not to have that light reduced to an

[93] *Carr-Saunders v Dick McNeil Associates* [1986] 1 WLR 922. Where parts of a building have been constructed at different times it is possible that some parts of the building, those constructed more than 20 years ago, may enjoy a prescriptive right of light and other parts constructed more recently may not enjoy such a right.

[94] *Davis v Marrable* [1913] 2 Ch 421.

unacceptable standard when an easement of light exists, irrespective of the effect on other parts of the building.

(b) It is not clear whether the offsetting improvement to other rooms in the building has to be such as to improve their light from an unacceptable to an acceptable standard. It may be that an improvement in light in a room is to be taken into account as an offsetting factor when that improvement is from a level of light which is already sufficient to a level of light which is even better.

(c) How the exact process of offsetting an area which obtains better lighting against an area which has imposed on it worse lighting is to be carried out is not clear. Possibly what is required is a valuation of the dominant building as a whole before and after the development on the servient land, on the principle that when a deterioration in the light to some parts of the building and an improvement in the light to other parts of the building are taken into account, there is no actionable injury if there is no decrease in the value of the building as a whole due to the development.

(d) There is the question of what is to happen if the light to areas of improved lighting is subsequently reduced. The answer given in *Davis v Marrable* is that in these circumstances, the later reduction would be a wrong.

(e) A further complication may arise where a landlord and a tenant own interests in the whole of the dominant building and the values of these interests are differently affected in overall terms by the increases and decreases in the light received to different parts of the building.

(f) There may of course be cases in which different persons have different interests in parts of the dominant building, and in such circumstances it would be patently unjust that the benefit to one owner should be used to offset or eliminate the injury to a different owner.

An allied question is whether in assessing damages an improvement to one part of a building can be offset against an injury to another part; this is discussed in Chapter 7.[95] 3.49

(C) ALTERATIONS TO WINDOWS AND REDEVELOPMENT

1. Introduction

Physical alterations to existing windows or other apertures have produced a body of case law on the question of what is the effect of such alterations on rights of light as enjoyed through the previous and unaltered windows. This question can arise in a number of situations and engenders a number of other issues. It is sometimes 3.50

[95] See ch 7, para 7.102 et seq.

necessary to consider whether the window, or the structure in which the window is contained, has been removed without any intention of effecting an early replacement of it. As regards lesser alterations to a window, it must be asked whether the alteration is in plan, ie whether the wall containing the window is moved back from or nearer to the servient land. A more frequent form of alteration is likely to be that the window is retained in its existing vertical structure, but there is an alteration in the position or the dimensions of the window. It is also relevant to consider the effect of a physical alteration to a window during the running of the prescription period, as opposed to after the end of that period.

3.51 If the removal or alteration of a window results in the loss of any right of light through that window then no further question arises. On the other hand, if a right of light through the window is not wholly lost then there arise further questions on what is the exact content and nature of the retained right and how the matter of a possible infringement of that retained light is to be resolved, having regard to the new dimensions or new physical structure of the window. The important question is how a loss of light to the altered window by reason of an obstruction erected on the servient land is to be measured for the purpose of deciding whether there has been an infringement of a right of light. There is also the question of how damages for such an infringement are to be measured in the situation of an altered window, assuming that damages are an appropriate remedy.[96]

3.52 The questions raised above may often resolve themselves into the single or initial question of whether by reason of the changes to a window the right of light through that window has been impliedly abandoned or released. If the alteration does bring about the ending of the right of light, then it is correct to describe that process as an implied abandonment. The implied abandonment of easements and of a right of light in particular is considered more generally in Chapter 8. The question of exactly when an alteration brings about an implied abandonment, the critical question of the content of the right of light which is retained if an alteration is effected but does not bring about an abandonment, and the effect of this last situation on the calculation of any loss of light and remedies for it, are all complex subjects and for that reason are dealt with in this chapter because of their connection with the central matter of the content of the right of light, if that right indeed remains in relation to an altered window.

2. Abandonment of Rights

3.53 The abandonment of a right is not easily implied from the actions of the owner of the right, and depends on proof of a firm intention to abandon the right.[97]

[96] The measurement of light is considered generally in ch 6 and remedies, including the assessment of damages, are considered generally in ch 7.

[97] See ch 8, paras 8.8–8.11, and see *Gotobed v Pridmore* (1971) 207 Estates Gazette 759; *Tehidy Minerals v Norman* [1971] 2 QB 528.

Where the right is an easement of light, the tendency of the courts has been not to imply an abandonment from physical alterations to the window, or even from the removal of the building containing the window, if it is proposed to replace the window in a new building. Nonetheless there will be an abandonment if the structure containing the window, such as a wall, or the whole or some part of a building containing the window, is removed and there is no intention to replace the window at an early stage in some new building.[98] There can presumably be an abandonment of the access of light through a part of a window where a part of the glazed area is permanently removed or boarded up or painted over. Once a right of light has been abandoned by reason of events such as just stated, the right is gone for ever, and cannot be revived in the same building or in some later new building.[99] An abandonment of a right of light through an aperture may also occur if the dominant owner himself erects an obstacle on his property, or alters his property, in such a way as substantially to reduce the amount of light received through the aperture.[100] If it were otherwise, the dominant owner could by his own actions increase the burden of the servient owner.[101] Where a building has been demolished and redeveloped and, in accordance with the principle explained below,[102] there is no substantial similarity in the cone of light received by the old and the new windows the rights of light appurtenant to the old windows are taken to have been abandoned.[103] It follows that once an abandonment has taken place, there can be no question of the dominant owner at some time in the future erecting a new building and claiming that the right of light which was appurtenant to the former building is resuscitated in the new building, even if a window in the new building is identical in its plane and dimensions to a window in the old building.[104]

3. Alterations to Windows: The General Principles

It was at one time thought that if a window was altered, so that for example the new window contained some but not all of the glazed area of the former window and contained in addition a new glazed area, the entitlement of the dominant owner might in practice be lost. This was at least considered to be the position 3.54

[98] *Moore v Rawson* (1824) 3 B & C 332; *Tapling v Jones* (1865) 11 HLC 290, 319 (Lord Chelmsford).

[99] Lord Chelmsford said in *Tapling v Jones* (1865) 11 HLC 290, 319: 'for a right once abandoned is abandoned for ever'. The point was put more succinctly in *Tyrringham's Case* (1584) Co Rep 16b when it was stated that any right of light which had been lost was 'tunc moritur' and could not be revived.

[100] *Ankerson v Connolly* [1967] 1 Ch 678: see para 3.58.

[101] The dominant owner can to some extent do this by changing the use of the dominant building or rearranging its internal structure: *Carr-Saunders v Dick McNeill Associates* [1986] 1 WLR 922.

[102] See para 3.66 et seq.

[103] *Heath v Bucknall* (1869) LR 8 Eq 1; *Carriers' Company v Corbett* 2 Dr & Sm 355, 359; *Newson v Pender* (1884) 27 Ch D 43, in which diagrams of the alterations to the windows are reproduced in the report.

[104] *Tapling v Jones* (1865) 11 HLC 290, 319 (Lord Chelmsford).

if the servient owner could not obstruct light to the new or altered window or part of a window without obstructing light to the former window. This reasoning found favour in the mid-nineteenth century in the Court of Queen's Bench, in the Court of Common Pleas, and in the Exchequer Chamber.[105]

3.55 This reasoning was disapproved and the general principles on the effect of alterations to windows were stated by the House of Lords in *Tapling v Jones*.[106] This decision concerned a house with three storeys, each containing a single window. The plaintiff had acquired rights of light by prescription in favour of these windows. He then altered the window in each of the two lower storeys so that the new apertures contained glazing which was in part coincident with the glazing in the former windows, and in part a new area of glazing. He also erected two further storeys to the building and inserted a window in each of those storeys. The servient owner erected a wall on his land which obstructed the access of light to all of the windows in the dominant building. It was impossible for the servient owner to block off light to the new windows without also blocking off light to the old windows. The principles laid down by the House of Lords can be summarised as follows.

(a) A dominant owner who has an existing right of light through windows does not in principle lose that light by altering the windows or by constructing new windows.[107]
(b) Following an alteration to a window the right of light remains, but is confined to the exact dimensions of the old window.[108]
(c) The servient owner therefore has a right to obstruct a wholly new window, or the newly glazed area of a previous window, but he cannot obstruct the glazing of a new window which is coincident with the glazing of a previous window. As Lord Chelmsford put it in *Tapling v Jones*,[109] 'It must always be borne in mind that it is no unlawful act for the owner of a house to open a new window, or to enlarge an ancient window, although in the latter case some difficulty may be thrown upon an adjoining owner to distinguish the old part from the new, and so to ascertain which party has a right to obstruct, and which is privileged from his obstruction.'
(d) If the servient owner erects an obstruction which is an actionable injury to the windows in the dominant building in their previous and unaltered state, he commits a wrong even though the practical result is that he is prevented from obstructing the area of new glazing in the altered windows, or

105 *Renshaw v Bean* (1852) 18 QBD 112; *Hutchinson v Copestake* (1861) 9 CB (NS) 863.
106 *Tapling v Jones* (1865) 11 HLC 290.
107 ibid, 318 (Lord Chelmsford).
108 ibid, per Lord Chelmsford at p318: 'The right thus acquired [by twenty years of enjoyment under s3 of the Prescription Act 1832] must necessarily be confined to the exact dimensions of the opening through which the loss of light and air has been permitted.'
109 ibid, 320 (Lord Chelmsford).

is prevented from obstructing a new window.[110] Thus in *Tapling v Jones* the erection of the wall by the servient owner was held to be a wrongful act because it infringed the rights of light of the dominant owner as attached to the original and unaltered windows.

4. Alteration to Windows: Application of Principles

It is possible to apply the above principles to the main factual situations which may arise when windows are altered. These situations are: 3.56

(1) the removal or blocking up of a window in the dominant building and the construction of a new window in a wholly different position;
(2) the carrying out by the dominant owner of works to parts of the dominant property not involving any alteration in its windows but which substantially reduce the light received through the windows;
(3) an increase in the dimensions of a window leaving the whole of the existing glazed area intact and so a part of the new window;
(4) an increase in the dimensions of a window where some of the existing glazing is removed and some of it is incorporated into the enlarged window;
(5) a decrease in the dimensions of a window; and
(6) the construction of a new window leaving any existing window or windows unaltered.

Naturally not every possible combination of events can be considered in this account, and there may be variations and combinations of the factual situations just described, but any set of circumstances should be examined in accordance with the principles laid down in *Tapling v Jones*. Other principles may sometimes become relevant in addition to those stated in *Tapling v Jones* such as that in some circumstances the dominant owner cannot alter his property so as to increase the burden on the servient land. The practical result in the various situations is sometimes intimately bound up with the question of what measurement or comparison of light has to take place in the determination of the question of whether there will be, or has been, an actionable infringement of the right to the access of light. This may sometimes involve a comparison between the light which provides illumination to a room with the previous and unaltered window in place and the light which provides illumination to the same room with the existence of the altered window. It is now proposed to examine the six factual situations summarised earlier in this paragraph.

The first situation is where the alteration to the dominant building is the removal or the blocking up of an existing window and the construction of a new window in 3.57

[110] ibid, 320 (Lord Chelmsford); *Frechette v La Compagnie Manufacturiere de St Hyacinthe* (1883) 9 App Cas 170, 186 (Sir Arthur Hobhouse).

the facade in a wholly different position, so that there is no coincidence of glazed area between the old and the new window. The result is clear. The right of light appertaining to the building is a right of access of light through the particular former aperture, and the destruction of that aperture with no intention to replace it in the same or a similar position amounts to an abandonment of the right of light. The servient owner can therefore obstruct the light which accesses the building through the new window as he wishes unless and until a right of light is obtained to that new window by the necessary 20 years of enjoyment of the access of light through it over the servient land.

3.58 The second situation to consider is one in which the dominant owner carries out alterations to his property, such as creating new boundary walls which themselves significantly reduce the access of light through the apertures in his property, even though the apertures are themselves unaltered. In *Ankerson v Connelly*[111] the plaintiff owned a small house with prescriptively acquired rights of light to two windows on the ground floor and to a small window in a shed. The plaintiff reconstructed his property by covering in a yard through which light entered over the servient land and by raising the height of a wall at the edge of his property and abutting the servient land. It was held by the Court of Appeal that by these actions the plaintiff had impliedly abandoned his right of light to the windows in question. It was emphasised that the Court was not supporting the proposition that any alteration in the physical nature of the dominant land amounted to an abandonment of a right of light, or that any alteration to windows in the dominant land necessarily had that effect. The decision is an example of the principle that where the owner of an easement carries out works which mean that the easement cannot thereafter effectively be enjoyed as it was, or only enjoyed to some minor extent, that may amount to an implied abandonment of the easement, and this principle was applied to a right of light. This decision of the Court of Appeal may therefore be regarded as elaborating the principle which emerges from *Tapling v Jones*, that an alteration to a window or other alteration to the dominant land does not of itself and necessarily result in the termination of a right of light to a window. The elaboration is that the alterations in question, whether to the window or to the remainder of the property, may be so great that the right of light to the window is impliedly abandoned. Alterations to the exterior or structure of the dominant building which may result in the implied abandonment of a right of light to windows in that building must be distinguished from alterations to the internal layout of that building which are unlikely to have that effect.[112]

3.59 The third situation, an increase in the dimensions of a window, such as by adding to the glazed area an area of further glazing but leaving intact the whole of the previous glazing, is not difficult to explain. If an obstruction is erected on the servient land, the question of whether that obstruction is an actionable injury to

[111] *Ankerson v Connelly* [1907] 1 Ch 678.

[112] See *Carr-Saunders v Dick McNeil Associates* [1986] 1 WLR 922. See para 3.41.

the dominant building should be resolved by comparing the room lit by the window in question, first, as it was lit with the former and smaller window in place but without the obstruction and, secondly, as it is or will be with the new and larger window in place and taking account of the obstruction. It is only if the comparison shows a decrease in the area of the room sufficiently lit, and a decrease to the necessary extent, that there will be an infringement of the right of light.[113] What appears would be wrong in principle is that when considering the effect of the obstruction the new window should be ignored. If the new window were ignored and the comparison confined to the effect of the obstruction on the glazed and smaller area of window as it previously was, the result could be that the dominant owner would obtain damages on the basis that his room was notionally ill-lit when in fact, and because of his decision to extend the window, the room is in fact adequately lit. In this type of situation the servient owner obtains the benefit of the new and extended window which the dominant owner has constructed, but there seems no injustice in that.

The fourth situation to consider is that in which an existing window is enlarged so that some of the glazing remains but part of the glazing is destroyed and the new window therefore contains a part of the glazing of the existing window and additional new glazing. A simple example would be an oblong window of 24 sq ft of glazed area, alone providing light to a room, which is replaced by a new window of 36 sq ft of glazing, but with 16 sq ft being coincident glazing within the old window and the new window. The right of light will appertain to the 16 sq ft of coincident glazing, and to that alone. There cannot be a right of light through the area of previous glazing removed or through the new area of glazing installed. 3.60

There should be no difficulty in applying rights of light principles to this situation if the correct analysis is carried out in order to determine whether an obstruction on the servient land is an actionable injury. It is necessary to look at the situation first on the assumption that the retained portion of glazing of the previous window (the 16 sq ft in the example) remained unaltered and that the obstruction had not been erected on the servient land. It is necessary then to take the situation in which the obstruction has been erected on the servient land but the room in the dominant building is lit through the whole of the new and enlarged window and is therefore likely to receive more light than through the previous and smaller window. The two situations can then be compared and, if the result is that there is a reduction in light such that the room becomes insufficiently lit when the second situation is compared with the first, there will be an actionable injury. 3.61

[113] See *News of the World Ltd v Allen Fairhead & Sons Ltd* [1931] 2 Ch 402 discussed in para 3.74. This decision concerned the construction in a new redeveloped building of a window with only a small part of the glazing coincident with the glazing in the former building, but the same principle seems applicable. The same general principle should apply when the dominant owner improves a window in some way without altering its dimensions such as by removing a mullion or improving the glazing. The effect of an obstruction on the servient land should be assessed taking into account the improved physical state of the window: see *Turner v Spooner* (1861) 1 Drew & Sm 467. See ch 6 for an explanation of how light is measured and how the comparison of the 'before and after' situation is carried out.

The only right of light is to the area of glazing which is coincident between the previous and the altered window, but in considering whether there is an obstruction to light which results in the room lit becoming insufficiently lit, the actual light received through the new window with its additional glazed area should be taken into account. As mentioned earlier,[114] if the additional and better light received through the enlarged new window were left out of account there could arise the anomalous situation in which the dominant owner received damages for a notional reduction in the light to his room and was compensated as though his room was inadequately lit whereas in reality, and through his own actions in altering and enlarging the window, he has a room which is sufficiently lit.

3.62 The fifth situation to consider in connection with alterations to existing buildings is that in which the dominant owner decreases the size of an existing window but does not otherwise alter it or carry out any other alterations which affect the lighting to the area lit by the window. This is not a very likely situation but, should it occur, principle suggests that the effect of an obstruction to the window should be judged solely by reference to the original window, so that one should compare the access of light to the whole of the previous window prior to the obstruction and then the access of light to the whole of that window after the obstruction. It is only if the change between the two degrees of access of light amounts to an actionable injury that there will be an infringement of the right of light. It would obviously be unfair and unsatisfactory that a dominant owner should for his own purposes decrease the size of a window so as to prevent a servient owner from carrying out a development which could have been lawfully carried out if the window had not been decreased in size.[115] This reasoning should apply whether the dominant owner has reduced the size of his window simply by removing a part of it, or has removed a part of a window and added a further area of glazing such that the total size of the window is less than it previously was. The reasoning stated in this paragraph may again be an example of the operation of a general and underlying principle that the dominant owner cannot by his own actions increase the burden on the servient land.[116] It seems in principle correct that a dominant owner should not be able to increase the burden on the servient land by actions which reduce the amount of light which may be transferred through a window, for example by

[114] See para 3.59.

[115] In *WH Bailey & Son Ltd v Holborn & Frascati Ltd* [1914] 1 Ch 598 Sargant J approved a passage in the 8th edn of *Gale on Easements*, in which it was said: 'It would seem clear that after an alteration in an ancient window whereby its size was decreased, the dominant proprietor would not be entitled to prevent the erection of buildings which, although obstructing the altered window, would not before the alteration, have caused an illegal obstruction within the rule laid down in *Colls' case*.'

[116] Support for this analysis may be found in the decision in *Smith v Evangelisation Society (Incorporated) Trust* [1933] Ch 515 in which a dominant owner was not permitted to increase the burden on the servient land from a prescriptively acquired right of light when that owner had removed skylights in the dominant building, and so by his own actions reduced the access of natural light, during the running of the prescription period. See para 3.30. Similar reasoning is implicit in the decision of the Court of Appeal in *Ankerson v Connelly* [1907] 1 Ch 678. See para 3.58.

painting over a part of the glazing or by changing the form of the glazing.[117] In such a case the effect of an obstruction on the servient land should be judged as though the glazing remained in its original form.

The sixth and final situation to consider is that in which a new window is inserted into the wall of a room leaving any existing window or windows unaltered. This situation has been considered earlier[118] where it is explained that in deciding whether an obstruction to a window is an infringement of a right of light appurtenant to that window, there may have to be disregarded any light received through any other window or windows which light the same area. The principle is that in such circumstances the light which enters the room through the other window or windows is to be disregarded unless those other windows have themselves a right of light to be received through them. The reason is that in such circumstances the continued access of light through the other window or windows could be reduced or removed at any time. Therefore if the dominant owner inserts a new window into a facade of his building which provides additional light to a room beyond that received through an existing window, then in considering whether an obstruction is an infringement to the right of light appertaining to that existing window the light received by the new window will normally have to be ignored. Of course, after 20 years of enjoyment of light through the new window, that window will itself obtain a prescriptive right of light. 3.63

A further possible alteration to a window is that its position as viewed in plan is changed. This arises if a window in a wall is replaced by a new window in a new wall but erected either further away from or nearer to the servient land than the previous wall. This situation will most often arise where there has been a complete reconstruction or redevelopment of a building, and so is considered in the next sub-section of this chapter, which is directed towards the effect of a complete reconstruction of a building. 3.64

A possible variation of the situations examined above which may arise is that the dominant owner has rights of light over servient properties A and B and consents to the erection of an obstruction to his rights on property A. By doing so he does not lose his rights of lights over property B, but it appears that in exercising his rights over property B he cannot increase the burden on property B by what he has agreed could be done on property A.[119] For instance, the reduced light to the dominant building resulting from the physical development on property A may have meant that a development on property B would be an infringement of the rights of the dominant owner, when there would have been no infringement if the dominant building had remained better lit as it was before the permitted development 3.65

[117] In *Newham v Lawson* (1971) 22 P & CR 852 Plowman J suggested that an unusually high amount of light through stained glass windows could not be acquired by prescription, since the dominant owner had reduced the light which would otherwise pass through the apertures by installing in them a type of semi-opaque glass. See para 3.22.

[118] See para 3.26 et seq.

[119] *WH Bailey & Son Ltd v Holborn & Frascati Ltd* [1914] 1 Ch 598.

on property A. In other words, in judging whether a development on property B would be an infringement of the rights of light of the dominant owner, it must be assumed that he has not agreed to an obstructive development on property A.

5. Redevelopments: The Principle

3.66 A building which enjoys prescriptive rights of light through its apertures may be completely demolished and a new building erected on the site. A good example of this process, and one which may give rise to rights of light issues, is redevelopments of offices in central London and other urban areas where offices built 40 or more years ago are often considered to be out of date today, in that they may not have features such as raised floors, suspended ceilings and modern forms of air conditioning. It is likely that there will be a degree of coincidence between areas of glazing in the previous building and in the redeveloped building. There is no principle of law which prevents a right of light received through apertures in the old building being transferred to apertures in the new building. The destruction of the old building including its windows does not give rise to an implied abandonment of the rights of light to the apertures, providing there is an intention to rebuild the building within a reasonable time.[120] Sometimes thought is given by developers to the transfer of rights of light, and this may affect the exact physical form of a new building. However, in order for there to be a transfer of rights of light in these circumstances to a new building it is not necessary that there should be a deliberately conceived plan to bring about this result.[121] Whether in any case there will be a transfer of existing rights of light to a redeveloped building depends upon the coincidence of glazing between the new and the old windows with that coincidence considered both in the horizontal plane and in the vertical plane (ie, as viewed in plan or as viewed in elevation).

3.67 The relevant principle to be applied to a redevelopment of the dominant building is derived from the decision of the Court of Appeal in *Scott v Pape*.[122] In that case the dominant building had rights of light through its apertures acquired by prescription. The former building was demolished and replaced by a new building which contained larger and more numerous windows. There was some coincidence in the glazing of the windows in the upper and lower floors of the former and the new building, but no rights of light were claimed in respect of those windows. The three windows in the middle floor of the new building differed from those in the old building in certain respects. There was a considerable degree of coincidence between the old and the new windows on this floor, as viewed in elevation. As viewed in plan, however, the new windows were moved forward and nearer to

[120] *Turner v Spooner* (1861) 1 Drew & Sm 467.
[121] *News of the World Ltd v Allen Fairhead & Sons Ltd* [1931] 2 Ch 402.
[122] *Scott v Pape* (1886) 31 Ch D 554.

the servient land. The issue for the Court of Appeal was whether the rights of light enjoyed through the old windows could be transferred to the new windows in the new building, notwithstanding these alterations in the plane of the relevant wall and in the dimensions of the windows. The Court of Appeal rejected the contention that the moving of the windows outwards towards the servient land as a result of the redevelopment necessarily resulted in an implied abandonment of rights of light enjoyed through those windows.

The Court declared the law in these circumstances as depending on the similarity of 'the cone of light' received by the old and the new windows. If the cone of light received by the new windows was sufficiently similar to the cone of light received by the former windows, then the rights of light were retained and transferred to the windows of the new building. Obviously this exposition of the law depends upon asking what precisely is meant by 'the cone of light', and in asking in each individual case whether there is sufficient similarity between the cone of light as received by the former windows and the cone of light as received by the new windows. 3.68

The expression 'cone of light' is itself in some ways curious, since most windows are rectangular in shape and receive light through what is not technically a cone. Nonetheless, the concept is reasonably apparent. It is possible for rights of light surveyors to look at a window in the previous building and to indicate the area within a room lit by that window which receives light directly from that window. This excludes, of course, light reflected from other parts of the room. The point at which such an exercise is done is usually taken as 850mm above the floor level of the room, since this is the height at which people normally need light for use at tables or desks. It is, therefore, possible to indicate an area of the room at 850mm above its floor level which received direct light from the former window and which does or will receive direct light from the new window. Thus by this means it is possible to establish a floor area which was lit by the cone of light from the old window and from the new window, and to compare the two. So far this is a technical exercise which can be carried out by experts in this area. 3.69

If the area lit by the previous cone of light and the new cone of light is exactly the same, then clearly in accordance with the principle established by the Court of Appeal there is a complete coincidence of cones of light, so that the rights to light enjoyed through the old window will, subject to any other relevant considerations, be transferred to the new window in the new building. 3.70

Obviously most cases are not as simple as this. The two cones of light to the room, from the previous window and from the new window, will differ to some extent in many cases. In an extreme case, if the window is moved back sufficiently from its position in plan as it previously was, then none of the cone of light which went to the floor area, or to 850mm above the floor area, of the room in the old building would be transferred to the equivalent room in the new building. In that case there would be no transferred right of light. But the crucial question of course is what is to happen in some intermediate situation. What one needs is a precise test, 3.71

even if expressed linguistically. That is not provided by the decision of the Court of Appeal in *Scott v Pape*. Cotton LJ considered that there would be a transfer of a right of light if the same cone of light, or a substantial part of that cone of light, which went to the old building went also to the new building.[123] Bowen LJ said that a person was not to be taken to have intended to abandon any of the old light he enjoyed if the building as rebuilt was such as to preserve evidently and without confusion of proof the enjoyment either of the whole of the volume of light which was enjoyed before, or some material part of it.[124] Fry LJ said that whereas the complete closure of a window might indicate an intention to abandon any right of light attached to that window, yet if there is a maintenance, either in its entirety or to a considerable part of it, of the old window it is difficult to suppose that you mean to give up a right to the light which that window or a portion of it enjoyed.[125] The best that can be done is to say that the Court of Appeal held that when the position of a window in the dominant building in plan was moved, either forwards or backwards, in relation to the servient land from its former position and the window was replaced in the new vertical structure either in the same or in a somewhat different position in that vertical structure the rights of light which were enjoyed through the previous window will continue to attach to the new window, provided that the room lit by the new window receives either the same, or a similar, cone of light as that received by the room lit by the old window. No one can pretend that this is a precise test but it is the best that can be elucidated from *Scott v Pape*, a decision which has endured for over a century.

3.72 All that can be said with certainty on the current state of the law is that when windows through which there is a prescriptive right of light are replaced by windows in a redeveloped building, the rights will be transferred to the new building if, and only if, there is a sufficient similarity in the cones of light received by a new window and the window which it replaces. The answer to this question will depend on the differences between the two windows when looked at in plan and in elevation, and on any other changes in configuration between the two windows.[126] It is of course possible that rights of light appurtenant to a building may be transferred to some windows in a new building, but not to other windows in that building.

3.73 Where an easement of light is created by implication from the circumstances of a deed[127] the same principles should govern the question of a transfer of rights on a redevelopment as apply to easements acquired by prescription. In the case of an easement acquired by an express provision in a deed, it will be necessary to consider the language of the deed, which may confine the easement to a particular building.

[123] *Scott v Pape* (1886) 31 Ch D 554, 570.

[124] ibid, 574.

[125] ibid, 576.

[126] See *CGIS City Plaza Shares Ltd v Britel Fund Trustees Ltd* [2012] EWHC 1594 (Ch) for a decision on which it was held that there was a sufficient coincidence between former windows and altered windows to permit an easement of light to attach to the new windows.

[127] See ch 4, section (B).

In the absence of such a provision the same principles as to the transfer of the easement to a redeveloped building should apply as apply to the transfer of prescriptive easements.

6. Redevelopments: Assessing an Infringement

Difficulties in the operation of these principles are illustrated by the decision in *News of the World Ltd v Allen Fairhead & Sons Ltd*.[128] The plaintiffs owned premises with rights of light and had redeveloped them. There was insufficient evidence as regards windows above the ground floor in the new building to enable a conclusion on whether rights of light had been transferred to these windows. On the ground floor there were substantial coincidences between the old and the new windows. The plaintiffs claimed that the redevelopment of the nearby premises of the defendants which was under way would constitute an infringement of the rights of light of the new ground-floor windows. Two issues therefore arose, the first being whether rights of light had been transferred to the ground-floor windows, and the second being, if there had been a transfer, how it was to be determined whether there had been an infringement of the transferred rights. Farwell J held on the first question that there had been a transfer of rights, even though there appears to have been no assessment of the similarity of the cones of light received by the old windows and the new windows. 3.74

The central issue was therefore how the question of whether there would be an infringement of these transferred rights was to be determined. The plaintiffs contended that the effect of the defendants' building was to be judged solely by the reduction of light caused by that building to the rooms as lit by the areas of glazing in the new windows which was coincident with that of the old windows on the assumption that the areas of coincident glazing remained, and disregarding entirely the light entering through the new areas of glazing. They founded this argument on the principle that as there were no rights of light appurtenant to the new and non-coincident areas of glazing, these areas had to be ignored in deciding whether there was an infringement of rights of light.[129] There was a degree of logic in this argument, but it was rejected by the court as leading to an unacceptable and unfair result when transferred rights are claimed. If the approach urged by the plaintiffs was correct, it would mean that a developer could arrange a degree of coincident glazing between the old and the new windows, and then claim that a development on the servient land was a violation of the transferred rights by considering the access of light to the coincident glazed areas only, and ignoring the access of light through the remainder of the windows. This was an unacceptable position since it could mean that the owner of the redeveloped dominant building 3.75

[128] *News of the World Ltd v Allen Fairhead & Sons Ltd* [1931] 2 Ch 402.
[129] See para 3.26 for this general principle.

could obtain damages on the basis that a room was badly lit, when in truth and reality it was well lit. The court therefore held that in considering the effect of the new development on the servient land, the access of light through the full areas of glazing in the windows which had transferred rights should be taken into account. A reason for this decision was that if a different conclusion had been reached it would have infringed the general principle that the dominant owner cannot by his own actions increase the burden on the servient land.

3.76 It follows that where there has been a transfer of rights of light from windows in an old building to windows in a new and redeveloped building, this arising because of the similarity in the cones of light, the correct method of determining whether an obstruction on the servient land is an infringement of the transferred rights of light is to compare two situations or scenarios:

(a) The access of light should be considered with the old windows (or such portion of their glazing as remains coincident with the glazing of the new windows) alone existing in the dominant building and with the obstruction on the servient land not having been erected.
(b) The access of light should then be considered with the whole of the new windows in the dominant building existing and receiving light and the obstruction having been erected on the servient land.

The floor areas sufficiently lit in the dominant building under the two scenarios can then be compared and a judgment made on whether the reduction in light amounts to an infringement.[130] If this process means that the access of light through a part of a window or windows which does not itself enjoy a right of light is taken into account, then it must be regarded as an exception to the principle that that cannot normally be done.

7. Partial Redevelopments

3.77 It is of course possible that the plane or position of a window is altered by works carried out to an existing building which do not involve a complete demolition and redevelopment of the building. A wall in a building might be moved backwards or forwards, or the inclination of a window changed from it being vertical to the ground to it being at an angle to the ground. The main principles which govern the transfer of rights from windows in a building to corresponding windows in a redeveloped building on the site were stated in *Scott v Pape*[131] in the Court of Appeal as just explained in connection with a complete redevelopment, but there were decisions prior to that decision in which it was held that changes in the plane or inclination of windows in an existing building did not destroy rights of light

[130] See ch 6 for how the details of this exercise are carried out.
[131] *Scott v Pape* (1886) 31 Ch D 554.

appurtenant to those windows.[132] It seems likely that as regards such alterations which do not result from a complete redevelopment the question now to be asked is the same as where there is a complete redevelopment, namely whether the cone of light received by the windows after the alterations are substantially the same as were previously received by those windows. It is only if there is a substantial similarity that rights of light will be preserved.

8. Tension Between Principles

The discussion in this section of the chapter on alterations to windows and the effect of such alterations on rights of light enjoyed through the unaltered windows has revealed more than once a tension between two principles of law. The tension arises when a window is altered such that the new or altered window contains a part, but perhaps only a small part, of the glazing which is coincident with the glazing of the former and unaltered window. This situation can occur when a window is altered in an existing wall or when a building is redeveloped and a new window is constructed in the new and redeveloped building.[133] The area of glazing which is coincident with the old glazing will often retain a right of light through that area, whereas there will be no right of light through the area of new glazing. The question is whether, when assessing the effect of an obstruction carried out on the servient land, the light received through the new area of glazing should be taken into account. One possible solution is that it should not. Such a solution is in accordance with the principle that when considering the effect of an obstruction on the access of light to a room through a window which enjoys a right of light through it, no account should be taken of light received through another window in the same room where there is no right of light.[134] This principle can be applied to different areas of glazing in a single window, an area with a right of light through it and an area without that right, as it can to two separate windows. The other principle is that the dominant owner should not be able by his own actions to increase substantially the burden on the servient land. The solution just stated infringes this principle, since if there is an obstruction on the servient land and account is taken of light which passes only through the concurrent area of glazing, which may be a small area, that obstruction is more likely to constitute a breach of the right of light than would be the case if light passing through the whole of 3.78

[132] *National Provincial Plate Glass Insurance Co v Prudential Insurance Co* (1877) 6 Ch D 757 (building redeveloped with dormer windows replaced by a skylight); *Barnes v Loach* (1879) 4 QBD 494 (position of a wall set back from the boundary of the property with windows in the new wall in much the same position as in the old wall); *Bullers v Dickinson* (1885) 29 Ch D 155 (windows in a redeveloped building in a position further back from the street as compared to the old building and at a different angle to the street).

[133] These situations are described in paras 3.54–3.73.

[134] This principle and the reason for it have been explained in paras 3.26–3.30.

the new area of glazing was taken into account. Furthermore if no account is taken of light which may pass through the greater part of the altered or new window, then the dominant owner may well be able to obtain damages for a reduction in light to a room which is well lit by reason of the new and non-coincident area of glazing. The answer given to this problem and to the clash of principles in the leading case on the subject[135] is that in the assessment of the effect on the access of light of an obstruction on the servient land, account is to be taken of light which passes through the new and non-coincident area of glazing as well as through the coincident area of glazing. This appears to be the preferable solution to the question and the test to be applied when the type of situation under discussion in this paragraph arises.

9. Summary

3.79 The law on the effect on established rights of light of alterations to windows through which light is received has been built up by a series of decisions, and sometimes by reference to general principles. The main principles were laid down by the House of Lords in *Tapling v Jones*[136] and by the Court of Appeal in *Scott v Pape.*[137] There are many different types of possible alteration to windows which can take place from a small extension to an existing window to the complete replacement of a window in one building by a window in a redeveloped building on the same site. It is impossible to provide the answer to the effect in law of every possible alteration, but the following general principles can be culled from the decisions.

(i) An alteration to a window can amount to an implied abandonment of a right of light appurtenant to that window, but there must be a firm intention to abandon the right which can be inferred before this occurs.

(ii) If a window in one position is blocked up and replaced by a window in a wholly different position where there is no coincidence of glazing, the right to the access of light through the blocked-up window is abandoned.

(iii) If a window is itself left unaltered but substantial changes are made to the dominant building or its curtilage which substantially reduce the access of light through the window, that may be enough to bring about an implied abandonment of a right of light through the window.

(iv) If a window is reduced in size, the effect of an obstruction erected on the servient land will be judged as though the previous window had remained.

[135] *News of the World Ltd v Allen Fairhead & Sons Ltd* [1931] 2 Ch 402.
[136] *Tapling v Jones* (1865) 11 HLR 290.
[137] *Scott v Pape* (1886) 31 Ch D 554.

(v) If a window is increased in size by the addition of a new glazed area, a right of light will remain for the access of light through the previous area of glazing (or so much of it as remains, if part of it has been removed), but no right of light will arise through the new area of glazing until that right is itself acquired by prescription.

(vi) An alteration in plan in the position of a window, eg the wall which contains the window is moved backwards or forwards, or a change in the inclination or angle of a window, eg it becomes a sloping window instead of a vertical window, will allow the retention of a right of light to the altered window, but only if the altered window receives the same or a substantial part of the same cone of light as did the previous window.

(vii) Where the dominant building is demolished and redeveloped, it is possible that a right of light through a window in the previous building is transferred to a window in the new building, but only if the new window receives the same cone of light, or a substantial part of the same cone of light as did the old window. Even then the right of light transferred will be enjoyed only through that area of glazing in the new window which is coincident with the glazing in the old window.

(viii) Where a right of light remains after a window has been enlarged, or after a building is redeveloped and there is a transfer of the right of light to a window in the new building, and an obstruction takes place on the servient land, it is generally correct to judge whether that obstruction constitutes an actionable injury by taking into account the light which enters the dominant building through the whole of the enlarged window, or through the whole of the window in a new building to which a right of light has been transferred.

4

Acquisition of Rights of Light by Deed

4.1 An easement of light can be created:

(a) by an express term of a deed;
(b) as an implied term of a deed; and
(c) by prescription.

Rights akin to an easement of light can arise under the doctrine of derogation from grant or as a result of a restrictive covenant.[1] This chapter is concerned with the creation of easements as an express or implied term of a deed. It also covers the creation of easements by reason of the words which are deemed to be included in a conveyance unless a contrary intention is shown by section 62 of the Law of Property Act 1925. The subject of easements which arise under the various forms of prescription or long use and enjoyment is explained in Chapter 5.

4.2 A further means by which an easement of light could conceivably arise is by virtue of the operation of the doctrine of proprietary estoppel. The underlying principle of estoppel is that when a person makes a statement which is acted upon by the recipient of the statement, the maker of the statement may be prevented in legal proceedings from contradicting what he has said or written. There are several varieties of estoppel and most of them, such as common law estoppel or estoppel by convention, have nothing to do with the creation of interests in land. The exception is proprietary estoppel, under which an interest in land, including an easement, can arise. In general terms a proprietary estoppel arises when the owner of land encourages someone else to act in some way, often by the expenditure of money, in the expectation that that person will be given an interest in the land. A leading definition of a proprietary estoppel is: if A under an expectation created or encouraged by B that A shall have a certain interest in land, thereafter, on the faith of such expectation and with the knowledge of B and without objection by him, acts to his detriment in connection with such land, a Court of Equity will compel B to give effect to such expectation.[2] A court has a discretion on what interest in land or other right to order so as to give effect to the estoppel. One order could be for the grant of an easement. It seems unlikely that an easement of light would be ordered, but it is not inconceivable. Proprietary estoppel is a subject in

[1] For derogation from grant and for restrictive covenants see ch 2, section (C).
[2] *Taylors Fashions Ltd v Liverpool Victoria Trustees Co Ltd* [1982] 1 QB 133n, 144 (Oliver J).

its own right and details of its operation may be found in textbooks on the law of real property and on the law of equity.[3]

(A) EXPRESS EASEMENTS

An express easement may be created by deed. A legal estate cannot be created *inter vivos* except by a deed.[4] If the easement is purported to be created by some other instrument it will take effect in equity only. A testator may create an easement by will, but a written assent from the personal representatives of the testator is necessary and until this occurs the easement takes effect in equity only.[5] An easement may take effect as a legal interest in land if it is granted for an interest equivalent to a fee simple absolute in possession, ie in effect in perpetuity, or for a term of years absolute.[6] Therefore an easement granted for some other period such as the life of the grantee or the life of some other person is necessarily equitable. If the servient land has a registered title, an easement created today by an express provision in a deed must be protected by a notice on the register of that title if it is to take effect as a legal estate. In addition, if the dominant land is registered the proprietor must be entered in the register as the proprietor of the easement.[7] An equitable easement is more fragile than a legal easement, in the sense that it may not be enforceable against a purchaser of the servient land either because of the provisions in the Land Registration Act 2002 or because of the rules relating to unregistered land. An easement created by prescription or by an implied term in a deed may take effect as a legal easement (providing it is created in perpetuity or for a term of years) despite the absence in the former case of a deed.[8] It is said that an easement cannot be created so as to take effect in reversion, that is at some time later than the date of the grant.[9] Easements were formerly subject to the rule against perpetuities[10] but easements created on or after 6 April 2010 are no longer subject to this rule.[11] The rules which apply to the creation of easements generally by deed apply equally to the easement of light. 4.3

No special words are necessary for the creation of an easement by a deed. The general rule on the construction of express contracts applies so that the intention of the parties is to be ascertained from the language used, read in the context of 4.4

[3] See *Megarry & Wade: The Law of Real Property*, 8th edn (London, Sweet & Maxwell, 2012) ch 16; *Snell's Equity*, 32nd edn (London, Sweet & Maxwell, 2010) ch 12.3.

[4] Law of Property Act, s 52(1).

[5] Administration of Estates Act 1925, s 6.

[6] Law of Property Act 1925, s 1(2)(a).

[7] Land Registration Act 2002, sch 2, para 7. Land registration is considered more fully in ch 11.

[8] See *R (Beresford) v Somerset County Council* [2003] UKHL 60, [2004] 1 AC 869 [36] for the status of an easement implied into a deed.

[9] See *Cable v Bryant* [1908] 1 Ch 259.

[10] *Dunn v Blackdown Properties Ltd* [1961] Ch 433; *Newham v Lawson* (1971) 33 P & CR 852.

[11] Perpetuities and Accumulations Act 2009.

all surrounding circumstances known to the parties at the date of the execution of the deed.[12] The same principle is applied to general words in a deed which refer to rights to be enjoyed by the property transferred.[13] Accordingly when a property is conveyed with a declaration that rights and easements and quasi-easements shall continue to be used as before, the effect may be the creation of express easements equivalent to what was previously enjoyed for the benefit of the land conveyed over land retained by the vendor.[14] In situations such as this, an easement may also be created as an implied easement or by the operation of section 62 of the Law of Property Act 1925, as is explained in later sections of this chapter. If nothing is said as to the duration of the easement granted, then it is likely to be taken to be an easement in perpetuity, and so capable of existing as a legal easement. It is possible that the easement is created for the benefit of a leasehold estate in the dominant building, or as against a leasehold estate in the servient land, in which case it will take effect as a legal leasehold interest. If the grantor of an easement of light has only a leasehold interest in the servient land, the easement will endure during the term of that lease and for no further period.[15]

4.5 An easement may be reserved for the benefit of the land retained by a vendor as against the land granted. There was once a technical conveyancing difficulty in bringing this about, since the grantor could not reserve to himself a right which did not exist at the time of the grant. Any difficulty is now resolved by section 65(1) of the Law of Property Act 1925, which provides that the reservation of a legal estate or interest shall operate without execution of the conveyance by the grantee, and without any regrant by him. Despite this provision, it appears that the rule that in case of doubt a grant shall be construed against the grantor is to be applied in the case of a reservation of an easement to the grantor, such that a provision of this nature in the deed is to be construed against the grantee, who is taken to be making a regrant.[16] This rule has been substantially criticised.[17]

4.6 It is essential to the nature of an easement that there is dominant land which is benefited by the easement, and servient land over which the easement exists, and

[12] *Investors Compensation Scheme Ltd v West Bromwich Building Society* [1998] 1 WLR 896; *Rainy Sky SA v Kookmin Bank* [2011] UKSC 50, [2011] 1 WLR 2900. Events which occurred after the date of the deed are not admissible as an aid to the construction of the deed, save where they are relevant to the determination of a boundary: *Wood v Waddington* [2015] EWCA Civ 538, [2015] 2 P & CR 11 [22] (Lewison LJ). There is a cogent explanation of the general principles which apply to the construction of contracts and other consensual documents in Lewison, *The Interpretation of Contracts*, 5th edn (London, Sweet & Maxwell, 2011).

[13] *Pitt v Buxton* (1970) 21 P & CR 127.

[14] *Pallister v Clark* (1975) 30 P & CR 84. For the meaning of quasi-easements, see para 4.23 and ch 2, para 2.21.

[15] *Booth v Alcock* (1873) 8 Ch App 663. See ch 8, section (B)4 for a fuller account of the termination of leasehold easements by reason of the termination by various means of the lease of the dominant or the servient property.

[16] See *St Edmundsbury and Ipswich Diocesan Board of Finance v Clark (No 2)* [1975] 1 WLR 468.

[17] See the view of the Law Commission expressed in Law Com CP No 186 (2008), paras 4.13 et seq and see *Megarry and Wade: The Law of Real Property*, 8th edn (London, Sweet & Maxwell, 2012) para 28-001. See also n 29.

this principle applies to easements of light as to other easements.[18] A well-drafted deed creating an easement will therefore specifically and clearly identify what are the dominant and servient areas of land. Even so, there is no legal necessity that a particular piece of land is specifically designated as the dominant land, and the court will consider, in accordance with the usual principles for the construction of contracts, the language of the deed and relevant surrounding circumstances in order to determine what exactly is the dominant land.[19] Nonetheless, if there is not in existence at the time of the grant some wholly identifiable area of land which is intended to and can constitute the dominant land, there will be no valid creation of an easement.[20]

An easement may of course be granted by a deed executed specifically and only for that purpose. More frequently, easements are created as part of a conveyancing transaction, either by a grant for the benefit of the land transferred or by a reservation for the benefit of land retained by the vendor. The same principles of construction and of law apply in either case. 4.7

(B) IMPLIED EASEMENTS

1. Introduction

Nearly all contractual or consensual arrangements, as well as containing their express terms, are capable of containing implied terms which can create rights and obligations beyond those stated in express provisions. Implied terms often arise under contracts of all types. Some implied terms are of a standard nature, such as a term that neither party will act so as to impede the obvious purpose of the contract. Other implied terms are specific to the subject matter of a particular contract. In general, a term will not be implied into a contract just because it is reasonable to do so[21] but only: 4.8

(a) if the implied term is necessary to give business efficacy to the contract; or
(b) if the need for the implied term is so obvious that if a bystander had suggested its inclusion in the contract as an express term the parties to the

[18] See ch 2, para 2.11 et seq.

[19] *Johnstone v Holdway* [1963] 1 QB 601; *The Shannon Ltd v Venner Ltd* [1965] Ch 682; *Thorpe v Brumfitt* (1873) LR 8 Ch App 650.

[20] *London & Blenheim Estates Ltd v Ladbroke Retail Parks Ltd* [1994] 1 WLR 31. An easement cannot benefit land subsequently to be acquired by the dominant owner, at least unless that further land is clearly specified and identified. Therefore a developer cannot create an easement for the benefit of land which he has not acquired at the date of the grant by him. See Year Books, 21 Edw 3, 2, p15 where a right of way to a mill was granted to a grantee who did not then own the mill as the dominant land. The grantee subsequently purchased the dominant land, but was not entitled to enforce the right of way so granted.

[21] *Liverpool City Council v Irwin* [1977] AC 239.

contract would have responded that plainly that must be so, ie the 'officious bystander' test.[22]

4.9 Certain types of property transactions attract the existence of standardised implied obligations in the sense that the obligation will always be implied in a particular form unless it is excluded or varied by an express term of the transaction. The best example of this process is the covenants by landlords for quiet possession and not to derogate from the grant, which are implied into all leases. The implied obligation not to derogate from grant applies to property transactions beyond the grant of leases and may give rise indirectly to what amount to rights of light.[23] The importance of implied terms for present purposes is that when a part of the property of an owner is transferred by a deed there may arise in favour of the transferee an implied easement over the part of the land retained, or there may arise in favour of the transferor an implied easement over the part of the land transferred. The processes by which this can occur are by the implication of an easement as an implied term in the deed or by the operation of section 62 of the Law of Property Act 1925.[24] The two processes lead to much the same result which is the creation of an easement. Normally the two processes must be considered and applied separately since the exact requirements for their operation are not the same. Section 62 can create an easement only in favour of a transferee of land whereas an implied easement can in principle arise in favour of a transferee or a transferor of land. The first process, the creation of an easement by implication, is covered in this section of the chapter.

4.10 The circumstances in which an implied easement may arise, and the tests to be applied to decide whether it does arise, are now well settled. Two preliminary observations are appropriate. First, the parties may by express language exclude the creation of an easement by implication, or may limit the scope of that easement. It would be irrational to impute to the parties to a disposal of land an intention to create particular rights and obligations when they have expressly stated that they do not wish to do so. Secondly, implied easements are more readily created in favour of the transferee for the benefit of the part of the land transferred to him than they are in favour of the transferor for the benefit of the part of the land retained by him. This result is said to derive at any rate in part from the principle that a grant is to be construed against the grantor.[25] Although it is of some antiquity, it is not easy to justify this rule and it has been suggested by the Law Commission that the determination of whether an easement has arisen by implication on a transfer of land should be governed by the same principles, whether

[22] For a full consideration of implied terms in contracts generally see *Treitel on the Law of Contract*, 13th edn (London, Sweet & Maxwell, 2011) 222 et seq.

[23] See ch 2, section (C)2.

[24] It may not be strictly accurate to describe an easement which arises by statutory process under s 62 as an implied easement. See para 4.40.

[25] See, eg *Neill v Duke of Devonshire* (1882) 8 App Cas 135, 149; *Wheeldon v Burrows* (1879) 12 Ch D 31, 49; *Bayley v Great Western Railway Co* (1884) 26 Ch D 434, 458; *Walby v Walby* [2012] EWHC 3089 (Ch), [2013] 1 EGLR 111 [28] (Morgan J).

the implication is in favour of or against the grantor.[26] Accordingly in this section of the chapter the creation of easements in favour of a transferee of land will be examined first, followed by an examination of the more limited circumstances in which an easement may be created by implication in favour of a transferor of land. The law can only be understood by reference to the general principles applicable to the creation of easements by implication and the particular application of those principles to easements of light. A leading case on the subject which has given its name to the general rule on implied easements, the rule in *Wheeldon v Burrows*, concerned a claim for an implied easement of light.[27]

Where a transferor transfers a part of the land owned by him, the creation of an implied easement against the land retained is described as an implied grant of the easement to the transferee. The circumstances in which there can be an implied grant of an easement are: 4.11

(a) under the principle of easements of necessity;
(b) under the principle of an intended use or development of the land transferred; and
(c) under the rule in *Wheeldon v Burrows*.[28]

The creation of an easement by implication in favour of the land retained over the land granted is termed an implied reservation of the easement.[29] The circumstances in which there can be an implied reservation of an easement are:

(a) under the principle of easements of necessity; and
(b) under the principle of an intended use or development of the land retained.

An easement can also be created in favour of the land transferred as against the retained land of the transferor under section 62 of the Law of Property Act 1925. This form of creation of an easement by statute is of considerable practical importance and is examined in the next section of this chapter. The exact operation of section 62 is of some complexity, and is in some ways uncertain. 4.12

The rules which apply to the creation of easements generally by implication and under section 62 of the Law of Property Act 1925 are in principle the same for the creation of easements of light as for the creation of other forms of easement. It is possible that in one instance an easement of light may be created under section 4.13

[26] Law Commission, *Making Land Work: Easements, Covenants and Profits a Prendre* (Law Com No 327, 2011). This report and other recent Law Commission documents relevant to rights of light are discussed in ch 12.

[27] *Wheeldon v Burrows* (1879) 12 Ch D 31.

[28] ibid.

[29] Prior to the Law of Property Act 1925 there were technical conveyancing difficulties in reserving an easement to the transferor or vendor. It was considered that since the easement was not a pre-existing right, it could not be excepted out of the grant and that there had to be a re-grant by the transferee. These difficulties have been removed by section 65 of the Law of Property Act 1925, and the process here being examined can properly be described as an implied reservation of an easement. See also para 4.5.

62 in circumstances which would not permit the creation under that section of a different type of easement and this is discussed below.[30]

2. Implied Grant: Easements of Necessity

4.14 An easement of necessity arises by implication when the land granted is landlocked, in the sense that it has no means of access to or from a public highway, save over the land retained. An implied easement of way then arises over the land retained. The requirement of the way over the land retained must be a matter of necessity and not of convenience.[31] Easements of necessity are nearly always easements of way, although it is possible that an easement of a different sort could arise by this means, such as an easement of support for a building, or an easement permitting the creation of a ventilation duct.[32] It seems very unlikely that an easement of light could arise as an easement of necessity, since the access of natural light to a particular standard cannot be necessary for the use of property in the strict sense needed to support the creation of an easement of necessity. There appears to be no reported instance of an easement of light arising by implication pursuant to the principle of easements of necessity.

3. Implied Grant: Intended Use

4.15 Where at the time of the grant the parties intend that the land transferred shall be used or developed in a particular way, there is implied an easement over the land retained where that is necessary for the carrying out of that use or development. In a leading decision on the subject, a lease was granted with the understanding that the tenant might carry out coal mining operations on the land demised. One type of easement which can exist is that of a right to commit what would otherwise be a nuisance. The tenant contended that because of the intended use, he became entitled to spread coal dust caused by the mining operation over land retained by the landlord without incurring any liability in the tort of nuisance. The claim to an easement failed only because the causation of this type of nuisance was not necessary for the carrying out of the mining operation.[33] The principle which justifies the implication of an easement in these circumstances is an emanation of the wider principle that a person who grants an interest in land cannot derogate

[30] See para 4.37.

[31] *Manjang v Drummer* (1991) 61 P & CR 194, in which an access by water was held to exclude the creation of an easement of necessity. See also *Kingfish Lodge (1993) Ltd v Archer* [2000] 3 NZLR 364.

[32] *Wong v Beaumont Property Trust Ltd* [1965] 1 QB 173.

[33] *Pwllbach Colliery Co v Woodman* [1915] AC 634. See n 36.

from his grant.[34] It does not often matter whether the obligation of the grantor not to use his land so as to render impractical or substantially less convenient an intended use of the land transferred is regarded as attributable to an obligation not to derogate from grant or to the existence of an implied easement.[35] Even so, the duty not to derogate from a grant may impose burdens on the retained land of the grantor which are wider than or different to those which could be the subject of an easement. The rights which accrue to a grantee as to what can be done on the land of the grantor may be more akin to the benefit of a restrictive covenant than an easement. An implied easement under this doctrine will arise where:

(a) at the date of the grant, which may be a sale or a lease, it was known to the parties that the land transferred was to be used or developed in some definite and specific way; and
(b) the easement was reasonably necessary to give effect to that particular purpose.[36]

An implied easement of light can be acquired by means of the principle of intended easements for the benefit of the land transferred over the land retained. A person may own a house with adjoining ground and may sell the house. In the ordinary course of events the house would benefit from an implied easement of light over the adjoining land retained so that the transferor will be prevented from carrying out a development on the land retained which infringes that intended easement.[37] If the part of the land transferred does not contain a house or other building but it is the common intention of the parties that it will be built upon the implied easement will arise so as to protect light through the apertures of the intended building when it is constructed.[38] It is not necessary for the creation of an intended easement that the land transferred immediately adjoins the land retained.[39] The critical matter is that the land transferred can benefit as regards its intended use from the passage of light to it over the land retained. 4.16

Since the application of the easement depends on the intention of the parties to the transfer the known proposals for the use or development of the retained or servient land will also be significant when it comes to the matter of an intended easement of light restricting the development of that property. The fact that it was intended at the time of the transfer that the retained land was itself likely 4.17

[34] See *Moncrieff v Jamieson* [2007] UKHL 42, [2007] 1 WLR 2620, 2657 (Lord Neuberger).

[35] An earlier leading decision on this subject, *Lyttleton Times Co Ltd v Warners Ltd* [1907] AC 476, is often cited as an authority on derogation from grant as applied to leases: see *Southwark Borough Council v Mills* [2001] 1 AC 1.

[36] As stated earlier in this paragraph, the claim failed in *Pwllbach Colliery Co v Woodman* [1915] AC 634 because there was no evidence that the spreading of coal dust was reasonably required for the carrying out of the mining activity on the land granted.

[37] *Swansborough v Coventry* (1832) 9 Bing 305; *Leech v Schweider* (1874) LR 9 Ch App 463.

[38] *Frederick Betts Ltd v Pickfords Ltd* [1906] 2 Ch 87.

[39] *Birmingham, Dudley and District Banking Co v Ross* (1888) 38 Ch D 295. In this case (ibid, 313) Bowen LJ referred to the land transferred which might in an appropriate case benefit from the implied easement of light as 'adjoining or neighbouring' the land retained.

to be developed in a certain way may prevent the implication of an easement of light against that property which would prevent that development.[40] An easement acquired by implication against retained land may therefore be limited in its effect by the intention and understanding of the parties at the time of the transfer, so as to have an effect or impose a restriction on the retained land not identical to that which would arise from an easement of light created by express words in a deed or by prescription. In one case where a railway company sold land, it was intended that the retained land of the company would be used for railway purposes, but this did not permit the company to block up railway arches through which light passed to a house on the land transferred.[41] Circumstances such as this emphasise the origin of intended easements of the present character as an aspect of the duty not to derogate from grant.

4. Implied Grant: The Rule in *Wheeldon v Burrows*

4.18 *Wheeldon v Burrows*[42] is a decision in which a person sold a piece of land adjoining his workshop and later claimed an implied easement of light in favour of the workshop, in order to prevent the obstruction of its windows by building carried out on the land sold. It was therefore a claim for the implied reservation rather than for the implied grant of an easement of light. The Court of Appeal, the judgment of which was delivered by Thesiger LJ, after a review of the authorities as they then stood, considered the general matter of the implication of easements on the transfer of property and laid down certain principles which governed all types of implied easement and which applied to the implication of easements by implied grant as well as by implied reservation. The following general principles were established.

(i) The principles are founded on the rule that a person shall not derogate from his grant, described as a maxim which was well established by authority and was consonant to reason and common sense. A similar origin to the principles has been stated by modern authority.[43]

(ii) Where a person grants an interest in land, he must expressly reserve to himself any easement which is to be created over the land granted. There are exceptions to this principle, of which an easement of necessity reserved by

[40] *Birmingham, Dudley and District Banking Co v Ross* (1888) 38 Ch D 295 (property let with the knowledge of the tenant that retained property was likely to rebuilt with a higher building). See also *Broomfield v Williams* [1897] 1 Ch 602; *Godwin v Schweppes Ltd* [1902] 1 Ch 926.

[41] *Myers v Catterson* (1889) 43 Ch D 470.

[42] *Wheeldon v Burrows* (1879) 12 Ch D 31.

[43] *Sovmots Investments Ltd v Secretary of State for the Environment* [1979] AC 144, 168 (Lord Wilberforce); *Moncrieff v Jamieson* [2007] UKHL 42, [2007] 1 WLR 2620, 2657 (Lord Neuberger). The principle that a grantor cannot derogate from his grant goes back at least to the seventeenth century: *Palmer v Fletcher* (1662) 1 Lev 122.

implication in favour of that land retained is one. It will be explained that an implied easement in favour of the land retained over the land transferred based on the intended use of the land retained is a further exception.[44]

(iii) Where a person grants an interest in land, there will be implied in favour of the land granted over the land retained by the grantor easements which correspond to what prior to the transfer were the use and enjoyment of the land retained for the benefit of the land transferred, provided (a) the use and enjoyment was continuous and apparent, (b) the use and enjoyment was reasonably necessary for the enjoyment of the land granted, and (c) the use and enjoyment had been, and was at the time of the grant, carried out by the grantor for the benefit of the land granted.[45]

There are some uncertainties about this rule. It is not clear from the original formulation of the principle as stated in sub-paragraph (iii) of the last paragraph whether the satisfaction of the first requirement is an alternative to the satisfaction of the second and third requirements, or that all three requirements have to be satisfied for an easement to be implied. Recent authority supports the latter view.[46] It seems that the expression 'continuous and apparent' is derived from French law.[47] In any event the enjoyment of the access of light through a window or other aperture in a building is continuous and apparent for present purposes.[48] Thus where the land transferred contains a building which has windows receiving light over the land retained, the three requirements of the rule are likely to be satisfied so that an implied easement of light for the benefit of the land transferred is likely to arise as against the land retained. There is a substantial degree of overlap between the operation of the rule in *Wheeldon v Burrows* and the operation of the rule relating to intended easements, and in many cases the creation of an implied easement in favour of land transferred can be justified under both heads. The overlap is not total. An easement of light can be created as an implied easement to benefit the land transferred where it is intended to construct a building on that land,[49] but this would not be possible under the rule in *Wheeldon v Burrows* since the enjoyment of the access of light to the proposed building would not exist at the date of the transfer. 4.19

An easement of light can arise under the rule in *Wheeldon v Burrows* where a grantor makes simultaneous grants of two parts of his land to two grantees.[50] Thus if 4.20

44 See para 4.24.
45 *Wheeldon v Burrows*, 49 and 58–59 (Thesiger LJ).
46 See, eg *Millman v Ellis* (1996) 71 P & CR 158.
47 *Dalton v Angus & Co* (1881) 6 App Cas 740, 821 (Lord Blackburn); *Wood v Waddington* [2015] EWCA Civ 538, [2015] 2 P & CR 11 [15] (Lewison LJ). The concept of a use which is continuous has moved from its original meaning in French law and today, for the purposes of the rule in *Wheeldon v Burrows*, includes the use of a right of way. The word 'continuous' appears to be all but superfluous within the expression 'continuous and apparent': *Wood v Waddington* [15].
48 *Phillips v Low* [1892] 1 Ch 47, 53 (Chitty J) citing the 4th edition of *Gale on Easements*; *Wood v Waddington*.
49 See para 4.16.
50 *Russell v Watts* (1884) 25 Ch D 559.

A owns a house and an area of open adjoining land and transfers the house to B and the adjoining land to C at the same time, it is possible that B will obtain an implied easement of light over the land of C so as to prevent the building on that land in a way which will unacceptably reduce the light to the house. The situation of B is the same as if the house had been transferred to him and A had retained the open adjoining land. For this principle to be applied, the two transfers need not be exactly simultaneous in time and it is enough if they are part and parcel of the same transaction.[51]

4.21 The creation of implied easements is not confined to dispositions of land for value. An implied easement can arise following a devise under a will[52] or appointments by trustees.[53]

4.22 The implication of an easement of light under the rule in *Wheeldon v Burrows* depends on the access of light being enjoyed at the date of the grant. When the grant is preceded by a contract, the circumstances necessary for the creation of the easement are judged as at the date of the contract.[54]

4.23 The application of the rule in *Wheeldon v Burrows* (as the operation of the principle of intended easements, and the operation of section 62 of the Law of Property Act 1925 considered in the next section of this chapter) gives rise to the concept of quasi-easements, an expression used by Thesiger LJ in his articulation of the rule in *Wheeldon v Burrows.*[55] What is meant by a quasi-easement is that a person who owns an area of land exercises some use or enjoyment over one part of the land for the benefit of another part. An owner may use a roadway on one part of his land as an access to a building on another part of his land, or an owner may rely on the unimpeded access of natural light over one part of his land to provide illumination to a building on another part of his land. The use or enjoyment of the road or of the access of light in circumstances such as those described cannot be the exercise of an easement since a person cannot have an easement against himself. The situation discussed is called a quasi-easement. It is the exercise of some use or enjoyment for the benefit of one part of a person's land over another part of his land, such that if the two parts of the land were in separate ownerships there could be the exercise of an easement. The application of the rule in *Wheeldon v Burrows* converts a quasi-easement into a true easement when the two pieces of land come into separate ownership, provided that the requirements of the rule are fulfilled.

[51] *Donaldson v Smith* [2007] 1 P & CR DG2 [16] (separate appointments by trustees four months apart held to be sufficiently 'simultaneous').

[52] *Phillips v Low* [1892] 1 Ch 47.

[53] *Donaldson v Smith* [2007] 1 P & CR DG2.

[54] *White v Taylor (No 2)* [1969] 1 Ch 150; *Beddington v Atlee* (1887) 35 Ch D 317.

[55] *Wheeldon v Burrows* (1879) 12 Ch D 31, 49.

5. Implied Reservation

4.24 As mentioned, a reservation of an implied easement for the benefit of a grantor is less easy to establish than a grant of an implied easement for the benefit of a grantee. The decision in *Wheeldon v Burrows*, itself a decision on an alleged implied reservation of an easement of light, states this rule on the basis of earlier authority.[56] In general, the two circumstances in which an easement may be implied by reservation in favour of a grantor are easements of necessity and implied easements. As stated in connection with implied grants, an easement of necessity of light can scarcely arise. An implied intended easement of light could arise in favour of a grantor as in favour of a grantee. There seems no rational reason in this instance for an implied easement by reservation being any easier or more difficult to establish than an implied easement by grant. If the owner of an open plot of land sells a part of it for the construction of a house, an implied easement of light is likely to arise for the benefit of the house when constructed against the open land retained. It should follow by parity of reasoning that if the owner had retained the land on which the house was intended to be built, and had sold the open land, there should be implied for the benefit of the house when constructed on the retained land an easement of light over the open land sold. The theoretical foundation of the principle of intended easements is the need to give effect to the intention and the purpose of the parties to a grant of land, and this need can operate in appropriate circumstance as much in favour of a grantor as in favour of a grantee.

(C) SECTION 62 OF THE LAW OF PROPERTY ACT 1925

1. Purpose and Effect

4.25 Prior to 1881 it was usual in a conveyance or other disposal of land to set out specifically each right appurtenant or ancillary to the interest in the land transferred which was to be transferred with that interest. It is probable that, when a property was sold, no specific reference was necessary in the conveyance to pass to the grantee easements over other property appurtenant to the property transferred.[57]

[56] *Wheeldon v Burrows* (1879) 12 Ch D 31, 49 (Thesiger LJ); *Bayley v Great Western Railway Co* (1884) 26 Ch D 434, 458 (Fry LJ); *Re Webb's Lease* [1951] Ch 808; *Adealon International Proprietary Ltd v Merton LBC* [2007] EWCA Civ 362, [2007] 1 WLR 1898 [14].

[57] *Godwin v Schweppes Ltd* [1902] 1 Ch 926. An easement 'legally appendant or appurtenant to the property' was said by Joyce J at p 932 to pass by a conveyance of the property without any additional words. In *Sovmots Ltd v Secretary of State for the Environment* [1979] AC 144, 178 Lord Edmund-Davies pointed out that on a compulsory purchase of property, a right of way appurtenant to the land acquired was passed to the acquiring authority.

Section 6 of the Conveyancing Act 1881 was enacted so as to include automatically in conveyances of land general words which removed the need to refer specifically to appurtenant and ancillary rights as things which were transferred. As a result of this statutory provision the need for elaborate phraseology in conveyances was removed, as was any doubt on what ancillary property and rights passed on a conveyance. This provision was replaced by the somewhat wider language to the same general effect in section 62 of the Law of Property Act 1926. Section 62(1) provides:

> A conveyance of land shall be deemed to include and shall by virtue of this Act operate to convey, with the land, all buildings, erections, fixtures, commons, hedges, ditches, fences, ways, waters, watercourses, liberties, privileges, easements, rights, and advantages whatsoever, appertaining or reputed to appertain to the land, or any part thereof, or, at the time of conveyance, demised, occupied, or enjoyed with, or reputed or known as part or parcel of or appurtenant to the land or any part thereof.

Section 62(2) contains a similar provision relating to the conveyance of land with buildings on it. The provisions apply to transfers of registered land in the statutory form. The provisions do not apply to contracts to dispose of land.[58]

4.26 The effect of section 62 is greater than that of ensuring the passing to a grantee of rights over the property of third parties. It may operate in certain circumstances to create for the benefit of the grantee of a part of the land of the grantor easements derived from what were before the grant quasi-easements in the sense explained earlier.[59] To this extent the section can operate alongside the rule in *Wheeldon v Burrows* and the principle of intended easements to create new easements of light for the benefit of property sold against the land retained by the grantor. In some ways section 62 operates more widely than the rule in *Wheeldon v Burrows*, and in some ways it operates more restrictively.[60] Section 62 may operate where there is a transfer of the freehold of land or where there is a lease of land. Because of its language and purpose, section 62 cannot operate so as to create rights for the benefit of a grantor. It is of course the case that where the grantor has only a limited interest in the land retained by him, the obvious case being a lease of that land,

[58] *Borman v Griffith* [1930] 1 Ch 493. Section 62 operates where there is a conveyance of land, as opposed to where there is a contract to convey land.

[59] See para 4.23. It seems that even before the Conveyancing Act 1881 the type of general words often inserted into conveyances could turn quasi-easements into easements. In *Booth v Alcock* (1873) LR 8 Ch App 663 the grantor of a lease himself held a leasehold interest in adjoining land. The grant of the lease contained the words 'together with all edifices, buildings, ways, lights, sewers, watercourses, rights, easements, advantages, and appurtenances thereto belonging, or used therewith, or enjoyed'. It was held that the words of the lease amounted to a grant of a right of light during the lease over the adjoining property held by the lessor.

[60] A right can only ripen into an easement under s 62 if it was enjoyed with the land sold at the date of the conveyance, whereas an intended easement can arise by implication where it is intended that the benefit of the easement shall be enjoyed in the future, such as an easement to protect the light to a property to be built on the land sold. See paras 4.24 and 4.29.

the right of light created by the operation of section 62 will bind only that limited interest. It will therefore end when the limited interest ends.[61]

2. Operation of Section 62

Section 62 applies by virtue of its language to a variety of benefits enjoyed by the land transferred such as rights, easements and advantages. They are said to appertain to the land transferred. The primary situation to be examined for the purposes of rights of light is that in which the grantor owns land and conveys a part of it, part A, to the grantee and himself retains a different part, part B, in circumstances in which a building on part A enjoys the access of light to its apertures over part B. The question is whether, following the grant, the enjoyment will ripen into an easement of light appurtenant to plot A and exercisable against plot B. In order for this to occur, four conditions have to be fulfilled. These conditions apply to the creation of all types of easements but are described here in the context of rights of light. 4.27

(a) The First Condition

The first condition is that the right or advantage which becomes an easement by the operation of section 62 must be capable of existing as an easement. A general use for recreation or exercise over land, an *ius spatiendi*, was thought at one time to be incapable of being an easement and so at that time could not have been created as an easement by the operation of section 62,[62] although under the modern law such a right has been admitted into the category of easements.[63] A right to the access of light is of course a recognised category of easements so that in the circumstances being considered, this condition would be fulfilled. 4.28

(b) The Second Condition

The second condition is that, in accordance with the language of section 62, at the time of the grant the right or advantage is enjoyed with the land granted.[64] In the case of the example given, the access of light to the building on part A, the land transferred, is enjoyed at the time of the grant so that this condition is readily 4.29

[61] *Booth v Alcock* (1873) LR 8 Ch App 663. See ch 8, section (B)4, for a fuller account of the termination of leasehold easements by reason of the termination by various means of the lease of the dominant or the servient property.

[62] *International Tea Stores Co v Hobbs* [1903] 2 Ch 165, 172.

[63] *Re Ellenborough Park* [1956] Ch 131.

[64] The requirement that a right is enjoyed 'at the time of conveyance' includes a reasonable period before the conveyance: *Wood v Waddington* [2015] EWCA Civ 538, [2015] 2 P & CR 11.

fulfilled.[65] The condition may mark a difference between the operation of section 62 and the operation of the principle of intended easements in respect of rights of light. If part A of the land was intended to have a building constructed on it, an implied easement of light to the apertures in that building when constructed might arise as an implied easement under the principle of intended easements, but could not arise under section 62, since the access of light was not enjoyed to those apertures at the time of the grant.[66] A difference between the operation of section 62 and the operation of the rule in *Wheeldon v Burrows* can also be noted. Under section 62 it is sufficient if the access of light over plot B to plot A was actually enjoyed at the time of the grant of plot A, whereas for an easement to be implied under the rule in *Wheeldon v Burrows* the access of light must also have been necessary for the reasonable enjoyment of plot A.[67]

(c) The Third Condition

4.30 The third condition is the most complex to describe, and may reveal a difference between easements of light and other easements which are created by the operation of section 62. It is a matter of common sense that a person cannot acquire rights against himself,[68] nor can he exercise against himself the privileges, liberties, advantages, etc as referred to in the torrential style of drafting used in sections 62(1) and (2) of the Law of Property Act 1925. It might therefore be thought at first that section 62 would be confined to ensuring that on a grant of land all rights appurtenant to the land over property not owned by the grantor should pass to the grantee with the purpose of section 62, and its predecessor in the Conveyancing Act 1881, being confined to removing the need, so far as it existed, for express words in a grant to that effect. If the operation of section 62 were so confined, the creation of an easement for the benefit of a part of a person's land granted over other land retained by him could be left to an express provision in the grant or the creation of an easement by implication under the rule in *Wheeldon v Burrows* and the principles of intended easements and easements of necessity. However, authority precludes any such simple approach.

[65] Ss 62(1) and 62(2) also refer to rights and advantages 'reputed or known as part or parcel of' the land granted so that enjoyment in the past but not subsisting at the time of the grant may be enough, since such past enjoyment may make the right or advantage a reputed right: see eg *Costagliola v English* (1969) 210 Estates Gazette 1425, in which a right of way arose by virtue of s 62 even though the way had not been much used for 11 months before the grant. This situation is more likely to arise in connection with easements such as rights of way where the enjoyment may be intermittent than it is with an easement of light, where the enjoyment is likely to be continuous. See also *Green v Ashco Horticultural Ltd* [1966] 1 WLR 889; *Pretoria Warehousing Co Ltd v Shelton* (1993), unreported.

[66] See paras 4.15–4.17 for easements implied from the intention of the parties.

[67] *Watts v Kelson* (1871) LR 6 Ch App 166; *Wood v Waddington* [2015] EWCA Civ 538, [2015] 2 P & CR 11. See para 4.18 for the requirements of the creation of an implied easement under the rule in *Wheeldon v Burrows*.

[68] See ch 2, para 2.2 for a discussion on the nature of rights relating to land.

The authorities establish that where a grantor owns an area of land and grants a part of it, retaining the remainder, an existing quasi-easement[69] for the benefit of the land granted can be created under section 62, so as to be exercisable by the grantee over the part of the land retained. Even so, there are limitations on the application of this process. For an easement to be created in this way it is necessary that at the date of the grant either (a) there was diversity of occupation of the two parts of the land, or (b) the quasi-easement was 'continuous and apparent'.[70] The third condition for the operation of section 62 therefore requires the satisfaction of one or other of what are usually stated as two alternative requirements. It should be noted that this third condition derives not directly from the express language of section 62, but from an interpretation of its meaning in decided case. The precise meaning now given to section 62 appears not to bear a close and direct relationship to the statutory language. 4.31

The first of the two alternative requirements was stated in the House of Lords in *Sovmots Investments Ltd v Secretary of State for the Environment*.[71] Lord Wilberforce referred to a separation of 'ownership or at least of occupation'. This was a decision on the application of section 62 where a part of an owner's land, maisonettes at the top of a high office building, had been compulsorily acquired, but the principle is of general application. The statement of Lord Wilberforce was based on earlier authority. In *Long v Gowlett* Sargant J observed: 4.32

> Mr Greene for the defendant was challenged to produce from the very many cases in which, on a conveyance of Whiteacre, an easement over Blackacre has been held to pass under the statutory words or their equivalent, a single case in which both the closes in question had been in common ownership and occupation, or in which there had not been an actual enjoyment over Blackacre on the part of an owner or occupier of Whiteacre who was not the owner and occupier of Blackacre. And neither from among the cases cited to me, nor from any other case in the books, was he able (with one solitary exception) to produce such a case as required.[72]

The solitary exception is referred to below.[73]

Applying the first of the two requirements, the operation of section 62 as regards rights of light is as follows. The grant of land which has a subsisting right of light over land of a third party not owned by the grantor and not the subject of the grant will pass the benefit of that easement over the land of the third party to the grantee. This will be so whether the easement has been created by a deed or by prescription. The reason is that there was a separation of ownership at the time of the grant. As mentioned earlier, this result would in most cases have come 4.33

[69] See para 4.23 for the meaning of a quasi-easement. It is the exercise of some use or advantage for the benefit of a part of a person's land over or against another part of the land of the same person which could amount to the exercise of a true easement if the two pieces of land were in separate ownership.

[70] *Wood v Waddington* [2015] EWCA Civ 538, [2015] 2 P & CR 11; *Alford v Hannaford* [2011] EWCA Civ 1099, [2012] 1 P & CR DG2.

[71] *Sovmots v Secretary of State for the Environment* [1979] AC 144, 169.

[72] *Long v Gowlett* [1923] 2 Ch 177, 201–02.

[73] See para 4.37.

about apart from section 62 by reason of express language in the grant or by the operation of the general law.[74] If a person owns and occupies the whole of an area of land and grants away a part of the land the first of the two alternative requirements will not be satisfied even if prior to the grant the part sold enjoyed the access of light over the part retained, the reason being that prior to and at the time of the grant there was no separation of either ownership or occupation. Therefore in these circumstances the grantee will not in reliance on this alternative acquire an easement of light in favour of his land over the land retained by virtue of section 62 of the Law of Property Act 1925. On the other hand if, prior to and at the time of the grant, the part sold or the part retained had been occupied by a tenant or tenants of the grantor the first of the alternative requirements would be satisfied since in those circumstances there would be a separation of occupation and as a result the grantee of the part transferred would gain an easement of light over the part retained under section 62.

4.34 The second of the two alternative requirements, that the use or enjoyment was continuous and apparent, is well established by authority. The expression 'continuous and apparent' is said to derive from French law and has become an ingredient in the rule in *Wheeldon v Burrows*.[75] It has been long established that the benefit of continuous and apparent quasi-easements passed on a conveyance of a part of the property for the benefit of which the quasi-easement was enjoyed, either by reason of express language in the conveyance such as is now stated in section 62 or by implication.[76] A distinction was drawn between on the one hand 'easements such as a right of way, or easements used from time to time, and easements of necessity, or continuous easements'. It was said that upon a severance of the land, easements in the second category passed to a grantee without any words of grant, but that appropriate express language was needed to pass easements in the first category.[77] It now appears clear from modern authority that a quasi-easement may be converted into an easement on a grant of a part of the land of the grantor which enjoyed the quasi-easement where the enjoyment was continuous and apparent, even though at the time of the grant there was no separation or diversity of occupation. In one case the owners and occupiers of a hotel and of moorings used for hotel guests sold just the hotel. It was held by the Court of Appeal that under section 62, the right to use the moorings passed to the purchaser of the hotel even though at the date of the sale there was no separation of occupation between the hotel and the moorings.[78]

4.35 It is not wholly easy to understand why continuous and apparent easements are put on a different footing to other easements when the effect and operation of

[74] *Godwin v Schweppes Ltd* [1902] 1 Ch 926, and see para 4.25.

[75] See para 4.18.

[76] *Nicholas v Chamberlain* (1606) Cro Jac 121; *Polden v Bastard* (1865) LR 1 QB 156; *Watts v Kelson* (1871) 6 Ch App 166.

[77] *Polden v Bastard* (1865) LR 1 QB 156, 161 (Earl CJ), delivering the unanimous judgment of the Exchequer Chamber.

[78] *P & S Platt Ltd v Crouch* [2003] EWCA Civ 1110, [2004] 1 P & CR 18 [42] (Peter Gibson LJ).

section 62 of the Law of Property Act 1925 is involved. In the leading modern decision in which the ambit of section 62 has been examined, the *Sovmots* decision,[79] neither Lord Wilberforce nor Lord Edmund-Davies mention any such wide and general exception to the principle that for section 62 to operate there must have been a separation of ownership or occupation of the land. Indeed Lord Edmund-Davies said in terms that section 62 could not operate 'unless there has been some diversity of ownership or occupation of the quasi-dominant and quasi-servient tenements prior to the conveyance.'[80] The point may therefore still be open to consideration in the Supreme Court. Assuming that section 62 does operate to create easements even where there was no diversity of ownership or occupation at the time of the grant provided the easement in question was continuous and apparent, this rule is of importance for easements of light. An easement of light is continuous and apparent,[81] so that a quasi-easement of light will pass to a grantee of a part of land sold which has enjoyed the access of light over the part retained under section 62 whether or not there was at the time of the grant a separation of occupation of the quasi-dominant and quasi-servient areas of land.

The important question for present purposes is how this somewhat confused situation is to be applied to the creation of easements of light under section 62. It is useful to take again the situation given earlier as an example[82] which is that the grantor owns land and conveys a part of it, part A, to the grantee and himself retains a different part, part B, in circumstances in which the building on part A enjoys the access of light to its apertures over part B. If at the time of the grant part A and part B, notwithstanding their common ownership, had been in separate occupation, for example part A had been let to a tenant, then the use and enjoyment of light over part B as a quasi-easement will become a full easement of light available to the grantee of part A since at the time of the grant there was separation of occupation. Even if there was no separation of occupation at the time of the grant then under the second of the two alternative requirements, as now applied by the Court of Appeal, the grantee of part A will obtain a full easement because the access and use of light is a quasi-easement which is continuous and apparent. 4.36

It is at this point that there arises a further and specific rule or relaxation applicable to the creation of rights of light but not other easements. Even if the second alternative requirement, that the quasi-easement is continuous and apparent, is not in general correct in law, it appears that the use and enjoyment of the access of light is an exception in its own right to the first alternative and so will ripen into a full easement on the sale of the quasi-dominant and even if prior to and at the time of the sale there was no separation of occupation of the quasi-dominant and quasi-servient areas of land. This was held to be so by the Court of Appeal in *Broomfield v Williams* in 1897.[83] In that case the owner of a house and of adjoining 4.37

79 *Sovmots v Secretary of State for the Environment* [1979] AC 144.

80 ibid, 176. *Long v Gowlett* [1923] 2 Ch 177 was cited as the authority for this proposition.

81 *Phillips v Low* [1892] 1 Ch 47.

82 See para 4.27.

83 *Broomfield v Williams* [1897] 1 Ch 602, citing *Swansborough v Coventry* (1832) 9 Bing 305.

land over which light had been received through the windows of the house conveyed the house but retained the adjoining land. It was held by the Court of Appeal that an easement of light for the benefit of the house sold arose under section 6(2) of the Conveyancing Act 1881. At the time of the grant there was no separation of ownership or occupation. This decision has twice been considered to be an exception in its own right to the requirement that there should be at the time of the grant a separation of occupation. It was so regarded by Sargant J in *Long v Gowlett*,[84] where the exception was said to apply to the access of light and to any other right which was on the same footing as the access of light, and by Lord Edmund-Davies in the *Sovmots*[85] decision, where it was pointed out that the easement of light had been said to be an exception to many rules.

4.38 Despite its uncertainties, the present law may therefore be stated as being that where a grantor owns a piece of land on a part of which is situated a building which enjoys the access of light over the remainder of the land and the grantor transfers the building, the grantee will obtain a full easement of light by the operation of section 62 of the Law of Property Act 1925 whether or not at the time of the grant there was a separation of occupation of the two areas of land owned by the grantor. This at least simplifies the operation of section 62 of the Law of Property Act 1925, where the matter under consideration is the access of light and a right to that access. If ever there was a need for a confused and logically untenable state of the law to be authoritatively determined by the Supreme Court it is this situation regarding an aspect of the operation of section 62 with its alternative requirements, not themselves readily defensible, and its illogical exception for rights of light, possibly not needed and in any event indefensible as an exception.

(d) The Fourth Condition

4.39 The fourth condition is that there is no expression of an intention that section 62 is not to apply to the grant. Section 62(4) states: 'This section applies only if and as far as a contrary intention is not expressed in the conveyance, and has effect subject to the terms of the conveyance and to the provisions therein contained.'

4.40 If the parties to a conveyance wish that section 62 is not to apply, they should state this in express terms referring to that section.[86] Conveyances of land frequently contain language which excludes certain matters from the grant, by the use of general phraseology. One form of words sometimes used is that no implied rights are to pass, or that no easements or similar rights are to be implied. Language of this nature would prevent the creation of a right of light by implication under the rule in *Wheeldon v Burrows* or under the principle of intended easements. It is less certain that such language would exclude the operation of sections 62(1) and (2)

[84] *Long v Gowlett* [1923] 2 Ch 177, 202.

[85] *Sovmots v Secretary of State for the Environment* [1979] AC 144, 176.

[86] This should be done in the form of transfer used for the transfer of the whole or a part of the title to registered land.

of the Law of Property Act 1925 by reason of a contrary intention being expressed. Although they may serve the same general purpose and often lead to the same result by way of the creation of an easement the rules as to implied easements arising on a grant of land and the operation of section 62 are separate legal routes to a result. Sections 62(1) and (2) refer to a conveyance being 'deemed to include' certain matters and being something which 'operates to convey' certain benefits. The creation of an easement resulting from the operation of these provisions may be conceptually different from an easement arising by way of an implied term. Indeed it has been said in the Court of Appeal that the words of the statute 'must not be looked upon as implied words or anything of that sort'.[87] It seems reasonable to suppose that some general language in a grant excluding the creation of implied rights against the grantor is intended to prevent the creation of rights whether by implication or by the operation of section 62, but the situation is far from clear, and for this reason an express reference excluding the operation of section 62 should always be included in a conveyance, if that is the wish of the parties.

Section 62(4) provides not only that section 62 may be excluded by express words, but that it shall have effect 'subject to the terms of the conveyance'. It is therefore possible that provisions in the conveyance may show an intention to exclude or limit the operation of section 62. An obligation in a conveyance to erect fencing may exclude the creation of a right of way under section 62.[88] It also seems that surrounding circumstances at the time of the grant may serve to exclude the operation of section 62. A statement in the sixth edition of *Megarry & Wade: The Law of Real Property* (2001), that a contrary intention may be implied from circumstances existing at the time of the grant, has been cited with approval in the Court of Appeal.[89] There may be circumstances existing at the time of the grant, for example a recent planning permission and a start on the laying of foundations for a house on the land retained by the grantor, which show that the creation of an easement of light under section 62 for the benefit of the land conveyed is excluded, at any rate in so far as it would prevent the construction of that house. It is uncertain whether such existing or surrounding circumstances at the time of the grant are to be regarded as a contrary intention expressed in the conveyance, or something in the terms of the conveyance within the meaning of section 62(4). The existence of such facts and events does not fall easily into either category. 4.41

The express grant of a limited right may not be enough to exclude the creation under section 62 of a wider right of a similar nature, in terms of area or use, where the wider right was actually enjoyed at the time of the grant. An express grant of a right of way over an area described on a plan in a deed has been held not to exclude 4.42

[87] *Gregg v Richards* [1926] Ch 521. On the other hand, in *Alford v Hannaford* [2011] EWCA Civ 1099, [2012] 1 P & CR DG2 [34], Patten LJ described the operation of s 62 as 'a species of implied grant'. In *Wood v Waddington* [2015] EWCA Civ 538, [2015] 2 P & CR 11, Lewison LJ described s 62 as operating 'by way of express grant'. The juridical basis of s 62 is far from certain.

[88] *Alford v Hannaford* [2011] EWCA Civ 1099 [40].

[89] *P & S Platt Ltd v Crouch* [2003] EWCA Civ 1110, [2004] 1 P & CR 18 [37].

the creation of a right of way under the statute where a wider right of way was used and enjoyed at the date of the deed.[90] It may therefore be by parity of reasoning that an express grant of a right of light to be enjoyed through one aperture in a building transferred would not prevent the creation under section 62 of a right of light to be enjoyed through other apertures in the building if light to those other apertures had passed over the retained land of the grantor prior to and at the date of the grant.

(D) SUMMARY OF IMPLIED AND STATUTORILY CREATED EASEMENTS

4.43 The rules on the creation of easements by implication and by the operation of section 62 of the Law of Property Act 1925 are not simple, and are in some respects still uncertain. The two methods of the creation of easements also substantially overlap. Nonetheless, as regards easements of light, the usual effect of the main provisions can be summarised quite briefly. It is helpful again to take the example described earlier.[91] An owner of land, comprising plot A with a building on it and plot B which is open land adjoining it, over which light passes to the building, transfers the whole of his land or transfers plot A or plot B only. The following general principles will govern what easement of light passes to or is created in favour of the grantee or is created in favour of the grantor. In all cases the principles give way to an express provision in the grant to a different effect.

(i) If at the time of the grant there is a subsisting easement of light against some other neighbouring land held by a third party for the benefit of the building, whether created by deed or by prescription, the benefit of that easement will pass to a grantee of the whole of the land or of plot A. The transfer of the easement occurs either automatically or by virtue of section 62 of the Law of Property Act 1925.

(ii) If plot A is granted away and the grantee retains plot B, there will normally arise for the benefit of the relevant apertures in the building on plot A as against plot B an easement of light. This will occur either (a) under the rule in *Wheeldon v Burrows* or (b) under the principle of intended easements or (c) under section 62 of the Law of Property Act 1925.

(iii) If plot B is granted away and the grantor retains plot A, an easement of light for the benefit of plot A may arise as an implied easement under the principle of intended easements. No implied easement can arise under the rule in *Wheeldon v Burrows* or by the operation of section 62, since both these rules or provisions apply only for the benefit of a transferee.

[90] *Gregg v Richards* [1926] Ch 521; *Snell & Prideaux Warehousing Co v Dutton Mirrors Ltd* [1995] 2 EGLR 359; *Wood v Warrington* [2015] EWCA Civ 538.

[91] See para 4.27.

5

Acquisition of Rights of Light by Prescription

(A) INTRODUCTION

Any advanced legal system is likely to have rules of prescription and limitation.[1] What this amounts to is that the occupation of land or the exercise of some types of limited enjoyment of land for a sufficient period without any right to do so may give rise in favour of a person who has acted in this way to, in the first case, the ownership of the land and, in the second case, the ownership of a right to enjoy the land in a limited way. Conversely, if a person has rights but neglects for a substantial period to enforce them when he could do so, he may be prevented thereafter from enforcing those rights. The law of adverse possession and the gaining of a possessory title to land are an example of the first type of case. The law of limitation, which generally prevents a right from being enforced by proceedings in a court commenced more than a certain period after the cause of action has arisen (often six years), is an example of the second type of case. The law of prescription is an aspect of this underlying principle and is a method by which easements generally, including easements of light, may be acquired without there being any express provision in a deed or any implication from the terms and circumstances of a deed. An easement such as a right of way comes into existence simply because a person who owns land has enjoyed access or some other benefit over another person's land without any right or permission to do so for the requisite period. Of course the enjoyment must be of a nature which is capable of forming the subject matter of an easement, if an easement is to arise in this way. A further aspect of the same underlying principle is that an established right may be lost by an implied 5.1

[1] In *R v Oxfordshire County Council, ex parte Sunningwell Parish Council* [2000] 1 AC 335, 349 Lord Hoffmann said: 'Any legal system must have rules of prescription which prevent the disturbance of long established de facto enjoyment'. Lord Hoffmann's observation was cited by Lord Hope and Lord Scott in *Bakewell Management Ltd v Brandwood* [2004] UKHL 14, [2004] 2 AC 519 [9] and [27]. On the other hand, prescription is not possible in some jurisdictions which certainly have an advanced legal system based substantially on English law. For example, prescription is not available in New South Wales or Queensland in Australia. In a recent decision Lord Neuberger described the effect of the law of prescription when eating into the power of an owner of land to use his land as he wished as *tempus edax rerum* ('time, the devourer of things') by reference to works of the Roman poet, Ovid: *Metamorphoses* 15.234: *R (Newhaven Port and Properties Ltd) v East Sussex County Council* [2015] UKSC 7, [2015] 2 WLR 601 [103].

abandonment after a sufficient period of a failure to enforce the right on the part of a person with the right to enforce it and with knowledge of the facts which give him that right.[2]

5.2 The legal concept of prescription goes back to Roman law and the ancient Twelve Tables, and was called *usucapio* by Roman lawyers.[3] The general concept was imported into medieval land law. Actions for recovery of land by the ancient writ of right were limited by reference to the date of the accession of Henry I in 1100; the statute of Merton of 1235 altered this date to the accession of his grandson, Henry II, in 1154. A later date of 1189, the accession of Richard I, was prescribed by the statute of Westminster I in 1275, and it is this date, 1189, which remains of significance for the prescriptive acquisition of easements today.[4]

5.3 The law of prescription was backed by theory, that theory being that the exercise of some enjoyment of land not owned by the person exercising that enjoyment such as a way over the land, if continued without protest for a sufficient period, must have originated in an express grant of a right to that enjoyment, even though no deed of grant could be produced. The theory was of course a fiction, since it was well understood that in reality in such cases no deed was likely to have ever been executed, and the presumed grant may have salved the conscience of courts and lawyers who allowed persons to acquire rights through their own persistent and wrongful acts.[5] The theoretical basis of prescription, that it is founded on a grant presumed to have been made some time in the past, remains today except for the acquisition of easements of light under section 3 of the Prescription Act 1832.[6]

5.4 As the law developed, it became possible to acquire easements, including easements of light, by three methods of prescription:

(a) by common law prescription;
(b) under the doctrine of lost modern grant; and
(c) under the Prescription Act 1832.

The doctrine of lost modern grant is itself in a sense a principle of common law since it does not depend on any statutory provision, but it is usually distinguished from common law prescription for reasons explained below. All three methods

[2] It is possible that this principle can give rise to an implied abandonment of an easement of light: see ch 8.

[3] See *Dalton v Angus* (1881) 6 App Cas 740, 794 (Lord Coleridge).

[4] For a summary of the history and an explanation of the theory and the process described, see the opinion of Lord Hoffmann in *R v Oxfordshire County Council, ex parte Sunningwell Parish Council* [2000] 1 AC 335, a decision relating to the establishment of village greens by long use for sports and recreation by the inhabitants of the area.

[5] See, eg *Mann v Brodie* (1885) 10 App Cas 378, 385–86 (Lord Blackburn). It seems that the acquisition of public rights of way by long user was exempted from the fiction of a presumed grant or dedication.

[6] *Bryant v Foot* (1867) LR 2 QB 161, 179 (Cockburn CJ); *Gardner v Hodgson's Kingston Brewery Co Ltd* [1903] AC 229, 239 (Lord Lindley); *R (Newhaven Port & Properties Ltd) v East Sussex County Council* [2015] UKSC 7, [2015] 2 WLR 601 [79] (Lord Neuberger). As to easements of light acquired under the Prescription Act 1832 where there is no fiction of a presumed grant, see para 5.34(f).

remain available today although for easements generally and for easements of light prescription under the 1832 Act is the most usual method relied upon. The law is of some antiquity and even the statutory intervention by the Prescription Act 1832 is now approaching two centuries of age. Since claims to prescriptive rights of light are today founded mainly on the Prescription Act 1832, a substantial part of this chapter is devoted to the operation of that Act, a subject far from bereft of its own difficulties in part due to the antiquated language of that Act, as well as the terse phraseology which was then the style in drafting legislation.[7]

The use of prescription as a method of the acquisition of easements of light has met with far from universal approval in recent times. The exercise of some easements involves the carrying out of positive acts over or on the servient land, such as regular access over it, or the passage of water through a pipe on that land. It should be obvious to the servient owner that such enjoyment of his land was regularly taking place over many years. The easement of light, sometimes called a negative easement, is different in that it involves no actions by either the dominant or the servient owner. Light simply passes naturally over the servient land to the dominant building and continues to do so unless some action to stop it is taken by the erection of an obstruction.[8] It is therefore easy for an easement of right to arise by inadvertence, in a way which does not apply to the acquisition by prescription of other easements such as rights of way. It is also easy to prevent the acquisition of easements of light by the registration in good time of a light obstruction notice as a local land charge under the Rights of Light Act 1959, but property owners often omit to take this sensible step.[9] Out of the main arguments against prescriptive easements of light is that, with their being so easy to acquire and with landowners so often failing to take available measures to prevent their acquisition, the carrying out of new development is unduly inhibited, especially in urban areas. 5.5

The existence of actual or possible easements of light acquired by prescription is a major impediment to the development of land in urban areas. In 2011 the Law Commission published a report on the general law of easements recommending general reform of the acquisition of easements by prescription.[10] In 2013 the Commission published a consultation paper on rights of light in which the abolition 5.6

[7] See the description of that Act as 'notoriously ill-drafted' by Lord Neuberger in *London Tara Hotel Ltd v Kensington Close Ltd* [2011] EWCA Civ 1356, [2012] 1 EGLR 33 [20]. A further example of the same difficulties is the Land Clauses Consolidation Act 1845 which, through its repetition in modern statutes in virtually similar words, forms the foundation of the current law of compensation for the compulsory purchase of land. It is debatable whether the convoluted style of some modern legislation is a substantial improvement: see *Transport for London Ltd v Spirerose Ltd* [2009] UKHL 44, [2009] 1 WLR 1797 [22] (Lord Walker).

[8] An easement of support for buildings on the dominant land by the servient land is a further example of an easement which can be acquired without positive action by either the dominant or the servient owner.

[9] For the procedure under the Rights of Light Act 1959 see ch 9.

[10] Law Commission, *Making Land Work: Easements, Covenants and Profits a Prendre* (Law Com No 327, 2011).

of prescription as a means of acquisition of rights of light was provisionally proposed.[11] This proposal was supported by some consultees, such as the Bar Council. However, in its report on rights of light in December 2014, the Commission reversed its view and concluded that any reform of prescription as applicable to rights of light should follow the same reform as would apply to the acquisition by prescription of easements generally.[12] It seems, therefore, that the possibility of the acquisition of easements of light by prescription is likely to remain part of the law for some time.

5.7 What is certainly unsatisfactory is that prescription is possible by each of the three methods described.[13] The requirements which underlie the three methods considerably overlap, and claims are sometimes asserted under more than one method as alternatives. For example, as will be explained, an easement of light can hardly ever be claimed relying on common law prescription, but may in some circumstances be asserted under the doctrine of lost modern grant, where no claim can be sustained under the Prescription Act 1832.[14] There are different rules which regulate the effect of unity of ownership or of possession of the dominant and the servient land during the running of the prescription period for rights of light dependent on whether the prescriptive right is claimed under the doctrine of lost modern grant or under the Prescription Act 1832. Special rules may impede the acquisition of rights by prescription against ecclesiastical land of the Anglican Church.[15]

(B) COMMON LAW PRESCRIPTION

5.8 The theory which underpins common law prescription is that the use or enjoyment of land which constitutes the easement has lasted since 'time immemorial'. As mentioned above, the statute of Westminster I of 1275 stated that a writ of right to recover possession (seisin) of land was to be subject to a limitation period which started with the accession of Richard I in 1189. If the dispossession of the claimant or his predecessor had been before that date, the claim was barred by limitation. When it came to a claim to acquire a right such as a right of way founded on long use, the medieval courts adopted the same date and required a claimant to show that the use of the land had started prior to 1189, in which case that use was presumed to originate from a grant made before that date.

[11] Law Commission Consultation Paper No 210 (2013), paras 3.10–3.48.

[12] Law Commission, *Report on Rights of Light* (Law Com No 356, 2014), para 2.71. An outline of the general proposals for reform in this area is given in ch 12, section (C).

[13] See *Tehidy Minerals Ltd v Norman* [1971] 2 QB 528, and see *London Tara Hotel Ltd v Kensington Close Hotel Ltd* [2011] EWCA Civ 1356, [2012] 1 EGLR 33 [20] (Lord Neuberger). The Law Commission in its 2011 Report (see n 10) recommended that there should be a single method of prescription based on 20 years of continuous qualifying use. The Government have taken no action on the Report.

[14] See para 5.14.

[15] See ch 2, paras 2.23 and 2.24.

The law was amended for actions to recover possession of land by later statutes. The Limitation of Prescription Act 1540 provided for not a fixed but a moving limitation period of 60 years for writs of right, and the Limitation Act 1623 shortened the period for actions to recover land to 20 years. Unfortunately no alteration was made to the period which had to be shown in order to establish a prescriptive claim to acquire incorporeal rights, which remained 1189.[16] 5.9

A rigid insistence on proof of use or enjoyment of a benefit such as a right of way since 1189 made the system impractical. Such proof could rarely be available. This was particularly so as regards rights of light, which had to have been enjoyed through a particular aperture in a particular building. The Normans and their Plantagenet successors were prolific castle-builders, but a law of the prescriptive acquisition of rights of light that was centred on the windows of a few remaining castles would have produced little public benefit. To meet these difficulties the courts produced a further presumption. It became established that if the use and enjoyment had been for the span of living memory, that use or enjoyment was presumed to have lasted since 1189. A further step was that by analogy with the 20-year limitation period for actions for possession of land established in the Limitation Act 1623, a period of 20 years of use and enjoyment was presumed to show use and enjoyment since 1189, and so a presumed grant before that date.[17] 5.10

While the courts were willing to presume a grant made prior to 1189 in circumstances in which there was no real likelihood of such a grant ever having been made, it was a step too far to presume such a grant of an easement when that grant could not have been made. Therefore if the servient owner could show that no grant could ever have been made before 1189 because the inception of the enjoyment of the use had been after that date the claim for an easement resting on common law prescription was defeated. This restriction on the use of common law prescription was and is of particular importance for easements of light which are enjoyed through particular apertures in buildings. If an easement is alleged to have been acquired for a building by common law prescription by reason of light having passed to an aperture in that building over the servient land for over 20 years it will very often be possible to show that the building and its aperture were constructed after 1189, with the result that the claim will fail. It seems that a claim based on common law prescription could also be defeated if the dominant and servient land had been in the same ownership and possession during any part of the prescription period.[18] To the extent that any claim for an easement of light 5.11

[16] For the meaning of incorporeal rights see ch 2, para 2.8.

[17] *Jenkins v Harvey* (1835) Cr M & R 393; *Aynsley v Glover* (1875) 10 Ch App 283.

[18] *Morris v Edgington* (1810) 3 Taunt 24, 30. This is consistent with the general principle referred to later in this paragraph that prescription operates between the fee simple owners of the dominant and the servient areas of land, the so-called fee simple rule, so that a person as the fee simple owner of an area of land cannot acquire a right against himself as the fee simple owner of another area of land. See para 5.22 et seq for the application of this principle to the doctrine of lost modern grant, and para 5.83 et seq for its limited application to prescription under the Prescription Act 1832.

today can still be made depending on common law prescription it will also be necessary for the claimant to show that the use has been 'as of right', a concept which is more usefully explained in connection with the two other methods of prescription which have now largely superseded prescription at common law. A further rule which applies to common law prescription and to prescription under the doctrine of lost modern grant is the fee simple rule, the principle that prescription operates only between the freehold owners of the dominant and the servient owners of land, and this rule is also explained when the doctrine of lost modern grant is considered.

5.12 In these circumstances, whereas in theory a claim for an easement of light can be founded on common law prescription, it is rarely if ever that such a claim can succeed today.[19] Common law prescription came to be replaced, at any rate as regards easements of light, by the two other forms of prescription available today, prescription under the doctrine of lost modern grant and prescription under the Prescription Act 1832. It is still necessary to understand the nature of prescription and its origins in common law prescription before examining these further areas of law both of which are important for the acquisition of easements of light.

(C) LOST MODERN GRANT

1. Origins and Use

5.13 The difficulties in the operation of common law prescription just explained were to some extent resolved by the emergence of the doctrine of lost modern grant. Where a claim by common law prescription was defeated by the date of the origin of the use or by way of unity of ownership and possession during some part of the prescription period, the courts were willing to presume a more modern grant with that presumption founded on only 20 years of use. Thus the fiction that an easement must have originated in a grant was preserved with the date of the fictional (and presumed lost) grant moving from before 1189 to a date at least 20 years before the issue arose. Prior to the last century, civil actions such as claims for an infringement of an easement were generally tried before a jury, and juries were told that if use could be shown during living memory, taken as 20 years, they might presume a lost grant or deed executed at some time prior to the 20-year period as the origin of the use. Juries were then recommended to make this presumption and as a final step they were directed that they must make the presumption.[20]

[19] For a modern case in which a claim resting in part on common law prescription was rejected because there was no history of the dominant building since 1189, see *Bowring Services v Scottish Widows Fund and Life Assurance Society* [1995] 1 EGLR 158.

[20] *Bryant v Foot* (1867) LR 2 QB 161, 181 (Cockburn CJ). However, if the approval of some person to the grant is needed and there is no evidence of that approval having been given, there may not be the

Consequently by way of what some would call the development of the common law and what others would call judicial legislation, the prescription period became in effect one of 20 years of use. The courts by this process assimilated the prescription period to the 20-year limitation period established by the Limitation Act 1623. Reliance on the doctrine of lost modern grant appears to have been available since at least the middle of the eighteenth century.[21]

The doctrine of lost modern grant is sometimes useful today as the foundation of a prescriptive easement, although generally the Prescription Act 1832 is relied upon. Under the Act, the period of 20 years' use has to be a period ending immediately before the legal proceedings in which the issue of the existence of an easement arises.[22] A person claiming an easement may be able to show the requisite 20 years of continuous use needed to establish the acquisition of an easement, but there may be a gap between the end of that period and the commencement of the legal proceedings to establish or enforce the alleged easement as so acquired. The gap may be caused by an obstruction erected on the servient land or by something done on the dominant land. Reliance on the Prescription Act 1832 will then not be possible, but the doctrine of lost modern grant, or common law prescription, can still be invoked. For the purpose of both of these methods of acquiring an easement by prescription, the 20 years of use can in principle occur at any time, and not necessarily immediately before the commencement of legal proceedings.[23] Rights of common of grazing were established in a modern case in reliance on both of these methods.[24] 5.14

presumed grant needed to support the doctrine of lost modern grant: *Oakley v Boxton* [1976] QB 270 (no evidence that the Ecclesiastical Commissioners had given their approval to the grant of a right of way over glebe land such as was required for a grant under the Ecclesiastical Leasing Acts of 1842 and 1858). A lost modern grant will not be presumed if the person who might have made the grant could not lawfully do so: *Bakewell Management Ltd v Brandwood* [2004] UKHL 14, [2004] 2 AC 519.

[21] *Lewis v Price* (1761), referred to by Lord Blackburn in *Dalton v Angus* (1881) 6 App Cas 812 as mentioned in a note by Sergeant Williams in his 1871 edition of the reports of Wms Saund (ie, the editions of Saunders' Reports of 1686 edited by Sergeant Williams in the nineteenth century). It is for this reason that the reports are commonly referred to as 'Wms Saund'.

[22] Prescription Act 1832, s 4. See para 5.39 et seq.

[23] An example of this situation is *Marine & General Mutual Life Assurance Society v St James Real Estate Co Ltd* [1991] 2 EGLR 178, in which windows had been bricked up for some years so that a claim for a prescriptive easement could not be established under the Prescription Act 1832 because of s 4 of that Act, but an easement was held to be established in reliance on the doctrine of lost modern grant. If there has been a long period of non-use of an easement since the end of the 20-year period, or some other relevant circumstances, this may show that the easement, although acquired, has then been impliedly abandoned. Where an easement is negative or passive in nature, such as an easement of light, non-use, unaccompanied by any physical change to the dominant or servient property, is obviously unusual and is unlikely to be the foundation of an implied abandonment of the easement. See ch 8. See *Finlay v Cullen* [2014] NICh 17 for a recent decision in Northern Ireland in which a right of way could not be established under the Prescription Act 1832 because there had been an interruption to the use of the way, but where the right of way was established under the doctrine of lost modern grant since there had been 20 years' use of the way prior to the interruption.

[24] *Tehidy Minerals Ltd v Norman* [1971] 2 QB 528. Other examples of the operation of the doctrine of lost modern grant have been the establishment of a right to discharge sewage into a river (*Somerset Drainage Commissioners v Bridgwater Corporation* (1904) 81 LT 729) and a right to ventilation through adjoining property (*Bass v Gregory* (1890) 25 QBD 481). See also *Healey v Hawkins* (1968) 1 WLR 1967; *Bridle v Ruby* [1989] QB 169; *Smith v Brudenell-Bruce* [2002] 2 P & CR 4.

5.15 It has been suggested in an Irish decision that the doctrine of lost modern grant does not apply to the acquisition of easements of light.[25] However, there is no reason why the doctrine should not so apply.[26] The doctrine may be of importance in some instances for establishing an easement of light where section 3 of the Prescription Act 1832 cannot be relied upon for the reason stated in the last paragraph. One unanswered question is the relationship between the doctrine of lost modern grant and the effect of a light obstruction notice under the Rights of Light Act 1959. As will be explained in Chapter 9, the procedure under that Act permits a servient owner to register a notice of notional obstruction of the access of light across his property to the dominant building as a local land charge, so preventing the acquisition of a right of light to the dominant building by prescription. What is not entirely clear is whether a light obstruction notice will have this effect if 20 years of the access of light has passed so that a right has been established under the lost modern grant doctrine.[27] Within the City of London, the custom of London may prevent the acquisition of an easement of light by lost modern grant.[28]

2. User as of Right

5.16 The general rule for the acquisition of an easement by prescription is that the period of time which founds the prescriptive claim must be a period during which the use was user as of right.[29] This is so as regards common law prescription and as regards prescription by lost modern grant. It is also the case as regards the acquisition by prescription of easements generally under section 2 of the Prescription Act 1832. That section provides that a claim under it can be defeated in any way, other than the 20-year period of use, in which the claim was formerly able to be defeated. A claim could be defeated before the Act if the use was not user as of right so that that requirement remains when easements generally are claimed under section 2 of the Act. Section 3 of the Act, which applies only to the acquisition of

[25] *Tisdall v McArthur & Co* (1951) IR 228. The court referred to the obiter statement of Farwell LJ in *Hyman v Van den Bergh* [1908] 1 Ch 167, 176–78 that the doctrine of lost modern grant did not apply to rights of light. The Irish Supreme Court did not in the end find it necessary to decide the questions: see ibid, 246 (MacGuire CJ).

[26] It was held to apply to the acquisition of an easement of light by Lightman J in *Marlborough (West End) Ltd v Wilks Head & Eve* [1996] New Law Digest 138. See also *Duke of Norfolk v Arbuthnot* (1880) 5 CPD 390 in which the Court of Appeal accepted in principle that a claim to an easement of light might be acquired under the lost modern grant doctrine but held that on the facts of that case it had not been so acquired. See also *Marine & General Mutual Life Assurance Society v St James Real Estate Co Ltd* [1991] 2 EGLR 178 in which a right of light was established in reliance on the doctrine of lost modern grant in circumstances in which a prescriptive right could not be claimed under the Prescription Act 1832.

[27] See ch 9, section (I).

[28] See section (E) of this chapter. The custom of London may also prevent the acquisition of a right of light by common law prescription.

[29] In legal terminology the words 'use' and 'user' are employed more or less interchangeably.

rights of light, contains no requirement that the 20 years of enjoyment must be as of right. As a result, when easements of light are claimed under section 3 of the Prescription Act 1832, as is usually the case, the matter of user as of right is largely irrelevant. The only remaining aspect of that requirement is that the enjoyment of the access of light over the servient land must not have been by the written consent of the servient owner.[30]

Since reliance on lost modern grant, or even conceivably on common law prescription, may be necessary in establishing an easement of light in some cases where section 3 of the Prescription Act 1832 cannot be relied upon[31] it is necessary to examine at least in outline what is meant by the expression 'user as of right'.[32] The language of the expression 'as of right' may itself be somewhat confusing. The use cannot be of right, since in its nature the use is not the exercise of a right but is a wrongful act, usually a trespass, which may in time lead to the creation of a right. A better expression might be 'user as if of right', which would encapsulate the underlying idea that the dominant owner acts as though he had a right, when in fact he had no right.[33] The meaning of user as of right, as the concept of prescription itself, goes back to Roman law and appears early in the common law as recorded in Coke on Littleton[34] in 1628; it is usually described by the latin words *nec vi, nec clam, nec precario*: 'not by force, not secretly, and not by consent'. The general principle of the law of prescription is that time does not run unless the activities of the owner of the putative dominant land can be objected to by the owner of the putative servient land.[35] The explanation now given need only be brief in part because user as of right today plays only a small part in the acquisition of easements of light as just explained, and in part because it is difficult to imagine the access of light being by force or in secret. 5.17

[30] See section (D) of this chapter for a full description of the operation of s 3 of the Prescription Act 1832.

[31] See para 5.14.

[32] A full explanation relating to easements generally will be found in *Gale on Easements*, 19th edn (London, Sweet & Maxwell, 2013). The Law Commission in its 2011 Report on Easements (see n 10) recommended that the requirement of user as of right should remain as a part of the new method of prescription proposed which would apply to easements of light as to other easements. See ch 12 for a fuller consideration of the Report.

[33] See *R (Beresford) v Sunderland City Council* [2003] UKHL 60, [2004] 1 AC 889 [72] (Lord Walker). The fact that the owner of the dominant land used an access to his land in the mistaken belief that he had a right of way when he did not have that right did not in itself prevent the use being as of right for the purposes of the doctrine of lost modern grant: *Bridle v Ruby* [1989] QB 169. For the distinction between 'use as of right' and 'use by right' see *R (Newhaven Port and Properties Ltd) v East Sussex County Council* [2015] UKSC 7, [2015] 2 WLR 601. The meaning of user as of right and use by right was further considered by the Supreme Court in *R (Barkas) v North Yorkshire District Council* [2014] UKSC 31, [2015] AC 195, in the context of the registration of a town or village green. It was held that where the public were entitled by a statutory provision to use land for recreational purposes, that user was 'by right' and not 'as of right', so that the use could not be relied on in support of the registration of the land as a town or village green.

[34] Co Litt 113b.

[35] *Lawrence v Fen Tigers Ltd* [2014] UKSC 13, [2014] 1 AC 822 [4?] (Lord Neuberger). This decision is considered more fully in ch 7 on remedies. In a right of light case the only 'activity' of the dominant

5.18 Use of force in relation to matters such as the use of a way may mean physical force, as when an obstruction lawfully erected by the servient owner during the prescription period is torn down by the dominant owner. If the use is continued by the dominant owner after clear and vigorous objection by the servient owner, that may amount to use by force even though no physical force is involved.[36] The underlying rule is that use will be *vi*, or by force, if it is violent or clearly contentious.[37] The period of prescription for the acquisition of an easement of light involves the passing of light over the servient land to the dominant building and it is difficult to see how this could occur by force. Perhaps an example of enjoyment '*vi*' in this context would be if the dominant owner entered the servient land and removed an obstruction lawfully erected by the servient owner. It would be an unusual case for the servient owner to raise a verbal objection to the dominant owner at the passage of light over the servient land to the dominant building, since it is not clear how the dominant owner could prevent his property receiving natural light in this way. In the unlikely event of the servient owner protesting about the access of light over his land, or putting up some form of notice relating to the access of light over his land, this would probably not mean that the access of light was by force. These are perhaps somewhat fanciful circumstances and unlikely to occur in practice. The servient owner has other means of preventing the acquisition of an easement of light by prescription, notably by the use of the procedure available under the Rights of Light Act 1959, which is explained in Chapter 9.

5.19 It seems even less likely that the access of light over the servient land to the dominant building could be *clam*, or in secret, and this aspect of user as of right needs no further consideration in relation to rights of light.

5.20 The third requirement of user as of right is that the use is not *precario*, that is it is not by the consent of the servient owner. When it comes to the acquisition of an easement of light by prescription under section 3 of the Prescription Act 1832, this is the only part of the user as of right requirement which remains. Even then, the only consent which prevents the running of the statutory prescription period is a consent in writing. It is therefore convenient to postpone a fuller consideration of the meaning of *precario* or by consent until section 3 is examined. Nonetheless if an easement of light is claimed in reliance on the doctrine of lost modern grant or common law prescription, the requirement that there is no form of consent by the servient owner applies as it does to the acquisition of any other easement. Consequently a consent to the access of light across his land to the dominant building given by the servient owner orally or as an implication from his conduct (as well

owner is that of the passive receipt of the access of light to his property over the servient land, a situation which is to be contrasted with that under most easements, where the prescription period only runs when there is some positive action by the dominant owner such as using an access to his land over the servient land, and so is something to which the servient owner can more readily object.

[36] See eg *Smith v Brudenell-Bruce* [2002] 2 P & CR 4.

[37] *R (Lewis) v Redcar and Cleveland Borough Council (No 2)* [2010] UKSC 11, [2010] 2 AC 70 [90].

of course as a consent give expressly and in writing) could defeat a claim to an easement of light founded on either of these methods of prescription.[38]

For the purposes of the general concept that the use which builds up a prescription period must not be by consent, the consent need not be granted by express words or by writing but may be inferred from overt acts of the servient owner.[39] The essential distinction to be drawn in law is between the consent of the servient owner and the acquiescence of the servient owner to the use in question. Consent involves some positive action by the servient owner such as the giving of written or oral consent or at least some positive acts from which it may be inferred that he is giving his consent. The consent need not be a part of a contract, although of course it can be. A consent means that the use is not as of right. Where a consent has been given, the dominant owner does not act as if he has a right to the use; rather he acts pursuant to the consent, which is only necessary if he does not have such a right. The former situation may be called user as of right and is a foundation of the law of prescription (although limited in its application to rights of light under section 3 of the Prescription Act 1832), whereas the latter situation is user by right and prevents the running of the prescription period (although under section 3 of the Prescription Act 1832 the consent must be in writing to have this effect). Acquiescence, on the other hand, is passive. It means that the servient owner with knowledge of the use by the dominant owner takes no action to prevent or impede that use. Far from preventing the running of the prescription period, it is acquiescence in this sense which is a foundation of prescription. 5.21

3. Prescription and Relevant Interests in Land

(a) The Dominant Building

As mentioned earlier, prescription at common law can only be by the fee simple owner of the dominant land and against the fee simple owner of the servient land.[40] As regards the dominant owner, the same rule applies to prescription by lost modern grant. The period of use runs against the servient owner, whether the use made of the servient land is by the freehold owner of the dominant land or by 5.22

[38] The concept of a use having to be as of right in order for rights to arise from that use continued for a 20-year period is maintained for the creation of town and village greens by s 15(4) of the Commons Act 2006. In *R (Newhaven Port & Properties Ltd) v East Sussex County Council* [2015] UKSC 7, [2015] 2 WLR 601, the distinction between use 'as of right' and use 'by right', that is *precario* or by permission, is explained in the context of a permission to the public to use part of the foreshore for leisure activities granted by byelaws made under statutory authority.

[39] *R (Beresford) v Sunderland City Council* [2001] EWCA Civ 1218, [2002] QB 874 [11]–[12], affirmed in the House of Lords at [2003] UKHL 60, [2004] 1 AC 889. This was a decision on the registration of a village green under s 22 of the Commons Registration Act 1965 where 20 years' use as of right was required. Lord Scott at para [34] warned that the principles may not be exactly the same as those applicable to the acquisition of easements.

[40] See para 5.11.

a tenant or sub-tenant of that owner who is in possession of the dominant land. However, for these purposes the possession of the dominant land by a tenant is taken to be the possession of his landlord, so that an easement created by 20 years of use enures for the benefit of the fee simple owner of the dominant land and may be asserted by him both before and after the tenancy ends.[41] This is an aspect of the fee simple rule that, except where statute has intervened, the theory of prescription is that it is normally by the owner of a fee simple of one area of land against the owner of the fee simple of another area of land. The only freehold estate in land which can exist today is the fee simple absolute in possession.[42] Until 1926 an entail (an interest under which property passed automatically to the heir of each successive owner) or a life interest could exist as a legal estate. After that, entails and life interests could only exist as equitable interests under a settlement. Entails have now been abolished and a life interest can exist only as an equitable interest under a trust for sale.[43] As a result of the fee simple rule an easement can only be created by common law prescription or by lost modern grant where there is a person who could be a grantee of the easement so that, for example, a right could not be so acquired by a fluctuating body such as the inhabitants of a particular area who would not be competent grantees of an easement.[44] Therefore if the dominant land is let to a tenant for, say, 50 years and an easement is acquired under the doctrine of lost modern grant by 20 years of use, it appears that the landlord as the freehold owner obtains the benefit of the easement and can enforce it, whereas the tenant cannot do so. In the same way, if a landlord lets a part of his property to A and a part of it to B, and A enjoys the access of light to his property over that of B for 20 years, no easement of light can be acquired by common law prescription or by lost modern grant, since A can prescribe only for the benefit of his landlord and the landlord cannot acquire an easement against himself.

5.23 Although a tenant of the dominant land cannot acquire an easement of light for his own benefit by common law prescription or by lost modern grant, it should not be supposed that a tenant of that land can never enforce an easement of light against servient land. Where the landlord of the dominant land has the benefit of an easement of light over servient land at the time of the grant of the lease, whether created by a deed or by prescription, the benefit of that easement will normally pass to the tenant as a part of that which was demised unless there are express words in the lease to the contrary effect.[45] There is nothing to prevent

[41] *Wheaton v Maple & Co* [1893] 3 Ch 48; *Kilgour v Gaddes* [1904] 1 KB 457; *Grimstead v Marlowe* (1792) 4 Term Rep 717; *Gayford v Moffatt* (1868) 4 Ch App 133; *Midtown Ltd v City of London Real Property Co Ltd* [2005] EWHC 33 (Ch), [2005] 1 EGLR 65 [15].

[42] Law of Property Act 1925, s 1(1)(a). The fee simple is regarded as being 'in possession' even though there is a letting to a tenant. The landlord's possession of the right to the rents and profits is enough.

[43] See *Megarry & Wade: The Law of Real Property*, 8th edn (London, Sweet & Maxwell, 2012) chs 6 and 12, for a full description of the development of this aspect of the land law.

[44] *Foxall v Venables* (1589) Cro Eliz 180.

[45] See ch 11, paras 11.74–11.77.

an easement of light being expressly created for the benefit of a leaseholder of dominant land.[46]

As regards the dominant land, the rules for the acquisition of easements, including easements of light, under the doctrine of lost modern grant when 20 years of the access of light over the servient land have been enjoyed by a tenant of the dominant land, are therefore as follows: 5.24

(a) An easement is acquired but enures to the benefit of the fee simple owner of the dominant building who may enforce the easement during or after the subsistence of the lease.
(b) The tenant of the dominant land has no right to enforce the easement.

The rules here described circumscribe the acquisition of easements of light by prescription at common law or under the doctrine of lost modern grant. As will be explained, the rules are now considerably relaxed when it comes to the acquisition of an easement of light by prescription under s 3 of the Prescription Act 1832. For example, an easement of light may be acquired under s 3 by one tenant against a different tenant of other land from the same landlord.[47] It should be understood that the rules apply only to the acquisition of easements of light by prescription. The owner of a lease of land can acquire an easement over other land by an express or an implied grant of the easement, and the easement will then be appurtenant to his leasehold interest. It will end when his lease expires.[48] 5.25

(b) The Servient Land

When it comes to the interest held in the land against which an easement is being acquired by lost modern grant, the servient land, the position is less clear. The orthodox view is that no acquisition of an easement by lost modern grant is possible while there is a lessee of the servient land. This has been held to be the law in earlier cases including a claim for an easement of light[49] and has been applied in recent authority.[50] As against this, other decisions and judicial observations suggest that 20 years of use could give rise to an easement even though the servient land was in the possession of a tenant especially where the period of use started before the grant of the tenancy and continued against the tenant after that grant.[51] 5.26

[46] See ch 8, paras 8.16–8.18 for the law on the determination of such an easement when the leasehold interest in the dominant land terminates.

[47] See section (D) of this chapter.

[48] See ch 8, paras 8.17 and 8.18, for the suggestion that an easement so created and appurtenant to a leasehold interest may survive the determination of that interest by surrender or merger.

[49] *Daneil v North* (1809) 11 East 372; *Barker v Richardson* (1821) 4 B & Ald 579. See also *Roberts v Jones* [1903] 89 LT 287 (right of way).

[50] *Simmons v Dobson* [1991] 1 WLR 720, citing *Wheaton v Maple & Co.* [1893] 3 Ch 48; *Derry v Sanders* [1919] 1 KB 223; *Kilgour v Gaddes* [1904] 1 KB 457. The law in Ireland is to the opposite effect: see *Flynn v Harte* [1919] 2 IR 322; *Tallon v Ennis* [1937] IR 549.

[51] *Cross v Lewis* (1824) 2 B&C 686, 690 (Littledale J); *Palk v Skinner* (1852) 18 QB 568; *Bright v Walker* (1834) 1 Cr M & R 211; *East Stonehouse UDC v Willoughby Brothers Ltd* [1902] 2 KB 318; *Pugh v Savage* [1970] 2 QB 373. See also for a summary of the principles *Williams v Sandy Lane (Chester) Ltd* [2007] 1 P & CR 27, and see *Llewellyn v Lorey* [2011] EWCA Civ 37.

The question has not been considered by the House of Lords or the Supreme Court for over a century.

5.27 The objection to allowing prescription by lost modern grant against servient land where that land is in the possession of a tenant has been said to be that it would be unjust to bind a landlord of the servient land when he might not have been in a position to prevent the use which gives rise to the prescription and when he may not even have known of that use. Covenants in leases often seek to protect landlords against the possibility of this happening by requiring the tenant not to allow the acquisition of rights against the property demised. While this objection is forceful, it is not a good objection against an easement being acquired so as to bind a tenant and his successors in title during the tenancy of the servient land, even though it may not bind the landlord after the end of the tenancy. For example, if land were let for 50 years and an adjoining owner exercised some use of it for the first 20 years of the term, it seems reasonable that an easement could be acquired against the tenant even though that easement would end at the expiration of the 50 years of the term or upon the earlier determination of the term. An express grant of an easement can be made by a tenant so as to bind his tenancy, and there seems no impediment to a grant being presumed to the same effect under the doctrine of lost modern grant. The rights of the dominant owner would be fragile since they would end at the ending of the tenancy in the servient land. The freeholder of the servient land would be free of those rights when he resumed possession at the end of the lease. It seems odd that an easement can be acquired by prescription against a freeholder of the servient land but not against a tenant under a 999-year lease of that land.

5.28 The above question was considered extensively by Lord Millett in his judgment in a decision of the Court of Final Appeal in Hong Kong in a case concerning the application of the lost modern grant doctrine as between two tenants of the same landlord.[52] It was held that in Hong Kong, an easement could be acquired by lost modern grant as against a tenant of the servient land, including by a tenant of the person who is the owner of the dominant land. The situation regarding land-holding in Hong Kong is significantly different to that in England, since all land, except the Anglican Cathedral, is held under leases formerly granted by the British Crown, and now by the Government of the Special Administrative Region of the People's Republic of China. Many former long leases that were due to expire in 1997 (the end of the lease of the New Territories held by the Crown) have been extended by Ordinance to 2047. If the more orthodox fee simple rule had been applied in Hong Kong there would therefore have been no prescription possible by lost modern grant. There is no Hong Kong Ordinance (statute) equivalent to the Prescription Act 1832.

5.29 Lord Millett concluded that there was no rational reason to prevent an easement arising by long user and under the doctrine of lost modern grant as between

[52] *China Field Ltd v The Appeal Tribunal (Buildings)* [2009] 12 HKCFAR 342.

lessees including lessees of the same landlord. He considered the fee simple rule in general terms and concluded that:

(a) a presumed grant derived from 20 years of use could bind a tenant of the servient land;
(b) an easement so derived would generally end on the ending of the tenancy of the servient land (although subject to (e) below);
(c) a tenant of the dominant land could acquire an easement by lost modern grant on behalf of his landlord so that the easement would remain enforceable by the landlord of the dominant land even after the end of the tenancy of that land (something which reflects the law in England);[53]
(d) these principles applied equally where the dominant land and the servient land were held by different tenants from a common landlord; and
(e) the reversioner of the servient land could be bound by the prescriptive easement if he was aware of the use on which that easement was based and was in a position to prevent it.

It remains to be seen whether this sensible approach will be applied in England, but it would probably take a decision of the Supreme Court reviewing the whole subject to make it so applicable.[54] If it is so applied, the scope for reliance on easements of light acquired by lost modern grant would be significantly increased. However, the question is of less importance for easements of light than it is for other easements, since the language of section 3 of the Prescription Act 1832 permits the acquisition of such easements as between tenants by statutory prescription, whereas the older rules are retained by section 2 of the Act for the acquisition of other easements by statutory prescription.[55]

4. Unity of Possession

A further aspect of the running of the prescription period, dependent on the use being as of right, is that the period will end if there is a substantial time during which there is unity of possession of the dominant and the servient land. The reason is that during such a period, the use is not as of right, in the sense that it is conducted as if a right existed, but is simply the inherent right which the person in possession of a whole area of land has to use or enjoy any part of it for the benefit of any other part. For instance, if there was separate possession for 15 years of the dominant and servient land, succeeded by five years of unity of possession, that would bring about the ending of the running of the prescription period at the 5.30

[53] See para 5.22 et seq.

[54] In its report on easements and other matters, *Making Land Work: Easements, Covenants and Profits a Prendre* (Law Com No 327, 2011), the Law Commission, having taken into account what Lord Millett said, was in favour of retaining the fee simple rule.

[55] See section (D) of this chapter for statutory prescription.

15th year. If separate possession resumed at a later date, it would not be possible to aggregate together the earlier and the later periods of separate possession. In one case a use of a way was commenced in 1860 and continued till 1900, but during the period 1877 to 1898 the same person was in possession of the putative dominant and servient areas of land. For this reason the claim to a prescriptive easement of way failed.[56] The principle that a substantial period of unity of possession of the dominant and the servient land prevents the running of the prescription period and defeats a claim applies to prescription at common law, to prescription under the doctrine of lost modern grant, and to prescription for easements generally under section 2 of the Prescription Act 1832, but, exceptionally, does not apply to the prescriptive acquisition of easements of light under section 3 of the Prescription Act 1832. In the case of easements of light claimed under section 3, a period of unity of possession, however substantial, does not end but merely suspends the period in question for the running of the prescription period, so that a time before the period of unity of possession and a time after the period of unity of possession, during which there is separate possession, may be aggregated in order to establish the full statutory period for the purposes of section 3.[57] A further important question is the effect of (a) unity of ownership and (b) unity of possession on an easement which already exists. The termination of easements of light by reason of one or other or both of these unities is examined in Chapter 8.[58]

(D) STATUTORY PRESCRIPTION

1. Introduction

5.31 The acquisition of all easements, including easements of light, is now accomplished mainly under the provisions of the Prescription Act 1832. This Act, and the Rights of Light Act 1959, are the only major statutory interventions into the subject of rights of light.[59] The Prescription Act 1832 (once known as Lord Tenterden's Act)

[56] *Damper v Bassett* [1901] 2 Ch 350.

[57] *Ladyman v Grave* (1871) 6 Ch App 763. See section (D) of this chapter for the operation of section 3 of the Prescription Act 1832. It is not possible to justify these complicated and anomalous rules on any rational principle. It may be that where reliance is placed on common law prescription a period of unity of possession will defeat the claim however long ago that period ended, since the period in question means that user as of right cannot have endured since 1189. See para 5.11.

[58] See ch 8, section (B)3.

[59] There are other relevant statutory provisions, such as those in the Land Registration Act 2002 requiring the registration of the grant of easements. See ch 11. The Law Commission in its report in 2011 included a draft Easements Bill with various reforms: see *Making Land Work: Easements, Covenants and Profits A Prendre* (Law Com No 327, 2011). Some of these are explained and discussed in ch 12. On the other hand, the allied subject of limitation has been the subject of successive Acts from the statute of Merton in 1235 to the current law which is wholly statutory and is now contained in the Limitation Act 1980. See para 5.2.

did not abolish the previous non-statutory methods of prescription, common law prescription and lost modern grant, and important elements of the previous law remain as a part of the Act including the general requirement, though not a requirement applicable to the acquisition under the Act of easements of light, that the use over the prescription period must be user as of right. A prescription period of 20 years was maintained. The Act dealt with easements of light partly by provisions applicable to them which also apply to other easements and partly by provisions which apply only to easements of light.

Apart from its special treatment of easements of light, it is not clear what the Act was designed to achieve. Section 2, which relates to easements generally, states that enjoyment for 20 years shall not be defeated as the basis of prescription by it being shown that the first enjoyment was at some time prior to the commencement of the 20 years. In other words the possibility of defeating a claim resting on common law prescription by showing that the enjoyment started after 1189 does not apply to prescription under section 2 of the Act (although it continues to apply to common law prescription). This alteration was scarcely necessary, since the fact that enjoyment commenced after 1189 could always be overcome by reliance on the doctrine of lost modern grant, under which this fact did not prevent the presumed existence of a grant in more modern times.[60] It has been suggested that the Act was intended to give comfort to courts, which had to presume the existence of a grant in the past when it was known that in all likelihood, no such grant had ever been made.[61] Even so the theoretical basis of prescription under the Act, except as regards the acquisition of easements of light under section 3, remains the presumption that an actual grant of the easement was made in the past. 5.32

Section 3 of the Prescription Act 1832 applies only to easements of light. It provides as follows:[62] 5.33

> When the access and use of light to and for any dwelling house, workshop, or other building shall have been actually enjoyed therewith for the full period of twenty years without interruption, the right thereto shall be deemed absolute and indefeasible, any local usage or custom to the contrary notwithstanding, unless it shall appear that the same was enjoyed by some consent or agreement expressly made or given for that purpose by deed or writing.

Section 4 of the Act, which applies to all easements including easements of light, provides as follows:

> Each of the respective periods of years hereinbefore mentioned shall be deemed and taken to be the period next before some suit or action wherein the claim or matter to which such period may relate shall have been or shall be brought into question; and no act or other matter shall be deemed to be an interruption, within the meaning of the statute, unless the same shall have been or shall be submitted to or acquiesced in for one

[60] See para 5.13.

[61] *Angus v Dalton* (1877) 3 QBD 85, 105 (Cockburn CJ).

[62] In *London Tara Hotel Ltd v Kensington Close Hotel Ltd* [2011] EWCA Civ 1356, [2012] 1 P & CR 13 [20], Lord Neuberger described the Act as 'notoriously ill-drafted'.

year after the person interrupted shall have had or shall have notice thereof, and of the person making or authorising the same to be made.

5.34 The main differences in the law relating to the acquisition by prescription of easements of light under the Act as compared to the previous law are as follows.

(a) The requirement that the use must not be *vi* (by force) or *clam* (in secret) is removed. In practice these requirements of the principle of user as of right had little significance for easements of light.[63]
(b) The acquisition of an easement of light is no longer defeated by showing that the enjoyment was by an oral consent from the servient owner, or by a consent from that owner inferred from circumstances. A consent in writing to the enjoyment is still a bar.
(c) Prescription is possible by the owner or a tenant of the dominant building against a tenant of the servient land and is possible by a tenant against his own landlord where that landlord also owns the servient land, whether or not he has granted a tenancy of that land. Thus under the Act a tenant can acquire an easement of light against his own landlord and against a different tenant of his own landlord.
(d) The 20-year prescription period has to be a period immediately before the question of the acquisition or existence of the easement is brought into question in legal proceedings.
(e) An interruption of the access of light may prevent the running of the prescription period, but only if (i) it has lasted for at least a year and (ii) there has been a submission to or acquiescence in the interruption by the dominant owner who has notice of the interruption and of the person making or authorising the interruption.
(f) As regards easements of light there is no presumption of a grant. The acquisition rests on the language of section 3 of the 1832 Act. The acquisition of the easement 'is a matter of *juris positivi*, and does not require, and therefore ought not to be rested on, any presumption of grant'.[64]
(g) Unity of possession of the dominant and servient land for any substantial part of the prescription period defeats a claim for easements generally, but as regards the acquisition of easements of light merely suspends the operation of the prescription period.

The first three and the last two of the alterations to the law are particular to easements of light. The fourth and fifth alterations apply to the acquisition of easements generally under the Act.

5.35 In order to explain the operation of the Act it is necessary to consider:

(a) the 20-year period;
(b) the rule that the period must be that immediately before any legal proceedings;

[63] See paras 5.18 and 5.19.

[64] *Tapling v Jones* (1865) 11 HLC 290, 304 (Lord Westbury); *Midtown Ltd v City of London Real Property Co Ltd* [2005] EWHC 33, [2005] 1 EGLR 65 [16].

(c) any interruption to the enjoyment of light;
(d) written consent;
(e) agreements permitting development;
(f) interests in land;
(g) the Crown;
(h) local usage or custom;
(i) persons with disabilities; and
(j) pleadings.

It should be noted that periods under the Act may be extended in some circumstances because of mediation in certain cross-border disputes.[65]

2. The 20-Year Period

Section 3 of the Prescription Act 1832 refers to 'the full period of twenty years without interruption'. There must be a reasonable continuity of the enjoyment of the light which passes over the servient land during the prescription period. Obviously some periods of discontinuity, such as when curtains are drawn, shutters closed to keep out sunlight, or a temporary obstruction to a window, will not prevent the running of the prescription period.[66] It is not necessary that the access of the light is used or received by persons in occupation of the rooms which are lit.[67] For example, the prescription period will continue to run in respect of a window in a spare bedroom in a house which is very intermittently used. The erection of scaffolding along a property to permit repairs or alterations, which interrupts the access of light to windows, would be unlikely to prevent the running of the prescription period. There may be circumstances in which windows in one building may be replaced in the same or a very similar position in a new building and the right of light attached to the window in the old building is transferred to the new window in the new building.[68] Plainly if this occurs, there will be a limited period when the old window has disappeared and the new window has not come into being. This gap will not in itself prevent the transfer of rights to the new windows. On the other hand where a window is stopped up for a substantial period of time by the installation of shutters which cannot be opened, this may be sufficient to prevent the running of the 20-year period.[69] A blocking-up of a window in the dominant building, unless it is clearly temporary and for a temporary purpose, may prevent 5.36

[65] Prescription Act 1832, s 8A. The disputes to which s 8A applies are cross-border disputes as defined in Directive 2008/52/EC of the European Parliament and the Council of 21 May 2008.

[66] *Smith v Baxter* [1900] 2 Ch 138; *Andrews v Waite* [1907] 2 Ch 500; *Tamares (Vincent Square) Ltd v Fairpoint Properties (Vincent Square) Ltd* [2006] EWHC 3589 (Ch), [2006] 3 EGLR 87.

[67] *Hollins v Verney* (1884) 13 QBD 304.

[68] See ch 3, section (C).

[69] *Courtauld v Legh* (1869) LR 4 Ex 126. *Glover v Coleman* (1874) LR 10 CP 108, 117 (Brett J). The blocking-up of windows, or a substantial part of windows, during the prescription period prevents the acquisition of a right of light by prescription: *Smith v* Baxter [1900] 2 Ch 138. By contrast it was held in the same case that the erection of shelving across a window during the prescription period did not

the enjoyment of the access of light during the prescription period being sufficiently continuous. The painting or covering-over of a window so that light cannot pass through it, at any rate in an ordinary quantity, may have a similar effect in the same circumstances. Sometimes windows are blocked off internally to preserve security or privacy, and this may prevent the running of the prescription period.[70] The overall principle to be derived from the authorities is that the blocking-off of the access of the whole or the greater part of the light passing through an aperture permanently or for a long period will prevent the running of the prescription period, whereas the creation by the dominant owner of an obstruction to the passage of light through his window which is either intended to last for only a temporary period or leaves a substantial amount of light still passing through the aperture will not prevent the running of the prescription period. As so often with legal rules, the governing principle can be briefly stated, but its application to a multitude of different possible factual circumstance may involve much dispute.

5.37 There is no precise or numerical test which will dictate whether the cessation of the access of light through an aperture for some period or periods of time results in the prescription period ending or the use being insufficiently continuous to found a prescription period. It is a question of fact and degree in all cases, with the primary criteria being the length and purpose of the blocking up of the access of light to a window. The use and enjoyment of the access of light over other land is passive and continuous in its nature, and does not involve the active use and enjoyment of some aspect of the servient land, such as is the case with a right of way and other positive easements. In the case of such positive easements a sufficiently irregular use may prevent the running of the prescription period. An instance would be the use of an easement for only alternate weeks.[71] In relation to such easements it is sufficient for the running of the prescription period if the use is of such a nature, and takes place at such intervals, as to afford an indication to the owner of the servient land that a right is claimed against him—an indication that would not be afforded by a mere accidental or occasional exercise.[72] Perhaps the best general expression of the principle to be applied to all easements is the statement of Lindley LJ in *Hollins v Verney* that

> A cessation of user which excludes an inference of actual enjoyment as of right for the full statutory period will be fatal at whatsoever portion of the period the cessation occurs;

prevent the running of the period, when a substantial amount of light could still enter the building through the window in question. See also ch 8, in which the possible abandonment by implication of an easement of light by reason of the blocking-up of a window is considered. See also para 5.38.

[70] It is said in Bickford-Smith, Francis and Weekes, *Rights of Light*, 3rd edn (Bristol, Jordan Publishing, 2014) at para 6.57 that the painting of the inside surfaces of windows in a night club in order to preserve a dark interior valued by the customers would prevent the access of light to those premises through those apertures being continuous.

[71] *Monmouthshire Canal Company v Harford* (1834) 1 Cr M & R 614.

[72] A passage to this effect in the 14th edn of *Gale on Easements* (London, Sweet & Maxwell, 1972), was approved by the Court of Appeal in *Ironside, Crabb and Crabb v Cook, Cook and Barefoot* (1981) P & CR 326.

> and, on the other hand, a cessation of user which does not exclude such inference, is not fatal, even though it occurs at the beginning, or the end of, the period.[73]

The principle therefore is that if there is a break in the enjoyment of the access of light such that the enjoyment ceases to be sufficiently continuous and there is later a resumption of the enjoyment, the measurement of the full period of 20 years has to start again from the date of the resumption.

The discontinuance of the access of light over the servient tenement to an aperture in the dominant building may have one of three different consequences in law. In the first place, if the discontinuance is a result of the actions of the dominant owner and occurs during the prescription period, then if the discontinuance lasts for a sufficient period or is subsequently repeated, it may mean that the enjoyment of light over the servient land has not been sufficiently continuous or regular to constitute the actual enjoyment and use of the access of light during the 20-year period immediately prior to the commencement of proceedings, as required by sections 3 and 4 of the Prescription Act 1832. The result is that no easement of light will be acquired under the Act. It is this possibility which has been discussed in the previous two paragraphs. Secondly, if the cessation of the enjoyment of the light occurs as a result of the actions of the dominant owner after the easement has been enjoyed by 20 years of previous use, for example by the permanent blocking-up of a window, the correct inference may be that the easement acquired has been impliedly abandoned.[74] It also appears that these circumstances may lead to the defeat of a claim under section 3 of the Prescription Act 1832, since the necessary 20 years of continuous use will not be that immediately before the question of the existence of the easement has been raised in legal proceedings, as is required by section 4 of the Act.[75] Thirdly, an obstruction of the access of light by the servient owner, whether a physical obstruction or the notional obstruction produced by a light obstruction notice registered as a local land charge under the Rights of Light Act 1959, if it is acquiesced in by the dominant owner for a year or more, will result in the prescription period ceasing to run if it has not yet been completed. Such an obstruction will result in the loss of the ability to enforce the easement under the Prescription Act 1832, even if the 20 years of previous enjoyment has been completed, since in those circumstances that 20 years of enjoyment of the access of light will not be immediately before the question of the existence of an easement has been raised in legal proceedings as required by section 4 of the Act.[76] 5.38

73 *Hollins v Verney* (1884) 13 QBD 304, 315. See *Mills v Silver* [1991] Ch 271 for observations on the degree of use of a way which may establish continuous user as of right when an easement of way was claimed under the doctrine of lost modern grant.

74 See ch 8 for the termination of easements by various means including abandonment.

75 See para 5.39 et seq.

76 See para 5.39 et seq and see ch 9 for the procedure under the Rights of Light Act 1959. It is not entirely clear what will be the effect of a notional obstruction under the 1959 Act if at the time the procedure under the Act is operated a prescriptive right of light has already been acquired under the doctrine of lost modern grant: see ch 9, section (I).

3. End of the Prescription Period: Legal Proceedings

(a) The General Rule

5.39 With common law prescription, and with the doctrine of lost modern grant, the conclusion of the 20-year prescription period brings an easement into existence. The easement is not then lost unless it is voluntarily released or abandoned.[77] If there is an obstruction to the access of light, the dominant owner may lose his opportunity to prevent the obstruction by injunction if he does not act promptly, since the grant of injunctive relief is discretionary. Subject to any question of limitation of actions the dominant owner may in principle enforce his right, for example by an action for damages, at any time. The position with claims under the Prescription Act 1832 is different. Section 4 of the Act, which applies to all easements, states that the 20-year period is 'the period next before some suit or action where the claim or title to which such period shall relate shall have been or shall be brought into question.'

5.40 Section 4 of the 1832 Act therefore contemplates a period after the 20-year prescription period has been completed and before legal proceedings are commenced during which the access of light has not been enjoyed with the result that by reason of that cessation of enjoyment an easement cannot be established or enforced in subsequent legal proceedings. It does not matter if these proceedings have been commenced by the dominant or the servient owner. The proceedings may be commenced by the dominant owner to establish or enforce an alleged right of light or they may be commenced by the servient owner, who may seek a declaration that no right of light exists against his property. The question of the existence or enforceability of a right of light may arise as a secondary or collateral matter in legal proceedings which are primarily concerned with other matters, such as the value of a piece of land the subject of an option or the value of land being compulsorily acquired, but where the existence or enforceability of the right of light is brought into question. In such proceedings section 4 of the Prescription Act 1832 operates in the same way as if the existence or enforceability of the right of light was the only or primary question in the proceedings.[78] It seems reasonable that a referral by the Registrar of HM Land Registry to the Property Chamber of the

[77] It is possible that an easement so acquired under the doctrine of lost modern grant may be terminated by the procedure under the Rights of Light Act 1959. An easement may also be lost by other means such as unity of ownership and possession of the dominant and servient land. See ch 8 for a general consideration of the termination of easements.

[78] In such cases there will usually be a valuation date, by reference to which values are to be ascertained. It will then generally be necessary to take into account facts and events as they were at that valuation date, so that in principle the existence or enforceability of an easement can probably be assessed in the light of the prospect of legal proceedings being taken at that date. The general principle of valuation of land is that in valuing the land, only those facts and events known at the valuation date, or reasonably anticipated at that date, may be taken into account in the valuation process: see *Penny's Bay Investment Co v Director of Lands* (2010) 15 HKCFAR 287.

First-tier Tribunal under section 73 of the Land registration Act 2002 should count as a suit or action for these purposes.[79] If it is to be relied upon, the 20-year period must always be a period immediately before the legal proceedings in question.

(b) *Types of Discontinuance*

In considering the legal effect of a discontinuance of the enjoyment and use of the access of light, it is necessary to have in mind what are three separate requirements of sections 3 and 4 of the Prescription Act 1832. First, the enjoyment and use must last with a reasonable degree of continuance over a period of at least 20 years. This requirement has been examined earlier in this chapter.[80] Secondly, the enjoyment and use must be for a period next before the legal proceedings in which the acquisition or existence of the easement is in issue. This requirement is the subject of the present discussion in this chapter. Thirdly, the period of enjoyment and use must be without interruption. This requirement is examined later in this chapter. It is helpful to analyse the three requirements separately in this way, although in practice there is a degree of merger, and a factual discontinuance of the enjoyment and use of the access of light may have implications for more than one of the requirements. A discontinuance of the enjoyment and use of the access of light over the servient land to the dominant building may occur in any circumstances, but it is useful at this point to refer to the four main types of events which bring about a discontinuance. The first two types of event are relevant to what has just been described as the first and second requirements, and the third and fourth types are relevant to the third requirement. It assists to classify the four types of discontinuance here and to summarise their legal consequences for the purposes of statutory prescription, but the main treatment of the third and fourth categories is in section (D)4 of this chapter. 5.41

The first type of discontinuance is at the instigation of the dominant owner who takes some step which prevents the access of light to his property, for what is usually a limited period. An example already given would be the erection of scaffolding or shuttering over apertures while repair works or decorations are carried out. As explained, such an event would not prevent the running of the prescription period and so has no further bearing on the present discussion and on prescription under the 1832 Act.[81] 5.42

The second type of discontinuance is again at the instigation of the dominant owner, and is the taking of some step which brings about a longer cessation of the access of light, and is of a more permanent nature. An example which has 5.43

[79] This was the view of the Adjudicator to HM Land Registry (the predecessor of the Property Chamber) as stated in *Wilkin & Sons Ltd v Agricultural Facilities Ltd* (Ref 2011/0420) [113]. For the jurisdiction of and the procedure before the Property Chamber, see ch 11, section (C). See also para 5.46.

[80] See para 5.36 et seq.

[81] See para 5.36.

been given is the erection of non-removable shuttering across an aperture, or the blocking-up or painting-over of a window. The erection of a high wall near a window, or of a roof which blocked the access of light to a window, or the erection of a structure within the curtilage of the dominant building which blocked the access of light to a window in that building, would be further examples.[82] A discontinuance of the access of light of this type prevents the running of the prescription period. It means that the previous period of enjoyment and use of the access of light cannot be relied upon for the purposes of prescription under the 1832 Act.[83]

5.44 The third type of discontinuance is where there has been an obstruction to the access of light by the servient owner, for instance the construction by him on his land of a new building, and the obstruction lasts at least a year and is acquiesced in by the dominant owner, who takes no action. In these circumstances, and as provided for in the last part of section 4, there will be an interruption which prevents the running of the prescription period. If the 20-year period has ended, the interruption will still prevent the assertion of the easement under the Prescription Act 1832 since in any proceedings to enforce it the requisite 20 years 'without interruption' would not have been immediately before the commencement of the proceedings.[84] The dominant owner may still be able to rely on prescription by lost modern grant where the statutory rule that the 20-year prescription period must be immediately before the commencement of proceedings does not apply. The use of the process available to a servient owner under the Rights of Light Act 1959, ie the registration as a local land charge of a light obstruction notice, has a similar effect to an actual obstruction. The dominant owner must take legal proceedings to challenge the notice within a year of its registration if he is to prevent the notional obstruction constituted by the notice operating as an interruption and so preventing his right to enforce his easement of light.[85]

5.45 The fourth type of discontinuance is an interruption to the access of light by the servient owner which has either lasted for less than a year or has not been acquiesced in by the dominant owner for a year. The dominant owner can prevent acquiescence taking place by sufficient protests at the interruption. In this type of case, if the statutory prescription period is still running at the beginning of the period of interruption it will continue to run, and if the prescription period has ended at the date of the interruption the interruption will not prevent legal proceedings to enforce the easement which has been acquired under the 1832 Act. These results are the effect of the particular meaning given to an interruption by section 4 of the 1832 Act. A dominant owner who has protested at an interruption should still be wary of waiting too long without commencing legal proceedings, since he might find that his continuing inaction leads to the conclusion that he has acquiesced for a year in the interruption, in which case the interruption will

[82] See *Ankerson v Connelly* [1907] 1 Ch 678 and see ch 3, para 3.58.

[83] See section (D)4 of this chapter; *Glover v Coleman* (1874) LR 10 CP 108, 117 (Brett J).

[84] See para 5.39.

[85] See ch 9.

prevent the running of the prescription period and will prevent the taking of legal proceedings to enforce any easement which had previously been acquired under section 3 of the Act. The reason is that in these circumstances the period of use and enjoyment of the access of light without interruption will not be immediately before the legal proceedings in which the issue of the acquisition or existence of the right is brought into question.

(c) Date of Commencement of Action

The prescription period under the 1832 Act is the 20 years next before a claim is brought into question in some 'suit or action', so that it is necessary to know what exactly is a suit or action, and when it is commenced. Proceedings to establish or resist a claim to an easement of light will normally be brought in the High Court, usually in the Chancery Division, or in the county court. The procedure for commencing such an action today is by the issue of a claim form under Part 7 or Part 8 of the Civil Procedure Rules. The necessary 20 years must therefore be measured back from the date of the issue of the form. A Part 7 claim is generally the appropriate procedure where there is a substantial issue of fact involved, and a Part 8 claim is more appropriate where there is no such issue. The existence of an easement can be established by a referral by the registrar of HM Land Registry to the Property Chamber of the First tier Tribunal under the Land Registration Act 2002.[86] It seems likely that for present purposes, such proceedings count as the bringing of a suit or action. Such proceedings have all the attributes of an action in that they may be commenced by a referral by the registrar to the Tribunal in order to obtain a decision on the existence or otherwise of an easement and result in a binding decision on that question.[87] Even if such proceedings were for some reason not a suit or action within the meaning of section 4 of the 1832 Act, the participation in the proceedings by a dominant owner seeking to establish an easement would be clear evidence that he was not submitting to or acquiescing in an obstruction which had interrupted the access of light to his property. It is possible that some other form of proceedings brought within a year of the interruption starting could defeat the effect of the interruption, for instance a reference to the Lands Chamber of the Upper Tribunal to assess the compensation for the compulsory acquisition of land in which the existence of an easement of light was one of the issues.[88] 5.46

[86] See ch 11, section (E).

[87] See *Wilkin & Sons Ltd v Agricultural Facilities Ltd* (Ref 2011/0420) [113].

[88] Such a reference is an action for the purposes of the running of a limitation period: *Hillingdon LBC v ARC Ltd (No 1)* [1999] Ch 139. See n 78 for the possibility that where in such a case land has to be valued at a previous valuation date the important question may be whether legal procedures to establish or enforce a prescriptive easement could have been initiated at that valuation date.

4. Interruption and Acquiescence

(a) The Interruption

5.47 An interruption to the enjoyment and use of the access of light is some physical obstruction or impediment to the passing of light over the servient land to the dominant building. The construction of a building on the servient land, whether the extension of an existing building or the erection of a new building or of some other structure, will be an interruption. A screen erected deliberately to prevent the passage of light may be an obstruction. This was sometimes done before the enactment of the Rights of Light Act 1959. Since that legislation, a process has been available which allows the registration as a local land charge of a notional obstruction which will have much the same effect as an actual obstruction in preventing the acquisition of a right of light.[89] Advertising hoarding along the boundary of the servient land would be a further example of a possible obstruction. A structure such as a building or a screen would constitute a permanent obstruction to the access of light. Impermanent structures, such as stacks of containers on land, could amount to an obstruction of the access of light. In the latter type of case if structures such as stacked levels of containers or stacks of timber were on the servient land only for irregular periods, and erected to irregular and fluctuating heights and in different positions, it might be that they would be held not to constitute an interruption of the access of light sufficient for the purposes of the Prescription Act 1832. Questions of this nature are matters of fact and degree and of common sense rather than the subject of any rigid rule. The commencement of legal proceedings by the servient owner is not in itself an interruption to the use and enjoyment of light by the dominant owner.[90]

5.48 An interruption to the access of light across the servient land will usually of course be by the deliberate actions of the servient owner. This need not always be so. An obstruction erected by a third party may interrupt the access of light to the dominant building over particular servient land, and so defeat an inchoate or established claim to an easement by reason of the length of the obstruction. The dominant building may have near to it two areas of land, one immediately adjacent to the dominant building and the other just beyond the first area, with an agreement between the owner of the dominant building and the owner of the nearer area of land that no rights of light should come into existence between them.[91] The erection of a building on the nearer area pursuant to the agreement could then act as an interruption to the access of light to the dominant building over the further area, so preventing an easement of light being acquired over that

[89] See ch 9.

[90] *Reilly v Orange* [1955] 2 QB 112.

[91] The effect of such agreements is discussed in para 5.65 et seq. Agreements of this nature may constitute a written consent given by the servient owner to the access of light over his land, and may in this way prevent the coming into existence of a prescriptive easement.

further area. It is also feasible that an obstruction erected on the further area of land could amount to an obstruction of light passing to the dominant building over the nearer area of land.

Whereas the interruption may be by the servient owner or by some third party, actions of the dominant owner on the dominant land cannot interrupt the access of light over the servient land, and cannot be an interruption of the access of light for present purposes. An interruption has to be capable of being acquiesced in or submitted to for it to count as an interruption for present purposes and a person cannot sensibly acquiesce in or submit to what he has himself done. In other words, the interruption referred to in sections 3 and 4 of the 1832 Act is an interruption to the passage of light over the servient land, and not an interruption to the ingress of that light into apertures in the dominant building after it has completed its passage across the servient land. Acts of the dominant owner which prevent the access of light to his premises, such as permanent shuttering placed against its windows, or the creation of some structure upon his land which prevents the access of light to his windows, may prevent the prescriptive acquisition of a right of light or may terminate a prescriptive right of light which has been acquired, but for other reasons.[92] 5.49

Sections 3 and 4 of the 1832 Act must not be applied too literally when it comes to an interruption. The dominant building may enjoy an excellent standard of light passing over the servient land, so that the floor areas of the rooms in the dominant building are, say, 80 per cent sufficiently lit. An obstruction erected on the servient land may reduce the light passing over it to the dominant building so that only 65 per cent of the floor areas of the rooms in the dominant building remains sufficiently lit. This reduction will in all likelihood not constitute an infringement of an easement which has been acquired in favour of the dominant building. The reason is that a room which enjoys a sufficiency of light to 65 per cent of its floor area would normally be regarded as being sufficiently lit as a whole.[93] Despite this consequence, the new building on the servient land would still be in literal terms an interruption of the access and use of light to and for the dominant building. It cannot be the case that in such a situation the running of the prescription period in favour of the dominant building is prevented, since the dominant owner would be unable to prevent the obstruction to his light even if he had acquired an easement by that time. It follows that an interruption to the access of light for the purposes of sections 3 and 4 must mean an interruption of such a nature that the dominant owner, if he had the benefit of an easement of light, would be able to prevent it. 5.50

[92] See para 5.36. For example, if a prescriptive easement of light has been acquired by 20 years of the access of light to a window and the window is then permanently blocked up the easement may then be impliedly abandoned.

[93] See chs 3 and 6 for the ascertainment of the degree of the reduction in light which constitutes an infringement of a right of light.

(b) Acquiescence or Submission and Notice

5.51 An interruption to the access of light to the dominant building is not itself enough to prevent the running of the prescription period, even if it has lasted for a year or more. For the interruption to have that effect, the dominant owner must have acquiesced in or submitted to it for at least a year. Where questions of the present nature arise in legal proceedings, it is for the servient owner to prove that there has been an interruption, but the burden is then on the dominant owner who claims the acquisition of an easement to prove either that the interruption has lasted for less than a year or that, if the interruption has lasted for a year or more, there is not a period of at least a year during which he acquiesced in or submitted to the interruption.[94] For example, after 25 years of the access of light over the servient land to the dominant building, an interruption may have occurred by reason of a structure erected on the servient land, which has been there for 18 months. The dominant owner may have acquiesced in or submitted to it for nine months but then ceased to do so. If at this point the dominant owner commences proceedings for a declaration that he has an easement of light, he should succeed since he can show over 20 years of the access of light and the interruption will not defeat him since, although it has lasted for a year or more, he will be able to show that he has not acquiesced in or submitted to it for a year or more. If in the above circumstances the dominant owner delays for the whole 18 months from the date on which the interruption first commenced before commencing proceedings, he will lose his entitlement to an easement under the Prescription Act 1832 since by then the interruption will have lasted for at least a year and he will have acquiesced in or submitted to it for at least a year.

5.52 For present purposes, and by reason of the closing words of section 4 of the 1832 Act, the dominant owner is not to be taken to have acquiesced in or submitted to an interruption unless he has had notice of the interruption and of the person making or authorising the making of it. Notice means some formal statement, which can be in writing or oral, that the interruption has occurred.[95] In the case of an interruption to the access of light, the existence of the physical obstruction and the interruption will normally be readily apparent to the dominant owner, but some independent notice is still required. Even the creation on the servient land of a 16-feet high wooden hoarding required notice to the dominant owner of its existence before he could be taken to have acquiesced in it as an interruption to light.[96] The notice must state the person who has made the interruption or the person who has authorised it. The notice should be given at the time of or prior to the erection of the obstruction. It seems that if the notice is not given until the

[94] *Dance v Triplow* (1991) 64 P & CR 1.

[95] *Glover v Coleman* (1874) LR 10 CP 108.

[96] *Seddon v Bank of Bolton* (1882) 19 Ch D 462, 468–69 (Fry J). If this principle is correct, it may seem somewhat curious that a dominant owner in occupation of a building can say that he has not had notice of, for instance, a 10-storey building erected opposite to his property.

obstruction has been in place for some time, the necessary one-year period of the obstruction will not start until the notice is given. The notice should be given to all persons with interests in and in occupation of the dominant building, since all such persons may have the benefit of any easement of light.

Acquiescence and submission appear to mean much the same thing, and probably no distinction is to be drawn between the meaning of the two words.[97] Whether in any particular situation there has been acquiescence in or submission to an interruption is a matter of fact. Certain principles pertinent to the question can be stated. It is for a dominant owner claiming the easement to show that, having had notice of the interruption and of the person making or authorising the interruption, he has made his opposition to the interruption clear to that person. Inactivity is not enough, and mere internal dissatisfaction or protests to third parties, such as complaints to a local planning authority, are not enough.[98] Therefore a dominant owner who receives notice of an interruption to the access of light over the servient land and does nothing, or communicates with others but not with the person who has made or authorised the interruption, is likely to find that he is taken to have acquiesced in or submitted to the interruption. If this situation continues for a year or more after the interruption has commenced, and after the dominant owner has received the requisite notice of it, the easement claimed under the Prescription Act 1832 will be lost. 5.53

It is not difficult to prevent acquiescence or submission. A sufficiently clear letter of protest will be enough, whether it comes from the dominant owner or from his advisers.[99] A protest may be oral, but it is obviously preferable that it should be in writing, if only to facilitate proof that it has been made. The clearest step that can be taken for preventing acquiescence or submission is the commencement of legal proceedings to enforce the easement and prevent the interruption. If the dominant owner knows that an interruption is imminent or likely, and protests at it in advance with sufficient clarity, his protest may be sufficient to prevent his acquiescence in or submission to the physical interruption when it occurs.[100] A protest may be withdrawn, in which case acquiescence or submission will commence from the date of the withdrawal. The servient owner, even when a protest has been formally withdrawn, may not feel safe in being able to resist reliance on a prescriptive easement until a year has passed from the withdrawal, since only then will there be acquiescence in or submission to the interruption for at least a year. In practice, in this type of situation there may arise an estoppel by convention, a common understanding of law or fact relied upon in some way by the servient owner, which would prevent the dominant owner subsequently going 5.54

[97] In *Glover v Coleman* (1874) LR 10 CP 108 Brett J appeared to be saying that acquisition and submission were the same thing and were to be contrasted with 'opposition', which was dissent or dissatisfaction manifested by some act.

[98] *Dance v Triplow* (1991) 64 P & CR 1.

[99] *Glover v Coleman* (1874) LR 10 CP 108.

[100] *Davies v Du Paver* [1953] 1 QB 184.

back on the understanding and seeking to have the obstruction removed or seeking damages.[101]

5.55 Presumably a protest can be retrospectively withdrawn. In such circumstances good practice would be that a formal agreement was drawn up between the parties recording what was their understanding of the situation. What is less clear is what may happen if, upon the interruption commencing, a formal protest is made by the dominant owner but nothing else is done, and either the interruption remains or becomes more pronounced by the erection of a building on the servient land to a greater height. Logic suggests that once the dominant owner has made his clear protest, and so has negatived the existence of acquiescence or submission by him, he has done enough and does not need to repeat his protests. Consequently in these circumstances, however long the interruption lasts, there will never be an acquiescence in or submission to it for the requisite year. A dominant owner who takes no further action except that of protesting may find that he is refused an injunction to compel the removal of an offending obstruction, but he is likely to remain able to continue to assert his rights by an action for damages. A servient owner who asserts that his interruption is lawful, for example because there has not been the requisite 20 years of the enjoyment and use of the access of light over his property, may himself bring proceedings to establish that that is the situation.

5.56 A question which may arise is what is the effect of non-acquiescence in an interruption by the dominant owner when that owner has no right to prevent the interruption. This situation may arise if there has been access of light to apertures in the dominant building for only a part of a necessary full 20 years. If the servient owner interrupts the access of light, the dominant owner may protest to an extent which shows that he is not acquiescing in or submitting to the interruption, but beyond protesting, there is no effective action that the dominant owner can take to prevent or secure the removal of the interruption. The question is whether in those circumstances the non-acquiescence prevents the interruption being something which after a year terminates the running of the prescription period. On a purely literal application of sections 3 and 4 of the 1832 Act, this would appear to be the result. It is scarcely a reasonable or practical result and it is likely that the legislation would be read as meaning that a non-acquiescence by protests of the dominant owner is only something which prevents an interruption having effect to end the running of the prescription period if the dominant owner is entitled to prevent the interruption by reason of an already acquired easement. Of course the servient owner can resolve any doubt by himself instituting proceedings for a declaration that he is entitled to interrupt the access of light to the dominant building.

[101] See the definition of an estoppel by convention given by Lord Steyn in *Republic of India v India Steamship Co (No 2)* [1998] AC 878, 913. For example, if the servient owner started to erect a structure on his land and the dominant owner protested, but then as part of an understanding between the two owners withdrew his protests, so that the servient owner acted on the understanding by continuing the erection of the structure, there might arise an estoppel by convention which prevented the dominant owner from resuscitating his protest.

(c) The '19 Years and a Day Rule'

The rule that an interruption is only effective to prevent the running of the statutory prescription period if it has lasted for at least a year has a consequence for the length of the prescription period, and leads to what has been called 'the 19 years and a day rule'. This can best be illustrated by an example. Suppose that the access and enjoyment of light to the dominant building across the servient land commenced on 1 April 1996. The 20-year prescription period will end on 31 March 2016. If an obstruction to the passage of light over the servient land is erected on 1 May 2015, the dominant owner can at that point do nothing to prevent it, since there will still be 11 months to elapse before the end of the 20-year prescription period. On the other hand, the interruption will not affect the running of the prescription period until it lasts for a year, until 30 April 2016. It follows that from 1 April 2016 the dominant owner will have a month during which he can claim an easement by 20 years of the access of light (with the interruption disregarded for this purpose, because it had not lasted for at least a year) and during which he can therefore commence proceedings and establish his right to an easement and can prevent the continuance of the obstruction. In practice, therefore, a dominant owner who is willing and able to act quickly and prudently can be confident of establishing his prescriptive easement after he has enjoyed at least 19 years and a day of the access of light over the servient land and can then regard himself as immune, again providing he acts promptly, from any subsequent interruption to his enjoyment of light over the servient land by the action of the servient owner.[102] 5.57

The law as stated in the last paragraph is illustrated by the decision in *Lord Battersea v Commissioners of Sewers for the City of London.*[103] In that case, former houses on the servient land had been removed between May and October 1875 and replaced by buildings with a low elevation. The owners of the servient land started in or about 1895 to build new offices on their land. The owners of the dominant land commenced proceedings for an injunction by a writ issued on 16 July 1895, claiming that the new development was in breach of their rights of light. It was held that at the date of the issue of the writ their rights were inchoate only, since the full 20 years of use and enjoyment of light following the removal of the former houses, as required by section 3 of the Prescription Act 1832, had not fully passed. It seems that if proceedings had been commenced in October 1895 the proceedings would have succeeded unless the obstruction created by the new office development had existed prior to October 1894, so as to constitute an interruption to light for at least a year.[104] 5.58

[102] A similar situation occurs with the registration of a light obstruction notice under the Rights of Light Act 1959. See ch 9. Because of a particular provision in that Act there is for the purposes of that Act in effect an 18 years and a day rule, as is explained in ch 9, section (H).

[103] *Lord Battersea v Commissioners of Sewers for the City of London* [1895] 2 Ch 708. See also *Bridewell Hospital v Ward, Lock and Co* (1892) 62 LJ (Ch) 270.

[104] This was a possible course suggested arguendo by Mr Swinfen Eady QC for the dominant owners. An interlocutory injunction was granted restraining the servient owners from building higher than the previous houses which had existed before they were demolished in 1875, although it is not clear exactly on what basis this was done.

5. Consent or Agreement

5.59 For the purpose of all acquisitions of easements by prescription, including common law prescription, prescription under the doctrine of lost modern grant, and prescription under section 2 of the Prescription Act 1832, save for easements of light under section 3 of the Act, the consent of the servient owner to the enjoyment of a use of his land means that the use is not user as of right, and no easement is acquired. The consent may be written or oral, or may arise as an inference from the facts.[105] As regards the acquisition by prescription of easements of light under section 3 of the 1832 Act, the only form of consent which prevents an acquisition of an easement is a consent or agreement to the access of light over the servient land to the dominant land made expressly by a deed or in writing. Consequently an oral consent by the servient owner, or a consent inferred from his actions, will not prevent the running of the prescription period.[106] This is the last remnant as regards the acquisition of easements of light under the Prescription Act 1832 of the full doctrine of user as of right which still applies to other forms of prescription, including that generally applicable to the acquisition of easements under section 2 of the Prescription Act 1832. The giving of written consent to the access of light over one property to another property is not a frequent occurrence, and when it does happen it is usually either a term of a transfer of some interest, such as the grant of a lease, or a term of a formal agreement between owners regulating the acquisition of rights of light. The provisions of documents of this nature are often interpreted as the giving of a written consent to the passage of light over a property, although the language of the document often contains no express reference to a consent.

5.60 There seems to be little difference between a consent and an agreement for the purposes of the passage of light over a property. The word 'agreement' may be more appropriate to the type of arrangement discussed below in this section of the chapter.[107] The reference to a deed adds nothing, since every deed must be in writing. It is not necessary that the servient owner has signed the written consent. It has been held that when a question arose of whether the use of land for lawful sports and pastimes was 'as of right' for the purposes of the Commons Act 2006, the making of byelaws relating to the land by statutory undertakers under statutory powers prevented the use being as of right.[108] A consent may be given for a limited period only or, unless its terms state otherwise, may be withdrawn such that after the end of the period of the consent the prescription period will start to run. If the consent is given during the running of the prescription period and the consent is then ended it is probable that the 20-year prescription period would

[105] *Mallam v Rose* [1915] 2 Ch 222.

[106] See para 5.33 for the text of s 3 of the Prescription Act 1832 and its description of a consent 'by deed or writing'.

[107] See para 5.65 et seq.

[108] *R (Newhaven Port & Properties Ltd) v East Sussex County Council* [2015] UKSC 7, [2015] 2 WLR 601. See section (F) of this chapter.

have to recommence since the period of consent may be a sufficient break in the continuity of the 20-year period, and so mean that the periods before and after the consent cannot be aggregated together as a 20-year period before any legal proceedings. Such circumstances will be rare when the enjoyment is the access of light, and not some other enjoyment of the servient land.

Normally, insofar as it occurs at all, a written consent by the servient owner will be as a result of a request for that consent. It would be unusual for the dominant owner to have any motive for obtaining such a consent when the access of light over the servient land to his land will simply occur by the force of nature unless interrupted. Possible circumstances in which a consent may be given by the servient owner to the access of light are where the servient owner is minded to carry out a redevelopment which would affect the access of light to the dominant land, and the dominant owner persuades him not to do so in return for the access of light in future being by consent, and so not being such as can build up an easement. 5.61

A question which could arise is what is to happen if the servient owner gives his written consent to the access of light over his property without any prior request or arrangement for him to do so. On the face of it this course might appear to be an easy way for a servient owner to prevent the running of the prescription period against his property. That owner could send an express written consent to the owners of all properties who might be able to acquire or be in the course of acquiring an easement of light over his property by virtue of the access of light across it, and so prevent the commencement or running of the prescription period. The creation of an obstruction to the access of light by the servient owner or the use of the process available under the Rights of Light Act 1959 would then be unnecessary. It seems unlikely that this possibility was intended under the 1832 Act, and it is probable that a purely unilateral written consent of the nature just indicated would not have any effect under section 3 of the Prescription Act 1832. If a dominant owner received such a unilateral consent, his best course would be to reply that he had not sought and did not require or accept such a consent for the access of light to his property over the servient land. 5.62

Easements of light may be somewhat unusual in this regard. For the purposes of other easements, notably rights of way, notices are sometimes erected on the servient land stating that the use of the land as a route is by consent. This is a sufficient consent to prevent the use of the route being as of right. Similar notices are erected so as to prevent land which is used for recreational purposes being registered as a town or village green under the Commons Registration Act 2006. Such notices are unilateral, as opposed to being the result of a request for permission to enjoy the use. The granting of an unsolicited consent to use an access has been held to prevent the use of the access being as of right and so to prevent the acquisition of a right of way under the doctrine of lost modern grant.[109] 5.63

[109] *Odey v Barber* [2006] EWHC 3109 (Ch), [2008] Ch 175; *Gardner v Hodgson's Kingston Brewery Co Ltd* [1903] AC 229.

In one recent decision the making of byelaws by a statutory port undertaker was held to be a form of consent which resulted in the use of a beach within the port area for lawful sports and pastimes having been by consent and so 'of right', instead of being 'as of right', as required for registration of the area as a town or village green under the Commons Act 2006.[110]

5.64 It may be that the most frequent instances of the giving of written consent to the access of light over the servient land are as an adjunct or effect of agreements permitting development on the servient land, a subject which is considered next.

6. Agreements Permitting Development

(a) The Effect of Agreements

5.65 It is not infrequent to find in leases or other documents a provision which allows a party to redevelop his land as he wishes, notwithstanding the effect on the passage of light to other property. A typical example would be a provision in a lease which gave to the landlord the right to carry out any development on land retained by him. The question is what effect this has on the acquisition by the tenant or other dominant owner of a right of light by prescription against the landlord or other servient owner. It is explained later that a tenant can acquire an easement of light by prescription under the Prescription Act 1832 against his own landlord.[111] It is plain that the intention of the parties to arrangements of the character described is that the servient owner shall have a right to carry out development unimpeded by its effect on the access of light to the dominant building. The courts have striven to give effect to that intention by interpreting a provision of the nature just described as meaning that the access of light over the servient land, perhaps adjoining land retained by a landlord, to the land let to a tenant is enjoyed by the written consent or agreement of the landlord, that consent or agreement being constituted by the deed or other arrangement, with the result that no prescriptive right of light can be acquired under section 3 of the Prescription Act 1832. For the same reason, no prescriptive right would be acquired under the doctrine of lost modern grant.[112]

5.66 An example of this process is *Haynes v King*.[113] The Ecclesiastical Commissioners let to the plaintiff premises on one side of a street for 60 years, retaining premises

[110] *R (Newhaven Port & Properties Ltd) v East Sussex County Council* [2015] UKSC 7, [2015] 2 WLR 601. It was held in *Betterment Properties (Weymouth) Ltd v Dorset County Council* [2012] EWCA (Civ) 250, [2012] P & CR 3, that the erection of signs stating that property was private land was sufficient to prevent the use of the land being as of right for the purposes of the Commons Registration Act 1965, even though some of those using the land may not have seen the signs.

[111] See para 5.87.

[112] As to lost modern grant in this context see *Marlborough v Wilks Head & Eve* [1996] New Law Digest 138.

[113] *Haynes v King* [1893] 3 Ch 439.

on the opposite side of the street. The plaintiff enjoyed access of light over the retained premises for over 20 years. The Commissioners then let the retained premises to the defendant, who erected on the land buildings which impeded the access of light to the plaintiff's premises. The lease to the plaintiff stated that the Commissioners (including their successors) might erect buildings on adjoining or contiguous properties whether or not the light enjoyed by the plaintiff was affected. Although there was no analysis in the judgment of section 3 of the Prescription Act 1832, the provision in the lease was said to be a bargain authorising what was done, so that the plaintiff failed in his proceedings. A similar situation arose in *Willoughby v Eckstein*,[114] that is leases of adjoining premises were granted by a common landlord with a provision in the lease to the plaintiff that adjacent premises might be rebuilt as agreed by the landlord. It was held that this provision rendered the access of light over the adjoining premises something which was enjoyed by consent or agreement so that no prescriptive right was acquired by the plaintiff under section 3 of the 1832 Act over the adjoining premises. These decisions and this line of legal reasoning have been uniformly followed in other and subsequent cases where there were provisions to the same general effect.[115]

On the other hand, an agreement will only prevent the running of the prescription period if it is intended that the access of light over the servient land is to be by the consent of the servient owner so as to have that effect. An agreement that the dominant owner will not enforce his right of light so as to prevent a development as proposed at a particular time will not amount to a general consent given by the servient owner to the access of light over his property, and so will not prevent the dominant owner enforcing his right against a subsequent proposed development.[116] A provision in a lease that rights were granted to the tenant 'except rights, if any, restricting the free use of any adjoining land' was held not to be a consent within the meaning of section 3 of the 1832 Act and so did not prevent the lessee from acquiring a right of light under section 3 by 20 years' enjoyment of light over the adjoining land of the landlord, and therefore did not stop the lessee from being able to prevent development on that adjoining land after the end of that 20-year period, when that development obstructed the passage of light to his land.[117] The purpose of the writing must be clear if it is to amount to a consent to the access of light. An inscription on a stone set into a wall has been held to be insufficiently 5.67

[114] *Willoughby v Eckstein* [1937] 1 Ch 167.

[115] *Blake and Lyons Ltd v Lewis Berger & Sons Ltd* [1951] 2 TLR 605; *Marlborough v Wilks Head & Eve* [1996] New Law Digest 138; *Paragon Finance Plc v City of London Real Property Company Ltd* [2001] 1 EGLR 97; *Midtown Ltd v City of London Real Property Co Ltd* [2005] EWHC 33 (Ch), [2005] 1 EGLR 65; *RHJ Ltd v FT Patten (Holdings) Ltd* [2008] EWCA Civ 151, [2008] Ch 341; *CGIS City Plaza Shares Ltd v Britel Fund Trustees Ltd* [2012] EWHC 1594 (Ch).

[116] *Salvage Wharf Ltd v G & S Brough Ltd* [2009] EWCA Civ 21, [2010] Ch 11. This decision of the Court of Appeal arose in the context of a challenge to the registration by the servient owner of a notice under the Rights of Light Act 1959. See ch 9.

[117] *Mitchell v Cantrill* (1887) 37 Ch D 56.

clear in its purpose to amount to a consent.[118] No express reference to the access of light is necessary before an agreement can constitute a consent under section 3.[119] Leases sometimes contain a provision that no rights of light are granted to the tenant. Such a clause merely ensures that existing rights of light over other property are not granted to the tenant, as would occur in the absence of such an express statement, and is unlikely to amount to a consent for the purposes of section 3.[120]

5.68 Agreements which amount to a consent under section 3 are often found in leases where the landlord wishes to ensure that the tenant shall not be able to prevent subsequent development on other land of the landlord, either by the landlord or by a purchaser of that other land from the landlord, or by a lessee of that other land. However, in principle an agreement sufficient to exclude the operation of section 3 can arise as a term of a purchase of property or as an agreement between adjoining owners unconnected with the disposal of an interest in property, providing the language and the intention are sufficiently clear.[121]

5.69 Where the agreement or provision in question does amount to a consent under section 3 of the 1832 Act, it is necessary to identify the servient land over which consent to the passage of light is given. It is only against that land that a prescriptive right of light is prevented from arising. The terms of the agreement will normally identify the servient land either specifically or by way of some general description, such as a reference to the adjoining land of the landlord. There may be some ambiguities. A simple reference to adjoining land to that let or sold may mean adjoining land in which the landlord or seller has a proprietary interest, or may mean any adjoining land. The former is the more likely intention and interpretation.[122] It is in any event doubtful whether a landlord could effectively give consent to the access of light over land in which he had no proprietary interest, and sometimes there would be no motive for him wishing to do so.[123] A further area of doubt

[118] *Ruscoe v Grounsell* (1903) 89 LT 426. The fact that the writing was in stone would not itself have prevented it being a written consent.

[119] *RHJ Ltd v FT Patten (Holdings) Ltd* [2008] EWCA Civ 151, [2008] Ch 341.

[120] ibid.

[121] Examples are *Ruscoe v Grounsell* and *Salvage Wharf Ltd v GRS Brough Ltd* (in neither case was there a sufficiently clear intention that there should be a consent for the purposes of s 3). Sometimes agreements between neighbouring landowners permit the construction on one property of a building of specified proportions notwithstanding its effect on the access of light to the other property. It is a matter of construction of the agreement whether such a provision authorises the initial construction of a building up to the stated dimensions or permits indefinitely further or redeveloped buildings within the stated dimensions. Since rights of light have a longstanding effect, it is likely that, subject to the exact contractual language, such agreements will be construed as having repeated effect: see *CEMP Properties (UK) Ltd v Dentsply Research and Development Corporation (No 2)* [1989] 2 EGLR 196.

[122] *Paragon Finance Plc v City of London Real Property Co Ltd* [2002] 1 EGLR 97.

[123] There could be occasions on which a landlord would wish to prevent his tenant acquiring a right of light by prescription against adjoining property in which the landlord had no present interest. The landlord might hope to acquire that property. The landlord might have a subsisting right of light over that property which was not passed to the tenant under the lease and the landlord might wish to preserve the ability himself to enforce that easement or the ability to release that easement without the participation of the tenant required under some subsequently acquired easement.

might be whether the consent as regards adjoining land owned by the landlord related to adjoining land owned by the landlord at the date of the agreement, or included land which the landlord might subsequently acquire. The answer must depend on the intention of the parties derived from the language used and the matrix of relevant facts at the date of the agreement.[124] A landlord might have an obvious interest in extending the consent to land which he might obtain in the future, since he might have a hope or expectation of acquiring other land in the area on which he might wish to carry out unhampered redevelopment.[125] In this context there is the same doubt on whether a person can effectively give consent to the access of light over land which at the time of the consent he does not own.

Where an agreement does constitute a consent to the access of light over some particular servient land, its effect on the dominant building will depend upon whether at the time of the agreement a prescriptive right of light has already been acquired for the benefit of the dominant building by 20 years or more of access of light without interruption over the servient land. If an easement of light has been acquired in this way, the giving of the consent is likely to mean that any subsequent reliance by the dominant owner on that easement under section 3 of the 1832 Act will be met by the defence that the necessary 20 years' enjoyment without written consent was not that next before the proceedings in which the question of the easement arose.[126] If at the time of the agreement the 20 years' enjoyment of the access of light in favour of the dominant building has not started or, although started, has not been completed, the effect of the consent will be to prevent any period or continuing period of the enjoyment of light without written consent so that no easement will be acquired under section 3 of the 1832 Act. 5.70

It is necessary to distinguish between (a) an agreement under which the owner of a potentially dominant building agrees that no right of light will be acquired by prescription against potentially servient land and (b) an agreement under which the owner of dominant land with the benefit of an easement of light agrees not to enforce this easement either generally against a particular area of servient land or not to enforce it against a particular development on that servient land. The first type of agreement is likely to be interpreted as the servient owner giving his written consent to the passing of light over his property to the dominant building so that no right can be claimed by prescription over the servient land. The second type of agreement operates simply in accordance with its stated terms. 5.71

A servient owner entering an agreement of the second type needs to take care. It often occurs that the rights of light which are appurtenant to a dominant building are enjoyed by more than one person with an interest in that building. In particular, such rights may be enjoyed by tenants. An agreement with the freehold 5.72

124 *Paragon Finance Plc v City of London Real Property Co Ltd* [2002] 1 P & CR 36.

125 See n 123.

126 It may still be possible for the dominant owner to assert a prescriptive easement of light under the doctrine of lost modern grant where the period of enjoyment relied upon does not have to be that immediately before the proceedings. See section (C) of this chapter.

owner will not prevent the tenants asserting their own rights. An agreement with the freehold owner and a number of tenants will not prevent a further tenant or under-tenant coming forward and asserting that the rights of light are enjoyed by him by virtue of his interest. A servient owner entering into such an agreement would therefore be well advised to be sure that he has dealt with and included within his agreement everyone with an interest in the dominant building who could have any right to assert a right of light. If there is uncertainty, then a servient owner, before parting with his money under an agreement, may wish to obtain an indemnity from those persons with interests in the dominant building to whom he is to pay a sum of money that there are no further persons with interests in that building who may be able to assert rights of light.

(b) Agreements and Transfers of Interests

5.73 A question which sometimes arises in the context of agreements permitting development is the continuing effect of such agreements if there is a transfer of the dominant building or of the servient land. For example, a landlord, A, might grant a 99-year lease of a part of his land to a tenant, B, with a provision in the lease that A shall be entitled to carry out any development on the remainder of his land notwithstanding any reduction in the access of light to the property let to B. As has been explained, this provision will normally be construed as a consent to the access of light across the retained land of A to the property let such that no prescriptive easement can arise in favour of the property let. The question which arises is what happens if, as is likely, at some time during the term of the long lease A sells his retained land or B sells his lease?

5.74 It is of course possible that the provision in the lease, or in any similar instrument, is expressly made personal to A or to B or to both. In that event the consent will end upon a transfer of the relevant interest and after that the prescription period can commence and run in the ordinary way.[127] Such a provision is unlikely, particularly in the context of commercial properties. Whether a particular provision confines a right or an obligation to an original party to an instrument is always a matter of the interpretation of the language used within the context of all relevant facts. In one case a provision in a conveyance of land conferred on the transferee the right to build on the land transferred without regard to any interference with air or light enjoyed by 'the buildings for the time being erected on any adjoining adjacent or neighbouring land owned by or vested in the Corporation [ie the

[127] An example of a licence or consent which was personal and to endure only during the ownership of the land benefited by the licensee is the decision in *London Tara Hotel Ltd v Kensington Close Hotel Ltd* [2011] EWCA Civ 1356, [2012] 1 EGLR 33. A licence was given to the owner of a property to use a road on the land of the licensor and was made personal to the licensee. The licence came to an end when the licensee transferred the land benefited to a different person. The continued use of the road after the end of the licence was therefore not by consent and was capable of leading to the commencement of the running of the prescription period.

transferor].' It was held that the right endured against successors in title of the original transferor. The court held that this interpretation was in accord with business common sense.[128]

It seems obvious that in the absence of a limiting provision of the nature mentioned in the last paragraph, the opportunity to develop the retained land of A in the example just mentioned is intended to subsist throughout the term of the lease to B, even though one or both of the freehold or leasehold interests is transferred during that period. If it were otherwise, the provision could be deprived of much of its effect, since B could transfer his lease at an early date and the prescription period could then start to run. 5.75

If B transfers his lease there seems no reason why the consent constituted by the redevelopment provision should not continue to operate such that the transferee of the lease will not be able to acquire an easement of light by prescription against the retained land of A. There seems no reason or principle of law which terminates the effect of the redevelopment provision or of the consent inferred from it just because the leasehold land is transferred. The correct analysis is not that of the burden of a contract passing to the transferee of the lease, but that of a written consent to the access of light to the demised land over the retained land having been given for a period of 99 years such that the transferee takes the land with the factual existence of that consent and of its consequences in law. 5.76

It has been suggested that the position may be different if A transfers the freehold of his retained land and that in such a case the consent terminates upon that transfer. The result would be that upon the transfer of A's land, either B or his successor in title to the long lease could commence the acquisition by prescription of an easement of light against the retained land of A. This suggestion, which appears to be directly contrary to the intention of the parties, seems to be founded on two possible lines of reasoning. 5.77

One line of reasoning is that the burden of a contract is not transferable, with the result that the contract cannot be enforced against a transferee of land such as a purchaser of the retained land of A. As has been explained, the existence of proprietary interests in land, which may bind a transferee of the land burdened by such an interest, is in a sense an exception to the above general principle.[129] The fallacy of this argument is that a contractual obligation normally involves a duty to do or refrain from doing something. In the example given earlier, there is no obligation on a transferee from A to do or not to do anything. The situation is no more than that a consent has been given by A to the access of light across his retained land to the land let to B and that consent is obviously intended, in the absence of some provision to the contrary, to last for the 99-year duration of the lease. The relevant 5.78

[128] *CGIS City Plaza Shares Ltd v Britel Fund Trustees Ltd* [2012] EWHC 1594 (Ch). The court applied the principles of the interpretation of commercial contracts stated by the Supreme Court in *Rainy Sky SA v Kookmin Bank* [2011] UKSC 50, [211] 1 WLR 2900.

[129] See ch 2, para 2.4 et seq.

event, the giving of consent, has happened at the time of the grant of the lease with the inclusion of the redevelopment provision and there is no transferred contractual burden after that date. In any event so far as one can speak of the burden of a contract in the present context the burden, the inability to take advantage of the rules on prescription, is on the tenant not the landlord.

5.79 A second line of reasoning is that the consent given by A amounts to a licence, and a licence cannot normally be enforced against a transferee of the land of the licensor who granted the licence.[130] This principle of law is well established but the difficulty in its application in present circumstances is that of describing the consent which arises out of the redevelopment provision as a licence. A licence is that which renders lawful what would otherwise be a trespass.[131] If a person parks his car on a neighbour's land, that act is a trespass, but if the neighbour has given his licence for that to occur, the act of course ceases to be a trespass. In the situation here under discussion involving the access of light to a building, there is no trespass or possibility of a trespass or other unlawful act occurring. The passage of light over servient land to a dominant building occurs by the force of nature and without the intervention of anyone. It is not apposite to describe a consent given by the servient owner to the passage of light over his building to other land as a licence, in the ordinary understanding in law of that word. If the light passes over the servient land and there is no consent from the servient owner then plainly there is no trespass or unlawful act involved on the part of the owner of the dominant building to which the light passes. The situation is much simpler. It is no more than that as a part of an agreement, a consent has been given in the above example by A to the passage of light over his retained land to the building let to B for a period of 99 years. That having been done, there is no more to be done. The consent plainly cannot be withdrawn since it has been given for a definite period with no provision for withdrawal. In these circumstances the fact that the retained land of A, the servient land, is transferred during the 99 years should make no difference to the effect of the consent given and to the effect of the redevelopment provision.

5.80 The intention behind a redevelopment provision, and behind the consent which is deemed or is inferred to exist as a result of that provision, is that in the above example A or his successors in title shall be entitled to redevelop the retained land during the 99-year period of the lease, notwithstanding any effect on the access of light to the property let to B. The law will seek to give effect to this agreement if it is consistent with general legal principles. There does not appear to be any legal principle which prevents the agreement having its ordinary and intended effect, whether or not the retained land is transferred during the 99 years and whether or not the leasehold land is transferred during the 99 years.

[130] *Ashburn Anstalt v Arnold* [1989] 1 Ch 1. This line of argument is suggested in the 19th edn of *Gale on Easements* (London, Sweet & Maxwell, 2012) para 4-35.

[131] *Thomas v Sorrell* (1673) Vaugh 330, 351.

It is also sometimes suggested that an agreement of the nature here under discussion may have effect as a restrictive covenant. This seems implausible. A restrictive covenant is a covenant which restricts the use of one piece of land for the benefit of a different piece of land. Rules have been worked out for the passing of the benefit and the burden of restrictive covenants. The type of agreement here being considered does not restrict the use of any land by any person. The agreement merely prevents the acquisition of an easement by prescription, which is quite different in its juridical effect. 5.81

The example here given has been a provision for redevelopment by a landlord in a lease, and that is an occasion in which such redevelopment provisions often occur. The same principle as to the continuing effect of an agreement permitting redevelopment on one piece of land notwithstanding its effect on the passage of light to another piece of land would apply if the provision was in a transfer of freehold land or was in an agreement between neighbouring landowners not involving a transfer of an interest in land. In the absence of some express temporal or other limitation the normal expectation would be that the provision, and the consent to the access of light implicit in it, was to have permanent effect. 5.82

7. Interests in Land

(a) Freehold and Leasehold Interests

It has been explained that for the purposes of prescription at common law and under the doctrine of lost modern grant where the dominant building is let under a lease, any right acquired for the benefit of that building is acquired for the benefit of the freehold and cannot be enforced by the tenant who is in possession during the period of the access of light to the building. It is also doubtful whether an easement by common law prescription or under the doctrine of lost modern grant can be acquired at all against the servient land when that land is in the possession of a tenant.[132] Where a right of light is claimed by prescription under s 3 of the Prescription Act 1832, the rules are substantially different, the differences being said to flow from the wide language of s 3, which does not require user as of right and refers to a right acquired being absolute and indefeasible. 5.83

If the dominant building is let and at that time the 20-year prescription period has been completed as against the servient land, it appears that the easement acquired under section 3 may be enforced by the tenant and also enures for the benefit of the landlord of the dominant building who may continue to enforce the easement after the end of the lease.[133] It is possible that there is a term of the lease of the 5.84

[132] See para 5.22 et seq.

[133] In *Forster v Lyons & Co* [1927] 1 Ch 219 the dominant building was let under a 99-year lease. Eve J at p 227 observed that it could not be doubted that the tenant, by the uninterrupted enjoyment of the

dominant building which provides that rights acquired against third parties are to be for the benefit of the landlord alone, in which case it seems that only the landlord would be able to enforce a right of light acquired under section 3 of the 1832 Act.

5.85 The effect of leases granted of the dominant building and in effect during the prescription period may be summarised as follows:

(a) The freeholder of the dominant building can rely on the access of light to his building during any period when the building is subject to a lease or a succession of leases, so that all the freeholder has to show to establish an easement of light under section 3 of the Prescription Act 1832 is the actual access of light over the 20 year period.
(b) A tenant of the dominant building can establish for himself the benefit of a right of light if he has enjoyed the access of light for 20 years during the tenancy which he holds (or a predecessor in title to him under that tenancy has enjoyed the access of light during a whole or a part of the period).[134] The tenant will not be able to rely on the access of light during a previous tenancy held by him which has expired.[135]
(c) A tenant can claim that a right of light established in favour of the landlord at the date of the grant of the lease has passed to him as a part of that grant. Of course for this to have occurred, the landlord must himself have established the easement at the date of the grant of the lease. If the landlord has established that right the benefit of the easement will pass to the tenant either automatically or under section 62 of the Law of Property Act 1925 in the absence of any provision to the contrary in the lease.[136]
(d) It seems that if a part of the prescription period has passed at the date of the grant of the lease, the benefit of the inchoate right can pass to the tenant under section 62 of the Law of Property Act 1925 so that the tenant can

access of light to the building for the statutory period, could acquire an absolute right to the access of light under s 3 of the Prescription Act 1832. It was held in that case that the right did not arise because of the particular language of the lease of the dominant land. See also *RHJ Ltd v FT Patten (Holdings) Ltd* [2008] EWCA Civ 151, [2008] Ch 341, in which an office building let to a tenant had enjoyed the access of light over adjoining land retained by the landlord for a period in excess of 20 years. A purchaser of the freehold of the land within the lease claimed the benefit of an easement under s 3 of the Prescription Act 1832. It was held in the Court of Appeal that he would have succeeded had it not been for a particular provision in the lease which operated as a written consent to the access of light over the adjoining land and so prevented an easement being acquired under s 3. For such agreements permitting development, see section (D)5 of this chapter. See also *Midtown Ltd v City of London Real Property Co* [2005] EWHC 33 (Ch), [2005] 1 EGLR 65 [15].

[134] *Midtown Ltd v City of London Real Property Co Ltd* [2005] EWHC 33 (Ch), [2005] 1 EGLR 65.

[135] Ibid. It is not clear why this should be so. The policy behind s 3 of the Prescription Act 1832 appears to be that there should be 20 years or more of the uninterrupted access of light if an easement of light is to be acquired by prescription irrespective of who holds interests in the dominant building during this period. There seems to be no reason why a tenant should not count towards the 20 years a period of the access of light during a previous tenancy which he has held.

[136] See ch 11, paras 11.74–11.77.

complete the remainder of the 20-year period of the access of light and can then at the end of the 20 years assert the right against the servient land in his capacity as a tenant of the dominant building.[137]

If the servient land is let during the prescription period, a right of light may be acquired for the benefit of the dominant building under section 3 which will enure for the benefit of the dominant building against both the tenant of the servient land and the landlord of that land when its lease ends.[138] In this respect also the rule for prescription under section 3 differs from that which applies to prescription at common law and under the doctrine of lost modern grant.[139] It seems that, as with other easements, an easement for a term of years cannot be acquired under section 3, so that the easement which arises by prescription against the servient land is necessarily an easement in fee simple which enures against the fee simple owner of the servient land. It is in order to prevent the acquisition of prescriptive rights in this way against property which is let that covenants are often inserted into leases which require the tenant not to allow the acquisition of rights against the demised property. The acquisition of rights of light may be prevented by the use of the procedure under the Rights of Light Act 1959.[140] A fee simple owner as landlord should be able to ascertain whether rights of light are in the course of being acquired by prescription against land which he has let and is himself entitled to operate the procedure under the Rights of Light Act 1959 needed to prevent the rights being acquired. 5.86

One consequence of these rules is that under section 3 a tenant can acquire an easement of light against other property of his own landlord. To this extent also the 'fee simple rule' is not applicable.[141] A situation which may arise is that a landlord lets land and retains adjoining land, and the tenant enjoys the access of light over the retained land of the landlord for 20 years. In principle in this situation the tenant will acquire an easement of light under section 3 over the retained land enforceable against his landlord.[142] If the retained land is itself let to a tenant, the tenant of the dominant building will acquire an easement enforceable against the tenant of the retained land and against the landlord at the end of the tenancy of the retained land. The easement will of course be effective against successors in title of the landlord. In order to prevent this type of situation arising, a provision is often included in leases to permit the landlord to develop land retained by him, irrespective of the effect on the access of light to the premises let. Such a provision will usually operate as a written consent by the landlord to the access of light 5.87

[137] *Midtown Ltd v City of London Real Property Co Ltd* [2005] EWHC 33 (Ch), [2005] 1 EGLR 65 [23].

[138] *Morgan v Fear* [1907] AC 425, citing *Frewin v Philips* (1861) 11 CB (NS) 449 and *Mitchell v Cantrill* (1887) 37 Ch D 56; *Pugh v Savage* [1970] 2 QB 373.

[139] See para 5.26 et seq.

[140] See ch 9 for the Rights of Light Act 1959.

[141] See para 5.22 for the fee simple rule.

[142] *RHJ Ltd v FT Patten (Holdings) Ltd* [2008] EWCA Civ 151, [2008] Ch 341; *Willoughby v Eckstein* [1937] Ch 167; *Foster v Lyons and Co Ltd* [1927] 1 Ch 219.

over the retained land, and so will prevent the acquisition of an easement under section 3.[143]

5.88 In the type of situation just described, where both the dominant building and the servient land are let by the same landlord and an easement is acquired under section 3 for the benefit of the dominant building, the position appears to be as follows. If the lease of the dominant building ends before that of the servient land, the benefit of the easement can continue to be enforced by the common landlord against the tenant of the servient land. If the freehold of only the dominant building has been sold by the landlord the successor landlord will be able to enforce the easement acquired against the tenant and the landlord of the servient land and other successors in title to that land. On the other hand if the lease of the servient land ends before that of the dominant building, the tenant of the dominant building will continue to be able to enforce the easement against his own landlord as the owner of the servient land and against any successor in title of his landlord to the servient land. When the lease of the dominant building does come to an end the landlord will be able to enforce the easement against his successors in title to the servient land if he has sold the land. This summary of possible situations which may arise is of course subject to any provision on the matter in any relevant transfer of land.

(b) Unity of Ownership or Possession

5.89 These rules should be read subject to the principle that a period of unity of ownership and unity of possession of the dominant and servient properties extinguishes any easement. This would occur if the landlord became the owner in possession of the freehold of both properties. It has been explained earlier that if there has been just unity of possession of the dominant and servient land during any substantial part of the prescription period, that fact will defeat any claim for an easement either under the doctrine of lost modern grant or where acquisition is claimed of any easements other than the easement of light under section 2 of the Prescription Act 1832.[144] However, under section 3 of the Act and in relation to rights of light the law is different. A period of unity of possession does not terminate the running of the prescription period but merely suspends it. Therefore if there is a period of 15 years of access of light over the servient land to the dominant building, and for five years thereafter there is unity of possession of the two properties followed by five years of separate possession, the first of the periods may be aggregated with the second of the periods, that following the period of unity of possession, so as to found a claim for an easement under section 3, which requires 20 years of use and enjoyment of the access of light.[145] There are difficulties in understanding this

[143] See para 5.65 et seq.

[144] *Damper v Bassett* [1901] 2 Ch 350. See para 5.30.

[145] *Ladyman v Grave* (1871) 6 Ch App 763, 768 (Lord Hatherley LC). In this case the total aggregated periods did not exceed 20 years, so that no easement was acquired.

statement of the law, which is not supported by any legal explanation, although it has remained unchallenged for well over a century. One difficulty is that in these circumstances there has not been enjoyment of the access of light for the full period of 20 years required by section 3 of the 1832 Act, which means a period of reasonably continuous enjoyment. Also, and perhaps more importantly, the reliance on the aggregated period of 20 years is not reliance on a period 'next before' any issue which arises in legal proceedings as required by section 4 of the 1832 Act. It has been observed that the easement of light is an exception to many rules[146] but it should surely be a principled exception, and it is difficult to see any principle which justifies this aggregation of periods.

8. The Crown

It is a general rule of law that statutes do not bind the Crown unless a particular statute contains an express provision that it, or some part of it, does apply to the Crown.[147] Section 2 of the Prescription Act 1832 refers to use or enjoyment of 'any land or water of our Lord the King … or being parcel of the Duchy of Lancaster or the Duchy of Cornwall.' As far as easements generally are concerned there may therefore be a prescriptive acquisition of the easement against the Crown under section 2 by 20 years of use. However section 3, dealing specifically with the access and enjoyment of light, does not mention the Crown. Consequently section 3 does not bind the Crown, and an easement of light cannot be acquired against the Crown by prescription in reliance on the Prescription Act 1832. This situation is obviously anomalous and unsatisfactory. It is all the more unsatisfactory in that the Crown may take the benefit of a statute even though not expressly referred to in it.[148] Consequently the Crown may obtain an easement of light by prescription against the land of some other person under section 3 of the Act. 5.90

The immunity of the Crown under section 3 may extend to properties owned by government departments, although it is unlikely that it would extend to bodies such as those industries which are still nationalised, or the privatised successors of nationalised industries. The immunity certainly does not extend to local government and other similar public official or administrative bodies. 5.91

In practice the Crown may voluntarily submit to the operation of section 3 of the 1832 Act against it. It has been suggested that the special position and immunity of the Crown may be a contravention of article 1 of the First Protocol to the European Convention on Human Rights and Fundamental Freedoms. That article 5.92

[146] *Sovmots Ltd v Secretary of State for the Environment* [1979] AC 144, 176 (Lord Edmond-Davies) quoting from the 4th edn of *Megarry and Wade: The Law of Real Property* (London, Sweet & Maxwell, 1975).

[147] See, eg, *Province of Bombay v Municipal Corporation of Bombay* [1947] AC 58.

[148] *Case of the King's Fine* (1605) 7 Co Rep 32a.

refers to the peaceful enjoyment by a person of his possessions. The question of Crown immunity from the operation of the burden of statutes and the impact on that immunity of the Human Rights Act 1998 is a wider one, going well beyond questions of easements of right and section 3 of the Prescription Act 1832.

9. Local Use or Custom

5.93 Section 3 of the Prescription Act 1832 states that the creation of an easement of light by the use of light enjoyed for 20 years shall be absolute and defeasible, 'any local usage or custom to the contrary notwithstanding'. It is explained below that there is a custom of London, applicable in the City of London, which prevents the acquisition of easements of light by common law prescription or under the doctrine of lost modern grant in certain limited circumstances so as to prevent new houses being built within the area of the foundations of existing houses. It is also possible that there was a similar custom of York, but no evidence of this exists. In any event, where an easement of light is claimed in reliance on section 3 of the Prescription Act 1832, neither of these customs prevents the acquisition of the easements, by reason of the words just mentioned.[149]

10. Persons Under Disabilities

5.94 Under section 7 of the Prescription Act 1832, periods during which the servient owner is a minor, a mental patient, a married woman (femme couvert) or a tenant for life may be excluded in the computation of the prescription period except where the right acquired by the period of enjoyment is declared to be absolute and indefeasible. This provision for excluding time does not apply to the acquisition of rights of light, since such a right is declared by section 3 to be absolute and indefeasible. Section 2 of the Act, which is applicable to easements generally, provides that where there has been 40 years' enjoyment, the right created is absolute and indefeasible unless the enjoyment was by written consent. In other words, the provisions which apply to the prescriptive acquisition of an easement of light by 20 years of enjoyment apply to the prescriptive acquisition of other easements where there has been 40 years of enjoyment. Thus the use where there is 40 years' enjoyment does not have to be user as of right and, as with the acquisition of rights of light, all that remains of the user as of right concept is that the enjoyment must not have been by written consent. By virtue of section 8 of the Act, where the servient land is held by a tenant for life or a tenant for a term of over three years in certain circumstances, and as regards certain types of easement, the period during

[149] See section (E) of this chapter for local customs. Modern authorities suggest that the Custom of London may apply to the rebuilding of commercial buildings as well as houses.

which the servient land is so held can be excluded in the computation of the 40-year period. Since the 40-year period does not apply to the acquisition of rights of light under section 3, no such exclusion is possible in rights of light cases. In summary, there are no disability provisions or periods which can be used against a claim to a prescriptive right of light made under the Prescription Act 1832.

11. Pleading

5.95 In the early nineteenth century, pleadings in legal proceedings were much more complex and rigid than is the case today.[150] A case could be lost because of inadequate pleadings, something which is very unlikely today when amendments to pleadings are regularly allowed as necessary to allow the true issue to be before a court, subject to payment of the costs of the other party which have been unnecessarily incurred by an inadequate pleading and a need to amend it.[151]

5.96 Section 5 of the Prescription Act 1832 sets out certain provisions on pleadings. It is stated that a claimant may allege his right generally without averring the existence of the right from time immemorial, and that a party who intends to rely on any proviso, exception, incapacity, disability, contract or agreement should specifically allege that on which he relies. The latter part of this provision remains good practice today. In addition, if any party relies on any cause or matter of fact or of law not inconsistent with the simple fact of enjoyment the same must be specifically alleged in answer to the allegation of the party making a claim.[152] It is today normally sufficient in a rights of light claim or defence to follow the general rules on pleading contained in the Civil Procedure Rules, so that little attention need be paid to the antique provisions of section 5 of the 1832 Act. The availability of remedies for an infringement of a right of light, generally an injunction or damages or a declaration, is explained in Chapter 7.

(E) THE CUSTOM OF LONDON

5.97 The long-established custom of London places some limitation on the acquisition of easements by prescription within the area of the City of London. There had arisen at least by the early years of the seventeenth century a custom within the

[150] A pleading is the formal Statement of Case of a party in civil litigation by which he sets out what is his claim or what is his defence to a claim. Until recent decades pleadings tended to be formal documents, sometimes using traditional phraseology. An example was a general traverse in a defence which might contain some such words as 'all facts and matters pleaded in the statement of claim are denied, save where herein expressly admitted or otherwise pleaded to, as if the same were herein set out seriatim and specifically traversed.' Modern pleadings are much more relaxed and are governed by Part 16 of the Civil Procedure Rules.

[151] Amendments to pleadings are governed by Part 17 of the Civil Procedure Rules.

[152] See *Beasley v Clarke* (1836) 2 Bing NC 705.

City that a person could build within the foundations of an existing house a new house to any height without incurring liability to the owner of any other house in the vicinity by reason of a reduction in light to that other house.[153] The extent of the custom was clarified by 1757 when the Recorder of London certified that the custom existed at law but was limited so that:

(a) the custom was confined to a right to rebuild one house even though it reduced the access of light to another house, ie it did not allow the rebuilding of any building to the detriment of any other building, so that the law seemed to be that the custom applied only if the property being rebuilt or extended was a house and the property whose light was reduced was a house;
(b) the right was confined to a rebuilding within the foundations of a former building, ie there could not be a lateral extension of the boundaries of the building; and
(c) the right could be removed by a written agreement to the contrary effect.[154]

The custom is predicated on the assumption that apart from the special custom, a reduction in light to an existing building caused by the rebuilding of a different existing building could give a right of action because of the reduction of the access of light to the building affected.[155]

5.98 The custom therefore placed a limit on the acquisition of easements of light within the City of London by common law prescription or lost modern grant. It does not apply where a prescriptive easement of light is claimed under section 3 of the Prescription Act 1832, since that provision contains the words 'any local custom or usage notwithstanding'. Today, prescriptive claims are mainly founded on the 1832 Act.[156]

5.99 Some doubt has been cast by more modern cases on whether the custom is confined to the effect of the rebuilding of a house on the light passing to another house, as opposed to the rebuilding of other types of premises.[157] This more modern development seems regrettable, since the custom of the City of London is a local anomaly and it seems sensible to circumscribe its operation as far as possible. Even if the custom is confined to houses, the question arises whether modern

[153] *Hughes v Keymish* (1610) 1 Bulstrode 115.

[154] *Plummer v Bentham* (1757) 1 Burr 248; *Wynstanley v Lee* (1818) 2 Swan 333; *Perry v Eames* [1891] 1 Ch 658 (see n 157 on the effect of this last decision).

[155] This appears to have been the case certainly by 1610: see *Aldred's* case (1610) 9 Co Rep 57(b).

[156] *Salters' Company v Jay* (1842) 3 QB 109; *Truscott v Merchant Taylors Co* (1856) 11 Exch 855. There may however still be cases where reliance is placed on the doctrine of lost modern grant, particularly where there has been some interruption in the access of light in the past, since the prescription period under sections 3 and 4 of the Prescription Act 1832 has to be for a period immediately prior to the legal proceedings in which the matter is brought into issue: see para 5.39 et seq.

[157] In *Perry v Eames* [1891] 1 Ch 658 it seems to have been assumed that the custom applied to the redevelopment of a site previously used for non-residential purposes. There was no detailed consideration of the point and no analysis of what was said in *Plummer v Bentham* in 1757. This view was

forms of residential buildings, such as blocks of flats, constitute houses within the custom.

It has been suggested that there is a similar custom in the City of York.[158] 5.100

(F) UNLAWFUL USES

It has been suggested that an easement of light cannot be acquired by prescription for the benefit of a building whose erection or use is in breach of planning control or is in some other way unlawful. The suggestion is apparently founded on a proposition of law that prescriptive rights cannot be gained by a use which is unlawful. The suggestion is sometimes extended so as to say that a prescriptive easement of light cannot be acquired where the use of the dominant building is unlawful in some other way. An associated question is whether an easement of light can be obtained by prescription when the existence of the right would be inconsistent with statutory purposes for which the servient land is held. 5.101

1. Breach of Planning and Similar Controls

The core of town planning law is that the carrying out of building or other operations on land, or the making of a material change in the use of land, is a breach of planning control unless it is authorised by a planning permission. There are time limits for the taking of enforcement action against breaches of planning control, which are generally four years from the date of the breach in the case of operations on land and 10 years from the date of the breach in the case of changes of use.[159] 5.102

The suggestion described in paragraph 5.101 as it relates to a case of the erection or use of the dominant building being in some way a breach of planning control is plainly unfounded for a number of reasons. 5.103

In the first place, the supposed principle that actions which are unlawful can never give rise to prescriptive rights, even if generally correct, cannot be applied to rights of light. The activity or situation which brings into being a prescriptive right of 5.104

followed in *Bowring Services Ltd v Scottish Widows Fund and Life Assurance Society* [1995] 1 EGLR 158 on the reasoning that it was appropriate to follow what had been said in 1891 rather than to look at the genesis of the custom.

[158] The authority for this appears to be *Bland v Moseley,* cited in Coke 9 pl fo, referred to in *Aldred's* case (1610) 9 Co Rep 57(b). A note in *Aldred's* case states that an alleged custom at York to stop lights (ie impede the access of light) by building on new foundations where no house previously existed was declared void. The implication may be that there was such a custom where a house was rebuilt on existing foundations. There appears to be no further authority on the existence or limits of any custom in York.

[159] Town and Country Planning Act 1990, ss 55, 57 and see Pt VII.

light is the passing of natural light over the servient land to apertures in the dominant building. There is no conceivable illegality, whether in public law or in private law, in this occurring. It simply happens by the force of nature.

5.105 Secondly, the whole theory of prescription, apart from certain easements such as rights of light, is that there are some tortious acts which because of their duration and nature become established as lawful rights. The owner of dominant land may use a route regularly and for over 20 years over adjoining servient land. His every use of the route is the tort of trespass until the de facto use of the route ripens by prescription into an easement of way and so ceases to be a tort. It is illogical to say that the acquisition of a right by prescription cannot occur because the use of the dominant land is unlawful when the very acts which found the prescription are generally unlawful.

5.106 Thirdly, the correct statement of law is not that actions which are unlawful, even criminal actions, cannot found a prescriptive right, but rather that there cannot be the presumed fictional grant which is said to be the origin of the prescriptive right (save for rights of light under section 3 of the Prescription Act 1832)[160] where the making of an actual grant would have been unlawful. The true principle is illustrated by a decision in which the use of land as a vehicular access was carried out in circumstances where it was a criminal offence unless done pursuant to lawful authority. A prescriptive right was established by the long use since the relevant rules of prescription, there the doctrine of lost modern grant, depended on an assumed grant and there was nothing unlawful in that grant being made.[161] In its 2011 report on easements and other rights in land, the Law Commission recommended that the qualifying use which would give rise to an easement, including an easement of light, should not be one which is contrary to the criminal law unless it could be rendered lawful by the dispensation of the servient owner. This recommendation was considered to reflect the existing law.[162]

5.107 Fourthly, there is nothing in the planning legislation or in planning or other policy which suggests that an operation on land carried out, or a use of land instituted, in breach of planning control cannot form the basis of the acquisition of ordinary private law rights. To suppose that a property erected without the requisite planning permission cannot acquire an easement for its benefit is as illogical as suggesting that a tenancy of the building cannot lawfully be granted. If there were any such rule preventing the acquisition of rights it is not known how long the inability to acquire an easement or other rights was to remain, ie whether it was to last for ever, or until the limitation period for the enforcement of planning

[160] See n 6.

[161] *Bakewell Management Ltd v Brandwood* [2004] UKHL 14, [2004] 2 AC 519. The use of the land which was common land as an access by vehicles was a criminal offence under s 193(4) of the Law of Property Act 1925 if carried out 'without lawful authority'.

[162] Law Commission, *Making Law Work, Easements, Covenants and Profits a Prendre* (Law Com No 237, 2011) paras 3.123 and 3.129. The report and its recommendations for reform of the law of easements are examined in more detail in ch 12.

control elapsed. The carrying out of certain works to a listed building without listed building consent may itself amount to a criminal offence under section 9 of the Planning (Listed Buildings and Conservation Areas) Act 1990, but to suggest that this would prevent the acquisition of an easement of light in favour of the building would be equally illogical. Where it is intended that actions which are in some way contrary to law are not to be used in support of the acquisition of certain rights or benefits there is usually a statutory provision to that effect.[163] There is no such provision in the case of breaches of planning law, and no such provisions as regards the acquisition of rights by prescription.

2. Breaches of Private Law Rights

If works are carried out to the dominant building or its use is changed in breach of some contractual or other right enforceable in private law, there is even less reason to believe that an easement of light cannot be claimed for that building. A person entitled to assert such a right, for example a landlord under the terms of a lease or a neighbour under the terms of a restrictive covenant, can do so equally well whether or not the prescription period is running in favour of the dominant building. If A has a property right enforceable against B there is no general principle of law that B cannot create a right in favour of C or acquire a right against C. An illustration of this principle is that a tenant who grants a sub-lease in breach of a covenant in his lease not to do so nonetheless vests a valid legal estate in the sub-tenant.[164] 5.108

3. Land Held for Statutory Purposes

A question which arises is what is the position if during the whole or a part of the prescription period the servient land was held for statutory purposes which were inconsistent with the existence of an easement of light against that land for the benefit of the dominant building. A similar question was recently addressed by the Supreme Court in *R (Newhaven Port and Properties Ltd) v East Sussex County Council*.[165] The company held and operated land as a port at Newhaven, which included a beach on the foreshore, under legislation going back to 1847, and made byelaws under statutory authority for the regulation of the port including the beach. The beach had been used for lawful sports and pastimes for over 20 years 5.109

[163] See eg rule (4) of s 5 of the Land Compensation Act 1961, which provides that in assessing the value of land for the purposes of compensation for compulsory purchase, no increase in value due to certain types of unlawful conduct shall be taken into account.

[164] *Sanctuary Housing Association v Baker* (1998) 30 HLR 809.

[165] *R (Newhaven Port and Properties Ltd) v East Sussex County Council* [2015] UKSC 7, [2015] 2 WLR 601.

and the Town Council applied to have it registered as a town or village green under the Commons Act 2006. The indulgence in the sports and pastimes had to be 'as of right' if registration was to be effected. It was held that since the use of the beach was regulated by byelaws, the recreational use by the public was a use by permission and so was not as of right, and the application for registration failed for that reason. The Supreme Court also held that the application for registration failed for a further reason, which was that the port was held and used for a specific statutory purpose which was incompatible with the registration of a part of it as a town or village green. Accordingly no registration under the Commons Act 2006 was possible.

5.110 This decision may have implications for the acquisition of easements by prescription under the Prescription Act 1832 and by other methods of prescription. The nature of use as of right is similar for the registration of town and village greens and for easements. If a right such as that of the inhabitants of a locality to use an area of land for recreation, which can be acquired by a form of statutory prescription, is not possible where the right would be incompatible with the statutory purposes governing the use of the land over which it is to exist, it would seem that an easement over a particular property should not be capable of acquisition by prescription where there exists the same incompatibility. The exercise of an easement of light may be incompatible with the use and operation of land for specific statutory purposes, just as may the use of that land for the purposes of public recreation. For instance, development of the land used for statutory purposes by the erection of structures may be impeded by or be inconsistent with an easement of light over that land. In the *Newhaven* case Lord Neuberger stated the law thus:

> Where Parliament has conferred on a statutory undertaker powers to acquire land compulsorily and to hold and use that land for defined statutory purposes, the 2006 Act [the Commons Act 2006] does not enable the public to acquire by use rights which are incompatible with the ordinary use of the land for those statutory purposes.[166]

It does not seem to be a large step to adapt this succinct statement of law so as to replace the words 'the public' by 'any person', and to replace the words 'the 2006 Act' by 'the Prescription Act 1832'. It should be noted that if such an incompatibility does prevent the prescriptive acquisition of easements, it would only do so where the servient land is held for a specific statutory purpose, and not when it is held by a public body such as a local authority for more general purposes.[167]

[166] ibid [93].
[167] ibid [100].

6

The Measurement of Light

(A) INTRODUCTION

Once it is established that a building, the dominant building, has acquired by some method an easement of light through an aperture or apertures against the servient land, it is necessary to determine whether some development, usually the erection of a new building or the enlargement of an existing building, on the servient land will infringe that easement of light and so constitute an actionable injury. The question is whether the development on the servient land would so reduce the access of natural light through an aperture in a room or rooms or other areas within the dominant building that the room or rooms or other areas of that building would no longer receive natural light through the aperture sufficient for their reasonable use in accordance with the ordinary notions of mankind. There may also be an infringement of a right of light if the light enjoyed by the dominant building is already below an acceptable standard and is further reduced, and the amenity of the dominant building further worsened, by an obstruction erected on the servient land.[1] 6.1

The question of whether there will be an actionable injury if development on the servient land is carried out, and of the remedies for any such injury or prospective injury, requires a consideration of six matters: 6.2

(i) It must be determined what is the amount of light received by the area lit through the aperture in the dominant building with only the existing development, if any, on the servient land.

(ii) It must be determined what will be the amount of light received by the same area lit by the same aperture in the dominant building after the new development on the servient land.

(iii) It must be determined what amount of light so received at any part of the area lit through the aperture amounts to a sufficiency of natural light.

[1] See chs 4 and 5 for the acquisition of easements by deed or by prescription and ch 3 for the standard of light protected by an easement, as established by the House of Lords in *Colls v Home and Colonial Stores Ltd* [1904] AC 179.

(iv) It must be determined whether the reduction in the amount of the light received through the aperture as a result of the development on the servient land will constitute an actionable injury.

(v) If there will be an actionable injury it must be determined whether the remedy should be an injunction or damages or both.

(vi) If damages are awarded the amount of the damages must be determined.

The same matters will have to be considered if the development on the servient land has already taken place. The main difference in the situation where that development has wholly or partly taken place is that a court may be more reluctant to grant a mandatory injunction to remove a building or a part of a building which has been erected than it would to grant a prohibitory injunction to prevent the construction of the offending development.

6.3 This chapter is concerned with the first four of these questions, which are addressed in sections (B)–(E) of this chapter. The last two questions are examined in Chapter 7 on remedies.

6.4 The determination of the first four questions requires an examination of a number of technical matters, such as the nature of light, luminous intensity, luminous flux and illuminance. These are scientific concepts and their details lie within the realm of general physics. They will be generally known to expert rights of light surveyors. A brief account of what is involved may be of assistance to others involved with rights of light and with disputes over rights of light such as lawyers, valuers, architects and developers. A similar area of expertise is the so-called sky factor and the production of 'Waldram diagrams'. These last matters are also well known to and are widely used by rights of light surveyors, but again a brief account may be of assistance to others who become involved as expert advisers with rights of light problems and disputes. While in principle these techniques for the measurement of light may be used by any surveyor or by others in professional practice, there has emerged a small group of expert surveyors who carry out the necessary measurements, often with the use of specialist computer programs, and who usually act as advisers to the parties in major rights of light disputes.

6.5 By way of introduction it can be stated that the use of the Waldram methodology rests on two assumptions. The first assumption is that a particular location in a room is sufficiently lit if it receives illumination from natural light of at least 10–11 lux at desk or table height (usually taken as 850 mm above floor level). The second assumption is that the room as a whole is sufficiently lit by natural light if at least 50 per cent of its area receives natural illumination to this standard. Both assumptions may be subject to question, as is discussed later in this chapter. The technical calculations which underride these assumptions are also explained. References in this chapter and elsewhere to the Waldram methodology are references to processes used applying one or both of the two above assumptions.

(B) BASIC CONCEPTS CONCERNING LIGHT

1. Light

It is appropriate to start with the concept and nature of light on which everything else depends.[2] Light is a form of electromagnetic radiation which generally arises from the movement of charged elementary particles of matter.[3] Radiation has a spectrum of wavelengths and frequencies. Radiation within the visible band of the spectrum, wavelengths of 4×10^{-7} metre to 7.7×10^{-7} metre, is perceived as visible light by the human eye and brain through the stimulation of electrical activity in the eye. The frequency of the radiation is the number of cycles or wave motions which pass a given point in a given time. It is usually measured in hertz, which is one cycle per second. Since light travels (in a vacuum) at a constant velocity of about 300,000 kilometres per second (186,000 miles per second), the frequency of light at a particular wavelength can be found by dividing its velocity by the wavelength. 6.6

Electromagnetic radiation, including light, is a form of energy. In quantum physics, radiation is regarded not as a wave but as distinct packets or particles, each of which has a quantum or amount of energy. The discrete particles are called photons. Each quantum of radiation or photon has an energy which is the frequency of the radiation multiplied by a universal constant, called Planck's constant.[4] Radiation or radiant energy is only one form of energy (another obvious form is the energy involved in the movement of matter called kinetic energy), and is the only form of energy which can exist in the absence of matter. The nature of light is the same whatever its source, for example the light received from the sun or from an artificial source such as an electric lamp. Therefore when one refers to light the reference is ultimately to units of energy. For example, a reference to a lumen as a unit of luminous flux, as mentioned below, is a reference to luminous energy per unit of time. 6.7

[2] See also ch 1, paras 1.1–1.14.

[3] It may also arise from the natural radioactivity of some elements and isotopes of elements (radioisotopes) or from the natural or man-produced fusion or fission of atomic nuclei. All fundamental particles bearing mass (fermions) have a positive or negative electric charge, save for neutrinos. The charges are a negative charge for an electron of 1 unit of electron charge, and positive or negative charges of ⅓ or ⅔ of the electron charge for quarks. Antiparticles of electrons and quarks have the opposite charges.

[4] Max Planck was the German physicist whose statement of the Planck constant in 1900 may be regarded as the main starting point of quantum physics. The essential idea is that measureable physical quantities such as energy exist not in a continuous spectrum but as small discrete and indivisible units called a quantum. Other quantities such as length and time are also quantised in this way. Energy may be measured in joules (a joule being the work done when the point of application of a force of one newton is displaced through a distance of one metre in the direction of the force). This is the SI (*Système Internationale*) unit of energy. Energy was formerly measured in much smaller units, called ergs, and an even smaller unit, the electron-volt, is used by nuclear and particle physicists. Luminous flux, as discussed in para 6.10, is an amount of light energy per second and so is a unit of power (for example a watt, also a unit of power, is one joule per second).

2. The Measuring Units of Light

6.8 Having described the nature of light, the next step is to see how light is measured. Without at least an outline understanding of this, calculations of the loss of light are difficult to follow. There are three concepts involved, the last two of which are essential to calculations of loss of light as carried out by rights of light surveyors. The three concepts are (a) luminous intensity, (b) luminous flux, and (c) illuminance. The second and third concepts are fundamental to the modern method of measuring a reduction of natural light to a room.

6.9 Luminous intensity is the amount of light emitted per second in unit solid angle from a point source of light in a given direction. A point source simply means that theoretically the whole of the light is emitted from a single point. The solid angle is the ratio which the area of the surface of a part of a sphere enclosed by the conical surface of the angle bears to the square of the radius of the sphere. The *Système Internationale* (SI) unit of luminous intensity is the candela. In 1979 the General Conference on Weights and Measures adopted the current definition of a candela, which is that it is the luminous intensity, in a given direction, of a source that emits monochromatic radiation of frequency 540×10^{12} hertz and that has a radiance intensity in that direction of $^{1}/683$ watt per steradian.

6.10 Luminous flux is an amount of luminous energy per unit of time. It is therefore a unit of power. The unit of luminous flux is the lumen. A lumen is the amount of light emitted per second in a solid angle of one steradian by a point source of one candela. A steradian is the solid angle that encloses a surface on a sphere equal to the square of the radius of the sphere. It is important to note that the lumen is a unit of 'luminous' flux. It measures electromagnetic radiation within those wavelengths perceivable by the human eye. A source of electromagnetic radiation such as the sun may radiate energy at other wavelengths so creating frequencies both above (ultra violet radiation) and below (infra red radiation) frequencies within the visible spectrum. Even within the visible spectrum the human eye is more sensitive to some wavelengths than others. The wavelength determines the colour of light as perceived, and the peak sensitivity of the human eye is to green light (a wavelength of 555 nanometres). Light as seen from the sun is a combination of radiation at wavelengths within the visible spectrum. A measurement of the whole of the electromagnetic radiation emitted by the sun would be a measurement of radiant flux. Ordinary electric lamps are now commonly labelled with their output of luminous flux stated in lumens.

6.11 Illuminance is the luminous flux or amount of light per second falling on a specified surface area. It is today measured in lux, with a lux being 1 lumen per square metre. A lux is sometimes called a metre candle.[5] Since a lumen is an amount of luminous energy (light) per second, a lux is an amount of energy falling on a

[5] See para 6.16 for the meaning of a foot candle, which is the older unit of illuminance.

square metre each second. The word 'lux' is used as a singular (one lux) or as a plural (eg 5000 lux). One thousand lux may be called a kilolux.

Putting these concepts and definitions together, if one wishes to know how much light from a particular source, such as the sun or a lamp, falls on the surface of a given area per second, the amount can be expressed in lumens per square metre, or lux. Thus 10 lux means that an amount of light of 10 lumens (an amount per second) falls on each square metre of the surface which is being lit. It is by the use of these definitions and measurements that the sufficiency of the lighting at a particular point in a room or over a part of a room by the receipt of natural light from the sun through an aperture can be measured. 6.12

As noted above, the only difference in its physical nature between light and other forms of electromagnetic radiation is the wavelength, and thus the frequency, of the radiation.[6] An easement of light is designed to protect the receipt of sufficient natural illumination for the reasonable use of buildings. It therefore protects only the access to a building of electromagnetic radiation within the visible spectrum. The receipt of man made radiation outside the visible spectrum within a building may be important for other purposes such as television signals or mobile phone reception, but this radiation is not protected by the easement of light.[7] 6.13

(C) THE SKY FACTOR

As viewed from the surface of the earth, the sky can be represented as a hemisphere. There is a slight irregularity in this description, due to the curvature of the earth, but this can be ignored. If one imagines a point on the earth where the whole of the sky is visible and unobstructed, there can be said to be a 100 per cent sky factor at that point. Such a sky factor would be found on top of a building higher than any other building in its vicinity, or in a field in a plain with no obstructions to the receipt of light, or on a raft at sea with no land or vessels in sight. 6.14

The number of lux (the illuminance measured in lumens per square metre) emanating from the sun which fall on the surface of the earth with a 100 per cent sky factor depends of course on a number of factors. 6.15

(a) During the night no lux from the sun reach the surface of the earth, save for a small amount of light reflected at times from the moon.
(b) Different numbers of lux reach a given area on the surface of the earth during different hours of the day as the earth spins on its orbit.
(c) Different numbers of lux reach a given area on the surface of the earth during different times of the year in the northern and southern hemispheres due to the tilt of the earth as it proceeds on its orbit around the sun.

[6] See para 6.6.
[7] *Hunter v Canary Wharf Ltd* [1997] AC 655. See ch 3, section (B) 1.

(d) Different numbers of lux reach different areas on the surface of the earth depending on their latitude.
(e) Weather conditions, particularly the presence of cloud, affect the number of lux which reach a given area on the surface of the earth at any particular time.

6.16 In order to make standard measurement possible, the number of lumens of light per unit area of the surface of the earth in this country received from the sun as a light source with a 100 per cent sky factor had to be ascertained on some average or standardised basis. This was done by the National Physical Laboratory in 1928 when an average condition was assumed such as might exist in Great Britain in spring and autumn and on wet days in the summer, which was said to produce an illuminance of 500 lumens per square foot.[8] This is not the same as 500 lux. A lux is 1 lumen of light per square metre, whereas the unit of measurement used at that time was a foot candle, which is 1 lumen of light per square foot.[9] A foot candle is equivalent to about 10.764 lux. Thus an area on the surface of the earth in Great Britain with a 100 per cent sky factor is taken to receive 500 foot candles (500 lumens per square foot) attributable to light from the sun. This is equivalent to 5,382 lumens per square metre, or 5,382 lux.[10]

6.17 Rooms or other areas in buildings lit through apertures do not enjoy a 100 per cent sky factor. Indeed an area of the cill immediately outside a window in the vertical wall of a building with no other obstructions may receive only about a quarter sphere of light, or at most a 50 per cent sky factor. A large part of the light from the sun will be obstructed by the building itself. The next step is to decide what amount of illuminance is needed for there to be sufficient natural light to a room or other area within a building.

6.18 A good deal of work on this subject was done in the early decades of the last century by Mr Percy Waldram, an eminent rights of light surveyor who gave evidence on the subject before the courts including in important reported cases.[11] His view was that there was a sufficiency of natural light at any point in a room if at a height of 850 mm (2 feet and 9 inches) above the floor an illuminance of 1 foot candle (1 lumen per square foot) was received. The height is that of the surface of a normal desk or table above the floor. This standard can be translated into a sky factor. If a 100 per cent sky factor provides 500 foot candles of illuminance, then a 0.2 per cent sky factor will provide 1 foot candle of illuminance. This is the same

[8] See para 6.39(iv) for the CIE standard overcast sky.

[9] Any idea that a foot candle is directly or precisely related to a candle one foot in length or one foot away from the observer should be firmly resisted.

[10] It is necessary to be extremely careful when referring to units such as foot candles, lumens and lux as errors of calculation can easily be made. For example, it is stated incorrectly in Bickford Smith, Francis and Weekes, *Right of Light*, 3rd edn (Bristol, Jordans, 2014), at para 14.11 that 500 foot candles (500 lumens per square foot) is approximately 500 lux. In fact 500 foot candles is equal to exactly 5,382 lux (ie lumens per square metre).

[11] See eg *Sheffield Masonic Hall Co v Sheffield Corporation* [1932] 2 Ch 17.

as 10–11 lux. It seems preferable today to measure illuminance in lux, which is the standard international unit of measurement. Consequently, and in accordance with these postulates, the question of whether a particular point in a room receives a sufficiency of natural light can be answered by determining whether at a height of 850 mm above floor level that point enjoys through an aperture or apertures a sky factor of at least 0.2 per cent.

(D) MEASUREMENT OF THE SKY FACTOR

The next question is how the sky factor enjoyed at a particular point in a room in the dominant building is to be measured. To carry out this exercise requires data on the shape and dimensions of the room lit, the position and dimensions of any aperture or apertures in the room, the dimensions of any structure on the servient land, and the dimensions of any other structures in the vicinity which impede the access of light to the aperture or apertures. It is possible that some feature of the dominant building or of a window may affect the sky factor. A building may have some overhanging feature which impedes a view of the sky. A window may give access to a balcony with surrounding walls. A window may be in a recess in a building. A window may have internal components such as astragals, glazing bars and muntins or dividers between panes, or between upper and lower parts, which obstruct the sky. Once all data which is likely to be used has been collated, it is possible to calculate the precise sky factor enjoyed at any point in the room. Before the advent of computers this process was carried out by the use of measurement instruments and trigonometry. Today, the data can be input into computer programs and a speedier and more accurate result obtained. The result is that it can be known, assuming the 10-11 lux or 1 foot candle standard, whether any point within the room at a height of 850 mm above the floor is adequately lit in the circumstances of the existing development on the servient land. 6.19

Assuming a room with one window, it is obviously likely that the sky factor enjoyed, and therefore the illuminance from the sun received, will reduce as one passes further into the room and away from the window. One is likely to reach a point in the room at which the sky factor falls below 0.2 per cent. Once a sky factor has been established for all points in the room, a line can be drawn which differentiates those parts of the room where the sky factor is 0.2 per cent or above and those parts of the room where the sky factor is below 0.2 per cent. By this process there can be determined the area of the room which is and is not sufficiently lit by natural light from the sun, and this can be shown on a diagram. This is a Waldram diagram. It is usual that the diagram shows that part of the room sufficiently lit with a sky factor of 0.2 per cent or more by red hatching. The red-hatched space is in most cases likely to be an irregularly bounded area running into the room from the window. This is the first diagram which shows the existing or before situation, ie the situation before the actual or proposed development on the servient land. 6.20

(E) SUFFICIENCY OF LIGHT

1. The 50-50 test

6.21 The purpose of the process being described is to decide whether a particular room which receives an amount of natural light is or is not sufficiently lit according to the ordinary notions of mankind. What is demonstrated by a Waldram diagram is that a part of a room is sufficiently lit if it enjoys a sky factor of at least 0.2 per cent. The important question as regards a possible infringement of a right of light is whether the room or other area served by the window or aperture is as a whole sufficiently lit. There is no way of answering this question as a generality except to conclude that a room as a whole is to be regarded as sufficiently lit if a certain minimum proportion of it is sufficiently lit. Again, a subjective judgment has to be made and it is often assumed by rights of light experts that a room taken as a whole is sufficiently lit if at least 50 per cent of its area is sufficiently lit, ie if at least 50 per cent of its area has a sky factor of at least 0.2 per cent.[12] This is sometimes called the 50 per cent test or rule, and sometimes the 50-50 test or rule. The differences of nomenclature do not affect the substance of the matter. There is no way of proving the correctness of this proposition on any objective test or by analysis, except that it seems to comply with what has often come to be accepted. Much of this area of law rests on the convenience of long convention, which some people criticise as avoiding the need for a more rigorous process. Just as the test for sufficiency of light, that generally acceptable according to the ordinary notions of mankind, is imprecise so the justification for the application of the 50 per cent test is imprecise. Nonetheless it is a process which can be regularly and uniformly applied. There is much to be said for certainty and regularity in the law; it is only in this way that owners of property can judge in advance with some degree of confidence what they can or cannot lawfully do. The question of the justification in principle of the established Waldram diagram method of examining rights of light and alleged infringements of rights of light will be discussed later.[13]

[12] The 50-50 dividing line is sometimes called the 'grumble line': see *Fishenden v Higgs and* Hill (1935) 153 LT 128 (Crossnan J). In *Midtown Ltd v City of London Real Property Co* Ltd [2005] EWHC 33 (Ch), [2005] 1 EGLR 65 [53] Peter Smith J described the 50-50 rule as a test that was regularly applied. Sometimes with larger rooms the analysis is confined to the area of a room which runs back 6 m from a window, on the argument that this is the area of a larger room in which adequate natural light can most reasonably be expected to exist. The analysis can most readily be applied to large open plan offices in this way.

[13] See section (F) of this chapter where an account is given of the criticisms which have been levelled at the use of the Waldram methodology.

2. The Waldram Diagrams

The central question to be addressed in connection with rights of light is usually whether an actual or proposed development on the servient land has or will constitute an infringement of a right of light appurtenant to the dominant building. This question is approached by preparing a further diagram, this time showing what will be the area of the room which will remain sufficiently lit with a sky factor of at least 0.2 per cent following the erection or extension of a structure on the servient land. The same process in the preparation of the drawing of this diagram is used as for the diagram showing the situation before the development on the servient land. The dimensions and layout of the room lit remain the same, the aperture remains the same, other structures in the vicinity which impede the access of light to the aperture remain the same. All that is altered is the new or extended building on the servient land. The second diagram will therefore show the area of the room which will be sufficiently lit with at least a 0.2 per cent sky factor with the new development having taken place on the servient land. 6.22

The second, or after situation, diagram is likely to be different from the first diagram in that the additional obstruction of the access of light caused by a new or larger structure on the servient land may reduce the sky factor for the whole or parts of the room lit in the dominant building. A likely result is that the part of the room which has a sky factor of 0.2 per cent or more will be reduced. The reduction in the area of red hatching on the second diagram as compared to the first diagram will show this situation. 6.23

A comparison must be made between the before and after diagrams. By this means the loss of area in the room which is sufficiently lit as a result of the new development on the servient land can be assessed. It is usual to provide a composite diagram which shows by red cross-hatching the area of the room sufficiently lit before the new development on the servient land and by green cross-hatching the area of the room which remains sufficiently lit after the development on the servient land. The reduction of area sufficiently lit is demonstrated diagrammatically in this way. 6.24

A typical but simple Waldram diagram for an area within a building is set out below. The overall rectangle shows a small room or area which is a part of a larger building extending to each side of it. It can be seen that the lighter and darker parts cross-hatched are the area sufficiently lit before the obstruction on the servient land, and comprise the whole or nearly the whole of the room. The darker area cross-hatched is the area which remains sufficiently lit after the obstruction. The latter area is about a fifth of the total area and is that nearest to the window. A similar diagram can be prepared for all relevant windows on all floors of the dominant building. The diagrams are often accompanied by three-dimensional representations of the existing buildings on the dominant and servient areas of land and of the proposed new building on the servient land which will bring about the reduction in light to the dominant building. 6.25

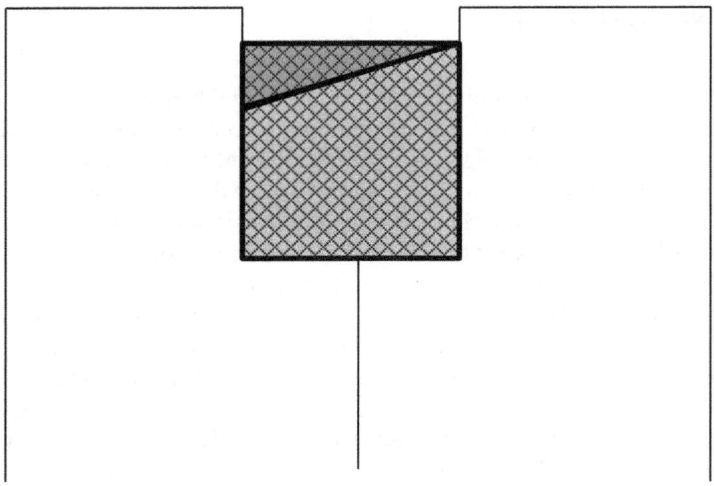

Form of Simplified Waldram Diagram

6.26 The diagram is simplified in order to give a general indication of its purpose and of what is done. In practice, two diagrams are usually produced: one showing the lighting of the room before the obstruction on the servient land and one showing the lighting after that obstruction. Also in many cases it is less than 100 per cent, or nearly 100 per cent, of the room which is sufficiently lit before the obstruction. It is also often the case that the line which divides the room into that sufficiently lit and that insufficiently lit is a curved or irregular line, rather than a straight line as here shown. In the diagram the window extends across the whole width of a wall of the room, and this creates the excellent light prior to the obstruction. Where a window extends across only a part of a wall the areas of the room immediately adjacent to the window and on each side of it may be poorly lit.

6.27 The loss of floor space sufficiently lit can be presented in a table. Three situations can arise.

(a) The proportion of the room in the building of the dominant owner sufficiently lit to the standard described, ie with a 0.2 per cent or higher sky factor, may have been 50 per cent or more before the development on the servient land and, albeit reduced after the effect of the development on the servient land is taken into account, may continue to be in excess of 50 per cent. In that event there will on the standard approach be no actionable injury, since the room as a whole will remain sufficiently lit. The essence of rights of light is that they protect the owner of the dominant building not against any reduction of the access of natural light to his property, but only against a reduction of the access of natural light which renders his property insufficiently lit according to the ordinary notions of mankind. Accordingly in this situation the room remains sufficiently lit and no actionable injury occurs.

(b) The room in the building of the dominant owner may have had a sky factor of 0.2 per cent or higher over 50 per cent or more of its floor area before the development on the servient land, but that development may have reduced the area with that sky factor to less than 50 per cent of the total floor area. The room as a whole will then on the standard approach become insufficiently lit. In this case, and on the application of the measurements and principles explained, there will be an actionable injury.

(c) The room in the building of the dominant owner may have had a sky factor of 0.2 per cent or higher over less than 50 per cent of its area before the development on the servient land so that the effect of that development may have been to reduce the area with that sky factor to an even lower proportion of the room with the result that the room, already insufficiently lit, becomes even more insufficiently lit. In this case also there will be an actionable injury.

A typical EFZ loss table is set out in Chapter 7.[14] It is based on the Waldram diagram depicted above. The table shows a reduction in the area of the room sufficiently lit from 99.02 per cent to 20.42 per cent. The situation as described falls into category (b) as described in the last paragraph, so that there is an actionable injury. The loss of area sufficiently lit is 118.74 sq ft which produces a weighted, or EFZ (effective first zone) loss of 85.18 sq ft. It is this last figure which is taken forward into the assessment of damages as described in Chapter 7.[15] It can therefore be seen that the Waldram methodology and the diagrams perform two functions. They provide a rational and standard basis on which it can be decided whether a development on servient land does or will constitute an actionable infringement of a right of light enjoyed by the owner of the dominant building. It is the use of the process for this purpose which is discussed in this chapter. The second function of the process is that, if there is an actionable infringement, it provides a basis for an assessment of the reduction in the value of the dominant building. Assessing such a reduction is one way of assessing damages for the wrong committed (something called 'book value' damages), although certainly not the only basis, and this is discussed in detail in Chapter 7. 6.28

The explanation just given has assumed that the room with the benefit of a right of light through an aperture has a single aperture only. In practice of course a room may have two or more apertures or windows in it, perhaps in different walls of the room. Rights of light are often acquired by prescription, by 20 years or more of the uninterrupted access of light over other land, and the right so acquired is the access of light through a particular window or other aperture. It has been explained earlier that in such a case, in estimating whether a development on the 6.29

[14] See ch 7, para 7.91.

[15] The weighting and the calculation of the EFZ loss are described in ch 7, para 7.88.

servient land which reduces the light received through one window constitutes an actionable injury,

(a) account may be taken of light entering the room through another window if that window also has a right of light and
(b) no account is to be taken of light entering through another window if there is no right of light appurtenant to that window.[16]

6.30 For example, a room on the corner of a building may have a window in its front wall which has acquired a prescriptive right of light, having been in place for 25 years, and a further window in a side wall which was installed 10 years ago, and so does not have a prescriptive right of light. If a building is erected on the servient land which reduces the access of light through the front window the question of whether the reduction of light constitutes an actionable injury must be assessed ignoring the light received through the side window. It would be otherwise if the side window had also been in existence for 25 years, by which time it would have acquired its own prescriptive right of light. The preparation of Waldram diagrams must take these principles into account. A more usual situation will be a room with two windows in one wall, each with a prescriptive right of light, in which case diagrams will be prepared showing the area of the room with a 0.2 per cent sky factor, taking into account light received through both windows, first before and then after a development on the servient land.[17]

3. Other Matters

6.31 In order to prepare a Waldram diagram for a room it is necessary to know the exact shape and dimensions of the room and of its aperture or apertures. Where a new development on the servient land is proposed, the owner of the dominant building will be able without difficulty to have prepared a diagram for the rooms in his building. He will know the dimensions of his own rooms and the position and size of his windows, and he will generally be able to find out the dimensions of the new or proposed new building on the servient land, if necessary by looking at the plans deposited with the local planning authority as part of an application for planning permission.[18] Most developments of a scale likely to amount to a

[16] See ch 3 for an explanation of the matters in this paragraph. The general rule as just stated applies where there are no alterations to the windows in the dominant building. If there is or has been such an alteration, whether to windows in an existing building or by reason of a redevelopment of the dominant building, somewhat different principles may apply as explained in ch 3, section (C).

[17] It is sometimes convenient to refer to an easement of light through a particular window. In strict law the easement is appurtenant not to a window but to a building which receives its light through a specified window or windows: see *Carr-Saunders v Dick McNeill Associates Ltd* [1986] 1 WLR 922.

[18] A local planning authority is required by s 69 of the Town and Country Planning Act 1990 to keep a register of applications for planning permission which may be inspected by the public. The application will contain plans of the buildings or structures proposed. The effect of the law and practice of town planning on rights of light and rights of light disputes is examined in ch 10.

breach of an easement of light appurtenant to neighbouring property are likely to require planning permission. The owner of the dominant building will also need to know the dimensions of any existing building on the servient land (when a redevelopment on that land is proposed) or of any former building on that land (when a redevelopment on that land has taken place) in order that a comparison can be made of the before and after effect on the access of light to the dominant building. The developer of the servient land may not be so easily able to discover the exact dimensions of the rooms in buildings near to his proposed development which have or may have rights of light affected by that development. Where they exist, such rights of light will usually have arisen by prescription. The developer may be reluctant to make a direct enquiry of the owners of such land, lest those persons are alerted to the possibility of rights of light and claims for infringements. General assumptions can be made by rights of light surveyors of the size and shape of rooms in nearby buildings likely to be affected by a development, and a general indication can be given to a developer on whether his development will infringe rights of light attached to nearby buildings and on the extent and gravity of any likely infringement.

In carrying out appraisals of the economic viability of a proposed development, a somewhat arbitrary sum is sometimes included for the risk of payments that may have to be made to persons with property in the vicinity of the development with rights of light. Such estimates can be prepared on the footing that any damages recoverable by a neighbouring owner will be assessed by reference to the diminution in the value of his property caused by an infringement of his right of light (the book value method) or by reference to the amount of money that would be agreed in a hypothetical negotiation for a voluntary release of the right of light (the voluntary release method). Today, damages are more likely to be assessed by the latter method.[19] A more difficult question may be to advise on whether a neighbouring owner whose right of light will be infringed is likely to be able to obtain an injunction to prevent, or even remove, a development on the servient land.[20] The proposed developers of servient land will sometimes appoint a rights of light surveyor, who will approach the owners and tenants of dominant buildings in the locality and invite them to obtain advice on and discuss rights of light matters. The aim is to try to reach agreement at an early stage, perhaps involving the payment of an agreed sum to persons with interests in dominant buildings. By this means, later disputes which arise during the course of the development can be avoided. Sometimes an offer is made to pay the costs of a dominant owner in obtaining specialist advice. 6.32

Purchasers or developers of land where there is a risk that adjoining owners have rights of light sometimes seek insurance policies against adverse claims. Such claims can gravely impede a development, by delaying it or even causing its form to be altered at a late stage. The attraction of obtaining insurance has been increased by 6.33

[19] See ch 7, section (C).
[20] See ch 7, section (B).

developments in the law of remedies in recent years. A major fear of a developer is that the development may be delayed or impeded by a claim for an injunction by a neighbouring landowner, especially at a time when the development is under way. A further consideration is the practice of the courts to assess damages for breaches of property rights, including infringements of rights of light, on the 'voluntary release' basis, which is the sum which would be agreed between parties negotiating reasonably for a voluntary agreement to permit the offending development.[21] Damages assessed by this method are likely often to exceed substantially damages assessed by the older and more traditional method of concentrating on the reduction in the capital value of the dominant building caused by the infringement.[22] In order for insurers to assess the risk which they take on under such policies, insurers need to know in reasonable detail the form of the proposed new development, and policies are normally not sought or issued until planning permission for the development has been sought and obtained. It is usual for the expert input of a rights of light surveyor to be sought before a policy is issued, and this may need to be supplemented by legal advice from solicitors or counsel.

6.34 In applying the Waldram methodology it may sometimes be necessary to have regard to the principle that the dominant owner is entitled to protection not only for the current use and layout of the dominant building, but also for any different use or layout which it can reasonably be anticipated will occur in the future.[23] Therefore in some cases diagrams may need to be prepared showing the effect of a development on the servient land on a future use and layout of the dominant building.

6.35 The preceding account has shown how the first four questions identified in paragraph 6.2 may be answered by the use of the Waldram methodology. In broad terms this methodology provides a standardised and to some extent scientific route towards deciding whether a development on servient land will amount to an actionable injury to a dominant building. The detailed results of Waldram diagrams can also be used as the foundation of a calculation of damages by reference to the amount of floorspace in the dominant building which has become inadequately lit (or even more inadequately lit). This is a subject which has its own complications. It is examined as a whole in Chapter 7 on remedies, where attention is given to (a) the somewhat arbitrary selection of the reduction in the rental value of the area of floorspace which becomes inadequately lit, and (b) the widespread preference of courts today for assessing damages on the 'voluntary release' basis,

[21] See ch 7, section (C). It is said that the apprehensions of developers over the prospect of an injunction were much increased by the decision of the High Court in *HKRUK II (CHC) Ltd v Heaney* [2010] EWHC 2245 (Ch), [2010] 3 EGLR 15 in which a mandatory injunction was granted ordering the removal of a part of a building erected in contravention of a right of light. The apprehension may today have been somewhat reduced (though not removed) by the recent decision of the Supreme Court in *Lawrence v Fen Tigers Ltd* [2014] UKSC 13, [2014] AC 822.

[22] See ch 7, para 7.108 et seq.

[23] See ch 3, section (B)5.

which has no direct connection with reduced rental value. The use of the Waldram methodology may also assist a court in deciding whether an injunction or damages is the appropriate remedy where an actionable injury is established since the severity of the reduction in natural light is likely to be one factor relevant to that decision.

(F) STATUS OF THE WALDRAM METHODOLOGY

1. Limitations on the Waldram Methodology

The attraction of the use of the Waldram methodology in measuring the natural light received in a room through an aperture, and in deciding whether that amount of light leaves the room sufficiently lit after a development on the servient land so that there is no infringement of an easement of light, is that it provides a standardised and objective method of reaching conclusions on these matters. The essentially subjective question of whether an amount of light is sufficient to light an area of a building in accordance with the ordinary notions of mankind is replaced by an objective and to some extent scientific test. The methodology as a whole may be described as an objective test, in that its application in each case leaves little or no room for subjective judgments even though the initial and underlying determination of important elements of the methodology, such as the adequacy of the light received when there is a 0.2 per cent sky factor, and the 50 per cent test, appears to be substantially subjective. A physical characteristic such as the presence or otherwise of a minimum 0.2 per cent sky factor at particular points in a room can be accurately and scientifically determined so that there is little scope for dispute on the application of the methodology especially when the parties to many questions or disputes rely on professional assistance from one of a small number of rights of light surveyors expert in the field. The experts do not often disagree on matters such as the preparation of Waldram diagrams using their computer programs, although there may be disputes on other matters such as whether a right of light to windows can be transferred to new windows in the same or a new building on the site. The experts usually accept and apply the two basic tenets of the Waldram methodology, namely (a) that a point in a room is sufficiently lit by natural light if it enjoys at least a 0.2 per cent sky factor and (b) that the room as a whole is sufficiently lit if at least 50 per cent of its area enjoys this minimum proportion of sky factor. That having been said, it is necessary to consider possible deficiencies in the methodology and to examine comments on the use of the methodology in decided cases. 6.36

The BRE Trust has published a Guide which offers advice and guidance to local planning authorities and others on the safeguarding of daylight to nearby buildings when designing a new building or an extension of an existing building. 6.37

A brief explanation of this guidance is given in Chapter 10.[24] The guidance is advisory only and is meant to be flexibly applied. It is stated that the guidance is not intended to replace, or to be a means of satisfying, the requirements of the law surrounding an easement of light. It is also stated that it should not be assumed that satisfaction of the guidelines means that a new development will not infringe an easement of light, or vice versa. The guidance recognises, in its own words, that 'The assessment of loss of light in rights of light cases is carried out in a different way to the matters given in this BRE Guide'.[25] An example of the differences in methodology and the process described in the BRE Guide for assessing whether there will be an unacceptable light to a building as compared to what has been described in this chapter is that the Guide introduces the concept in relation to the vertical plane of a window of the vertical sky component[26] which may be found by using a Waldram diagram as described in Appendix B of the Guide, but which is different from the Waldram diagrams used in rights of light calculations as described in this chapter.[27]

6.38 Despite these caveats, it remains the case that the BRE Guide is aimed at the same general purpose as the traditional Waldram diagram methodology, which is to conclude whether a proposed new or extended building will unacceptably reduce the natural light received in an existing building through its windows. It seems sensible that dominant owners concerned with protecting their rights of light, and servient owners concerned lest their development will infringe rights of light, should at least obtain a preliminary indication of the probable answer to their concerns from applying the process described in the Guide. Furthermore there is no reason why a party to litigation should not gain some assistance from the fact that compliance or non-compliance with the guidance assists his case.

6.39 A number of criticisms or doubts have been levelled at the use of the Waldram methodology.

(i) An obvious point is that there is no objective way of determining whether an illuminance of 1 foot candle (1 lumen per square foot) or its equivalent of 10–11 lux (10–11 lumens per square metre) is enough to provide reasonable conditions over an area of the room which receives that amount of natural illuminance. Recent experiment has suggested that 2.5 foot candles, or about 25 lux, may be required for reading in reasonable comfort.[28]

[24] Paul Littlefair, *Site Layout and Planning for Daylight and Sunlight—A Guide to Good Practice*, 2nd edn (Watford, BRE Trust, 2011) ('the BRE Guide').

[25] ibid, para 2.2.18.

[26] ibid, para 2.2.6, and see ch 10, para 10.36.

[27] ibid, Appendix E, para E5.

[28] See Defoe, 'Waldram Was Wrong' 27, 3 (2009) *Structural Survey* 186–99, and see *Gale on Easements*, 19th edn (London, Sweet & Maxwell, 2012) paras 7.30–7.31. It is observed in Appendix E, para E9 of the BRE Guide (see n 24) published in 2011, that there was an active debate by experts in the field of rights of light regarding the legal measure of the adequacy of natural light and that this might result in a change in approach within the next few years. The dispute was said to concern the use of a non-uniform sky in the calculation process, the 0.2 per cent sky factor for the criterion, and the use of a working plane at 850 mm above floor level. No general change of approach by rights of light surveyors has yet been discerned.

This standard suggests a required minimum sky factor of 0.5 per cent, rather than the 0.2 per cent previously assumed. The application of this higher standard of a sufficiency of light could make a major difference in many rights of light disputes, both as to the existence of an actionable injury and as to the assessment of damages.

(ii) The 50 per cent test is also open to query. An owner of a building might be unreasonable in complaining if there were only small corners or alcoves in a room which received less than adequate natural light for ordinary activities such as working or reading. He might feel more aggrieved if he was told that the ordinary notions of mankind always, and by tradition, required that he be satisfied if only 50 per cent of his room received adequate light. He might be surprised at the tradition, and might pertinently ask why he should be satisfied and have no redress if his room, previously well lit over 90 per cent of its area, became well lit over only, say, 55 per cent of its area, as a result of a profitable commercial redevelopment of neighbouring land.

(iii) The calculation in the methodology takes no account of natural light received by reflection from external structures or from surfaces and objects within a room. For example, an external structure may to some extent cut off the passage of light to the dominant building directly from the sun, but light from the sun may reach the façade of a structure facing the dominant building and be reflected back to the dominant building, so as to reach it indirectly and form a part of the total illumination of the dominant building. Light received at points within a room at 850 mm above floor level may be in part reflected from surfaces within the room. Different surfaces absorb or reflect different amounts of light, the differences depending upon the sub-atomic structure of the surface materials. The amount of natural light which passes through a window may vary with different physical characteristics of the glazing used. Up to 16 per cent of the photons of light which reach the outer surface of the glazing of a window may be reflected back, and so never illuminate the interior of the room. These matters may all affect the actual illuminance of a point in a room measured in lux, but are not taken into account in the determination of the sky factor. The critical consideration for a person living or working in a room is how much natural light he receives and not the exact physical process by which that light is received.[29]

(iv) The concept of a standard day and standard weather conditions to be applied throughout the year and in all actual weather conditions in England and Wales is obviously crude. There are likely to be many winter days with a great deal of cloud when a 0.2 per cent sky factor will not provide light to a point in a room of 1 foot candle or 10–11 lux such as it is assumed would be provided to that point on the standard day. There exists

[29] The argument against taking into account reflected light is that the structure which reflects the light, certainly if it is an external structure, may be moved or altered in ways or at times over which the owner of the dominant building may have no control. See ch 3, section (B)3.

today a CIE (*Commission Internationale de l'Eclairage*) standard overcast sky for which for a completely overcast sky the ratio of its luminance at an angle of elevation above the horizontal to the luminance at the zenith (vertically overhead) is given by a formula.[30]

(v) The 50-50 test has a crudity of application within it. For example, if a development on the servient land reduces the access of natural light to a room in the dominant building so that that room changes from being 85 per cent adequately lit to 52 per cent adequately lit, there will be no actionable infringement, whereas if the reduction is from 52 per cent of the room being adequately lit to 48 per cent being adequately lit there will be an actionable infringement. Problems of this nature are inherent in the application of a rigid arithmetical criterion such as the 50 per cent test.

(vi) Rooms in the dominant building may be used for a variety of purposes, such as residential purposes (with different rooms in a house or flat used for different purposes), office purposes, industrial purposes, storage purposes, or as corridors or stairs or circulation space. For example, bathrooms in blocks of modern flats may have no windows and be ventilated by electrical fans. Different areas put to different purposes may require different amounts of light for their ordinary beneficial use. On the face of it, the Waldram methodology takes no account of this, although an exception to its standard approach may be urged in particular cases where a particular room is used for a particular purpose.[31]

(vii) Measurement of light received on a working plane level of 850 mm above floor level is no doubt a useful general approach, but it takes no account of activities which may be needed to be carried out at a higher level in some rooms, or of people who may be sitting at a lower level in armchairs reading, so that again an element of rigidity is found in the methodology. The BRE Guide uses the concept of the 'no sky line'. This involves drawing a straight line from the highest point of a new or extended building to the top of the window of an existing building and continuing it to the working plane within the room in the existing building illuminated by that window. The working plane, assumed to be horizontal, used is 850 mm above floor level in residential properties, but only 700mm above floor level in offices. The Guide points out that in special buildings such as hospitals or hospital wards a different height may be appropriate.[32] The usual application of the Waldram methodology uses a working plane of 850 mm above floor level for all properties.

[30] The formula is set out in the BRE Guide glossary. For the Guide see n 24.

[31] The BRE Guide states that windows to bathrooms, toilets, storerooms, circulation areas and garages need not be analysed. See para 2.2.2 of the Guide.

[32] Para 2.2.8 of the Guide. The application of the 'no sky line' test is described in more detail in ch 10, para 10.38.

(viii) The methodology takes no account of the orientation of a window or windows in a room, for example a northerly or southerly orientation, which may affect the amount of light received through the window.

(ix) An accurate assessment of the light received through a window should take account not only of the dimensions of the aperture into which the window is fitted, but also the construction of the window. Thus a window, instead of containing a single area of unobstructed glazing, may contain a mullion (a vertical bar dividing areas of glazing within the window) or a series of small panes, or may be obstructed by external security bars.[33]

(x) Less light per unit area of the surface of the earth is received in the northern hemisphere as one proceeds to more northerly latitudes, and the hours of daylight are less in winter as one so proceeds. There could therefore be a difference in the amount of natural light received from a 0.2 per cent sky factor between the most southerly and the most northerly parts of England and Wales.

(xi) The use of the Waldram methodology makes no allowance for changing standards in the amount of light required. A court is entitled to have regard to the higher standards expected for comfort as the years go by.[34] In other words, the ordinary notions of mankind may change in this as in other areas of life. The methodology remains dependent on figures established in the 1920s.

(xii) It is arguable that a higher standard of natural light may reasonably be expected in some localities, such as rural areas, as compared to densely developed urban areas. The Waldram methodology takes no account of this consideration.[35]

These criticisms should not be exaggerated. The use of Waldram diagrams is a numerical process for arriving at a numerical conclusion. Its use cannot in the final analysis deprive a court of its power to decide whether an obstruction to light would leave less light than that reasonably acceptable for the enjoyment of a building, so that other factors such as the locality or orientation of windows or use of a building can be taken into account by a court. 6.40

2. The Approach of the Courts

The use of the Waldram methodology may be attractive to courts. The methodology provides a coherent and unfluctuating standard to be applied from case to case. 6.41

[33] See *Turner v Spooner* (1861) 1 Drew & Sm 467, discussing windows with such characteristics which were subsequently improved. In *Davis v Marrable* [1913] 2 Ch 421 the ground floor window in the dominant building, used as a jeweller's shop, was said to be 'a good deal darkened' by a close network of thick security bars in front of it.

[34] See *Ough v King* [1967] 1 WLR 1547 (Lord Denning MR).

[35] See ch 3, para 3.19.

It has the merit that generally persons cannot complain that a small area of a room is not well lit.[36] Since experts in the subject generally agree on the production of Waldram diagrams, courts may be reluctant to decline to accept the conclusions drawn from such diagrams.[37] If the parties with the benefit of expert advice are agreed on the use of a particular approach or methodology, and in the conclusion to be drawn from the use of that approach, it will be very rare for a court to refuse to accept that which is agreed. Nonetheless, the Waldram methodology is certainly not a rule of law, and conclusions drawn from it are open to dispute. A court may prefer to rely on its own common sense and it has been suggested that the drawings may be 'exceedingly misleading'.[38] In one case a judge in the county court held that a room was not sufficiently lit according to the ordinary notions of mankind, although 51.27 per cent of it enjoyed a sky factor of 0.2 per cent or higher. The Court of Appeal refused to overturn this ruling and it was said that the 50-50 rule was something which had since the 1920s come to constitute no more than 'a convenient rule of thumb'.[39] Property owners and developers should not therefore assume that the retention of a 0.2 per cent or higher sky factor in 50 per cent or more of a room rules out a claim for an infringement of an easement of light any more than it should be assumed that there is automatically an infringement of a right of light if less than 50 per cent of a room is left enjoying a sky factor of 0.2 per cent or more. This observation may be particularly true when the proportion of the room which retains a sky factor of 0.2 per cent is slightly more or slightly less than 50 per cent. With large rooms in the dominant building, there may be disputes on whether the EFZ loss derived from a Waldram analysis should be confined to the first 6 m of the room running back from the window through which the access of light is obstructed.[40]

[36] *Carr-Saunders v Dick McNeil Associates Ltd* [1986] 1 WLR 922 (Millett J), citing the similar observations of Meredith J in *Smyth v Dublin Theatre Co Ltd* [1936] IR 692.

[37] For example in *Midtown Ltd v City of London Real Property Co Ltd* [2005] EWHC 33 (Ch), [2005] 1 EGLR 65, the experts on each side were agreed (see paras 51–53 of the decision). The Waldram approach was upheld by Upjohn J in *William Cory & Son Ltd v City of London Real Property Co* (1954), unreported.

[38] See *Sheffield Masonic Hall Co v Sheffield Corporation* [1932] 2 Ch 17, 24 (Maugham J) (Mr Percy Waldram, after whom the methodology is named, gave evidence in this case); *Fishenden v Higgs and Hill* (1935) 153 LT 128, 143–44. In *Price v Hilditch* [1930] 1 Ch 500, Maugham J heard the experts on both sides as well as a series of lay witnesses. He observed that in cases where the obstruction had actually occurred he preferred to depend on the evidence of ordinary members of the public who had used the dominant building before and after the obstruction. Of course such evidence is only practical if the alleged infringement of the easement has occurred by the erection of an obstruction on the servient land. In many cases the issue of whether a particular development on the servient land would be an infringement of the easement has to be decided before the development is carried out, possibly because an injunction is being sought to prevent it. See also para 6.43.

[39] *Ough v King* [1967] 1 WLR 1547, 1553 (Diplock LJ). See also para 6.43 for the evidential value of a view of the dominant building by a judge. In *Regan v Paul Properties DPF Ltd* [2006] EWCA Civ 1391, [2007] Ch 135 [22], Mummery LJ described 50 per cent of a room being well lit as the 'conventional minimum'. In *Deakins v Hockings* [1994] 1 EGLR 190, 193 HH Judge Cooke said that save in an extreme case, it would be difficult to say that once a living room fell below the 50 per cent criterion the remaining light was adequate.

[40] Ch 7, para 7.86.

6.42 A further question which arises in connection with the 50-50 test is whether it should be applied to premises irrespective of their use. The formulation of the basic rule as to a sufficiency of natural light does distinguish in its language between sufficient light according to the ordinary notions of mankind for 'the comfortable use and enjoyment' of residential property and 'the beneficial use and occupation' of commercial property.[41] The dichotomy suggests that a greater amount of natural illumination might be expected in a residential property. A person might reasonably be more aggrieved at a reduction of light to the house in which he and his family live and enjoy their times of rest and relaxation and in which he may have a substantial financial interest than he would at the same reduction of light to the office in which he works.[42] One way of accommodating such a distinction in needs and expectations would be to adopt a more stringent numerical test for residential properties, such as a requirement of a 0.3 per cent sky factor as sufficient light at any part of a room, or a requirement that a room as a whole is sufficiently lit only if 60 per cent enjoys light in accordance with the specified sky factor. There is no authority for such a mechanistic approach, and perhaps the inherent flexibility in the basic criterion, sufficiency of light according to the ordinary notions of mankind, would allow courts more readily to conclude that for some residential properties there is an infringement of an easement of light even though at least 50 per cent of the area of a room continues to enjoy a sky factor of 0.2 per cent or more. It is also of course the case that different rooms in a house can readily be said to require different amounts of natural light. As mentioned, the BRE Guide on the effect of new buildings on the light enjoyed by neighbouring existing buildings does not include bathrooms, toilets, storerooms and circulation space in its analysis.[43] Owners and occupiers of some circulation space may consider natural light to parts of that space important; for example good light to stairs may be important from a safety point of view, or may avoid the need to use artificial light during daylight hours.

6.43 If there is a dispute, a judge will often be well advised to view the premises himself so as to form his own impression or judgment.[44] Such evidence is sometimes called real evidence. In past days, disputes concerning obstructions to light were normally decided by juries following a direction from a judge, and juries sometimes viewed the premises. This occurred in *Back v Stacey* in 1826, in which Best CJ told a jury who had viewed the premises that they were to judge from their own ocular

[41] *Colls v Home and Colonial Stores Ltd* [1904] AC 179, 208 (Lord Lindley). See ch 3, para 3.3 for the statement of the principle.

[42] In *Lawrence v Fen Tigers Ltd* [2014] UKSC 13, [2014] AC 822 [168], Lord Mance, in connection with a noise nuisance and the issue of injunctions, said that the right to enjoy one's home without disturbance was one which most people value for reasons largely if not entirely independent of money. This observation is as true for a loss of amenity by a reduction of natural light as it is true for a loss of amenity, as was in issue before the Supreme Court, due to noise nuisance.

[43] See n 31.

[44] *Ough v King* [1967] 1 WLR 1547. A judge may sometimes say that he has inspected premises not to obtain evidence but with a view to understanding better the evidence that has been given: see *Davis v Marrable* [1913] 2 Ch 421, 428 (Joyce J).

observation rather than from the testimony of any witnesses, however respectable, the degree of diminution which the plaintiff's ancient lights had undergone.[45] Of course courts in those days did not have the benefit of the Waldram methodology and experts who apply that process. Also a view of a property may not be on a 'standard day'. Plainly a view may have more evidential value if the obstruction on the servient land has already been erected so that its impact on the lighting of the dominant building can be directly and visually perceived.

[45] *Back v Stacey* (1826) 2 C & P 465, 466.

7

Remedies

(A) INTRODUCTION

The owner of an interest in the dominant building who is threatened with or has suffered work on the servient land which will violate or has violated his right of light has three possible remedies to prevent or redress the wrong. First, he may seek an injunction to prevent the obstruction being erected or to remove it if it has been erected. Secondly, he may seek an award of damages. Thirdly, he may exercise a right to abate the nuisance, that is himself proceeding to remove it without an order of the court. The first two are important remedies. The third is of little practical significance for rights of light. The remedies are not, of course, exclusive and a person may obtain damages for the effect of an obstruction which has occurred, and an order for the removal of that obstruction. The first two of these remedies are the remedies generally available for the redress of civil wrongs, mainly torts and breaches of contract. The third remedy, that of abatement, is confined to nuisances and is relevant to rights of light, since an infringement of that right is in law a nuisance. The aim of this chapter is to explain the general nature and availability of the remedies and to discuss their particular application to infringements of rights of light. 7.1

An essential difference between damages and an injunction is that a person who suffers a wrong such as a nuisance to his property is entitled as of right to be compensated for his loss by an award of damages to be paid to him by the perpetrator of the nuisance. An injunction is an equitable remedy and, like all equitable remedies, it is discretionary, and a court may or may not issue an injunction in any particular case. There are two main issues which arise when remedies are sought for the violation of a right of light. One issue is the exact principles which guide a court in exercising its discretion on whether or not to grant an injunction. The other issue is whether the damages awarded to the dominant owner should be confined to the reduction in the value of his land caused by the unlawful obstruction to light erected on the servient land, or may comprise or include the amount of money which the dominant owner could have obtained in a hypothetical negotiation with the servient owner for the voluntary release of the right of light. This chapter considers the remedies available to the dominant owner and addresses, among other things, the two issues just mentioned. 7.2

7.3 There is nothing inherently special about claims for remedies for an infringement of rights of light when it comes to an examination of the availability of remedies. The decisions on the subject, including on the two important questions identified in the last paragraph, span the spectrum of wrongs to property, and beyond.[1] Naturally in the following description the focus will be upon the application of general principles to rights of light claims. There are a number of general principles relating to remedies which apply to remedies for a breach of rights of light as they do to remedies available for other wrongs, for example the general principle that a person who seeks an equitable remedy must come to the court with 'clean hands', ie he must have behaved responsibly and properly.[2]

7.4 The remedies considered in this chapter are those available where a violation of a right of light is threatened or has been carried out. There may arise circumstances in which no work on the servient land is currently proposed, but either the dominant owner or the servient owner or both have a legitimate need to ascertain whether an easement of light exists. An instance of such a need might be where the servient owner proposes to sell his land for development, and the price is affected by the existence or otherwise of an easement of light which might limit that development. Proceedings for an injunction or damages would not be appropriate in such circumstances, but a party may seek a declaration from the court on the existence or otherwise of the right. A court may make a binding declaration whether or not any other remedy is claimed.[3] This procedure is therefore available in appropriate cases to both dominant and servient owners.[4] A declaration may be made by consent in an appropriate case.[5]

7.5 A further example of a case where a declaration might be sought is where an easement of light is agreed to exist, and the only issue is whether the reduction of light to the dominant building caused by a particular proposed development will constitute an actionable injury. A declaration could then be sought on whether an injury would be created. The court has a discretion on whether or not to make a declaration and will not do so unless it would serve a useful purpose; obviously a

[1] Two of the leading cases on the principles which guide the decision on whether to grant an injunction concerned nuisance by noise and vibration (*Shelfer v City of London Electric Lighting Co* [1895] 1 Ch 287) and nuisance by noise from a stadium used for motor sports (*Lawrence v Fen Tigers Ltd* [2014] UKSC 13, [2014] AC 22). The decision which initiated the modern line of cases on voluntary release damages concerned a breach of a restrictive covenant (*Wrotham Park Estates Co v Parkside Homes Ltd* [1974] 1 WLR 798). A recent case in the Privy Council which summarised the effect of earlier decisions on voluntary release damages arose out of a breach of a confidentiality agreement relating to oil exploration (*Pell Frischmann Engineering Ltd v Bow Valley Iran Ltd* [2009] UKPC 45, [2011] 1 WLR 2370). It is the principles of law derived from these leading cases which apply to remedies or claims following an infringement or alleged infringement of rights of light.

[2] See *Snell's Equity*, 33rd edn (London, Sweet & Maxwell, 2015) para 18.039. See also para 7.35 on the doctrine of clean hands.

[3] Civil Procedure Rules, Pt 40.20.

[4] For example, in *Ankerson v Connolly* [1907] 1 Ch 678, the servient owner sought a declaration that his property was not bound by an easement of light.

[5] *Haym v Couch* [2009] EWHC 1040 (Ch); *Animatrix Ltd v O'Kelly* [2010] EWCA Civ 788 (an intellectual property case).

party should make every effort to seek agreement, before bringing an action for a declaration before a court.[6] A declaration may be sought together with other relief such as an injunction, for example, where there is an issue on whether an easement of light exists and, if so, whether the effect of a proposed development on the servient land would be an infringement of the easement. A person who has carried out a development which he accepts is an infringement of a right of light appurtenant to another property may seek a declaration that an injunction requiring him to remove the development would not be an appropriate remedy, and that the only liability on him should be to pay damages. The motive for seeking such a declaration might be to bring about certainty on whether the development can remain.[7] A declaration is the appropriate remedy in proceedings under the Rights of Light Act 1959.[8]

This book is not concerned with the details of procedure in legal actions. The general rules of procedure in the High Court and the county court are now contained in the Civil Procedure Rules (the CPR) and Practice Directions issued as a supplement to many of the Rules. The Rules are published with an extensive commentary in 'the White Book' and in 'the Green Book'.[9] Proceedings must be commenced by way of a claim form, which must state the remedy sought or the question which the claimant wishes the court to determine. There are two alternative procedures: that under Part 8 of the CPR, where the claimant seeks the court's decision on a question which is unlikely to involve a substantial dispute of fact, and that under Part 7 in other cases. The main difference is that under Part 7, formal pleadings by way of a particulars of claim and a defence are usually necessary so that the precise allegations and issues of fact can be elucidated. Proceedings relating to rights of light disputes are likely to be commenced in the Chancery Division rather than in the Queen's Bench Division of the High Court, or to be commenced in the county court. The early stages in the proceedings are likely to be controlled in the High Court by a master who will give procedural directions such as the exchange of reports of experts, where necessary further particulars of what is alleged, and the disclosure by each party of relevant documents. A litigant is entitled to present his case in person, but rights of light cases usually involve questions of law, and expert evidence and the employment of lawyers to assert or defend a claim in the courts is usually necessary. The evidence of an expert rights of light surveyor may be necessary in many cases. Where an easement of light is claimed by prescription in 7.6

[6] The principles on the appropriateness of granting declaratory relief were considered by the Court of Appeal in *Nokia Corporation v InterDigital Technology Corporation* [2006] EWCA Civ 1618.

[7] Such a declaration was sought in *HKRUK II (CPC) Ltd v Heaney* [2010] EWHC 2245 (Ch), [2010] 3 EGLR 15. The court decided that an injunction was appropriate and ordered the demolition of a recently erected extension to a property. See para 7.15. See also *Greenwich Healthcare NHS Trust v London and Quadrant Housing Trust* [1998] 1 WLR 1749; *Messier-Dowty Ltd v Sabena SA* [2000] 1 WLR 2040.

[8] See ch 9.

[9] These books are published regularly, usually annually, by Sweet & Maxwell (the White Book) and Lexis/Nexis (the Green Book).

reliance on the Prescription Act 1832, there are certain specific pleading provisions in section 5 of that Act, but these are of little, if any, practical significance today.[10]

(B) INJUNCTIONS

1. Introduction

(a) The Nature of Injunctions

7.7 An injunction is an equitable remedy, issued at the discretion of the court, which orders a person who threatens to commit a wrong not to do so, or orders a person who has committed a wrong or is in the course of committing or continuing a wrong to take measures to remedy that which has been wrongfully done, or to cease that which is being wrongfully done. The first type of injunction is called a negative or prohibitory injunction, and the second type is called a positive or mandatory injunction. The first type of injunction which prevents a threatened wrong which is not actually existing or present is often called a *quia timet* injunction. In the field of rights of light, a negative injunction may prevent the erection of a structure on the servient land which, if it were erected, would infringe an easement of light appurtenant to the dominant building. A mandatory injunction may require a servient owner, who has erected or is in the course of erecting an unlawful obstruction, to remove that obstruction. A deliberate failure to comply with an injunction is a contempt of court, and a punishment by way of a fine or a committal to prison may be imposed on a defendant, or on directors or officers of a corporate defendant, who acts or fails to act in accordance with the injunction.[11]

7.8 Sometimes the dispute between the parties is whether an easement of light exists, or whether a particular obstruction is or will be an infringement of an easement, and, if these matters are decided in favour of a dominant owner, a servient owner may give an undertaking to the court as to his future actions which may be accepted by the court in place of an injunction. A breach of such an undertaking is also a contempt of court.[12] A breach of an undertaking which is alleged to be a contempt of court must be proved in accordance with the standard of proof applicable in criminal proceedings: that is, beyond reasonable doubt so that the court is certain.[13] A further remedy available to enforce an injunction or an undertaking is a sequestration of the property of a party in breach, including the property of

[10] See ch 5, section (D)11.

[11] See eg *Biba Ltd v Stratford Investments* [1973] Ch 281 for the liability of directors of companies for a breach of an injunction or undertaking which binds the company.

[12] *Milborn v Newton Colliery* (1908) 52 SJ 317; *Biba Ltd v Stratford Investments* [1973] Ch 281.

[13] *Re Bramblevale Ltd* [1970] Ch 128.

directors or officers of corporate bodies. Sequestration means the seizure of the assets of the party in question.[14]

A further distinction between types of injunctions is between a permanent injunction (sometimes called a perpetual injunction) and an interim injunction (sometimes called an interlocutory injunction). A permanent injunction has permanent effect. An interim injunction is granted until some further order of the court.[15] 7.9

Obviously a court will need to scrutinise carefully the exact form of an injunction, and a mandatory injunction may sometimes specify a time within which acts ordered are to be carried out. A prohibitory injunction often contains the words that a defendant is restrained from carrying out certain acts by himself or his servants or agents. Since an injunction is a discretionary remedy, the court also has a discretion to discharge an injunction which it has issued. The discharge of an injunction is unlikely often to occur in rights of light proceedings, but it could happen, for instance where an injunction has been obtained by the suppression of material facts or by an error, a possible instance being an agreement as to rights of light which has been overlooked. This principle illustrates a difference between damages and an injunction. An order for an amount of damages cannot be altered save by way of an appeal.[16] 7.10

(b) The Historical Basis of Injunctive Relief

It is necessary to state briefly the historical basis of the equitable remedy of an injunction, since this is relevant to a full understanding of the current law. The normal remedy available to a person aggrieved by a civil wrong committed against him such as a tort or a breach of contract, as developed by the medieval common law courts, was an award of damages, a monetary sum to compensate that person for the wrong committed towards him. Proceedings could only be commenced following the issue of a writ in the appropriate form by the Lord Chancellor, and these writs became known as forms of action. The common law courts had no power to issue orders requiring or preventing specific actions by specific orders, such as an injunction or an order for the specific performance of a contract. In these circumstances there grew up a second source of legal remedies and proceedings. Petitions for specific relief could be addressed to the King's Council, and the Lord Chancellor, acting on behalf of the King and the Council, came regularly to issue such orders. This procedure became available at least since the reign of Edward III (1327–77). The law as administered by the Lord Chancellor became known as the law of equity, and the courts which administered this jurisdiction became called Chancery courts. There therefore came into existence two systems of justice. The common law courts could award damages but not specific relief. 7.11

[14] *Steiner Products Ltd v Willy Steiner Ltd* [1966] 1 WLR 986 (fine imposed in place of sequestration).
[15] See section (B)6 of this chapter.
[16] *Fitter v Veal* (1701) 12 Mod Rep 542; *Derrick v Williams* [1939] 2 All ER 559.

Courts of equity could in general award only specific relief (although some jurisdiction to award damages in limited circumstances seems to have been exercised by these courts). It was an obvious inconvenience that a person who sought damages had to proceed in a common law court, and a person who sought a specific remedy had to proceed in a court of equity. A person who sought both remedies, for example damages for a past wrong and an injunction to prevent a continuation of the wrong, had to proceed in both courts.

7.12 The availability of the two alternative forms of remedy reflects a juridical or even social dispute on the function of legal remedies which has persisted ever since the controversy in the seventeenth century between Sir Edward Coke, a prominent common lawyer who became Chief Justice of the Court of King's Bench in 1613, and Lord Ellesmere, who became Lord Chancellor in 1603. Coke regarded persons as having a fundamental freedom to choose whether to commit a civil wrong, in the light of an expectation of the amount of money which they would have to pay as damages if they did commit that wrong. The election of a person to abstain from a wrong or pay a sum of money if he did commit it would of course be removed if an order could be made by the Chancery courts restraining him from committing or continuing the act.[17] The view of Lord Ellesmere, settled at the time by James I in favour of the Chancery courts, has subsequently in general prevailed.

7.13 This unsatisfactory situation has now changed. The Common Law Procedure Act 1854 conferred power on the common law courts to grant an injunction in certain circumstances. More importantly, the Chancery courts were given power by the Chancery Amendment Act 1858 (Lord Cairns' Act) to award damages in addition to or in place of an injunction or specific performance. Damages awarded in lieu of an injunction or specific performance are sometimes called equitable damages.[18] There was a limitation in this power, in that if there was no jurisdiction to grant an injunction, for example because there was no threat to continue a wrong which had been committed in the past but which had ended, no injunction could be granted and thus no damages could be awarded by a Chancery court.[19] As a result of the Judicature Acts 1873 and 1875 there was created a new High Court of Justice divided into Divisions. All Divisions of the High Court, and the county court, can today enforce legal and equitable rights and can award damages

[17] See *Co-operative Insurance Society Ltd v Argyll Stores (Holdings) Ltd* [1996] Ch 286, 304 (Millett LJ). Points of a somewhat similar philosophical nature can arise today. For example, where six people have rights of light which will be violated by a proposed development and five of them are willing to release their rights in return for a substantial monetary payment, a court may have to decide whether an injunction to prevent the development should be issued at the behest of a sixth person who is unwilling to bargain away his rights. See para 7.44.

[18] The meaning of equitable damages and the distinction between common law and equitable damages are considered in more detail in section (C)2 of this chapter.

[19] *Proctor v Bayley* (1889) 42 Ch D 390. The position is different if a court could have granted an injunction but has not done so either because an injunction was not sought or because there was no prospect of an injunction being granted having regard to the conduct of the claimant. In such a case damages can be awarded in substitution for an injunction. See para 7.120.

or equitable remedies.[20] The right to enforce an easement of light is a common law right which can today be enforced in any civil court and by the primary remedies of damages and an injunction.[21]

(c) Current Guidance

Any court which has jurisdiction to entertain a claim for the infringement of a right of light may, therefore, today grant an injunction, a negative or positive injunction or a permanent or interim injunction. In all cases when a threatened infringement of a right of light or an actual infringement of a right of light occurs, the court has a discretion on whether to grant an injunction or to leave the claimant to his remedy in damages. The important practical question is when an injunction will be granted or, put another way, what are the principles which govern the decision of the court on whether or not to grant an injunction. 7.14

It had long been difficult to find clear guidance on the principles to be applied by a court in exercising its discretion. It had often been thought that a dominant owner who knew that a building was being erected in breach of his easement of light would be unlikely to obtain a mandatory injunction to remove the building if he had not at least sought an interim injunction to prevent the construction going ahead. However, in *HKRUK II (CPC) Ltd v Heaney*[22] the dominant owner of residential premises had known of, and had protested against, the erection of a two-storey extension to a commercial building, which he claimed infringed his right of light. In proceedings brought by the developer a month after completion of the works, the dominant owner sought a mandatory injunction for the removal of the extension. The servient owner admitted that the extension was in breach of the claimant's rights, but contended in the proceedings which he brought that in the circumstances an injunction was an inappropriate remedy. The High Court issued an injunction requiring the removal of the extension. This decision caused some surprise to developers and to those practising in the field and perhaps strengthened the negotiating position of dominant owners seeking compensation for a reduction in their light. Developers are said to have felt 'dissatisfaction' at the decision.[23] The decision should perhaps have caused little surprise, having regard 7.15

[20] This is commonly called the fusion of law and equity. The Acts of 1873 and 1875 were replaced by the Judicature Act 1925 and then by the Supreme Court Act 1981, now called the Senior Courts Act 1981 (the change in name was due to the creation of the United Kingdom Supreme Court by the Constitutional Reform Act 2005). The power to issue an injunction is today stated in sections 37(1) and 50 of the Senior Courts Act 1981. The county court has jurisdiction to issue an injunction under section 38 of the County Courts Act 1984.

[21] The concept of equitable damages remains and is considered below. See section (C)2 of this chapter.

[22] *HKRUK II (CPC) Ltd v Heaney* [2010] EWHC 2245 (Ch), [2010] 3 EGLR 15.

[23] Law Commission Consultation Paper No 210 (2013), para 5.42. The recommendations of the Law Commission on injunctions in rights of light cases are discussed in paras 7.49 and 7.50, and more generally in ch 12.

to the recent assertion by the Court of Appeal of the right of a residential owner to obtain an injunction against a threatened obstruction to his light in *Regan v Paul Properties DDF No 1 Ltd*.[24] It is difficult to feel much sympathy for a defendant who admits he has acted unlawfully in the face of and despite protests made and is then required by a court to put right his unlawful acts.

7.16 For over a century the main guidance on the exercise of the discretion to grant an injunction was what was said in the decision of the Court of Appeal in *Shelfer v City of London Electric Lighting Co*,[25] a case concerned with nuisance caused by noise and vibration. Four tests of a somewhat imprecise nature were suggested in that case, but both the application of the tests and their exact status as guidance for courts in subsequent cases remained less than certain. The *Shelfer* decision was considered, and some degree of new guidance given, by the Supreme Court in the recent case of *Lawrence v Fen Tigers Ltd*.[26] It is appropriate now to go on to consider the guidance recently given by the Supreme Court in this last case and the principles which apply today on the question of whether an injunction will be ordered.

2. Exercise of the Discretion: General Approach

7.17 When a court has to decide what is on the face of it a stark question, such as the exercise of a discretion on whether or not to grant an injunction once a violation of a property right has been established, the initial matter to consider is whether there is any general presumption one way or the other. There are many situations in law in which a court will exercise its discretion in a particular way, or take a particular course unless there is some special or particular reason in an individual case not to do so. An example is the rule that costs are generally awarded in favour of a successful party in litigation, unless there is some special reason not to do so.[27] Even when there is such a rule or presumption its strength, or put another way, the strength of the reasons needed to rebut the presumption, varies from subject to subject.

7.18 It had been considered for a century and a half that if the existence or threatened existence of a nuisance is established, the normal course of events is that an injunction will be granted to prevent the commission or the continuance of the nuisance. In *Imperial Gas Light and Coke Co v Broadbent*, the tenant of premises used for the cultivation of flowers, fruit and vegetables established that noxious fumes emitted

[24] *Regan v Paul Properties DDF No 1 Ltd* [2006] EWCA Civ 1319, [2007] Ch135. In this case the development on the servient land had been commenced and the injunction granted was to prevent a further part of it which would constitute an infringement of the claimant's right of light.

[25] *Shelfer v City of London Electric Lighting Co* [1895] 1 Ch 287.

[26] *Lawrence v Fen Tigers Ltd* [2014] UKSC 13, [2014] AC 822.

[27] This rule is now stated as regards litigation in Pt 44.3 of the Civil Procedure Rules.

from a nearby property used to manufacture gas was a nuisance to his premises. He obtained the award of an arbitrator that the activity of the defendants was a nuisance and then sought an injunction to prevent its continuance. An injunction was granted. In the House of Lords Lord Campbell, the Lord Chancellor, observed: 'I cannot doubt for a moment that under such circumstances, upon proof that the nuisance continued, an injunction would follow as a matter of course.'[28]

Perhaps unfortunately, the simplicity of this approach has given way to what is described as a more nuanced approach. There is clearly a distinction to be drawn between circumstances in which the offending acts constituting a nuisance can be prevented before they commence or can be required to cease (for example, the emission of fumes from an industrial process) and circumstances, such as in some rights of light cases, where a newly erected building would have to be wholly or partly demolished if the nuisance was to cease. It was the first type of case which was considered in *Lawrence v Fen Tigers Ltd.*[29] The defendants had committed a noise nuisance through their activities of running a stadium used for motor sports. The Supreme Court, reversing the Court of Appeal, restored the order of the judge which limited the activities carried out at the stadium.[30] 7.19

The *Lawrence* decision is important since, although an injunction to prevent a wrong was granted, it propounds a more limited approach to the issue of injunctions compared with that stated in the House of Lords in *Broadbent's* case in 1859. Lord Neuberger said that when a claimant had established that the defendant's activities amounted to a nuisance, prima facie the remedy to which the claimant was entitled, in addition to damages for past nuisance, was an injunction to restrain the defendant from committing such a nuisance in the future. He added that the prima facie position is that an injunction should be granted, so that the burden was on the defendant to show that the injunction should not be granted.[31] So stated, the rule appears to be not much different to that stated by Lord Campbell in *Broadbent's* case, since clearly Lord Campbell would have accepted that there might be circumstances which disentitled a claimant to the injunction which, as he said, in general circumstances would normally be granted as a matter of course. However, after the statement of the principle on the location of the burden there then appears the nuance. A different view to that taken in *Broadbent's* case as regards infringement of rights of light had emerged. In *Colls v Home and Colonial* 7.20

[28] *Imperial Gas Light and Coke Co v Broadbent* (1859) 7 HLC 600, 609. The *Shelfer* rules as promulgated by the Court of Appeal at the end of the nineteenth century in a nuisance case (see paras 7.16 and 7.23) seems to have been predicated on the proposition that an injunction to prevent the creation or continuation of a nuisance would normally be granted, in the absence of special circumstances. In the *Shelfer* decision AL Smith LJ said that the plaintiff who was suffering from a nuisance was prima facie entitled to an injunction to prevent the nuisance.

[29] *Lawrence v Fen Tigers Ltd* [2014] UKSC 13, [2014] AC 822.

[30] The defendants were given liberty to apply to have the injunction discharged and damages awarded in its place. For a further decision of the Supreme Court on other aspects of this litigation, such as the liability of a landlord for nuisances committed by a tenant, see [2014] UKSC 46.

[31] *Lawrence v Fen Tigers Ltd* [2014] UKSC 13, [2014] AC 822 [101] and [121].

Stores Ltd,[32] a leading case on the content of rights of light,[33] Lord Macnaghten stated that if the defendant had acted fairly and not in an unneighbourly spirit, he was disposed to think that a court ought to incline to damages rather than an injunction. This, of course, was different to the approach of the Lord Chancellor in *Broadbent's* case. Lord Neuberger, commenting on this, said that it was right to emphasise that, when a judge was called upon to decide whether to award damages in place of an injunction, he did not think 'that there should be any inclination either way (subject to the legal burden discussed above): the outcome should depend on all the evidence and arguments'.[34]

7.21 Courts of first instance and practitioners advising persons on rights of light problems and disputes need above all to have clear guidance on the overall approach to the exercise by courts of the power to grant injunctions.[35] A useful starting point would be that there was a clear presumption one way or the other, in favour of an injunction being granted or the opposite, on this matter. As it is, the statement of principle approved by Lord Neuberger does not offer such guidance, possibly because it was not thought practical or appropriate to do so. The fact that a person who suffers a nuisance, including a violation of a right of light, is prima facie entitled to an injunction is small comfort if, once the defendant opposes the grant of an injunction, there is to be no initial inclination one way or the other towards upholding that opposition. Furthermore there are many who would argue that where a wrong is established, or agreed to have been committed or about to be committed, and a court has power to prevent or redress the wrong it should do so wherever it reasonably can, instead of awarding only damages, a course which in effect allows the wrongdoer to buy himself out of the consequences of his wrong.[36]

32 *Colls v Home and Colonial Stores Ltd* [1904] AC 179, 193.

33 See ch 3.

34 *Lawrence v Fen Tigers Ltd* [2014] UKSC 13, [2014] AC 822 [122]. Lord Mance agreed with what he described as the 'nuanced approach of Lord Neuberger': see para 168. Lord Clarke indicated that he would not lay down any general principles which should be followed in the future but that such principles must be developed on a case-by-case basis and that each case would depend on its circumstances: see para 171. One of the difficulties before the Supreme Court was that at first instance the defendants accepted that if a nuisance was established, an injunction should follow, apparently because they had taken the view that on the authorities, any resistance to an injunction as the appropriate remedy would have been doomed to failure. The Law Commission in its recent *Report on Rights of Light* (Law Com No 356, 2014), had the benefit of being able to consider the *Lawrence* case and concluded in para 5.3 that in rights of light cases an injunction was still the primary remedy for an infringement but that the decision of the Supreme Court had weakened the primacy. The recommendations of the Law Commission on this subject are discussed in section (B)4(i) of this chapter and more generally in ch 12.

35 The responses of property developers and others to the recent consultation exercise on rights of light carried out by the Law Commission illustrate this need: see Law Commission, *Report on Rights of Light* (Law Com No 356, 2014).

36 In *Lawrence v Fen Tigers Ltd* [2014] UKSC 13, [2014] AC 822, Lord Sumption described any repugnance that might be felt at a wrongdoer being able to buy his way out of his obligations as 'an unduly moralistic approach to disputes'. There seems no reason to believe that, within reasonable limits, a moralistic approach to disputes (presumably as opposed to a pragmatic or financial approach) should not be adopted by our courts.

The decision of the Supreme Court, in the judgment of Lord Carnwath, contains an elaborate examination of planning processes, first introduced in this country on a general basis in the Town and Country Planning Act 1947, but in the generality of the decision there is less examination of the older principle that a person whose rights are to be or have been infringed should, save in exceptional circumstances, expect the assistance of a court administering the law of equity in prohibiting the continuation of a wrong. Lord Sumption suggested that consideration should be given to a principle that an injunction should not normally be issued to restrain an activity for which planning permission had been granted. It may not be acceptable to owners of property that the just and ancient protection of their rights by an effective remedy issued by the courts is made subordinate to the transitory views and fashions of town planners.[37] 7.22

3. Exercise of the Discretion: The *Shelfer* Rules

(a) The Development of the Shelfer *Rules*

With regard to one matter, the decision of the Supreme Court in *Lawrence* has shed considerable light on what was previously unsatisfactory and unclear. This is the status and application of the rules stated by the Court of Appeal in *Shelfer v City of London Electric Lighting Co* in 1895.[38] In that case the Court of Appeal upheld the decision of the judge to restrain by injunction the causing of noise and vibration from electricity generation, which constituted a nuisance. AL Smith LJ said that when a plaintiff's rights had been invaded, he was prima facie entitled to an injunction, but that there were cases in which damages might be awarded in substitution. The Lord Justice then added: 7.23

> In my opinion it may be stated as a good working rule that—(1) if the injury to the plaintiff's legal rights is small, (2) And is one which is capable of being estimated in money, (3) And is one which can be adequately compensated by a small money payment, (4) And the case is one in which it would be oppressive to the defendant to grant an injunction:- then damages in substitution for an injunction may be given.[39]

The application of this 'working rule' or rules (or tests) to all cases of nuisance and all types of nuisance is not straightforward. Nor is it straightforward when applied to rights of light. Presumably, in the case of an invasion of a right of light, the injury is small if the amount of light obstructed is small. This rule was stated before the methodology of measuring loss of light by way of Waldram diagrams was 7.24

[37] There are indications in the judgments of Lord Mance and Lord Clarke that this will not be allowed to happen. See para 7.40 et seq on the relevance of the existence of a planning permission to the exercise of the discretion to issue an injunction. See also ch 10 on town planning.

[38] *Shelfer v City of London Electric Lighting Co* [1895] 1 Ch 287.

[39] ibid, 322–23.

developed.[40] It is uncertain when a loss is one which is capable of being estimated in money. If damages are to be assessed by the reduction in the value of the dominant building (the 'book value' method of assessment, as described below),[41] it is often difficult to translate a reduction in light into a precise reduction in rental or capital value of the dominant building, as is required by the second rule. The difficulty may be greater when the reduction in light is small, so that logic suggests that the smaller the injury, the less likely it is that the second rule will be satisfied, which leads to the curious result that a smaller injury, because it does not satisfy the second test, is more likely to be restrained by an injunction than a larger injury.[42] Turning to the third test, today damages are often assessed not by the book value method but by the voluntary release method, which is in effect an estimate of the amount which would be agreed in a negotiation for the voluntary release of the right of light.[43] Monetary payments and damages assessed by this method may be substantial even though the injury to the dominant building in terms of reduced capital value is small. In other words, the third working rule or test may be out of touch with the more modern approach to the assessment of damages which has been applied in rights of light cases and has been generally approved by the House of Lords.[44] The fourth test in itself provides no guidance on when it would be oppressive to grant an injunction, although the test seems to create a separate requirement which is distinct from the other three tests.

7.25 The way in which the rules or tests were formulated by AL Smith LJ suggests that if an injunction is not to be granted, all four rules or criteria must be satisfied. This has led to the rules being regarded not so much as guidance but as a checklist to be applied by courts.[45] Such a mechanical approach does not distinguish between the different forms of nuisance which may arise. In addition, such a mechanical approach may not be as helpful when what is sought is an injunction to demolish a recently erected building as it may be when an injury is caused by some noisy or offensive leisure activity on land. There arose in the cases following *Shelfer* a tension between those who regarded the four rules as close in status to a statutory provision on the subject of the discretion to grant an injunction in nuisance cases and those who regarded the rules as of some assistance but as something which could be departed from by a court in appropriate circumstances.

7.26 It is not surprising that, having regard to the imprecision in the nature of the four working rules, the approach to the rules and their application have differed widely in the century and more that followed the decision of the Court of Appeal

[40] For a discussion of this methodology, see ch 6.

[41] See section (C)4 of this chapter.

[42] See *HKRUK II (CPC) Ltd v Heaney* [2010] EWHC 2245 (Ch), [2010] 3 EGLR 15.

[43] The voluntary release method of assessing damages is explained in detail in section (C) of this chapter.

[44] See *Attorney General v Blake* [2001] 1 AC 268: see para 7.116.

[45] In *Jaggard v Sawyer* [1995] 1 WLR 269, 287 Millett LJ referred to the four working rules as 'AL Smith LJ's checklist'.

in *Shelfer* in 1895. Since general guidance has now been given by the Supreme Court which is very different to the *Shelfer* rules, there is little purpose in drawing elaborate attention to the various decisions and to the various linguistic descriptions of the status and application of the *Shelfer* rules which emerge from decided cases. As just mentioned, one line of cases supports the application of the working rules of AL Smith LJ, sometimes in a mechanistic fashion with a requirement that an exceptional case has to be shown before damages are awarded in place of an injunction.[46] On the other hand, a different line of cases suggests a more flexible and open approach, with the working rules regarded as only general guidance and with the court free to depart from them in particular circumstances and having regard to the conduct of the parties.[47]

(b) *The Guidance in* Lawrence

The Supreme Court in *Lawrence* has downgraded the status and importance attaching to the *Shelfer* decision. Certainly the four working rules can no longer be applied in the rigid and mechanistic way which has sometimes been favoured. Unfortunately the conclusions of the members of the Court are not fully consistent with each other. Lord Sumption considered that the decision in *Shelfer* was out of date, and that it was unfortunate that it had been followed so recently and so slavishly.[48] Lord Clarke agreed with this observation.[49] These statements suggest that little attention need today be paid to *Shelfer* and the four working rules. However, Lord Neuberger put the matter in a rather different way. He stated a modified version of the status to be accorded today to the rules, which he encapsulated in three propositions.[50] First, the application of the four rules or tests must not be such as 'to be a fetter on the exercise of the court's discretion'. Secondly, it would, in the absence of additional relevant circumstances pointing the other way, normally be right to refuse an injunction if those four tests were satisfied. Thirdly, the fact that those tests are not satisfied does not mean that an injunction should be granted. What this last analysis seems to amount to is that the *Shelfer* rules may remain as a sort of negative threshold. If all four tests are satisfied then there should not be an injunction. If one or more of the tests is not satisfied then the question of an injunction remains at large (although the satisfaction of others 7.27

[46] Decisions broadly within this category include *Slack v Leeds Industrial Co-operative Society Ltd* [1924] 2 Ch 475; *Miller v Jackson* [1977] QB 966; *Kennaway v Thompson* [1981] QB 88; *Regan v Paul Properties DPF No 1 Ltd* [2006] EWCA Civ 1319, [2007] Ch 135; and *Watson v Croft Promosport Ltd* [2009] EWCA Civ 15, [2009] 3 All ER 249. The *Shelfer* principles have been applied in New Zealand: *Bank of New Zealand v Greenwood* [1984] 1 NZLR 525.

[47] *Kine v Jolly* [1905] 1 Ch 480; *Fishenden v Higgs & Hill Ltd* [1935] 153 LT 128.

[48] *Lawrence v Fen Tigers Ltd* [2014] UKSC 13, [2014] AC 822 [161].

[49] ibid [171].

[50] ibid [123]. Lord Carnwath at para 245 said that he agreed with the observations of both Lord Neuberger and Lord Sumption, although these observations are scarcely consistent with each other. He considered that the opportunity should be taken to signal a move away from the strict criteria in *Shelfer*: see ibid [239].

of the tests may still be relevant). This guidance may not be abundantly helpful to courts of first instance which have to decide whether or not to issue an injunction. Courts will still have to grapple with the uncertainty of what the practical application of the tests means.

7.28 The important question is where does that leave the *Shelfer* rules today as guidance. Many will think that the description of the rules as out of date is well founded, and that the rules should henceforth offer little assistance on the question of whether an injunction should or should not be granted, whether in rights of light disputes or in other cases. Undoubtedly a rigid and mechanical or 'check list' adherence to the rules is no longer sustainable. Nonetheless, if the propositions of Lord Neuberger are taken to be the law there is still some substantial significance in the rules, and the difficulties over exactly what they mean will still have to be considered by courts and practitioners. That is probably the best guidance that can be given. It may be that in view of the trenchant observations of at least two members of the Supreme Court the four working rules will in the future play only a small part, if any real part at all, in the exercise of a discretion on whether to grant an injunction to prevent or remove an unlawful obstruction to a right of light.

7.29 There has not yet been time to assess the impact of such guidance as the Supreme Court gave in *Lawrence*. In a subsequent right of way case the Court of Appeal referred to the injury to the dominant land as being not small, and that it was not such as could be compensated by a small monetary payment.[51] The Court went on to consider the question of the grant of an injunction both under the four *Shelfer* working rules and on the basis of an exercise of a more general discretion.[52] What is perhaps illustrated is the uncertainty which still remains on the utility of the *Shelfer* rules and a feeling that it might have been preferable if the Supreme Court had unanimously concluded that the rules were not of any further utility or guidance.[53]

4. Exercise of the Discretion: Other Considerations

7.30 The only general guidance which can be given on the exercise of the discretion over the grant of an injunction is that all relevant circumstances should be considered by the court which takes the decision. Provided that the court which makes the decision pays real regard to all matters which are relevant, it is unlikely that its decision will be overruled on an appeal unless it is plainly wrong. There are many

[51] *Higson v Guenault* [2014] EWCA Civ 703, [2014] 2 P & CR DG 13.

[52] ibid [51] (Aikens LJ). See also *Comic Enterprises Ltd v Twentieth Century Fox Film Corporation* [2014] EWHC 2286 (Ch) [15] (a decision in an intellectual property case).

[53] The Law Commission has recently suggested that there is a real risk of the courts sliding back into a variant of the *Shelfer* test: see the Law Commission *Report on Rights of Light* (Law Com No 356, 2014). It is not clear what variant of the four rules might be adopted.

occasions in which courts of first instance are required to exercise a discretion, and the circumstances in which an appellate court will interfere are limited. A useful statement of principle is that the court will interfere only if it is shown that the judge has either erred in principle in his approach, or has left out of account or has taken into account some factor which he should, or should not, have considered, or that his decision was wholly wrong, so that the court is forced to the conclusion that he has not balanced the various factors fairly in the scale.[54] A challenge by way of appeal to the decision of a court to grant or not grant an injunction will therefore normally be on the ground that the judge has taken into account a wrong consideration or has failed to take into account a relevant consideration or, even if all relevant considerations have been taken into account and all irrelevant considerations rejected, the judge has balanced the relevant considerations in a way which is plainly wrong. It is apparent that different considerations will arise in different cases, and the same consideration may deserve greater weight in different cases. In rights of light cases the factors now to be mentioned may be of particular relevance in any particular case.

(a) Delay

Delay by a claimant in asserting a claim to an injunction is always a relevant factor, and may be sufficient to prevent the grant of an injunction.[55] Claims for damages are subject to a statutory limitation period, usually six years from the accrual of the cause of action. Limitation in this sense is wholly statutory and was created by a series of statutes starting with the Limitation Act 1623 and now contained in the Limitation Act 1980. These statutory periods do not apply to equitable relief such as an injunction. Equity developed its own doctrine, which was that a court would not exercise its discretion in favour of a party who had slept upon his right and had not proceeded with reasonable diligence. The technical expression used by equity for delay in pressing a claim is laches, this being an old French word for slackness or negligence, or not doing.[56] Delay is important in any case where a 7.31

[54] *Phonographic Reproductions Ltd v AEI Rediffusion Music Ltd* [1999] 1 WLR 1507, 1523 (Lord Woolf MR). See also *G v G (Minors): (custody dispute)* [1985] 1 WLR 647, 652 (Lord Fraser). In *Lawrence v Fen Tigers Ltd* [2014] UKSC 13, [2014] AC 822 [120], Lord Neuberger adopted on this subject what Millett LJ had said in *Jaggard v Sawyer* [1995] 1 WLR 269 at p 288, which was as follows: 'Reported cases are merely illustrations of circumstances in which particular judges have exercised their discretion, in some cases by granting an injunction, and in others by awarding damages instead. Since they are all cases on the exercise of a discretion, none of them is a binding authority on how the discretion should be exercised. The most that any of them can demonstrate is that in similar circumstances it would not be wrong to exercise the discretion in the same way. But it does not follow that it would be wrong to exercise it differently.'

[55] *Smith v Clay* (1767) 3 Bro CC 639n, 640n. The latin expression of this principle, as contained in Coke's Institutes 690, is *vigilantibus, non dormientibus, jura subservient* ('the law serves and protects those who are vigilant, not those who sleep'). For a modern illustration of delay preventing the obtaining of an injunction, see *Bracewell v Appleby* [1975] Ch 458, discussed in para 7.110, and *Jaggard v Sawyer* [1995] 2 WLR 269, where a factor in the refusal of an injunction was delay by a claimant.

[56] Co Litt 380b.

discretionary remedy is sought, but it may be particularly important in rights of light cases where the result of delay may be that a servient owner presses on with plans for his development and may commence or even complete construction of an offending development. It is unlikely that a court would issue a mandatory injunction compelling a servient owner to remove a building or part of a building which had been constructed if the dominant owner was well aware of the construction proceeding but made no protest and took no effective action until the works were under way or completed. Of course a good deal depends upon what knowledge the dominant owner had of a proposed development. If the development on the servient land is proceeding, then a dominant owner can scarcely say that he did not have knowledge of what was going on. On the other hand, there may be circumstances in which the dominant owner does not know of the extent of the proposed development until he sees its completion or is informed of its proposed extent. An instance of this last situation might be where the owner of a house had let it when he was abroad, and on his return a neighbour had erected an extension which obstructed his light but of which the tenants had told him nothing.

7.32 In circumstances where a servient owner proposing a development is uncertain whether a dominant owner or owners have a prescriptive right of light, or where it is uncertain whether and to what extent the proposed development on the servient land will violate any right of light, servient owners and developers often find themselves in a dilemma. On the one hand if they bring their proposals to the attention of dominant owners or possible dominant owners at an early stage they may encourage rights of light investigations and claims by dominant owners which would not otherwise happen. On the other hand, if the servient owner or developer does nothing and simply proceeds with his development he may open himself to the prospect of an injunction during the course of the development and he will find difficulty in pleading delay on the part of the dominant owner, since the dominant owner may have had no knowledge of what was to occur until he saw the building on the servient land being constructed.

7.33 Many developers in this situation take the prudent and expedient course of bringing their proposals to the knowledge of their neighbours and providing some reasonable details of it. On occasions, developers instruct a rights of light surveyor and offer to pay the costs of neighbouring owners appointing their own specialists so that the experts can meet and hope to arrive at an amicable settlement of any difficulties relating to the access of light. One possible arrangement is of course that a sum of money is paid to those with interests in neighbouring properties whose rights of light may be infringed. The expense of having to remove or alter a building when it is in the course of construction or has been constructed can obviously be very large, and the risk to a developer of proceeding without providing full information to neighbours is sometimes substantial. The risk of an injunction being sought during the course of a development or after its completion is understandably of particular concern to developers. To meet this concern, the

Law Commission has recently recommended a 'Notice of Proposed Obstruction' procedure, the essence of which is that a developer proposing to develop servient land could give notice of his proposals to the dominant owner, who would then have eight months in which to commence proceedings seeking an injunction. If the dominant owner did not commence such proceedings within the time allowed, he would lose any entitlement to an injunction.[57]

Most developments which could constitute a violation of a right of light require planning permission and it is likely that notification of an application for permission will be given by the local planning authority to those persons with property in the vicinity of it who might be affected. Local planning authorities are required to keep a register of planning applications which can be inspected by the public, and from this the details of any proposed development including plans of it can be scrutinised.[58] A dominant owner who believes that a development is proposed which will violate his right of light is entitled to apply for an interim injunction to prevent the allegedly offending development until a final decision is made on matters in dispute in a court. The failure of a dominant owner to apply for an interim injunction is not necessarily fatal to a claim for a permanent injunction to prevent or even remove a structure, but is certainly a relevant consideration in the exercise of the court's discretion.[59] The prospect of a claimant obtaining a mandatory injunction is reduced if the defendant has offered to delay his proposed works pending the final determination of the issue provided the claimant gives the usual undertaking as to damages but the claimant refuses to do so.[60] 7.34

(b) Clean Hands

It is a general maxim of equity that a person who seeks the discretionary assistance of the court in obtaining an equitable remedy should come to the court with what are described as 'clean hands'. Courts are here concerned not with the general character of a claimant, but with conduct which has immediate reference to the subject matter of the dispute. For instance, the fact that a spouse has committed adultery during a marriage will not prevent him or her subsequently obtaining an injunction to prevent breaches of confidentiality relating to events during the marriage.[61] In a rights of light case the relevant conduct of a claimant for an 7.35

[57] *Rights of Light* (Law Com No 256, 2014) ch 6. The proposal is explained in more detail in ch 12, paras 12.32 et seq.

[58] See s 69 of the Town and Country Planning Act 1990, and see generally ch 10 for the relationship between town and country planning law and principle and rights of light.

[59] See section (B)6 of this chapter for interim injunctions. See *HKRUK II (CPC) Ltd v Heaney* [2010] EWHC 2245 (Ch), [2010] 3 EGLR 15, in which a mandatory injunction to remove an extension to a building was issued, even though no application for an interim injunction had been made. See *Mortimer v Baley* [2004] EWCA Civ 1514, a decision on a breach of a restrictive covenant in which an application for an interim injunction had been refused but a mandatory injunction was granted ordering an extension to a building which was in breach of the covenant to be removed.

[60] *Snell & Prideaux Ltd v Dutton Mirrors Ltd* [1995] 1 EGLR 259 (a case concerning a right of way).

[61] *Duchess of Argyll v Duke of Argyll* [1967] Ch 302.

injunction will therefore be his conduct in relation to the rights of light dispute itself. A claimant who has refused to cooperate in any way with the defendant in discussing the matters in dispute, or the possibility of monetary compensation for a wrong, may find a court reluctant to assist him by issuing an injunction. It has been held that such conduct by a dominant owner may mean that his damages have to be assessed on the basis of a reduction in the value of the dominant building, rather than on the usually more generous basis of voluntary release damages,[62] and the same principle would apply to the seeking of an injunction. The lesson to be derived is that a person with an interest in the dominant building should take steps to make his position and concern known as soon as he is aware of a proposal to carry out development on the servient land which may infringe his right of light, and should make every effort to cooperate with the developer by discussing the matter, by seeing whether any amendment to the proposed development could be made, and in some cases by at least discussing the possibility of some monetary settlement. A claimant who has acted in this way, as opposed to relying on inactivity or truculent protest, may find that his prospects of obtaining an injunction are increased. There may be some cases in which a dominant owner, acting reasonably and properly, would in principle not be satisfied with monetary compensation, for example a householder who finds a substantive reduction in light to his property unacceptable. A person in this position can scarcely be blamed for making his position clear as soon as possible. A servient owner who behaves in a reasonable fashion and offers reasonable monetary compensation is likely to reduce the prospect of an injunction being ordered against him.

(c) Completed Building

7.36 It is obvious that a potent factor in respect of the exercise of the discretion is whether the offending building on the servient land has been constructed or is in the course of construction. A court will always have regard to the waste of resources involved in requiring that which has been recently constructed to be demolished, and will also have regard to the burden on a developer in having to remove recent development. It is at this point that the public interest becomes an important consideration.[63] That having been said, it would be most unwise for any servient owner or developer to believe that simply because he has pressed on speedily with construction of a building, despite the protests of a dominant owner, he will avoid the possibility of a mandatory injunction which requires the removal of the structure. It appears wrong in principle that a developer who continues regardless of protests, and attempts to ride roughshot over the rights of his

[62] *Forsyth-Grant v Allen* [2008] EWCA Civ 505, [2008] EGLR 1. See para 7.127 et seq. The reason may be that voluntary release damages are to be regarded as 'quasi-equitable': see *Lunn Poly Ltd v Liverpool & Lancashire Properties Ltd* [2006] EWCA Civ 430, [2006] 2 EGLR 29 (Neuberger LJ) and see para 7.74(ii).

[63] See the next paragraph.

neighbours of which he may have full knowledge, should be able to retain any part of the gain from his wrongful acts. To some extent the retention of such a gain can be avoided by an award of damages on a voluntary release basis, where the damages may be a proportion of the gain which may be made by the servient owner from his wrongful development, but of its nature in such a case the servient owner still benefits to a substantial extent, by retaining the remainder of his gain. A recent decision in which an order was issued for the removal of a newly constructed offending development, carried out despite the protest of a neighbour, is said to have caused some surprise at the time among practitioners.[64]

(d) *Public Interest*

A rights of light dispute, whatever remedy is sought, is a dispute in private law between private parties. Even so, it is undoubtedly the case that when it comes to the exercise of a discretion on whether to grant an injunction, the court should have regard to the public interest whenever that may be relevant. By the public interest is meant the interests of the public generally, or of particular members of the public, in particular actions or activities being permitted to be carried out or to remain undisturbed. It is hard to think of any circumstances in which the public interest arose yet could not, as a matter of law, be a relevant factor.[65] A somewhat more extreme view of the relevance of the public interest was expounded by Lord Sumption in *Lawrence v Fen Tigers Ltd*,[66] which was that damages are ordinarily an adequate remedy for nuisance and that an injunction should not usually be granted in a case where it is likely that conflicting interests are engaged other than the interests of the parties. He said that in particular it may well be that an injunction should as a matter of principle not be granted in a case where a use of land to which objection is taken requires and has received planning permission. These observations were not endorsed by other members of the Supreme Court,[67] and Lord Sumption recognised that all that he was doing was identifying matters which called for consideration in a case in which they arose. A view which once prevailed was that the public interest could only be relevant where the damages were minimal.[68] This suggestion is now to be regarded as incorrect.[69] 7.37

The public interest which is to be taken into account may have a number of aspects. Where a building which may constitute an infringement of a right of light is 7.38

[64] *HKRUK II (CPC) Ltd v Heaney* [2010] EWHC 2245 (Ch), [2010] 3 EGLR 15.

[65] *Lawrence v Fen Tigers Ltd* [2014] UKSC 13, [2014] AC 822 [121] (Lord Neuberger). An obvious aspect of public interest would be the defence of the realm, such as the need to operate military aircraft despite the nuisance which they might cause: *Dennis v Ministry of Defence* [2003] EWHC 793 (QB), [2003] 2 EGLR 121.

[66] ibid [161].

[67] ibid [168] (Lord Mance) and [127] (Lord Neuberger).

[68] See *Watson v Croft Promosport Ltd* [2009] EWCA Civ 15, [2009] 3 All ER 249.

[69] *Lawrence v Fen Tigers Ltd* [2014] UKSC 13, [2014] AC 822 [118] (Lord Neuberger) and [239] (Lord Carnwath).

concerned, one aspect of the public interest may be the use to which the building is to be put, and the need for property put to such a use in the public interest. Another aspect of the public interest, certainly if a building exists, is the continuation of employment for those who work within it. Even where the building is to be used for some purpose such as a form of public entertainment, the interests of those who seek and enjoy such entertainments may be of significance.

7.39 Public interest considerations will often militate against the issue of a mandatory injunction to remove a building which has been completed in breach of a right of light. In *Wrotham Park Estate Co Ltd v Parkside Homes Ltd*[70] an injunction was refused to demolish houses which had been erected in breach of a restrictive covenant, one reason being that it would have been an unpardonable waste of much needed houses to direct that they be pulled down. In deciding whether to order the demolition of a building, courts are aware of the potential advantage which such an injunction will offer to claimants, since it could deliver to the claimant the defendant 'bound hand and foot to be subjected to any extortionate demands the plaintiff might make.'[71] A court may suspend the operation of a mandatory injunction for a period to give the parties an opportunity to reach an agreement.[72]

(e) Planning Permission

7.40 An associated question is the relevance of the fact that planning permission has been granted for a particular development. The existence of a planning permission can be a relevant factor in favour of refusing an injunction and compensating the claimant in damages.[73] It is nonetheless necessary to be cautious on this point. The grant of a planning permission may indicate no more than that the local planning authority can see no objection in the public interest to the development being carried out, and does not necessarily mean that that authority has concluded that there is some particular public interest in the development. There is no principle that an applicant for planning permission has to demonstrate some particular public interest in favour of his development before he is granted planning permission. On the other hand, the circumstances of a grant of planning permission may show that the planning authority perceives there to be a considerable public interest in a development proceeding, and this situation may add weight to the assistance the court obtains from the grant of a permission.

[70] *Wrotham Park Estate Co Ltd v Parkside Homes Ltd* [1974] 1 WLR 198. This case was a seminal decision in the rise of the voluntary release method of assessing damages, as is explained in section (C) of this chapter.

[71] *Jaggard v Sawyer* [1995] 1 WLR 269, per Millett LJ at p288, adopting the very similar description of the situation used by the Lord Chancellor in *Isenberg v East India House Estate Co Ltd* (1863) 3 De G J & S 263.

[72] *Achilli v Tovell* [1927] 2 Ch 243.

[73] *Lawrence v Fen Tigers Ltd* per Lord Neuberger at para 122 and per Lord Clarke at para 169.

One of the matters taken into account by planning authorities in deciding whether to grant planning permission is the effect of the development proposed on the access of natural light to other properties in the vicinity of the development. If the planning authority has carefully evaluated this matter in deciding to grant planning permission, then the weight which a court will give to the grant is likely to increase. As against this, it should be understood that planning is concerned with the public interest and not with private interests and rights. Therefore the fact that there is a restrictive covenant or an easement which would prevent the implementation of a planning permission should not in itself justify the refusal of permission. If the development is in the public interest, or if there is no public interest which is adverse to the development, it is a matter for the developer how he overcomes private rights which might prevent it. If the local planning authority is sufficiently concerned at the public interest in a scheme of development for which it has granted planning permission, it can consider the wide powers available for the making of a compulsory purchase order under the Town and Country Planning Act 1990, or possibly the use of the procedure under section 237 of that Act.[74] In short, the existence of a planning permission is a matter to be taken into account by a court when it considers rights of light disputes and the availability of an injunction, but the weight to be accorded to the existence of a planning permission in the making of the decision on whether to grant an injunction is likely to vary from case to case, and in many cases the existence of a planning permission may be of little significance at all. This topic is considered further in Chapter 10, where the impact and relevance of town planning controls on rights of light and of the guidance given to planning authorities on the overshadowing of existing properties by new developments are examined more generally and in greater detail. 7.41

(f) Seriousness of Injury

A more important consideration is likely to be the extent and the seriousness of the reduction in light to the dominant building. It is sometimes thought that because the reduction in light, albeit constituting an actionable injury, is small, an injunction will necessarily not be granted. This is an incorrect view of the law.[75] While the fact that the injury is not serious will not in principle and in all cases preclude the grant of an injunction, it may nevertheless be a consideration which in any specific case will weigh heavily against the court exercising its power to grant an injunction.[76] On the other hand, the fact that the reduction in natural light to the dominant building is large may certainly be a potent factor in leading the court 7.42

[74] See ch 8, section (C)2, for s 237 of the Town and Country Planning Act 1990 and for the circumstances in which a compulsory acquisition of land may override easements such as rights of light.

[75] It is described in para 4.2 of the Law Commission *Report on Rights of Light* (Law Com No 356, 2014) as 'a misconception'.

[76] *Price v Hilditch* [1930] 1 Ch 500 in which a mandatory injunction was refused when a room affected, a scullery, could continue to be used without great inconvenience after the obstruction.

to issue an injunction. It has been said in the context of a nuisance arising from noise that particular attention should be paid to the right of a person to enjoy his home without disturbance, and it may be by close analogy that the right of persons to rest and relaxation in their home with a sufficiency of natural light where an easement of light exists in favour of the home is a consideration which should weigh heavily in favour of the grant of an injunction to prevent a violation of the easement of light, certainly where the home owner acts promptly to protect the right in question.[77]

(g) Number of Persons Adversely Affected

7.43 A corollary of the significance as a consideration of the public interest, and of the number of persons who might be affected if a particular building was prevented from being erected or had to be removed, is the importance which should be attached to the number of persons whose light will be affected by an offending development. Each person with an interest in a building which has appurtenant to it a right of light is often entitled to assert or not to assert the easement as that person wishes. Where different people have separate properties all of which have easements of light and all of which are affected by a proposed nearby development, some may seek to prevent the development and some may not. If a number of people are affected and join together in a concerted action to prevent a development which will affect the access of light to all of their properties, then the court is likely to be influenced by that fact in favour of the grant of an injunction. A situation may arise in which one person brings proceedings and seeks an injunction even though there are a number of others whose rights will be affected by a particular development but have not themselves chosen to assert their right at any rate by legal proceedings. It seems that the fact that other neighbours in addition to a claimant may be badly affected by a nuisance is to be regarded as a factor in favour of granting an injunction even though those other persons have not initiated or joined in proceedings.[78]

7.44 Another situation which may occur is one in which a proposed development will infringe the rights of light of a number of people in the vicinity, and most of them are willing to come to an agreement with the developer to release their right to the extent needed to permit the development to go ahead, but in return for payment of a sum of money. The question which then arises is whether one particular person who has an interest in a dominant building but is not willing to come to an agreement should nonetheless be entitled to an injunction. One view could be that such a person is being unreasonable and recalcitrant in not coming to an arrangement of a nature acceptable to his neighbours. On the other hand an

[77] *Lawrence v Fen Tigers Ltd* [2014] UKSC 13, [2014] AC 822 [168] (Lord Mance) and [247] (Lord Carnwath). In *Isenberg v East India House Estate Co Ltd* (1863) 3 De G J & S 263 reference was made by the court to the importance of protecting the rights of light of an ancient mansion or family seat.

[78] *Lawrence v Fen Tigers Ltd* [124] (Lord Neuberger).

opposing view, and a view of substantial force, is that each person is entitled to assert his own individual right as he wishes, and that each person's opportunity to obtain an injunction at the discretion of the court should not be affected by reason of the fact that other people are willing to bargain away their rights in return for money. Many courts may feel inclined towards the second view. A further question which may arise when a number of persons assert their rights of light and damages are awarded on a voluntary release basis, is how the damages are to be divided between the various claimants. This question is considered below.[79]

(h) *Light as a Special Case*

7.45 There are indications in *Lawrence* that the general principles which apply to the grant of an injunction in other nuisance cases and other circumstances may not necessarily be applicable to infringements of rights of light.[80] The very general guiding principle, that a person who has his property rights violated is prima facie entitled to an injunction, but that when the issue arises the court should have no prior inclination either way, appears to be as applicable to rights of light cases as to other cases. It is difficult to see why factors which apply generally to the grant of an injunction in any particular dispute, such as the effect of delay by a claimant, or unmeritorious conduct in relation to the dispute on the part of a claimant, should have a different impact in principle in rights of light claims as compared to any other claims. One major feature of rights of light claims which may in individual cases affect the decision on whether an injunction should be granted is the existence of a building or extension to a building or other obstruction at the date when the matter comes before a court. A court will often be more ready to order the cessation of some activity which causes a noise or other nuisance, than to order the demolition of a newly erected structure. In cases of noise and similar nuisances an injunction can be a more flexible instrument than it is in rights of light disputes, since it can impose limits on an offending activity rather than preventing it altogether.[81] Matters such as the benefit to the public of a particular activity to be carried out, whether it is the creation of a commercial leisure activity or the creation of an extension to an office or other commercial building, seem in principle to be the same as possible relevant considerations in a decision on whether to grant a discretionary remedy whatever the subject matter of the dispute. Considerations such as the particular regard which is paid to the protection of a person's home, whether it is threatened by excessive noise from some activity or by an unacceptable reduction in natural light to it, also seem in principle to be the same whatever the type of nuisance threatened.

[79] See para 7.142 et seq.

[80] *Lawrence v Fen Tigers Ltd* [2014] UKSC 13, [2014] AC 822 [168] (Lord Mance). However, Lord Neuberger said at para 122 that he did not see rights of light cases as involving special rules.

[81] ibid [167] (Lord Carnwath).

(i) Other Considerations

7.46 The considerations explored in the preceding paragraphs are, of course, no more than illustrative of the type of factors which arise in a number of cases. There will inevitably be other individual factors, often concerning the conduct of the parties, which arise in particular cases and which should be taken into account. The need for a claimant seeking an injunction to come to the court with clean hands has already been explained.[82] The conduct of a defendant is also relevant.

7.47 Various aspects of the conduct of a defendant may increase or decrease the prospect of an injunction being granted against him. In one case the defendant continued to erect a building which obstructed a right of way even though a judgment had been given against him establishing that the right of way existed. A mandatory injunction was issued requiring the removal of the obstruction.[83] The same considerations might apply to a continued erection of an obstruction to a right of light. The fact that a defendant continues with a building in spite of protests that it will affect his neighbour's right of light and despite advice from his own expert that this would be so may encourage a court to order that what has been done is removed.[84] No court wishes to be presented with a fait accompli. On the other hand, there are instances in which even an acceleration by a defendant of works after a warning to him but before the commencement of the proceedings did not lead to a mandatory injunction to remove what had been done.[85]

7.48 The law is less clear on the relevance of the fact that a servient owner has received advice from surveyors or lawyers that his building will not infringe the rights of light of other persons. It seems hard that a dominant owner should be prejudiced in pursuing an injunction to remove an unlawful obstruction by the fact that the servient owner has received incorrect advice. The fact that the advice is incorrect seems to be a matter for the servient owner alone.[86] If the advice received has been negligent, the servient owner is likely to have a cause of action for damages for professional negligence against the adviser. On the other hand the fact that the servient owner has at least sought and received the advice of experts, albeit advice which in the end turns out to be incorrect, shows that he has behaved to some extent responsibly and may assist him in resisting a mandatory injunction.[87]

[82] See para 7.35.

[83] *Krebl v Burrell* (1879) 11 Ch D 146.

[84] *Pugh v Howells* (1984) 48 P & CR 298.

[85] *Isenberg v East India House Estate Co Ltd* (1863) 3 De G J & S 263; *Kilbey v Haviland* (1871) 24 LT 353; *Sharp v Harrison* [1922] 1 Ch 502.

[86] *Regan v Paul Properties DDF No 1 Ltd* [2006] EWCA Civ 1319, [2007] Ch 135.

[87] This was a view taken in *Snell & Prideaux Ltd v Dutton Mirrors Ltd* [1995] 1 EGLR 259 and in *Tamares Ltd v Fairpoint Properties Ltd* [2006] EWHC 3589 (Ch), [2007] 1 WLR 2148.

(j) Law Commission Recommendation

The Law Commission has recommended a new statutory test to guide the decision of a court on whether to issue an injunction or award damages.[88] The recommendation was reached after a Consultation Paper and the receipt of responses.[89] Account was taken of the decision of the Supreme Court in *Lawrence*. The recommendation is that a court must not grant an injunction to restrain the infringement of a right of light if doing so would be a disproportionate means of enforcing the dominant owner's right of light. It is recommended that in reaching its decision the court should take into account all of the circumstances, including: 7.49

(a) the claimant's interest in the dominant land;
(b) the loss of amenity attributable to the infringement (taking into account the extent to which artificial light is relied upon);
(c) whether damages would be adequate compensation;
(d) the conduct of the claimant;
(e) whether the claimant delayed unnecessarily in claiming an injunction;
(f) the conduct of the defendant;
(g) the impact of an injunction on the defendant; and
(h) the public interest.

This recommendation abandons the prima facie position that an injunction should be granted with its corollary that the burden is on the defendant to show that the injunction should not in the particular circumstances of the case be granted.[90]

Proportionality is a concept much discussed in public and administrative law and may have its origin in continental European jurisprudence (the doctrine is Prussian in origin). In this field its essence is that any interference by governmental bodies with the rights of citizens in the public interest should be confined to that which is strictly necessary to protect or achieve a particular public interest or desired result.[91] The Law Commission described proportionality as a powerful and pervasive idea: 'not that one consideration should outweigh another if it is simply greater; rather, it is that one consideration should outweigh another only if it is so *much* greater that it is right for it to outweigh the other.'[92] It seems that this particular test is intended to apply specifically and solely to infringements of rights of light rather than to infringements of easements generally or to nuisances generally or to breaches of other property rights such as breaches of restrictive covenants. It seems uncertain why this particular guidance is required 7.50

[88] Law Commission, *Rights of Light* (Law Com No 356, 2014), para 4.116.
[89] Law Commission Consultation Paper No 210 (2013).
[90] See para 7.20.
[91] See *Wade and Forsyth on Administrative Law*, 10th edn (Oxford, Oxford University Press, 2009) 305 et seq. The doctrine is applied by the European Court of Human Rights in Strasbourg and by the European Court of Justice in Luxembourg.
[92] Law Commission, *Rights of Light* (Law Com No 356, 2014), para 4.22. The recommendations of the Commission, including this recommendation, are explained and discussed more generally in ch 12.

solely in rights of light disputes, and the various specified circumstances appear to be factors which under the existing law and practice a court would in any event be likely to take into account where relevant. The Law Commission seems to have paid close regard to the protests of developers and commercial property owners at having their wrongs redressed by injunctions; for instance, Transport for London, which controls major sites available for development partly as a result of above-ground works associated with the Crossrail scheme, represented that injunctions in rights of light cases should only be considered in the severest of cases.[93]

5. Real Threat of Injury

7.51 The type of injunction which restrains an injury which is anticipated but has not yet taken place is called a *quia timet* injunction.[94] Before a court will grant an injunction in these circumstances there must be a real and immediate prospect of an injury. Thus the dominant owner seeking such an injunction must show that something is to be done imminently on the servient land which, if it is allowed to be carried out, will or may infringe his right of light. It is not enough that there is merely some apprehension that some indefinite scheme may be carried out at some time in the future.[95] An illustration of that principle is a case in which an injunction was refused when the defendant had stated that he did not currently intend to carry out the works complained of, and that if he formed such an intention in the future he would give to the plaintiff two months' notice of his proposal.[96] The rigour of this rule is tempered by three considerations. First, a dominant owner may in an appropriate case seek a declaration that he has the benefit of an easement of light, so that at least that issue is resolved.[97] Secondly, and as a corollary of the rule, if it is known that some development is to commence on the servient land at an early date but it is uncertain as to whether it will constitute an actionable injury against the dominant owner, either because the existence of an easement of light is in issue or because it is not accepted that the reduction in light caused by the proposed development will constitute an actionable injury, the dominant owner can seek an interim injunction which, if granted, will prevent the commencement or continuation of the development on the servient land until it is determined by a court whether that development will constitute an actionable

[93] ibid para 4.45.

[94] Literally 'because he fears'.

[95] *Crowder v Tinkler* (1816) 19 Ves JR 617; *Celsteel Ltd v Alton House Holdings Ltd* [1986] 1 WLR 512; *CIP Property (AIPT) Ltd v Transport for London* [2012] EWHC 259 (Ch), [2012] BLR 202; *CGIS City Plaza Shares Ltd v Britel Fund Trustees Ltd* [2012] EWHC 1594 (Ch).

[96] *Lord Cowley v Byass* (1877) 5 Ch 944.

[97] See para 7.4. An owner of land contemplating a development of it may in an appropriate case seek a declaration either that there is no easement of light appurtenant to some specific neighbouring property which binds his land or that, if there is such an easement of light, the proposed development would not infringe that easement. See n 6.

wrong. It is therefore necessary to consider next the valuable remedy of an interim injunction. Thirdly, a declaration of a person's rights may be obtained if there is a real dispute between the parties even though no wrong has been committed or is threatened.[98] An instance of this situation might be that a person wishing to sell his land might reasonably wish to establish whether a right of light existed over his land for the benefit of adjoining land since the answer would affect the price obtainable for the land to be sold.

6. Interim Injunctions

(a) The Nature and Purpose of Interim Injunctions

The power of a court to issue an interim injunction is an important procedural tool in rights of light disputes.[99] The purpose of an interim injunction is to preserve the status quo until the rights of the parties and an appropriate remedy can be established at a full trial. The importance of an interim injunction is in circumstances where a servient owner proposes to carry out a development on his land, asserting that the dominant owner has no easement of light or that the development would not infringe any easement of light or that an injunction to prevent the development would not be an appropriate remedy, and is unwilling to delay the carrying out of the development until these matters can be resolved by the court at a full trial. In the days of Lord Eldon (1751–1838) there were great delays in obtaining a final judgment from a court,[100] but even today it can take a considerable time to obtain a final judgment in a case involving significant issues of law, and the need for expert evidence such as may arise in rights of light disputes, save in cases of great urgency.[101] If the case could have been heard and determined at once, the dominant owner might obtain a permanent injunction to prevent the development. Yet if the development has been completed by the date in which a final judgment is obtained from the court a court might be reluctant to issue a mandatory injunction requiring the demolition of a recently constructed building. It follows that without the availability of an interim injunction, a defendant might be able to some extent to ride roughshod over the true rights of a claimant. 7.52

Faced with circumstances of this nature, a dominant owner as the claimant may apply to the court for an interim injunction. An application for an interim injunction should be made with three clear days' notice given to the other party.[102] An application can be made ex parte, that is not on notice, in a case of sufficient 7.53

[98] *Pavledes v Hadjisawa* [2013] EWHC 124 (Ch), [2013] 2 EGLR 123.

[99] For the power to issue an interim injunction see CPR, Pt 25.1(1)(a).

[100] See the fictional case of *Jarndyce v Jarndyce* in Dickens's *Bleak House*.

[101] Such disputed cases may take a year or even longer between the commencement of the action and a final judgment at trial.

[102] CPR, Pt 23.7(1)(b).

urgency but such a situation is most unlikely to arise in rights of light disputes. If an interim injunction is granted its effect is that it prevents the servient owner as defendant from commencing or further carrying out the proposed development until there has been a full trial and final judgment on the claim. The content of the interim injunction may be tempered to fit the facts of the case. If it is common ground that a development on the servient land can lawfully be carried out up to, say, six storeys in height but that a higher development might infringe the rights of light of the claimant, then an interim injunction might prevent any development above six storeys. A mandatory, as opposed to a prohibitory, interim injunction may be ordered in an appropriate case although where such an interim injunction is sought it may be more difficult to show that the balance of convenience requires some interim action such as the removal of a building.[103] It is hard to envisage many circumstances in which a court would issue an interim order for the removal of a building on the ground that it might constitute a breach of a right of light.[104] Even if a claimant fails at trial to establish his rights or to obtain an injunction it is possible that he can then obtain an interim injunction to preserve the position pending an appeal by him.[105] Either the court of first instance or the Court of Appeal may grant an interim injunction in these circumstances. An appeal requires the permission to appeal of the Court of first instance or of the Court of Appeal, and permission will not be granted unless the court considers that the appeal has a reasonable prospect of success or that there is some other reason why permission should be granted. There is a possible further appeal to the Supreme Court, but this also requires permission which in practice is not readily granted.

(b) Undertakings as to Damages

7.54 If in the circumstances just described a court issues an interim injunction, then if matters stopped at that point there could be a potential injustice to a defendant. A defendant might be prevented from commencing or carrying on with his development for a substantial period until there was a final determination of the rights of the parties at a trial, only to find that at trial the claimant failed to make out his case. On this hypothesis the defendant would have suffered what may be a considerable financial burden in perhaps a year of delay to his project, with no recompense. Because of these considerations it has become the general, indeed the almost invariable, practice of a court which issues an interim injunction in favour of a claimant to require that claimant to give what is called an undertaking as to

[103] *Commercial Bank Jamaica Corporation v Olint Corporation* [2009] UKPC 16, [2009] 1 WLR 1405; *Films Rover Ltd v Cannon Film Sales Ltd* [1987] 1 WLR 670.

[104] An instance where something of this nature occurred in a right of light case is *Daniel v Ferguson* [1891] 2 Ch 27, in which a person proposed to build a wall which would infringe his neighbour's right of light. He took steps to complete the wall quickly when he had notice that an interim injunction was sought against him. An injunction was granted to remove the wall.

[105] *Erinford Properties Ltd v Cheshire County Council* [1974] Ch 261.

damages. What that means is that the claimant has to undertake that he will pay to the defendant such damages as the court may order and determine if in the end the claimant fails to establish the whole or a part of his claim. The damages which may be ordered to be paid to the defendant are likely to be compensation to him for the delay in carrying out his project during the period of the operation of the interim injunction.

Whereas an undertaking as to damages is nearly always required, the court still has a discretion when it has finally determined the issues between the parties on whether to order payment of compensation to the defendant pursuant to the undertaking, and as to what matters that compensation should cover. There could be cases in which a defendant, even though he succeeds in the litigation, has concealed matters or behaved otherwise unmeritoriously in which the court might think it proper not to require a sum to be paid by the claimant under the undertaking. The amount to be paid by the person who has given the undertaking and then fails in the action will normally be assessed by the application of the general rules which govern the assessment of damages for a breach of contract, such as the rules relating to causation, remoteness and the duty to mitigate.[106] However, a degree of latitude is permissible and, for example, in an appropriate case compensation may be awarded for mental distress caused to a defendant by reason of an interim order against him, despite the general rule that damages for mental distress are not recoverable for a breach of contract.[107] The undertaking is therefore not in absolute terms to pay any loss occasioned to the defendant but only to pay loss if so ordered by the court, and to the extent ordered by the court. If a claimant is willing to give an undertaking in acceptable terms, then a defendant may himself give an undertaking not to proceed with what may be the offending development (the undertakings are often then called cross-undertakings). If this is done, the enforcement by the defendant of the cross-undertaking by the claimant will proceed in the usual way. If the Crown brings proceedings to enforce its proprietary rights it may be required to give an undertaking in the ordinary way, but this is in contrast to a case where the Crown seeks to enforce duties under general public statutes, in which case no such undertaking is normally required.[108] 7.55

The law and practice as just described may present problems for a dominant owner claiming an injunction. His dilemma may be as follows. If he seeks and obtains an interim injunction but at trial fails to make out his case, he is at substantial risk of having to compensate the defendant under the undertaking as to damages. On the other hand, if the claimant elects not to seek an interim injunction and the offending development goes ahead even if the claimant makes out his case at trial then, as previously stated, a court may be reluctant to order a new building to be 7.56

[106] *Hoffmann-la-Roche & Co AG v Secretary of State for Trade and Industry* [1975] AC 295, 361 (Lord Diplock).

[107] *Abbey Forwarding Ltd v Hone* [2012] EWHC 3525 (Ch), [2013] 2 WLR 1386.

[108] *Hoffmann-La-Roche & Co AG v Secretary of State for Trade and Industry* [1975] AC 295; *Attorney General v Wright* [1989] 1 WLR 164.

demolished, so that the claimant is at risk of losing his primary remedy, which is a permanent injunction. This will not necessarily occur, and providing that he has protested at what is to go on or is going on, and providing he has proceeded as quickly as he can to assert his claim to a permanent injunction, a claimant in an appropriate case may still obtain a permanent injunction, notwithstanding his failure to apply for an interim injunction.[109] The decision on whether to apply for an interim injunction may therefore be a delicate one for a claimant, and may depend upon how strong he believes his case is and how strong he believes are the prospects of ultimate success, as well as the importance to the claimant of obtaining a permanent injunction. Of course, even if a claimant does not seek an interim injunction and does not obtain a permanent injunction, provided he proves a breach of his rights, he will still have his remedy in damages.

7.57 An undertaking in damages is only of real value to a defendant if he can be confident that in the event of the claimant being called upon to honour and pay a sum under his undertaking, the claimant will have sufficient means to do so. A claimant seeking an interim injunction should therefore provide evidence of his means to meet the obligations under an undertaking as to damages in order to show that the defendant can have reasonable confidence that the undertaking will be honoured at the time of trial, even if the claimant fails and even if the claimant as a result of his failure has to bear his own costs and pay the defendant's costs. In a suitable case a court might make it a condition of ordering an interim injunction that the claimant gave some form of security, such as a bank guarantee or a charge on property, so as to ensure that there will be funds available to meet the claimant's undertaking as to damages if it is called upon. A defendant who wishes to resist an interim injunction might adduce evidence of the likely loss or expense to him if his development process is unjustifiably delayed. There may be ways in which a court can obviate the grant of, or even the need for, an interim injunction in rights of light disputes. If the dispute depends upon, to give an example, the correct meaning of a provision in a deed that question can be ordered to be tried quickly and as a preliminary matter so that if the claimant fails on that matter his case as a whole may fail and there will be no need for an interim injunction. The converse case is where a trial will involve substantial questions requiring expert evidence so that no quick or summary decision can be made.

7.58 An undertaking as to damages is an undertaking given to the court, and this emphasises the rule that the court has a discretion whether or not to enforce the undertaking and to what extent to enforce it.[110] If the claimant wholly succeeds at the full trial and obtains a permanent injunction, then of course no question of

[109] See *HKRUK II (CPC) Ltd v Heaney* [2010] EWHC 2245 (Ch), [2010] 3 EGLR 15. While the failure of a claimant to seek an interim injunction does not in principle prevent him from obtaining a permanent injunction it may be an adverse factor to be taken into account against him even if he establishes an injury against him when it comes to how the court is to exercise its discretion on whether to issue a permanent injunction or to confine a successful claimant to a remedy in damages.

[110] *Cheltenham & Gloucester Building Society v Ricketts* [1993] 1 WLR 1545.

enforcing the undertaking arises. If the claimant wholly or partly fails at the full trial, for example in a rights of light case he fails to establish any wrong towards him, or establishes a wrong but fails to obtain an injunction as the appropriate form of remedy, the exercise of the discretion by the court is governed by certain principles.

(a) The general principle is that unless the claimant succeeds in obtaining a permanent injunction, his undertaking as to damages will be enforced against him unless there are special circumstances which lead to a different conclusion.[111] In such circumstances whatever the reasons for the claimant's failure, the defendant has been prevented for a period from doing that which a court is in the end unwilling to prevent him doing, and he will normally be entitled to compensation for any delay or other loss caused to him.
(b) The special circumstances which justify the undertaking not being enforced may be generally inequitable conduct by the defendant, or some more specific matter such as delay by him in seeking to enforce the undertaking.[112]
(c) The fact that the claimant has established liability, for example a breach of his right of light, even though he is refused an injunction, is unlikely by itself to prevent his undertaking as to damages being enforced, but it may be a relevant factor when combined with other matters such as poor conduct by a defendant which in the end prevents the defendant from obtaining the benefit of the undertaking.[113]

(c) Exercise of the Discretion

Assuming that the claimant seeks an interim injunction and is willing to offer an undertaking as to damages, the question of cardinal importance will be how and on what principles a court is to exercise its discretion on whether to issue an interim injunction. General guidance on this question was given by the House of Lords in *American Cyanamid Co v Ethicon Ltd.*[114] As with most questions of the exercise of a discretion, the principles stated are guidance only, not rules of law such as might be found in a statute, and a court must always in the final analysis seek to do justice in the light of conflicting considerations and special facts in any particular case before it.[115] 7.59

[111] ibid.
[112] *Smith v Day* (1883) 21 Ch D 421; *Ex parte Hall* (1883) 23 Ch D 644; *Modern Transport Co Ltd v Duneric Steamship Co* [1917] 1 KB 370; *Regan v Paul Properties DPF No 1 Ltd* [2006] EWHC 1591 (Ch), [2007] Ch 135.
[113] *Lunn Poly Ltd v Liverpool and Lancashire Properties Ltd* [2006] EWCA Civ 430, [2006] 2 EGLR 29; *Regan v Paul Properties DPF No 1 Ltd* [2006] EWHC 2052 (Ch).
[114] *American Cyanamid Co v Ethicon Ltd* [1974] AC 396.
[115] *R v Secretary of State for Transport, ex parte Factortame* [1991] 1 AC 603, 671.

7.60 Two preliminary matters can be stated.

(i) A claimant seeking an interim injunction must show at least that he has a real possibility of success in the proceedings. Therefore in a claim relating to rights of light the claimant must show, so far as it is disputed, that he has a real possibility of succeeding in showing that he has the benefit of an easement of light and that the works to be carried out on the servient land are such that there is a real possibility that they will constitute an infringement of his rights.

(ii) In the context of a claim relating to rights of light, the claimant must also show that there is at least a real possibility that the appropriate remedy for any violation of his rights will be an injunction and not merely damages. If it occurred that the claimant had not either protested against what was being done on the servient land with full knowledge of it or had sought no remedy against it at a reasonably early stage then a court might conclude that, even if he succeeded in establishing that the completed development would be an infringement of his rights when the matter came to trial, he would still be most unlikely to be granted an injunction to remove the development or to prevent its completion and in those circumstances a court might conclude that as there was no real possibility of a permanent injunction being granted it would be purposeless and inappropriate to issue an interim injunction.

7.61 If a claimant can establish that he has a real possibility of showing that the proposed development on the servient land would be an actionable injury against him, and that he also has a real possibility of obtaining a permanent injunction to prevent that development being carried out, it is still necessary for the court to consider what is usually called the balance of convenience. Convenience is a curious word to be used in this context, and the function of the court in striking any balance between the competing needs and aspirations of the parties will not be to arrive at a result which is convenient so much as to arrive at a result which does justice as best it can be done in what are *ex hypothesi* uncertain circumstances with an uncertain outcome. It has been said that in deciding whether to issue an interim injunction and on what terms a court should take whichever course seems likely to cause the least irremediable prejudice to one party or the other.[116]

7.62 It is likely that a claimant who can show (a) that he has a real possibility of establishing that the proposed development on the servient land will constitute an infringement of his rights of light, (b) that he also has a real possibility of obtaining a permanent injunction to prevent that infringement to his rights, (c) that he has acted reasonably promptly and that there are no other special circumstances concerning his conduct which should be held against him, and (d) that he offers an undertaking as to damages which he could meet if the case went against him,

[116] *National Commercial Bank Jamaica v Olint Corporation* [2009] UKPC 16, [2009] 1 WLR 1405, 1409 (Lord Hoffmann).

will obtain an interim injunction. It would generally be unjust in these circumstances that a claimant should not obtain an interim order. The defendant can suffer no substantial loss if the claimant fails at trial since the defendant will then obtain compensation for any loss to him under the terms of the undertaking as to damages.

The most difficult situation when an interim injunction is sought is one in which a claimant can establish all the matters just mentioned save the last one, since his financial position is such that he is not able to show that his undertaking as to damages will necessarily compensate a defendant for every loss which that defendant may suffer if in the end the claimant does not establish his right. The significance of this in rights of light cases is that defendants often wish to carry out major developments and have all the resources of large property owners and developers. The amount of loss which they will suffer if they are unjustifiably prevented from carrying out a development, or a part of a development, for a period which may be a year or more if an interim injunction is granted may be great. The financial penalties for a developer in halting a development where he has a contract with a building contractor may be high. In addition there is the risk to the developer that if the development is delayed for a year, rents and property values may have fallen so that the development that he sells on at the end of his project will be substantially less valuable. These sums can in some cases be measured in many millions of pounds. It is very difficult for a dominant owner of moderate means to offer an effective undertaking which would compensate a developer for these losses. Thus the court may be in a situation in which it realises that the developer may never be fully compensated if the case goes in his favour when finally determined. In practice claimants in this situation may not offer an undertaking as to damages the result of which could be to deprive them of the whole of their property, their assets, their homes, and their livelihood. However if this situation arises the court must consider the balance of convenience or justice. In such a case, as in other circumstances, the court may look to the consideration that in general there is much to be said for the status quo being preserved for a limited period.[117] 7.63

In general, in regard to interim injunctions the relative strength of the cases of the parties is not a central consideration, since all that the applicant for an interim injunction has to show is that he has a real possibility of success, and that is different from showing that his case is very strong or very much stronger than that of the defendant. Nonetheless, in the difficult balance which emerges in the sort of situation discussed in the previous paragraph, the relative strengths of the cases of the parties, so far as that can be ascertained by the court at the stage at which it grants or does not grant an interim injunction, could play a part.[118] 7.64

[117] *American Cyanamid Co v Ethicon Ltd* [1974] AC 396, 408 (Lord Diplock). See *Century Projects Ltd v Almacantar (Centre Point) Ltd* [2014] EWHC 394 (Ch) for a recent decision in which an interim injunction was refused because there was a real risk that if it failed at the trial, the claimant would not be able fully to fulfil its undertaking as to damages.

[118] *National Commercial Bank Jamaica v Olint Corporation* [2009] UKPC 16, [2009] 1 WLR 1405.

(C) DAMAGES

1. Introduction

7.65 If proceedings are brought to enforce an easement of light and either an injunction is not sought or is refused by the court, the only remedy available from the court is an award of damages. Damages are, of course, a frequent remedy for breaches of contract and for the commission of a tort or other civil wrong, and a large corpus of learning and decided authorities has been built up on the principles which apply to the assessment of damages.[119] The infringement of an easement of light is the commission of the tort of nuisance, and general rules as to assessing damages apply to the assessment of damages for this wrong.

7.66 The overall purpose of damages has traditionally been said to be to order the payment to a person who has suffered an injury to his rights of a sum which will, so far as money can do so, put that person in the position in which he would have been if the injury had not been committed.[120] In some cases such as severe physical injuries money can never be adequate compensation and the law must simply do the best it can. In other cases where the loss is monetary or a reduction in the value of an asset, including a property asset, an award of damages can be calculated in a fashion which corresponds much more closely to the true loss suffered by an injured party. Awards of damages for an infringement of a right of light fall within the latter type of assessment.

7.67 This statement of the purpose of damages leads to the often-stated proposition that damages are compensatory in nature. Damages are designed to compensate a claimant for the loss he has suffered, not to punish a wrongdoer for what he has done. A person who is crippled by a road accident will obtain the same damages if the defendant has acted in a way which was unfortunate although negligent as he would if the defendant had driven recklessly while drunk. If a person sells goods for £100 and fails to deliver them because he has found a different buyer who offers £120, it is said that the purchaser will obtain no damages if he could have purchased alternative goods for £100.[121] The profit made by the contract breaker is considered not to be relevant, since it does not create or involve a loss to the injured party. While this strict interpretation of the compensatory principle is at the root of the assessment of damages, its operation in the case of an infringement

[119] A full account of the assessment of damages is found in *MacGregor on Damages*, 19th edn (London, Sweet & Maxwell, 2014) and in Burrows, *Remedies for Torts and Breach of Contract*, 3rd edn (Oxford, Oxford University Press, 2004).

[120] *Robinson v Harman* (1848) 1 Ex 850, 855; *Livingstone v Rawyards Coal Co* (1880) 5 App Cas 25. This principle may be elementary law, but it is significant in connection with the award of 'voluntary release' damages in rights of light claims as is discussed subsequently in this chapter: see, eg para 7.127.

[121] The law may be different where the subject matter of the sale is an interest in land, probably because a specifically enforceable contract for the sale of land creates a trust between the contractual vendor and the contractual purchaser. See para 7.77.

of rights of light and of other proprietary rights is now less clear than might on an initial impression be supposed.[122] Even so, the root principle remains valid and, save in the exceptional instances of restitutionary and exemplary damages, both of which are most unlikely to have a part in rights of light cases, an award of damages is firmly compensatory. The real question, as will be examined later in this section of this chapter, is not whether damages for a violation of a right of light are compensation for a loss, but rather what exactly is the loss to be compensated.

There are certain other important principles which apply to the assessment of damages generally and which could be significant in claims for damages relating to easements of light. One such principle is that of mitigation. A person who suffers an actionable injury of any sort must take all reasonable steps to reduce or mitigate his loss. If he fails to do so, he will not recover damages for any element of loss which he could have avoided by taking proper steps in mitigation. A corollary of this rule is that the injured party will be able to recover the costs incurred by him in taking reasonable steps in mitigation. The mitigation principle could come into play in rights of light cases. If a claimant whose light has been reduced could mitigate his loss by some minor change which he could readily carry out, for example by cutting back some bushes on his property or by making minor physical changes which would not harm his property, he might fail to recover damages for any component of his loss which could have been avoided by such measures. 7.68

A further general aspect of the law of damages in tort is remoteness of damage. In very general terms, damages will not be recoverable for a loss which is of a type which could not have been reasonably foreseen by the wrongdoer at the date of the commission of the tort.[123] The damages normally awarded for an infringement of a right of light are either for a reduction in the value of the dominant building or for a loss by the dominant owner of the opportunity to negotiate a payment for the voluntary release of his rights. Neither of these two types of loss could be categorised as too remote. There could occur some other or particular loss suffered by a dominant owner, such as the loss of a potential advantageous opportunity to sell his land due to a threatened reduction in light, and in such cases the ordinary rules on remoteness of damage might have to be applied in order to decide whether damages were recoverable for the item of loss.[124] Care must always be taken to ensure that there is no double counting in the assessment of damages by any means. Thus if damages were awarded as the reduction in the capital value of 7.69

[122] This question is discussed at para 7.124 et seq.

[123] *Overseas Tankship (UK) Ltd v Morts Dock and Engineering Co. (The Wagon Mound)* [1961] AC 388. This very general statement of principle has led to a body of further law which qualifies and elaborates the general principle: see *McGregor on Damages*, 19th edn (London, Sweet & Maxwell, 2014).

[124] Damages for the loss of an opportunity to sell a house because of the obstruction of an easement of way were awarded in *Owers v Bailey* [2007] 1 P & CR DG 17. Damages for a loss of the prospect of selling a property as a result of a nuisance to it were contemplated as acceptable in *Battishill v Reed* (1856) 18 CB 696, 715–16 (Cresswell J).

the dominant building due to a loss of light, it would be wrong to award a further sum for loss of amenity since that would be to award compensation twice for the same thing.[125]

2. Common Law and Equitable Damages

(a) The Distinction in Theory

7.70 Many people concerned with rights of light and the assertion of those rights may be uncertain as to the distinction between common law damages and equitable damages, and what is the practical significance of any distinction. The answer is historical. Common law damages were developed by the medieval common law courts as the primary remedy to redress a wrong. The Chancery courts, administering a system of equity, could make specific orders such as an injunction to prevent or redress a wrong but could not award damages for the wrong. The Chancery Amendment Act 1858 gave power to Chancery courts to award damages in addition to or in place of a specific order such as an injunction, and the damages awarded pursuant to this jurisdiction became known as equitable damages. Following the Judicature Acts of 1873 and 1875, and today under section 50 of the Senior Courts Act 1981, all Divisions of the High Court have power to award any remedy and so may award both kinds of damages.[126] Rights of light proceedings are sometimes brought in the county court, and this court also has power to award both kinds of damages.

7.71 Two characteristics which differentiate common law damages and equitable damages need to be mentioned. First, common law damages were available as compensation for a wrong committed in the past but not for future anticipated wrongs. If there had been an infringement of the right of light of a dominant owner by an obstruction on the servient land the dominant owner could obtain damages at common law for the effect of the obstruction up to the date of the award of damages by the courts. He could not obtain damages for the effect of the future loss which would arise if the obstruction remained in place as a continuing injury.[127]

[125] *Raymond v Young* [2015] EWCA Civ 456. The point of course is that the loss of amenity was something which itself caused or contributed to the reduction in the value of the property.

[126] See paras 7.11–7.13 for a fuller explanation of the development of law and equity as relevant to remedies for rights of light matters. The Chancery Amendment Act 1858 referred in s 2 to damages 'in lieu' of an injunction, and this expression is retained in much legal writing.

[127] *Battishill v Reed* (1856) 18 CB 696, 714 in which Jervis CJ observed: 'Every day that the Defendant continues the nuisance, he renders himself liable to another action' (claim for damages by an owner for the erection of eaves and a gutter over his property). The claimant was not entitled to damages for the reduction in the value of his property since the loss would have been caused by the effect of subsequent nuisance. The law on this matter was explained by Lord Nicholls in *Attorney General v Blake* [2001] 1 AC 268, 281. See also *Jaggard v Sawyer* [1995] 1 WLR 269, 276 where Sir Thomas Bingham MR said that historically, common law damages afforded retrospective compensation for past wrongs.

A new cause of action arose each day that the nuisance caused by the obstruction remained so that the dominant owner could bring subsequent claims for damages subject only to the operation of statutory limitation periods.[128] It is important to be clear that common law damages were and are available for the future effect of a wrong already committed, but not for the effect of an anticipated future wrong. Thus if a claimant is personally injured by the negligent actions of a defendant, the claimant may be awarded common law damages for the future effect of the wrong already committed, such as a continuing physical disability or a continuing loss of the capacity to earn. The inhibition of common law is as to the award of damages for a wrong not yet committed. Since a nuisance, such as a noise nuisance or an obstruction to light, is a continuing wrong, which is committed each day that the offending acts are committed or the offending obstruction remains in place, common law damages are confined to the effect of the wrong or wrongs as committed up to the date of the award of damages by the court. A continuing trespass is treated in the same way.

The second differentiating characteristic between common law and equitable damages flows from the legislation which conferred a power on Chancery courts to award damages. That power is to award damages in addition to or in place of an injunction. It follows that where there is no power to issue an injunction no equitable damages can be awarded. A situation in which there is no power to award an injunction could be where a wrong had been committed but had ceased, such as where an activity creating a noise nuisance had ended with no prospect of its resumption or an obstruction which infringed a right of light had been erected but then removed. No injunction could be granted in these circumstances so that no equitable damages could be awarded for the loss caused in the past by the nuisance.[129] Of course common law damages could be awarded as redress for the past nuisance and the loss caused by it. It is important here to be clear that the inhibition on the award of equitable damages exists only where the court has no power to issue an injunction, such as in the circumstances just mentioned. There is jurisdiction to order equitable damages where the court has power to issue an injunction but does not do so either because an injunction is not sought or because the case is not one in which an injunction would be appropriate.[130] In such a case equitable damages can be awarded. The inhibition on the jurisdiction to award 7.72

[128] *Shadwell v Hutchinson* (1831) 2 B & Ald 97. Limitation periods have been imposed by successive statutes since the Limitation Act 1623, and the statutory provision in force today is the Limitation Act 1980, which by s 2 provides a limitation period of six years for claims in tort such as nuisance claims. Therefore a claim for damages for the effect of an unlawful obstruction in the past will be confined to claims for losses suffered in the six years from the accrual of the cause of action to the date of the commencement of the proceedings.

[129] *Lavery v Pursell* (1889) 39 Ch D 508 (no equitable damages could be awarded when specific performance of a contract for the sale of an interest in land could not be enforced because of the operation of the Statute of Frauds of 1677).

[130] See *Pell Frischmann Engineering Co v Bow Valley Iran Ltd* [2009] UKPC 45, [2011] 1 WLR 2370 [47(5)].

equitable damages just described arose from the language of the Chancery Amendment Act 1858 but continues to apply today despite the repeal of that statute.

(b) Practical Consequences of the Distinction

7.73 While the differences between common law and equitable damages are of historical interest in the development of the law of remedies, it might be queried what practical effect they have on the assessment of damages today for breaches of easements of light. Common law and equitable damages can be awarded as necessary by the Chancery and Queen's Bench Divisions of the High Court and in the county court when rights of light proceedings are heard, and the availability of one or both forms of damages appears to cover all factual situations which may arise.

(a) If an infringement of a right of light is threatened, a court can award damages for the loss which will be caused by the infringement if an injunction to prevent it is not granted.
(b) If an obstruction has taken place and no injunction ordering its removal is granted, damages can be awarded for the loss which will be caused by it in the future and for any loss which has already been caused by it.
(c) If an obstruction has been erected and has been removed prior to the proceedings, damages can be awarded for any loss caused during the period of the obstruction.

It does not seem of great significance whether the overall award of damages in these cases requires a combination of common law and equitable damages. The policy of the law has been said to be to remove all differences which may exist between the assessment of common law and equitable damages.[131]

7.74 There are probably three circumstances in which the distinction between common law and equitable damages may have a modern significance when damages are sought in rights of light claims.

(i) Where a building exists and is in breach of a person's right of light, that person may elect to claim damages only for the effect of the obstruction up to the time of the proceedings. This seems an unlikely course, but if it did occur a claimant could then bring further proceedings for further damages up to the date of those further proceedings since the nuisance continues and is renewed each day as long as the obstruction exists. The damages in these circumstances would be common law damages. Any attempt to proceed in this way would be likely to be met by the answer that the further proceedings should be struck out as an abuse of the process by reason of the principle that a person should bring forward the whole of his claim in one

[131] *Johnson v Agnew* [1980] AC 367, 400, a decision on damages for breach of a contract for the sale of land.

action where that can reasonably be done,[132] and in the circumstances postulated a claim for equitable damages for the future effect of the obstruction could have been brought in the first proceedings.

(ii) As will be explained in detail, damages for an infringement of a right of light are assessed either as the diminution in the value of the dominant building caused by the obstruction (commonly called 'book value' damages)[133] or as the amount which would have been agreed between the parties in a hypothetical negotiation for the release of the right of light (commonly called 'voluntary release' damages). It has been said that an award of damages on the usually more generous voluntary release basis is at the discretion of the court and that this discretion may arise from the nature of voluntary release damages as 'quasi-equitable'.[134] A further consequence of voluntary release damages being said to be quasi-equitable is that, although the assessment of the damages is said to be by way of a hypothetical negotiation for the release of the right of light at a date before the commencement of development on the servient land, it is acceptable in exceptional circumstances to have regard to events which occurred after that date.[135] A different view may be that the power to award damages on a voluntary release basis does not depend on the Chancery Amendment Act 1858 or on the concept of equitable damages but is something which exists as common law.[136] This aspect of the distinction between common law and equitable damages is today probably the most significant of the distinctions as far as rights of light disputes are concerned.

(iii) It is suggested that a reason why the voluntary release basis of damages was rejected by the Court of Appeal in *Surrey County Council v Bredero Homes Ltd*[137] was that only common law damages were claimed in that case.[138] It seems preferable today to regard the *Bredero* decision as not establishing any point of principle on the assessment of damages, but as impliedly overruled following the criticism of it by the House of Lords in *Attorney General v Blake*.[139]

132 *Johnson v Gore Wood & Co* [2002] 2 AC 1.

133 This expression is used in the RICS publication *Rights of Light—Practical Guidance for Chartered Surveyors in England and Wales* (Warwick, RICS, 2010) 11.

134 *Lunn Poly Ltd v Liverpool & Lancashire Properties Ltd* [2006] EWCA Civ 430, [2006] 2 EGLR 29 [21] (Neuberger LJ). It is not clear what is the distinction between equitable and quasi-equitable damages or why, if voluntary release damages are equitable or quasi-equitable, that justifies the claimant being sometimes deprived of compensation for what amounts to a part of his loss, namely the loss of his ability to negotiate a sum for the voluntary release of his rights. This matter is explored further in para 7.127 et seq.

135 ibid. See para 7.149 et seq for a further discussion of this question.

136 See *WWF World Wide Fund for Nature v World Wrestling Federation Inc* [2008] 1 WLR 445 [54] (Chadwick LJ).

137 *Surrey County Council v Bredero Homes Ltd* [1993] 1 WLR 1361 (breach of a restrictive covenant in a planning agreement).

138 See *Jaggard v Sawyer* [1995] 1 WLR 269, 281 (Sir Thomas Bingham MR).

139 *Attorney General v Blake* [2001] AC 268, 283 (Lord Nicholls). See para 7.116.

3. The Compensation Principle

7.75 A loss which a dominant owner may suffer when there is an unlawful obstruction to the access of light to his property is that the market value of his property is reduced. There is no doubt that the owner is entitled at least to the amount of that reduction in value as damages. An assessment of damages in these circumstances can be said to accord with the principle that the purpose of compensation is to place the injured party in the position he would have occupied if there had not been an actionable injury suffered by him. This method of assessing compensation for the violation of a right of light was at one time the normal and accepted method of doing so.

7.76 The reduction in market value method of assessment is not necessarily the only way of providing monetary compensation to a dominant owner. It forms a bed-rock below which damages are unlikely ever to fall. In addition to this basic method of assessment it is necessary to consider, or at least mention, as alternative methods (a) 'voluntary release' damages, (b) restitutionary damages, sometimes described as an account of profits, and (c) exemplary damages. The first of these further methods of assessment, voluntary release damages, is of cardinal practical importance. The other two are not normally likely to be appropriate in rights of light claims. A possible characteristic of these three further methods of assessing damages is or may be that on one view of what is done they go beyond providing compensation to the claimant for his loss and involve some consideration of the wrongful gain which had been made by the developer of the servient land. Restitutionary damages and exemplary damages certainly have this effect. Put in its starkest terms, the question to be asked is, if the servient owner has carried out a development which makes him a profit of £10 million, and in doing so wrongfully infringes the rights of light of an owner of adjoining property, why should the owner of that property be confined to the diminution in the value of his property, which may be, say, £1 million, so leaving the wrongdoer with a profit of £9 million gained from his wrong? Put another way, the question is whether the law should insist that the developer of the servient land in these circumstances should disgorge to the owner of the dominant land by way of damages the whole or at any rate some proportion of the gain which he has made from his wrongful actions.

7.77 There are certainly circumstances involving property transactions outside the area of rights of light in which a defendant may be required to give over to the claimant a profit which he has made from his own wrong. An example is where a person has agreed to sell his land at a specified price and then in breach of contract sells it at a higher price to a third party. The contractual purchaser is entitled to recover the profit which the vendor has made from the sale to the third party in breach of contract even though that profit may exceed the loss which the purchaser has himself suffered.[140] A reason for the result in this type of case, which differs from the

[140] *Lake v* Bayliss [1974] 1 WLR 1073. The situation may be different where the sale is of goods as opposed to land: see para 7.67.

position where goods are sold, may be that the vendor is taken from the date of the formation of a contract which is specifically enforceable to hold the land under a species of trust for the benefit of the purchaser. Before coming to voluntary release damages, which may be regarded as the most usual method today of assessing damages for a violation of a right of light, it is necessary to consider the older, and once generally applied, method of damages assessment which was the diminution in the value of the dominant building caused by the violation. However, it will be explained that voluntary release damages can be justified and accommodated firmly within the compensation principle.[141]

4. Diminution in Value Damages

(a) General Description: The Four Stages

As previously mentioned it was once assumed that the correct, and perhaps the only generally recognised, method of assessing damages for an infringement of a right of light was to assess the diminution in the value of the building of the dominant owner caused by the infringement. That diminution would normally be a reduction in the rental value of the interest held by the claimant in the dominant building. The reduction in rental value can readily be converted into a reduction in the capital value of the interest and that latter reduction in value will then constitute the damages. The amount of the reduction was seen as the loss to the dominant owner and, in accordance with the classic definition of the purposes of damages, this was the amount which it was thought would put the person wronged in the same position as he would have been if there had been no wrong committed against him.[142] This method of assessing damages is still frequently used and may be seen as a base or bedrock below which the damages cannot fall. Indeed there is some suggestion that it may still constitute the normal method of damage assessment.[143] 7.78

There are major criticisms of the general assessment of damages for a loss of light on this basis. The major objection to it as a method of assessment is that it provides no recompense to the dominant owner for the loss of opportunity to him of not being able to negotiate for an agreement with the servient owner for the 7.79

[141] It is explained in para 7.124 et seq that on a true analysis, when voluntary release damages are awarded the assessment of damages as a part of the gain to the wrongdoer is not a breach of the compensation principle, and that on the contrary, damages awarded on that basis may be the only way of giving true effect to the compensation principle. Restitutionary damages certainly and avowedly go beyond any question of compensation, and focus on the gain made by the wrongdoer. Restitutionary and exemplary damages are considered in section (C)12 and 13 of this chapter.

[142] For a statement of the general purpose of awarding damages, see *Robinson v Harman* (1848) 1 Ex 850, 855: see n 120.

[143] See *Lawrence v Fen Tigers Ltd* [2014] UKSC 13, [2014] AC 822 [128] (Lord Neuberger).

payment to him of a sum of money for the voluntary release of his right of light so far as necessary to render lawful the development which the servient owner wishes to carry out or has carried out. A second, and cogent, criticism is that it may sometimes be difficult for the dominant owner to show that he has suffered any substantial reduction in the value of his property due to the unlawful development carried out by the servient owner, so that if the diminution in value basis is the only method to be used for the assessment of damages the servient owner may make a substantial gain from his wrongful action and the law will do nothing to deprive him of the fruits of that unlawful gain.[144] It is these powerful criticisms that have led to the widespread adoption of the voluntary release method of assessing damages.

7.80 The diminution in value method of assessment is simple in concept. Damages assessed in this way are often called 'the book value' or 'book value damages' among rights of light practitioners. The value of the interest in land of the dominant owner is assessed first on the assumption that the offending development on the servient land has not taken place and never could take place. The value of that same interest is then assessed on the assumption that the offending development on the servient land has taken place. The difference between the two values is the book value and the amount of the damages.

7.81 A valuation of land only makes sense if there is a valuation date. If there are court proceedings the valuation date will be the date of the hearing if the obstruction on the servient land has not then taken place. If the obstruction has taken place then the valuation date will usually be the date when the unlawful obstruction was erected. The general principle is that damages are assessed as at the date of the commission of a tort, but the court has a discretion to substitute a later date in exceptional circumstances.[145]

7.82 It is not easy to assess the reduction in the capital value of a property caused by a reduction in the natural light received through one or more of its apertures. What are required for this purpose are 'before' and 'after' valuations, a valuation of the dominant building before the reduction in light and a valuation of the same building on the same date after the reduction in light. Such before and after valuations are frequently carried out for various purposes. Where a part of a person's land is compulsorily acquired a valuation of the retained land may have to be carried out before and after the severance of that land from the land acquired in order to assess the compensation payable for severance as part of the compensation for the compulsory acquisition.[146] Where land is injuriously affected by the removal of some valuable ancillary right such as a right of way or the right of access to the

[144] See, eg the observation to this effect in a different jurisdiction of Fuller CJ in *Union Pacific Railway Co v Chicago, Rock Island and Pacific Railway Co* (1896) 163 US 564, 600.

[145] *Alcoa Minerals of Jamaica v Broderick* [2002] 1 AC 371.

[146] See s 7 of the Compulsory Purchase Act 1965. The valuation process to be used for this purpose is explained in the decision of the Lands Tribunal in *Abbey Homesteads Group Ltd v Secretary of State for Transport* [1982] 2 EGLR 198.

sea, valuations of the land before and after the removal of the right may have to be carried out.[147]

In principle this valuation process with its two valuations has to be carried out for the dominant building, if the book value compensation is to be determined. In practice there may be substantial difficulties in carrying out such valuations on a coherent basis. Valuations are generally carried out with the assistance of comparable transactions, that is sales or lettings of other properties where the agreed price or rent per unit area can be applied to the subject property the value of which is being assessed after appropriate adjustments are made. It may not be difficult for a skilled valuer to carry out this process if, say, it is necessary to find the rental or capital value at a specified valuation date of a large modern city centre office building, for instance for the purposes of a rent review under a lease. Such a process may be impossible to apply where, for instance, a 12-storey office building has to be valued before and after a reduction in light to two or three of its many windows and where the rooms lit by the windows in question have their natural light reduced from a situation where 65 per cent of the area is sufficiently lit to a situation where 45 per cent of the area is sufficiently lit. The process may also be difficult for a residential building, when sometimes the best that a valuer can do is to say that the building is reduced in value due to the loss of light by some arbitrary figure, such as 5 per cent of its previous value. The only way in which a reduction in value could be calculated by hard evidence derived from comparables is if the rents or prices of two similar properties in the vicinity of the dominant building let or sold at about the same time, one well lit and one in part poorly lit, could be compared. Such evidence of comparable transactions is not often available. Even if such comparables did exist, it might be difficult to ascertain whether a small difference in rent or price between the buildings was due to poor natural light as opposed to other differing characteristics of the properties such as their age or exact location. 7.83

Given these difficulties, rights of light surveyors have developed a methodology which is workable and provides a uniform way of calculating book value damages. The methodology does not aspire to anything approaching scientific accuracy. The calculation proceeds by four stages. 7.84

(a) The reduction in the amount of the floor area in a room which is sufficiently lit brought about by the obstruction is assessed. This assessment is effected using the 0.2 per cent sky factor criterion and the Waldram diagram methodology which has been described in detail in Chapter 6.[148] The result is the amount of the reduction expressed in square feet.

[147] See, eg the declaration proposed by Lord Hoffmann in the Court of Final Appeal in Hong Kong in para 47 of his judgment in *Penny's Bay Investment Co Ltd v Director of Lands* (2010) 13 HKCFAR 287 (injurious affection caused by extinguishment of a right of access to the sea). In England and Wales a similar process may have to be carried out when a right of light or other easement is overridden by a compulsory acquisition of the servient land and compensation to the dominant owner becomes payable under s 10 of the Compulsory Purchase Act 1965. See ch 8, section (C)2.

[148] See ch 6, sections (C), (D) and (E).

(b) The reduction in area sufficiently lit in the room is then recalculated as the EFZ (effective first zone) loss. This is also an amount expressed in square feet.
(c) A reduction in rental value per square foot of the EFZ loss is then calculated. The figure chosen is often £5 per square foot per year. This reduction per square foot is multiplied by the EFZ loss so as to give the overall reduction in rental value for the room caused by the obstruction.
(d) The reduction in annual rental value for the room is capitalised so as to determine the reduction in the capital value of the dominant building caused by the obstruction, and it is this last figure which is the book value damages. Of course if more than one room is affected, the process is carried out for each room so that a total loss of EFZ, a total reduction in rental value, and a resultant total reduction in capital value are calculated.

The second, third and fourth stages within this methodology must now be described in rather greater detail. It is possible that different rights of light surveyors will adopt somewhat different means of calculation within the ambit of the overall methodology.

7.85 The general account here given of book value damages has concentrated on the usual method of establishing and assessing a diminution in the value of the dominant building caused by the obstruction of light and of awarding damages pursuant to that assessment. There could be other items of loss which attract an award of damages on the compensatory principle, for example a loss of an opportunity to sell the dominant building due to the actions of the servient owner in erecting an obstruction to light[149] or the fact that a tenant operates a break clause in his lease and leaves the property vacant because of an obstruction to light. The recovery of any such other item of damages would be subject to the general rule on remoteness of damage in tort.[150] It could happen that during a part of the time when the light to the dominant building was unlawfully obstructed that building was unoccupied, so that no damage was suffered by anyone with an interest in the building. In that case the book value damages should in principle be assessed so as not to include any loss of amenity or letting value during that period.[151]

(b) The Second Stage

7.86 The second stage, the calculation of the EFZ loss, requires that the floor area of the room in which the light is reduced is divided into four zones of an equal depth running back from the window which receives the light. The process is commonly terminated at 6 m back from the window if the depth of the room exceeds 6 m, such as in large open plan office floors. Therefore in a regularly shaped room such

[149] *Owers v Bailey* [2007] 1 P & CR DG 17.
[150] See paras 7.68 and 7.69.
[151] See *Dobson v Thames Water Utilities* [2009] EWCA Civ 28, [2009] 3 All ER 319.

as a square or a rectangular room, each zone is a successive strip of floor of 1.5 m back from the window. Obviously in such a case each zone embraces 25 per cent of the total floor area if the room is at least 6 m deep, and the process is terminated at 6 m. If the room is only, say, 4.2 m deep the measurement would never get beyond the third zone back from the window. If the room is irregularly shaped it may be preferable to take successive zones of an equal amount of floor area, but with each zone not going the same distance back from the window. If there is more than one window in the room then a more complicated method of zoning may need to be adopted. The zones are traditionally called the front zone (that immediately back from the window), the first zone, the second zone, and the makeweight (MKWT) zone. It is not clear why the zones are not simply numbered one to four.

It is important at this stage of the book value assessment to be clear just what floor areas should go into the calculation of the EFZ loss.[152] 7.87

(i) Where less than 50 per cent of the floor area of a room was sufficiently lit before the obstruction on the servient land the additional floor area that becomes insufficiently lit as a result of the obstruction on the servient land should be taken into the calculation.

(ii) Where 50 per cent or more of the floor area of a room was sufficiently lit before the obstruction on the servient land, and as a result of that obstruction the area sufficiently lit is reduced to less than 50 per cent, under this method of carrying out the process the reduction in floor area sufficiently lit insofar as it is below 50 per cent should be taken into the calculation. For example, if a room of 500 sq ft had 400 sq ft sufficiently lit before the obstruction but had only 150 sq ft sufficiently lit after the obstruction, the floor area to be taken into the calculation of the EFZ loss should be 100 sq ft (ie 50 per cent of the floor area is 250 sq ft, so that the area beyond that which becomes insufficiently lit is 100 sq ft). The rationale is of course that on the Waldram diagram methodology the room only becomes insufficiently lit, and there is only an actionable injury, if less than 50 per cent of the total floor area receives natural light from a sky factor of less than 0.2 per cent. Rights of light surveyors often use an alternative method of calculating the EFZ loss when there is an actionable injury, this alternative method being to include in the loss the whole of the floorspace which becomes less than sufficiently lit in accordance with the 0.2 per cent sky factor criterion and the Waldram diagram methodology as explained in Chapter 6. If this approach is used the loss in the above example, to be attributed to the relevant zones, would be 250 sq ft (400 sq ft less 150 sq ft). The example given in the table

[152] The explanation in this paragraph is founded on the twin assumptions which underlie the Waldram diagram method of measuring a reduction in light to a room through an aperture as described in detail in ch 6. These assumptions are (a) that a point in a room is sufficiently lit if it receives natural light through an aperture from at least a 0.2 per cent sky factor and (b) that a room as a whole is sufficiently lit if at least 50 per cent of its area is sufficiently lit by this standard.

in paragraph 7.91 follows the second or alternative method of calculation just described since this is the method most often used but a further explanation of the two methods and their merits and demerits is given following the table.

(iii) Therefore if there are any rooms in the dominant building where the obstruction on the servient land neither reduces the area sufficiently lit below 50 per cent of the total floor area nor, if the area sufficiently lit is already below 50 per cent, reduces that area further, there is no floor area in that room to go into the EFZ loss calculation. An example would be a room where 70 per cent of the floor area sufficiently lit is altered by the obstruction on the servient land to a room where 60 per cent of the floor area is sufficiently lit. There is in such a case no infringement of the right of light through a window in that room.

(iv) It is possible that the principle of parasitic damages may have to be applied to the calculation.[153] Parasitic damages arise where some windows in a building owned by one person enjoy a right of light over the servient land but other windows in other parts of the building or in another building owned by the same person do not enjoy a right of light over the servient land. If there is an infringement of the right of light to the first category of windows, the damages may be assessed by reference to not only the reduction in light to areas lit by those windows but also to the reduction in light to areas lit by windows in the second category. The damages for the infringement therefore extend to the reduction in light in rooms with windows in the second category, provided that the reduction would be an actionable injury in its own right if those windows had also enjoyed rights of light. To take an example, suppose that a building within one ownership enjoyed rights of light to windows A and B but not to windows C and D. If the obstruction on the servient land did not constitute an actionable injury to the rooms lit by windows A and B then no claim arises. If there is an actionable injury to one or both of the rooms lit by windows A and B, then the damages may be calculated by reference to the EFZ loss for those rooms and to the EFZ loss to the rooms lit by windows C and D. Of course the reduction in light to the rooms lit by windows C and D will only come into the calculation of the EFZ loss if that reduction would have been an actionable injury to the areas lit by those windows had those windows enjoyed rights of light.

7.88 The total amount of floorspace established as that which has become insufficiently lit, or more insufficiently lit, is then divided into that amount which falls within each of the zones. A multiplier is applied to the amount of floorspace within each zone. The multiplier is 1.5 for the front zone, 1 for the first zone, 0.5 for the second zone, and 0.25 for the MKWT zone. For example, suppose that a room has

[153] See para 7.152 et seq for the law on parasitic damages. Although it is supported by authority, there are severe criticisms which can be levelled against the principle involved.

400 sq ft of floor area with 200 sq ft sufficiently lit before the obstruction and as a result of the obstruction only 100 sq ft remain sufficiently lit. The 100 sq ft which becomes insufficiently lit may be located with 10 sq ft of this in the front zone, 20 sq ft in the first zone, 30 sq ft in the second zone, and 40 sq ft in the MKWT zone. The calculation will then be (10 x 1.5 = 15) + (20 x 1 = 20) + (30 x 0.5 = 15) + (40 x 0.25 = 10), so giving an EFZ loss of 60 sq ft. The purpose of this process is to attribute greater weight in calculating the reduction in value to the part of the room where natural light is thought to be most important which is the area nearest the window which is the source of the natural light. Consequently, since in this example 70 per cent of the floor area which loses a sufficiency of natural light is in the second and MKWT zones which attract a lower weighting, the EFZ loss is only 60 sq ft, as compared to an actual loss of sufficiently lit floor area of 100 sq ft.

A somewhat simplified Waldram diagram appears in Chapter 6.[154] The diagram relates to one room on the fourth floor of a building, described as room 1 (R1). 7.89

The following details relate to that room and the obstruction to its light. Its floor area is 151.06 sq ft. Prior to the obstruction on the servient land, 149.57 sq ft or 99.02 per cent were sufficiently lit. After the obstruction, 30.84 sq ft or 20.42 per cent remained sufficiently lit. After the obstruction, the loss of a sufficiently lit area was 118.74 sq ft. When the weighting is applied, this translates to a weighted or EFZ loss of 85.18 sq ft. The reduction is because most of the area which loses a sufficiency of light is in the zones away from the window and towards the rear of the room. The situation as described, with a reduction in area within the room sufficiently lit from 99 per cent to 20 per cent, shows that there is an actionable injury. The situation in all relevant rooms in the dominant building is tabulated in this way so as to show an overall or total EFZ loss. 7.90

The table below sets out the EFZ calculation in a form in which it is often presented. 7.91

Fourth floor

ROOM DATA		ROOM AREA	BEFORE CONTOUR		AFTER CONTOUR		LOSS	EFZ
LEVEL	ROOM NAME	SQ FT	SQ FT	%	SQ FT	%	SQ FT	EFZ FT
Fourth	R1	151.06	149.57	99.02	30.84	20.42	118.74	85.18
							Total	85.18

Where the floor area of a room with a sky factor of at least 0.2 per cent exceeds 50 per cent prior to the development on the servient land and is reduced to less than 50 per cent by that development, so that there is likely to be an actionable injury as already indicated, there is a question of how the EFZ loss calculation 7.92

[154] See ch 6, para 6.24.

is to be carried out. There are in principle two methods of doing so. One is by taking into account the whole of the reduction of floor area which is sufficiently lit. For example, if 70 per cent of the room enjoyed a 0.2 per cent or higher sky factor before the obstruction and 40 per cent of the room enjoyed a 0.2 per cent of higher sky factor after the obstruction, the reduction to be taken into the weighting calculation would be 30 per cent of the floor area. The calculation in the example given in the last paragraph has followed this method of working. It appears to be the method generally adopted.

7.93 The other method is to use in the calculation only that part of the total floor area below 50 per cent of the total area which has a sky factor reduced to below 0.2 per cent. To use again the above example, the floor area to be taken into the EFZ loss calculation will on this method of working be 10 per cent of the floor area, not 30 per cent of it.

7.94 There is much to be said for the second method being used in assessing book value compensation. The dominant owner with his easement of light is entitled to be protected against a reduction in the amount of light to a room which renders the room as a whole not adequately lit according to the ordinary notions of mankind. If this standard is interpreted as meaning that the room is adequately lit as long as 50 per cent or more of its floor area receives a sky factor of at least 0.2 per cent, it seems logical to confine any calculation of the loss to that part of the room below 50 per cent of the total floor area of the room which, following an obstruction, receives less than the requisite standard of light. If it were otherwise, the dominant owner would be compensated for a loss of light to a part of his room where the loss of light to that part did not in itself render the room as a whole inadequately lit. The use of the first method seems to some extent to harken back to the theory, once supportable in law but now no longer supportable, that an easement of light offers protection against any loss of natural light, and not just against a loss of light which renders a room inadequately lit according to ordinary notions. The difficulty in using the first method can be illustrated by an example. Suppose that there are two rooms affected by an obstruction. For the first room the obstruction reduces the floor area adequately lit, that is with a sky factor of 0.2 per cent or greater, from 80 per cent to 40 per cent, whereas for a second room the reduction in floor area adequately lit is from 55 per cent to 15 per cent. The second room is clearly more grievously affected than the first room, yet in the EFZ loss the calculation is based on a reduction of 40 per cent of floor area for both rooms. The simplicity of this example and the point being made may be affected by the EFZ weighting process, but the principle behind what is said is apparent.

7.95 Which method is the more appropriate in arriving at a just level of compensation using the book value method of calculation is a matter for expert surveyors. Plainly the use of the second method is likely to result in some cases in a lower level of compensation than is the first method. Of course if the area of the floor adequately lit was less than 50 per cent prior to the obstruction, and following the obstruction falls to an even lower level, then there will be no difference between the application of the first and second methods of calculation. Other variations and adjustments of the weighting attributed to various areas of a room are possible depending on the particular circumstances of a room or a building and in each case the expert surveyor using the Waldram methodology must decide on the appropriate exact use of that methodology and must be prepared to justify and defend his method of calculating the EFZ loss.

(c) *The Third Stage*

7.96 The third stage is to translate the EFZ floor area loss into a reduction in annual rental value per square foot. It is at this stage that traditional valuation techniques, such as a valuation by the use of comparables, breaks down. As stated there are rarely comparables which will assist in determining by how much the rental value of an area of reduced light within a room is diminished by the reduction in light or by how much the rental value of the room as a whole is diminished by the same cause. In these circumstances rights of light surveyors often have recourse in the absence of any other method to the arbitrary solution of applying a rental sum per square foot of EFZ loss, which rests more on tradition and the absence of any other method than on a disciplined or rational valuation approach. For commercial floorspace the figure often used is a reduction in rental value of £5 per square foot of the EFZ loss per year.[155] Thus in the example in the table set out above the rental loss would be £5 x 85.18, or £425.90 per year for the room in question.

7.97 It is easy to pick theoretical holes in this third stage of the overall calculation. An initial question is of course why £5 per square foot, or any other particular figure, is taken. A further point is that it is difficult to believe that the same reduction in rental value due to a particular reduction in light occurs irrespective of the location of the dominant building. An office building in the central area of the City of London is likely to have a very much higher value than an office building on the outskirts of London or on the fringe of some other city. Consequently the same reduction in light would be likely to have a greater effect in absolute terms on the rental value of the City building. It might be argued that a more appropriate method of finding the reduction in rental value would be to apply a proportion of the rental value at any particular time of the floor area which becomes insufficiently lit as the reduction rather than an absolute figure such as £5 per square foot. The age and specification and attraction of the building will dictate its rental value, so that again it is difficult to believe that a figure such as £5 per square foot as the reduction in rental value due to a reduction in light is the same for buildings of very different ages and specifications. The position of floors in buildings such as office buildings significantly affects the rent, with a higher rent usually

[155] The rate is sometimes said to be £3–£5 per square foot, dependent on location. See the Law Commission, *Rights to Light* (Law Com No 354, 2014), para 5.6, citing the 19th edn of *Sale on Easements* (London, Sweet & Maxwell, 2012) para 14-126.

being attributable to higher floors, whereas it is normally lower floors of a building which are most affected by an obstruction to the access of light to the blinding. Consequently it is arguable that the reduction in value due to the reduction in light should have regard to the position in the building of the room which suffers the reduced light. Rental values of commercial property may change rapidly. For example, the annual rents obtainable for prime City of London offices were about £57.50 per square foot in the summer of 2008, but had moved down to about £44 per square foot nine or 10 months later following the banking and liquidity crisis which started with Lehman Brothers going into administration in the United States in September 2008. Such changes upwards and downwards in rental values may be caused by general economic circumstances and the balance of supply and demand at any particular time. It is plainly arbitrary to adopt the same figure for the reduction in rental value due to diminished light at all times, having regard to these fluctuations in commercial rental values which are cyclical and are well known to the market. Leaving aside cyclical changes, the effect of inflation and real increases in property value may be felt over time, so requiring a reconsideration of a particular figure such as £5 per square foot. A further criticism of the calculation is that the same loss of rental value per square foot is applied whatever the degree of the reduction of light occurs to a particular area of the room. Thus if a part of a room has its natural light reduced from that received with slightly above a 0.2 per cent sky factor to that received with slightly below that sky factor, the loss of £5 per square foot is the same as if the reduction had been much more severe and to a much lower sky factor.[156] The use of an arbitrary figure for a reduction in rental value such as £5 per square foot may be the most difficult component of the traditional method of calculating book value damages to justify or defend.

7.98 All of these considerations may be cogent grounds of attack on an arbitrary figure such as £5 per square foot for a reduced rental value due to loss of light (or on any other figure used that is not based on hard evidence of real transactions and the actual characteristics of the dominant building), but there are two other major considerations in favour in carrying out the third stage of the process in the manner described. One is that it produces a degree of uniformity. It assists those involved in actual or potential rights of light disputes to have some real idea of what are likely to be the book value damages in a particular case. An arbitrary but generally accepted method of calculation, despite its manifest imperfections, does assist this objective. The second consideration is that if the method just described is not adopted, it is incumbent on anyone criticising it to find a better and more rational means of calculating a reduction in value due to a loss of natural light in any particular case, and that is something which it will often be difficult to achieve. In practice, rights of light surveyors advising the parties to a dispute frequently adopt the same overall methodology of assessing a book value, including this third stage in the process, and it would be difficult for a court not to accept

[156] For an explanation of the 0.2 per cent sky factor see ch 6, section (C).

such an agreed method of working in the absence of some plausible and preferable alternative.

(d) The Fourth Stage

The fourth stage is the calculation of the reduction in capital value of the dominant building. It is this reduction which will constitute the damages assessed by the book value method. Annual rental values are converted into capital values by the use of a years purchase (YP) multiplier, and that multiplier is determined by the appropriate yield. The yield simply means the percentage return per year which a person would require on his investment if he were acquiring a property. For example, a person might require a 5 per cent yield, that is a 5 per cent annual return, on the amount he expends in purchasing a property. The years purchase multiplier is 100 divided by the yield. Consequently if the required yield is 5 per cent, then the years purchase multiplier is 20. Taking again the above example,[157] a loss of annual value of £425.90 can be converted into a loss of capital value if the required yield is 5 per cent by multiplying it by 20 so that the loss of capital value becomes £8,518. The critical element of this calculation is of course the required yield. The correct yield depends on many considerations such as the financial standing of a tenant or tenants of the property, the hope for rental growth, and general financial circumstances and interest rates within an economy at a particular time. The general principle is that the better the quality of the investment and the more certain it is that the full rent will continue to be paid the lower will be the yield or return which an investor will accept on his investment (and so the higher the years purchase multiplier will be). A purchaser acquiring a multi-tenanted older office building on the fringes of Greater London would be likely to require a significantly higher yield on his investment than would the purchaser of a recently constructed office building in the core of the City of London let to a single high-quality tenant. 7.99

At this final stage the surveyor must therefore determine the appropriate yield and the appropriate years purchase multiplier derived from the yield. The circumstances as at the date of the obstruction must be taken into account for this purpose. When it comes to yields it is more likely that comparables will be available calculated from the relationship between the amount of money which has been paid to acquire a property subject to tenancies and the total rental income from that property at the date of the acquisition. The duration of the interest of the dominant owner in the dominant building will be important in carrying out the capitalisation process. If the dominant owner owns a freehold interest in the dominant building then his interest is one which will in principle last for ever, so that the capitalisation will be in perpetuity. The example given in the last paragraph is a capitalisation in perpetuity. As against this the interest of the dominant owner may be a limited leasehold interest. For example, if the claimant holds a 7.100

[157] See the table in para 7.91.

lease with seven years to run, then his loss due to a reduction in light will last for seven years only. The capitalisation process will take account of this.

7.101 The position may be more complicated, in that a landlord and a tenant may both have claims to book value damages for a reduction in light to the property of which one is the owner and the other is the tenant. If the rent is fixed for, say, the next five years, the landlord will not be affected during that time by a reduction in rental value, since he will continue to receive the same rent. The tenant will be affected by the reduction in rental value because he will continue to pay the same rent but will occupy premises with a lower value due to the reduction in light. At the end of the five years, assuming the lease ends at that date, the burden of a reduced value in the future and in perpetuity will become that of the landlord assuming that he is a freeholder. In such a case it would be appropriate to capitalise the reduction in rental value over a five-year period when assessing the book value damages due to the tenant and then capitalising the reduction in rental value in perpetuity, but deferred for a period of five years, when calculating the book value damages due to the landlord. There are many permutations of such situations and the surveyors and valuers involved will apply traditional techniques making use of valuation tables in their calculations.[158]

(e) *Offsetting a Benefit*

7.102 A situation may arise in which a development takes place on servient land which affects the dominant building where that building as a whole enjoys an easement of light against that servient land. The development on the servient land may reduce the access of light to certain rooms in the dominant building so that there is an actionable injury. On the other hand the development on the servient land may be such that the access of light is improved to other rooms in the dominant building in comparison to the previous position. This could occur if a building on the servient land was demolished and it was replaced by a new building which was taller and bulkier at some points but was smaller at other points. In Chapter 3 the question has been considered of whether in such circumstances the benefit and improvement to certain rooms can be offset against the injury to other rooms, so that taken as a whole it can be concluded that there is no actionable injury at all to the dominant building.[159] One view taken is that in the circumstances postulated, there is no actionable injury to the dominant building as a whole and, if that is indeed the law, then there is no question of damages or of offsetting any item against damages. However there is considerable doubt on whether the law is as just stated, and it may be that in circumstances of the sort here under consideration it can be established that there is an actionable injury to a particular room or rooms,

[158] For example, the dates and terms of rent reviews under a lease or the existence of an option to determine the lease may have to be taken into account in the calculation.

[159] See ch 3, para 3.46 et seq.

even though there is a benefit created by the development on the servient land to other rooms by way of increased light to those rooms as compared with the previous situation. If this latter approach to the law is correct it is necessary to consider here the separate question of whether in assessing the damages for the injury to a room adversely affected a benefit arising from the same development on the servient land to a different room in the same building by reason of an increase in the light which that second room receives can be taken into account.

There is a general principle of law that when a wrong committed by a defendant adversely affects the claimant in some respect, then in assessing the damages for that wrong, account must be taken of benefits which accrue to the claimant from the actions which constitute the wrong, provided there is sufficient connection between the actions in question and the benefits to be taken into account.[160] The application of this principle suggests that in the assessment of damages for an actionable interference with a right of light the overall effect on the dominant building should normally be considered, so that benefits to some parts of it can be offset against the injury to other parts of it. 7.103

The application of this principle is not difficult in a simple case. If room A in the dominant building has its area sufficiently lit reduced from 70 per cent to 30 per cent an EFZ loss calculation can be carried out as described above so as to arrive at a sum of book value damages. If room B in the same building has its area sufficiently lit increased from 30 per cent to 50 per cent a similar 'EFZ gain' can be carried out to arrive at a sum. The second sum can then be deducted from the first sum (assuming that the second sum is smaller than the first) so as to arrive at the overall effect on both rooms and an ultimate sum of book value damages. Of course if the EFZ gain to room B is greater than the EFZ loss to room A there will on that hypothesis be no loss and therefore no damages. 7.104

Other calculations are likely to be more complicated. 7.105

(a) There may be a series of rooms, some with reduced and some with increased light. The calculation can then be carried out so as to offset a cumulative gain against a cumulative loss.
(b) It may not be correct that the reduction in the rental value or the capital value of property due to reduced light corresponds in any simple arithmetical fashion to an increase in the rental or capital value of the same property due to some increase in the access of natural light.
(c) It is uncertain when an increase in light to a room is to be reflected in the overall calculation. One question is whether the increase in light in the room which obtains the benefit of better light can only be taken into account if the increase takes the light from the situation in which the room had less than an adequate amount of light to a situation in which it obtains an adequate

[160] See eg *Stanniforth v Lyall* (1830) 7 Bing 169; *British Westinghouse Co v Underground Electric Railways of London* [1912] AC 673; *Hussey v Eels* [1990] 2 QB 227.

amount of light, ie where it passes the 50-50 test or 'grumble line'. If a room is very well lit, say 85 per cent of its area is well lit, it seems curious that an addition of natural light to make it 95 per cent well lit should be taken into account.

7.106 It may be the situation that different people own different interests in different parts of the dominant building. Obviously in such a situation there could be no question of offsetting a gain made by a person with one interest by reason of improved light to his rooms against a loss suffered by a different person by reason of a reduction in light to his rooms.

7.107 The situation under discussion is therefore uncertain in the correct legal answer to the circumstances which arise. In fact the overall situation being discussed is not one which is likely to arise in many circumstances, something which perhaps explains the absence of any line of decided authority on the matter, if only because most developments either create a new building on a previously undeveloped site, or increase generally the height and size and bulk of existing developments. The most that can be said is that as a matter of general principle, where a person owns a building with more than one room which is affected, the overall effect of a development on the servient land relating to the access of light should in principle and as a matter of law be taken into effect in assessing book value damages, with the possibility of offsetting the different effects on different rooms. Subject to this general observation the working out of how that principle should be applied in particular cases will involve considering particular circumstances and concatenations of fact, so that little is to be gained from doing more than stating the general principle.

5. Voluntary Release Damages: The Principle

(a) An Origin of the Principle

7.108 Despite the compensation principle, or probably more accurately as an elaboration of that principle, there has emerged over the last few decades a method of assessing damages for breach of rights affecting land which relates to the gain made by the wrongdoer from his breach as opposed to the loss to a claimant due solely to a reduction in the value of the claimant's land caused by the breach. The seminal decision, which led to a chain of consistent authority ultimately approved by the House of Lords, was that of Brightman J in *Wrotham Park Estate Co Ltd v Parkside Homes.*[161] In that case, damages rather than an injunction were the remedy given for development which had taken place in breach of a restrictive covenant. The owners of an estate with the benefit of the covenant could not show any reduction in the value of the land benefited by the covenant due to the breach. This

[161] *Wrotham Park Estate Co. Ltd v Parkside Homes* [1974] 1 WLR 798.

may often be the situation where an estate as an entity protects itself by covenants against development on neighbouring land. It was held that the damages should be a sum equal to 5 per cent of the profit made by the developer as a result of the breach of covenant. Damages assessed in this manner have been given various descriptions, including 'Wrotham Park damages', voluntary release damages', 'fair negotiation damages', 'gain-based relief', 'release fee damages', 'negotiating damages', and 'buy-out damages'. The concept is the same whatever expression is used.[162] Although the decision of Brightman J was seen as innovatory at the time, there had been decisions going back to the nineteenth century in which damages had been awarded as a reasonable recompense to the person whose rights had been wrongfully overridden.[163] It is explained later why the voluntary release method of assessing damages is compensatory in nature; indeed it may in many cases be a more accurate way of assessing the true monetary loss to a person whose rights have been violated than is the book value method of assessment.[164]

The principle that damages for the breach of property rights should bear some relation to the gain made by the wrongdoer by his wrong, because this gain may be relevant to the true loss suffered by the person whose rights have been violated, has been applied and explained in a series of subsequent cases. The property rights involved which have resulted in an award of damages on this basis have varied from rights of way to rights of light and to the right to enforce restrictive covenants and the right to freedom from trespass. The decisions reveal a chain of consistent authority in favour of an award of voluntary release damages in all but exceptional cases. 7.109

(b) The Chain of Consistent Authority

Following the *Wrotham Park* decision, and relying on it as an authority, in *Bracewell v Appleby*[165] an injunction to prevent the obstruction of a right of way by a house built across the way was refused on the ground that the plaintiff had delayed in bringing proceedings until construction of the house was under way. The defendant had made a profit of about £5,000 from the erection of the house and Graham J awarded damages of £2,000, or 40 per cent of the profit, calculated as a sum which he considered the defendant would have been willing to offer, and which those with the benefit of the right of way would have been willing to accept, 7.110

[162] All of these expressions should be understood to be by way of contrast to restitutionary damages or exemplary damages, which are conceptually separate methods of assessing damages and which are briefly referred to later in sections (C)12 and 13 of this chapter. The essential difference is that voluntary release damages aim to embrace what is a true loss to the person wronged whereas restitutionary or exemplary damages are intentionally and overtly outside this method of assessing damages.

[163] See n 175. The concept of a reasonable recompense is of course not entirely the same as the concept of the result of a hypothetical negotiation such as underlies the assessment of voluntary release damages.

[164] See para 7.124 et seq.

[165] *Bracewell v Appleby* [1975] Ch 408.

for a voluntary release of the right of way so as to permit the construction of the house. The damages were divided equally between the five persons entitled to the right of way, so that each received £400. By this point, therefore, the voluntary release basis or justification for an award of damages had been established as the sum which would have been agreed in a hypothetical negotiation for the release of a right and a proportion of the profit gained by the wrongdoer, 40 per cent, had been awarded as damages calculated in this way, substantially in excess of the 5 per cent of the profit awarded in the *Wrotham Park* case.

7.111 Both of the above decisions were cited to Millett J in a rights of light case, *Carr-Saunders v Dick McNeill Associates Ltd.*[166] In that case a prescriptive right of light appurtenant to a property used as a number of consulting rooms was infringed. The judge accepted evidence that the loss of capital value to the dominant property was £3,000. However, he applied the principle that account should be taken of the loss to the plaintiff of bargaining position so that the loss to him of the capacity to obtain by negotiation a part of the gain to the defendant should feature in the assessment of damages in the case of a loss of light. There was no evidence before the court of what was the profit to the defendant obtained from his wrongful action, but the judge, doing the best that he could and regarding the £3,000 as an absolute minimum figure, assessed the damages at £8,000.

7.112 This decision has given rise to an unfortunate practice among rights of light practitioners. Since the damages awarded by Millett J were two to three times the reduction in value of the dominant property, a multiplier of two or three times that reduction in value has been adopted as what are sometimes called 'enhanced damages'. What this practice ignores is the legal and theoretical justification for an award of damages on the voluntary release basis. Such damages are not some sort of arbitrary punishment or rap over the knuckles to a servient owner but, as the decisions generally explain, are compensation for the loss by the dominant owner of the ability to obtain a negotiated sum for the voluntary release by him of his rights to the extent necessary to permit and so render lawful the acts which the servient owner has wrongfully carried out or wrongfully intends to carry out. Whilst the reduction, if any, in the value of the property of the dominant owner may be germane to the likely result of such a voluntary negotiation one would expect the primary factor in such a negotiation to be the gain made or to be made by the servient owner for what is *ex hypothesi* his wrongful act. The only reason that Millett J made an award of damages of two to three times the reduction in value of the consulting rooms was that he had no evidence of the amount of gain made by the defendant. In other words, simply to multiply the reduction in the capital value of the dominant property by an arbitrary figure of two or three is wrong in law and in principle when an estimate of the gain to the servient owner can realistically be made and there is evidence of this gain.[167] It might be impossible for

[166] *Carr-Saunders v Dick McNeill Associates Ltd* [1986] 1 WLR 922.

[167] One of the principles suggested for the calculation of voluntary release damages in *Tamares (Vincent Square) Ltd v Fairpoint Properties (Vincent Square) Ltd* [2006] EWHC 212 (Ch), [2007] 1

the dominant owner to prove any substantial loss of capital value to his property (as in the *Wrotham Park* case) and the application of this enhancement damages technique would then logically result in no damages being awarded, however great the gain to the servient owner and however much of that gain would have been likely to have been disgorged in a voluntary negotiation for the release of the right of light.

It is equally illogical and misleading to suggest that 'enhanced damages' are some sort of halfway house between book value damages and voluntary release damages, suitable perhaps when the injury to the dominant building due to a reduction in light is small. The law does not proceed in such an inconsistent fashion. If a claimant can establish that he has an easement of light which is infringed, he is entitled to damages to compensate him for his loss. If those damages are awarded on a voluntary release basis in order to compensate the claimant for the loss of his opportunity to negotiate a voluntary release of his rights, the damages should be founded on the amount which would have been obtained in a reasonable negotiation for the release. The main factor which is likely to determine that amount is the gain which the servient owner anticipates making if he can negotiate a release. The book value loss, or an arbitrary multiple of the book value loss, is unlikely to play a major part in the hypothetical negotiation. The dominant owner will reasonably demand a share in the gain irrespective of the amount of the book value loss.[168] 7.113

A further right of light decision was that in the Mayor's and City of London County Court in *Deakins v Hockings*.[169] A mandatory injunction was awarded to compel the removal of a rear extension to a house which infringed the plaintiff's right of light. The judge indicated that if an injunction had not been awarded, he would have assessed the damages as 15 per cent of the benefit to the defendant from his wrongful act. The 5 per cent of profits awarded in the *Wrotham Park* case was said to be too low. 7.114

The question of voluntary release damages came before the Court of Appeal in *Jaggard v Sawyer*[170] in which the defendant had committed a breach of a restrictive covenant by the construction of a driveway, and was continuing to commit a trespass by the use of a private road as an access to his newly constructed house. An injunction was refused mainly because of the delay by the plaintiffs in commencing proceedings. The principle of awarding damages as the amount which a claimant could reasonably have been expected to receive for the voluntary release of rights was upheld. The sum awarded as damages by the judge at first instance 7.115

WLR 2167 [22] was that if there was no evidence of the likely size of the profit, the court could do its best by awarding a suitable multiple of the damages for loss of amenity. This emphasises that the 'enhanced damages' technique should only be used in the absence of data on the gain or likely gain to the wrongdoer.

168 There is an allied notion that, if the award of voluntary release damages is discretionary, damages so assessed should be refused where the injury to the dominant building is small. See para 7.131.

169 *Deakins v Hockings* [1994] 1 EGLR 190.

170 *Jaggard v Sawyer* [1995] 1 WLR 269.

was £6,250, and this was split between the nine persons entitled to the benefit of the restrictive covenant and the use of the private road. The sum of £6,250 was arrived at as a figure between a quarter and a third of the hypothetical profit.[171] It was emphasised by the Court of Appeal that, although the damages in cases of the sort before the court were not confined to the diminution in the value of the land of the person whose rights had been infringed, the damages were still compensatory in nature.

7.116 There is strong support for the principle which starts with the *Wrotham Park* decision in the decision of the House of Lords in *Attorney General v Blake*.[172] The traitor George Blake, who had been sentenced to 42 years' imprisonment, escaped from prison and fled to the Soviet Union. He entered into a contract with a publisher to write and publish a book with an account of his activities as an officer with the British Secret Intelligence Service (MI6). In doing so he was in breach, inter alia, of his contract of employment with the Government. No monetary loss could be proved by the Government. The House of Lords held that exceptionally damages for breach of contract could be assessed by way of an order that the defendant should pay the whole of the profits made by his breach of contract. It should be noted that damages assessed as the whole of an amount of profits gained are restitutionary in nature. Such damages require that the defendant pays over as damages the whole of his wrongful gain. Damages calculated on this basis are therefore different in principle and concept to the voluntary release damages here under consideration where the defendant is required to pay over as damages that part of his wrongful gain which would be agreed in a reasonable negotiation for the voluntary release of rights exercisable against him. This discloses a fundamental difference of approach and it is this difference which, as will be explained, renders voluntary release damages compensatory in nature.[173] Nobody suggested that Blake should be required to pay as damages a sum which the Government would have agreed with him for a voluntary release of his obligations.

7.117 In *Attorney General v Blake* Lord Nicholls, with whom Lord Goff and Lord Browne-Wilkinson agreed, described the voluntary release method of assessing damages as having been adopted on many occasions for violations of property rights, citing some of the decisions referred to above. He described the *Wrotham Park* decision as rather a 'solitary beacon', stating that in contract as well as in tort damages are not always narrowly confined to recoupment of financial loss.[174] The *Wrotham Park* approach was said to be correct in applying by analogy the cases concerning the assessment of damages where a defendant had violated another

[171] [1993] 1 EGLR 197, 203.

[172] *Attorney General v Blake* [2001] 1 AC 268.

[173] See para 7.159.

[174] *Attorney General v Blake* [2001] 1 AC 268, 281–83. This last observation was described as 'rather surprising' by Lord Walker in *Pell Frischmann Engineering Ltd v Bow Valley Iran Ltd* [2009] UKPC 45, [2011] 1 WLR 2370 [48(3)]. See para 7.120 for this decision.

person's property rights but without diminishing the value of the property of that person.[175] Lord Nicholls described the assessment of damages in this type of case as damages for loss of a bargaining opportunity.[176] He also described the decision in the Court of Appeal in *Surrey County Council v Bredero Homes Ltd*, in which voluntary release damages were refused as a difficult decision which had attracted criticism from academic commentators and in later cases, and as espousing a principle which would be a sorry reflection on the law. Insofar as the decision in *Bredero* is inconsistent with the voluntary release or *Wrotham Park* approach, the latter approach was to be preferred.[177] The voluntary release or loss of bargaining opportunity approach to the assessment of damages in cases involving violations of property rights has therefore received the endorsement of a majority of the opinions delivered in the House of Lords.

The use of the voluntary release method of assessment has continued and grown in pace since *Blake*. In *Midtown Ltd v City of London Real Property Co Ltd*[178] this method was accepted in a rights of light case as appropriate by counsel for the servient owner. In *Lunn Poly Ltd v Liverpool & Lancashire Properties Ltd*[179] there was a claim by a tenant against his landlord for damages for the landlord's wrongful act in bricking up a door. The judge in the county court ordered that the damages should be fixed at a figure to represent the result of a hypothetical negotiation between reasonable parties in the position of the landlord and the tenant for a voluntary release of the tenant's right to prevent the landlord from blocking up and relocating the door in question. This decision was upheld in the Court of Appeal. The leading judgment, that of Neuberger LJ, concentrates on the question of whether in deciding the result of the hypothetical negotiation, events after the date of that negotiation can be taken into account.[180] 7.118

The claimant in *Forsyth-Grant v Allen*,[181] who had suffered an infringement of a right of light, claimed that the damages should be on a restitutionary basis, that 7.119

[175] *Attorney General v Blake* [2001] 1 AC 268, 281. See eg *Whitwham v Westminster Brymbo Coal and Coke Co* [1896] 2 Ch 538, in which the Court of Appeal held that when one person unlawfully used the property of another, he should pay as damages not the diminution in the value of that property but the value of the property for that unlawful use; *Penarth Dock Engineering Co Ltd v Pounds* [1963] 1 Lloyd's Rep 359.

[176] *Attorney General v Blake* [2001] 1 AC 268, 281.

[177] ibid 283. *cf Surrey County Council v Bredero Homes Ltd* [1993] 1 WLR 1361, see para 7.74(iii). It has been suggested that the *Bredero* decision is explicable on the footing that the court was assessing only common law damages and not equitable damages: see para 7.74(iii).

[178] *Midtown v City of London Real Property Co Ltd* [2005] EWHC 33 (Ch), [2005] 1 EGLR 65. A further decision applying the *Wrotham Park* approach is *Amec Developments Ltd v Jury's Hotel Management (UK) Ltd* (2001) 82 P & CR 22, a case involving the construction of a building beyond an agreed line in which there is a valuable discussion on the various factors which are relevant to the decision on the result of a hypothetical negotiation for a voluntary release.

[179] *Lunn Poly Ltd v Liverpool & Lancashire Properties Ltd* [2006] EWCA Civ 430, [2006] 2 EGLR 29.

[180] This question is discussed in para 7.149 et seq.

[181] *Forsyth-Grant v Allen* [2008] EWCA Civ 505, [2008] 2 EGLR 16. In this case the unhelpful conduct of the claimant in asserting his rights was a factor which motivated the court in confining him to book value damages.

is that, as in *Blake*, the defendant should be required to provide an account of all profits obtained from the infringement and to pay the whole of them over as damages to the claimant. The Court of Appeal regarded this as inappropriate. The damages as awarded in the court of first instance and upheld by the Court of Appeal were on a diminution in value of the dominant building basis, but it was said that on the authorities, a claimant could in appropriate cases obtain an award calculated by reference to the price that the person carrying out the violation of the rights might reasonably be required to pay for the relaxation of those rights so as to avoid an injunction. In *Stadium Capital Holdings (No 2) Ltd v St Marylebone Co Plc*, a case of damages for trespass, the Court of Appeal allowed an appeal from the court of first instance which had awarded damages as 100 per cent of the profit earned by the wrongdoer, ie damages assessed on a restitutionary basis. On a subsequent reassessment of the damages, a lower sum of 50 per cent of a licence fee was awarded.[182] In *Tamares (Vincent Square) Ltd v Fairpoint Properties (Vincent Square) Ltd (No 2)*, also a right of light case, it was said that in deciding the result of the hypothetical negotiation, the court had to be satisfied that 'the deal feels right' before arriving at its award of damages.[183] The damages were assessed as a little under one third of the anticipated profit. In *HKRUK II (CPC) Ltd v Heaney*[184] an injunction was awarded in the High Court to require the removal of development which infringed a right of light, but the judge indicated that if an injunction had not been granted he would have awarded damages on a voluntary release basis.

7.120 Powerful and general support for the use of the voluntary release method of assessing damages is found in the decision of the Privy Council in *Pell Frischmann Engineering Ltd v Bow Valley Iran Ltd*.[185] This case concerned the assessment of damages for breach of a contractual duty of confidentiality entered into between two companies in connection with the development of an offshore oil field. Lord Walker summarised the law on the subject of what he described as *Wrotham Park* damages after a citation of a series of cases most of which are referred to above. The first of two general principles stated was as follows.[186]

> Damages under this head (termed 'negotiating damages' by Neuberger LJ in *Lunn Poly* [2006] 2 EGLR 29, para 22) represent 'such a sum of money as might reasonably have been demanded by [the claimant] from [the defendant] as a *quid pro quo* for [permitting the continuation of the breach of covenant or other invasion of right]': *Lunn Poly*, at para 25.

[182] *Stadium Capital Holdings (No 2) Ltd v St Marylebone Co Plc* [2010] EWCA Civ 952 (CA); [2011] EWHC 2856 (Ch), [2012] 1 P & CR 7 (Vos J).

[183] *Tamares (Vincent Square) Ltd v Fairpoint Properties (Vincent Square) Ltd (No 2)* [2007] EWHC 212, (Ch) [2007] 1 WLR 2167. This decision also contains a discussion on the factors to be taken into account in deciding the likely result of a hypothetical negotiation for the voluntary release of a right.

[184] *HKRUK II (CPC) Ltd v Heaney* [2010] EWHC 2245 (Ch), [2010] 3 EGLR 15.

[185] *Pell Frischmann Engineering Ltd v Bow Valley Iran Ltd* [2009] UKPC 45, [2011] 1 WLR 2370. See ibid [47]–[50] (Lord Walker). This case was an appeal from the Channel Islands.

[186] ibid [44(4)] and [49].

The second principle was stated in the following way.

> Several of the recent cases have explored the nature of the hypothetical negotiation called for in the assessment of Wrotham Park damages. It is a negotiation between a willing buyer (the contract-breaker) and a willing seller (the party claiming damages) in which the subject matter of the negotiation is the release of the relevant contractual obligation. Both parties are to be assumed to act reasonably. The fact that one or both parties would in practice have refused to make a deal is therefore to be ignored; *Wrotham Park* [1974] 1 WLR 798, 815, *Jaggard* [1995] 1 WLR 269, 282–283.

It was also made clear that the jurisdiction to award damages on the voluntary release basis in place of an injunction, as conferred by the Chancery Amendment Act 1858 and now section 50 of the Senior Courts Act 1981, depended on the court having power to award an injunction, and it was not necessary that in the case before a court an injunction had been sought or that there was any prospect of an injunction actually being granted.[187]

(c) Lawrence v Fen Tigers Ltd

The most recent word on the present subject is the decision of the Supreme Court in *Lawrence v Fen Tigers Ltd*,[188] sometimes referred to as *Coventry v Lawrence*. In this case there was a claim for an injunction to prevent noise nuisance caused by the use of a stadium for motor sports, and the decision is of considerable importance to the question of the principles which apply to the discretion of the court to order an injunction.[189] The decision is of little assistance, and is not designed to offer much assistance, on the question of voluntary release damages. Lord Neuberger observed that it was at least arguable that, where a claimant has a prima facie case for an injunction to restrain a nuisance, and the court decides to award damages instead, those damages should not always be limited to the amount of the consequent reduction in the value of the claimant's property. He said that the damages might well, at least where it was appropriate, also include the loss of the claimant's ability to enforce rights, which may often be assessed by reference to the benefit to the defendant of not suffering an injunction. He stated that support for that approach was found in the reasoning in *Jaggard v Sawyer*. The only reservation of Lord Neuberger was that in the absence of argument on the issue it would not be appropriate for the court to decide whether, and in what circumstances, damages on this voluntary release basis could be recoverable in a nuisance claim.[190] Lest there should be any misunderstanding, it should be noted that it had 7.121

[187] ibid [47(5)].

[188] *Lawrence v Fen Tigers Ltd* [2014] UKSC 13, [2014] AC 822. A further decision of the Supreme Court in this case is reported at [2014] UKSC 46, [2015] AC 106, and is concerned with the liability of a landlord for nuisance committed by his tenant and questions of costs (the costs question was adjourned for further hearing).

[189] This aspect of the case has been discussed in section (B) of this chapter.

[190] *Lawrence v Fen Tigers Ltd* [2014] UKSC 13, [2014] AC 822 [128] and [131].

become well established in earlier authorities that an award of voluntary release damages does not depend on an injunction being sought in the proceedings or on there being any prospect of an injunction being granted if it were sought.[191] Lord Mance, having also cited *Jaggard*, said that if voluntary release damages could be awarded in a trespass case such as *Jaggard*, he did not see why it could not in principle be done in a nuisance case, but he was also unwilling to reach a final conclusion, in the absence of full argument.[192] Lord Carnwath mentioned that where there was a clearly defined interference with a specific property right, it was not difficult to imagine a hypothetical negotiation to establish an appropriate 'price' as the basis of an award of damages. Curiously, he stated that the voluntary release approach had not hitherto been extended to interference with rights of light. In fact voluntary release damages have been awarded or considered appropriate in a substantial number of previous rights of light decisions which have been mentioned earlier.[193] It has not been suggested in the line of decisions in which voluntary release damages have been applied that infringements of rights of light should be treated differently to infringement of other rights. The two leading cases in the House of Lords and the Privy Council have not suggested any such distinction.[194]

7.122 There is, therefore, nothing in this most recent decision which militates against the general, and now very widely accepted, proposition that voluntary release damages may be awarded for the infringement of many varieties of property rights, including an easement of light. Fashions and received views in the property industry and among its advisers tend to fluctuate as new decisions of the courts emerge in ways which are not always justified by those decisions and which do not always reflect the nature of the legal process. In accordance with this practice the decision of the Supreme Court in *Lawrence* has been read as throwing doubt on the

[191] See *Pell Frischmann Engineering Ltd v Bow Valley Iran Ltd* [2009] UKPC 45, [2011] 1 WLR 2370, and see para 7.120.

[192] *Lawrence v Fen Tigers Ltd* [2014] UKSC 13, [2014] AC 822 [173].

[193] ibid [248]. The cases in which voluntary release damages have been awarded or accepted as applicable for an infringement of a right of light include *Carr-Saunders v Dick McNeill Associates Ltd* [1986] 1 WLR 922; *Deakins v Hockings* [1994] 1 EGLR 190; *Midtown v City of London Real Property Co* [2005] EWHC 33 (Ch), [2005] 1 EGLR 65; *Tamares (Vincent Square) Ltd v Fairpoint Properties (Vincent Square) Ltd (No 2)* [2007] EWHC 212 (Ch), [2007] 1 WLR 2167; *HKRUK II (CPC) Ltd v Heaney* [2010] EWHC 2245 (Ch), [2010] 3 EGLR 15. The only decision referred to by Lord Carnwath was *Forsyth-Grant v Allen* [2008] EWCA Civ 508, [2008] 2 EGLR 16, in which damages were not awarded for a violation of a right of light on a restitutionary basis, i.e on the basis that the damages included the whole of any gain made by the wrongdoer from his wrong, but the Court of Appeal specifically recognised that in a rights of light case damages on a voluntary release basis might be awarded in appropriate circumstances. The reluctance of Lord Neuberger to decide on when voluntary release damages would be the appropriate method of assessment is perhaps understandable when none of the decisions in this footnote appear to have been cited to the Court, save for *Forsyth-Grant v Allen*. There can be no criticism of Lord Carnwath, since what this process illustrates is the fragility of the system of litigation in England even in the highest courts. The procedure before the Supreme Court includes the submission of full written arguments prior to the hearing of the case, yet it seems that a series of cases relevant to rights of light and voluntary release damages were not cited to the Court. The situation in the Court of Appeal in cases involving serious points of law is even less satisfactory, since the opportunity to submit prior written arguments by way of 'skeleton arguments' is even more constrained.

[194] *Attorney General v Blake* [2001] 1 AC 268; *Pell Frischmann Engineering Ltd v Bow Valley Iran Ltd* [2009] UKPC 45, [2001] 1 WLR 2370.

general acceptance of voluntary release damages in nuisance cases and property cases generally. It is nothing of the kind. The question of voluntary release damages was not for decision before the Court and the most that can be derived from the decision is that when and if the Supreme Court has before it the general question of this method of assessing damages, it will review the question. It would be unwise of those giving legal advice to read into the decision any more than this, which is what the Supreme Court explicitly said. Judges of first instance are likely to continue to award voluntary release damages in appropriate cases, including rights of light cases, as they have done for some years.

6. Voluntary Release Damages: Issues

As is demonstrated by the above review of the authorities, the use of the voluntary release method of assessing damages has now become well established as a method of compensating persons who have suffered an unlawful invasion of their property rights where an injunction is not granted so as to prevent or reverse the wrongful actions of the defendant. Even so, there remain significant uncertainties in the application of this method of damages assessment, such as the exact circumstances in which it will be applied and its exact theoretical basis. This section of the chapter therefore goes on to consider: 7.123

(a) the true compensatory nature of voluntary release damages;
(b) the question of whether damages on a voluntary release basis are always appropriate where there is a violation of a right of light but no injunction is granted;
(c) the ascertainment of the proportion of any gain to the servient owner to be payable as damages, its division among more than one claimant, and the factors which are relevant to the determination of this proportion; and
(d) the date of the hypothetical negotiation for a voluntary release of the right of light.

All of these matters may be of significance when damages assessed by the voluntary release method are claimed for the violation of a right of light. It is difficult to discern from the authorities or from any principle why the various considerations should operate differently in rights of light cases as compared to property cases generally.

7. Voluntary Release Damages: Compensatory Nature

It should be made clear at the outset that damages assessed in this way are compensatory in nature. There is a natural tendency to think that in having to pay as damages some part of his unjustified gain, the defendant is being punished for his 7.124

wrongful act. This is a misconception. If the defendant was being punished in this way he would be required to pay over the whole of his wrongful gain, and perhaps even some additional sum as a sort of punishment, but that is not the basis or the purpose of voluntary release damages. It is possible that in some cases an assessment of damages by the method just mentioned could be made, but doing so enters the realm of restitutionary or exemplary damages, subjects which are referred to briefly later but which have little, if any, place in rights of light proceedings.[195]

7.125 The reason that voluntary release damages are truly compensatory in nature is that they compensate the dominant owner for a part of what he has lost. If the servient owner had not wrongfully and for his own gain erected an obstruction to light, the dominant owner could have negotiated with him for the payment of a sum of money in return for the removal or release or variation of the easement of light such as would be necessary to render lawful that which had been done or was about to be done by the servient owner. Voluntary release damages are therefore a means of compensating the dominant owner for what he has in truth and reality lost, namely the opportunity to obtain a sum of money by negotiating for the voluntary release by him of his rights. Loss of opportunity is a traditional item of compensatory damages for contractual and other wrongs and there is no reason why it should not figure as the basis of compensatory damages in cases involving a violation of property rights, including rights of light.[196] The reason that the damages may be calculated by reference to the amount of financial gain which the servient owner makes by his wrongful acts arises not from the need to punish the servient owner, but from the fact that in any negotiation for the release of the rights of the dominant owner the amount of any gain anticipated to accrue to the servient owner would be likely to play a central part in the reaching of an agreement.

7.126 There cannot be any doubt that the ability of the owner of one piece of land to facilitate development on some other land, either by granting a right to the owner of that other land or by releasing some restriction which binds the owner of that other land, may add to, and may be a component of, the value of the first piece of land. That this is so has been the commonplace of valuations of land for the purposes of compensation for compulsory acquisition for many years, where it is sometimes called the *Stokes v Cambridge* principle.[197] This principle is applied where by statute and for the purposes of compensation the value of the land

[195] See section (C)12 and 13 of this chapter.

[196] For example, a person who is deprived of a contractual right to participate in a form of beauty competition may be awarded damages for this loss of opportunity: *Chaplin v Hicks* [1911] 2 KB 786. In *Lunn Poly Ltd v Liverpool & Lancashire Property Ltd* [2006] EWCA Civ 430, [2006] 2 EGLR 29 [29], Neuberger LJ pointed out that damages of the present nature were meant to be compensatory. The compensatory nature of the damages was also mentioned by the Court of Appeal in *Jaggard v Sawyer* [1995] 1 WLR 269, a leading decision in the development of the voluntary release method of assessing damages: see para 7.115.

[197] *Stokes v Cambridge Corporation* (1962) 13 P & CR 77. This is a decision of the Lands Tribunal on the valuation of land acquired compulsorily. Its facts are examined in more detail at para 7.136.

must be taken to be the amount which the land, if sold in the open market by a willing seller, might be expected to realise.[198] The opportunity to gain a sum by way of negotiation for the creation or release of a right over other land is therefore regarded as part of the value of a piece of land for the purposes of its valuation. If this is so in the context of land valuation generally, and in the particular context of the valuation of land for the purposes of assessing compensation for compulsory acquisition, it is difficult to see why as a matter of principle this same component of value, the ability to agree a sum for conferring some benefit on the owner of a different piece of land by the grant or release of rights, should not be considered to be a part of the value of the dominant building in rights of light cases and therefore something for the loss of which the dominant owner should in principle be compensated by an award of damages.

8. Voluntary Release Damages: Discretion

The next question is whether the voluntary release method of assessment is to be used in all cases where damages are awarded for the infringement of a right of light. Logic and ordinary principle suggest that the voluntary release method is applicable at least unless there are exceptional circumstances. Damages are not a purely discretionary remedy in the same way as an injunction, so that if a person is entitled to damages, and if his loss includes the loss of an opportunity to obtain a sum for a voluntary release of his rights by negotiation, it is difficult to see on what basis he can be denied that element of his loss as a part of the damages awarded to him. The root purpose of an award of damages is to put a person in the same position as he would have been had a wrong not been committed against him, so far as a monetary payment to him can achieve that aim.[199] Where a person whose rights of light are violated is deprived of a bargaining opportunity, a real and quantifiable loss, to refuse to award him damages equivalent to that loss seems to be a denial of the fundamental purposes of damages. It may not be easy to apply this method of damages assessment where the servient owner has not made and does not anticipate making any monetary gain from his wrongful act. For example, an unsightly extension to a building may obstruct light to a neighbouring building without adding any identifiable capital value to the building extended. Damages cannot be awarded as a proportion of a non-existent monetary gain. Nonetheless a servient owner who erects an obstruction will normally have some motive for doing so, and the voluntary release principle can still be applied by asking what that owner would pay for the release of a restriction which prevents him doing that which he wishes. The fact that a person will not make a monetary gain out of what he 7.127

198 Land Compensation Act 1961 s 5, rule (2).
199 See para 7.66.

intends to do does not mean that he will not pay a sum, and perhaps a substantial sum, for the ability to fulfil his wish by lawful means.

7.128 Although the voluntary release methodology has been applied or considered appropriate in a substantial number of cases, including cases involving claims for damages for an infringement of rights of light, the only decision in which it has been rejected as a method in a rights of light claim is the decision of the Court of Appeal in *Forsyth-Grant v Allen*.[200] This was an unusual case in which damages were claimed on a restitutionary basis which is quite different from the voluntary release basis[201] and in which the claimant had behaved in an unsatisfactory fashion in not being willing to discuss matters in dispute with the servient owner. The claimant was confined to damages calculated as the reduction in the value of his property. Even so the court accepted that there might be rights of light claims in which voluntary release damages would be appropriate.[202] It may be that because voluntary release damages are regarded as equitable, or as it was put in one decision quasi-equitable,[203] a court should be regarded as having a discretion as to whether to award damages on this basis. The theoretical explanation of the discretion to award damages assessed by the voluntary release method may be that as the damages relate to the future and continuing wrong constituted by the erection or retention of an obstruction to light on the servient land those damages are necessarily equitable (or quasi-equitable) in nature and the power to award equitable damages in place of an injunction, as originally conferred by the Chancery Amendment Act 1858, is a power the exercise of which is discretionary. However, the reduction in the rental and capital value of the dominant building caused by the future or continuing obstruction is also something which follows from future or continuing wrongs which are not prevented or redressed by an injunction and so can also be considered an aspect of equitable damages and on this basis should also presumably be considered discretionary. The distinction between common law damages and equitable damages is mainly historical and has been considered more fully earlier in this chapter. As mentioned earlier, the apparent discretion to refuse voluntary release damages and to confine a claimant to book value damages on the reasoning that voluntary release damages are equitable or quasi-equitable

[200] *Forsyth-Grant v Allen* [2008] EWCA Civ 505, [2008] 2 EGLR 1. See para 7.119. The decision in *Surrey County Council v Bredero Homes Ltd* [1993] 1 WLR 1361, which was a refusal of the Court of Appeal to apply this method in a claim for damages for breach of covenant, should probably be regarded as incorrect following the observations made on it in the House of Lords in *Attorney General v Blake* [2001] 1 AC 768. See para 7.117. The *Bredero* decision may also be explicable on the footing that the claim in that case was for common law damages and not equitable damages: see para 7.74(iii).

[201] See section (C)12 of this chapter for the restitutionary basis of the assessment of damages.

[202] *Forsyth-Grant v Allen* [2009] EWCA Civ 505, [2008] 2 EGLR 1 [32] (Patten J).

[203] *Lunn Poly Ltd v Liverpool & Lancashire Properties Ltd* [2006] 2 EGLR 29, [2006] EWCA Civ 430 [21] (Neuberger LJ). It is a characteristic of forms of equitable relief such as an injunction or specific performance that a court always has a discretion on whether to grant the relief, and the conduct of a claimant, whether, as it is said, he comes to the court with clean hands, is relevant to the decision on the grant of an injunction: see para 7.35.

in nature may be one of the few significant practical consequences of the distinction between common law and equitable damages in rights of light claims.[204]

7.129 In *Lawrence v Fen Tigers Ltd* Lord Neuberger contemplated that there might be some circumstances in which voluntary release damages were appropriate and some in which they were not appropriate. He declined to lay down any principles in the absence of full argument on the subject.[205] However, such reasoning cuts across the principle that where possible the assessment of equitable damages, in the sense of damages in lieu of an injunction, should be on the same basis as the assessment of damages generally or at common law.[206] If a person suffers a physical injury for which damages of, say, £50,000 are appropriate on general principles of assessment so as to compensate that person for the loss so far as money can do so, there is no question of the damages being reduced to only a part of the loss, because the claimant behaves unhelpfully in asserting his right or in seeking to agree the amount of the damages. There is a similar lack of clarity in the circumstances in which restitutionary damages may be awarded.[207] While it appears that the conduct of a person who claims damages may be such as to disentitle him to voluntary release damages, it has been held that once the court decides that voluntary release damages are to be awarded, the conduct of a party will not be held against him so as to reduce the sum determined as the result of the hypothetical negotiations.[208] The reason may be that the hypothetical negotiations are taken to be conducted between reasonable persons without a disposition to difficult conduct such as might oppress or benefit one or other of the actual parties to the litigation.[209]

7.130 It seems likely that courts will continue to regard the award of damages on the voluntary release principle as discretionary, with damages based on the diminution of the capital value of the dominant building caused by the loss of natural light as a minimum figure below which the damages cannot fall. However, given that the loss of bargaining opportunity is a real loss which, like any other loss which is not too remote, should be reflected in the damages awarded, given the

[204] It was held in *Battishill v Reed* (1856) 18 CB 696 that common law damages for a continuing nuisance (overhanging of property by eaves and a gutter) could not be awarded for a reduction in the value of the property, since that would be to award damages not for the nuisance which had occurred at the date of the award of the damages but for future and continuing nuisances. This reasoning supports the view that book value damages may on a strict analysis be as much equitable damages as are voluntary release damages.

[205] *Lawrence v Fen Tigers Ltd* [2014] UKSC 13, [2014] AC 822 [128] and [131].

[206] *Johnson v Agnew* [1980] AC 367, [1979] 2 WLR 487, 400 (Lord Wilberforce).

[207] See para 7.161.

[208] *Amec Developments Ltd v Jury's Hotel Management (UK) Ltd* [2001] 1 EGLR 81. However, delay by a claimant in asserting a claim, which is surely an aspect of his conduct, may be something which reduces the amount of voluntary release damages: see *Pell Frischmann Engineering v Bow Valley Iran Ltd* [2009] UKPC 45, [2011] 1 WLR 2370 [54] (see para 7.120 of this chapter). There are still inconsistencies of approach to be resolved in this area of the law.

[209] See *Pell Frischmann Engineering Ltd v Bow Valley Iran Ltd* [2009] UKPC 45, [2011] 1 WLR 2370, and see para 7.134.

natural disinclination to allow a wrongdoer to benefit from a large gain achieved by his wrongful acts but paying only small damages, and given the approval of the voluntary release method of damage assessment by the highest courts, it also seems likely that an award of damages on the basis of the result of a voluntary and hypothetical negotiation for the release of rights can be expected to be made in all but exceptional cases when an injunction is not issued. A possible example, mentioned later, of when a claimant may be confined to book value damages is when a number of properties suffer an actionable injury but the owners of some of them delay in making a claim for damages.[210] It is at least established that in principle, voluntary release damages can be awarded even if a claimant does not seek an injunction or even if the circumstances are such that there is no prospect of an injunction being granted. It should be for a defendant who wishes to avoid paying damages on the voluntary release basis to establish the exceptional circumstances which would justify refusing damages on that basis.

7.131 A theory which has grown up amongst some of those who advise or report on rights of light matters is that if the reduction of light to the dominant building is small and there is no question of an injunction, that situation also means that voluntary release damages are inappropriate. An owner of land is entitled to the protection of the law to compensate him for a violation of his rights as much when the violation is small as when it is large. A landowner is as much entitled to prevent someone trespassing on his land by taking a short cut over it for 10 minutes as he is to prevent someone unlawfully taking possession of the whole of his land for a week. The fact that the reduction in light to the dominant building caused by works on the servient land is small may be relevant to (a) the question of whether there has been an actionable injury or (b) the question of whether an injunction should be granted to prevent or remove the obstruction or (c) the amount of money which might be obtained in a voluntary negotiation to permit the obstruction.[211] It cannot in all logic and justice lead to the conclusion that there should be no damages at all for a real loss to the dominant owner caused by the removal of his ability to negotiate a sum to be paid for the release by him of his rights.[212] A similar misconception, mentioned earlier, is that where the reduction in light is small an injunction will necessarily be refused.[213]

[210] See para 7.144.

[211] In *Tamares (Vincent Square) Ltd v Fairpoint Properties (Vincent Square) Ltd (No 2)* [2007] EWHC 212 (Ch), [2007] 1 WLR 2167, the damages awarded were reduced from a third of the anticipated development value to a slightly lower figure because the infringement of the right of light was small. This approach can be justified on the reasoning that a dominant owner who realised that the loss of value to his property would be small is more likely to accept a smaller proportion of the development gain than he would if the loss in value would be large. This reasoning, solid and sensible in itself, is of course quite different from the suggestion that because the injury to the dominant building is small, voluntary release damages should not be awarded at all.

[212] The fact that a reduction in light is small is sometimes thought to justify the assessment of 'enhanced damages' that is damages which are some multiple of the book value loss. As explained in para 7.113, there is no justification in logic or authority for this proposition.

[213] See para 7.42.

It has been held by the Court of Appeal that when a right such as a right of way or a right of light appurtenant to a property is overridden by a statutory power to carry out a project, and compensation is payable to the owner of the right under section 10 of the Compulsory Purchase Act 1965, no account of loss of bargaining opportunity is to be taken into account in assessing the compensation.[214] This decision was at a time when the use of voluntary release damages in private law disputes was not as well established as it is today. It seems a harsh and scarcely logical approach to say that if a person's rights are infringed by another citizen he can claim damages which truly recompense him for his loss, but if the same rights are taken away by a public body and in the public interest no compensation is to be paid for an important component of the loss of the landowner.[215] 7.132

9. Voluntary Release Damages: Determining the Amount

(a) The Hypothetical Negotiations

The theory behind the assessment of voluntary release damages is that there is a hypothetical negotiation between the owners of the dominant and the servient properties which results in a fair settlement of a sum to be paid to the dominant owner for the release of his right of light to the extent necessary to allow the servient owner lawfully to erect or maintain a specified obstruction. The concept of a hypothetical negotiation to arrive at a value of land or of an interest or right in land is familiar to the law. Valuations of land are required for a variety of purposes from assessing compensation for compulsory purchase to the valuation of land for the purposes of capital gains tax or inheritance tax. For example, for the purposes of assessing compensation for compulsory purchase the compensation is equal to the value of the land acquired and statute directs that the value is to be the amount which the land if sold in the open market by a willing seller at a specified valuation date might be expected to realise.[216] Such a provision necessarily enjoins a hypothetical negotiation leading to a hypothetical sale of the land. The determination of an open market rent as required by most rent review clauses in leases also requires the assumption of a hypothetical negotiation. 7.133

There is a possible difference between a hypothetical sale of land required for a land valuation and a hypothetical negotiation for the release of a right such as a right of light. In the first type of case the parties are hypothetical: a hypothetical willing seller and a hypothetical willing purchaser. They are not any real person 7.134

[214] *Wrotham Park Settled Estates v Hertsmere Borough Council* [1993] 2 EGLR 13. This decision concerned the overriding of an easement under s 237 of the Town and Country Planning Act 1990, a subject examined in ch 8.

[215] This matter is further considered in ch 8, section (C)1(b) and 2(b).

[216] Compulsory Purchase Act 1965, s 7; Land Compensation Act 1961, s 5, rule (2), replacing the same language in rule 2 in s 2 of the Compulsory Purchase (Assessment of Compensation) Act 1919.

or any actual corporate entity.[217] In the second type of case the negotiators are real, although the negotiation itself is, of course, hypothetical. In any negotiation between real persons the personalities and strengths of those involved may be an important factor in determining the result of a negotiation. For the purposes of the hypothetical negotiation between the two actual owners of land needed to assess voluntary release damages, both of them are for present purposes taken to act fairly and sensibly and reasonably, whether or not they would in reality do so. Thus the fact that one party may have a dominating personality or high experience of commercial negotiation not shared by the other party should not influence the result.[218] On the other hand the personal circumstances of the two parties can probably be taken into account where this would be relevant to their negotiating strength, for instance the fact that one party was a person of limited means. This may represent a difference between the two types of case distinguished at the beginning of this paragraph since in the hypothetical sale or letting enunciated for the purpose of valuing land in cases of compensation for compulsory purchase or rent reviews personal attributes of parties, eg that a person is pressed by his creditors for money, are normally disregarded.[219] The practical result of this approach is that the judge is given a good deal of latitude in imposing a result of the hypothetical negotiations which accords with that which he believes would be reached by two reasonable people. Any difference between the hypothetical sale or letting envisaged in valuing land and the hypothetical negotiation envisaged in assessing voluntary release damages may not be great. In the first case the assumed negotiation is between hypothetical parties taken to act reasonably and in the second case the assumed negotiation is between actual parties taken to act reasonably. Any difference is in most cases a fine one.

7.135 The hypothetical negotiation is one in which the two parties have competing, but in one sense similar, interests. The servient owner plainly has an interest in being permitted to erect a structure which will provide for him a gain. Without an agreement with the dominant owner, he cannot achieve that gain. The dominant owner is in the position in which, unless he can come to an agreement with the servient owner, he will be left without any form of participation in the potential gain. In such a situation courts and tribunals have often reasoned that the logical result of a negotiation is that the amount of the gain will be split on an equal basis between the two negotiating parties. Unless there is some particular reason to depart from that proportion it appears to be the logical and fair result of the negotiation.

7.136 The well-known *Stokes v Cambridge*[220] principle, referred to earlier, proceeds on just this footing. In that case, a piece of land was valued for the purposes of

[217] The classic explanations of the meaning of hypothetical parties are those of Hoffmann LJ in *Executors of Lady Fox v IRC* [1994] 2 EGLR 185 and of Donaldson J in *Evans (Leeds) Ltd v English Electric Co* [1978] 1 EGLR 93.

[218] *Pell Frischmann Engineering Ltd v Bow Valley Iran Ltd* [2009] UKPC 45, [2011] 1 WLR 2370 [49] (Lord Walker).

[219] *Evans (Leeds) Ltd v English Electric Co* [1978] 1 EGLR 93.

[220] *Stokes v Cambridge Corporation* (1962) 13 P & CR 77.

compensation for compulsory acquisition. The land in question had a value for industrial development, but that development could only be achieved by the acquisition of a right of way over adjoining land. The starting point of the Lands Tribunal when assessing the compensation was that the owner of the land acquired and being valued would be willing to pay to the owner of the adjoining land 50 per cent of the development value released by the grant of the right of way in order to obtain that grant. There were, however, special circumstances in that particular case in that the person over whose land a right of way was required would, if development of the land being valued took place for industrial purposes, obtain a further benefit in that the expectation of permission to develop his own land for a similar purpose would be enhanced. It was decided that in these special circumstances the owner of the land over which the grant of the right of way was required would have been willing to agree to grant the necessary right of way in return for not a half but only one third of the development value released by that grant. This decision and its reasoning illustrate the way in which the particular negotiating strengths and weaknesses of the parties to a hypothetical negotiation should be carefully evaluated by persons who prognosticate the likely result of that hypothetical negotiation.

The particular facts of the *Stokes* decision sometimes lead to some misunderstanding. The decision supports a 50-50 division of the development value released by an agreement in the absence of any special circumstances. This is logical, since if a particular gain will accrue dependent on the agreement of two parties, reason and common sense indicate that in the absence of other considerations the parties are likely to agree to divide the actionable gain equally between them. Because of the special facts of the situation in *Stokes*, the normal division is sometimes represented as being on a one-third/two-thirds basis. Neither logic nor what was said by the Lands Tribunal in *Stokes* supports this last form of division.[221] 7.137

The underlying principle is, therefore, (a) that in the absence of special circumstances two parties to a negotiation needed to release a development value of land would be likely to share that development value equally between them in an agreement which they reached and (b) that special circumstances may operate to reduce (or possibly even enhance) the amount of the development value which would be agreed to be paid by the person who needed a right or the release of a right in order to realise a development value. These principles have been applied in a number of subsequent authorities relating to the valuation of land for compulsory purchase.[222] Despite the attractions of a 50-50 split of the value which would be 7.138

[221] This apparent error appears in, for example, the recent Law Commission report, *Rights to Light* (Law Com No 356, 2014) para 5.52. It seems that a similar misunderstanding may have occurred in *Tamares Ltd v Fairpoint Properties (No 2)* [2007] EWHC 212 (Ch), [2007] 1 WLR 2167, 2173.

[222] See, eg *Ozanne v Hertfordshire County Council* [1991] RVR 229 (see [1991] 1 WLR 105 for the subsequent decision of the House of Lords); *Batchelor v Kent County Council* [1990] 1 EGLR 32. A similar 50 per cent division of the value released has been adopted when valuing the reversion on a lease where there was a marriage value to be obtained by the merger of the landlord's and the tenant's interests and the amount which the tenant as a potential bidder in the market for the landlord's interest

obtained by the release of a right of light which prevented development, the courts have usually concluded that a more modest proportion of the gain from the development would be agreed between the two parties and so would become payable as the voluntary release damages.

7.139 It is inherently extremely unlikely that the servient owner would be willing to agree to pay 100 per cent of the gain which he was to make from the offending development. There would be no purpose from his point of view in reaching such an agreement, since he would be giving up the whole of any gain which he could make. In one case the Court of Appeal overturned a judgment in the court of first instance which had awarded 100 per cent of the gain as voluntary release damages, and on remission of the case for further consideration an amount of damages at a 50 per cent level was awarded.[223] An award of 100 per cent of the gain as voluntary release damages would be an award of damages on a restitutionary rather than a voluntary release basis.[224]

(b) General Considerations

7.140 There are certain general considerations which may assist in the prognostication of the result of the hypothetical negotiation. It is necessary to be careful to avoid double-counting.[225] A dominant owner may suffer a diminution in the value of his property and may seek compensation for this as well as for a share in the development gain brought about by the offending obstruction on the servient land. It is for a court to consider how these two elements of loss, a reduction in value of land and the loss of an opportunity to obtain a sum for a voluntary release, should be reflected in the result of the hypothetical negotiation between the parties. It is certainly not necessarily the case that a servient owner in a fair negotiation would always be willing to compensate the dominant owner by paying the amount of the reduction in the value of his land and a substantial proportion of the gain. There are likely to be instances in which a part of a development on the servient land could be carried out without an actionable injury being caused to the dominant owner and it is only some additional or particular element of that development which causes the actionable injury. In these circumstances the hypothetical negotiation is likely to concentrate on not the whole of the gain which the servient owner will make from the whole of his development, but only on that additional gain which he will make from that part of the development which causes the actionable injury to the dominant building. For example, the servient owner

would agree to pay has been held to be a half of that marriage value: see *Norfolk v Trinity College Cambridge* (1976) 32 P & CR 147; *Lloyd Jones v Church Commissioners* [1983] RVR 89 (decisions on s 9 of the Leasehold Reform Act 1967 prior to its amendment).

[223] *Stadium Capital Holdings (No 2) Ltd v St Marylebone Co Plc* [2010] EWCA Civ 952 (CA); [2011] EWHC 2856 (Ch), [2012] 1 P & CR 7 (Vos J).

[224] See para 7.159 et seq for restitutionary damages.

[225] *Lawrence v Fen Tigers Ltd* [2014] UKSC 13, [2014] AC 822 [128] (Lord Neuberger).

may wish to erect a building of eight storeys on his land in circumstances in which a six-storey building would create no actionable injury to the dominant land, but the extra obstruction to light caused by the additional two storeys would cause the injury. The hypothetical negotiation will then concentrate on the value to the servient owner of becoming entitled lawfully to erect the additional two storeys.

It is not possible for parties to an actual rights of light dispute or negotiation to estimate with any certainty the proportion of the gain to the servient owner from his potential or actual wrongful actions which a court will award as voluntary release damages. Indeed, and as mentioned earlier, while an estimate and a division of a potential development gain may play a part in the estimate of voluntary release damages, that is not the only way in which the amount of such damages may be calculated. There will be cases in which no identifiable monetary gain has been or will be made by the servient owner, but that fact does not prevent a court looking to the result of a hypothetical negotiation.[226] Actual awards of damages have varied between 5 per cent of the profit made by the offending development, as in the *Wrotham Park*[227] decision which commenced the general award of damages on a voluntary release basis, to substantially higher awards of up to 50 per cent of the development gain in a later case. A summary of the proportions of the gain which have led to various assessments of damages in relation to different forms of breach of property rights is found in the current edition of *Gale on Easements.*[228] It can be argued that in the absence of any special facts a central figure which emerges from this record of decided cases and from the theoretical basis of a hypothetical negotiation is that awards of damages of something in the area of 25 to 40 per cent of the monetary gain which accrues to a servient owner from his wrongful obstruction may be the order of damages which are awarded. However, actual decisions show a span of 5 to 50 per cent of the gain. It is assumed 7.141

[226] See para 7.112.

[227] *Wrotham Park Estate Co Ltd v Parkside Homes* [1974] 1 WLR 798.

[228] See *Gale on Easements*, 19th edn (London, Sweet & Maxwell, 2012). Some of the main decisions on the subject resulted in the following proportions of the gain to the wrongdoer forming the damages (or forming what would have been the damages if no injunction had been granted): *Wrotham Park Estate Co Ltd v Parkside Homes Ltd* [1974] 1 WLR 798: 5 per cent (breach of a restrictive covenant); *Bracewell v Appleby* [1975] Ch 408: 40 per cent (obstruction of a right of way); *Carr-Saunders v Dick McNeill Associates Ltd* [1986] 1 WLR 922: 2–3 times the book value (infringement of a right of light); *Deakins v Hookings* [1994] 1 EGLR 190: 15 per cent (infringement of a right of light); *Jaggard v Sawyer* [1995] 1 WLR 269: 25–35 per cent (breach of a restrictive covenant and a trespass); *HKRUK (CHC) Ltd v Heaney* [2010] EWHC 2245 (Ch), [2010] 3 EGLR 15: 16 per cent (proportion of the anticipated profits that would have been awarded if an injunction had not been granted) (infringement of a right of light); *Stadium Capital Holdings (No 2) Ltd v St Marylebone Co Plc* [2011] EWHC 2856 (Ch), [2012] 1 P & CR 7: 50 per cent of the income which a landlord had obtained for the erection of hoardings which were in part on the claimant's land and so were a trespass (erection of hoardings without permission); *Tamares (Vincent Square) Ltd v Fairpoint Properties (Vincent Square) Ltd (No 2)* [2007] EWHC 212 (Ch), [2007] 1 WLR 2167: 33 per cent, then a reduction because the infringement was small (infringement of a right of light); *Kettel v Bloomfield Ltd* [2012] EWHC 1422 (Ch), [2012] 2 P & CR DG16: 50 per cent of gain after deduction of 25 per cent for developer's profit (infringement of an easement to park vehicles); *Enfield LBC v Outdoor Plus Ltd* [2013] EWCA Civ 608, [2012] 2 EGLR 105: 50 per cent of notional licence fee for the erection of hoardings (erection of hoardings as a trespass).

that the parties will reach agreement and the possibility of their failing to do, which in actual negotiations may exist, is to be disregarded.[229]

(c) Multiple Claimants

7.142 Cases may occur in which there is more than one person with an interest in the dominant building having the benefit of a right of light and able and willing to sue for damages. The indication from the authorities is that in these circumstances the correct process may be first to estimate what sum would be obtained in a negotiation for the voluntary release of a right of light and then to apportion that sum equally between those persons who have a claim for damages.[230] This may be an entirely acceptable approach where all those persons whose interests have been infringed have a similar interest, for example a series of householders equally affected by a breach of a restrictive covenant. The situation may be significantly different where different persons with different interests in the dominant building assert a right of light. It often occurs that rights of light acquired in favour of the apertures in the building are passed to different tenants of different parts of the building simply because on the grant of the leases there is no exclusion of the benefit of the accrued rights of light. The position of a landlord of the whole building may be very different from that of a short-term tenant of a part of the building whose lease is nearing its end. Conversely, a tenant of a building may have a long lease at a low rent, which means that any damage to the landlord's reversionary interest may be long delayed. Circumstances of this nature suggest that an equal division between claimants of an overall sum may not be always the correct way of awarding damages. In such cases it may be necessary to envisage some claimants in their hypothetical negotiation having a stronger bargaining position than others or having more to lose than others and so being entitled to a higher share of some overall amount of damages.

7.143 It is possible to envisage two different types of situation where there are multiple claimants. The most obvious case is where a development infringes the rights of light of different persons with different properties, for instance a new office block which affects a number of surrounding houses. The other type of situation is where different persons have different interests in a single property which is affected by a new development, for instance the various tenants of a dominant building used

[229] *Wrotham Park Estate Co Ltd v Parkside Homes Ltd* [1974] 1 WLR 798, 815; *Jaggard v Sawyer* [1995] 1 WLR 269, 282–83; *Enfield LBC v Outdoor Plus Ltd* [2012] EWCA Civ 608, [2012] 2 EGLR 105. In accordance with the same principle when it has to be determined what would be the result of a negotiation between hypothetical parties for a letting of demised premises for the purposes of a rent review under a lease, it is assumed that agreement would be reached: see *Evans (FR) Leeds Ltd v English Electric Co Ltd* [1978] 1 EGLR 93 (Donaldson J).

[230] See *Jaggard v Sawyer* [1995] 1 WLR 269 (damages divided equally between nine persons); *Bracewell v Appleby* [1975] Ch 408 (damages divided equally between five persons); *Small v Oliver and Saunders (Developments) Ltd* [2006] EWHC 1293 (Ch), [2006] 3 EGLR 141 (equal division of a percentage of the development profit between 48 persons entitled to enforce a restrictive covenant).

as multi-let offices or as flats. The theory appears to be that in the latter type of case, loss to the building as a whole is assessed and is then divided between the various occupiers of the building, with the corollary that the total amount paid as damages cannot exceed the total loss to the building.[231] The rationale behind this principle is not obvious. Where persons have different leasehold interests in a property, each of them may have a separate easement of light over servient land acquired separately by prescription. One might then suppose that the damages, however assessed, for each individual claimant depended on the circumstances of his lease, rather than on some division of an overall loss to the building. It is not apparent how the overall loss to the building is to be calculated in such circumstances, unless for this purpose there is taken to be a freehold owner in possession of the whole of the building.

The extent of the reduction in light and the injury caused to different claimants may vary. A property close to the obstruction may be affected more seriously in its loss of light than a property further away, even though both properties endure actionable injuries, and in such a case the owner of the closer property might expect to obtain a higher sum in the hypothetical negotiation for the release of rights. It may be that where there is more than one claimant who is awarded voluntary release damages, the hypothetical negotiation is to be envisaged as carried on by all of the claimants acting together as a body, although with each claimant not necessarily agreeing the same sum as the others. It could occur that there are, say, six property owners likely to suffer an injury, but only three bring their claims for damages before the court. Probably in such circumstances the voluntary release damages should be assessed on the hypothesis of an agreement between the three claimants and the servient owner, with the other persons ignored.[232] On the other hand the amount that the servient owner would be willing to pay to those persons who made a claim might be reduced because of his apprehension that others with a potential claim might later come forward and demand a similar sum. If it is the case that voluntary release damages can be denied to claimants in certain circumstances, then it could occur that some claimants but not others are denied any part in damages assessed on this basis and are confined to the diminution in the value of their interest in the dominant building brought about by the unlawful obstruction. It has been said that delay in bringing a claim might result in a reduction in the damages assessed on a voluntary release basis.[233] 7.144

[231] *Rust v Victoria Graving Dock Co* (1887) 36 Ch D 113, 130 (Cotton LJ); *Hunter v Canary Wharf Ltd* [1997] AC 655, 606–07 (Lord Hoffmann).

[232] There would be nothing to prevent the other dominant owners bringing an action for damages in the future. It may be that if the award of voluntary release damages is discretionary, the later claimants would be confined to book value damages because of their delay in asserting their rights.

[233] *Pell Frischmann Engineering Co v Bow Valley Iran Ltd* [2009] UKPC 45, [2011] 1 WLR 2370 [54]. See however para 7.129 of this chapter.

(d) Expert Evidence

7.145 There may be a substantial role for expert evidence when damages are assessed on a voluntary release basis. Such evidence may be valuable in relation to two matters. The first matter is an estimate of the gain which the servient owner will make from the erection of an unlawful structure on the servient land. For example, if the unlawful structure is the increase in the height of a building on the servient land the gain to the servient owner may be the increase in value of his property when the extended building has been completed less the costs of carrying out that extension. Expert evidence may be necessary to gauge the extent of the gain to the servient owner. Such evidence may come from a valuer in connection with the value of the extended building and from other experts, such as a quantity surveyor, in connection with the cost of constructing the extension. In *Tamares (Vincent Square) Ltd v Fairpoint Properties (Vincent Square) Ltd (No 2)*[234] the court heard conflicting evidence from experts on the anticipated profit and held that the result of the hypothetical negotiation would have been that the parties would have agreed a figure for the voluntary release of the right of light which was one third of the half way point between the views of the experts with a subsequent downwards adjustment because the infringement was small. The approach of the judge in this case illustrates an important principle in respect of voluntary release damages. The function of the court is not necessarily to decide which evidence is correct or more correct when there is conflicting expert evidence of the anticipated gain but is rather to decide what sum the parties would have agreed for a voluntary release of the right of light in view of the conflicting expert evidence on the likely gain which they might have presented to each other.

7.146 The second area in which expert evidence may assist the court is an estimate of what would be likely to be the result of the hypothetical negotiation for the release of the rights of the dominant owner. Those with experience of such negotiations and with experience on matters of how a division of the development potential of land or the marriage value of two interests in land or two pieces of land is reached may be able to give assistance to the court. When land has to be valued for various purposes and the *Stokes v Cambridge* principle is applied, expert valuation evidence is often given to establish what would be the result of a hypothetical negotiation to divide a gain in the value of land brought about by a grant or a release of rights.[235] It must, however, be understood that the final judgment of what would be the result of hypothetical negotiations and of what the court feels right as the likely result of those negotiations is a matter for the judge.

[234] *Tamares (Vincent Square) Ltd v Fairpoint (Vincent Square) Ltd (No 2)* [2007] EWHC 212 (Ch), [2007] 1 WLR 2167.

[235] See para 7.136 for the *Stokes v Cambridge* principle. There may be a common knowledge that the sum to be paid for some consent, such as a licence to permit advertising hoardings to be erected on a person's land, was commonly agreed at 50 per cent of the income from letting space for hoardings, and if so evidence of this could be adduced: see *Stadium Capital Holdings (No 2) Ltd v St Marylebone Co Plc* [2011] EWHC 2856 (Ch), [2012] 1 P & CR 7.

(e) Guidance from Decided Cases

7.147 In principle any factor which would be relevant to the hypothetical negotiation between reasonable parties should be taken into account by the court. One factor to be left out of account is a possible reluctance to reach an agreement, or any intransigence of one or other of the parties. The parties are assumed to act as reasonable persons would act. It is only if such an assumption is made that this method of assessing damages can operate sensibly at all. In one case the fact that one of the parties was a very determined, or even recklessly determined, negotiator was said to be something to be disregarded.[236]

7.148 Some guidance on the correct approach and the matters to be taken into consideration can be derived from the decided cases.[237] The following general guidance can be noted.

(i) The parties are taken to agree a proper or reasonable sum. This sum is said to be contrasted to a 'ransom sum'.[238] In general valuation practice and terminology a price which a person agrees in order to confer a right or release a right to enable development to take place is often called a ransom sum, and probably all that is meant by the rejection of a ransom sum is that the dominant owner who exerts the ransom is taken to act reasonably in the negotiations.

(ii) The parties are assumed to carry out and complete their negotiation before the offending obstruction has been erected.[239] This assumption deprives the dominant owner of the bargaining advantage he might have if he could threaten to seek the removal of a building already erected or in the course of erection with the additional cost which would then be borne by the servient owner. The logic of this principle suggests that the award of damages as a part of the anticipated gain may exceed the gain ultimately made by the defendant since that gain may in the event be substantially less than was anticipated.[240] Therefore even if the development on the servient land has been completed and sold when the damages are assessed so that the amount of the gain to the servient owner is known the assessment should take place by reference to the gain expected prior to the development rather

[236] *Pell Frischmann Engineering Ltd v Bow Valley Iran Ltd* [2009] UKPC 45, [2011] 1 WLR 2370 [49] (Lord Walker).

[237] There is a useful general discussion on what is relevant in *Amec Developments Ltd v Jury's Hotel Management (UK) Ltd* [2001] 1 EGLR 81 (Anthony Mann QC sitting as a Judge of the High Court) and in *Tamares (Vincent Square) Ltd v Fairpoint Properties (Vincent Square) Ltd (No 2)* [2007] EWHC 212 (Ch), [2007] 1 WLR 2167 (Gabriel Moss QC sitting as a Judge of the High Court).

[238] *Jaggard v Sawyer* [1995] 1 WLR 269, 282 (Sir Thomas Bingham MR). A further expression which has gained currency in this context is a 'ransom strip'. This means a small piece of land which has little or no intrinsic value except that it holds the key to the development or use of some other piece of land, for instance by providing the only practicable means of access from the other land to a public highway. The value of the strip is often termed a ransom value.

[239] *Amec Developments Ltd v Jury's Hotel Management (UK) Ltd* [2001] 1 EGLR 81 [35].

[240] *Pell Frischmann Engineering Co v Bow Valley Iran Ltd* [2011] 1 WLR 2370.

than by reference to the actual gain. To this extent, and because of the theoretical basis of voluntary release damages, there is a possible exception to the general law of damages that all relevant facts known to the court at the date of the assessment of the damages are to be taken into account in the assessment.[241] The correct analysis may be to say that the actual gain is not a fact relevant to the voluntary release method of assessing damages. There are exceptional circumstances in which the court may take into account events after the date of the assumed negotiation.[242]

(iii) The dominant owner is taken to know the anticipated amount of the gain which would accrue to the servient owner if the obstruction was permitted and his development was carried out. This appears to be a reasonable assumption since it allows a realistic negotiation on a level playing field for a division of the gain between the parties. In practice, such details are not necessarily made available in negotiations and a dominant owner may have to produce his own estimate of the likely gain to the servient owner. At the very least the dominant owner will not necessarily accept the servient owner's estimate of the likely gain and will make his own estimate or obtain advice on it. As mentioned above, it may be necessary for the court to hear conflicting valuation evidence on this question.[243]

(iv) The assumed deal 'has to feel right'. An intellectual justification of what ought to be the likely result of a hypothetical negotiation, perhaps based on data and valuation principles and experience from other negotiations, must not be preferred to that which the court feels would be likely to have happened in the particular circumstances of the case before it.[244] It is perhaps for this reason that the theoretical equal division between the parties of the gain to the servient owner from the offending development is not often adopted by a court.[245] That amount may simply not feel right.

(v) Where a profit can be gained from the unlawful development the dominant owner can expect to receive a fair proportion of that profit.[246] This of course leaves open the question of what is a fair proportion.

(vi) The size of the award of damages should not be so large that the development of the servient land, or of the unlawful part of that development, would not have taken place if such a sum had to be paid by the servient

[241] See, eg *Lesschke v Jeffs & Faulkner* [1955] Queensland Weekly Notes 67.

[242] See para 7.149 et seq.

[243] *Amec Developments Ltd v Jury's Hotel Management (UK) Ltd* [2001] 1 EGLR 81; *Tamares (Vincent Square) Ltd v Fairpoint Properties (Vincent Square) Ltd (No 2)* [2007] EWHC 212 (Ch), [2007] 1 WLR 2167. A conflict of expert evidence on the likely gain from the offending acts occurred in both cases.

[244] *Amec Developments Ltd v Jury's Hotel Management (UK) Ltd* [2001] 82 P & CR 72 [35]; *Tamares (Vincent Square) Ltd v Fairpoint Properties (Vincent Square) Ltd (No 2)* [2007] EWHC 212 (Ch), [2007] 1 WLR 2167 [22].

[245] For the equal division principle and the *Stokes v Cambridge* principle: see para 7.136.

[246] *Tamares (Vincent Square) ltd v Fairpoint Properties (Vincent Square) Ltd (No 2)* [2007] EWHC 212 (Ch), [2007] 1 WLR 2167.

owner.[247] This proposition is inherent in the nature of the hypothetical negotiation. No servient owner expecting to make a commercial gain from a development would agree to pay a sum which would make it not worthwhile to carry out the proposed project.

10. Voluntary Release Damages: Subsequent Events

The general rule in the valuation of land is that when a value of land has to be determined at a certain date by way of a hypothetical sale of the land at that date all that can be taken into account are those facts and matters and events which had occurred up to that date and any reasonable anticipation of events beyond that date.[248] Since the assessment of voluntary release damages depends upon a hypothetical negotiation, of its nature much the same as that which is required in a valuation of land, the same principle should apply and no account should be taken, when determining what would be the result of that hypothetical negotiation, of events which have occurred after the date on which the negotiation is assumed to take place. That date is the date immediately prior to the creation of the unlawful obstruction even if in fact that obstruction is in existence when the matter comes before the court. 7.149

Despite this fairly obvious reasoning, suggestions have emerged that later events may be taken into account. Thus in one case it was said that post-negotiation date events could be taken into account because the negotiation analysis was not to be pursued rigorously to its logical end.[249] In a subsequent case the same suggestion was made in the context of a submission that the damages might be assessed not by reference to the result of a voluntary negotiation but by reference to a reasonable payment in respect of the whole of the benefit gained by the wrongdoer. As explained earlier such a basis of damages would not be compensatory but would be akin to damages assessed on a restitutionary basis. Nonetheless the matter was considered by the Court of Appeal and it was said that voluntary release damages were meant to be compensatory and were normally to be assessed or valued at the date of breach, so that principle and consistency indicated that post-valuation events were normally irrelevant. This was qualified by a statement that the quasi-equitable nature of the damages meant that the judge might, where there were good reasons, direct a departure from that norm. It seems that this may 7.150

[247] ibid [22(7)].

[248] This is a fundamental precept of land valuation. See, eg *Penny's Bay Investment Co Ltd v Director of Lands* (2010) 13 HKCFAR 287 [43] (Lord Hoffmann).

[249] *Amec Developments Ltd v Jury's Hotel Management (UK) Ltd* [2001] 1 EGLR 81. In *Stadium Capital Holdings (No 2) Ltd v St Marylebone Co Plc* [2011] EWHC 2856 (Ch), [2012] 1 P & CR 7 it was held that events after the date of the hypothetical negotiation were irrelevant.

be done either by selecting a different valuation date or by directing that a specific post-negotiation date or event should be taken into account.[250]

7.151 The law on this particular point is therefore left, perhaps unfortunately, on an uncertain basis rather than on a basis of principle. What is not known is what could constitute the good reasons which would justify the taking into account of subsequent events. If the court decided that the case before it is not an exceptional case which justifies taking post negotiating events into account it is possible that the proportion of the gain awarded as damages will exceed the actual gain eventually made. This could occur if the anticipated gain at the date of the hypothetical negotiations was substantially greater than the gain actually made.[251] There is perhaps an at any rate tenable theoretical basis on which a consideration of the gain actually made by a servient owner from his works could be taken into account. It is that that sum, albeit it could not be known to the negotiating parties, may help in ascertaining what they would have agreed. In the general valuation of land, while post-valuation date events may not be taken into account, consideration can be given to comparable transactions on other properties which took place after the valuation date.[252] The reason is said to be that such transactions may give some indication of what the parties to the hypothetical transaction would have agreed on the valuation date. There may be some analogy in the two situations.

11. Parasitic Damages

(a) The Parasitic Damages Principle

7.152 There has arisen in connection with damages for an infringement of a right of light a principle which has been given the unattractive name of parasitic damages. What is meant is that if a dominant owner has the benefit of an easement of light in favour of one or more apertures in a building owned by him, but he has no easement for the benefit of other apertures in that building or other buildings which he owns, and there is an infringement of the easement in respect of the apertures with the benefit of the easement, the damages which the dominant owner will obtain extend not only to the effect of the reduction in the access of light to those apertures but also to the effect of any reduction in the access of light

[250] *Lunn Poly Ltd v Liverpool & Lancashire Properties Ltd* [2006] EWCA Civ 430, [2006] 2 EGLR 29 [29] (Neuberger LJ), approved in *Pell Frischmann Engineering Ltd v Bow Valley Iran Ltd* [2009] UKPC 45, [2011] 1 WLR 2370 [50].

[251] *Pell Frischmann Engineering Ltd v Bow Valley Iran Ltd* [2009] UKPC 45, [2011] 1 WLR 2370. See also para 7.148.

[252] *Segama NV v Penny Le Roy Ltd* [1984] 1 EGLR 169; *Melwood v Commissioner of Main Roads* [1979] AC 426; *Electricity Supply Nominees Ltd v London Clubs Ltd* [1988] 2 EGLR 152. There is a full discussion on post-valuation date evidence, including the use of post-valuation date comparables, in Barnes and Bignell, 'Valuation Evidence: A Principled Approach' (2009) 13(1–3) *Landlord & Tenant Review*.

to the other apertures which would be an actionable injury if those other apertures had enjoyed easements of light.

The origin of the principle is the decision of the Court of Appeal in *London Tilbury & Southend Railway Co v Gowers Walk School Trustees.*[253] In that case a right of light attached to windows in a former building which, on the demolition of that building, had been transferred to certain windows, but not to all windows, in a new building.[254] It was held that the damages which were payable for an infringement of the rights attached to the new windows which had transferred rights should include an element for the damage caused by a reduction of light to the other windows. The principle appears to be applicable whenever some windows of an owner enjoy a right of light and others do not, such that the damages can encompass loss caused by a reduction of light to the other windows.[255] 7.153

It is hard to support this principle. Suppose that a person has acquired a right of light to the apertures in the two storeys of a building by 20 years of the enjoyment of the access of light over the servient land to those windows. He then constructs an extension of three storeys over the existing building, or constructs a lateral extension to the existing building. If the servient owner a year after the new development on the dominant land carries out a development on his land which infringes the rights of light to the two-storey original building, he has to pay damages for a reduction of light to the apertures not only in that building but to the apertures in the extensive newly built structures which have existed for only a year. Such a conclusion appears to cut across the nature of easements being acquired for the access of light to a building through a particular aperture and across the nature of prescriptive rights which depend on long enjoyment of the access of light to an aperture. A truer analysis of legal principle was stated by Lord Denning MR in *Spartan Steel Alloys v Martin & Co*, when the parasitic damages principle relating to rights of light cases was put before the Court of Appeal by way of analogy. Lord Denning said:[256] 7.154

> I do not believe that there is any such doctrine [of parasitic damages]. The cases on ancient light stand in a category by themselves and are to be explained in this way: if a house has ancient lights which are threatened by a new building, the owner, if he moves promptly, may obtain an injunction to restrain the erection of the new building. The court, however, may refuse an injunction and award him damages in lieu of an injunction: see *Leeds Industrial Co-operative Society Ltd v Slack* [1924] AC 851. These damages

[253] *London Tilbury & Southend Railway Co v Gowers Walk School Trustees* (1889) 24 QBD 326.

[254] For the transfer of rights of light from a former building to a new building where there is a coincidence of apertures see ch 3, section (C)5.

[255] *Griffiths v Richard Clay & Sons* [1912] 2 Ch 291; *Wills v May* [1923] 1 Ch 317. See the statement of the principle said to be derived from the authorities as stated by Buckley LJ in *Horton v Colwyn Bay and Colwyn UDC* [1908] 1 KB 327, 341 in the context of the laying of sewers under the Public Health Act 1875. The principle of parasitic damages in a rights of light case has received support from the majority decision of the Supreme Court of Ireland in *Scott v Goulding Properties* [1973] IR 200.

[256] *Spartan Steel Alloys v Martin & Co* [1973] QB 27, 35.

> would be, in effect, buying a right to put up the new building. If the owner, however, delays and allows the new building to go up without making any objection—so that he cannot seek an injunction—I do not think he should recover damages for his big new windows (for which he has no right). He ought only to recover damages for the small old windows (for which he has a right).

(b) Practical Impact of the Principle

7.155 Despite these last trenchant comments, courts may feel that they are bound to follow the ratio of the *London Tilbury Railway* decision. Even so, the practical impact of that decision and of parasitic damages as a principle and as just described is probably limited today. This is so for a number of reasons.

7.156 One reason is that the principle is of no significance if an injunction is granted to prevent or redress an infringement of an easement of light. If an easement of light attaches to windows A, B and C within a building and an injunction is issued to prevent an obstruction on the servient land to the access of light to those windows then the fact that the injunction also benefits rooms which are lit by windows X, Y and Z which have no easement of light is incidental and has nothing to do with parasitic damages. A second reason is that if parasitic damages are to have any application, the person who seeks and obtains damages must be the owner of the areas lit by the apertures which do not have attached to them an easement of light. If a tenant of two floors of a building with windows through which easements of light are enjoyed seeks and obtains damages for an infringement of those easements caused by an obstruction on the servient land that will be of no avail to some other tenant of other areas of the building where the windows do not have easements of light. There is no question of that tenant, a person with a different interest in different premises, somehow attaching his claim to that of the person who owns an interest which entitles him to obtain damages.

7.157 A further consideration can again be illustrated by the example of a person who has an easement of light attached to his windows A, B and C but does not have the benefit of an easement of light attached to his windows X, Y and Z. If there is an obstruction on the servient land which infringes the right of light of that person through windows A, B and C that person will not be entitled to damages for a reduction of light to windows X, Y and Z if that reduction of light does not reduce the access of natural light to rooms lit by windows X, Y and Z below that which is acceptable according to the ordinary notions of mankind. The principle of parasitic damages cannot elevate that which is not an actionable injury on any basis to something which is treated as if it were an actionable injury.[257]

7.158 Lastly, there is a consideration of high importance today, but which may not have been of significance when the authorities concerning parasitic damages

[257] The application of this reasoning when assessing book value damages is illustrated in para 7.87(iv).

were decided, which is that today damages will often be awarded on the voluntary release basis, described earlier.[258] Voluntary release damages depend upon the result of a hypothetical negotiation between the dominant owner and the servient owner for the voluntary release of rights of light. To take again the same example, if the owner of a building has rights of light enjoyed through windows A, B and C within his building but not through windows X, Y and Z and there is an infringement of the rights of light through windows A, B and C, so that the owner obtains voluntary release damages calculated on the above basis, it may well be that the damages are calculated by reference to a proportion of the gain which the servient owner would make from the erection of his obstruction. In that event the fact that the dominant owner also has rooms lit by windows X, Y and Z may have little impact on the result of the hypothetical negotiation. In other words where damages are assessed on a voluntary release basis the principle of parasitic damages may have little or no impact on the assessment of damages.

12. Restitutionary Damages

There is sometimes a confusion between voluntary release damages, as described above, and which are important in rights of light claims, and restitutionary damages. Discussion is not helped by the wide variety of descriptions given to voluntary release damages.[259] The two methods of assessing damages are different in concept. The purpose of voluntary release damages is to compensate the dominant owner for the loss of the amount of money which he could have obtained in return for a voluntary release of his rights. It is in effect damages for a loss of opportunity. The damages are often calculated by reference to a proportion of the profit which the servient owner anticipates making by the obstruction to light erected or to be erected by him, although there is no legal necessity for the damages to be calculated in this way.[260] Restitutionary damages are different in principle since their purpose and effect is to require the wrongdoer to pay to the claimant the whole of the gain which he has made from his wrongful actions. There is no question of a hypothetical negotiation for a voluntary release of rights, and no division of the gain by the wrongdoer such as would often characterise voluntary release damages. Exemplary damages may certainly provide an element of compensation to a person who has suffered an actionable wrong, but their purpose and rationale is in no sense compensatory. 7.159

[258] See sections (C)5–9 of this chapter.

[259] See para 7.108.

[260] For example, if the court has no evidence of the profit made or anticipated to be made by the servient owner it may adopt the crude expedient of assessing voluntary release damages by multiplying the reduction in the value of the dominant building by an arbitrary figure of 2 or 3: see *Carr-Saunders v Dick McNeill Associates Ltd* [1986] 1 WLR 922; and see para 7.111 et seq.

7.160 An award of restitutionary damages is not new to the law. Damages on such a basis may be awarded where a defendant has broken a duty of confidentiality or where a breach of contract is also a breach of a fiduciary obligation, that is an obligation which arises where one person stands in the position of a trustee towards another in relation to certain matters.[261] The leading modern case on restitutionary damages is *Attorney General v Blake*,[262] which arose out of the publication of a book written by the traitor George Blake, and which has been explained above.[263] Blake was ordered to pay over as damages the whole of the gain made from the publication of the material which was in breach of his obligation to the Government which had employed him in the Secret Intelligence Service. The House of Lords took the opportunity to commend the practice of awarding damages on the voluntary release basis for the breach of property and other obligations.

7.161 While the nature of restitutionary damages and their availability in principle in an appropriate case are clear it is not apparent what are the exact circumstances which will justify such an award. The circumstances of *Blake's* case were plainly exceptional. In the House of Lords in *Blake* Lord Nicholls declined to lay down any fixed rules to determine when restitutionary damages would be ordered and referred to such damages being available when the claimant has a legitimate interest in preventing the profit-making activity of the wrongdoer.[264] This observation may not take the matter much forward since no principles were stated which would help a court to know when that legitimate interest does or does not exist.[265]

7.162 It is unlikely, though not impossible, that restitutionary damages could be ordered in a rights of light claim. In one case such damages were claimed but held to be inappropriate, although it was said in the Court of Appeal that voluntary release damages might be awarded in a suitable case.[266] In one rights of light claim damages were awarded as 100 per cent of the profit made by the wrongdoer, but this decision was overruled by the Court of Appeal, which ordered that the damages be reassessed, and on the reassessment only 50 per cent of the gain was awarded, ie by the application of the voluntary release method.[267] All that can safely be said is that it would take unusual and exceptional circumstances for restitutionary damages to be awarded in a claim for a breach of an easement of light.

[261] *Mathew v TM Sutton Ltd* [1994] 1 WLR 1455.

[262] *Attorney General v Blake* [2001] 1 AC 268.

[263] See para 7.116.

[264] *Attorney General v Blake* [2001] 1 AC 268, 285.

[265] Subsequent decisions involving commercial disputes have not greatly clarified the matter. See *Experience Hendrix LLC v PPX Enterprises Inc* [2003] EWCA Civ 323 (restitutionary damages not awarded for breach of an agreement concerning licences to market recordings of music) and *Esso Petroleum v Niad* [2001] All ER (D) 324 (restitutionary damages awarded for breach of an agreement concerning the price for the sale of petrol which could be charged by a garage owner).

[266] *Forsyth-Grant v Allen* [2008] EWCA Civ 505, [2008] 2 EGLR 16.

[267] *Stadium Capital Holdings (No 2) Ltd v St Marylebone Co Plc* [2011] EWHC 2856 (Ch), [2012] 1 P & CR 7.

13. Other Types of Damages

The law is replete with expressions which indicate different bases of the assessment of damages. References are made to aggravated damages, exemplary damages, punitive damages, retributory damages, vindictive damages, and vindicatory damages. These are in addition to book value damages and voluntary release damages and restitutionary damages, the first two of which are important in rights of light disputes. It is unlikely that any basis of damages except book value damages and voluntary release damages will be of significance in rights of light cases and it is proposed to mention only briefly the other methods of assessment just mentioned. 7.163

Exemplary damages (which is the description preferred today in place of the expressions 'punitive damages', 'vindictive damages', or 'retributory damages') are damages awarded when the conduct of the wrongdoer is sufficiently reprehensible or outrageous to justify his being ordered to pay damages over and beyond any compensation for loss to the claimant and as a form of punishment. Such damages have been available in law since the middle of the eighteenth century, when they were awarded in actions relating to the conduct of John Wilkes in his criticisms of the King and the Government.[268] There is considerable dispute whether such damages are ever justifiable in law, but modern authority indicates that exemplary damages may still be awarded in two types of case, the first being where there has been oppressive or arbitrary or unconstitutional conduct by a public or governmental body, and the other being where the conduct of the wrongdoer has been calculated by him to result in profit.[269] There is no record of damages being awarded on either of these bases in a rights of light case, although such damages have been awarded in property-related cases.[270] Vindicatory damages have the purpose of preserving the reputation of a claimant by means of a substantial award of damages which go beyond that which is wholly compensatory. Misconduct by a police force, including inhumane or degrading treatment, might be a justification for damages being awarded on this basis.[271] It is extremely unlikely that damages so assessed could have any relevance to a rights of light case. 7.164

It is necessary finally to mention aggravated damages. This component of damages compensates a claimant for the mental distress and affront to dignity which 7.165

[268] *Huckle v Money* (1763) 2 Wills KB 206; *Wilkes v Wood* (1763) Lofft 1.

[269] *Rookes v Barnard* [1864] AC 1129; *Broome v Cassell & Co* [1972] AC 1027; *Kuddus v Chief Constable of Leicestershire* [2001] UKHL 29, [2002] 2 AC 122. Exemplary damages have a wider scope in Australia and New Zealand: see, eg *A v Bottrill* [2002] UKPC 44, [2003] 1 AC 449 (a decision of the Privy Council on appeal from New Zealand). The Law Commission has recommended that exemplary damages should be retained as a part of English law and indeed expanded: see *Aggravated, Exemplary and Restitutionary Damages* (Law Com No 247, 1997).

[270] See, eg *Drane v Evangelou* [1978] 1 WLR 455 (exemplary damages awarded where a landlord had unlawfully evicted a tenant of residential premises).

[271] *Attorney General of Trinidad and Tobago v Ramanoop* [2005] UKPC 5, [2006] 1 AC 328.

is the result of certain wrongful actions. The offensive nature of the defendant's conduct is relevant to the ordering and assessment of an amount of aggravated damages. Such damages find their most frequent expression in publications which are a wrong towards well-known persons.[272] Aggravated damages can be awarded in a case involving the infringement of an easement such as when the defendant effected an obstruction to a right of way and behaved in an intimidatory and malicious fashion.[273] Similar circumstances could arise in a right of light case. Aggravated damages are entirely compensatory in nature, since distress caused by intimidating or unjustified behaviour can be a real loss, albeit a loss difficult to quantify in money. Aggravated damages should not be confused with exemplary damages, where the damages are overtly not founded on monetary compensation for a loss suffered, and can only be awarded in limited circumstances.[274]

(D) ABATEMENT

7.166 There is a long-standing rule of law that a person who suffers a nuisance to his property is entitled in certain circumstances to take steps to abate or remove the nuisance without obtaining an order or sanction of a court. This is a form of self-help, and a person who abates a nuisance within the limits of the rule does not commit a trespass when he enters the property of the perpetrator of the nuisance for this purpose. The rule applies to all forms of nuisance and similar wrongs against property including an interference with an easement.[275] An obstruction to a right of way may be removed in this fashion.[276] However, the law does not favour self-help save in exceptional cases, and today there are severe restrictions on the circumstances in which an abatement of the nuisance can lawfully take place and restrictions on the form of the exercise of the right. For reasons which will become apparent, a right of abatement is unlikely to be available in modern conditions for the removal by self-help of an obstruction to an easement of light.

[272] In *Campbell v MGN Ltd* [2002] EWHC 449 (QB) aggravated damages were awarded as a consequence of a newspaper article, whereas in *Douglas v Hello! Ltd* [2003] 3 All ER 996 aggravated damages were not awarded in a case involving unauthorised photographs taken at the marriage between Michael Douglas and Catherine Zeta-Jones.

[273] *Owers v Bailey* [2007]1 P & CR DG 17.

[274] The distinction can be seen in *Mosley v News Group Newspapers Ltd* [2008] EWHC 1777 (QB) in which the judge awarded aggravated damages but was not willing to order exemplary damages.

[275] *Baten's case* (1610) 9 Rep 54b, in which it was held to be lawful for a person to enter the property of his neighbour to remove a part of a building which jutted over the boundary of the property.

[276] *Chamberlain v Lindon* [1998] 1 WLR 1252, in which the removal of a wall obstructing a right of way was held not to be an offence under the Criminal Damage Act 1971. In *Tapling v Jones* (1865) 11 HLC 290 Lord Cranworth said: 'Where a person has wrongfully obstructed another in the enjoyment of an easement, as, for instance by building a wall across a path over which there is a right of way, public or private, any person so unlawfully obstructed may remove the obstruction; and if any damage thereby arises to him who wrongfully set it up, he has no right to complain.'

The leading modern decision on the subject of abatement is *Burton v Winters*,[277] which concerned a wall erected in part on the plaintiff's property. The principle of law laid down by the Court of Appeal was that an abatement was only justified in two cases. One case is where the abatement is a simple act, such as the lopping off of an overhanging branch, which does not justify the expense of legal proceedings, and the other case is where the removal of the nuisance is urgent and requires an immediate remedy.[278] The occurrence of the second type of case will be rare, since it is possible today to obtain an order of the court very quickly, if necessary on an ex parte basis (without prior notice to the defendant of the application), even by a telephone application to a judge in appropriate circumstances. 7.167

Even if the abatement can be brought within one or other of the two permissible circumstances, there are other limitations on the exercise of the right. Acts of abatement cannot take place if a court has refused an injunction to remove the nuisance and an abatement will not be lawful if it is not exercised promptly.[279] In addition, acts of abatement must be exercised in the most limited fashion practicable, must cause as little damage as possible to property entered, and must be carried out with prior notice to the persons affected if that is practicable.[280] 7.168

There is old authority for saying that a dominant owner may enter the servient land and remove a building such as a stable which obstructs a right of light.[281] However, today it is extremely unlikely that the exercise of an abatement so as to remove a built obstruction to light on the servient land would be lawful. Such an action would be very unlikely to fall within either of the sets of circumstances in which an abatement is now permissible.[282] If a structure has been erected or is in the course of erection on the servient land which is or will be an infringement of a right of light, the proper remedy of the dominant owner is to seek a mandatory injunction from the court to remove that which has been done, or a prohibitory injunction to prevent the continuation of what is being done. It will sometimes be appropriate for a dominant owner to seek an interim injunction.[283] An injunction 7.169

[277] *Burton v Winters* [1993] 1 WLR 1077; *McNab v Richardson* [2008] EWCA Civ 1631 (removal of a fence erected as a trespass not justified as an act of abatement because the matter was not urgent).

[278] See also *Blackstone's Commentaries*, Book III, ch 1.

[279] *Burton v Winters* [1993] 1 WLR 1077; *Moffatt v Brewer* (1848) Iowa 1 Greene 348, 350. The question of whether an abatement is permissible after the refusal of an injunction by a court was left open in *Lane v Capsey* [1891] 3 Ch 411 and was answered in the negative in *Burton v Winters*. On the other hand if a right of abatement did exist, the fact that it was not exercised would not prevent the bringing of legal proceedings in respect of the wrong: *Leaky v National Trust* [1980] QB 485.

[280] *Roberts v Rose* (1865) LR 1 Ex Ch 82; *Lemmon v Webb* [1895] AC 1; *Delaware Mansions v Westminster City Council* [2001] UKHL 55, [2001] 1 AC 321 (encroachment onto property by roots of a tree); *McNab v Richardson* [2008] EWCA Civ 1631.

[281] *Thompson v Eastwood* (1852) 8 Ex 69. This decision of Baron Alderson is concerned mainly with now obsolete points of pleading, but the right to remove the offending building was not doubted by the court. In *Davies v Williams* (1851) 16 QB 546 it was decided that there was a right to pull down an inhabited house which was a nuisance by reason of it obstructing rights of commoners. See also *Lane v Capsey* [1891] 3 Ch 411.

[282] See para 7.167.

[283] See para 7.52 et seq.

may be obtained to prevent a threatened obstruction if the threat is immediate, but no act of abatement is lawful merely to prevent an apprehension of a wrong.[284] Therefore if a dominant owner believes that there is an imminent threat or prospect of an unlawful obstruction being erected on the servient land, his proper remedy is to seek a prohibitory injunction from the court, including if necessary an interim injunction.

(E) SUMMARY

7.170 A person faced with an infringement or threatened infringement of his easement of light has in principle three potential remedies: an injunction, damages or an act of abatement. Abatement is extremely unlikely to have any practical utility in a rights of light case. The remaining two remedies are important.

7.171 It goes without saying that, if it is disputed, a claimant must establish that he has an easement of light created expressly in a deed, or implied from the circumstances of a deed, or created by a form of prescription, usually in the last case under section 3 of the Prescription Act 1832. Once these matters are admitted or established a claimant will usually seek an injunction, either a negative injunction to prevent the obstruction to his light if it has not occurred or a mandatory injunction to remove it if it has occurred. There is often little disadvantage to the claimant in seeking injunctive relief even if in the end it is not obtained.

7.172 Where an injunction is sought and resisted, the central question for the parties and the court will be the principles which guide the exercise of the discretion to grant or refuse the injunction. Following the decision of the Supreme Court in *Lawrence v Fen Tigers Ltd*[285] it seems unlikely that a great deal of attention will be paid to the 'four working rules' which had to some degree held sway for over a century in guiding courts on this matter since the decision of the Court of Appeal in *Shelfer v City of London Electric Lighting Co.*[286] The best guidance that can be given to the parties on the matter of the general approach today, which emerges from the *Lawrence* decision, is (a) that a claimant has a prima facie entitlement to an injunction, (b) that the burden is on the defendant to show that no injunction should be granted, (c) that the court should not approach the question with any inclination either to grant or refuse an injunction, and (d) that the decision will depend on all of the relevant considerations in each individual case.

7.173 It is impossible to produce a catalogue of all possible relevant considerations or of the weight to be attached to any particular consideration in any particular case and both of these matters will vary from case to case. The best that can be done by

[284] *Morrice v Baker* [1616] 3 Bulst 196, 197.
[285] *Lawrence v Fen Tigers Ltd* [2014] UKSC 13, [2014] AC 872.
[286] *Shelfer v City of London Electric Lighting Co* [1895] 1 Ch 287.

way of general guidance to the parties is to say that in any particular case certain considerations are likely to be of significance where they arise on the facts of that case including (a) whether the claimant has delayed in seeking injunctive relief, (b) the conduct of both parties in relation to the dispute, (c) whether the development or other obstruction has been erected or is in the course of erection, (d) whether an interim injunction has been sought in a case appropriate for such relief, (e) any public interest in the construction or retention of an offending development and whether planning permission has been obtained for it, (f) the extent and seriousness of the reduction of light to the claimant's property, (g) the use made of the claimant's property, particularly if it is as a home, (h) whether other persons as well as the claimant are adversely affected by the actual or potential obstruction to light, and (i) whether, if no injunction is granted, the damages are likely to be on a scale which can be considered a sufficient remedy.

If damages are the only remedy, either because an injunction is not sought or it is refused, the primary question is likely to be whether the damages should be assessed on a book value basis (the reduction in the value of the claimant's property caused by the wrongful obstruction of light) or on a voluntary release basis (the sum which would be agreed between reasonable parties in a hypothetical negotiation for the voluntary release of the right of light). It seems both likely and fair that generally a court will award voluntary release damages unless there is a particular reason for the court to exercise its discretion to refuse damages on this basis where that discretion is said to arise because voluntary release damages are quasi-equitable in nature. 7.174

In assessing voluntary release damages the court will have to prognosticate on the likely result of the hypothetical negotiation between reasonable persons just mentioned. Although this will not necessarily be so in every case in many cases this process will involve determining the gain which the defendant is likely to make from the unlawful obstruction and awarding to the claimant a proportion of that gain. The decided cases indicate proportions of up to 50 per cent of the gain, but a proportion of the gain of 25 per cent to 40 per cent may indicate the boundaries or brackets of the proportion most likely to be awarded in many cases. 7.175

8

Extinguishment and Overriding of Rights of Light

(A) INTRODUCTION

8.1 An easement of light, whether created expressly or by implication from the circumstances of a deed or by prescription, may be extinguished or overridden. The easement is said to be extinguished when it is brought permanently to an end and cannot be revived. An easement is said to be overridden when it is rendered unenforceable so that it does not prevent works carried out on the servient land under statutory authority. In the case of overriding, the easement is not wholly and permanently ended but remains in existence so as to prevent immediately or in the future any works on the servient land which constitute an infringement of the easement and are not authorised to be carried out pursuant to the statutory authority. Compensation is payable for the overriding of an easement by statute.

8.2 An easement of light may be extinguished by (a) an express release, (b) an implied release or abandonment, (c) unity of ownership and possession of the dominant and servient properties, and (d) in the case of a leasehold easement, the determination of a lease of the dominant or servient property.

8.3 An easement of light may be overridden by (a) the carrying out of work on the servient property pursuant to statutory powers and (b) the operation of section 237 of the Town and Country Planning Act 1990. Compensation to the dominant owner is payable in both of these circumstances.

8.4 An easement of light which has been acquired by prescription, at any rate where the prescription is under section 3 of the Prescription Act 1832, may be brought to an end by the operation by the servient owner of the procedure available under the Rights of Light Act 1959. The procedure under this Act is designed mainly to prevent the acquisition of easements during the 20-year prescription period, rather than the termination of easements which have been acquired following the end of the prescription period, although the procedure can have the latter effect. A general explanation of the Act, its procedures, and the effect of those procedures is provided in Chapter 9.

The Lands Chamber of the Upper Tribunal has power to modify or discharge restrictive covenants on certain grounds under section 84 of the Law of Property Act 1925. The grounds are: 8.5

(a) that following a change in the character of the neighbourhood or other circumstances the restriction ought to be deemed obsolete;
(b) that the continued existence of the restriction impedes some reasonable user of the land and either does not give those entitled to it any practical benefits of substantial value or advantage or is contrary to the public interest, where money will be an adequate compensation for any loss or disadvantage suffered;
(c) that all those entitled to the benefit of the restriction have agreed by their acts or omissions to its discharge or modification; and
(d) that the proposed discharge or modification will not injure those entitled to the benefit of the restriction.[1]

Compensation can be ordered to be paid to the person with the benefit of the covenant if a covenant is modified or discharged. It is generally considered that a modification or discharge of a restrictive covenant is not easily obtained under these provisions. There is no jurisdiction to modify or discharge an easement. The Law Commission has recommended that the jurisdiction be extended to enable the Lands Chamber to make an order for the modification or discharge of easements and profits whether created before or after the enactment conferring the new power comes into operation. No recommendation was made for extending the grounds for a modification or discharge as regards easements generally or as regards easements of light.[2]

(B) EXTINGUISHMENT OF RIGHTS OF LIGHT

1. Express Release

It is perhaps obvious that an existing easement of light may be terminated by the agreement of the dominant and the servient owners. If such an agreement is put into effect by an appropriate instrument the easement comes to an end. The process is usually called a release of the easement. The document will release the servient owner from his obligations under the easement.[3] The same principle 8.6

[1] The power, created in 1925, was extended by the Law of Property Act 1969.

[2] Law Commission, *Rights of Light* (Law Com No 356, 2014), paras 7.74 and 7.87. There has been no response by the Government to this and other recommendations of the Law Commission on rights of light and easements generally. The various proposals in this area of the Law Commission are considered in ch 12.

[3] It may therefore be that the process is best described not as a release of rights, although it is often described as such, but as a release of obligations. However rights and obligations are correlative to each other in law and it is not practical to terminate one without the other. See ch 2, n 1.

as to a release operates whether the easement of light was created expressly by deed or as an implication from the circumstances of a deed or by the operation of section 62 of the Law of Property Act 1925 or by prescription.

8.7 In order to have effect in law, a release of an easement has to be effected by deed.[4] Section 52(1) of the Law of Property Act 1925 states that all conveyances of an interest in land are void for the purpose of conveying a legal estate unless made by deed. Section 205(1) of the Act defines a conveyance as including a release. However, an imperfectly created release would be treated in equity under the doctrine of *Parker v Taswell*[5] as an agreement to release the easement of which specific performance could be granted in an appropriate case. A contract for the release of an easement must be in writing.[6]

2. Implied Release

8.8 There is a general doctrine of law that rights over property may be impliedly released or abandoned as a result of the conduct of the person who owns the right. For example, a landlord may be taken to have impliedly abandoned a right to enforce a restriction in a covenant in a lease which prohibits building or a certain type of building on the land demised if he has stood by for many years while buildings have been erected on parts of the land in breach of the covenant.[7] The principle applies to the abandonment of easements generally and to easements of light. As regards easements, an implied abandonment will not be lightly or readily inferred. The burden is on the person who alleges an abandonment by implication to show conduct by the dominant owner which makes it clear that neither he nor any successor in title intends in the future to make any use of the easement.[8] It has been said that an implied abandonment occurs only when the person owning the easement has by his actions demonstrated a fixed intention never in the future to assert the easement himself or to attempt to transfer it to some other person.[9] Mere non-use of the easement, such as non-use of a right of way, even for

[4] See Co Litt 264b. In *Lovell v Smith* (1857) 3 CB (NS) 120 it was held that the intention of the parties was not to effect a release, but Willes J added: 'I do not think that this court meant to lay it down that there cannot be an abandonment of a positive right like this without a deed or evidence from which the jury can presume a release of it.'

[5] *Parker v Taswell* (1858) 2 De G & J 559; *Frogley v Earl of Lovelace* (1859) John 333; *Davies v Marshall* (1861) 10 CB (NS) 697, 710 (Erle CJ) where an acquiescence to alterations to the servient land was treated in equity as amounting to a release of a right of light; *Robinson Webster (Holdings) Ltd v Agombar* [2002] 1 P & CR 20.

[6] Law of Property (Miscellaneous Provisions) Act 1989, s 2.

[7] *Attorney General of Hong Kong v Fairfax* [1997] 1 WLR 149.

[8] *Gotobed v Pridmore* (1971) 217 EG 759.

[9] *Tehidy Minerals Ltd v Norman* [1971] QB 528. This test was applied in the Mayor's and City of London Court in *Marine & General Mutual Life Assurance Society v St James Real Estate Co Ltd* [1991] 2 EGLR 178, in which it was held that a bricking-up of a window space but in a way which retained the

a substantial period is unlikely to be enough to support an intention permanently to abandon the easement.[10] The expressions 'implied abandonment' and 'implied release' appear to be used interchangeably in the present context.

A right of light appurtenant to a building is a negative easement the enjoyment of which does not involve any positive action by the dominant owner. It is therefore difficult to envisage circumstances in which non-use of the access of light to the dominant building over the servient land could occur unless there was the creation of some physical impediment so as to prevent light entering or passing through an aperture or apertures in the dominant building. A possible instance of an implied abandonment of a right of light would be when the dominant owner himself erected within the curtilage of the dominant building some obstruction, for example a new building or a hoarding or a roofing in of a part of the land, which prevented the access of much of the access of light which passed over the servient land to an aperture within the dominant building. The most obvious instance of an implied abandonment would be the permanent blocking-up of a window.[11] Even then it has been said that there might be no abandonment unless the servient owner had himself erected buildings in reliance of the blocking-up of windows or similar activities where those buildings erected by the servient owner would have infringed the right of light which was appurtenant to the blocked-up windows.[12] The demolition of the dominant building will amount to an implied abandonment of rights of light appurtenant to that building if there is no intention to replace the building, but if there is an intention to rebuild the building there will be no abandonment simply by virtue of the demolition of the former building.[13] Whether a right of light appurtenant to a building can be transferred to windows in a new building following the demolition of the former building is a question of some difficulty and is considered in Chapter 3.[14] An alteration of a building which preserves the apertures which have the benefit of a right of light but which so alters the building that the access of light through those apertures is 8.9

apertures and permitted the brickwork to be removed was not an implied abandonment of an easement of light through the apertures. See *Williams v Sandy Lane (Chester) Ltd* [2007] 1 P & CR 27 in the context of a right of way.

[10] *Snell & Prideaux Ltd v Dutton Mirrors Ltd* [1995] 1 EGLR 259; *Ward v Ward* (1852) LR 17 Ex 838; *Crossley & Sons Ltd v Lightwater* (1866) LR 2 Ch App 478, 482 (Lord Chelmsford); *James v Stevenson* [1893] AC 162; *Dwyer v City of Westminster* [2014] EWCA Civ 153, [2014] 2 P & CR 7.

[11] In *Moore v Rawson* (1824) 3 B & C 332 it was held that a right of light through windows had been abandoned when the wall containing the windows had been taken down and replaced by a blank wall which had stood in place for 17 years. In *Scott v Pape* (1886) 31 Ch D 554, 567 Cotton LJ said that the entire blocking-up of a window was sufficient to show an abandonment of any right of light to that window.

[12] *Moore v Rawson* (1824) 3 B & C 332 (Abbott CJ); *Cooke v Mayor and Corporation of Bath* (1868) LR 6 EQ 177, 279 (Malins VC). It is not apparent why there should be such an additional requirement, which seems more apposite to estoppels than to an implied abandonment. See also *Stokoe v Singers* (1857) 8 EL & BL 31.

[13] *Staigt v Burn* (1869) 5 Ch App 163; *Ecclesiastical Commissioners for England v Kino* (1880) 14 Ch D 213.

[14] See ch 3, section (C)5.

largely prevented may amount to an abandonment of the right of light.[15] The Law Commission has recommended that where an easement of light has not been used for a continuous period of five years, there should be a rebuttable presumption that it has been abandoned.[16]

8.10 A question which may arise is whether a dominant owner can be taken to have abandoned or released an easement of light because an obstruction to light has been constructed on the servient land and he has not protested at it. It seems that an abandonment cannot be inferred from such circumstances. It is true that an implied abandonment of a right to prevent an unlawful development which would be a breach of covenant can be inferred from a long-standing failure by the owner of the right to enforce it.[17] An easement of light may be different, in that every day that the obstruction on the servient land remains it is said to be a further nuisance which creates a further right of action in respect of that nuisance.[18] There may not be any possibility of an abandonment of a right potentially enforceable in the event of a specific infringement by a cause of action until that infringement and that cause of action arises. A failure to raise an effective protest against an obstruction may have other consequences in law, such as:

(a) it may mean that an easement which was otherwise claimable under section 3 of the Prescription Act 1832 by reason of 20 years' enjoyment of the access of light may cease to be claimable because there has been an obstruction to the access of light for a year with acquiescence in that obstruction;[19] or
(b) the prospect of obtaining a mandatory injunction to remove the obstruction may be lost;[20] or
(c) the prospect of obtaining voluntary release damages may be lost.[21]

8.11 There can in theory be an implied abandonment or release of an easement of light as there can be of any other easement or any other property right. In practice, in the case of rights of light an implied abandonment is likely to occur only if:

(a) an aperture receiving the ingress of light is permanently blocked up; or
(b) the dominant building or a part of it containing an aperture or apertures is demolished without any proposal for its early rebuilding; or
(c) alterations are carried out to the dominant building or within its curtilage which, although retaining in place the apertures through which light passes to the dominant building, substantially reduce that light.

More difficult questions arise when the dominant building is demolished with a proposal for the early rebuilding of that building. Although there may be an

[15] *Ankerson v Connelly* [1907] 1 Ch 678. See ch 3, section (C)2.
[16] Law Commission, *Rights of Light* (Law Com No 356, 2014), para 7.47. See ch 12, para 12.44.
[17] *Attorney General of Hong Kong v Fairfax* [1997] 1 WLR 149.
[18] *Shadwell v Hutchinson* (1831) 2 B & Ad 97; *Battishill v Reed* (1856) 18 CB 696.
[19] See ch 5, section (D)4.
[20] See ch 7, section (B)4(a).
[21] See ch 7, para 7.128.

implied abandonment of a right of light to the former windows in this situation the subject is best considered under the general heading of redevelopment of that building, and that general question is examined in Chapter 3. The critical factor is likely to be the extent to which the apertures in the redeveloped building are the same in the vertical and horizontal plane as those in the former building so as to allow the transfer of rights of light to apertures in the new building.[22] There is no reason why an implied abandonment of an easement or in particular of an easement of light should be treated in any way differently from the implied abandonment of any other property right and a general reconsideration of the principles applicable in this specific area of property law is much needed.

3. Unity of Ownership and Possession

As with other easements a right of light is extinguished if unity of ownership and unity of possession of the dominant and the servient properties occur. This rule derives from the obvious proposition that a person cannot have a right against himself.[23] Once an easement has been extinguished in this way it is gone forever and cannot be revived. As it was put in *Coke on Littleton* in 1628: 'They [easements, etc.] are said to be extinguished when they are gone forever, *et tunc moriuntur*, and can never be revived; that is, when one man hath as high and perdurable an estate, as shall make an extinguishment'.[24] The ownership of the freehold interest which, when combined with unity of possession, brings about the extinguishment of an easement must be of the fee simple absolute in possession and not of a determinable fee.[25] By virtue of section 1(1) of the Law of Property Act 1925, the only form of fee simple which can exist as an estate in land today is a fee simple absolute in possession. Having stated this rule it is now necessary to proceed to state what occurs in law where there is unity of ownership but not of possession, or there is unity of possession but not of ownership, of the dominant and servient properties. 8.12

Unity of ownership of the dominant and servient properties alone does not extinguish an easement. In *Richardson v Graham*[26] the freehold owner of property A owned a prescriptive easement of light over property B. He let property A to a tenant and subsequently sold the freehold reversion to the owner of property B. It was held that the easement of light was not extinguished. The tenant continued to be entitled to assert his right of light against the person who had become his own landlord during the remaining period of his lease. 8.13

[22] See ch 3, section (C)3.

[23] See *Sovmots Investments Ltd v Secretary of State for the Environment* [1979] AC 144, 169 (Lord Wilberforce).

[24] Co Litt 113a; *Tyrringham's Case* (1584) 4 Co Rep 36a.

[25] *R v Inhabitants of Hermitage* (1692) Carth 239.

[26] *Richardson v Graham* [1908] 1 KB 39. A passage from *Buckby v Coles* (1814) 5 Taunt 311 was not followed.

8.14 Unity of possession of the dominant and servient properties does not extinguish an easement. It may suspend its operation and exercise while the unity of possession continues.[27] Therefore if property A has an easement of light over property B, the two properties having different owners, and both properties are let to the same tenant, the easement is not enforceable by the tenant during the period of the lease (it will not be possible for a person to enforce a right of light against himself) and so is said to be suspended but it comes back into full effect when the lease ends.[28] There seems no reason in principle why the freehold owner of property A should not assert his easement over property B if the tenant carries out a development on property B. The owner of property A may have good reason in wishing to protect his investment in this way especially if the lease is nearing its expiry date.

8.15 It is said that the inability to create or to hold an easement where there is unity of ownership and possession of the dominant and servient properties creates difficulties when estates are being developed with an intention of selling off parts of the estate to various purchasers. It might be convenient to the developer of the estate to have in existence easements during and at the end of his development so that portions of the estate can be sold off with the benefit of those easements. The Law Commission has suggested that where the dominant and the servient properties have registered title, the existence of common ownership and possession in one person should not prevent the creation or the continued existence of an easement.[29]

4. Determination of Leases

8.16 A legal easement may be created for an interest equivalent to a term of years absolute, so that there may be a leasehold easement.[30] A leasehold easement may arise in a number of ways.

(a) The freehold owner of land may grant an easement over his land for the benefit of his neighbour for a fixed period of years.
(b) The freehold owner of land may grant an easement over his land for the benefit of his neighbour who has only a leasehold interest in the neighbouring land.

[27] *Canham v Fisk* (1831) 2 Cr & J 126.

[28] *Thomas v Thomas* (1835) 2 CM & R 34. See also *Simper v Foley* (1862) 2 John & H 555, 563 (Page Wood VC).

[29] Law Commission, *Making Land Work: Easements, Covenants and Profits a Prendre* (Law Com No 327, 2011), para 4.44.

[30] Law of Property Act 1925, s 1(2)(a). Such an easement may take effect as a legal easement. If the easement is granted for some other limited period, eg for the life of the grantee, it can take effect only as an equitable interest, and this may affect its enforceability against purchasers of the servient land: see ch 11.

(c) The freehold owner of land may grant a lease of a part of it and as a term of the lease may grant an easement to the tenant over the retained land of the landlord. An instance of this situation would be where an owner of a block of flats lets the individual flats to tenants and grants rights of way to each tenant over land retained by him.

(d) The leasehold owner of land may grant an easement to his neighbour.[31] If the freeholder does not join in the grant the easement will be exercisable only against the leasehold interest.

Where an easement is appurtenant to a lease, one would suppose that it would end upon the determination of the lease of the dominant land by whatever means that determination took place. Clearly when a lease granted for a term certain comes to an end, an easement granted with that lease comes to an end. An obvious example, as just mentioned, would be a lease of a flat in a block with a right of way over the grounds of the block of flats where the easement of way would come to an end with the determination of the lease. Most leases are subject to forfeiture, that is the landlord can end the lease upon a breach of covenant by the tenant subject to certain restrictions such as in some instances the need for the service of a notice under section 146 of the Law of Property Act 1925 and subject to the power of the court to give relief against forfeiture. Where an easement has been granted as part of a lease, the easement comes to an end when the lease is brought to an end by forfeiture.[32] Equally, if a lease is granted for a term certain and the lease is then surrendered, any right of way created in favour of the tenant as a leasehold easement by the lease comes to an end.[33]

A lease may determine by a number of means. The expiry of a fixed term and a forfeiture, as just mentioned, are perhaps two of the most frequent means of determination. A surrender occurs when the tenant surrenders his lease to his landlord, and a merger occurs when the freehold and the leasehold interests come into the same ownership, something which may occur if the tenant acquires the freehold or a third party acquires both the freehold and the leasehold interests. A surrender or a merger determines the lease subject to the parties declaring that notwithstanding the common ownership of the two interests the lease is to continue to have a continued subsistence. The parties may do this for the financial or other convenience of the person who owns both of the interests. 8.17

It should follow that where a lease, which contains the benefit of a leasehold easement as part of its terms so that the leasehold easement is appurtenant to the leasehold estate, comes to an end, the easement should come to an end. 8.18

[31] An easement of light created by the operation of s 62 of the Law of Property Act 1925 against retained land of the grantor may be a leasehold interest when the grantor held only a lease in the retained land: *Booth v Alcock* (1873) LR 8 Ch App 663 (on the general words often included in a lease the need for which has been taken away by the Conveyancing Act 1881 and today s 62 of the Law of Property Act 1925).

[32] *Beddington v Atlee* (1887) 35 Ch D 317.

[33] *MRA Engineering Ltd v Trimster Co Ltd* (1988) 56 P & CR 1. See however the next two paras.

This is in accordance with logic and decided authority. It should not matter by whatever means the lease comes to an end. Some confusion may have been thrown into this simple approach by the decision in *Wall v Collins.*[34] In that case there were two adjoining houses, both subject to 999-year leases. The 999-year lease of the dominant property included a right of way over the servient property. The owner of the 999-year lease of the dominant property acquired the freehold of that property, so that there was a merger of the long leasehold and freehold interests. It was held that notwithstanding the determination of the long lease to which the easement was appurtenant, the easement continued in the hands of the former owner of that lease after he had become the freeholder. No particular reason was given for this decision, which seems to be contrary to principle, and no earlier authority, which is to the contrary effect as far as the determination of leases is concerned, was considered by or even cited to the Court of Appeal. The decision is therefore of dubious authority and may be considered technically to be *per incuriam.*[35] It is possible that the same result, that is the continued subsistence of the easement, could have been reached by the application of section 62 of the Law of Property Act 1925 to the conveyance of the freehold of the dominant property to the former long lessee of that property.[36] The Law Commission has, not surprisingly, recommended the reversal by statute of the first ground of the decision.[37]

8.19 It was accepted by counsel in *Wall v Collins*[38] that a leasehold easement over the servient land does not end by the merger of the freehold and leasehold interests in that land and this was said by the court in an obiter dictum[39] to be right as a matter of common sense. The common sense is not apparent. An express easement over a leasehold interest in land may be created as a legal easement and will

[34] *Wall v Collins* [2007] EWCA Civ 444, [2007] Ch 390.

[35] *Per incuriam* means that a decision has been taken by a court without knowledge or notice of a previous decision which may be binding on it. The Court of Appeal is bound by its own previous decisions, and in *Wall v Collins* the Court should at least have taken proper cognisance of the previous decision of the Court of Appeal in *MRA Engineering Ltd v Trimster Co Ltd* (1988) 56 P & CR 1. See (2007) *Conveyancer* 464. For a statement of the operation of the doctrine of precedent, see *Howard de Walden Estate Ltd v Aggio* [2008] Ch 26. It is possible that in exceptional circumstances the language of a grant or reservation of an easement for the benefit of a person with only a leasehold interest in the dominant land could extend to enure to any interest which that person would in the future acquire, such as a tenant acquiring the freehold, but clear wording would be needed for the grant or regrant to have such an unusual effect: see *Rymer v McIlroy* [1897] 1 Ch 528. The decision in Year Books, 21 Edn 3, 2, P1.5, which may be to the contrary effect (where the grantee of a right of way had no interest in the dominant land), may reflect a sounder principle.

[36] S 62 of the Law of Property Act 1925 as a means of creating easements is considered in ch 4, section (C).

[37] Law Commission, *Making Land Work: Easements, Covenants and Profits a Prendre* (Law Com No 327, 2011), paras 3.232–3.263.

[38] *Wall v Collins* [2007] EWCA Civ 444, [2007] Ch 390.

[39] An obiter dictum is a statement of law by a court which is not necessary for the decision in the case. Thus in *Wall v Collins* an issue for decision was whether the surrender or merger of a leasehold interest in the dominant land to which an easement was appurtenant terminated that easement. It was not necessary for that decision to determine whether a surrender of a lease of the servient land would terminate an easement over that leasehold interest.

normally come to an end when the lease ends.[40] If a sub-lease is granted out of a lease at common law when the lease is surrendered or merged into the freehold, the covenants in the sub-lease are rendered unenforceable.[41] Thus if the lease of the servient land ends by the expiration of the term or by forfeiture, a sub-lease derived out of that lease ends and the same should surely be true of an easement derived out of that lease.[42] It is not readily apparent why common sense suggests that a different rule operates where the lease of the servient land ends by merger. The only explanation given by the court was that the owner of a servient tenement should not be able to escape the burden of an easement by dealings to which those interested in the dominant tenement are not parties. However the owner of the dominant tenement would not be a party to the forfeiture of a lease of the servient land or the termination of that lease by the operation of a landlord's break clause, yet it seems contrary to principle that an easement appurtenant to the dominant land should survive such a forfeiture or determination by other means. Since the observation made in the Court of Appeal was obiter, and was in any event made on a concession by counsel and not after proper argument, the statement so made does not constitute a binding precedent in law.

The explanation and discussion of the law in this section of the chapter concerns 8.20
easements of light created expressly by deed. The same principles should apply when an easement is created by an express provision in a deed and by implication from the terms of a deed. Different principles apply when an easement of light is acquired by prescription under section 3 of the Prescription Act 1832. For example, if the servient land is let during the 20-year prescription period, the easement of light acquired for the benefit of the dominant building will prevail against the tenant of the servient land and against the landlord of that land when the lease ends.[43]

[40] A leasehold easement created by the operation of s 62 of the Law of Property Act 1925 comes to an end on the expiry of the leasehold interest of the grantor in the land over which the easement so created subsists: *Booth v Alcock* (1873) 8 Ch App 663 (a decision on the form of words used in conveyances and leases and which were intended to be replaced by the provisions of the Conveyancing Act 1881 and today s 62 of the Law of Property Act 1925). See ch 4, section (C).

[41] *Webb v Russell* (1789) 3 Term Rep 393. The position has had to be reversed by statute in the case of sub-tenancies: see Law of Property Act 1925, s 139.

[42] As was said by Romer LJ in *Bendall v McWhirter* [1952] 2 QB 466, 487: 'Every subordinate interest must perish with the superior interest on which it is dependent'. See as regards sub-leases when the head lease is forfeited *Great Western Railway Rly v Smith* (1876) 2 Ch D 235; *Viscount Chelsea v Hutchinson* [1994] 2 EGLR 61.

[43] *Morgan v Fear* [1907] AC 425. See ch 5, section (D)7, for an account of the operation of s 3 of the Prescription Act 1832 as regards different interests in land.

(C) OVERRIDING OF RIGHTS OF LIGHT

1. Statutory Powers and Compulsory Acquisition

(a) The General Principle

8.21 Where a body is given a statutory power to carry out works on land or to use land in a certain way, that power may lawfully be exercised even though the carrying out of the works or the inception of the use would, in the absence of the statutory power, be a violation of a proprietary right vested in the owner of other land such as a breach of a restrictive covenant or an infringement of an easement. An illustration of the principle is the decision of the Court of Appeal in a case where land was acquired by a school board for the purposes of erecting a school on it under the Elementary Education Act 1870. The land was subject to a restrictive covenant that no building should be erected without the consent of an adjoining owner within a specified distance of the boundary of the land of that owner. It was held that the school board was entitled to erect the school within the specified distance pursuant to statutory authority and that no action in private law lay for damages against the authority.[44] This was a case concerning a restrictive covenant, but the same principle would have applied if the carrying out of the development authorised by statute had been an infringement of an easement including an easement of light. The right over the land developed pursuant to statutory authority which is overridden may be described as an *ius tertii*, or right of a third party.[45]

8.22 Rights rendered unenforceable in this way are not wholly extinguished but are overridden only so far as necessary to permit the actions which are authorised by statute. An illustration of this principle is *Marten v Flight Refuelling Ltd*[46] in which land subject to a restrictive covenant confining its use to agricultural purposes was compulsorily acquired by the Air Ministry for defence purposes. The Air Ministry permitted a commercial company to occupy the land. An injunction was issued to prevent use of the land by the company in breach of the restrictive covenant, but the injunction was framed in such a way as not to prevent use for the defence purposes which were authorised by statute and for which the land had been acquired. In principle the overridden right may still be enforced or become enforceable against anything done on the burdened land not authorised by the statutory powers or anything done when the exercise of the statutory powers has ended.

[44] *Kirby v School Board for Harrogate* [1896] 1 Ch 437. See *Long Eaton Recreation Ground Co v Midland Rly Co* [1902] 2 KB 574; *Greenwich Healthcare NHS Trust v London and Quadrant Housing Trust* [1998] 1 WLR 1749.

[45] In *Clark v School Board for London* (1874) LR 9 Ch App 120 the principle was said by Lord Selborne LC to be that the legislation which gave a right to acquire land compulsorily gave the acquiring authority that land 'absolutely free from any *ius tertii* which would control their domination over it for the purpose of the duty which they have to discharge'.

[46] *Marten v Flight Refuelling Ltd* [1962] Ch 115.

It follows that pursuant to these general principles, a right of light enjoyed over servient land may be overridden by the carrying out of works pursuant to statutory authority on that servient land. If the works in question are of a permanent nature such as the erection of a permanent new building interfering with the rights of light of the dominant owner then, although technically the right of light is still only overridden and not extinguished, the permanent nature of the obstruction means that in practice the right may usually be taken as having been extinguished. There could occur circumstances in which the exercise of statutory powers on the servient land meant that a particular development was carried out pursuant to those powers and had a limited effect on the access of light to the dominant building. The easement of light appurtenant to the dominant building would be overridden to the extent of permitting that development to take place, subject to the payment of compensation as explained below. At the same time as this development, or following it, there might occur a commercial development on the servient land permitted by the public body. The profit gained from the disposal of a part of the land or a grant of an interest in the land so as to assist the carrying out of the commercial development might financially assist the public authority which bore the costs of acquiring the land and carrying out the public project under statutory powers. The easement of light would not be overridden as regards the further development and in a suitable case the further development could be prevented by an injunction sought by the dominant owner. The dominant owner could of course also seek damages for the effect of the further development if it violated his easement of light. 8.23

(b) *Compensation*

An acquiring authority may acquire land for the purpose of carrying out development. If the land acquired is burdened by the rights of a third party such as an easement of light the authority cannot normally separately acquire the benefit of that easement as such. The position is that the easement of light (and other easements or restrictive covenants which might impede the development) are overridden to the extent that they impede the development, subject to compensation payable to those with the benefit of the easement, as explained below.[47] 8.24

Compensation for the overriding of an easement of light is payable to the dominant owner under section 10 of the Compulsory Purchase Act 1965 for any injurious affection to the dominant land. Section 10 reproduces, with only minor amendments, the language of section 68 of the Lands Clauses Consolidation Act 1845. The language of section 10 is difficult to understand and has been said to have received an interpretation which fixes upon it a meaning having little 8.25

[47] On occasions statutes which authorise a specific project provide for the extinguishment, subject to compensation, of certain third party rights such as rights of way over the land on which the project is to be carried out: see, eg s 8 of the Crossrail Act 2008.

perceptible relation to the words used.[48] Where an easement of light is overridden, or in practice extinguished, by the exercise of statutory powers, it is usually as a result of the acquisition, by agreement or compulsorily, of the servient land. It is said that a claim under section 10 can be made if the package of statutory powers which authorise the project being carried out includes a power of compulsory purchase over the land burdened by the *ius tertii*.[49] Given the existence of this power, section 10 may still be engaged even though the acquisition of the burdened land was voluntary.[50] In most cases the assessment of the compensation for injurious affection will involve valuing the dominant land prior to the overriding or extinguishment of the easement of light over the servient land, then valuing the dominant land again on the same date after the overriding or extinguishment of the easement of light. The difference between the two valuations will constitute the compensation for injurious affection. There is no valuation date as such for the carrying out of the two valuations but the date on which the body with the statutory powers commences, or possibly completes, the development which constitutes the obstruction is the usual date taken for the before and after calculations.[51] Of course if there is a dispute over the compensation the process of determination, normally before the Lands Chamber of the Upper Tribunal, may take place at a later date but the valuation should still be by reference to the date on which the development which constitutes the overriding of the easement took place.

8.26 Unfortunately the assessment of compensation under section 10 for the loss of a right of light or other easement is less than satisfactory. It is explained in Chapter 7[52] that where damages are awarded for an infringement of a right of light, the damages are today usually assessed on a 'voluntary release' basis. This method of assessing damages is now in general use for the infringement of property rights such as easements or the benefit of restrictive covenants. What this means is that the damages are equal to the amount which the parties acting reasonably would have agreed in a hypothetical negotiation for the voluntary release of the right of light. This basis of assessment is to be compared with the 'book value' basis of assessment, which is simply the reduction in the value of the land of the dominant owner ignoring the right to bargain for a voluntary release of the right of light. Damages assessed on a voluntary release basis often result in damages which are equal to a significant proportion of the gain or profit which the person who has infringed a right of light is anticipated to make from his wrongful act and for that

[48] *Argyle Motors (Birkenhead) Ltd v Birkenhead Corporation* [1975] AC 99, 129 (Lord Wilberforce).

[49] *Moto Hospitality Ltd v Secretary of State for Transport* [2007] EWCA Civ 764, [2008] 1 WLR 2822.

[50] *Kirby v School Board for Harrogate* [1896] 1 Ch 437.

[51] *Wildtree Hotels Ltd v Harrow LBC* [2001] 2 AC 1, in which it was held that the compensation for injurious affection could be assessed by way of loss of an annual rental value over a limited period where the activities of the public body which gave rise to the right for compensation, their works to and temporary closure of roads, were not of a permanent nature. For a statement of the 'before and after' valuations which have to be carried out in order to assess compensation for injurious affection to land due to the permanent removal of rights appurtenant to it, see para 47 of the judgment of Lord Hoffmann in *Penny's Bay Investment Co Ltd v Director of Lands* (2010) 13 HKCFAR 287 (removal of rights of access to the sea).

[52] Ch 7, paras 7.108 et seq.

reason are often substantially greater than book value damages. Logic and justice suggest that where a right of light is overridden or extinguished by the acts of a public body on the servient land, the compensation payable under section 10 of the Compulsory Purchase Act 1965 should be equal to the amount of damages which would have been obtained if the acts of the public body had been the acts of a private person so that there was no statutory authorisation and damages were payable. Unfortunately it has been held in the Court of Appeal that the compensation under section 10 is to be confined to the reduction in the value of the dominant land assessed on what is in effect a book value basis.[53] The unsatisfactory nature of the position in law may be of less concern in some instances than might otherwise be the case since projects carried out by public authorities under statutory powers, sometimes after the compulsory acquisition of land, are usually carried out otherwise than for profit or gain so that in many cases it might in any event not be easy to apply the voluntary release method of assessing damages to the assessment of compensation.

2. Section 237 of the Town and Country Planning Act 1990

(a) The General Principle

A right of light may be overridden, or on many occasions in effect be extinguished, by the operation of section 237 of the Town and Country Planning Act 1990. Section 237(1) provides: 8.27

> Subject to sub-section (3), the erection, construction or carrying out, or maintenance of any building or work on land which has been acquired or appropriated by a local authority for planning purposes (whether done by the local authority or by a person deriving title under them) is authorised by virtue of this section if it is done in accordance with planning permission, notwithstanding that it involves—
>
> (a) interference with an interest or right to which this section applies,
>
> or
>
> (b) a breach of a restriction as to the user of land arising by virtue of a contract.

[53] *Wrotham Park Settled Estates v Hertsmere Borough Council* [1993] 2 EGLR 15. The claim for compensation considered in this case by the Court of Appeal was under s 237 of the Town and Country Planning Act 1990 which applies s 10 of the Compulsory Purchase Act 1965. S 237 of the 1990 Act is considered below. See also *Ward v Wychavon District Council* [1986] 2 EGLR 205; *Holliday v Breckland District Council* [2012] UKUT 193 (LC), [2012] 3 EGLR 95. A complaint was made to the European Court of Human Rights that compensation in these circumstances assessed purely on a book value basis and without regard to the voluntary release basis was contrary to art 1 of the First Protocol to the European Human Rights Convention in *S v United Kingdom* [1984] 41 DR 226, but was rejected by the Commission under the procedural system then in force. The reasoning in the *Wrotham Park* case also seems out of accord with the established principle that compensation under s 10 of the Compulsory Purchase Act 1965 is to be assessed on the same principles as apply to the assessment of damages in tort: *Clift v Welsh Office* [1999] 1 WLR 796. See also ch 12, para 12.52.

The interests and rights to which section 237 applies, and so which may be overridden, are any easement, liberty, privilege, right or advantage annexed to land and adversely affecting other land, including any natural right to support. It is apparent that an easement of light may be overridden under these provisions.[54]

8.28 In order for a right of light to be overridden under section 237 it is necessary

(a) that the servient land has been acquired or appropriated by a local authority for planning purposes;
(b) that planning permission is in existence which authorises works on the servient land;
(c) that works are carried out on the servient land in accordance with that planning permission; and
(d) that the works are carried out by the local authority which has acquired or appropriated the land for planning purposes or by a person deriving title under that authority.

The acquisition of land by the authority may be by agreement or under a compulsory purchase order. Appropriation is a decision by the authority that land it owns shall be held for planning purposes. It involves no formal procedure except a resolution to appropriate the land by the authority or by a committee of the authority or other persons with delegated powers. The reference to planning purposes refers to the purposes for which land may be acquired under section 226 of the Town and Country Planning Act 1990 which is to facilitate the carrying out of development or redevelopment in or in relation to the land or to achieve the proper planning of the area. An authority can only acquire land under this provision if the acquisition is likely to contribute to achieving the promotion or improvement of the economic, social or environmental well-being of their area.[55] The opportunity for the exercise of powers under section 237 is therefore wide.

8.29 It appears that the operation of section 237 may have a continuing effect and is not confined to a first development following the acquisition or appropriation of land for planning purposes. Therefore if land is acquired by a local authority for planning purposes, and a development is carried out on it, it appears that if a later redevelopment of the building constructed is carried out section 237 is still available to permit that later development to be carried out, notwithstanding that it would otherwise be contrary to rights of third parties.[56] A right of light, or other right, may be overridden notwithstanding that it is a right granted by the local authority itself.[57]

[54] The two leading cases on the operation of s 237 referred to in n 56 concerned the overriding of rights of light in the City of London or its fringe.

[55] Town and Country Planning Act 1990, ss 246(1), 226(1), 226(1A).

[56] *R v City of London Corporation and Royal Mutual Insurance Society ex parte Mystery of the Barbers* (1997) 73 P & CR 59; cf *Midtown Ltd v City of London Real Property Co Ltd* [2005] EWHC 33 (Ch), [2005] 1 EGLR 65, and see n 58.

[57] *R v City of London Corporation and Royal Mutual Insurance Society, ex parte Mystery of the Barbers* (1997) 73 P & CR 59.

The heading of section 237 is 'Power to override easements and other rights'. The effect of the provision is not to extinguish easements and other rights, but rather to override them so far as necessary to permit the carrying out of the works authorised by the planning permission. It follows that an easement, including an easement of light, will remain available to prevent other works on the servient land. An illustration of this situation might be that a local authority acquired or appropriated land for a public project for which planning permission existed so that a right of light exercisable over that land could not prevent the carrying out of that work. However if the land was subsequently sold by the authority for some other form of development for a different purpose then the right of light might still operate to prevent that other development.[58] 8.30

(b) Compensation

Compensation is payable for any overriding of rights under section 237. It is payable under section 7 or section 10 of the Compulsory Purchase Act 1965.[59] The compensation will usually be assessed under section 10 of the 1965 Act and will be for the injurious affection caused to the land with the benefit of the right which is overridden. Section 10 of the 1965 Act applies where a right such as an easement is overridden pursuant to the exercise of statutory powers which is akin to what normally occurs under section 237 of the Town and Country Planning Act 1990. Section 7 of the 1965 Act applies where a part of a person's land is compulsorily acquired and he suffers a reduction in value to the part of the land retained by him by reason of its severance from the land acquired or by reason of some other form of injurious affection, with the result that section 7 does not seem the appropriate provision to apply at any rate to most cases where the operation of section 237 of the Town and Country Planning Act 1990 gives a right to compensation. The assessment of compensation has been considered above.[60] Particular attention is drawn to the fact that the compensation is not to be assessed by the same method as applies to the assessment of voluntary release damages in the case of an ordinary infringement of a right of light.[61] Where the works have been carried out by a person deriving title from a local authority it is that person who is liable to pay the compensation but, if that person is unable to do so, the person whose rights have 8.31

[58] In the *Midtown* case Peter Smith J said at para 47 that in his view, if a local authority or a successor of a local authority wished to rely upon the power to override rights under s 237, the proposed development which it sought to impose on adjoining owners must be related to the planning purposes for which the land was acquired or appropriated.

[59] Town and Country Planning Act 1990, s 237(4)(c).

[60] See para 8.26 for the assessment of compensation.

[61] *Wrotham Park Settled Estates v Hertsmere Borough Council* [1993] 2 EGLR 15. This case was a claim for compensation under s 237 of the Town and Country Planning Act 1990 and the application by that section of s 10 of the Compulsory Purchase Act 1965. See also *Ward v Wychavon District Council* [1986] 2 EGLR 205; *Holliday v Breckland District Council* [2012] UKUT 193 (LC), [2012] 3 EGLR 95. See para 8.26.

been overridden and who claims compensation may obtain the compensation from the local authority.[62]

(c) Assistance to Private Developers

8.32 Section 237 is sometimes operated by local authorities to assist private developers to carry out a development which the authority considers to be in some way in the public interest. This is done even though the land is not held initially by the authority for any planning purpose. What typically seems to happen is that the local authority acquires the land from the private developer for a nominal consideration, then appropriates it for planning purposes, and then promptly returns it to the developer for the same nominal consideration. This scheme relies upon the fact that under section 237 a right may be overridden even though the development in question is carried out by a private developer who derives title from the local authority which has acquired or appropriated the land for planning purposes. Sometimes agreements exist between local authorities and developers under which the local authority undertakes to carry out this procedure if required by the developer and if it proves necessary. The process is sometimes called 'cleansing the title', a description which might not always be appreciated by the owners of rights and interests such as easements of light which are allegedly 'cleansed' away. The result of the procedure, if it is effective, is that a private developer is in effect able to override private law rights such as easements and the benefit of restrictive covenants vested in other landowners. Recourse to this arrangement under section 237, if it is permissible, may be of particular use to developers who fear that their project will be prevented or delayed by owners of neighbouring property who assert prescriptively acquired rights of light. The existence of such rights is not always easy for developers to ascertain, and developers sometimes acquire land or commence a development on the assumption or hope that such rights will never be asserted.[63]

[62] Town and Country Planning Act 1990, s 237(5).

[63] It is said that the prospect of the use of the power under s 237 by the Corporation of London brought about compensation agreements between developers and neighbours with rights of light which facilitated a recent major development at Fenchurch Street. Responses from developers to a recent consultation exercise by the Law Commission have suggested that some local authorities are reluctant to use the s 237 procedure to assist in bringing about developments and that divergent approaches were adopted by different authorities: see *Rights of Light* (Law Com No 356, 2014), paras 7.98–7.114. It had been suggested by consultees to the prior Law Commission Consultation Paper, 'Rights to Light' (Law Com No 210, 2013), that the Department for Communities and Local Government should issue guidelines on the use of s 237 powers by local authorities. There are analogies between powers under s 237, which in effect involve the compulsory purchase of existing third party rights, and the power to purchase compulsorily both corporeal interests in land and new rights over land under the general law of compulsory purchase and it may be that in deciding whether to use s 237 powers local authorities should note the guidance on the use of compulsory purchase powers issued by the Office of the Deputy Prime Minister in Circular 06/2004, 'Compulsory Purchase and the Crichel Down Rules'. The operation of s 237 under the type of arrangement here being discussed includes an appropriation by the local authority and it has been suggested that an appropriation is in some ways 'the equivalent of compulsory purchase': see *R v Leeds City Council, ex parte Leeds Industrial Co-operative Society Ltd* (1997) 73 P & CR 70, 77 (McCullough J).

The validity of this process in terms of public and administrative law has not been tested in the courts. If it were tested there must be some doubt as to whether the validity of the process would be upheld if only because of the argument that a power vested in a public authority by statute has to be exercised strictly for the purposes intended by the legislation[64] and providing assistance to private developers to override third party rights may not be the purpose of section 237. A court would look carefully at the vires of an arrangement between a local authority and a private developer which involved a quick shuffling of interests and which was designed to deprive persons of their private law rights which the courts might otherwise protect by an injunction and with the result (as explained earlier) that the payment of compensation might be substantially lower than the damages which might otherwise be recoverable even if an injunction was not granted.[65] 8.33

One particular further point may be noted which is that if section 237 is to operate so as to override a private right the works must be carried out on land 'which has been acquired or appropriated by a local authority.. '. If the works have already been carried out and someone then claims that there is an infringement of a third party right such as a right of light, a subsequent acquisition or appropriation by a local authority under the type of arrangement just discussed will be of no effect since it will be too late. It is said that some local authorities are willing to hold the section 237 process, and the assistance it may give to developers, in reserve in that if there is a protest about an infringement of rights of light after the development has been carried out the authority will then go through the process of acquiring and disposing of the servient land in order to defeat the claim. If this is so the local authorities involved, and the developers involved, appear to be proceeding under a misconception. 8.34

[64] *Galloway v Mayor and Commonalty of London* (1886) LR 1 HL 34, 43 (Lord Cranworth LC); *Merravale Builders v Secretary of State* (1978) 36 P & CR 87.

[65] The Supreme Court in *R (Sainsbury's Supermarkets Ltd) v Wolverhampton City Council* [2010] UKSC 20, [2011] 1 AC 437, has recently held to be *ultra vires* a compulsory purchase order made to assist a developer but made by a local authority which took into account an irrelevant consideration. However there is nothing to prevent a local authority acquiring property compulsorily under powers in planning legislation with a view to transferring the property to a private developer who will carry out the development and will indemnify the authority against the cost of the acquisition: *Standard Commercial Property Securities Ltd v Glasgow City Council* [2006] UKHL 50, [2007] JPL 758.

9

The Rights of Light Act 1959

(A) THE BACKGROUND

9.1 It has been explained that the acquisition of a right of light by long user or prescription depends on the uninterrupted enjoyment of the access of light across the servient property to an aperture or apertures in a building on the dominant property for at least 20 years, in the case of prescription under the Prescription Act 1832 and under the doctrine of lost modern grant, and since time immemorial in the rare cases in which common law prescription can be relied on for the acquisition of this type of easement.[1] For the purposes of prescription under the Prescription Act 1832, which is the predominant source of claims to a right of light created by prescription, the requirements under section 3 of the Act are

(a) that there has been actual enjoyment of the access of light for at least 20 years;
(b) that consent to the access of light over the servient property has not been given in writing or in a deed by the owner of the servient property; and
(c) that the enjoyment has been without interruption.

Section 4 of the Act introduces two further rules, which are:

(a) that the period of enjoyment is that immediately before the proceedings in a court in which the right is claimed; and
(b) that an interruption of the enjoyment only counts for present purposes if it has lasted and has been submitted to or acquiesced in for at least one year.

The purport and effect of the Rights of Light Act 1959 can only be understood in the context of these five statutory rules.

9.2 To take a simple example, suppose that a building on property A has enjoyed the access of light over property B (which may or may not itself contain a building) for 15 years. A question is how the owner of property B is to create an interruption of the light passing over his property to property A so as to prevent a right of light over his property coming into existence within a few years under the 1832 Act. It may well be the case that the owner of property B can only prevent the continued enjoyment of the access of light over his property for a further five years, so that an easement of light is prevented from coming into existence, by himself erecting

[1] See ch 5.

a structure or extending a structure on his property which obstructs the passage of light across his property. The general rules in section 4 of the 1832 Act relating to an obstruction apply to the acquisition by prescription of all types of easement (although important differences on other matters apply to the acquisition of rights of light). When the easement which is being acquired by the running of the prescription period is a positive easement such as a right of way the course to be adopted by the owner of property B to prevent the continued running of the prescription period is apparent. He can physically obstruct or prevent passage over his property or can bring an action to prevent the enjoyment of the access by the owner of property A. Since a right of way has not by then been acquired by prescription the actions of the owner of property A in using the right of way will be a trespass and can be prevented and interrupted in the usual way by an injunction or other remedy issued by a court. When it comes to the access of light it is not possible to bring such an action. The owner of property A commits no wrong by simply enjoying the passage of light to his building over property B, and no court has power to stop him continuing that enjoyment. Therefore the only recourse of the owner of property B, if he is to prevent the access of light ripening into an easement by prescription, is to obstruct by some physical means the passage of light across his property to property A.[2]

The owner of property B can of course create the necessary obstruction by erecting a building, or a larger and higher building than that which is already there, or some other physical obstruction on his property. However, he may not wish to do so, or the time may not be commercially convenient for him to do so, in the few years which may remain to him before the end of the prescription period. In order for the obstruction to effect its purpose it would have to be extensive enough to reduce the light passing to property A such that property A was no longer sufficiently lit for its reasonable and comfortable use. He could deliberately erect a screen of a sufficient size at the edge of his property with the sole purpose of preventing the continued passage of light over that property, but in many cases such an action could be awkward or unacceptable. First, the owner of property B will need planning permission to erect a screen, and this may well be refused by the local planning authority whose concern is the public interest in development and the appearance and amenities of the area and not the prevention of the acquisition of private rights. Secondly, there is the trouble and expense of erecting and maintaining such a screen. Thirdly, if property B contains a building, a large physical screen on its boundary may adversely affect the attraction or utility of that building. Prior to the enactment of the Rights of Light Act 1959, such actual physical screens were sometimes erected. It is difficult to imagine what such a screen would be like in the case of a modern multi-storey office building. 9.3

[2] It has been suggested that the owner of property B could prevent the running of the prescription period by unilaterally signifying his consent to the passage of light over his property such that the access of light became by written consent, but this seems unlikely: see ch 5, para 5.62.

9.4 It was to investigate problems of the above nature that a committee under the chairmanship of Harman J, then a Judge of the Chancery Division of the High Court, was appointed in March 1957. The committee in its report described the problems just mentioned which arose under the present aspects of the law of rights of light. A further matter of concern at that time was the sites which remained vacant following war damage and which were not likely to be developed in time to prevent the passage of light over them to other properties for 20 years, and so the creation of an easement by prescription against the site. It was the report and recommendations of the committee to the Lord Chancellor which brought about the enactment of the Rights of Light Act 1959, an Act which aimed to address problems of the type just described. The Act is sometimes stated to be one of the methods by which an existing easement of light can be extinguished, and certainly the Act can sometimes be operated to bring this about, but its main purpose was to provide a convenient method which could prevent the acquisition of rights of light by prescription. A measure of the success of the Act may be that over the half century since it was enacted it has been the subject of little litigation. On the other hand, the procedure is undoubtedly cumbersome and this may explain why the procedure is not used as much as one would expect to prevent the acquisition of rights of light by prescription. It is explained in Chapter 12 that the Law Commission has recently proposed an essentially similar but much simpler procedure which would have the same effect of preventing prescriptive rights of light arising.[3]

(B) THE GENERAL EFFECT OF THE ACT

9.5 The essence of the solution recommended by the Harman Committee, and the core of the Rights of Light Act 1959, is that a person in the position of the owner of property B in the example just given, instead of erecting an actual obstruction to the passage of light across his property, should be able to register with the local authority for the area as a local land charge a notice of notional obstruction in a position and with dimensions chosen by him. Persons who would have been affected if there had been an actual obstruction can bring proceedings in the courts to challenge the lawfulness of the notional obstruction. If they fail to challenge the notional obstruction within a year, or if that challenge is unsuccessful, the notional obstruction will then operate for the purposes of sections 3 and 4 of the Prescription Act 1832 as an actual obstruction which had lasted for a year and had been known to the owner of property A and had been acquiesced in by him for that year. By this means the running of the prescription period will be prevented and no easement will arise by prescription under section 3 of the Prescription Act 1832. There are provisions for ensuring that prior to the registration

[3] See ch 12, para 12.39 et seq.

of a notional obstruction, notice has been given of the intended registration to all persons likely to be affected by that registration.

To revert to the example in paragraph 9.2, the owner of property B may register his notional obstruction after 15 years of the prescription period. If the owner of property A takes no proceedings in the court to challenge the registration during the subsequent year he will be taken to have submitted to and acquiesced in that obstruction as if it was an actual obstruction so that at the end of the 20-year prescription period he will not be able to claim that a prescriptive easement of light has been created. If the owner of property A sought to challenge the registration he would fail, since an actual obstruction at that time would not have been an infringement of any right which he then held. The result would then also be that the registration of the notice of the notional obstruction would prevent the running of the prescription period and prevent the acquiring of an easement of light by prescription. 9.6

Of course, if the circumstances had been different and at the time of the registration of the notice there had already been, say, 22 years of unobstructed access of light to property A over property B, the erection of an actual obstruction on property B would have constituted an infringement of the right of light to property A created by the long enjoyment of the access of light. In these circumstances the owner of property A would have a year from the date of the registration of the notice to bring proceedings in the court to challenge the legality of the notice and the notional obstruction. His proceedings would succeed. If the owner of property A failed to initiate proceedings in the year open to him, the notice would operate as an interruption for a year submitted to or acquiesced in by him so that he would lose the right to claim an easement of light by prescription under section 3 of the Prescription Act 1832. The owner of property A could point to the previous 22 years of uninterrupted access of light over property B but that period would be of no avail to him since it would not be the period immediately before any proceedings in a court in which the right was claimed. In other words, in some circumstances the 1959 Act can operate not only to prevent the creation of an easement but also to destroy an easement which has been established under section 3 of the Prescription Act 1832.[4] 9.7

The 1959 Act operates by reference to rights of light which may be appurtenant to a specific and identified dominant building. There is no procedure for some general notice to, or effect on, properties which are near the property of the servient owner. It is therefore incumbent on the servient owner who wishes to operate the statutory procedure to identify at the outset the dominant building or buildings. Thereafter an application to the Lands Chamber of the Upper Tribunal for a certificate that adequate notice has been given of a proposed application for registration of a light obstruction notice, a registration as a local land charge of a 9.8

[4] It is possible that on the facts described the easement could still be claimed under the doctrine of lost modern grant where the prescription period does not have to be a period immediately before the right is claimed in court proceedings. See para 9.71 et seq.

notice following the grant of a certificate, and the effect of a notice so registered, all relate to the identified dominant building or buildings and to no other property.[5]

9.9 It should be clearly understood that the operation of the rights of Light Act 1959 can affect only the acquisition or the continuation of rights of light obtained by prescription under section 3 of the Prescription Act 1832. The 1959 Act has no effect on rights of light which have been created expressly by a deed or by implication from the circumstances of a disposal of land.[6]

(C) THE DETAILED OPERATION OF THE ACT

9.10 While the general operation of the Rights of Light Act 1959 is easy to describe, there are some complexities in its detailed operation and these must now be explained.

1. Prior Publicity

9.11 The persons who may be affected by the procedure under the 1959 Act are those with interests in property who have acquired an easement of light by prescription where enjoyment of the access of light during the full prescription period has been completed or who may be in the process of establishing such an easement of light by the enjoyment of the access of light during the 20 year prescription period. Persons in the latter category are sometimes said to have inchoate rights. The result of the registration of a notice may be that a right of light established by prescription is lost by reason of the year of the notional interruption or that the running of the 20 year prescription period is brought to an end by that notional interruption so that no right of light will be established by prescription. It is obvious that parties with an interest in property who may be adversely affected in either of these two ways should receive adequate notice of the use or proposed use of the procedure under the 1959 Act.

9.12 The only person who can apply for the registration of a notice of a notional obstruction is the owner of the property on which the notional obstruction is to be placed. For these purposes an owner of property is either

(a) the owner of the fee simple freehold interest in the property; or
(b) a person entitled to a lease of the property with seven years or more of the term unexpired; or
(c) a mortgagee in possession of either of these interests.[7]

[5] Rights of Light Act 1959, ss 1(1), 1(2), 3(1).
[6] It is not wholly clear what is the effect of the Act on rights of light acquired by prescription under the doctrine of lost modern grant: see para 9.71 et seq and n 4.
[7] Rights of Light Act 1959, ss 2(1), 7(1). In the remainder of the notes to this chapter this Act is called 'the 1959 Act'.

The assumption is that persons with tenancies having less than seven years to run will have little interest in preventing the acquisition of rights of light by prescription against the property in which their tenancy subsists. The successful operation of the Act by a tenant of the servient property may of course enure to the benefit of a freeholder and vice versa.

The mechanism used in the 1959 Act to ensure that proper notice is given of the proposed application to the local authority to register a light obstruction notice as a local land charge is that prior to the application for registration the person intending to make that application must obtain from the Lands Chamber of the Upper Tribunal a certificate certifying that adequate notice has been given to the persons likely to be affected by the registration of a notice.[8] The Lands Chamber of the Upper Tribunal is the successor of the former Lands Tribunal under the Tribunals, Courts and Enforcement Act 2007. The form and content of the proposed light obstruction notice must be determined before an application is made to the Lands Chamber for a certificate since that application has to be accompanied by copies of the proposed notice. The notice of the notional obstruction which is registered with the local authority is usually described as a light obstruction notice although that expression is not used in the 1959 Act. It is used in the Local Land Charges Rules 1977 which contain the procedure for the registration of a notice as a local land charge.[9] The Act describes the land over which light passes and on which the notional obstruction is placed as the servient land and the property to which the light passes as the dominant building and this terminology is adopted in the remainder of this explanation of the procedure. The reason that the dominant property is called the dominant building is that only a building with apertures letting in light can acquire or enjoy an easement of light. 9.13

The 1959 Act states that the certificate which the Tribunal issues is that adequate notice has been given to all persons who, in the circumstances existing at the time when the certificate is issued, appear to the Tribunal to be persons likely to be affected by the registration of a light obstruction notice.[10] The procedure is supplemented by the Tribunal Procedure (Upper Tribunal) (Lands Chamber) Rules 2010.[11] The application for a certificate is made to the Registrar of the Tribunal. The application must be accompanied by three copies of the application, with any attached plans, proposed to be made to the local authority for the registration of a light obstruction notice. A fee is payable. 9.14

[8] 1959 Act, s 2(3).

[9] See r 10 of the Local Land Charges Rules 1977 and see para 9.28.

[10] 1959 Act, s 2(3). Obviously the identification of the dominant building or buildings is necessary before an application for a certificate can be made to the Tribunal and before a certificate can be issued.

[11] Tribunal Procedure (Upper Tribunal) (Lands Chamber) Rules 2010, SI 2010/2600. The Upper Tribunal has published guidance by way of its 'Explanatory Leaflet for Applications for Rights of Light Certificates' (October 2014).

9.15 The application to the Tribunal does not have to be in any prescribed or specified form, but

(a) must be signed and dated;
(b) must state the name and address of the applicant and of any representative of the applicant;
(c) must state whether the applicant is the owner of the servient land or is a tenant of that land for a term of years certain and, if so, when the term will expire, or is the mortgagee in possession of the servient land;
(d) must give a description of the servient land (presumably this can be given by reference to a plan such as the plan filed with HM Land Registry as part of the certificate of title but probably some description of any building or buildings on the land should also be given);
(e) must state the local authority which keeps the register of local land charges for the dominant building; and
(f) must state the names and addresses of all persons known by the applicant, after conducting all reasonable inquiries, to be occupying the dominant building or to have a proprietary interest in it.[12]

The final requirement means that the applicant should take steps to ascertain the freehold owner and any tenant of any part of the dominant building. These details can usually be obtained from the Land Registry, save that tenants with a term of seven years or less cannot obtain a registered title. The practical way of finding the names and addresses of such short-term tenants, as of other occupiers, is by postal or personal inquiry at the dominant building, or by inquiries of the landlord. It is, of course, with buildings in multiple occupation, such as blocks of flats, that these difficulties are most likely to arise. An attempt should certainly be made to find the identity of mortgagees (for example of flats held on long leases), since mortgagees have interests the value of which could be diminished by the loss of a right of light. Persons with third party rights such as rights of way have proprietary interests, but here the problem of identification may be less acute. There may of course be more than one dominant building and this may particularly be the case where the procedure is being used as a precursor to a redevelopment of the servient land. In these circumstances the above requirements of the application to the Tribunal should be observed for each dominant building.

9.16 The servient owner will need to consider what are the dominant building or buildings. In an urban area when a major new development is proposed, there are likely to be a number of neighbouring buildings which have acquired or are in the process of acquiring rights of light. Servient owners would be well advised to cast their net widely. Any property near to the servient land to which the access of light may be affected by the proposed development on the servient land should be regarded as a dominant building. The 1959 Act operates on rights of light to dominant buildings. If a building is not identified as a dominant building, the

[12] ibid, r 41.

process under the Act will have no effect on persons with interests in that building. Consequently the identification of any dominant building or buildings at an initial stage is essential. Clearly if there is any doubt on whether the access of light to a particular building will be affected by a proposed development, it will be prudent to include that building as a dominant building.

Upon receipt of an application for a certificate in the proper form and with the required accompanying documents and information, there are four steps which the Registrar of the Tribunal can or must take. It is important to ensure that proper notice of the proposed application to register a light obstruction notice is given since once a notice has been registered all persons interested in the dominant building are deemed to have notice of the registration and of the person who has effected the registration. 9.17

The first step is that the Registrar should satisfy himself that adequate steps have in fact been taken to identify the names and addresses of the persons with a proprietary interest in or in occupation of the dominant building. There may of course be more than one dominant building affected. Neither the 1959 Act nor the Rules specify in direct terms that this must be done. However, the function of the Registrar doing so is implicit in the nature of the certificate which the Registrar is being asked to issue and in the power of the Registrar to require the production of documents and information.[13] The selection of the dominant building or buildings is for the applicant and the Registrar should direct his attention only to this building and interests in it. 9.18

The second step is that the Registrar has power to issue a written direction that notice of the proposed application to register the light obstruction notice is given by advertisement to the persons who appear to have an interest in the dominant building.[14] Notice by advertisement may be in addition to or in place of any other form of notice. Presumably the giving of notice of the proposed application by advertisement will be appropriate when the dominant building is in fragmented occupation and it is difficult to establish the names and addresses of all occupiers. It is important to be clear on one point at this juncture. It is unlikely that short-term tenants of a building can have gained a right of light by prescription through 20 years of access of light over the servient land during their tenancy or previous short tenancy but such a right may have been gained by the landlord and have passed to the occupying short term tenants on the grant of their tenancy.[15] Short-term tenants may therefore themselves have a right to prevent an obstruction to the access of light to the building or part of the building which they occupy. This makes it all the more important that notice of the proposed application for 9.19

[13] ibid, r 5(3)(d).

[14] ibid, r 42(1)(c).

[15] On the grant of a tenancy of any length, rights of light owned by the landlord normally pass to the tenant, unless expressly excluded, either by reason of an express provision in the lease granting such rights or under s 62 of the Law of Property Act 1925. For s 62 of the 1925 Act see ch 4, section (C). For the transfer generally of the benefit of easements of light, including on the grant of a tenancy, see ch 11, section (E).

registration of the light obstruction notice is given to all occupiers of the dominant building. The nature of an advertisement is not specified. An advertisement by the placing of a notice in a local newspaper may be required, but some other step such as the placing of a notice in the entrance or lobby of a multi-tenanted or multi-occupied building may be appropriate.

9.20 The third step is that the Registrar must deliver written directions to the applicant specifying what notices are to be given to persons who appear to the Tribunal to be likely to be affected by the registration of a light obstruction notice, and the time by which such notices shall be given.[16] There is no prescribed or suggested form of notice. The Practice Directions of the Tribunal give no guidance on the form of notice which may be required.[17] A difficulty about notices is that the law of easements acquired by prescription, and the provisions of the Rights of Light Act 1959 which may prevent the acquisition of such easements, are scarcely likely to be general knowledge to the owners and occupiers of property. It seems therefore that an adequate notice should at least give some general indication of these matters. It is suggested that a notice should:

(a) enclose a copy of the proposed application for registration to be made to the local authority;
(b) contain a statement that if the recipient does not make an application to the court within a certain time he may lose certain rights relating to light which he holds or which may become available to him;
(c) contain a statement that by applying to the applicant or his solicitor at a named address answers to any reasonable query or further factual information may be available (although no advice can be given on legal matters); and
(d) contain a statement that the recipient of the notice may be well advised to seek independent legal advice on his position.

A notice by advertisement may need to be less detailed, but should still contain some of the elements just mentioned. Guidance on these matters in a Practice Direction of the Tribunal would be helpful. One matter to note is that particularly as regards residential properties a person occupying the property with a proprietary interest such as a tenant may have living with him or her family members or others such as lodgers who do not themselves have a proprietary interest. It seems sensible in such circumstances to regard the tenant, or holder of another proprietary interest, as the occupier. It may be good practice that the notice given to an owner or occupier of the dominant property, or a letter accompanying the notice, should ask that the recipient should draw the notice to the attention of any other persons resident in the property.

[16] Tribunal Procedure (Upper Tribunal) (Lands Chamber) Rules 2010, r 42(1)(a).

[17] The current directions are the Practice Directions of the Lands Chamber of the Upper Tribunal, issued on 20 November 2010.

The time specified for the giving of the notices need not be long, since all details will be or should be known to the applicant when he applies to the Tribunal for a certificate. A period of 21 to 28 days might be reasonable. Again it would be helpful if a standard time was specified in a Practice Direction issued by the Tribunal, which could be deviated from in special cases. 9.21

The fourth step is that the Registrar must issue a certificate of adequate notice when he is satisfied that any notices which he has directed should be given have been given.[18] The Rules do not say anything about the method of the giving of notices although there is nothing to prevent the Registrar specifying that notices shall be served using a postal service with recorded delivery or some equivalent system. The Registrar will only issue the certificate when the applicant has notified the Tribunal in writing that the notices have been served, setting out full particulars of the steps taken to serve the notices. The applicant must do this as soon as reasonably practicable.[19] A certificate issued in these circumstances is called a definitive certificate in the Rules.[20] An application to the Tribunal for a certificate involves only one party, the servient owner. If a person whose rights are affected by the issue of a certificate or any other aspect of the proceedings and the actions of the Tribunal is aggrieved, his only ultimate resort may be an application for judicial review to challenge what has been done. The Upper Tribunal is in principle subject to remedies in judicial review proceedings.[21] A party to a decision of the Registrar of the Tribunal may apply within 14 days of the decision for the decision to be considered afresh by a Judge of the Tribunal.[22] 9.22

2. Form of a Light Obstruction Notice

It is necessary for an applicant to draft his light obstruction notice before he applies for a certificate of adequate service from the Upper Tribunal. It is this form of notice which, after receipt of a definitive certificate from the Tribunal, he may register with the local authority as a local land charge. There is no prescribed form of light obstruction notice. The description of what a notice must contain is found in the Rights of Light Act 1959, which states that the notice must show an obstruction to the access of light to the dominant building across the servient land which would be caused by the erection in a position specified of an opaque structure of such dimensions, which may be of unlimited height, as is specified.[23] 9.23

[18] Tribunal Procedure (Upper Tribunal) (Lands Chamber) Rules 2010, r 44.

[19] ibid, r 42(2).

[20] ibid, r 44.

[21] *R (Cart) v Upper Tribunal* [2011] UKSC 28, [2012] 1 AC 663.

[22] The Tribunal Procedure (Upper Tribunal) (Lands Chamber) Rules 2010, r 4(3). This procedure was followed in *In The Matter of an Appeal. Against A Decision of the Registrar by Anglo Suisse Holdings* (unreported) 9 March, 2009 in connection with an emergency certificate. See para 9.55.

[23] 1959 Act, s 2(2)(b).

9.24 The important point is of course the description of the position of the notional opaque structure. There are five points to consider.

(a) The structure will normally be a form of screen. There is no need to specify any particular thickness of this screen since, being necessarily opaque, it will prevent the passage of light through it.
(b) The lateral dimension of the screen should be specified as sufficient to prevent so far as possible the access of light to the dominant building. Thus a screen which runs along a complete boundary of the servient land may be specified. If there is more than one dominant building, or if light could reach the dominant building otherwise than across the particular boundary on which a screen could be notionally erected, it may be necessary to specify a screen or screens which run along more than one boundary, or along all boundaries, of the servient land. The owner of the servient land may accept that rights of light are appurtenant to certain of his neighbouring buildings, perhaps created expressly by deed, and may wish only that a right of light to one particular neighbouring building, possibly one recently erected, shall not acquire a prescriptive right of light. In these circumstances the owner of the servient land may wish to confine his notional obstruction to a structure which prevents the passing of light only to that building.
(c) The Act states that the screen may be of unlimited height, and in practice the structure is usually specified as one of unlimited height, so as wholly to prevent the access of light over it.
(d) The structure is normally specified as erected along the boundary of the servient land with the highway or with another property. Of course any existing building on the servient land may be set back from the boundary. It is possible that there is some projection or overhang of a building on the servient land at a higher level over the boundary with the highway or over the ground level boundary with adjoining land. In that case the structure may need to be more carefully specified as one which contours around any such projection or stops at the bottom of the projection and starts again at the top of the projection.
(e) There may be occasions on which apertures on lower floors of the dominant building have already obtained rights of light expressly or impliedly by a deed or by prescription, but there has been a recent upwards extension of the building as regards the apertures in which no prescriptive or other right of light has been obtained. In such a case the notional structure may need to be more precisely specified so as to be one which, if that can be established, blocks out light to the apertures in the upper part of the dominant building only. If this is not practical (ie, because such a structure would seriously block light to the lower apertures with their rights of light), then a structure starting at ground level can be specified but with it being made clear in the publicity notice to persons in the lower parts of the dominant building that the process is not intended to affect their existing rights of

light. Even if that is done, the persons with interest in the lower parts of the dominant building would be well advised to commence legal proceedings in the year available for doing so, in order to be sure of protecting their rights. Similar considerations apply when the dominant building has been extended laterally so that the older part of the building has clearly obtained an easement of light by prescription whereas the newer part has not. In such a case it may be possible to design and specify a screen which blocks out the access of light over the servient land to only the apertures in the newer part of the dominant building.

It may be prudent for the owner of servient land to take advice from a rights of light surveyor or other expert on the exact specification of the notional structure, especially in cases which fall within the last two sub-paragraphs of the last paragraph. The prescribed form of application to the local authority for the registration of a light obstruction notice assumes that the usual type of notional obstruction will be a screen or screens of unlimited height along all boundaries of the servient land, but provides an opportunity for a screen or screens of different dimensions to be specified. 9.25

3. Registration of a Light Obstruction Notice

A light obstruction notice must be registered as a local land charge. The application for registration should be made to the district council or county borough council or Welsh county council outside London, or the council of the London borough or Common Council of the City of London within London, in which the dominant building is situated.[24] The requirement of registration as a local land charge is obviously sensible. A requirement for some form of registration or notice on the register within the land registration legislation would not be appropriate since, certainly in 1959, by no means all titles to land were registered and even today leases of seven years or less cannot obtain a registered title. Registration as an ordinary land charge under, today, the Land Charges Act 1972 would also not be wholly satisfactory, since the only searches which can be made would be in relation to the names of owners of land rather than the land itself, and this creates obvious difficulty in establishing the name of the owner of a property when the charge was registered.[25] 9.26

The local land charges register, maintained by local authorities, can be readily searched. The owners and occupiers of the dominant building when the procedure under the 1959 Act is initiated should be notified of what is occurring by the 9.27

[24] Local Land Charges Act 1975, s 3(1).

[25] Registration is effected in the name of the estate owner at the time of registration: Land Charges Act 1972, s 3(1). No search can be made against the land itself. The operation of land charges is explained in ch 11, section (D).

requirement for prior notification, which has been explained. A purchaser of an interest in land will search the local land charges register as a matter of normal conveyancing practice and can by doing so ascertain whether a light obstruction notice has been registered. He can then satisfy himself as to the effect on the existence of a prescriptive easement in favour of the property which he is buying of any registered light obstruction notice. The effect may be (a) that an easement of light which might otherwise have been gained by prescription has ceased to be available due to the interruption for a year attributable to an unchallenged registration of a notice, or (b) that the running of an uncompleted prescription period has been ended by the same interruption.[26] As explained earlier, where a property is bought with the benefit of an easement of light expressly or impliedly created by a deed, the registration of a light obstruction notice has no effect on the continued validity of the easement.

9.28 An application for the registration of a light obstruction notice must be in the prescribed form and must identify the servient land and the dominant building in the prescribed manner. The prescribed form is form A in Schedule 1 to the Local Land Charges Rules 1977.[27] The form requires that a description of the servient land and of the dominant building is inserted and states that wherever practicable, a map or plan of the dominant building should be attached. In many cases full descriptions of the two areas of land with an appropriate plan will be apparent from the light obstruction notice itself. In addition the application for registration must state that the registration of a notice in pursuance of the application is intended to be equivalent to the obstruction of the access of light to the dominant building across the servient land which would be caused by the erection, in the position on the servient land specified in the application, of an opaque structure of such dimensions as may be so specified.[28] The prescribed form contains a statement of this nature and contemplates that the usual case will be the erection of an opaque structure on all boundaries of the servient land to an unlimited height. The form also accommodates the possibility of this description of the notional erection being limited both in its lateral and its vertical dimension. This statement is the only description in the legislation of what exactly a light obstruction notice must contain. An application for registration must be accompanied by a definitive certificate issued by the Lands Chamber of the Upper Tribunal.[29] There is no time limit for an application to the local authority to register a notice as a local land charge following the issue of a definitive certificate by the Lands Chamber. This is perhaps a defect in the procedure, since persons with an interest in the dominant building do not have to be notified of an application to register a light obstruction notice as a local land charge or of the actual registration. Such persons must

[26] See paras 9.5–9.7.

[27] 1959 Act, s 1(2); Local Land Charges Rules 1977, r 10(1).

[28] 1959 Act, s 2(2)(b).

[29] 1959 Act, s 2(3)(a). See para 9.51 et seq for the exceptional case of the issue by the Upper Tribunal of a temporary certificate which permits the registration of a light obstruction notice to have effect for a temporary period until a definitive certificate is issued.

obtain their information searching the local land charges register (or from queries to the owner of the servient land) and a challenge to the courts has to be begun within a year of the registration. If a substantial period elapses between the issue of a definitive certificate by the Lands Chamber and the effecting of the registration of a notice as a local land charge persons with interests in the dominant building may become incautious and fail to challenge the registration by seeking a declaration from the courts within the one year available. This danger may be particularly acute since if the interest in the dominant building has been transferred following notification of that proposal.

Providing that a proper application has been made to the local authority for registration with an accompanying certificate of adequate notice the authority must register the light obstruction notice in the appropriate local land charges register and the notice when so registered is a local land charge.[30] No notice of the application to the authority for registration or of the registration has to be given to persons with an interest in the dominant building. It is considered that the notification of a proposal to register a light obstruction notice as a land charge and the definitive certificate given by the Lands Chamber of the Upper Tribunal constitute sufficient notification of the process to persons with interests in the dominant building. 9.29

(D) THE EFFECT OF REGISTRATION

1. The Effect in Law

The general purpose and effect of registration of a light obstruction notice have already been described.[31] It is now necessary to explain the effect in rather greater detail. 9.30

The primary effect of a notice is that for the purposes of determining whether a person is entitled to a right of light to the dominant building over the servient land the access of light to the dominant building across the servient land shall be treated as obstructed to the same extent as it would have been obstructed if the erection described in the notice registered had actually been erected on the date of the registration and had remained in position while the notice had effect.[32] A notice will normally cease to have effect one year after the date of registration.[33] In other words the notional obstruction is for this purpose equivalent to an actual obstruction. As explained an obstruction which lasts for a year may be fatal to the acquisition of a right of light by prescription. This effect of the registration of a 9.31

[30] 1959 Act, s 2(4).
[31] See paras 9.5–9.7.
[32] 1959 Act, s 3(1).
[33] See section (G) of this chapter for the cessation of the effect of registration.

notice applies to the acquisition of easements of light by prescription. It is of no relevance to easements created by express or implied grant or by the operation of section 62 of the Law of Property Act 1925, since an obstruction of light for a year will not affect the continued enforceability of an easement created by these means. The effect on easements created by lost modern grant is considered separately below. The main impact of the obstruction is on the acquisition of an easement of light under section 3 of the Prescription Act 1832.

9.32 The statutory assumption of an obstruction to the access of light to the dominant building would not by itself be sufficient to stop the running of the prescription period under the Prescription Act 1832. Section 4 of that Act provides that an obstruction only has that effect if it is submitted to or acquiesced in for at least a year by a person having notice of the obstruction. The 1959 Act therefore provides that until an action is brought in the courts to challenge the light obstruction notice all persons interested in the dominant building are deemed to have notice of the registration of the notice and of the person who has effected the registration and are deemed to acquiesce in the notional obstruction. The deemed acquiescence of any person ends when and if an action is brought by him. If an action is brought but the court decides against the claim to a right of light, the court may direct that the above provisions shall apply in relation to the notice as if that action had not been brought.[34] The notional obstruction and the deemed acquisition therefore apply to all owners and occupiers of the dominant building, whether or not they have received the prior publicity of the proposal to register the notice which has been required and whether or not they have received a copy of the notice and whether or not they know of the registration of the notice. Of course the purpose of the prior publicity and of the need for a certificate from the Upper Tribunal is to ensure that so far as possible a situation of persons not being notified does not arise, but it may do so, for example where a property or a part of a property is vacant at the relevant time or where buildings have a multiplicity of occupiers.

9.33 It was necessary to provide for a mechanism by which light obstruction notices could be challenged by persons with an interest in the dominant building. If an actual obstruction had been erected on the servient land, any person with an interest in the dominant building who claimed that his right of light over the servient land had been infringed by the obstruction could have brought proceedings in the courts for either an injunction to remove the obstruction, or for damages, or for both. Such proceedings are not appropriate as regards a notional obstruction. Accordingly the 1959 Act specifies its own procedure which is available for challenging the light obstruction notice and preventing the effect which the notice might otherwise have.

9.34 It is provided that any person who would have had a right of action in respect of an actual obstruction of the description specified in the notice on the ground of an infringement of his right of light has the same right of action in respect

[34] 1959 Act, s 3(6).

of the registration of the notice. An action cannot be begun after the notice has ceased to have effect.[35] A notice will generally cease to have effect one year after its registration (unless the court has ordered its cancellation before the year has expired) so that an action must be begun within one year of the registration. The remedy which may be sought in such an action is a declaration.[36] The court can make such declaration as it thinks appropriate, and in addition may order that the registration of the notice may be varied or cancelled.[37] If the proceedings are successful the court is likely to declare the existence of the right of light of the claimant and is likely to order the variation or cancellation of the notice. The proceedings will be brought in accordance with the Civil Procedure Rules.[38] It has been explained that if the proceedings fail, the court may direct that the provisions of the Act as to deemed notice of the registration and deemed acquiescence in the obstruction shall apply as if the action had not been brought.[39]

2. Practical Considerations

Those who advise persons with interests in property need to consider the practical implications of the legislation in the Rights of Light Act 1959. These implications can be considered from the point of view of a person considering the service of a light obstruction notice and from the point of view of a person who is notified of a proposed registration of a notice or discovers the existence of a notice from a search of the local land charges register. 9.35

Persons with an interest in the dominant building with knowledge of a light obstruction notice will fall into three categories. It is important that persons in this position who have received notification of a proposal to register a notice as a legal land charge should make regular subsequent searches of the local land charges register.[40] 9.36

The first category is the owner of an interest in the dominant building who has the benefit of a right of light over the servient land created expressly by a deed or by an implication from a deed or by the operation of section 62 of the Law of Property Act 1925. A person in this position is not required to take any action. The notional obstruction and the deemed acquiescence in that obstruction will not prejudicially affect the existing easement of light. There appears to be no question of the easement being abandoned by reason of the obstruction since the registration, and thus the notional obstruction, lasts only one year from the date of the registration 9.37

35 ibid, s 3(3).

36 ibid, s 3(5).

37 ibid.

38 The proceedings may be brought under Pts 7 or 8 of the Civil Procedure Rules. A claim under Pt 8 is appropriate where a decision is sought on a question unlikely to involve a substantial issue of fact: CPR, Pt 8.2.

39 See para 9.32.

40 See para 9.28.

as a local land charge. Nonetheless the person with the benefit of the easement is entitled to commence proceedings under the 1959 Act for a declaration that his right of light exists and that person may sometimes as a matter of prudence decide to do so if his rights are not agreed to subsist. It seems likely in such a case that the person who has registered the notice will often voluntarily accept the existence of and validity of the expressly or impliedly created right of light. If not the matter can be decided by the court.

9.38 A person with an express or implied easement appurtenant to the dominant building who becomes aware of a light obstruction notice may wish to consider his position in regard to his seeking an injunction at some future date to prevent a development on the servient land which may violate his easement of light. A dominant owner is not entitled to seek an injunction until there is an immediate threat of an obstruction.[41] The registration of a light obstruction notice and no more is unlikely to constitute such a threat. However, the owner of the dominant building may be wise if he makes known to the person serving the notice his rights since if he needs in the future to seek discretionary relief from a court by way of an injunction to prevent an offending development on the servient land an early statement of his rights may assist his case.

9.39 The second category is the owner of an interest in the dominant building who has enjoyed the access of light over the servient land for only a part of the prescription period, say for 15 years. There is little purpose in a person in this position challenging the light obstruction notice by legal proceedings. If he does so he will inevitably fail, since he will not be able to show the enjoyment of light over the 20-year period needed to establish his easement by prescription. The notice will operate as a notional obstruction for a year during which the person with the interest in the dominant building will be deemed to have notice of and to have acquiesced in the obstruction and so will prevent that person acquiring an easement by prescription at the end of what would otherwise be the prescription period. His only prospect of establishing an easement by prescription will be a further 20 years of enjoyment of the access of light after the end of the one-year period of the notional obstruction.

9.40 The third category of person is the owner of an interest in the dominant building who has established an easement of light by prescription by reason of the uninterrupted access of light over the servient land for the requisite period of 20 years or more. It is imperative that a person in this position takes legal proceedings to challenge the notice within a year of its registration. That person should have received prior notification of the proposal to register a notice and can find the date of the actual registration by searching the local land charges register. There appears to be no specified period which has to elapse between the issuing of a definitive certificate by the Upper Tribunal and the registration of the light obstruction notice over the land affected so that a number of searches of the register may be necessary.

[41] See ch 7, para 7.51.

If a person in this category does not challenge the notice by legal proceedings within a year from its registration the notice will operate as a notional obstruction to the access of light of which that person is deemed to have had notice and in which he is deemed to have acquiesced for a year. The result will be that the ability of that person to establish an easement in reliance on section 3 of the Prescription Act 1832, which previously existed, will end. It is of course for this reason that the issue of proceedings seeking a declaration that the easement has been acquired is vital. If the necessary period of 20 years or more of the enjoyment of the access of light over the servient land can be shown then a declaration of the existence of the easement will be obtained from the court. If there is a dispute as to the enjoyment for the requisite period it will be decided by the court on evidence in the usual way. Mere protests to the servient owner or informal objections are not enough; proceedings must be issued. It may be that persons in this category who can obviously show the enjoyment of the access of light for the requisite period will be able to obtain from the person who has registered a light obstruction notice an acceptance that this is so without the necessity for disputed proceedings. Even so in the absence of a clear and binding acceptance of the existence of the easement the issue of proceedings within good time is necessary.

Turning to persons with an interest in the servient land, the registration of a light obstruction notice is rarely of disadvantage to the owner of that land save for the trouble and expense of doing so including the prior notification and the obtaining of a definitive certificate from the Upper Tribunal. There are two main sets of circumstances in which the registration of a notice can result in considerable benefit to such an owner. 9.41

The first occasion is when the owner of the servient land knows that a substantial part of the prescription period has passed with the enjoyment of the access of light to the dominant building and wishes to prevent the completion of that period and the resultant acquisition of an easement by prescription. It is to this situation that the Rights of Light Act 1959 is primarily directed. In such a case the owner of the servient land would be well advised to register a notice in good time and so prevent the continued running of the prescription period and the acquisition of the easement. In practice in many cases the expedient of acting in this way is ignored by the owners of servient land to their later disadvantage when they decide to redevelop that land. 9.42

The second occasion on which the registration of a notice may be important is where a development of the servient land is proposed and it is unclear who has acquired the benefit of an easement of light by prescription over that land. In densely developed urban areas a site which becomes available for redevelopment is likely to have a number of buildings on or near its boundaries and in its vicinity some of which may or may not have acquired easements of light. The registration of a light obstruction notice brings clarity to the situation. Those persons who can claim an easement of light by prescription or by other means are likely to make themselves known so that the situation can be clarified at an early date 9.43

before funds are committed to development of a certain nature. There is always the prospect that persons, even though they have acquired an easement by prescription under section 3 of the Prescription Act 1832, will fail to take effective action by bringing proceedings to challenge the light obstruction notice within the year available for such a challenge. In such a case the existence of their easement, acquired under section 3, will end. Clearly this could be of advantage to a prospective developer of the servient land.

9.44 There is of course a possible disadvantage from the point of view of a potential developer in giving general notice of a proposal to register a light obstruction notice. To do so may alert persons notified of the possible availability to them of rights of light, something which they might not otherwise know or investigate. As against this if a development on the servient land proceeds, with no process under the Rights of Light Act 1959 having been initiated, there is always the risk that a person or persons may assert rights of light and threaten an injunction with major adverse consequences to the developer. The prudent course for a potential developer may be to implement the statutory process under the 1959 Act, especially in cases of uncertainty, in order to find out the position at an early stage. A prospective developer who proposes to use the procedure under the 1959 Act should do so at an early stage. The procedure is not a speedy process. Apart from the initial period of serving notices the developer must wait a year from the registration of a light obstruction notice as a local land charge before he can be certain that persons with interests in adjoining properties will not commence proceedings to establish a right of light.

9.45 There are limits to what a servient owner can achieve by using the procedure under the Rights of Light Act 1959. If a person with an interest in the dominant building fails to assert his rights by legal proceedings commenced within a year after the registration of the light obstruction notice, or if he fails in his attempt to establish a right of light in such proceedings, the servient owner can proceed with the knowledge that his development will be unaffected by that person on the grounds of a prescriptive right of light gained under section 3 of the Prescription Act 1832. If a person with an interest in the dominant building establishes a prescriptive right of light, by agreement or by legal proceedings, the situation may be more uncertain. There will remain the questions of (a) whether a proposed development of the servient land would reduce the access of light to the dominant building to such an extent as to constitute an actionable injury, and (b), if so, whether an injunction or damages would be the appropriate remedy available to the person who has established his right of light. It may be that at the time of the light obstruction notice the servient owner has no, or no specific, proposed development project on his land. In that event the notice and any response to it can do no more than establish that persons with interests in the dominant building do or do not enjoy rights of light acquired prescriptively under the Prescription Act 1832 against the servient land. However, if the servient owner has a specific and immediate proposed development to be carried out on his land, and believes that even if rights of light are established against his land for the benefit of the dominant building his development will not infringe those rights, he can seek a declaration that the development would not be an infringement of any rights of light established. This could be done in the proceedings which the owner of the dominant building has commenced in order to establish his rights.[42] By this means it should be possible in an appropriate case to have it determined in one set of proceedings (a) whether the dominant owner has a right of light over the servient land, (b), if so, whether a specific and proposed development would infringe those rights, and (c), if so, whether the dominant owner is entitled to an injunction to prevent the development. While all of this is theoretically possible, in practice the procedure under the 1959 Act is not often used in the fashion just described.

(E) ACTION OF THE COURT

The Rights of Light Act 1959 provides that in an action brought under the Act the remedies available are the making of a declaration by the court and an order directing the registration of the light obstruction notice to be cancelled or varied.[43] Of course, the court may make an order as to costs in addition to this and presumably may make ordinary ancillary orders such as an order for disclosure of documents or the granting of permission to appeal to the Court of Appeal which today is required but was not required at the date of the Rights of Light Act 1959. There is no possibility of an injunction or damages being awarded to the dominant owner in an action brought under the 1959 Act.[44] 9.46

The simplest case is where there is one owner and occupier of the dominant building and he brings proceedings to challenge a light obstruction notice registered against that building. If the owner of the dominant building establishes that, notwithstanding the effect of the notice, he has an easement of light by prescription under section 3 of the Prescription Act 1832 then the court will make an appropriate declaration of that right. In those circumstances it would be appropriate for the court also to cancel the registration of the notice.[45] On the other hand, if when the proceedings are heard by the court the owner and occupier of the dominant building cannot establish that he has acquired a right of light by prescription under section 3 of the Prescription Act 1832 by the date of the registration of 9.47

[42] The servient owner may assert his right by a separate action or by a counterclaim in the proceedings brought by the dominant owner: see CPR, Pt 20.4.

[43] 1959 Act, s 3(5).

[44] If the servient owner has a special and immediate proposed development project on his land and a dominant owner takes proceedings under the 1959 Act to establish that he has a prescriptive right of light it would be open to the servient owner himself to take proceedings to demonstrate that if the right of light was established it would not be infringed by the proposed development: see para 9.45.

[45] A recent example of such a remedy being obtained is *G & S Brough Ltd v Salvage Wharf Ltd* [2009] EWCA Civ 21, [2010] Ch 11.

the light obstruction notice, then the court may wish to make a declaration that as at the date in question no right of light had been so established by prescription. In those circumstances the court will presumably not cancel or vary the light obstruction notice which will have its ordinary effect of preventing the subsequent acquisition of an easement of light under section 3 of the 1832 Act such as would have in due course occurred had there been no light obstruction notice. A person with an interest in the dominant building has a year from the date of registration of the notice to commence his proceedings in the court.

9.48 The position may be more complex where there are a number of persons with interests in the dominant building. If all of those persons join together in challenging the light obstruction notice then their various claims can be considered by the court together. In practice it may be that only one or more persons with particular interests in the dominant building do challenge the notice and others do not. In those circumstances the court will of course determine whether those who have raised a challenge to the notice have established a right of light by prescription under section 3 of the Prescription Act 1832 and will make a declaration accordingly. It may be uncertain whether other persons who have not initiated or joined in proceedings to challenge the notice can establish a right of light. There may be a building a part of which has existed for many years but a part of which is of fairly recent construction. The rights of light which enure to different parts of the building by virtue of prescription may then be different. Obviously it would not be correct that any order made by the court should either prejudice those persons who have not initiated or joined in any proceedings before the court or should prejudice the validity of the light obstruction notice and its effect as regards such persons. It may be that in such circumstances the most attractive order will be that the court declares what rights of light have or have not been established by prescription under the 1832 Act in favour of those persons who have initiated proceedings, and then decides whether to cancel or not cancel the notice as regards those persons. However, if the light obstruction notice is cancelled or varied to any extent as regards those persons who have initiated or joined in proceedings, it would be appropriate that any cancellation or variation should not affect those persons who have not joined in the proceedings. The power of the court to cancel or vary the registration of a light obstruction notice presumably extends to a partial cancellation or variation of it in the sense that it is cancelled or varied in relation to certain persons with an interest in the dominant building or in relation to certain parts of the dominant building but not as regards other persons or other parts of that building.

9.49 To take a practical example, there might be a building which has existed for 40 years and has enjoyed the access of light for that period over the servient land. In those circumstances a light obstruction notice should not prevent the existence and continued existence of the right of light acquired by prescription in favour of that long existing part of the building. However, there may have been an addition to the building completed only 12 years ago. The apertures in that additional part of the building will not have enjoyed the necessary period of the enjoyment of light to give rise to an easement by prescription under the Prescription Act 1832. If proceedings are brought by the person owning or with an interest in the part of the dominant building which has existed for 40 years, the court would be likely to declare that that person did have an easement of light acquired by prescription under the 1832 Act and may vary the registration of the light obstruction notice so that it no longer applies to that older part of the building. The registration of the notice can then remain in full effect as regards the newer part of the building which has existed for only 12 years. As regards that newer part of the building the registration of the notice will have the effect of preventing an easement of light being acquired by prescription under section 3 of the 1832 Act. Where, therefore, there is more than one owner or occupier of a building, the order of the court will need to be carefully tailored to deal with the circumstances of the different parts of the building, possibly with different ages and circumstances and with different persons with interests in it.

The situation may be somewhat more complex when more than one person has an interest and the benefit of a prescriptive easement in the whole of the dominant building. Suppose that the building is 40 years old and has a freeholder and a tenant with a 21-year lease with seven years to run. Both are likely to have the benefit of a prescriptive easement of light. The freeholder may bring an action challenging a light obstruction notice, but the tenant may not. The court will be likely to cancel the notice as regards the freeholder but then has two courses open to it. It may cancel the notice as regards the freeholder only (a course which is suggested may be more appropriate),[46] or it may cancel the notice entirely. If the latter course is taken, a developer of the servient land will need to come to an agreement, usually involving the payment of a sum of money, with the freeholder and with the tenant if his development would infringe the easement. If the former course is taken, the tenant will lose the benefit of his easement and the developer will have to come to terms only with the freeholder whose easement is preserved. Naturally there are numerous combinations of circumstances which could in practice occur, and this analysis can only give a general guide as to how a court may seek to exercise its powers. The fact is, that although the Rights of Light Act 1959 has been in the statute book for over a half a century, there is very little guidance from decided cases on its operation. 9.50

(F) EMERGENCY OR TEMPORARY CERTIFICATES

This narrative has so far described the system of obtaining a certificate from the Lands Chamber of the Upper Tribunal followed by the registration of a light obstruction notice as a local land charge. It is this procedure which must 9.51

[46] See para 9.48.

be followed in the great majority of cases. The certificate so obtained is called a definitive certificate. The Rights of Light Act 1959 contains an associated procedure for obtaining an 'emergency certificate' (although this is not an expression used in the legislation).[47]

9.52 The owner of the servient land may apply to the Upper Tribunal for a certificate certifying that in the opinion of the Tribunal the case is one of 'exceptional urgency' and that accordingly a notice should be registered forthwith as a temporary notice for such period as may be specified in the certificate. The effect of a light obstruction notice registered pursuant to such a certificate has, at any rate for a temporary period, the same effect as a notice registered following a definitive certificate. The notice operates as a notional obstruction of the access of light to the dominant building over the servient land and all persons with an interest in the dominant building are deemed to have notice of the registration and to have acquiesced in the interruption to the access of light caused by that obstruction.[48]

9.53 The Act contains no indication of what are the factual circumstances which may make the case one of exceptional urgency. It seems that any circumstances can be prayed in aid as fulfilling this description. It seems likely that what the draftsman of the Act had in mind was that there might be cases in which the passing of the prescription period was so far advanced that if the process of notifying any persons likely to be affected by the registration of a light obstruction notice was properly put in hand the registration of the notice following that process and following a definitive certificate issued by the Upper Tribunal might be too late to prevent the acquisition by persons in the dominant building of an easement of light under section 3 of the Prescription Act 1832. The report of the Harman Committee does not contain an explanation of the temporary certificate procedure.

9.54 It seems therefore that what was intended was that there could arise circumstances in which if the owner of the servient land could immediately register a light obstruction notice, he might be able to prevent the passing of the full prescription period by an interruption to the access of light brought about by the registration of a light obstruction notice pursuant to the temporary certificate, whereas the later registration of a light obstruction notice pursuant to a definitive certificate, obtained after full notification of persons who might be affected, might mean that the registration of the notice was too late to prevent the running of the full prescription period and thus too late to prevent the acquisition of a prescriptive easement of light. Obviously this situation could or might occur if at the time when the processes under the Act were being considered by the owner of the servient land the prescription period was drawing towards its end. The question which arises is why it was thought appropriate to provide for this emergency procedure to prevent the acquisition of an easement under section 3 of the Prescription Act 1832 over the servient land. In the nature of things the owner of the servient land,

[47] 1959 Act, s 2(3).
[48] ibid, s 3(1).

or his predecessors in title, would already have had a decade and a half or more to operate the ordinary procedure under the Rights of Light Act 1959. Thus it is not easy to see why they are accorded this last moment emergency opportunity of operating the Act. Possibly the situation was thought to be different at the end of the 1950s, when the legislation was under consideration. Nonetheless temporary or emergency certificates are issued by the Tribunal in the circumstances postulated which are considered by the Tribunal to be cases of exceptional urgency.

The Tribunal must issue a temporary certificate if it is satisfied that the case is one of exceptional urgency that requires the immediate registration of a temporary notice in the register of local land charges and if a certificate is issued by the Tribunal under this emergency procedure the certificate of the Tribunal must state that a notice should be registered forthwith as a temporary notice for such period as may be specified in the certificate.[49] The Tribunal has held that it had no power to extend the time specified in a certificate.[50] Obviously the period in question should be such as to enable the owner of the servient land to give appropriate prior publicity of the proposed registration of a notice such as would be required in an ordinary case and then to obtain a definitive certificate which can be lodged with the registering authority. What is the requisite period will depend upon the circumstances and the property and the number of persons who may have an interest in the dominant building or buildings. The procedure is of its nature one of exceptional urgency and it is to be expected that the Tribunal will not unduly prolong any period. A period of four or six weeks for the operation of the temporary light obstruction notice should in most cases be sufficient. The Tribunal Procedure (Upper Tribunal) (Lands Chamber) Rules 2010 provide that a temporary certificate shall last no longer than four months.[51] A shorter period may often be appropriate. The application for a temporary certificate must state the grounds upon which it is claimed that the case is one of exceptional urgency.[52] It is difficult to imagine any grounds except the shortness of time before the coming to an end of the prescription period. 9.55

The 1959 Act provides that rules made for the purposes of these matters shall include a provision in connection with an emergency certificate for enabling a further certificate to be issued in accordance with the normal procedure.[53] No specific rules appear to have been made for this purpose. The Act provides that where the temporary certificate specifies a period for which a notice may be registered, as a temporary certificate must do, then if that period expires without a definitive certificate having been issued and lodged with the registering authority, the registration of a light obstruction notice pursuant to the temporary certificate ceases 9.56

[49] 1959 Act, s 2(3)(b); Tribunal Procedure (Upper Tribunal) (Lands Chamber) Rules 2010, r 43(1).

[50] *In the Matter of an Appeal Against a Decision of the Registrar by Anglo Suisse Holdings Ltd* (unreported) 9 March, 2009.

[51] r 43(2).

[52] r 41(1)(g).

[53] 1959 Act, s 2(5)(c).

to have effect at the end of the period specified by the Tribunal.[54] In concrete terms what this amounts to is that if, for example, the Tribunal is persuaded that the case is one of exceptional urgency and issues a temporary certificate requiring that, say, the registration of a light obstruction notice pursuant to the temporary certificate shall be for a period of six weeks, then unless within that six weeks the Tribunal issues a full or definitive certificate, having been satisfied that adequate notice has been given to all persons likely to be affected by the registration of a light obstruction notice and unless that definitive certificate is lodged with the registering authority within the same six weeks, the registration of a light obstruction notice pursuant to the temporary certificate will cease to have effect. Its effect in such circumstances will, therefore, be that of a notional interruption of the access of light over the servient land to the dominant building for the period specified by the Tribunal, but for no longer.

9.57 If a light obstruction notice is registered pursuant to a temporary certificate and a definitive certificate is obtained and lodged with the registering authority within the period specified in the temporary certificate the period of 12 months allowed for a challenge to the notice runs from the date of its registration, and not from the date of the issue of the definitive certificate.[55]

(G) CESSATION OF REGISTRATION

9.58 A light obstruction notice registered as a local land charge is cancelled or ceases to have effect in four circumstances.

9.59 The first circumstance is that a year has elapsed beginning with the date of the registration. The light obstruction notice then ceases to have effect. It is unnecessary for the registration to have effect beyond one year. Its effect during that year will be as a notional interruption of the access of light over the servient land to the dominant building with that interruption deemed to have been acquiesced in by persons with an interest in the dominant building. Consequently any passing of the prescription period which is being built up but has not yet been completed will be brought to an end by the one year of the interruption as provided by section 4 of the Prescription Act 1832.

9.60 The second circumstance is where the registration of the notice is cancelled by an order of the court. The occasions on which this may happen have been considered earlier.[56]

9.61 The third circumstance is where the registration is in pursuance of a temporary certificate issued by the Upper Tribunal that the case is one of exceptional urgency

[54] ibid, s 3(2)(c).
[55] *Bowring Services Ltd v Scottish Widows Fund and Life Assurance Society* [1995] 1 EGLR 158.
[56] See section (E) of this chapter.

and the period specified in the certificate has expired without a full or definitive certificate having been issued. The light obstruction notice then ceases to have effect. This also has been explained earlier.[57]

The fourth circumstance is where the local authority with which the notice has been registered as a local land charge is required to record amendments or cancellations to the registration. It must do so if a copy or order of a judgment of a court requiring the light obstruction notice to be varied or cancelled is received by it. The local authority must cancel the registration of a notice registered pursuant to a temporary certificate where no definitive certificate has been issued within the period specified by the Tribunal. If a definitive certificate is lodged within the period specified the authority must file the definitive certificate with the application and must amend the registration accordingly. In any event registration must be cancelled within 21 years from the date of the registration.[58] It is necessary that a registration of a notice should remain on the local land charges register for 21 years, unless previously cancelled, although the notice has ceased to have effect as a notional interruption of the access of light over the servient land after one year following its registration, in order that persons with interests in the dominant building, and persons acquiring interests in that building, can know of the effect of the year of the notional interruption which may be to have prevented the creation of a prescriptive easement of light or to have destroyed an easement of light which had arisen under section 3 of the Prescription Act 1832. 9.62

It is important in this last context to note the distinction between a registered light obstruction notice ceasing to have effect and the registration being cancelled. A notice will normally cease to have effect after one year from its registration. The notional obstruction and interruption of the running of the prescription period which is the effect of the notice therefore lasts for one year. This is a sufficient period under section 4 of the Prescription Act 1832 to prevent the acquisition of an easement by the future running of the prescription period or to destroy an easement which has been created due to the passing of the full prescription period. The registration will remain for the full 21 years from the date of registration, so that persons searching the local land charges register, such as potential purchasers of the dominant building, can find out that a notice was registered with the effect just described. The registration is cancelled after 21 years because by that time a further 20 years of a prescription period will have passed since the notional interruption ended, and the passing of that further prescription period without a further interruption may found the basis for a new acquisition of an easement by prescription. 9.63

[57] See para 9.56.

[58] Local Land Charges Rules 1977, r 10.

(H) THE EXACT PRESCRIPTION PERIOD

9.64 Section 3 of the Prescription Act 1832 refers to the access and use of light having been actually enjoyed for the full period of 20 years without interruption. Section 2 of the Act, applying to the acquisition by prescription of other easements, also refers to the way or other easement having been actually enjoyed without interruption for the full period of 20 years. It might appear at first glance that what the person claiming an easement of any sort under the Act has to demonstrate is 20 years of uninterrupted use or enjoyment of the subject matter of the easement.

9.65 In fact a claimant can normally establish the existence of an easement acquired under the 1832 Act if he can prove anything in excess of 19 years of use and enjoyment. It is useful to consider first the law on the operation of the Act as regards easements generally, the principle of which applies to the operation of easements of light, and then come to the special relaxation which is allowed for the acquisition of easements of light. The special relaxation can only be fully understood in the context of the general rule.[59]

9.66 To take an example, suppose that a way has been used for 19 years and six months by the owner of neighbouring land. After a further six months of use an easement of way will be gained under section 2 of the Prescription Act 1832. During the last six months of the twentieth year the owner of the land over which the way exists can lawfully block it up and prevent its use. The neighbouring owner can do nothing to stop him, since at this stage he has not used and enjoyed the way for the full 20 years. At the end of the six months an easement of way will arise under the 1832 Act since the interruption, having lasted for less than a year, will not be taken into account and will not prevent the use and enjoyment for the full period of 20 years for the purposes of the Act.[60] What this amounts to is that the use of a way for 19 years and a day is sufficient to gain the prescriptive easement at the end of the 20th year, providing that the person acquiring the easement acts speedily and efficiently. The same is true of other rights, such as the passage of water through a pipe.

9.67 If there is an actual obstruction to the access of light over the servient land, ie as opposed to the notional obstruction brought about by the registration of a light obstruction notice, the same principles apply. If the owner of the dominant building has enjoyed the access of light over the servient land for, say, 19 years and two months, the owner of the servient land may physically obstruct the passage of light across his land and the owner of the dominant building will not be able to take any effective action for the next 10 months. However, in the first two months of the 21st year the owner of the dominant building will be able to assert an easement of light established under the Prescription Act 1832, because in calculating

[59] The general rule, sometimes called the 19 years and a day rule, is further explained in ch 5 on prescription: see ch 5, paras 5.57 and 5.58.

[60] This is the effect of s 4 of the Prescription Act 1832.

the necessary 20 years of enjoyment the 10 months of the interruption will not be counted since that period is less than a year. On the other hand if the owner of the dominant building takes no action until after the end of the first two months of the 21st year he will fail to establish an easement under the Act since there will then have been an interruption which has lasted for a year and in which he has acquiesced. There is no difference in the operation of the 1832 Act between the enjoyment of a way and the enjoyment of access of light over another property when the interruption is by way of an actual physical obstruction of the use of the way or an actual physical obstruction of the access of light over the servient land.

One would have expected that when it comes to the registration of a light obstruction notice under the Rights of Light Act 1959 the same principles would apply. The theory of the Act is that the notional interruption to the access of light is to have generally the same effect as an actual interruption would have. Any such sensible expectation is removed by section 3(4) of the 1959 Act which states that after a light obstruction notice has been registered a person claiming a right of light has a right of action in a court as if the access of light to the dominant building had begun one year before the date on which it actually began. 9.68

It is best to illustrate the operation of section 3(4) by a further example. Suppose that on 1 January 1996 a building was erected on property A and started to enjoy the access of light to its apertures over property B. The 20-year prescription period will end on 31 December 2015. An actual obstruction erected on property B on 1 July 2015 would fail to prevent the operation of the 20-year prescription period, and thus the acquisition of an easement of light, on 1 January 2016. It does appear that a light obstruction notice registered on 1 July 2015 would have the same consequences. If an actual obstruction was erected on property B on 1 July 2014 and it remained for a year it would prevent acquisition of an easement of light. However, if a light obstruction notice was registered on 1 July 2014, that would not prevent the acquisition of an easement of light in the same way as would an actual obstruction erected on that date. Following the registration of the light obstruction notice the owner of property A can wait until January 2015 and then commence proceedings to establish the existence of his easement. The enjoyment of the access of light to the apertures of property A will be taken for the purposes of the 1959 Act and the light obstruction notice to have begun a year earlier than it did actually begin and so will be taken to have begun on 1 January 1995 and not on 1 January 1996. In January 2015 there will be taken to have been the access of light for 20 years (1 January 1995 to 31 December 2014) and the interruption constituted by the registration of the light obstruction notice will have lasted from 1 July 2014 to the date of commencement of proceedings in January 2015, that is for less than a year, so that the obstruction would not prevent the running of the prescription period up to the date of the commencement of the proceedings. 9.69

It might pertinently be asked why the Act contains what appears to be an anomalous provision. There was nothing in the report of the Harman Committee or in the Bill as it was originally presented to Parliament which had this effect. 9.70

Section 3(4) was introduced into the Bill by an amendment proposed in the House of Lords by the then Lord Chancellor, Viscount Kilmuir, on 5 May 1959 following the proposal for such a provision made to a committee of the House by Lord Granville-West on 12 February 1959. A consideration of the record of the Parliamentary proceedings suggests that the supposed need for section 3(4) may have been the result of a misunderstanding as to the operation of the rules governing prescription. Nonetheless, the law must of course be taken to be that which is stated in the statute, whatever the confusion which may have engendered it.[61]

(I) LOST MODERN GRANT

9.71 It has been explained in Chapter 5 that the doctrine of lost modern grant is a method of prescription which arose before the Prescription Act 1832 and which applies to easements of light as it applies to other easements.[62] The doctrine permits the acquisition of an easement by 20 years use or enjoyment as of right and rests on the fiction that such a period of use must have originated in a grant. The question which arises is how the Rights of Light Act 1959 operates when an easement of light is claimed in reliance on the doctrine of lost modern grant. The 1959 Act is founded closely on the language and operation of sections 3 and 4 of the Prescription Act 1832 and so fits uneasily into the operation of the common law lost modern grant doctrine. There is surprisingly no decided authority on this potentially important question.

9.72 The doctrine of lost modern grant has a number of important features which differentiate it from statutory prescription relating to rights of light under sections 3 and 4 of the Prescription Act 1832. First, there is nothing in the lost modern grant doctrine exactly equivalent to the provision in section 4 of the Prescription Act 1832 that the period of enjoyment must not have been interrupted for a year or more with the interruption known to and acquiesced in by the dominant owner. Secondly, section 4 provides that the statutory 20-year prescription period must be next before some action in which the claim is brought into question. For instance, if the dominant owner can show access of light over the servient land for 20 years and there is then an interruption for a year known to and acquiesced in by him he will not be able to rely on the 1832 Act in proceedings which are started after that period of interruption and in which the easement is in issue. Under the lost modern grant doctrine he will be able in these circumstances to rely on the 20 years of enjoyment even after an interruption has lasted for a year or more unless the

[61] A fuller discussion and explanation of s 3(4) of the 1959 Act and of what is stated in this and the last paragraph will be found in an article by Barnes and Bignell, 'A fiction too far' (2009) *Conveyancer and Property Lawyer* 474.

[62] See ch 5, section (C) and see *Marlborough (West End) Ltd v Wilks Head & Eve* [1996] New Law Digest 138.

interruption has been sufficient to amount to an abandonment of the easement. In other words, the easement acquired under the doctrine of lost modern grant by the necessary 20 years of enjoyment of the access of light solidifies and is not lost, save by an abandonment. With these differences between the doctrine of lost modern grant and the statutory provisions in mind, it is possible to examine the question of the effect of the Rights of Light Act 1959 on the doctrine of lost modern grant in two situations.

The first situation is where a light obstruction notice is registered during the course of the 20-year prescription period. As explained, the effect of the 1959 Act is that the registration will have the same effect as an actual obstruction which lasts a year so that the dominant owner will lose his opportunity to complete the statutory 20-year prescription period and claim an easement under the Prescription Act 1832. Although this is not expressly stated in the Prescription Act 1832, the period of actual enjoyment referred to in section 2 of that Act (easements other than easements of light) and section 3 of the Act (easements of light) means that during the 20-year prescription period there must have been a continuity of use. For example, if a window was boarded-up for a substantial and continuous time during the 20 years, there would not be the necessary continuity of enjoyment during the prescription period.[63] The same principle and requirement of a continuity of use applies to prescription under the doctrine of lost modern grant. The critical question is whether the notional interruption created by the registration of a light obstruction notice under the Rights of Light Act 1959 means that for the purposes of the doctrine of lost modern grant the enjoyment of the access of light is not continuous during that period so that the running of the prescription period for the purposes of that doctrine is ended. When describing the effect of registration of a notice section 3(1) of the 1959 Act states that the period of one year's notional interruption operates for the purposes of deciding whether a person is entitled to a right to the access of light 'by virtue of the Prescription Act 1832 or otherwise'. It appears from this that the legislation is intended to apply to a claim initiated under the lost modern grant doctrine. The better and more plausible view is that the notional obstruction for a year operates to render the enjoyment of the access of light to the dominant building non-continuous for the purposes of a claim based on a lost modern grant just as it operates as an interruption for a year for the purposes of the Prescription Act 1832. Indeed if it were otherwise, the dominant owner could often evade the effect of a light obstruction notice by founding his claim on the lost modern grant doctrine. If this is correct, the registration of a light obstruction notice in, say, the 15th year of the prescription period would prevent an easement being acquired at the end of 20 years, whether the claim to the easement was made under the Prescription Act 1832 or under the doctrine of lost modern grant. 9.73

[63] See ch 5, para 5.36 et seq.

9.74 The second situation is where the light obstruction notice is registered after the access of light has been enjoyed for a full prescription period of 20 years or more. The registration, unless it is successfully challenged by court proceedings begun in the year following the date of the registration, will then prevent reliance on sections 3 and 4 of the Prescription Act 1832 because the interruption for a year will mean that the 20 years of enjoyment is not next before the claim to an easement is brought into question in legal proceedings. However, this last requirement of a claim does not apply to the doctrine of lost modern grant as just explained.[64] Consequently, logic suggests that the dominant owner will be able successfully to found his claim under the lost modern grant doctrine despite the registration of the light obstruction notice and uninhibited by the provisions of the Rights of Light Act 1959. While logical, this seems an unhappy conclusion, and not that which is likely to have been the purpose of the 1959 Act. The true answer to a conundrum of this sort is that reform is required of the system of acquisition of easements, including easements of light, by prescription and an aspect of that reform should be the abolition of the doctrine of lost modern grant.[65]

[64] See para 9.73.

[65] The Law Commission has in recent reports in 2011 and 2014 recommended that the lost modern grant doctrine is abandoned for all purposes of prescription, and that for easements of light a new and simplified system is introduced to replace the Rights of Light Act 1959. These and other recommendations are explained in ch 12. The Government have not as yet responded to either report.

10

Town Planning

(A) INTRODUCTION

Town and country planning in England and Wales goes back to the period before the two world wars, but was first introduced on a comprehensive basis on 1 July 1948 pursuant to the Town and Country Planning Act 1947. It has since grown into an increasingly complex and costly system. Its foundations are the two principles that it is unlawful to carry out development on land without the grant of planning permission, and that development means the carrying out of any building, engineering, mining or other operations in, on, over or under land, or the making of any material change in the use of any buildings or other land.[1] The current legislation is contained mainly in the Town and Country Planning Act 1990, which has itself been substantially amended since it was enacted. There is a host of further provisions on other matters, such as the making of applications for planning permission, appeals against a refusal of planning permission, enforcement of planning control, and a separate system for the protection of buildings listed as of special architectural or historic interest. Planning permission for certain types of operations and changes of use, such as extensions to houses within specified limits, is given automatically and without the need for an application by the Town and Country Planning (General Permitted Development) Order 1995. The rights to carry out such permitted development are colloquially referred to as 'GDO rights'. 10.1

The public law system of planning control and other statutory controls and the system of private law rights attaching to land have grown up and operate to a large extent independently of each other.[2] A person may apply for and obtain planning permission to develop land even though he has no interest in or rights over that land. The fact that some right over land exists, such as an easement or a restrictive covenant, which prevents development of land, does not prevent the grant of planning permission to carry out development which would infringe that right. However, the owner of the restriction may be able to exercise his right and so prevent the implementation of the planning permission. Town planning is concerned with the public interest in regulating the development of land, not with private interests and private rights in or over that land. 10.2

[1] Town and Country Planning Act 1990, ss 55 and 57. There are, of course, important exceptions and qualifications to these two principles as stated.

[2] See *Barr v Biffa Waste Services Ltd* [2012] EWCA Civ 312, [2013] QB 455 and see para 10.8.

10.3 Nonetheless, there is inevitably some element of overlap between the operation of the two systems, and this can be seen in relation to rights of light. When a local planning authority, or the Secretary of State or an inspector on an appeal, has to decide whether to grant planning permission for a development one relevant consideration may be the effect which the development would have on the access of light to neighbouring properties. This consideration operates in the same way, whether or not a neighbouring property has a right of light over the land on which the development is proposed. In order that this consideration can be taken into account on a rational and consistent basis, local planning authorities may pay attention to published guidance on the standards of light required for buildings and the way in which proposed new development may or may not comply with those standards. The main such publication is *Site Layout and Planning for Daylight and Sunlight—A Guide to Good Practice*, published by the BRE.[3] Chapter 2 of this publication gives detailed guidance on how to assess whether a proposed new building is likely to cause an unacceptable loss of light to existing buildings. It should be emphasised that the BRE Guide is not binding on local planning authorities or anybody else, and does not purport to establish whether any proposed new development would violate easements of light appurtenant to existing buildings. It is an adjunct to one aspect of the public law system of planning control. A description of the guidance given in the BRE document is given in section (C) of this chapter. Control of buildings under public law statutes which have the incidental effect of reducing the impact of new buildings on the light of existing buildings, goes back to the nineteenth century.[4]

10.4 It is important in the context of the access of light to property to distinguish clearly between what are two quite separate matters.

(i) A right of light is a right in private law. It arises usually as an easement, although it may sometimes arise from the effect of the doctrine that a vendor or lessor of land cannot derogate from his grant or from the effect of a restrictive covenant. The existence of the right, and the question of whether a proposed or completed development would or has violated that right, are unaffected by the grant of planning permission for the development. It is possible that the availability of the particular discretionary remedy of an injunction to prevent or reverse an infringement of an easement of light may be affected by the existence of a planning permission.[5]

(ii) The grant or refusal of a planning permission, by a local planning authority or by a Minister on appeal, is a matter of public law to be decided in the public interest. What may be a relevant consideration in making the

[3] Paul Littlefair, *Site Layout and Planning for Daylight and Sunlight—A Guide to Good Practice*, 2nd edn (Watford, BRE Trust, 2011) ('the BRE Guide').

[4] See the Metropolitan Management Amendment Act 1862, s 85 and see ch 3, para 3.6.

[5] This matter is discussed later in this chapter in para 10.18 et seq and is also considered in ch 7, section (B)4(e), in connection with remedies.

decision to grant or refuse a permission is the extent to which neighbouring properties may be overshadowed by a development where that can be seen to be a matter of public interest. The facts (a) that some or all of those persons affected may have easements of light and (b) that the development may be an infringement of those easements of light are not as such relevant to the planning decision.[6]

The principles to be followed in respect of the above matters have been clearly stated by Ouseley J in *R (Freud) v Oxford City Council* in the following way.[7] 10.5

> The role of rights of light and sunlight in planning concern the planning effect which such diminutions have on an interest which the public interest in planning needs to serve: for example, the protection of residential amenity or more particularly, here, the protection of the setting of and interest in the listed building of Freud's which is possessed of very fine Victorian stained glass from the master of this art, Mr Kemper. It is said it will no longer receive the light which it previously enjoyed to the diminution of those who appreciate the stained glass from the inside.
>
> This is a matter which I shall turn to in a moment. The diminution of light and sunlight is relevant, for example, to that issue but in my judgment it is not arguable that the planning authority should have to rule upon a private law matter in order to conclude whether planning permission should be granted. Its view of what the private law rights and wrongs should be could not in any event usurp the position of a civil court. It may be that even if there is very clearly a nuisance, there might be a grant of permission.
>
> It is important that the functions of civil courts in protecting private rights is respected and the function of planning authorities and administrative courts in ensuring that public law is properly upheld, and it is important that their different spheres be recognised.

(B) THE RELEVANCE OF PLANNING MATTERS

This book is not concerned with the law or practice of town and country planning.[8] Town planning may impact on the private law of rights of light in a number of ways, however, and these are discussed in this chapter with a brief explanation of the general guidance in the BRE Trust publication just mentioned. This guidance may have some impact on aspects of rights of light disputes. 10.6

[6] *Brewer v Secretary of State* [1988] JPL 480 (an inspector wrongly took into account the existence of a private law right of light); *R (White) v Secretary of State* [2001] EWHC 897 (Admin) (inspector correctly concluded that the existence of a right of light was a civil matter between the parties which did not affect her conclusion on the effect of a development on the living conditions of neighbours). See also para 10.27 and n 35. It has been suggested that in extreme circumstances, an interference with the access of light to properties authorised by a planning permission might constitute an infringement of the right of persons to respect for their private and family life and their home under art 8 of the European Convention on Human Rights.

[7] *R (Freud) v Oxford City Council* [2013] EWHC 613 (Admin) [22]–[24].

[8] For full details of this, see the nine volumes of the *Encyclopaedia of Planning* (London, Sweet & Maxwell).

1. The Relevance of a Planning Permission to the Existence of an Infringement

10.7 The first possible relevance of planning matters to rights of light is that the existence of a planning permission for a development on the servient land could be argued to support the contention that development which was the putting into effect of the planning permission would not for that reason be an infringement of a right of light and a nuisance in law. There would be formidable arguments in the way of any such contention. A planning permission should generally be granted unless there is some reason in the public interest why it should be refused. An authority deciding a planning application may take into account the general effect of the proposed development on the access of natural light to neighbouring properties; indeed, since this is a relevant consideration, the authority considering the application is bound to have regard to any information which is before it on this matter. However, this is only one of the many considerations which should be weighed by the deciding body. The development may have other effects on neighbouring properties, such as a loss of privacy or a loss of a view, which are not protected by and will not be germane to rights of light.[9] On the other hand the deciding body may consider that there would be a significant loss of light to neighbouring properties from the development proposed but conclude that in the overall balancing of relevant considerations, that adverse factor is outweighed by the public benefit which would flow from the development in terms of, for example, increased employment or better transport facilities or fulfilling a need for housing.

10.8 It is unlikely that a local planning authority, or officers who provide advice to the authority or to its committees by way of reports, would consider the exact question which has to be asked when judging whether a development on the servient land would constitute a violation of rights of light appurtenant to nearby properties. It may not even be known to the local planning authority whether rights of light exist in favour of such properties, and in any event, for reasons which have been mentioned, it is not likely to be relevant to their decision whether they do or not have information on such rights. The precise test for the infringement of a right of light, whether the access of light to the dominant building will be reduced below that acceptable for the reasonable enjoyment of the building according to the ordinary notions of mankind, may not be known to or may not be of concern to the authority. In any event the decision on the application of this test to a particular property in a disputed case is for the court deciding the matter, reached on the basis of expert evidence and often after a view of the property, and not for a planning authority or other body taking a decision in planning matters.[10]

[9] See ch 3, para 3.9.

[10] See ch 3, para 3.1 et seq for the origin and meaning of this test. See also the citation from the judgment of Ouseley J in *R (Freud) v Oxford City Council* [2013] EWHC (Admin) set out in para 10.5 of this chapter.

The recent decision of the Supreme Court in *Lawrence v Fen Tigers Ltd*[11] contains a substantial analysis of the assistance which may be obtained by a court from the existence of a planning permission when the court has to decide whether a particular activity or action constitutes a nuisance.[12] The case before the Supreme Court concerned an alleged nuisance caused by noise from the operation of premises for motor sports including speedway racing and stock car racing which was conducted in a stadium which had received planning permission, first by way of temporary permissions and then by a permanent permission. Such an activity is very different from the erection of a permanent building on servient land, and plainly caution should be applied in transferring principles stated in respect of a noise nuisance to an alleged interference with an easement of light. Nonetheless certain valuable insights can be gained to be applied in circumstances where the servient owner has planning permission for his building work, which will normally be the case, and prays this in aid in refuting the allegation that the development is in breach of an easement of light. 10.9

An important and central statement of principle, which is of relevance to rights of light disputes, is the reiteration of the obvious point that a grant of a planning permission for a particular development does not mean that the development is lawful (save of course in planning terms). An associated principle it is that it is wrong that, through the grant of a planning permission, a planning authority should be able to deprive a property owner of his right to object to what would otherwise be a nuisance, without providing that person with any compensation. The planning legislation contains no provision for the payment of compensation in such circumstances.[13] The Supreme Court approved a recent statement in the Court of Appeal in which it was said: 10.10

> The common law of nuisance has co-existed with statutory controls, albeit less sophisticated, since the 19th century. There is no principle that the common law should 'march with' a statutory scheme covering similar subject matter. Short of express or implied statutory authority to commit a nuisance … there is no basis, in principle or authority, for using such a statutory scheme to cut down private law rights.[14]

These principles are of importance to rights of light and they make it difficult for a servient owner to obtain much, if any, assistance from the existence of a planning permission in asserting that his development was not in breach of a right of light.

[11] *Lawrence v Fen Tigers Ltd* [2014] UKSC 13, [2014] AC 822.

[12] This question had been considered in a number of previous decisions: see *Gillingham Borough Council v Medway (Chatham) Dock Co Ltd* [1993] QB 343; *Hirose Electrical UK Ltd v Peak Ingredients Ltd* [2011] EWCA Civ 987, [2011] Env LR 34; *Wheeler v JJ Saunders Ltd* [1996] Ch 19; *Watson v Croft Promosport Ltd* [2008] EWHC 759 (QB), [2008] 3 All ER 1171, [2009] EWCA Civ 14, [2009] 3 All ER 249.

[13] *Lawrence v Fen Tigers Ltd* [2014] UKSC 13, [2014] AC 822 [89]–[90] (Lord Neuberger).

[14] *Barr v Biffa Waste Services Ltd* [2013] QB 455 [46(2)] (Carnwath LJ). See also *Hunter v Canary Wharf Ltd* [1997] AC 655, 710 (Lord Hoffmann).

10.11 A number of general considerations stated in the Supreme Court judgments, although in a different factual context, are applicable to the relevance of the existence of a planning permission in rights of light disputes. The decisions of local planning authorities are made after a weighing or balancing of a number of factors relevant to the public interest which may have no part in the decision on whether a nuisance has been committed, including the type of nuisance caused by a deprivation of the access of light. Political and economic considerations may loom large in planning decisions, overtly if not expressly, and these would be of no concern to a court in private law proceedings.[15] If it were the case that a decision by a planning authority to grant permission for a new building or an extension of an existing building had a significant effect on the question of whether the implementation of that permission would infringe a right of light then it would be inevitable that the planning authority should concern itself with, and perhaps make decisions on, the questions of whether a right of light existed and whether, as a matter of private law, the implementation of the permission would be an infringement of that right of light. It would be thoroughly unreasonable that local planning authorities should have the burden of these considerations placed upon them in making planning decisions in the public interest.[16]

10.12 There is then a brief catalogue of considerations mentioned by the Supreme Court in the context of a noise nuisance but which have significance in respect of an alleged nuisance by the erection of a building obstructing the access of light. Planning authorities have before them, and properly take into account, objections to the grant of planning permission for various reasons. There is rarely, if ever, any opportunity for persons to be cross-examined as to their objections to a grant of a permission, or even as to their support for it, when a decision is taken by a planning committee. The situation is of course quite different to the situation in a court, where witnesses can be cross-examined and tested. This point is particularly apposite in the case of some rights of light disputes, where the existence or otherwise of an easement of light may depend on witnesses of fact giving evidence of past events if the easement is claimed by prescription. In the Supreme Court Lord Neuberger said that he was very dubious about the notion that it would always be safe to assume that the reasons given by planning officers for recommending that planning permission be granted were the actual reasons which the members of a planning authority had in mind when they took a decision to grant permission. There may often be no grounds for thinking that members of the deciding committee or other body, or even the majority of those members, fully agreed with the reasons given in a report of officers or did not have other important reasons. These considerations could figure with equal impact in a case where a planning permission had been granted to erect a building on servient land.[17]

[15] *Lawrence v Fen Tigers Ltd* [95] (Lord Neuberger).
[16] ibid [95] (Lord Neuberger).
[17] ibid [97]–[98].

The conclusion of Lord Neuberger was encapsulated in the following statement. 10.13

> Accordingly, I consider that the mere fact that the activity which is said to give rise to the nuisance has the benefit of a planning permission is normally of no assistance to the defendant in a claim brought by a neighbour who contends that the activity causes a nuisance to her land in the form of noise or other loss of amenity.[18]

This succinct statement could be applied with equal force to a case where the loss of amenity in question was a reduction in the amount of light which reached a building which had appurtenant to it an easement of light.

It can therefore be safely said that the decision to grant planning permission for a development on the servient land, whether taken by a local planning authority or as a result of an appeal against a refusal of permission by a local planning authority, is, in itself and without further considerations, unlikely in most cases to play any significant part in the decision by a court on whether a development on the servient land which is the putting into effect of the planning permission would constitute, or has constituted, an infringement of an easement of light appurtenant to the dominant building. 10.14

2. The Relevance of Planning Standards

The second matter of possible relevance also relates to the question of whether there has been an infringement of a right of light. It is the matter of whether or not there has been compliance with the standards and guidance suggested in the BRE Guide. This matter applies whether or not the local planning authority or other deciding body has taken into account and applied the Guide when making its decision on granting planning permission. If it has done so, and if it has done so carefully, then the decision of the local planning authority and the assistance it has obtained from the Guide could be of some assistance to a court. On the other hand, even if the local planning authority has not had regard to the guidance, the existence of the Guide as a standard and as general advice still stands. The Guide issued by the BRE Trust offers a fairly simple, coherent and sensible approach to the question of whether there has been, in the words of the document, a situation in which daylighting to a particular property is 'likely to be significantly affected'. If the application of the guidance is brought to the attention of the court, with calculations having been done by one or other or both parties in accordance with the Guide, then it would be unusual for a court wholly to ignore this matter. The help which a court may obtain from the Guide is likely to be all the greater if, in accordance with the Waldram diagram methodology, the effect on the light of the dominant tenement is somewhere on or near the boundary of that which would constitute an actionable infringement. 10.15

[18] ibid [94].

10.16 If a rights of light expert acting for a claimant is confident that the effect of a development on the servient tenement brings the access of light to the dominant building well below that which is acceptable in accordance with the ordinary notions of mankind, or, if it is already below that standard, brings it even lower, then recourse to the BRE Guide may be of little significance. Equally, if an expert acting for a defendant is of the view that the amount of light available to a room in the dominant building affected by the development on the servient land is and will remain after the development is completed well above that which is acceptable in accordance with the ordinary notions of mankind then, again, recourse to the Guide may be of little assistance. It has been explained in Chapter 6 on the measurement of light that there is a general view taken by rights of light surveyors that if a room in the dominant building enjoys an amount of natural light, calculated in accordance with the 0.2 per cent sky factor methodology, over at least 50 per cent of its floor area, then it is sufficiently lit. If the result of the development on the servient land will be either to reduce the area sufficiently lit in a room in the dominant building to well below 50 per cent of its floor area, or to leave the floor area sufficiently lit well above 50 per cent, in accordance with the 0.2 per cent sky factor standard, then it is unlikely that rights of light experts or a court will be influenced to reach a conclusion, other than that dictated by the application of these criteria, as a result of the application of the Guide.

10.17 What, therefore, can be concluded is that, whereas the application of the Guide may always be a relevant consideration, and it may be worthwhile bringing the result of the process recommended in that document to the attention of the court, it is unlikely that a result obtained in accordance with the application of the Guide will supplant a conclusion reached by the application of the Waldram methodology which has embedded itself for decades into the expert thinking and advice of rights of light surveyors. The Guide itself emphasises that it does not attempt or purport to provide an answer to rights of light questions in private law.[19]

3. Planning Permission and Injunctions

10.18 The third possible area of relevance of planning control and planning permissions is probably the most important. It is the effect of the existence of a planning permission for the development on the servient land on the decision of a court on whether to issue an injunction to prevent or remove that development if it constitutes a violation of a right of light.[20] It is of course necessary that it should be either admitted or established that the development is a breach of the easement of

[19] See para 2.2.18 of the Guide.

[20] The principles which apply to the exercise of the discretion to grant an injunction are considered generally in ch 7, section (B).

light appurtenant to the dominant building before any question of an injunction as a remedy becomes pertinent.

The existence of a planning permission for the offending development is undoubtedly a matter to be taken into consideration by a court when dealing with the issue of an injunction. This rule is a part of the wider principle that the public interest generally is a relevant factor in a decision on this question.[21] In *Lawrence v Fen Tigers Ltd*, Lord Sumption went much further in the following passage.[22] 10.19

> There is much to be said for the view that damages are ordinarily an adequate remedy for nuisance and that an injunction should not usually be granted in a case where it is likely that conflicting interests are engaged other than the parties' interests. In particular, it may well be that an injunction should as a matter of principle not be granted in a case where a use of land to which objection is taken requires and has received planning permission. However, at this stage, in the absence of argument on these points, I can do no more than identify them as calling for consideration in a case in which they arise.

This suggestion in support of one possible result of the necessary further consideration of the question—it was avowedly no more—did not find general approval in other judgments in the case. Lord Neuberger said that he could see much merit in the proposals proffered but added that there might be objections, qualifications and alternatives to the suggested approach which should be considered before the law on the topic was developed further.[23] Lord Mance said that he was not presently persuaded either by the view that damages were ordinarily an adequate remedy for a nuisance or by the proposition that an injunction should not usually be granted when a use of the land had received planning permission. He also said that in his view a grant of planning permission could not give rise to any presumption that there should be no injunction.[24] Lord Carnwath also said that he would not regard the grant of a planning permission for a use as in itself giving rise to a presumption against the grant of an injunction.[25]

The present law on this aspect of planning control can be stated as that, whereas the existence of a planning permission for the development proposed or carried out on the servient land is a relevant factor to be taken into account in deciding whether an injunction should be granted, it is not a decisive factor and does not create a presumption that an injunction should not be granted. Any servient owner proposing to carry out a development would be ill advised to assume that he avoids the risk of an injunction to prevent his project, or of an injunction to compel its removal if he carries it out, simply because there exists a planning permission for the development in question. Plainly the weight to be given 10.20

[21] *Lawrence v Fen Tigers Ltd* [2014] UKSC 13, [2014] AC 822, [124]–[126] (Lord Neuberger) and [169] (Lord Clarke).

[22] ibid [161].

[23] ibid [127].

[24] ibid [167], [168]. Lord Neuberger, perhaps qualifying the merits which he saw in the suggestion of Lord Sumption, said at para 127 that he saw real force in the opposite view of Lord Mance.

[25] ibid [246].

to the grant of a planning permission depends on the circumstances of each case. Nonetheless there are four matters which as a generality may influence the weight that a court will attribute to the existence of a planning permission in deciding whether to issue an injunction.

10.21 The first matter is the degree of consideration which has been given by the local planning authority, or an inspector or the Secretary of State on an appeal against the refusal of planning permission, to the effect of the development permitted on the access of light to neighbouring properties. If the consideration by the authority has involved no examination, or only a scant examination, of this matter, then this may indicate that little weight should be given to its decision. On the other hand, if the matter of the access of light to neighbouring properties has been given full consideration, perhaps with the benefit of some expert advice and appraisal on the matter, then obviously the weight to be given to the grant of planning permission is likely to be that much greater. Where the decision to grant planning permission is that of a local planning authority the degree of consideration which it has given to access of light matters may be gauged from the report which it has received from a planning officer or other expert and from any record of the discussion by the committee of the authority which takes the decision. The fact that there have been objections to the grant of the planning permission raising the effect of the proposed development on the access of light to existing properties which have been taken into account by the authority may also be a significant factor.[26] On occasions, local planning authorities take decisions which are contrary to the advice and recommendation of their planning officers and this will be something to be borne in mind. If the permission has been granted by the Secretary of State or an inspector on an appeal, or by the Secretary of State on a 'called-in' application, then the decision letter of the Secretary of State or the inspector is likely to explain what weight, if any, has been given to access of light considerations.[27]

[26] However, note should be taken of the observation of Lord Neuberger in *Lawrence v Fen Tigers Ltd* [2014] UKSC 13, [2014] AC 822 [97]–[98] to the effect that there may be no way of knowing to what extent members of a local planning authority who made a decision to grant planning permission took into account all that was said in the reports prepared by officers or of knowing what other considerations of an economic or political nature may have motivated their decision.

[27] The Secretary of State is entitled under s 77 of the Town and Country Planning Act 1990 to require that an application for planning permission made to a local planning authority should be referred to him for his decision. Such applications are often called 'called-in' applications. If an application is called in the Secretary of State will usually hold an inquiry into the application and the proceedings at the inquiry will then indicate the extent to which access of light matters have been considered. Most ordinary planning appeals are today decided by inspectors. The decision may be made on written representations or following a public local inquiry or a hearing. Members of the public may attend inquiries or hearings and make their views known. The owners or occupiers of a dominant building may wish to attend and make known their views. Written representations by objectors to or supporters of a proposed development may also be made and are taken into account in the decision-making process. While the decision is that of the Secretary of State, an inspector who has held an inquiry will present a report of the inquiry to the Minister and the Minister will then issue a decision letter. If the decision is that of an inspector, he or she will issue a decision letter.

The second matter is that the consideration of a planning application by a local planning authority or other body may indicate that there is a significant public interest in the development for which permission is granted going ahead. For instance, one reason for the grant of a permission for residential development is that there is a deficiency of land available for new housing in the area of the local planning authority. As indicated above, the public interest in a development is a material factor in deciding whether an injunction to prevent that development should be granted. 10.22

A third matter is that in rights of light disputes, the situation as regards planning permission may be rather different from that which arises where the alleged nuisance is caused by factors such as noise or vibration or fumes, for example, the noise nuisance from motor sports activities which was in issue in the *Lawrence* case. A development by way of a new or extended building on servient land is a specific and definite event, the nature and boundaries and appearance of which are known from a planning permission which is granted. The exact details of the development, including its height and bulk and size, will be known from the terms of the planning permission either because that permission is a full permission which requires that the development is carried out precisely in accordance with drawings submitted with the application or because the permission is an outline planning permission but with approval of details obtained pursuant to a condition requiring those reserved matters to be approved. If a planning permission is granted for some commercial or recreational activity which may create a degree of nuisance through noise or other matters because of the way in which it is carried on the planning authority may not be aware of the extent or risk of this when granting planning permission. The authority may assume that the activity will be carried on responsibly and with consideration for neighbours. Of course if there are conditions attached to a planning permission which restrict the impact of the activity permitted then the fact that there is a breach of those conditions may induce enforcement action from the local planning authority and may encourage the court to issue an injunction if that enforcement action is not taken or proves ineffective. On the other hand, where a new building or an extension to an existing building is permitted on the servient land with full details known to the local planning authority that may be a situation which results in greater weight being attributed to the existence of the permission since the impact on the access of light of the development is something which can be fully assessed by the authority at the date when it grants permission. 10.23

The final matter is that the inception of a use or a change of use which creates a nuisance may in some cases not require a planning permission. The use as a whole may have been established through a long period of use so that no planning permission is required for it, or a permission may have been granted for the use but that use is intensified in a way which does not require a further permission but creates a nuisance to neighbours. In contrast to this type of situation a planning permission following an application for permission is nearly always required for the 10.24

erection of a building or an extension to a building which is of a scale likely to have a material effect on the access of light to neighbouring properties. It is, therefore, more likely that in rights of light disputes, and where the grant of an injunction is in issue, the existence of a planning permission may be more relevant than with other forms of nuisance. In addition, in rights of light disputes a relevant planning permission is likely to have been granted fairly recently. In most cases planning permissions contain conditions that the development shall be commenced within a limited period from the grant of the permission, usually three years for a full planning permission, or two years from the approval of reserved matters such as the details of the development in the case of outline planning permissions.[28] On the other hand the commencement of the development can occur by the carrying out of some fairly minor operation and thereafter the permission remains in existence and may be completed at any time in the future.[29] The date on which a permission was granted could be of relevance to the weight which is to be attached to it.

4. Publicity for Planning Applications

10.25 The fourth relevant aspect of planning control to rights of light is the publicity which has to be given to applications for planning permission. The Town and Country Planning Act 1990 requires that notice of an application for a planning permission has to be given to certain persons in certain circumstances,[30] and local planning authorities have a practice of notifying persons with property in the vicinity of the site of a planning application, who may be affected by the development proposed, of the making of the application and may invite comments and representations to the authority. Notices of applications for planning are often exhibited at points where they can be seen by the public and by persons with property in the vicinity of the proposed development. It is likely that by this means a dominant owner will have notice of a proposed development which may affect his right of light. Upon receiving such a notification a dominant owner may make further enquiries as to the exact nature and height and bulk and position of the proposed development so that he can gauge its effect on his right of light. This information can be obtained from the developer or from the local planning authority. The local planning authority is required to keep a register of planning applications made to it and this register may be inspected and the exact nature and dimensions of a proposed development ascertained from the register and from the terms of the application for permission and the plans and other information

[28] Town and Country Planning Act 1990, s 91 et seq.
[29] ibid, s 56.
[30] ibid, s 62.

which will accompany such an application.[31] Registers today are often kept in a computerised form.

5. Representations by Dominant Owners

The fifth relevant aspect of planning control is that it offers an opportunity for a dominant owner who objects to a proposed development which will or may infringe his right of light to seek to prevent the development going ahead at the planning stage. A dominant owner may object to the grant of planning permission, giving as his reason the effect which the proposed development will have on the access of light to his property. Of course a neighbouring owner can make such protests and representations even if he has no right of light. The planning authority would take such representations into account whether a right of light exists or not. However, as explained, the fact that a right of light exists or even the fact that such a right of light will be infringed will not necessarily prevent the grant of planning permission. The reason is the distinction between the duty of a local planning authority to consider the public interest and the existence of private law rights.[32] 10.26

It will normally be preferable for a dominant owner with a right of light to prevent a development on the servient land proceeding by encouraging a refusal of a planning permission rather than by going through the courts in order to seek a remedy by way of an injunction or damages. If the development project can be halted at the planning stage the risk and expense of legal proceedings are avoided. Where an easement of light has been acquired by prescription under sections 3 and 4 of the Prescription Act 1832, there is always a danger to the dominant owner that there will be an interruption to the access of light to his property for a period in excess of a year to which he has submitted or in which he has acquiesced. Protests by the dominant owner made known to the servient owner, such as an objection to the grant of planning permission, may be sufficient to prevent there being a submission or acquiescence by him.[33] An objection made to the local planning authority when an application for planning permission is made may stand to the credit of a dominant owner if permission is granted and that owner later seeks relief from a court to an infringement of his rights. If planning permission is granted for a development despite the objection of a person or persons whose light will be adversely affected, there is not normally much more that those persons can do in the area of town planning. Their private law rights, if any, would remain. Their only remaining town planning remedy would be to apply for judicial review to quash the planning permission on the ground that the local planning authority 10.27

[31] ibid, s 69.

[32] See paras 10.2–10.15.

[33] See ch 5, para 5.53. A mere complaint to the local planning authority may not prevent there being a submission or acquiescence: *Dance v Triplow* (1991) 64 P & CR 1.

had acted in some way unlawfully, for example by not taking into account material considerations relating to the overshadowing of neighbouring properties.[34] Such proceedings are not easy to pursue, and the permission of the High Court is needed before an application for judicial review can be made.[35] There is a time limit of six weeks from the date on which the decision to make the claim first arose for applications relating to planning decisions.[36]

(C) PLANNING GUIDANCE AND STANDARDS

1. Purpose and Status of Guidance

10.28 Planning authorities in carrying out their statutory planning function of deciding planning applications are required to have regard to the provisions of the development plan and other material considerations.[37] Development plans have changed greatly since they were first introduced by the Town and Country Planning Act 1947. Different plans for different local planning authorities contain different policies as regards amenity and the sufficiency of the access of light to individual properties. It is likely that many plans will contain general provisions about development not being permitted to the detriment of the amenity of existing properties, particularly residential properties. At any particular time, plans may be in the course of preparation to replace or amend an existing plan, and such plans and amendments are not the statutory development plan but may be material considerations in the determination of any planning decision with the weight to be given to them depending upon the stage to which their preparation has reached in accordance with the statutory process.

[34] The principles of law underlying such challenges to the validity of administrative actions are explained in *Associated Provincial Picture Houses Ltd v Wednesbury Corporation* [1948] 1 KB 223. A failure to understand a particular relevant policy may be a ground for impugning the validity of a planning decision: *Tesco Stores Ltd v Dundee City Council* [2012] UKSC 13, [2012] 2 P & CR 9. In *Marshall Street Regeneration Ltd v Westminster City Council* [2013] EWHC 2764 (Admin) there was an unsuccessful attempt to challenge a planning permission in the High Court by judicial review, where one ground was that the local planning authority had not had proper regard to the adverse effect of the proposed development on the daylight which reached neighbouring flats. In *R (Malster) v Ipswich Borough Council* [2001] EWHC 711, an application by judicial review to quash a planning permission, one of the grounds of which was that a redevelopment of a part of the premises of a football club would cause a loss of light to nearby properties, failed. See also *R (Norton) v London Borough of Lambeth* [2007] EWHC 3476; and see *R (Freud) v Oxford City Council* [2013] EWHC 4613 (Admin) in which the distinction between the relevance of the access of light in public law and private law is explained (see para 10.5). See also paras 10.4 and 10.5.

[35] Civil Procedure Rules, Pt 54.4.

[36] ibid, Pt 54.5(5). This limit is more strict than the time limit of three months which applies generally to applications for judicial review. An extension of time may be granted under Pt 3.1(2)(a).

[37] Town and Country Planning Act 1990, s 70(2).

Regard must also be paid to the national planning policy guidance issued by the Government.[38] That document removed a number of planning guidance notes and similar advice previously issued by the Government. In addition, many local planning authorities produce supplementary planning documents which are not part of the statutory development plan but provide additional guidance as to aspects of development control. It is possible that such supplementary planning documents will provide particular guidance on the effect of developments on the access of light to other properties and, if so, that guidance is likely to be a material consideration in deciding planning applications where the effect on the access of light to neighbouring properties is relevant. A number of published documents exist on matters pertaining to the adequacy of lighting in buildings and the access of light to buildings. Two such documents, which are important in the design of new buildings, are the BSI *Code of Practice for Daylighting*,[39] and the Chartered Institution of Building Services Engineers' Lighting Guide, *Daylighting and Window Design*.[40] 10.29

These documents are important for the design of new buildings, but are unlikely to play a major part in rights of light disputes. The content of an easement of light, and so the right protected by such an easement, is the access of light sufficient for the ordinary and reasonable use of the dominant building, and this does not compare directly with the recommendations in a document such as BS 8206-2:2008. 10.30

Of greater relevance for the present discussion is the BRE Guide already referred to.[41] This document gives advice on a number of subjects, such as site layout planning to achieve good daylighting and sunlighting within buildings and in open spaces between them, and on solar energy. 10.31

A purpose of the BRE Guide is to assist designers and developers and local planning authorities deciding planning applications for new developments or extensions of existing buildings to assess that which is necessary to safeguard daylight to nearby properties. Certain numerical values are suggested, but these are purely advisory.[42] The BRE Guide is not designed to resolve issues concerned with easements of light and the possible infringement of those easements. There are general comments in Appendix E of the Guide on rights of light, where it is stated that according to legal 10.32

[38] National Planning Policy Framework, published by the Department for Communities and Local Government on 27 March 2012. For requirements of good design see para 56 et seq.

[39] British Standard BS 8206-2:2008 *Lighting for Buildings—Part 2: Code of Practice for Daylighting* (London, British Standards Institution, 2008).

[40] CIBSE, Lighting Guide LG10:1999 *Daylighting and Window Design* (London, The Chartered Institution of Building Services Engineers, 1999).

[41] See n 3.

[42] See para 1.6 of the Guide. There is therefore no duty in law on local planning authorities to apply the Guide. They are free to have regard to other guidance on policies on daylighting questions provided they give proper consideration to the matter. See *R (Hewitson) v Guildford Borough Council* [2011] EWHC 3340 (Admin), [2012] JPL 951. As with all policies or guidance applied by deciding authorities, the decision of the authority may be challenged on the ground that it has failed properly to understand the policies or guidance being applied: *Tesco Stores v Dundee City Council* [2012] UKSC 13; *R (Norton) v London Borough of Lambeth* [2007] EWHC 3476 (Admin) (on BRE guidance).

precedent if more than a half of a room has a sky factor of less than 0.2 per cent then the room as a whole is inadequately lit.[43] The Guide advises developers to exercise extreme caution in the area of rights of light, as the law is said to be very complex.[44] It is pointed out that the sky factor in rights of light cases is often calculated using a Waldram diagram but that this is different from the Waldram diagram illustrated in the Guide, and it is said that the diagram in the Guide should not be used in calculating the sky factor for rights of light purposes.[45] The Guide advises that rooms, including living rooms, kitchens and bedrooms, in adjoining dwellings should be considered. However it is stated that windows to bathrooms, toilets, store rooms, circulation areas and garages need not be analysed. Easements of light may protect lights to rooms within a dwelling in these latter categories, but note will be taken of the use of the room in question when deciding whether there is an infringement of a right of light. The Guide is said to be applicable to non-domestic buildings where the occupants have a reasonable expectation of daylight, and that this would normally include schools, hospitals, hotels and hostels, small workshops and some offices.[46] It seems uncertain why it may be the case that the occupants of some offices do not have a reasonable expectation of daylight. Rights of light under easements can protect windows and other apertures in buildings used for any purposes, and the protection of office buildings may be important and has certainly been something which has engendered a number of disputes.

2. The BRE Guide

10.33 The methodology used in the Guide is in general that of applying a sequential test process. If the relevant circumstances of a new building and an existing building satisfy one test, then it is unnecessary to go further. If the first test is not satisfied, then it is necessary to go on to apply a further test, which in turn may or may not be satisfied. The process continues generally in this way. A brief account of the methodology is given here, but this is no substitute for a full consideration of the Guide, with its fuller description and useful diagrams.

10.34 The Guide offers an initial and threshold test. The centre of an existing ground floor window is taken and the distance from the ground is measured (say 1.5 m). The height of the new building is measured (say 10 m). The first figure is subtracted from the second (10 m−1.5 m = 8.5 m). This last figure is multiplied by 3 (8.5 m x 3 = 25.5 m). If the horizontal distance of every part of the new building is greater than this last figure, greater than 25.5 m in the present example, no further analysis need be carried out and it is assumed that the new building will not

[43] BRE Guide, para 2.2.3.
[44] ibid, Appendix E, para E6.
[45] ibid, para E9.
[46] ibid, para 2.2.2

create any unacceptable loss of daylight to the existing building.[47] This is an easy calculation to carry out from plans and elevations of the two buildings, and it may be a useful initial check to be applied by the owners of a dominant building faced with proposals to develop nearby property.

The second test is also easy of description. The centre of the lowest window in the existing building is taken, and a horizontal line is drawn from it towards the new building. A diagonal line is then drawn from the centre of the window to the highest part of the new building and the angle between the horizontal and diagonal lines is measured. If the angle is less than 25 degrees, then it is assumed that the new building will not have a substantial effect on the daylight enjoyed by the existing building.[48] A diagram illustrating the test is included below. Obviously the higher the new building and the nearer it is to the existing building, the greater the angle is likely to be. The angle shown in the diagram exceeds 25 degrees, so that the second test is failed. 10.35

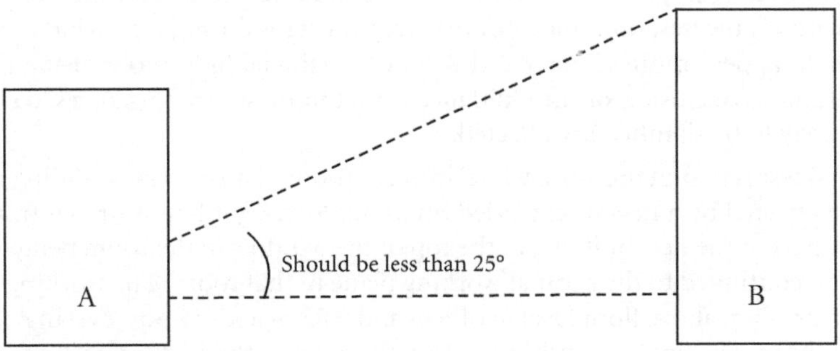

A = Dominant Building
B = New Building on Servient Land

The BRE Guide's second test

If the new development fails to satisfy both of the first two tests as regards an existing building it is necessary to continue to the third test. This test involves assessing the vertical sky component (VSC). The VSC is defined as 'Ratio of that part of illuminance, at a point on a given vertical plane, that is received directly from a CIE standard overcast sky, to illuminance on a horizontal plane due to an unobstructed hemisphere of the sky'.[49] The vertical plane to be taken is a point 1.6 metres above ground level on the surface of the main windows in the existing building. The VSC for this purpose is calculated using the sky light indicator as shown in Appendix A in the Guide, or a Waldram diagram as shown in Appendix B in the Guide, or by 10.36

[47] Ibid., para 2.2.4.

[48] ibid, para 2.2.5. This can be called a 25 degree test. A 45 degree test, perhaps found on s 85 of the Metropolitan Management Amendment Act 1862, had some influence in the late nineteenth century: see ch 3, para 3.6.

[49] ibid, glossary.

the use of computer software. The direct sky illuminance falling on the relevant window at this point is then compared to the simultaneous horizontal illuminance under an unobstructed sky, ie such as would exist on a flat roof of the building if it were higher than, and so unobstructed by, any other buildings or other obstruction. If the vertical illuminance at the window is greater than 27 per cent of the simultaneous horizontal illuminance under an unobstructed sky, then it can be concluded that enough skylight will continue to reach the window of the existing building notwithstanding the construction of the new building.[50]

10.37 The structure of the recommended process is such that if the first or the second or the third of the three tests described is satisfied by a new or extended development when assessed in relation to an existing building the daylighting of the existing building is unlikely to be significantly affected. If the VSC with the new building in place is less than 27 per cent then a comparison should be made between that VSC and the former VSC value without the effect of the new building. If the VSC with the new building in place is below 27 per cent and is less than 0.8 times its former value without the new building, the area receiving light through the window tested is likely to appear more gloomy and will need artificial light more of the time.[51] The ultimate conclusion of the Guidance is that in these circumstances, daylighting is likely to be significantly affected.[52]

10.38 The final test is to plot the 'no sky line' in every room of an existing building which may be affected by a new or extended building. A straight line is drawn from the highest part of the new building to the top of the window in the room being tested and then continued to the normal working plane in that room. The working plane is taken as 0.7 m above floor level in offices and 0.85 m above floor level in residential buildings. The line as continued within the room is the no sky line. The area of the room below the no sky line and between it and the window receives direct skylight. The area above the no sky line and away from the window does not receive direct skylight. The no sky line is drawn before and after the new building is in place. If after the obstruction created by the new building the area which receives direct sunlight is less than 0.8 times its former value, obviously more of the room will appear poorly lit, and this will be noticeable to the occupiers.[53]

10.39 The sequential tests are not entirely straightforward to apply in all circumstances so as to reach a conclusion. The recommended process may be summarised as follows.

(i) If the first test (the ratio of the height of the new building to its distance from the existing building: see para 10.34) is satisfied, then daylighting to the existing building is unlikely to be significantly affected. It is unnecessary to go any further.

[50] ibid, paras 2.2.6, 2.2.7.
[51] ibid, para 2.27.
[52] ibid, fig 20.
[53] ibid, paras 2.2.8, 2.2.9.

(ii) If the second test (the angle above the horizontal plane of the highest part of the new building being 25 degrees or less: see para 10.35) is satisfied, then daylighting to the existing building is unlikely to be significantly affected. It is unnecessary to go any further.

(iii) If the third test (the vertical sky component of 27 per cent or more: see para 10.36) is satisfied, that is not quite the end of the process. If the VSC for any main window is 27 per cent or more, it is still necessary to go on and assess for the room lit by that window whether the area of the working plane of the room which sees the sky is at least 80 per cent of the area of the working plane which saw the sky before the erection of the new building (the no sky line test: see para 10.38). Only if (a) the VSC is 27 per cent or more and (b) the area of the working plane which can see the sky is at least 80 per cent of the area of the working plane which could do so before the new building, can it be said that the daylighting for the room is unlikely to be significantly affected.

(iv) If the third test discloses a BSC of less than 27 per cent for a main window, then two further tests, the fourth and fifth tests have to be applied. These are (a) the fourth test of whether the VSC is at least 80 per cent of its former value, and (b) the fifth test of whether the area of the working plane which can see sky is at least 80 per cent of the area which could formerly do so. It is only if both these tests are satisfied that the daylighting can be said to be unlikely to be significantly affected.

A useful summary is provided in the Guide of the application of the process just described. It is as follows. If any part of a new or extended building measured in a vertical section perpendicular to a main window of an existing building, from the centre of the lowest window, subtends an angle of less than 25 degrees to the horizontal then the daylighting of the existing building may be adversely affected. There will be an adverse effect if either (a) the VSC measured at the centre of an existing main window is both less than 27 per cent and less than 80 per cent of its former value, or (b) the area of a working plane in a room which can receive direct skylight is reduced to less than 80 per cent of its former value.[54] 10.40

A potent origin of rights of light disputes is the building of extensions to houses. Neighbours are sometimes aggrieved at this being done. The grievance is sometimes at an obstruction to a view which is not of relevance to easements of light, but in other cases the objection is that the extension causes a reduction of natural light to a window in the neighbouring property. In such cases the positioning of the extension is often perpendicular to the window of the neighbouring property which is affected. The BRE Guide offers a quick method of assessing whether an unacceptable loss of light is likely to be caused by the construction of such a perpendicular extension. 10.41

[54] ibid, fig 20: summary.

10.42 The procedure suggested is as follows.

(a) Suppose that house A has a window facing out from its rear wall. The owner of adjoining house B erects an extension outwards from the rear of his house and so perpendicular to the rear wall of house A with its window (this would be a typical situation, but of course there could be many variants).

(b) A downwards diagonal line at an angle of 45 degrees is drawn from the top inner corner of the extension of house B along the elevation of the rear wall of house A.

(c) The houses are considered in plan and a line is drawn back at an angle of 45 degrees from the outer bottom corner of the extension. If the centre of the window of house A lies on the extension side of both of the 45 degree lines, the extension may cause a significant reduction in the natural light received by the window in house A. This process is only one of general guidance which may give a quick answer to any dispute between the owners of properties A and B. If the dispute cannot be resolved in this way, then a full Waldram diagram analysis may be appropriate.[55]

[55] ibid, paras 2.2.8, 2.2.9.

11

Registration and Transfer of Easements of Light

(A) INTRODUCTION

Easements of light are usually created to last permanently, or for a substantial period of time. If the easement is to have any real effect it must therefore normally be possible for the benefit of it to be transferred with the ownership of the dominant building, and for the burden of it to bind successors in title of the servient land to the person who owned that land when the easement was created.[1] There is not normally any difficulty in the benefit of the easement passing to a transferee of the dominant building. The transfer of the burden of the easement to a transferee of the servient land may pose more problems. 11.1

It has been explained that easements generally, including easements of light, are proprietary interests in land, in the sense that they are capable in principle of binding successors in title of the servient land.[2] Before the advent of modern systems of statutory registration, the principles which determined when an interest in land bound transferees of that land were not difficult to state. A legal interest in land such as a lease bound all persons into whose hands the landlord's interest came, irrespective of the knowledge of that person of the lease. An equitable interest in land such as the benefit of a restrictive covenant bound all persons into whose hands the land burdened by the covenant came, save for a bona fide purchaser for value of a legal estate in that land without notice of the equitable interest. Notice could be actual or constructive, constructive notice being that notice which would be obtained by a person who made reasonable investigation. Whether a proprietary interest in land was legal or equitable depended on whether its reception into the categories of proprietary interests was by the common law courts, as with leases in late medieval times, or by courts of equity, as, for example, with the 11.2

[1] It is of course possible for an expressly created easement of light to be confined by the express terms of the deed creating it so as to benefit or burden only the original parties to the deed or only one of them or to be limited in some other way. Such limitations are uncommon. Similar questions may arise in connection with agreements which permit development on land despite the effect on the access of light to adjoining premises. See ch 5, para 5.74, and see *CGIS City Plaza Shares Ltd v Britel Fund Trustees Ltd* [2012] EWHC 1594 (Ch).

[2] See ch 2, section (A).

benefit of restrictive covenants following the decision in *Tulk v Moxhay* in 1848.[3] An interest in land, albeit in principle capable of being a legal interest, might have effect as an equitable interest because of some non-compliance with the formalities required for its creation.

11.3 An easement was a legal interest in land, and so would bind transferees of the servient land in accordance with the above principles. It did not matter for these purposes how the easement was created, whether expressly or by implication or by prescription. Interests that were normally legal interests could sometimes exist as equitable interests where they were supported by some equitable principle. Thus a specifically enforceable agreement to grant a lease or to create an easement could create an equitable lease or easement in favour of the proposed grantee, so that its enforceability was dependent on the rule applicable to equitable interests.[4]

11.4 Changes brought about by the 1925 property legislation have radically altered the above principles and system. The Law of Property Act 1925 provided that easements could exist as legal interests in land only if created in perpetuity or for a term equivalent to a term of years absolute.[5] In effect, legal easements could exist as equivalent to freehold or leasehold estates. Any other easement was necessarily equitable. Of perhaps greater significance for present purposes, systems of registration of interests in land or encumbrances on interests in land were introduced by the Land Charges Act 1925 and the Land Registration Act 1925. The two systems are entirely different.

11.5 The essence of the land charges system was that certain encumbrances on interests in land were designated as land charges and could be registered on a central register against the name of the owner of the land burdened by the charge when it was created. If the charge was not registered, a subsequent purchaser of the burdened land could take free of it. A purchaser of land could search the register and by this means find either that the interest was registered, in which case he would be bound by it, or was not registered, in which case he would acquire the land free of that interest. The system as first enacted was expected to have a temporary life while registration of title was gradually introduced across the country. To some extent this has happened although the spread of registration of title was much slower than had originally been anticipated. Land charges are still of significance in relation to some easements of light. The current legislation is contained in the Land Charges Act 1972 and is explained in section (C) of this chapter.

[3] *Tulk v Moxhay* (1848) 2 Ph 774. An account of these basic principles in the development of the land law is contained in chs 1–5 of *Megarry & Wade, The Law of Real Property*, 12th edn (London, Sweet & Maxwell, 2013).

[4] The best example of this process is the rule in *Walsh v Lonsdale* (1882) 21 Ch D 9 as regards equitable leases. Thus an easement such as a right of way granted as part of an equitable lease is itself necessarily equitable: see *Celsteel Ltd v Alton House Holdings Ltd* [1985] 1 WLR 204.

[5] See Law of Property Act 1925, s 1(2)(a).

Registration of title or land registration is a wholly different system. It aims not just to register charges or encumbrances over land, such as third party proprietary interests, but rather to provide a central register of titles to land. There are various types of freehold and leasehold titles which may be registered, and the registered proprietor of a title to a particular interest in a particular area of land has a state-guaranteed and indefeasible title to that interest in the land.[6] Charges and encumbrances are treated differently. The underlying principle was that a person who took a disposition of the registered land and became registered as the new proprietor took free from all encumbrances unless the encumbrance was noted on the register of the title or was one of a number of categories of overriding interest. This system was far from a comprehensive guarantee to purchasers of land, since there were a number of overriding interests, including easements, which bound a purchaser even though he had no notice of them. Following a review and recommendations by the Law Commission in 2001,[7] major changes were made in a new statement of the law contained in the Land Registration Act 2002 which came into force on 13 October 2003. The present land registration system as it affects easements of light is described in section (B) of this chapter.[8] 11.6

Despite the important changes in property law just outlined, the fundamentally important question often remains the same. It is whether an easement of light binds purchasers of the servient land. The answer to this question today normally depends not so much on the distinction between legal and equitable interests as built up for centuries (although, as will be explained, this may still be significant) as on the rules under the Land Registration Act 2002 and, to a lesser extent, on the rules applicable to land charges. The date on which the easement was created may also be important for these purposes. As will be seen later in this chapter, it is necessary in explaining the continuing effect of an easement of light against a purchaser of the servient land to categorise easements in accordance with whether they are legal and equitable easements, and in accordance with whether they were created before or after the Land Registration Act 2002 came into effect on 13 October 2003. 11.7

[6] Indefeasibility is not absolute, since there are provisions under which the register can be altered in limited circumstances.

[7] Law Commission, *Land Registration for the twenty-first century—post-consultation report and draft bill: A Conveyancing Revolution* (Law Com No 271, 2001).

[8] Other systems of land registration exist in the common law world, the most important example being the Torrens system which operates in Australia, New Zealand and parts of the Caribbean. The Torrens system was first introduced in Australia by Sir Robert Torrens and had its first expression in the South Australian Real Property Act 1858. Its genesis appears to have been in part a need to create clear titles to land in the gold rushes which occurred in parts of Australia, as in California and the South Island of New Zealand, in the middle decades of the nineteenth century. It is in many ways similar to the English system and is in some ways simpler.

(B) LAND REGISTRATION

1. General Principles

11.8 It is not possible to understand the impact of land registration on easements of light without a brief explanation of the registration system. A register of titles is kept by the Chief Land Registrar at Her Majesty's Land Registry.[9] A register is kept of the title to a specific area of land. A number is attributed to the title, and the register for that title is divided into the property register which describes the land, usually by reference to red edging on an attached plan, the proprietorship register which contains the name of the current registered proprietor, and the charges register which contains details of encumbrances noted against the land. There are various categories of freehold and leasehold titles which may be registered, including a possessory title. For example, an absolute freehold title may be registered if the Registrar is of the opinion that the title of the registered proprietor of the estate is such as a willing buyer could properly be advised by a competent professional adviser to accept.[10] The details of the system are contained in rules, mainly in the Land Registration Rules 2003.[11]

11.9 Not all land has a registered title. A landowner of unregistered land is not required to register his land unless he deals with the land in some way, and about a third of the land in England and Wales does not have registered title. Compulsory registration on the occurrence of certain dealings in land as triggering events was applied at first to certain areas, and then extended to cover the whole country. Today, an interest which qualifies for registration may be registered voluntarily[12] at any time and must be registered on the happening of certain triggering events.[13]

11.10 Interests which may be registered are called qualifying estates. They are either a freehold estate or a lease for a term with more than seven years to run at the time of its transfer, grant or creation.[14] Compulsory first registration applies where there is a transfer of the freehold, or the grant or transfer of a lease with an unexpired duration exceeding seven years.[15]

[9] Land Registration Act 2002, ss 1, 99. In the remainder of the footnotes in this chapter this Act is referred to as LRA 2002.

[10] LRA 2002, s 9.

[11] The practical and detailed operation of the land registration system depends to a significant extent on the practice of HM Land Registry. Details of the system are explained in *Ruoff & Roper, Registered Conveyancing* (London, Sweet & Maxwell, looseleaf) and Harpum & Bignell, *Registered Land: The New Law: A Guide to the Land Registration Act 2002* (Bristol, Jordans, 2002).

[12] LRA 2002, s 3.

[13] ibid, s 4.

[14] ibid, s 4(2).

[15] ibid, s 4(1). Under the Land Registration Act 1925 only leases for a term in excess of 21 years were registrable. This was reduced to leases for a term in excess of seven years by the Land Registration Act 2002, and it is expected in due course that leases for a term in excess of three years will become registrable.

The registered proprietor of a registered estate is entitled to dispose of it as he wishes. Certain dispositions are required to be completed by registration of the disposition. These dispositions include a transfer of the freehold or of a registered leasehold estate, the grant of a lease for a term of more than seven years from the date of its grant, and the express grant or reservation of an easement including an easement of light.[16] A disposition must be effected by the execution of a form as issued by the Land Registry. The transferee or lessee is then required to apply to the Land Registry for registration. It is only when the registration requirements of a disposition are met that the registered legal estate vests in the transferee or lessee.[17] If registration is not properly effected, then only an equitable interest vests in the person taking the disposition. For example, if A sells the whole of his registered freehold interest to B, the transfer must be effected by the execution of form TR1 and B must apply for registration of the disposition. B is then entered on the register as the new proprietor, and the freehold legal estate vests in him. B can obtain an official copy (called an office copy) of the register of title.[18] It is this office copy of the relevant entry on the register that a landowner often regards as his certificate of title. 11.11

A vital question in this process is what encumbrances or third party interests do or do not bind the transferee following a registered disposition. The ultimate aim of land registration is that any encumbrances which are to bind the transferee should appear on the register prior to the disposition so that he can be aware of them. The Land Registration Act 2002 has moved the system further towards this ideal but the position is still far from perfect, and as regards easements there are a number of complex rules. The general principle is that a transferee is bound only by encumbrances which are either protected by a notice on the register of the title he is acquiring or are overriding interests. This latter expression is not used in the legislation but is an expression which denotes an interest which in certain circumstances may bind a person taking a registered disposition, even though it is not protected by notice on the register. The application of these principles to easements of light is explained in more detail later.[19] Prior to the introduction of general land registration in 1925 a purchaser of land had two burdens. He needed to establish that the seller had a good title to pass to him. This was achieved by finding a good root of title, such as a previous transfer or a devolution under a will, and then tracing the devolution of the title from that time onwards. At one time a root of title at least 60 years old was required, but this was successively reduced so that the period is now 15 years. Secondly, the purchaser had to investigate what encumbrances would bind the land in his hands. The land registration system removed the first burden, in that the registered title is a state-guaranteed title which does 11.12

[16] ibid, s 27(2).
[17] ibid, s 27(1).
[18] ibid, s 67.
[19] See para 11.20 et seq.

not need further investigation. The system has also moved towards a lessening of the second burden, but not to the full extent which is ultimately desirable.

2. Registration and the Creation of Easements of Light

11.13 It is necessary to state how the general system of land registration just described applies to the creation of easements of light. In this respect easements of light are no different from other easements. Four situations may be distinguished.

11.14 First, an easement of light cannot obtain its own registered title. The only interests which may be registered are an estate in land, a rentcharge, a franchise, and a profit a prendre in gross.[20] Therefore an easement cannot obtain its own registered title whenever it was created or by whatever process, including creation expressly by a deed, it came into being.

11.15 Secondly, an easement expressly created before 13 October 2003 did not require any form of registration of its creation. This was an aspect of the law which was altered by the Land Registration Act 2002.

11.16 Thirdly, an easement created by prescription, by implication, or by the operation of section 62 of the Law of Property Act 1925, does not require any form of registration, whenever created.

11.17 Easements of light created in the circumstances mentioned in the previous two paragraphs simply take effect as legal interests, providing they are of permanent duration or are for a term of years equivalent to a term of years absolute.[21] This does not of course mean that they necessarily bind a purchaser of the registered title to the servient land, and this subject is considered later in this chapter.

11.18 The fourth situation is one which came newly into effect under the Land Registration Act 2002. Where there exists a registered legal estate one of the dispositions which, since 13 October 2003, is required to be completed by registration is the express grant or reservation of an interest of a kind falling within section 1(2)(a) of the Law of Property Act 1925. and this includes the express grant or reservation of a legal easement including an easement of light.[22] It is provided that an express grant in the context of this rule does not include a grant as a result of the operation of section 62 of the Law of Property Act 1925.[23] It should be noted that when

[20] LRA 2002, s 3(1).

[21] See Law of Property Act 1925, s 1(2)(a). Any easement granted for a different period is necessarily equitable. Equitable easements, which may also arise for reasons other than their duration, are examined in para 11.47 et seq below.

[22] LRA 2002, s 27(2)(d).

[23] ibid, s 27(7). It is not entirely clear whether the creation of an easement by the operation of s 62 is by implication or simply by the operation of statute. In any event, it is made clear that the requirement of registration does not apply to easements created in this way. The creation of easements under s 62 is explained in section (C) of ch 4.

a lease is granted and an easement over the retained land within the registered title of the landlord is granted as a term of the lease, the easement will require registration even though the lease, if granted for a term not in excess of seven years, will not be registrable. Until the relevant registration requirements are met, the easement cannot have effect as a legal easement but has effect in equity only.[24]

In the case of an express grant or reservation of an easement of light, the way in which the registration requirements of a disposition are satisfied is as follows. A notice must be entered in the register of the title of the servient land. The notice will appear in the charges register. If the servient or burdened land does not have a registered title then the registration requirements cannot be met. In that case the grant or reservation of the easement is not a registrable disposition and the easement will have effect as a legal easement (and will qualify as an overriding interest) without the need for registration. If the building for which the benefit to the easement is created, ie the dominant building, is a part of land with registered title, the proprietor of that title must be registered in the register as also the proprietor of the easement.[25] These requirements ensure that a transferee of the dominant building with registered title will see that he is acquiring the benefit of the easement over the servient land, and a transferee of servient land with registered title will know that the land which he is acquiring will be burdened by the easement for the benefit of the dominant building. 11.19

3. Enforcement of Easements of Light: Priority and Postponement

Where an easement of light exists against servient land which has a registered title, the important question is whether the easement can be enforced against a transferee of the servient land. The general rule is that where a registered disposition of the servient land has been completed by registration in accordance with the registration requirements, any interest affecting the servient land immediately before the disposition is postponed to the interest under the disposition unless its priority is protected at the time of registration.[26] To translate these concepts of priority and postponement into simple terms, suppose that A has acquired by some means an easement of light in favour of plot A against B, who is the registered freehold proprietor of plot B. B transfers the freehold estate to C (who is sometimes described as the disponee) for valuable consideration and the registration is completed by C who becomes the registered proprietor of plot C in the register of its title. The easement of A is not enforceable against C unless the priority of the easement was protected at the time of the completion of the registration by C of the disposition by B to C. 11.20

[24] ibid, s 27(1).

[25] ibid, sch 2, para 7(2). Provisions for the entry of such benefits is made by r 50(b)(ii) of the Land Registration Rules 2003. The application to register should be made using Form AP1.

[26] ibid, s 29(1).

11.21 An important question is of course to know how priority can be protected. There are two means of protecting priority of interests. An interest is protected if it is the subject of a notice in the register. An interest is also protected if it is amongst those interests specified in Schedule 3 to the Land Registration Act 2002. Interests in the latter category are generally called overriding interests.[27]

11.22 It might be asked why the legislation is expressed in this way in the language of priority and protection of priority with the temporal connotations of these expressions. The answer is in the way in which the Land Registration Act 2002 is structured on the present subject. The statutory provisions proceed by stages.

(a) The provisions are introduced by what is described as the basic rule.[28] The basic rule is that the priority of an interest affecting a registered estate is not affected by a disposition of that estate. An interest affecting an estate is an interest adverse to that estate.[29] The basic rule is therefore that where there are two proprietary interests in an area of land the priority of the two interests is determined by the date of the creation of each interest. The first interest has priority. At this stage of the analysis, reverting to the example in paragraph 11.20, the easement of light acquired by A has priority over the freehold estate vested in C since that easement was created prior to the disposition to B, because it adversely affects the registered estate of B, and because its priority is not affected by the disposition of the registered estate to B.

(b) The next stage qualifies the basic rule by what is in effect an equally fundamental rule. Where the registered estate is disposed of by the completion of a registrable disposition for valuable consideration the priority of the interests as determined by the basic rule is partly reversed. An interest adversely affecting a registered estate is postponed to, or loses its priority over, the interest under the disposition unless the previously created interest was protected at the time of the registration of the disposition.

(c) The final stage is that protection will be obtained, ie the effect of the basic rule is preserved, if the interest affecting the registered estate is protected by notice on the register or is an overriding interest. To revert again to the example in paragraph 11.20, the easement of light of A will lose its priority, and so will not be enforceable against C, unless at the time of the registration by C of the disposition to him of the freehold estate the easement had obtained protection by one of the above means. The legislative structure just described may be attributable to the expectation that a general system of electronic conveyancing of registered land may ultimately be introduced.

11.23 Certain general matters need to be borne in mind relating to these principles. The capacity of a completed registered disposition to gain priority for the interest the

[27] ibid, s 29(2)(a). However, the expression 'overriding interest' is not used in the legislation.
[28] ibid, s 28.
[29] ibid, s 132(3)(b).

subject of the disposition over an interest the priority of which is not protected exists only when the disposition is for valuable consideration. No priority is gained by a registered disposition of a gift. The gaining of priority by a registered disposition arises only at the completion of the disposition, that is registration upon an application made by the disponee. The principles do not distinguish between legal and equitable interests although this aspect of an encumbrance may be significant when it comes to the effect of and limitations on easements as overriding interests. The principles do not vary in accordance with the date when the encumbrance was created although this again will be relevant when the principles are applied to easements created expressly by deed. Finally, it is irrelevant whether a disponee had notice of the encumbrance or has acted in good faith. The concept of a bona fide purchaser without notice has been replaced by a more mechanical system. It is therefore necessary to examine next how an easement of light can obtain protection by notice in the title of the servient land or by having the status of an overriding interest.

4. Protection by Notice

The priority of an interest is protected if that interest is the subject of a notice in the register at the time of the completion of the registration of a disposition. The statutory definition of a notice is that it is an entry in the register in respect of the burden of an interest affecting a registered estate. An easement including an easement of light may obviously be such a burden. The notice is entered in relation to the registered estate affected by the interest.[30] A notice may be entered so as to protect any proprietary interest subject to certain exceptions not relevant to the present explanation. 11.24

A notice is entered in the register of the registered estate affected by the registration on the making of an application to the Registrar by the person claiming to be entitled to the benefit of an interest. Notices are agreed or unilateral. An agreed notice requires the consent of the registered proprietor of the registered estate affected.[31] A unilateral notice may be entered with the consent of the Registrar, provided the application for the registration contains the necessary particulars. If he enters a unilateral notice, the Registrar must give notice to the registered proprietor of the registered estate to which it applies.[32] That registered proprietor may then apply for the cancellation of the notice. If the beneficiary of the notice does not exercise his right to object, the Registrar must cancel the notice.[33] The validity or binding nature of the interest sought to be registered by a notice may 11.25

[30] ibid, s 32.
[31] ibid, s 34.
[32] ibid, s 35.
[33] ibid, s 36.

be determined in this way. If agreement cannot be reached the Registrar must refer the objection to the Property Chamber of the First-tier Tribunal where the question in dispute may be determined in accordance with the procedure described in section (C) of this chapter.[34]

11.26 Where on or after 13 October 2003 a legal easement has been created expressly by deed, a notice in respect of the easement must be entered in the register of the title to the servient land in order that the disposition constituted by the creation of the easement is completed in accordance with the registration requirements.[35] Unless this component of the registration requirements is satisfied the easement cannot have effect as a legal easement. Accordingly as regards easements so created which have effect as a legal easement there is necessarily protection by notice and such easements (provided that the proprietor of the registered estate which contains the dominant building is entered in the register as the proprietor of the easement, which is a further registration requirement) will therefore bind a transferee of the servient land.

11.27 The above requirement for registration did not apply to easements expressly created before 13 October 2003 and does not apply to easements created by prescription, by implication, or by the operation of section 62 of the Law of Property Act 1925 whenever created.[36] Such easements are therefore more vulnerable to loss of priority on a transfer of the servient land, and may be dependent for their protection on the conditions which render an interest an overriding interest. It would therefore be a prudent step for the owner of the dominant building to ensure that such easements are protected by an agreed or unilateral notice entered in the register of the servient land, so as to avoid any possible dispute. Equitable easements are separately considered later.[37]

5. Protection as an Overriding Interest

11.28 If an easement is not protected by notice in the registered title of the servient land it may still enjoy protection, so as to bind a transferee for valuable consideration of the servient land, if it is an overriding interest. Under the system of registration in the Land Registration Act 1925 most easements were overriding interests however created.[38] The position has substantially changed under the Land Registration Act 2002 and the status of easements as overriding interests is now more confined.

[34] ibid, s 73.

[35] See paras 11.18 and 11.19. If the servient land does not have a registered title then of course no notice can be registered. In that case the deed creates a legal easement in the ordinary way: see para 11.19.

[36] See para 11.46.

[37] See para 11.47 et seq.

[38] Land Registration Act 1925, s 70(1)(a). See para 11.47 et seq for equitable easements, which under the 1925 Act were also overriding interests.

It is generally only legal interests which can be overriding interests. Equitable easements are never overriding interests if created on or after 13 October 2003, and are considered separately below.[39] 11.29

The statutory language in section 29 of and Schedule 3 to the Land Registration Act 2002 is somewhat tortured in its structure, with negative exceptions and an exception to the exceptions. It is preferable to state the substance of the matter in terms which are as simple as possible. There are three principles. 11.30

First, a legal easement will be an overriding interest if the person entitled to the interest proves that it has been exercised in the year preceding the day of the disposition.[40] 11.31

Secondly, even if it is not an overriding interest by virtue of the first principle, a legal easement will be an overriding interest if it was within the actual knowledge of the disponee at the time of the disposition.[41] 11.32

Thirdly a legal easement, even if it is not an overriding interest by virtue of the first principle, will be an overriding interest if it would have been obvious on a reasonably careful inspection of the land over which it is exercised.[42] The second and third principles appear to reintroduce to some extent in this context the concepts of actual and constructive notice of encumbrances which played a central part in the law before the 1925 property legislation.[43] 11.33

It is obvious that easements which were overriding interests prior to 13 October 2003 under the provisions of the Land Registration Act 1925, which rendered most easements overriding interests, might lose that status if they were equitable easements or could not be brought within the three principles just stated. This potential injustice is avoided by a transitional provision which preserves the overriding status of such easements.[44] Such easements therefore continue to have the status of overriding interests and to bind a disponee, even though not exercised in the year prior to the disposition and even though the disponee did not know of them at the time of the disposition, or they would not have been obvious to him on a reasonably careful inspection of the servient land. 11.34

A further general category of overriding interests is interests of persons in actual occupation of land.[45] This category has no relevance to easements since the limited use and enjoyment of land available to the owner of an easement is not actual occupation of the servient land.[46] 11.35

[39] LRA 2002, Sch 3 para 3(1). See para 11.47 et seq.
[40] ibid, Sch 3, para 3(2).
[41] ibid, Sch 3, para 3(1)(a).
[42] ibid, Sch 3, para 3(1)(b).
[43] See para 11.2.
[44] LRA 2002, Sch 12, para 9.
[45] ibid, Sch 3, para 2.
[46] *Celsteel Ltd v Alton House Holdings Ltd* [1985] 1 WLR 204. Obviously the exercise of an easement of light over servient land is not actual occupation of that land.

6. Easements of Light

11.36 It has been necessary to state the general principles of priority and protection of easements before coming to the application of these principles to the specific case of easements of light. There are no statutory provisions in this area of the law specifically applicable only to easements of light but the nature of easements of light makes it easier to apply certain of the general principles to these easements. The impact of the general principles can be examined (a) as regards legal easements created before 13 October 2003, (b) as regards legal easements expressly created by deed on or after that date, (c) as regards legal easements created by other means on or after that date, and (d) as regards equitable easements.

(a) Pre-13 October 2003 Legal Easements

11.37 If an easement in this category has been protected by an entry in the register of title of the servient land then its priority against a transferee for valuable consideration of that land will be secured. It may be that expressly created easements will have been protected in this way. It is less likely that easements acquired by prescription or by implication or by the operation of section 62 of the Law of Property Act 1925 have been protected by the entry of a notice. In that case, protection and the maintenance of priority against a transferee will depend on the easement being an overriding interest.

11.38 Paragraph 9 of Schedule 12 to the Land Registration Act 2002 provides that an easement which was an overriding interest prior to 13 October 2003, but which would not be such an interest if created on or after that date, retains its status as an overriding interest. Consequently an easement which was created, and which was an overriding interest, prior to 13 October 2003 is an overriding interest for the purposes of the 2002 Act. It is therefore necessary to look at the law under the Land Registration Act 1925 which stated what were overriding interests up to 12 October 2003. Under section 70(1)(a) of the Land Registration Act 1925, easements were overriding interests unless they were "equitable interests required to be protected by notice on the register".[47] Equitable interests are considered as a separate category below.[48] Prescriptive easements and easements created by implication or under section 62 of the Law of Property Act 1925 were always, or nearly always, legal easements and so, if created before 13 October 2003, were overriding interests prior to that date. The result is that all legal easements of light created by whatever means prior to 13 October 2003 remain as overriding interests on and after that date for the purposes of the 2002 Act. Such interests will remain protected and will maintain their priority and will remain enforceable against transferees of the servient land.

[47] For a fuller explanation of the law under the Land Registration Act 1925 in effect until 12 October 2003 see *Megarry & Wade, The Law of Real Property*, 6th edn (London, Sweet & Maxwell, 2000).

[48] See para 11.47 et seq.

The above rule may make it important to establish exactly when a prescriptive easement came into existence since the transitional provisions apply only to easements in existence on 13 October 2003. What will be needed in order to obtain the benefit of the transitional provision is that the 20 years of the use and enjoyment of the access of light to the dominant building over the servient land as required by section 3 of the Prescription Act 1832 had been completed prior to 13 October 2003. If only a part of that period had elapsed on 13 October 2003 it may still be possible to claim a prescriptive easement by the later completion of the 20-year period, but the protection of that easement on a disposition of the servient land will then depend upon the principles explained below. 11.39

(b) *Legal Easements Expressly Created by Deed on or After 13 October 2003*

As explained earlier, when a legal easement is created expressly by a grant or reservation in a deed on or after 13 October 2003, the owner of the dominant building must be entered in the register of his title as the proprietor of the easement and a notice of the easement must be entered in the register of the title to the servient land.[49] If these registration requirements are not met then the easement created will be equitable only. It follows that a legal easement of light so created in accordance with the requirements will bind a transferee of the servient land because that easement will be protected by a notice in the registered title of the servient land. 11.40

(c) *Legal Easements Created Otherwise than Expressly by Deed on or After 13 October 2003*

This category comprises all legal easements created on or after 13 October 2003 by prescription, by implication or by the operation of section 62 of the Law of Property Act 1925. The obvious way of protecting such easements is by notice on the registered title of the servient land. Often the existence of an easement in this category is not realised until some development project commences or is due to commence on the servient land and the owners of neighbouring property seek ways of preventing it. In such cases it is unlikely that an easement of light will have been protected by notice, and a disposition of the servient land may have occurred before the registration of a unilateral notice can be effected.[50] 11.41

In these circumstances it will be necessary to investigate whether the easement of light is protected by reason of its being an overriding interest. The circumstances in which any easement created after 13 October 2003 will rank as an overriding 11.42

[49] LRA 2002, s 27(2)(d), Sch 2, para 7. See paras 11.18 and 11.19. If the servient land does not have a registered title, then the easement granted expressly by deed has effect as a legal easement but its protection against a transferee of the servient land will depend on the operation of the system under the Land Charges Act 1972, as explained in section (D) of this chapter. See para 11.19.

[50] See para 11.25 for the registration of notices.

interest have been described.[51] The nature of easements of light makes it very likely that they will be overriding interests. The first principle, as described earlier, is that an easement will be an overriding interest if it has been exercised within the year prior to the disposition of the servient land. An easement of light is 'exercised' by the passage of light over the servient land to apertures in the dominant building. It is very likely that this will have occurred during the year prior to the disposition of the servient land. Indeed it is not easy to see circumstances in which it would not have occurred, unless the access of light to the dominant building has been prevented in the year by an obstruction on the servient land or by some actions taken on the dominant building such as the blocking up of windows in that building. Satisfaction of this first principle will generally be sufficient to establish an easement of light within this category as an overriding interest and so as an interest which will bind a transferee of the servient land.

11.43 The second and third principles, the application of which may result in an easement being an overriding interest even if the first principle cannot be satisfied,[52] may be more difficult to apply to easements of light. A purchaser of the servient land would normally be aware of neighbouring buildings. In the absence of any claim being made, prior to the transfer to him, of a right of light appurtenant to such a neighbouring building created by prescription or by means other than an express grant, the purchaser may not have knowledge of the existence of the easement. Persons buying a house are not normally property lawyers or rights of light surveyors, and it may simply not occur to or be known to them that a neighbouring property which has been there for a substantial time has acquired an easement of light under the Prescription Act 1832. Purchasers of sites for substantial commercial development in urban areas are likely to be better informed, but this consideration may be more apposite to the third principle. It should be kept in mind that what is required under the second principle is not just knowledge that light passes over the land purchased to a neighbouring property, which may be obvious, but knowledge that an easement of light exists in favour of that neighbouring property, which may be far from obvious.

11.44 The third principle involves asking whether the existence of the easement of light would have been obvious on a reasonably careful inspection of the servient land. This principle may be readily applicable in respect of easements the existence of which should be apparent from physical marks on the servient land, such as a right of way over a marked track which leads across the servient land from the dominant land to a public highway adjoining the servient land. A reasonably careful inspection of the servient land may show that light passes, and in the past has passed, across it to neighbouring buildings, but what has to be shown under this principle as obvious on a reasonable inspection is not the passage of light, but the existence of an easement which is appurtenant to a dominant building. If an easement has been created by implication or by the operation of section 62 of the Law

[51] See paras 11.31–11.33.
[52] See paras 11.32 and 11.33.

of Property Act 1925 as a result of some previous transaction it is unlikely that this will be apparent from an inspection of the servient land. The only way in which a prescriptive easement in favour of neighbouring property could become obvious would be if the transferee of the servient land or his advisers have entered into a process of reasoning involving a knowledge of the law of prescription, a knowledge of the age and structure of the dominant building and its apertures, and a knowledge of other relevant events such as whether there had been an obstruction in the past to the access of light. It seems unlikely that in most circumstances the existence of implied or prescriptive easements will be obvious merely from an inspection of the servient land.

Where properties are acquired for major development in towns and cities a survey by a rights of light surveyor is often obtained prior to the purchase of the property. Even such a surveyor will often do no more, and usually can do no more, than point out the possibility of rights of light being vested in the owners of neighbouring buildings. It seems doubtful whether this process could result in an easement of light in favour of adjoining premises being obvious merely from an inspection of the land however well informed were those who carried out the inspection on behalf of the proposed transferee of the servient land. 11.45

Although every case would have to be looked at in its particular circumstances, it seems very likely that in most cases the owner of a dominant building which has the benefit of an easement of light created by prescription or by implication or by the operation of section 62 of the Law of Property Act 1925 will be able to establish that his easement of light is an overriding interest by reason of the operation of the first principle since the easement, that is the passage of light over the servient land to apertures in the dominant building, is very likely to have been exercised in the year ending with the day of the disposition of the servient land to a purchaser. If in exceptional circumstances this first principle cannot be relied upon, it will be much more difficult, and probably in most cases impossible, to establish that the easement of light is an overriding interest by way of the application of either the second or the third principles. That, of course, will not matter if the first principle can be relied upon. Therefore as a generality it can be said that most legal easements of light acquired other than expressly by a deed since 13 October 2003 are likely to rank as overriding interests by reason of the application of the first principle. 11.46

(d) Equitable Easements

Equitable easements may arise in a number of circumstances. The most important are: 11.47

(a) an easement expressly created by deed on or after 13 October 2003 where the requirements of registration have not been complied with;[53]

[53] See para 11.18.

(b) an easement created which is not for an interest equivalent to a freehold or a term of years (for instance an easement created for life);[54]
(c) the benefit of a specifically enforceable but uncompleted contract to create a legal easement; and
(d) an easement which is appurtenant to an equitable interest such as an equitable lease.

11.48 An equitable easement created on or after 13 October 2003 cannot be an overriding interest.[55] It must therefore be protected by notice on the register of title of the servient land if that land has a registered title. Consequently if the servient land has registered title but the equitable easement is not protected by notice in the charges register of that title and the servient land is disposed of for valuable consideration the disponee will acquire the land free of that easement.

11.49 It remains to consider equitable easements created before 13 October 2003. Of course such easements could be protected by notice but those that existed may often not have been so protected. It is necessary in such a case to apply the transitional provision in paragraph 9 of Schedule 12 to the Land Registration Act 2003. That provision applies to an easement which was an overriding interest prior to 13 October 2003. Such an easement will continue as an overriding interest after that date even though it does not fall within the types of easement, legal easements only, which can be overriding interests if created on or after that date. The critical question is therefore whether an equitable easement created prior to 13 October 2003 was an overriding interest under the Land Registration Act 1925. It might at first sight appear that a pre-13 October 2003 equitable easement could not have been an overriding interest within section 70(1)(c) of the Land Registration Act 1925 which designates certain rights as overriding interests but concludes with the words 'other easements not being equitable easements required to be protected by notice on the register'. However, rule 258 of the Land Registration Rules 1925 stated that rights appertaining to land were overriding interests within section 70 of the Land Registration Act 1925 and it was held that this was sufficient to render an equitable right of way an overriding interest.[56] The position therefore is that equitable easements created before 13 October 2003 will retain their status of overriding interests and for that reason will bind purchasers of the servient land.

11.50 In summary, therefore, equitable easements of light created before 13 October 2003 will be overriding interests and so bind purchasers for value of the servient land with registered title whereas equitable interests created on or after 13 October 2003

[54] Law of Property Act 1925, s 1(2)(a).

[55] LRA 2002, Sch 3, para 3(1).

[56] *Celsteel Ltd v Alton House Ltd* [1985] 1 WLR 204 (Scott J). The easement of way in that case was equitable because it was contained in an agreement for lease of the dominant building which had not been completed by the grant of the lease. There seems to be no reason why an easement of light should not be treated in the same way as an easement of way for present purposes. The decision of Scott J was reversed on appeal but not so as to affect this point: see [1986] 1 WLR 512. For a fuller account of this point see *Megarry & Wade, The Law of Real Property*, 6th edn (London, Sweet & Maxwell, 2000) para 6-042.

will not bind such purchasers unless the easement is protected at the time of the disposition by a notice in the charges register of the registered title of the servient land.

(C) THE PROPERTY CHAMBER

Anyone may object to an application to the Registrar at HM Land Registry The Registrar must give notice to the applicant of the objection and may not determine the application until the objection has been disposed of, unless he is satisfied that the objection is groundless. If the objection cannot be disposed of by agreement the Registrar must refer the matter to the Property Chamber of the First-tier Tribunal.[57] Prior to 1 July 2013 the reference was to the Adjudicator to HM Land Registry.[58] The functions of the Property Chamber remain broadly the same as those of the Adjudicator. The transfer of functions was as a consequence of the reorganisation of tribunals into an Upper Tribunal and First-tier Tribunal following the Tribunals, Courts and Enforcement Act 2007.[59] 11.51

The procedure before the Property Chamber offers a reasonably speedy and simple method of determining some disputes concerning rights of light. For example, if a person alleges that he has an easement of light over the land of his neighbour, he may seek to protect this right by a notice in the registered title of his neighbour and in some cases he may be well advised to take this step. He may seek to enter a unilateral notice in the register to which his neighbour may object by an application to cancel the notice. The beneficiary of the unilateral notice may then object to the application for cancellation (and if he does not do so the Registrar will cancel the notice).[60] Unless agreement is reached, the Registrar must then refer the objection to the Property Chamber, which will adjudicate on the merits. In essence the Chamber will determine whether the alleged easement of light does or does not subsist and is binding on the land of the neighbour The process of determination may include the construction of a deed or a decision on factual matters such as whether there has been access of light over the property alleged as the servient land during the 20-year prescription period. 11.52

The Property Chamber procedure is not a substitute for a decision of the courts. In the circumstances mentioned in the last paragraph there is nothing to stop either of the parties to the dispute seeking a declaration as to their rights in the High Court or in the county court. 11.53

[57] LRA 2002, s 73(1). There are exceptions under s 18 of the Act relating to cautions, and under s 36 relating to the cancellation of unilateral notices. See para 11.52.

[58] LRA 2002, ss 73(4)–(6).

[59] See the Transfer of Tribunal Proceedings Order 2013, Sch 1(3), para 226.

[60] LRA 2002, s 36(3).

11.54 The procedure before the Property Chamber is not possible or suitable for all disputes relating to rights of light. The jurisdiction of the Chamber is dependent on the operation of the land registration system and on there being an application to the Registrar made under the Land Registration Act 2002 and an objection to that application.[61] Many rights of light disputes will fall outside these boundaries. An obvious source of dispute is whether a proposed development on the servient land will infringe what is accepted as an existing easement of light and, if it does, what is the appropriate remedy. Such a dispute would not involve any application to the Registrar and would have to be determined by ordinary proceedings in ordinary courts.

11.55 The referral of the matter by the Registrar to the First-tier Tribunal is governed by rules.[62] The Registrar is required to produce a case summary and to send a copy of this with accompanying documents to the Property Chamber. The parties are to be given a copy of the proposed case summary and to have an opportunity to comment on its content before it is sent by the Registrar to the Chamber.[63]

11.56 An initial step which may be taken by the Property Chamber is, instead of deciding the matter itself, to direct a party to commence proceedings in the court for the purpose of obtaining the court's decision on a point.[64]

11.57 The detailed procedure before the Property Chamber is governed by the Tribunal Procedure (First-tier Tribunal) (Property Chamber) Rules 2013. The Rules apply generally to proceedings before the Chamber which has many further functions as well as determining matters referred by the Registrar of HM Land Registry. The Rules give many powers to the Chamber such as, for example, ordering the production of documents, deciding the form of any oral hearing, and deciding preliminary issues[65] or striking out the case of a party.[66] The Tribunal must hold a hearing of a matter unless the parties agree that the matter can be determined by written representations.[67]

11.58 It is the general practice of tribunals to require written statements of case from the parties. In matters referred by the Registrar the Property Chamber will determine which party is to be the applicant and which is to be the respondent.[68] The party designated as the applicant must submit a statement of case which states the reasons for supporting or objecting to the application which has been made to the Registrar.[69] A similar statement of case must be served by the party designated as the respondent.[70]

[61] ibid, s 36. See para 11.52.

[62] The Land Registration (Referral to the Adjudicator of HM Land Registry) Rules 2003, SI 2003/2114.

[63] ibid, rr 3, 5.

[64] LRA 2002, s 110(1).

[65] The Tribunal Procedure (First-tier Tribunal) (Property Chamber) Rules 2013, SI 2013/1169, r 6.

[66] ibid, r 9.

[67] ibid, r 31.

[68] ibid, r 28(3)(c).

[69] ibid, r 28(4).

[70] ibid, r 30(1).

The decision of the Tribunal may be given orally or in writing. In the case of an oral decision, written reasons for the decision must subsequently be given.[71] 11.59

There is an appeal on a point of law from a decision of the Property Chamber to the Upper Tribunal (Tax and Chancery Chamber) with the permission of either Tribunal.[72] A further appeal lies to the Court of Appeal on a point of law with the permission of the Upper Tribunal or of the Court of Appeal.[73] 11.60

(D) LAND CHARGES

1. Outline of System

Since about a third of the land in England and Wales does not have registered title, the system of land charges which applies to unregistered land remains of importance although that importance is likely to diminish as more land obtains registered title. The land charges system is now contained in the Land Charges Act 1972 and the Land Charges Rules 1974. 11.61

There are a number of registers, of which only the land charges register is important for present purposes. The land charges register is administered by the Land Charges Department of HM Land Registry at Plymouth The essence of the system is that an interest which falls within one of the categories of land charges may be registered against the estate owner, that is the owner for the time being of the land burdened by the land charge. There are classes of land charges. A legal easement is not within the classes and so cannot be a land charge. The land charges system therefore does not affect legal easements however or whenever created. An equitable easement which was created or arose on or after 1 January 1926 is a Class D(iii) land charge, and so can be registered against the owner of the servient land.[74] 11.62

If an equitable easement was created or arose after 1925 and is not registered as a land charge, it is void against the purchaser of a legal estate in the servient land for money or money's worth.[75] The principle of invalidity is somewhat different to other classes of land charges which may be void against a purchaser of any interest in the land burdened with the charge for valuable consideration. The land charges system is a mechanical system which is not dependent on actual notice or constructive notice. A purchaser of the burdened land will take free of a land charge 11.63

[71] LRA 2002, s 111.

[72] Tribunals, Courts and Enforcement Act 2007, s 11. For the making of applications for permission to appeal see rr 52 and 53 of the Tribunal Procedure (First-tier Tribunal) (Property Chamber) Rules 2013.

[73] ibid, s 13.

[74] Land Charges Act 1972, s 2(5).

[75] ibid, s 4(6).

which has been registered even if he knows of the charge and irrespective of any considerations of good faith by him.[76]

11.64 The effect of registration of an equitable easement as a Class D(iii) land charge is that the registration is deemed to constitute actual notice of the easement to all persons and for all purposes connected with the land affected from the date of registration.[77] The proper course for a purchaser of the servient land is therefore to search the charges register. If an equitable easement created after 1 January 1926 has been registered then it will bind the purchaser. If it has not been registered then it will be void against the purchaser.

11.65 There is a major defect in the land charges system of registration. The registration is not against an area of land or a title to land, but is against the name of the owner of the burdened land at the time of the registration. A purchaser of the burdened land can therefore search the register of charges against the name of the seller of the land to him. If the land charge is an equitable easement it may have been created at any time on or after 1 January 1926 and so may have been registered against the owner of the servient land at the time of its creation. Conveyancing of unregistered land requires the investigation of a good root of title to the land, which is a past transaction in the land such as a sale or an assent by a personal representative. The seller, having produced a good root of title in this sense, then proves the steps by which the title has come to be vested in him since the transaction which constitutes the root of title. At one time a good root of title of at least 60 years in the past had to be proved, but this has been reduced by stages until the current period of 15 years was stipulated in the Law of Property Act 1959.[78] The difficulty is that an equitable interest may have been created after 1925 but before the date of the transaction which constitutes the good root of title. In such circumstances there is no easy method by which a purchaser can obtain the names of persons who participated in transactions prior to the root of title but after 1925, yet an equitable easement may have been registered as a land charge against the name of such a person and so will bind the purchaser. Thus a purchaser today of unregistered land may be bound by an equitable easement registered as a land charge against the owner for the time being of that land even though the purchaser today has no practical means of searching the register of land charges so as to ascertain the existence of that registration. Obviously this difficulty may become more acute as an ever-greater period comes to elapse between 1 January 1926 and the date, at least 15 years prior to the purchase, at which a good root of title is established.

[76] *Midland Bank Trust Co v Green* [1981] AC 513; *Hollington Brothers v Rhodes* [1951] 2 TLR 691.

[77] Law of Property Act 1925, s 198.

[78] Law of Property Act 1959, s 25. The contract of sale may provide for the production of an earlier root of title.

2. Easements of Light

11.66 The effect of the land charges system on easements of light may be summarised as follows.

- (i) If the easement is a legal easement it will bind all purchasers of interests in the servient land.
- (ii) If the easement is an equitable easement created on or after 1 January 1926 then (a) if it has been registered against the name of the person who was the estate owner of the servient land at the time of its creation it will bind all purchasers of an interest in the servient land, and (b) if it has not been so registered it will be void against a purchaser of a legal estate in the servient land for money or money's worth.
- (iii) If the easement is an equitable easement created before 1 January 1926 it will bind any purchaser of an interest in the servient land except a bona fide purchaser of a legal estate in that land without actual or constructive notice of the easement.

The distinction between legal and equitable easements of light is therefore of cardinal importance for the purposes of the operation of the land charges system.[79]

(E) TRANSFER OF EASEMENTS

11.67 It is useful to summarise the general principles which apply to the transfer of the dominant or servient land where the dominant land has the benefit of an easement of light and the servient land is bound by an easement of light.

1. Unregistered Land

11.68 A transfer of the dominant land will pass to the transferee the benefit of an easement of light appurtenant to that land unless it is expressly excluded from the transfer. The transfer of the benefit takes effect either by an express term of the transfer or by reason of the operation of section 62 of the Law of Property Act 1925 or automatically.[80] The transfer will normally be a triggering event which brings about a requirement for the first registration of the dominant land.[81]

11.69 If the title to the servient land is not registered and that land is transferred, a legal easement of light will bind the transferee whenever it was created. An equitable

[79] Examples of equitable easements of light are given in para 11.47.
[80] See ch 2, para 2.15.
[81] LRA 2002, s 4.

easement of light created on or after 1 January 1926 will bind any transferee if it has been registered as a Class D(iii) land charge, but if not so registered will not bind a purchaser of a legal estate in the servient land for money or money's worth. An equitable easement created before 1 January 1926 will bind all transferees of the servient land except a bona fide purchaser of a legal estate in that land for valuable consideration without actual or constructive notice of the easement.

2. Registered Land

11.70 Where title to the dominant land is registered, a transfer of that land in the correct form will pass the benefit of an easement of light appurtenant to that land unless that easement is expressly excluded from the transfer. Section 62 of the Law of Property Act 1925 applies to transfers of land with registered title.[82]

11.71 Where title to the servient land is registered an easement of light appurtenant to the dominant land and created before 13 October 2003 will bind any transferee of the servient land, since it has effect as an overriding interest.

11.72 A legal easement appurtenant to the dominant land created on or after 13 October 2003 will bind a transferee of the servient land with registered title if either (a) it is protected by notice in the charges register of the servient land or (b) it is an overriding interest by virtue of the operation of the three principles described earlier.[83] Normally an easement of light will achieve the status of an overriding interest, and so bind a transferee of the servient land, because it has been exercised in the year preceding the day of the disposition of the servient land.

11.73 An equitable easement of light created on or after 13 October 2003 will not bind a purchaser of the servient land with registered title unless the easement is protected at the time of the disposition of the servient land by a notice in the charges register of the registered title of that land.

3. Grants of Leases

11.74 If a landlord's interest has the benefit of an easement of light, whether created by deed or by prescription, the grant of a lease of the property or any part of it will normally transfer the benefit of that easement to the tenant. Such a transfer as a part of the lease will have effect by virtue of section 62 of the Law of Property Act 1925 unless there is an express provision in the lease to the contrary effect. The same will be true of an underlease which will pass to the underlessee any rights of light held by the underlessor. However, if the headlease has expressly excluded the

[82] See ch 4, section (C) for the operation of s 62.
[83] See para 11.47 et seq.

grant to the lessee of any rights of light over other property, the lessee will not have any such rights to pass to an underlessee, so that none will pass.

It appears that if the landlord of the dominant building is in the course of establishing the 20-year period of enjoyment of light over the servient land needed to acquire an easement by prescription under section 3 of the Prescription Act 1832, and grants a lease of the dominant building, the tenant can complete the residue of 20 years of enjoyment and then assert a right of light over the servient land for the benefit of his leasehold interest. A reason is said to be that the inchoate right of the landlord passes to the tenant under section 62 of the Law of Property Act 1925.[84] Whether in truth a tenant in the situation here described needs to rely on section 62 in order to be able to complete the 20 years and acquire an easement by prescription is doubtful, and this matter is discussed below.[85] 11.75

This situation can cause difficulties where a prescriptive easement of light has been acquired in respect of the apertures in a building which is divided or sub-divided into a number of units, each of which is let on tenancies including short tenancies. An instance of this situation would be a house or other building which has been converted into a number of flats and let on short-term or periodic tenancies. If the property as a whole has gained an easement of light by prescription through its apertures then, unless a particular lease of a particular part contains an express exclusion of the transfer of that easement, the benefit of the easement will be transferred to each tenant. The difficulty which may arise is that a developer of neighbouring property may be able to come to terms with the owner of the whole building, but each of the tenants will in principle be entitled himself individually to assert the easement of light which appertains to that part of the whole building which is let to him. On the face of it, each individual tenant has an equal right and opportunity to assert his easement of light and to take steps to prevent or limit the offending development. This situation may create practical difficulties for a developer, who may have to deal with a substantial number of people. It also may make it difficult for the landlord as the owner of the whole building, since any rights which he may be willing to give up may not be satisfactory to the developer unless each of the tenants is willing to join in the necessary arrangement or release of rights. The prudent course is that landlords granting leases, particularly short-term leases, of property or parts of property should consider carefully whether the transfer of any subsisting easement of light is to pass to each individual tenant, and should take steps to see that if this is not intended there is an express exclusion of such a transfer and of the operation of section 62 of the Law of Property Act 1925 in the lease or tenancy agreement. 11.76

There is a possible element of confusion on this matter. Where the dominant building has the benefit of a right of light over adjoining property created expressly or by implication or by the operation of section 62 of the Law of Property Act 1925, 11.77

[84] *Midtown Ltd v City of London Real Property Co Ltd* [2005] EWHC 33 (Ch), [2005] 1 EGLR 65 [23].
[85] See para 11.77.

it is a matter of choice whether the dominant owner when he grants a lease of the whole or a part of the dominant building passes the benefit of that easement to a tenant. The law as explained is that the right of light so created will be passed to the tenant unless there is an express statement to the contrary within the lease. The situation is less clear where the right held by the lessor of the dominant tenement has been acquired by prescription. One would expect that in the absence of some express provision in the lease, the benefit of that prescriptive right would pass to a tenant either automatically or by the operation of section 62 of the Law of Property Act 1925. The question is whether the tenant would need to rely on any transfer of the right to him. The acquisition of a prescriptive easement depends on 20 years of the enjoyment of the access of light to the dominant building. The enjoyment does not have to be by the same person throughout the period or even by persons who hold throughout the period the same interest or title.[86] All that section 3 of the Prescription Act 1832 requires is that the access and use of light 'shall have been enjoyed therewith [with the dominant tenement] for the full period of twenty years without interruption'. Section 3 of the Act says nothing about who has to hold a particular interest in the dominant building during the 20 years. It refers only to the actual existence of the enjoyment of the access of the light for the 20-year period. Therefore, if a lease is granted to a tenant after a prescriptive right has been acquired by his landlord in reliance on the 20 years of enjoyment by the landlord or by a predecessor in title of the landlord or by an earlier tenant of the property, there seems no reason in principle why the tenant should not himself be able to claim the benefit of the prescriptive easement relying on the simple fact of the 20 years of the enjoyment of light (together with any period of enjoyment by him after the grant to him of the lease) without the need to show that the benefit of the easement had been passed to him expressly or impliedly by any deed or transfer.

11.78 In the same way, if at the date of the grant of the lease only a part of the 20 years of the enjoyment of light had passed, the tenant should be able to rely on the previous period of enjoyment of the light and to aggregate that period to any further period during which he enjoyed the light so as to be able to claim a prescriptive right of light at the end of the so aggregated 20-year period.[87] The only way in which the landlord could prevent a tenant relying on the previously acquired prescriptive right of light, or relying on the period of less than 20 years during which the acquisition of the right was inchoate, would be by way of a clear express provision in the lease that these benefits could not accrue to the tenant.

[86] *Midtown Ltd v City of London Real Property Co Ltd* [2005] EWHC 33 (Ch), [2005] 1 EGLR 65.

[87] If this line of reasoning is correct it would be unnecessary for the tenant to rely on the passing of the benefit of the 'inchoate' rights under s 62 of the Law of Property Act 1925, as was held to occur in the *Midtown* decision.

12

Reform

(A) PROPOSALS FOR REFORM

1. General

The purpose of this book is to describe the current law of rights of light. It is a subject which has been part of the law for centuries and it is generally recognised that this area of the law of property has played and will continue to play an important part in protecting property rights. Even so, considerable dissatisfaction is sometimes voiced at aspects of the law, and this has engendered some pressure for change. There has in recent years been considerable support for reform and significant changes are likely to occur in future years, so that it may be helpful to practitioners and property owners to mention briefly the main areas of dissatisfaction and the way in which reform is likely to proceed. 12.1

Few would argue for a complete abolition of legally protected rights of light and it is generally accepted that such rights should continue to be protected as a part of the law of easements. Yet a proposal has been put forward for the abolition of the further creation of easements of light by prescription, which is the main source of new easements of light, and this proposal got so far as to obtain the provisional support of the Law Commission.[1] As is explained later the Law Commission subsequently changed its mind on this fundamental matter. A good starting point for a consideration of reform is to mention the main areas of dissatisfaction with, and criticism of, the current law. Six such areas can be identified. 12.2

The first matter is the general test for the standard of natural light which is protected by an easement of light. That which is protected is a sufficiency of light for the reasonable enjoyment of property according to the ordinary notions of mankind.[2] The very language of the test indicates its uncertainty and its subjective nature and the question is whether something more precise could be devised as a general criterion. 12.3

The second matter follows from the first and is the method used for the detailed application of the general test. A powerful tool which has been developed and used 12.4

[1] See para 12.21 et seq.
[2] See ch 3 and see *Colls v Home & Colonial Stores Ltd* [1904] AC 179.

for three-quarters of a century to determine whether the amount of light which remains after an obstruction is sufficient to satisfy the general test is the Waldram diagram methodology with its 'sky factor' and '50-50' rule.[3] While this methodology is widely used by rights of light surveyors and is often used in courts, it is not without its critics.

12.5 The third matter, and one of cardinal importance, is the acquisition of rights of light by prescription.[4] Prescription is of course a feature of the acquisition of all types of easement (as well as other rights, such as those over village greens), but such has been the level of criticism of it when it is applied to easements of light that an outright abolition of the prescriptive acquisition of rights of light has attracted considerable support, including at one time that of the Law Commission in a consultation paper. A strong driver of the criticism is the impediment which prescriptively acquired rights of light are said to constitute to new development in urban areas. The latest proposals of the Law Commission have stepped back from the radical solution of outright abolition, but much-needed reforms to the unwieldy law on prescription generally are now proposed and these will affect rights of light.

12.6 The fourth matter is the Rights of Light Act 1959, the chief effect of which is to provide a statutory method of preventing the running of the prescription period and so preventing the acquisition of rights of light by prescription.[5] A sensible reform here involves retaining a statutory mechanism for preventing the acquisition of rights of light by prescription but without the procedural complications in the current legislation.

12.7 The fifth matter is that which, after the question of prescription, is the main criticism about the impact of rights of light. The matter is the availability and nature of remedies for an infringement of a right of light. Developers are understandably concerned about the risk of an injunction, which could cause large financial loss if a development is prevented in whole or in part or if it is substantially delayed. Certainty is sought, but this is perhaps unobtainable, given the nature of an injunction as a discretionary and uncertain remedy. If an injunction is not sought or not granted, the general tendency of the courts over recent decades has been to award damages for a breach of a right of light on a 'voluntary release' basis, that is the amount of money that would have been agreed between parties negotiating reasonably for the voluntary release of the easement of light to the extent necessary to permit the unlawful development. The general result of this trend has been uncertainty on the likely amount of damages and a likelihood that the damages will be substantially higher than would previously have been the case. More certainty in the law is sought on these aspects of the law of remedies, although certainty is not easy to obtain.[6]

[3] See ch 6.
[4] Prescription is explained in ch 5.
[5] See ch 9 for a description of the operation of the Rights of Light Act 1959.
[6] Remedies are explained in ch 7.

The sixth matter is the termination of rights of light.[7] An easement of light may be extinguished or overridden by an agreed release or by the operation of statutory powers. However, an implied release by way of abandonment is difficult to establish and the power of the Lands Chamber of the Upper Tribunal under section 84 of the Law of Property Act 1925 to order the discharge or modification of restrictive covenants does not extend to easements. This situation is regarded as defective and there are proposals for reform in both of the areas of law just mentioned. 12.8

All of these matters have been considered in recent years as subjects for possible reform either by provisions specifically applicable to rights of light or as part of a wider reform of the law of easements. In some cases detailed reforms have been proposed, while in other cases it has been said that the development of the law or of the practical application of the law is for the courts or for the surveying profession. The remainder of this chapter summarises and comments on the main proposals for change as well as mentioning certain other areas where no reforms are proposed but to which alterations in the current law could profitably extend. 12.9

2. Law Commission Proposals

Over recent years the Law Commission has produced a number of papers and reports on easements generally and, most recently, on rights of light in particular with proposals for reform on a number of the topics just mentioned. The relevant documents are as follows. 12.10

(i) *Consultation Paper on Easements, Covenants and Profits a Prendre* (Law Com No 186, 2008).
(ii) *Making Law Work, Easements, Covenants and Profits a Prendre* (Law Com No 237, 2011). This report contained a draft Bill. In this chapter it is sometimes referred to as the Easements report.
(iii) *Rights to Light—A Consultation Paper* (Law Com No 210, 2013).
(iv) *Rights to Light* (Law Com No 356, 2014). This report included a draft of provisions to be added to the draft Easements Bill of 2011 and a draft of a separate Rights of Light Bill.

The Government have not yet responded to the 2011 Easements report of the Commission, or to the 2011 draft Easements Bill. In the 2014 report the Commission stated that the separate Rights to Light Bill should not be enacted without the prior, or simultaneous, enactment of the 2011 Easements Bill as amended by the 2014 report. It is therefore not known how or when the Government will deal with the various recommendations presented to them.[8] Some of the recommendations 12.11

[7] See ch 8.

[8] The Government do not necessarily implement by legislation the whole or parts of all recommendations of the Law Commission. For example, no action was taken on the report of the Commission on the *Law of Compulsory Purchase and Compensation* (Law Com No 286, 2003).

of the Law Commission may be contentious but others have been widely welcomed, such as the rationalisation of the present unsatisfactory and confused law of prescription. It is inevitable that any discussion of reform should concentrate on those aspects of the current law of rights of light considered in the reports of 2011 and 2014 and on the recommendations of the Law Commission.

(B) THE STANDARD OF LIGHT

1. The General Test

12.12 There is a frequently held view that a person with the benefit of a right of light is entitled to prevent any reduction in the light which he receives over the property against which the right exists. Although there may have once been authority for this view, it has been established since the *Colls* decision in 1904 that the entitlement is not to an absolute amount of light, but only to that amount of light which is sufficient for the reasonable use of the dominant building.[9] The law has been established in this sense for well over a century. The only criticism of it is one of lack of certainty.

12.13 It is difficult to see what could sensibly replace this admittedly imprecise test. It has been suggested in a response to a consultation carried out by the Law Commission that the whim of the judiciary should be replaced by a fixed proportion of a room which has to be sufficiently lit before the room as a whole can be said to be sufficiently lit.[10] The Bar Council has suggested to the Law Commission that there should be a definitive and statutory list of factors to be taken into account by a court when deciding whether a room is sufficiently lit in any given situation.[11] A plea has been made for harmonising the techniques used by courts to decide whether there has been a violation of a private right of light and the policy advice on which local planning authorities work in deciding whether to grant permission for a development which may have an adverse effect on the light which passes to nearby properties.[12]

12.14 It is sometimes not practical to achieve objective criteria and certainty in areas of the law and, despite the intellectual attraction of producing such a certain and objective test as opposed to the uncertain *Colls* criterion, it is unlikely that

[9] *Colls v Home & Colonial Stores Ltd* [1904] AC 179.

[10] *Rights to Light* (Law Com No 356, 2014), para 3.29. The suggestion begs the question of what is meant by 'sufficiently lit' for the proportion of the room selected.

[11] ibid, para 3.30.

[12] ibid, para 3.33. See ch 10 for the BRE Guide and the advice given in it to local planning authorities. There may be a degree of practical harmonisation in the view tentatively advanced in the Supreme Court by Lord Sumption in *Lawrence v Fen Tigers Ltd* [2004] UKSC 13, [2014] AC 822 [161] that an injunction to prevent an infringement of a right of light should not generally be granted when planning permission has been given for the offending development. See ch 7, para 7.37.

in practice that can be done. The view of the Law Commission, both before and after consultation on the question, is that no change should be made to the general test.[13]

A further suggestion within the same general context is that a different test should be prescribed for residential and commercial properties. In fact a linguistic distinction is drawn between the two categories of buildings in the classic formulation of the test in *Colls*.[14] In practice, courts are able to understand that in some circumstances a residential property, particularly in a quiet or secluded area, may reasonably require greater protection from loss of natural light than a large office in a busy urban area. Any attempt to formulate a different linguistic test for the two types of property would run into various difficulties, including: 12.15

(a) that it would be difficult to draft with any precision the different formulations;
(b) that a property may be changed from one category of use to the other; and
(c) that certain types of commercial property may require light as much as do residential properties.

2. Alterations to the Dominant Building

The present law is that the owner of the dominant building can alter the use or the internal layout of that building so as to increase the burden on the servient land, with the possible result of reducing the capacity of the servient owner to carry out a redevelopment of the servient land. Furthermore it appears that in deciding whether a proposed new structure on the servient land will constitute an actionable injury, regard must be not only to the use and layout of the dominant building at the date of the proposed development but also to any different use and layout of that building which can be reasonably anticipated in the future.[15] There is some understandable dissatisfaction at this state of affairs and the burden which it casts on the servient land. There is much to be said for the protection afforded by a right of light, at least when acquired by prescription,[16] being confined so as to protect only the same or substantially the same use and internal layout of the 12.16

[13] *Rights to Light* (Law Com No 356, 2014), paras 3.20 and 3.72.

[14] *Colls v Home & Colonial Stores Ltd* [1904] AC 179, 208 (Lord Lindley).

[15] See ch 3, para 3.40 et seq, and see *Carr-Saunders v Dick McNeill Associates* [1986] 1 WLR 922. The protection will not extend to a use of the dominant building which requires an extraordinarily high amount of light. Obviously if a development is carried out on the servient land and the dominant owner does not seek to prevent this development, perhaps because it will not have a sufficiently adverse effect on the current use or layout of the dominant building, the dominant owner cannot later seek the removal or modification of the development on the ground that it will have a more severe effect on a different use or layout of the dominant building commenced or proposed by him.

[16] If the easement has been created by an express provision in a deed then the parties can themselves prescribe the extent of the right and protection afforded to the dominant land.

dominant building as existed at the time of the acquisition of the easement by the completion of the prescription period.[17]

12.17 A further form of alteration which may be carried out to the dominant building is alterations to windows within it. The courts have built up a significant body of case law on the effect of various types of alterations to windows which has been discussed earlier.[18] The position reached appears broadly sensible and the best way of dealing with alterations of this nature is probably by further consideration in decided cases as different combinations of facts arise. The question of the transfer of rights of light to new windows in a new redeveloped building is mentioned later in this chapter.[19]

3. Application of the General Test

12.18 Rights of light disputes generally centre on two issues, which are (a) whether the dominant building has an easement of light over the servient land, and (b) whether a development on the servient land will constitute, or has constituted, an infringement of that easement. The second issue is to be determined by the application of the general test as stated in the *Colls* decision.[20] The critical question is often the detailed application of the test to the particular physical circumstances of the two properties. There are several sources of evidence by which a court can decide whether the dominant building will retain sufficient light for its reasonable use after the erection of an obstruction on the servient land. The judge can view the property himself, but if the proposed work on the servient land has not been carried out it may not be possible to gauge its effect by visual inspection alone. The general impression of experts on the effect of the proposed development can be heard, but except in obvious cases this may not be very helpful especially in the event of dispute between the experts. What in practice usually occurs is that an analysis is carried out using the Waldram methodology.[21]

12.19 This methodology offers considerable advantages. It is an objective method of answering the essentially subjective question posed by the general test established in *Colls*. There is general agreement among rights of light surveyors on the

[17] The general test for the survival of prescriptive and implied easements after changes in the use of the dominant property has been explained by Neuberger LJ in *McAdams Homes Ltd v Robinson* [2004] EWCA Civ 214, [2004] 3 EGLR 93. It should be borne in mind that in this area of the law there are two logically separate questions. The first question is whether, in deciding that an obstruction on the servient land is or is not an actionable injury, changes to the dominant building made since the easement of light was acquired can be taken into account. The second question is whether for the same purpose any future change to the use of the dominant building which can be reasonably anticipated can be taken into account.

[18] This subject is examined in ch 3, section (C)3 and 4.

[19] See paras 12.46–12.49.

[20] *Colls v Home & Colonial Stores Ltd* [1904] AC 179.

[21] This methodology is described in ch 6.

application of the measurements and calculations. However, there is no overall agreement on the efficacy of the test as something which provides a satisfactory answer to the question of whether a room will remain sufficiently lit after an obstruction to its light. There have been recent suggestions that the Waldram methodology, with its 0.2 per cent sky factor criterion, provides a substantial under-estimate of the light necessary for the reasonable use of premises. It has been suggested that the situation could be remedied by using a higher required sky factor, say 0.4 per cent, as the criterion, but this might substantially increase the burden on servient land and make redevelopments substantially more difficult. A further suggestion is that the vertical sky component test, as explained in the BRE Guide, should be used as a more satisfactory criterion.[22]

Statutory reform cannot solve these technical problems. What is needed is a definitive agreement and guide by the surveying profession on the use of the Waldram methodology and the standard of light required by the application of that methodology as a means of answering the general test established by the courts and on the use of other methods of deciding what is a sufficiency of light.[23] Even then it must be remembered that a court is not bound to accept the judgment of experts, whatever methodology is used. 12.20

(C) PRESCRIPTION

1. Prescription Generally

The acquisition of easements by prescription has a long history in English law, going back to medieval times.[24] In many ways the process has become unsatisfactory, notably by reason of the unsatisfactory language of the Prescription Act 1832 and the existence of three separate forms of prescription: common law prescription, the doctrine of lost modern grant, and prescription under the Prescription Act 1832. The situation is further complicated by the existence within the Prescription Act 1832 of different provisions for the acquisition of easements generally under section 2 and of easements of light under section 3. The Law Commission made general and welcome recommendations for the reform of the law of prescription in its 2011 Easements report, and these were to apply to rights of light.[25] 12.21

[22] These criticism are explained in greater detail in ch 6, section (F). The BRE Guide is Paul Littlefair, *Site Layout and Planning for Daylight and Sunlight—A Guide to Good Practice*, 2nd edn (Watford, BRE Trust, 2011). It is explained in ch 10, section (C).

[23] The various criticisms of the Waldram methodology are also discussed elsewhere, such as in *Gale on Easements*, 19th edn (London, Sweet & Maxwell, 2012), paras 7.30–7.31 and in the recent report of the Law Commission, *Rights of Light* (Law Com No 356, 2014), paras 3.8–3.13.

[24] See ch 5, para 5.1 et seq.

[25] Law Commission, *Making Law Work, Easements, Covenants and Profits a Prendre* (Law Com No 237, 2011). The Government have not responded to the report or the draft Bill included in the report.

The essence of the new proposals is that there should be a single new statutory method of prescription founded on 20 years of continuous qualifying use which would apply only between freehold owners.

12.22 There are those who say that while prescription should still apply to the acquisition of easements generally, albeit with the modifications and reforms proposed by the Law Commission, prescription should be abolished as regards rights of light or, possibly, be amended or limited in some way as regards such rights. When in 2013 the Law Commission published its consultation paper, which proposed the abolition of the acquisition of rights of light by prescription, responses from consultees were divided.[26] For example, the Bar Council stated that prescription should be abolished for rights of light but the Property Litigation Association considered that to remove the prescriptive acquisition of rights of light would be considered arbitrary and unnecessary. About a third of those who responded were in favour of abolishing prescription for rights of light.

12.23 It may seem surprising that the radical step of the abolition of an aspect of the law established for centuries, acquiring a right of light in favour of property by 20 years of use and enjoyment of that light, should have received the provisional support of the Law Commission in its consultation paper and the support of a third of those who made their views known in the consultation process. There were a number of arguments for abolition. It was said that for easements of light the prescription process happened by chance, since it involved no positive actions by the dominant owner known to the servient owner, such as were necessary to establish a positive easement such as a right of way. It was also said that the law was not generally understood. However, the first observation is true of any negative easement such as an easement of support for buildings, and as to the second observation, it can hardly be supposed that the law of easements generally has a widespread understanding. The other main thread of criticism of prescription and rights of light was its inhibiting effect on redevelopment of land. An allied point was that the existence of easements of light was used as a means of extracting ransom sums which increased the cost of developments. In fact the operation of rights of light by prescription has been preventable for many years by the use of the mechanism under the Rights of Light Act 1959 and the Law Commission has proposed a simpler and more effective statutory process to be used for the same purpose, which is described below.[27]

12.24 Having received responses to consultation and having weighed the competing arguments, the Law Commission has recently altered its provisional view and has recommended that rights of light should remain capable of being acquired by prescription.[28] It appears that both the balance of opinion and the merits are in

[26] Law Commission, *Rights to Light—A Consultation Paper* (Law Com No 210, 2013).

[27] See paras 12.39–12.41.

[28] Law Commission, *Rights to Light* (Law Com No 356, 2014). Ch 8 of the report contains a discussion on the economic impact of rights of light disputes.

favour of this course. The Commission has also rejected the suggestion that some special form of prescription should apply to rights of light.

2. The Proposed New Principles

As stated earlier, it is generally accepted that the present law on the acquisition of easements by prescription is unsatisfactory. The law is ancient and complex, and the attempt at reform in the Prescription Act 1832, now nearly two centuries old, was unsatisfactory and introduced problems of its own.[29] The main perceived deficiencies are as follows. 12.25

(a) There are three separate methods of prescription, each with its own rules, common law prescription, the doctrine of lost modern grant, and prescription under the Prescription Act 1832. The methods may be relied upon as alternative ways of establishing a prescriptive right. This is obviously unsatisfactory.
(b) There are different rules for prescription as regards easements generally and as regards rights of light. There is no good reason for special rules to apply to the acquisition by prescription of an easement of light.[30]
(c) Under the Prescription Act 1832 the prescription period has to be a period immediately before an issue relating to the matter arises for decision in a court. This requirement does not apply to the two other methods of prescription.
(d) There is uncertainty on whether and to what extent the various forms of prescription can operate only as between freeholders.
(e) Prescription is generally founded on the fiction that at some time in the past there was a grant of the right even though it is not now available.[31] There is no need to cling to this legal fiction. The Law Commission in its report in 2011 on easements and other property rights proposed comprehensive reform.[32]

Assuming that prescription is to be continued as a means of the acquisition of easements, an initial question is the length of the prescription period. A 20-year period may have had its origin in the 20-year limitation period established by the 12.26

[29] The rules governing prescription are explained in ch 5.

[30] One of the consequences of the special treatment of rights of light under the Prescription Act 1832 is that rights of light have come to be regarded as 'an exception to many rules': see *Sovmots Investments Ltd v Secretary of State for the Environment* [1979] AC 144, 176 (Lord Edmund-Davies), citing *Megarry & Wade, The Law of Real Property*, 4th edn (London, Sweet & Maxwell, 1975) 838, and referring to *Broomfield v Williams* [1897] 1 Ch 602.

[31] It appears that this fiction does not apply to the acquisition of easements of light by prescription under s 3 of the Prescription Act 1832. See ch 5, para 5.33(f).

[32] Law Commission, *Making Land Work: Easements, Covenants and Profits a Prendre* (Law Com No 237, 2011). The report contained a draft Bill.

Limitation Act 1623. This period was applied to the doctrine of lost modern grant, and 20 years is the period required under the Prescription Act 1832.[33] It seems unnecessary to alter this period, and the Law Commission has recommended its retention for the purposes of the new principles.[34]

12.27 The Commission has also recommended that the same rules for prescription should apply to rights of light as apply to easements generally.[35]

12.28 The use of the servient land which is to give rise to a prescriptive easement is described as a qualifying use. That use, as well as having to be for a period of 20 years, must have the characteristics that is continuous and is without force, without stealth and without permission. In addition, the use must not be a use which is contrary to the criminal law unless it can be rendered lawful by the dispensation of the servient owner.[36]

12.29 Under section 4 of the Prescription Act 1832 the use which creates a prescriptive easement under the statute has to be 'next before some suit or action where the claim or matter to which such period may relate shall have been or shall be brought into question'. This requirement does not apply to the acquisition of easements by common law prescription or under the doctrine of lost modern grant. There are arguments for retaining this rule since if a period of 20 years ending at any past time may be relied upon there may be evidential problems in establishing the period of use or in rebutting the existence of the period of use. Nonetheless the Law Commission did not favour the retention of the rule and the 20-year period of continuous qualifying use may end at any time.[37]

12.30 The qualifying use for 20 years must be continuous, as under the existing law. There would therefore be no possibility of combining together different periods, such as one period of 15 years of use and then a later separate period of five years of use, to create the required 20-year prescription period. The use over the 20-year period need not have been by the same person, and successive periods of continuous use by different owners of the dominant property can be relied upon, as under the existing law.

12.31 It is proposed that the qualifying use must be carried out by and against a freeholder. If a prescriptive easement arises when the servient land is let it can be enforced against the tenant and the freeholder.[38]

[33] The Prescription Act 1832 also refers to a 40-year period for certain purposes, but this has no application to rights of light.

[34] The Easements report, para 3.123(1).

[35] ibid, paras 3.119, 3.154–3.160.

[36] This is the modern language which replaces, although does not alter the sense of, the present requirement that, save for easements of light acquired under the Prescription Act 1832, the use has to be as of right, which is often described by the latin words *nec vi, nec clam, nec precario*. The newly stated requirement is to apply to rights of light in the same way as to other easements. See ch 5, section (C)1, and see paras 3.123(2) and 3.132(3) of the Easements report. The recommendation as to a use in breach of the criminal law is said to correspond to the existing law: see ch 5, section (F).

[37] Easements report, paras 3.131–3.133.

[38] ibid, paras 3.144–3.151.

3. Notices of Proposed Obstruction

It is said that one of the greatest problems for developers who apprehend rights of light claims is the uncertainty not only on whether an injunction may be granted to prevent their development but also on when an application may be made for an injunction and an injunction may be granted. One apprehension is that an injunction may be granted when a development is under way, or even after it has been completed. The concern is said to derive in part from the decision in *HKRUK II (CHC) v Heaney*[39] in which an injunction was granted ordering the removal of the two top storeys of a recently constructed development even though there had been a previous period of negotiation between the parties and even though the claimant had not sought an interim injunction. In fact there was nothing in the previous authorities which suggested that a mandatory injunction could never be granted in these circumstances. It is suggested that the decision of the Supreme Court in *Lawrence v Fen Tigers Ltd*[40] in 2014 makes it less likely that a mandatory injunction would be granted in similar circumstances today. 12.32

In order to meet this perceived difficulty for developers, the Law Commission in its 2014 report recommended a notice of proposed obstruction procedure.[41] The essence of the proposed procedure is that a developer intending to develop servient land will be able to serve on the owner of any dominant building or buildings which he selects a notice of proposed obstruction (NPO) which will describe the proposed development. The dominant owner will then have eight months to commence proceedings for an injunction to prevent the proposed development. If the dominant owner fails to do so he will lose any entitlement to an injunction but any right to damages will remain. The object is to let the developer know that a time has come after which there is certainty that all risk of an injunction has passed.[42] 12.33

The persons who can serve an NPO will be the freehold owner, or a tenant with more than five years outstanding, of the servient land. It is recommended that the exact content of an NPO will be prescribed by regulations but obviously a notice will have to describe the proposed development on the servient land. The description may be by way of a precisely detailed building with exact dimensions or by way of a three dimensional envelope within which any development must take place. Other material will have to be contained in the notice including a description of the dominant and the servient land and the consequence of the dominant owner not being able to claim an injunction if he does not commence proceedings for an injunction within a time to be specified in the notice which must be not less than eight months. 12.34

[39] *HKRUK II (CHC) v Heaney* [2010] EWHC 2245 (Ch), [2010] 3 EGLR 15.

[40] *Lawrence v Fen Tigers Ltd* [2014] UKSC 13, [2014] AC 822. See ch 7 for a discussion of this recent authority, which was a case on noise nuisance.

[41] Law Commission, *Rights to Light* (Law Com No 356, 2014), ch 6.

[42] In the current vernacular, the dominant owner will be required 'to put up or shut up', at least as far as the threat of an injunction goes.

12.35 An NPO must be served on a person with a freehold or leasehold interest in the dominant building. These categories are thought to encompass everyone who may have an interest in the dominant building which is capable of being protected by a right of light.

12.36 There would be provision for the withdrawal of an NPO. However, multiple NPOs served on a dominant building would be prohibited so that if one NPO is served, and the period for the commencement of proceedings for an injunction has not expired and a further NPO is served, both NPOs would be deemed to be withdrawn. It will be possible to register an NPO as a local land charge, and this will make it binding on successors in title of the person originally served.

12.37 As stated, the minimum time which could be specified in an NPO for the effective commencement of proceedings for an injunction will be eight months. A notice may specify a longer period. The parties would be able to agree in writing to extend the period for commencing proceedings. Such an agreement would be useful if the expiry date for commencing proceedings was approaching and serious discussions were under way. The protection given to the servient owner by the service of an NPO is that if no proceedings for an injunction are commenced within the eight months or other longer specified period, the servient owner knows that there is no risk that an injunction will be granted to prevent the development on the servient land specified in the notice. This immunity is not permanent and would end 10 years after the deadline for responding to the notice.

12.38 The proposed NPO procedure was the subject of substantial consultation by the Law Commission and is regarded as broadly fair, while providing a degree of welcome certainty to developers. The position of the parties under the procedure, if and when it is embodied in legislation in accordance with the recommendations of the Law Commission, may be summarised as follows.

(a) A developer will not be bound to serve an NPO. If he does not do so he will lose the prospect of immunity from an injunction. Of course, if he did not serve a notice and an injunction was sought against him he could still contend that the court should in its discretion refuse an injunction. It may be that the fact that no NPO has been served will be one of the factors to be taken into account by a court in favour of the grant of an injunction.
(b) A person serving an NPO would incur a statutory obligation to pay to a recipient the reasonable costs of obtaining legal and surveying advice on matters arising from the notice.
(c) There would be nothing in law to prevent a developer starting his development within the period prescribed in the NPO for the commencement of injunction proceedings. However, if the servient owner does interfere with the rights of light of the dominant owner during the period allowed that will not prevent the grant of an injunction to restrain that interference even after the end of the permitted period.[43]

[43] It seems that in para 6.84 of the 2014 report of the Law Commission the words 'the dominant owner' in the third line are an error for 'the servient owner'. The position is clarified in Sch 10 to the draft Bill published with the report.

(d) A dominant owner (or his successor in title, if the NPO has been registered as a local land charge) will be prevented from seeking an injunction against the development specified in the notice if he does not commence proceedings claiming an injunction within the eight months or longer period specified in the notice or within any extended period agreed in writing.[44]

(e) The immunity against an injunction will benefit the servient land for 10 years from the end of the period specified for commencing proceedings.

(f) A dominant owner is not prevented from seeking damages for an infringement of his right of light. Damages on the voluntary release basis (which are sometimes called equitable damages) in lieu of an injunction may be awarded even though the period during which an injunction can be claimed has expired.

4. Light Interruption Certificates

Prior to the Rights of Light Act 1959, the only way in which a servient owner could prevent the establishment against him of an easement of light by prescription was to erect an actual obstruction on the servient land. The 1959 Act permitted the notional obstruction of light by a light obstruction notice, but the procedure is cumbersome, involving an application to the Lands Chamber of the Upper Tribunal for a certificate that proper notice has been given to those affected and allowing a year for the notice to be challenged by legal proceedings. The procedure under the 1959 Act is linked to the provisions in sections 3 and 4 of the Prescription Act 1832 for the acquisition of easements of light by prescription.[45] The procedure under the Rights of Light Act 1959 appears to be used less extensively than would be in the interests of landowners, perhaps because of its complexity and perhaps because of a simple absence of knowledge of its availability and protective effect. 12.39

The Law Commission has proposed in its 2014 report a much simpler and more effective procedure. The freeholder or a tenant with a lease having more than seven years to run of any land can create a light interruption certificate. The certificate specifies the land of the person making it and the land over which the acquisition of rights of light by prescription is intended to be prevented. The certificate is registered as a local land charge as against the latter land. The effect of the certificate is to terminate the running of the prescription period in favour of the land identified in the certificate as against the land of the maker of the certificate. There is no need for notification to the owner of the former land since there is nothing that he can do. The certificate will have no effect on easements of light already in existence (unlike the procedure under the 1959 Act which may have such an effect). 12.40

[44] Proceedings are commenced by issuing a claim form in the High Court or the county court under the Civil Procedure Rules.

[45] See ch 9.

Purchasers of land which may have acquired a right of light by prescription will be able to ascertain by searching the local land charges register whether that acquisition has been prevented by a registered light interruption certificate. Equally purchasers of land against which a right of light may have been acquired by prescription will be able to search the register to ascertain whether that acquisition has been prevented by the registration of a certificate.

12.41 The proposal is a simple and effective procedure. The acquisition by prescription of easements of light can readily be prevented. If the reform is enacted it will presumably become standard conveyancing practice on the development of new buildings and the purchase of buildings less than 20 years old in urban areas to ensure that certificates are issued and registered as local land charges. Owners of land at any time will be able to establish whether an easement of light has been created by prescription in favour of or against their land by searching the local land charges register. This reform is dependent on the more extensive reform of prescription applicable to easements generally proposed in the draft Bill published by the Law Commission in its Easements report in 2011.

5. The Custom of London

12.42 As explained in Chapter 7,[46] there exists within the City of London a long-established custom which is a part of the law and the effect of which is that existing houses may be rebuilt within the boundaries of the foundation of the former house without there being an infringement of rights of light acquired by common law prescription or prescription under the doctrine of lost modern grant, whatever degree of obstruction to the access of light to other houses is created. The ambit of this particular custom is uncertain. In its origin it appears to have been confined to the effect of the rebuilding of one house as against another house or houses, but more modern authority suggests that it may apply to the rebuilding of commercial buildings. The custom does not apply to the enforcement of prescriptive easements of light which have been acquired under section 3 of the Prescription Act 1832 by reason of the specific language of that statute. There appears to be little justification for retaining an anomalous rule of this nature with a limited geographical extent, with the uncertainty as to its precise impact, and with no application at all to the most frequent instances of the acquisition of prescriptive rights under the 1832 Act. A brief but desirable reform would be to move towards a general law applicable to the whole country by way of the abolition of the custom of London.

[46] Ch 7, section (E).

(D) TERMINATION OF RIGHTS OF LIGHT

12.43 It has been explained in Chapter 8 that rights of light may be extinguished by two methods and may be overridden (and often in effect extinguished) by two statutory methods.[47] Certain of these methods suggest opportunities for reform or clarification and a new statutory method of alteration or discharge of easements generally including rights of light has been suggested.

1. Implied Release

12.44 It is difficult to establish the implied release or abandonment of easements including rights of light.[48] The authorities suggest that even such an act as the blocking-up for a long period of a window in the dominant building may not necessarily amount to an implied release of an easement of light. The unreality of this state of the law creates unnecessary uncertainty. Any implication which depends on an intention to be inferred from facts and events is inherently uncertain as compared to an express statement of intention but a presumption of abandonment derived from a minimum period of non-use would at least introduce an element of certainty. The Law Commission in its Easements report in 2011 proposed that an easement should be presumed to be abandoned after 20 years of non-use. The Commission has now proposed in its 2014 Rights of Light report that the Easements Bill as drafted in its 2011 report should be amended to provide that where a right of light has not been used for a continuous period of five years there should be a rebuttable presumption that the right has been abandoned.[49]

12.45 This appears to be a sensible and welcome reform. It could create a degree of certainty. It would still leave it open to a servient owner to contend that an implied abandonment had occurred for other reasons or by a shorter period of non-use and for a dominant owner to contend that in special circumstances even five years or more of non-use did not lead to an implied abandonment.

2. Redevelopment of the Dominant Building

12.46 The present law is that when a dominant building is redeveloped, rights of light appurtenant to the previous building can in principle be transferred to a new building, provided that there is a sufficient similarity in the cone of light which has passed and will pass to the different windows in the two buildings. The difficulties

[47] Ch 8, paras 8.2 and 8.3.

[48] Ch 8, section (B)1.

[49] Law Commission, *Rights to Light* (Law Com No 356, 2014), paras 7.41–7.48.

in knowing what exactly is the correct legal test and in applying that test have been mentioned.[50] Support for reform has focused on either an arithmetical test which would establish the required degree of similarity between the old and the new windows, or a registration scheme.

12.47 It would be very difficult to formulate an arithmetical test, for instance a requirement that the new window must be in a position not more than one metre forward or back from the old window or that the dimensions of the new window must not differ from those of the old window by more than a stated amount, and the Law Commission has found itself unable to frame such a test which would cater for all possible situations.[51]

12.48 The registration suggestion is that where a window is altered, whether as part of a redevelopment or not, the dominant owner must register his altered right of light as appurtenant to the new or altered window, so that in the absence of registration the new or altered window will not take the benefit of the right of light. There are formidable objections to such a scheme such as the level of detail of the proposed alteration which would require registration and the fact that, while registration might be a prerequisite for a transfer of rights from a previous window to an altered or new window, it could not itself determine whether a transfer was effected as a matter of law. It seems unlikely that this suggestion will find favour, and it is not a part of the most recent proposals of the Law Commission.[52] It is not at present clear what period may elapse between the end of the access to light through windows in the former building and the time at which light enters equivalent windows in a redeveloped building so as to allow rights of light to be transferred. In difficult economic conditions sites can remain demolished and awaiting redevelopment for a considerable time. The presumption of abandonment after five years of non-use of light may be significant when questions of this sort arise.

12.49 The current law on the effect of alterations to existing windows has been worked out in a series of cases concerning different factual situations and a reasonably clear set of guiding principles has emerged. The law on the replacement of windows in a new and redeveloped building is less clear. There are at least three areas of uncertainty which are (a) the exact test to be applied regarding the similarity of cones of light, (b) how long may elapse between the demolition of the old windows and their replacement in a new building, and (c) how the principle that a prescriptive or implied easement does not survive where the character of the dominant building is changed and the burden on the servient land is substantially increased operates in conjunction with the principle that rights of light can be transferred to a new building.[53] The most likely means of clarification of these questions will be when they are further considered by the higher courts.

[50] Ch 3, para 3.67 et seq.

[51] Law Commission, *Rights to Light* (Law Com No 356, 2014), para 7.28.

[52] ibid, paras 7.31–7.40.

[53] See ch 3, section (C)5, for a consideration of these questions.

3. Overriding or Extinguishment by Statute

The Law Commission has proposed that easements including easements of light shall be capable of discharge or modification under section 84 of the Law of Property Act 1925 by the Lands Chamber of the Upper Tribunal and that the grounds for the exercise of this power shall be the same for easements as they now are for restrictive covenants. The existing grounds are not easy to satisfy and the exercise of this power of discharge or modification by the Lands Chamber, or its predecessor, the Lands Tribunal, has been sparing for restrictive covenants. 12.50

The use of the power of local authorities under section 237 of the Town and Country Planning Act 1990 to override easements so as to permit development to go ahead has its own uncertainties. It is uncertain whether and to what extent the power can lawfully be used to assist private developers to override private law rights. It is also less than certain to what extent the power under section 237 once exercised can be used so as to enable not only an initial development but also a further and later development on the land affected to go ahead.[54] There are no proposals for statutory intervention on these questions, and both questions must await further clarification from the higher courts. 12.51

One further matter, however, does require further consideration and probably reform. It has been explained that when there is an infringement of a property right, and an injunction is not granted to prevent or reverse the actions which are unlawful, the damages today are often assessed on a voluntary release basis, that is the amount of money which would be agreed between reasonable parties in a voluntary negotiation for the release of the rights so far as necessary to render that which is to be done or has been done lawful.[55] The overriding of an easement or other rights by the exercise of statutory powers, including by the operation of section 237 of the Town and Country Planning Act 1990, brings about an entitlement to compensation paid to the person with the benefit of the right in question. The compensation will normally be assessed under section 10 of the Compulsory Purchase Act 1965 (a provision which is applied by section 237 of the Town and Country Planning Act 1990). It has been held in the Court of Appeal that in such circumstances the compensation should be confined to the reduction in value of the land with the benefit of the right which has been overridden and should not be equivalent to voluntary release damages.[56] It has also been held that where a restrictive covenant is discharged or modified under section 84 of the Law of Property Act 1925 the compensation should not normally be assessed on a voluntary release basis.[57] It seems incongruous that where a person owning a right such 12.52

[54] See ch 8, paras 8.29 and 8.32 et seq, for an examination of these matters.

[55] See ch 7, section (C), for an explanation of the current law on this subject and see para 12.57 et seq of this chapter for suggestions which have been made for the general reform of this aspect of the law.

[56] *Wrotham Park Settled Estates v Hertsmere Borough Council* [1993] 2 EGLR 15.

[57] *Winter v Traditional and Contemporary Contracts Ltd* [2007] EWCA Civ 1088, [2008] 1 EGLR 80; *Re Stupinsky's Application* [2005] RVR 269.

as a right of light has his right violated and is awarded damages that should be done on a voluntary release basis, so bringing about an award of damages which is often very much greater than that which would be arrived at simply by looking at the reduction in value of the land with the benefit of the right, but where a right of light is overridden by statutory process the compensation has to be confined to the reduction in value, and often lower, basis.[58] A reconsideration of this judge-made element of the law is due.

(E) REMEDIES

12.53 There are two main questions on the availability of remedies to enforce easements of light which have attracted discussion over recent years. The questions are (a) the circumstances in which an injunction will be granted to prevent or reverse a breach of the easement, and (b) the availability and calculation of voluntary release damages if no injunction is sought or granted. The law on injunctions and damages, including voluntary release damages, has been explained in Chapter 7.[59] A recent decision of the Supreme Court in *Lawrence v Fen Tigers Ltd*[60] contains observations on both questions in the context of an action to prevent a nuisance caused by noise.

1. Injunctions

12.54 The recommendations of the Law Commission in its 2014 Report on rights of light have been summarised in Chapter 7.[61] The Commission considered the *Lawrence* decision and the essence of its recommendations on injunctions was that a court should not grant an injunction to prevent or reverse the infringement of a right of light if doing so would be a disproportionate means of enforcing the right. The Commission set out eight specific considerations as those which, together with all other relevant considerations, should guide courts in deciding whether the grant of an injunction would be disproportionate.

[58] The loss of a bargaining opportunity is a part of the compensation as generally assessed under the law of compulsory purchase. See Barnes, *The Law of Compulsory Purchase and Compensation* (Oxford, Hart Publishing, 2014) ch 4.

[59] Other relevant remedies include the making of a declaration by a court, abatement (a form of self-help), and a determination by the Property Chamber of the First-tier Tribunal upon a referral by the Registrar of HM Land Registry. This last remedy is considered in ch 11, section (C).

[60] *Lawrence v Fen Tigers Ltd* [2014] UKSC 13, [2014] AC 822.

[61] Ch 7, section (B)4(i).

The Government have not as yet responded to the 2014 report.[62] There are a number of observations which can be made on the proposals of the Law Commission relating to injunctions in rights of light cases. 12.55

(a) It is not apparent why separate statutory provisions are necessary to govern the exercise by courts of their discretion on whether to grant an injunction in rights of light cases. The jurisdiction to issue an injunction exists in respect of most breaches of property rights, and indeed in respect of most civil wrongs, and there is no obvious characteristic of rights of light disputes which requires special statutory provisions.
(b) The concept of proportionality is derived from continental European law and plays a significant role in public law and administrative law proceedings including the application of the European Convention on Human Rights. It is uncertain what would be gained by the introduction of the concept as a statutory provision into one limited aspect of property law.
(c) In any event, and following the rejection by the Supreme Court in the *Lawrence* decision of the straightjacket of the *Shelfer* rules,[63] it is unlikely that a court would exercise its discretion to grant an injunction if it thought it 'disproportionate' to do so. If the idea of proportionality is as powerful and pervasive as the Law Commission suggests then Judges experienced in the law and its development are well able to take that idea into account.
(d) The principle that a person who suffers a wrong is prima facie entitled to a specific remedy to protect his rights such as an injunction would be abandoned. This may be unfortunate since it deprives courts of a universal and specific starting point in the exercise of their discretion.
(e) It is plainly the law that when a court decides how it is to exercise its discretion, on the grant of a particular remedy or on anything else, that court should take into account and weigh the strength of all relevant considerations. There does not seem to be much to be gained by having eight particular items as a statutory checklist, some of which may not arise in any specific case and some of which, even if they do arise, may have little weight in that case. Other items are of such generality, for instance the conduct of the claimant and the conduct of the defendant, that they could hardly be ignored by any court in any circumstances.[64]

[62] Nor has the Government responded to the 2011 Report of the Commission, Law Com No 237, on easements and other property interests. For a list of Law Commission publications since 2008 relevant to rights of light, see para 12.9.

[63] The *Shelfer* rules are four rules laid down by the Court of Appeal in *Shelfer v City of London Electric Lighting Co* [1895] 1 Ch 287 which stated the circumstances in which an injunction would be refused in nuisance cases. The rules were sometimes applied as though they were mandatory statutory provisions. As explained in ch 7, section (B)3, the Supreme Court in the *Lawrence* decision has now deprived the *Shelfer* rules of that status, if indeed they ever had that status, and this latest development and clarification of this aspect of the law is much to be welcomed.

[64] The authors of *Rights of Light: The Modern Law*, 3rd edn (Bristol, Jordan Publishing, 2014) comment at para 20.19 that the proposal of the Law Commission will be difficult to apply in practice and is unlikely to make the task of the courts and advisers a great deal easier.

12.56 A sensible way forward regarding rights of light and the availability of an injunction would be to state the clear principle as a starting point that a person who establishes that a violation of his property right will occur or has occurred should prima facie be entitled to an injunction and that the burden should be firmly on the wrongdoer to establish why in any particular case and in any specific circumstances an injunction should not be granted against him. The considerations to be taken into account in the exercise of the discretion of the court and in its examination of reasons put forward against an injunction by a defendant can be garnered from the application of common sense and the general guidance given in previous cases by appellate courts. To take an obvious example, the fact that the dominant owner has stood by and watched a development being carried out without protest on the servient land would be a powerful, and often decisive, consideration which would prevent the issue of an injunction to require the removal of the new building. This is an obvious instance of the conduct of one of the parties, here the claimant, being of relevance and of considerable weight and it does not need a statutory provision to tell courts that they should take it into account.

2. Voluntary Release Damages

12.57 It has been explained in Chapter 7 how damages assessed on a voluntary release basis have been awarded in cases involving violations of property and other rights and how this process has received the approval of the highest courts.[65] The decision of the Supreme Court in *Lawrence v Fen Tigers Ltd*[66] in 2014 can be regarded as adding further limited approval to this process although, as the exact issue was not before it, the Court declined to give definitive guidance on when voluntary release damages were an appropriate remedy.

12.58 Damages assessed as the amount which would be agreed in a negotiation between reasonable parties for the voluntary release or modification of a right have much to commend them. As explained damages assessed by such a method provide a real element of compensatory damages[67] and prevent or mitigate the affront that a person can benefit from his own wrong.[68] This last point may appear to some to be unduly moralistic, but there is much to be said for courts articulating in legal rules that which may people would think to be just, especially when that can be done within the compensation principle which underlies the law of damages.

[65] See ch 7, section (C)5.

[66] *Lawrence v Fen Tigers Ltd* [2004] UKSC 13, [2014] AC 822.

[67] See ch 7, section (C)7.

[68] Since voluntary release damages will generally be awarded as some proportion, not exceeding 50 per cent, of the gain made by a defendant from his wrongful acts there is obviously still an element of gain to that defendant from his unlawful conduct. The only way in which this gain could be eliminated would be by an award of restitutionary damages, but that is unlikely ever to happen in rights of light disputes: see ch 7, section (C)12.

Despite these considerations there seems to be a reluctance, particularly among property developers, to disgorge as damages even a modest proportion of the gain which they anticipate making from their wrongful action. The Law Commission considered this area of the law extensively in its 2014 report on *Rights of Light*.[69] One important point in discussing the question in connection with rights of light is that voluntary release damages have been regularly awarded and justified in respect of a variety of property rights and other rights and there seems no particular or logical reason for treating the subject differently for the purposes of rights of light disputes as compared to interferences with other property rights or with private law rights generally. The two most powerful endorsements of voluntary release damages as correct in legal principle have come from a case on breach of a contract of employment, that of the traitor, George Blake, with the Government,[70] and a dispute connected with offshore oil drilling.[71] It does not seem to have been suggested that different principles or methods of calculation should be applied depending on the type of property right in dispute, and no logical reason for such a differentiation has been put forward. 12.59

The Law Commission described 'book value' damages (the reduction in the open market value of the dominant land) as common law damages and voluntary release damages as equitable damages. It is unclear why this distinction is made since equitable damages in their origin mean damages assessed to take account of future wrongs when an injunction is not granted to prevent those future wrongs,[72] and book value damages and voluntary release damages are equally available for the effect of the later wrongs constituted by the erection, or retention, of the unlawful obstruction to light.[73] In any event, and whatever the correct juridical analysis, the Law Commission in its Report considered a number of suggestions all designed to limit in some way the amount of the voluntary release damages which could be awarded. 12.60

The first suggestion was that of limiting voluntary release damages to some arbitrary multiplier (a range of two to five was mooted) of the book value damages. This was an arbitrary and intellectually unsupportable proportion and was rejected as not viable.[74] 12.61

The second suggestion was that voluntary release damages should be capped as either the total value of the dominant property or a percentage of that value. It is particularly difficult to see what logical justification there could be for such a statutory cap and it also was rejected by the Law Commission.[75] 12.62

[69] Law Commission, *Rights to Light* (Law Com No 356, 2014), ch 5.

[70] *Attorney General v Blake* [2001] 1 AC 268 (where restitutionary damages were awarded).

[71] *Pell Frischmann Engineering Ltd v Bow Valley Iran Ltd* [2009] UKPC 45, [2011] 1 WLR 2370.

[72] Originally such damages were authorised by the Chancery Amendment Act 1858 and today are authorised by s 50 of the Senior Courts Act 1981. Neuberger LJ has trodden his own path by describing voluntary release damages as 'quasi equitable': see *Lunn Poly Ltd v Liverpool & Lancashire Properties Ltd* [2006] EWCA Civ 430, [2006] 2 EGLR 29 [29].

[73] See ch 7, section (C)2.

[74] Law Commission, *Rights to Light* (Law Com No 356, 2014), para 5.70.

[75] ibid, paras 5.71–5.73.

12.63 The third suggestion was that voluntary release damages could be based on a percentage of the estimated profit to the wrongdoer from erecting an unlawful obstruction but some lower percentage than had sometimes been decided in the cases should form a fixed percentage or a cap on the level of the percentage. The percentages awarded in the authorities on voluntary release damages relating to infringements of property rights have varied from 5 per cent to 50 per cent. Inevitably each case depends upon the factual circumstances particular to that case and the assumed result of the negotiation between the reasonable parties. It is impossible to see on what rational basis some specified fixed percentage, or maximum percentage, could be fixed. The Law Commission regarded this suggestion as 'the most viable option', but was not prepared to adopt it.[76]

12.64 It has also been pointed out, sensibly and rationally, that if damages are arbitrarily limited in some way so as to constitute less than the true amount due to a claimant when applying the voluntary release method of assessment as an aspect or the compensatory nature of damages then the result may be that the courts would be the more inclined to order an injunction since the adequacy of damages is one of the considerations to be taken into account in the exercise of the discretion on whether or not to issue an injunction.

12.65 In the event, the Law Commission in its 2014 report said that it could not safely make a recommendation for reform at that point. It recommended that the Government should review the question of reform of the level of equitable damages when other recommendations of the Commission had been enacted and that there should be a decision on the desirability of capping equitable damages either as a percentage of the profit share or as a multiplier of the book value diminution in value damages. The reason for the latter recommendation was said to be 'a matter of economic policy'. The economic policy is presumably to make it easier for commercial developments to take place at a profitable level to the detriment of those who have built up property rights to protect their property, including the amenity and value of their property. This somewhat vague proposal is made in circumstances in which, both under the existing law and even more so as a result of the recommendations of the Law Commission if they are enacted, the acquisition of prescriptive easements of light can or could be readily and easily protected by notices under legislation, that is the existing legislation in the Rights of Light Act 1959 or the replacement system of light interruption certificates proposed in the 2014 report.[77] The courts have developed a practical and theoretically coherent system of assessing damages for violations of property rights by the voluntary release method. It is possible to think that suggestions for arbitrary limits to be applied in the area of the law of rights of light alone give undue weight to the protests of property developers at having to pay a fair recompense to those whose rights they violate.

12.66 The truth is that as a result of developments by the courts over the last few decades, now underpinned by the commendation of the highest courts, voluntary release damages represent a fair and reasonable way of protecting those whose proprietary

[76] ibid, paras 5.74–5.75.
[77] See paras 12.39–12.41.

rights, including rights of light, are violated when an injunction is not granted to prevent the violation or the continuation of the violation. As mentioned earlier, such damages are truly compensatable in nature and fall within the general conception of damages as compensation for loss caused by a wrong and go some way to prevent the type of situation in which people can in effect buy themselves out of the consequences of their wrong. The courts are perfectly able on the basis of the experience and evidence of experts and others put before them to determine how exactly the voluntary release damages, the assumed result of a fair voluntary negotiation, should be assessed and have shown that they are able to do so in many fields including the assessment of damages and the assessment of compensation for compulsory purchase. No one has ever suggested a rational reason why there should be some special rule or limitation or cap on voluntary release damages in the particular case of rights of light. Many aspects of the law of rights of light are in need of reform but it reduces the prospect of sensible reform if suggestions are made for changes when there is no real need for those changes.

3. Parasitic Damages

Under the current law parasitic damages may be payable where some apertures in a building have acquired prescriptive rights of light by 20 years or more of the access of light to them and other windows or parts of the building owned by the same person have not, possibly because the latter parts of the building were built only recently. If there is an infringement of the rights of light through the older windows the damages are measured by reference to the reduction in light not only to the areas lit by those older windows which have enjoyed the access of light for over 20 years but also by reference to any diminution in light to the newer windows which, if those windows had been in existence long enough, would have been an independent actionable infringement. The latter element of the damages may be called parasitic damages.[78] 12.67

There has been considerable criticism of this rule and the merits and justification of it are, to say the least, not wholly apparent. The matter was considered by the Law Commission in its 2014 report but the conclusion reached was that the Commission did not feel that it would be appropriate to recommend reform in this area.[79] It may be that parasitic damages in rights of light cases are aspects of a wider rule on the measure of damages. It may also be that the rule does not create much practical difficulty and there appear to be no decided cases in which the principle has been considered with direct application to rights of light for over a century. Nonetheless it might be advantageous if this somewhat anomalous rule were to be abandoned as far as rights of light claims are concerned. 12.68

[78] See ch 7, section (C)11, for a fuller description of the law and the relevant authorities.

[79] Law Commission, *Rights to Light* (Law Com No 356, 2014), para 5.92. The report does not go into any detail on why exactly no reform was recommended.

Appendices

APPENDIX 1—PRESCRIPTION ACT 1832

1832 (2 and 3 Will. 4 C. 71)

UK Statutes Crown Copyright. Reproduced by permission of the Controller of Her Majesty's Stationery Office.

Table of Contents

An Act for shortening the time of prescription in certain cases.

[1st August 1832]

Whereas the expression "time immemorial, or time whereof the memory of man runneth not to the contrary," is now by the Law of England in many cases considered to include and denote the whole period of time from the Reign of King Richard the First, whereby the title to matters that have been long enjoyed is sometimes defeated by shewing the commencement of such enjoyment, which is in many cases productive of inconvenience and injustice;

1

Notes

1 Short title "The Prescription Act 1832" given by Short Titles Act 1896 (c. 14); Act saved by Law of Property Act 1925 (c. 20), s. 12: amended by Commons Registration Act 1965 (c. 64), s. 16(1); Words of enactment and certain other words repealed by Statute Law Revision (No. 2) Act 1888 (c. 57) and Statute Law Revision Act 1890 (c. 33); This Act is not necessarily in the form in which it has effect in Northern Ireland

Extent

Preamble: England, Wales, Northern Ireland

☑ Law In Force

1. Claims to right of common and other profits à prendre, not to be defeated after thirty years enjoyment by merely showing the commencement; after sixty years enjoyment the right to be absolute, unless had by consent or agreement.
No claim which may be lawfully made at the common law, by custom, prescription, or grant, to any right of common or other profit or benefit to be taken and enjoyed from or upon any land of our sovereign lord the King, or any land being parcel of the duchy of Lancaster or of the duchy of Cornwall, or of any ecclesiastical or lay person, or body corporate, except such matters and things as are herein specially provided for, and except tithes, rent, and services, shall, where such right, profit, or benefit shall have been actually taken and enjoyed by any person claiming right thereto without interruption for the full period of thirty years, be defeated or destroyed by showing only that such right, profit, or benefit was first taken or enjoyed at any time prior to such period of thirty years, but nevertheless such claim may be defeated in any other way by which the same is now liable to be defeated; and when such right, profit, or benefit shall have been so taken and enjoyed as aforesaid for the full period of sixty years, the right thereto shall be deemed absolute and indefeasible, unless it shall appear that the same was taken and enjoyed by some consent or agreement expressly made or given for that purpose by deed or writing.
1

Notes

1 Short title "The Prescription Act 1832" given by Short Titles Act 1896 (c. 14); Act saved by Law of Property Act 1925 (c. 20), s. 12: amended by Commons Registration Act 1965 (c. 64), s. 16(1); Words of enactment and certain other words repealed by Statute Law Revision (No. 2) Act 1888 (c. 57) and Statute Law Revision Act 1890 (c. 33); This Act is not necessarily in the form in which it has effect in Northern Ireland

Commencement

s. 1: December 1, 1832 (1832 c. 71 s. 10)

Extent

s. 1: England, Wales, Northern Ireland

Law In Force

2. In claims of right of way or other easement the periods to be twenty years and forty years.

No claim which may be lawfully made at the common law, by custom, prescription, or grant, to any way or other easement, or to any watercourse, or the use of any water, to be enjoyed or derived upon, over, or from any land or water of our said lord the King, or being parcel of the duchy of Lancaster or of the duchy of Cornwall, or being the property of any ecclesiastical or lay person, or body corporate, when such way or other matter as herein last before mentioned shall have been actually enjoyed by any person claiming right thereto without interruption for the full period of twenty years, shall be defeated or destroyed by showing only that such way or other matter was first enjoyed at any time prior to such period of twenty years, but nevertheless such claim may be defeated in any other way by which the same is now liable to be defeated; and where such way or other matter as herein last before mentioned shall have been so enjoyed as aforesaid for the full period of forty years, the right thereto shall be deemed absolute and indefeasible, unless it shall appear that the same was enjoyed by some consent or agreement expressly given or made for that purpose by deed or writing.
[1]

Notes

1 Short title "The Prescription Act 1832" given by Short Titles Act 1896 (c. 14); Act saved by Law of Property Act 1925 (c. 20), s. 12: amended by Commons Registration Act 1965 (c. 64), s. 16(1); Words of enactment and certain other words repealed by Statute Law Revision (No. 2) Act 1888 (c. 57) and Statute Law Revision Act 1890 (c. 33); This Act is not necessarily in the form in which it has effect in Northern Ireland

Commencement

s. 2: December 1, 1832 (1832 c. 71 s. 10)

Extent

s. 2: England, Wales, Northern Ireland

☑ Law In Force

3. Claim to the use of light enjoyed for 20 years.

When the access and use of light to and for any dwelling house, workshop, or other building shall have been actually enjoyed therewith for the full period of twenty years without interruption, the right thereto shall be deemed absolute and indefeasible, any local usage or custom to the contrary notwithstanding, unless it shall appear that the same was enjoyed by some consent or agreement expressly made or given for that purpose by deed or writing.
1 2

Notes

1 Short title "The Prescription Act 1832" given by Short Titles Act 1896 (c. 14); Act saved by Law of Property Act 1925 (c. 20), s. 12: amended by Commons Registration Act 1965 (c. 64), s. 16(1); Words of enactment and certain other words repealed by Statute Law Revision (No. 2) Act 1888 (c. 57) and Statute Law Revision Act 1890 (c. 33); This Act is not necessarily in the form in which it has effect in Northern Ireland

2 S. 3 explained by Rights of Light Act 1959 (c. 56), s. 4(2)

Commencement

s. 3: December 1, 1832 (1832 c. 71 s. 10)

Extent

s. 3: England, Wales, Northern Ireland

☑ Law In Force

4. Before mentioned periods to be deemed those next before suits.

Each of the respective periods of years herein-before mentioned shall be deemed and taken to be the period next before some suit or action wherein the claim or matter to which such period may relate shall have been or shall be brought into question and that no act or other matter shall be deemed to be an interruption, within the meaning of this statute, unless the same shall have been or shall be submitted to or acquiesced in for one year after the party interrupted shall have had or shall have notice thereof, and of the person making or authorizing the same to be made.
1 2

Notes

1 Short title "The Prescription Act 1832" given by Short Titles Act 1896 (c. 14); Act saved by Law of Property Act 1925 (c. 20), s. 12: amended by Commons Registration Act 1965 (c. 64), s. 16(1); Words of enactment and certain other words repealed by Statute Law Revision (No. 2) Act 1888 (c. 57) and Statute Law Revision Act 1890 (c. 33); This Act is not necessarily in the form in which it has effect in Northern Ireland

2 S. 4 amended by Rights of Light Act 1959 (c. 56), s. 3(6) and Commons Registration Act 1965 (c. 64), s. 16(2)

Commencement

s. 4: December 1, 1832 (1832 c. 71 s. 10)

Extent

s. 4: England, Wales, Northern Ireland

Law In Force

5. In actions on the case, the claimant may allege his right generally, as at present. In pleas to trespass and certain other pleadings, the period mentioned in this Act may be alleged. Exceptions, &c. to be replied to specially.

In all actions upon the case and other pleadings, wherein the party claiming may now by law allege his right generally, without averring the existence of such right from time immemorial, such general allegation shall still be deemed sufficient, and if the same shall be denied, all and every the matters in this Act mentioned and provided, which shall be applicable to the case, shall be admissible in evidence to sustain or rebut such allegation; and that in all pleadings to actions of trespass, and in all other pleadings wherein before the passing of this Act it would have been necessary to allege the right to have existed from time immemorial, it shall be sufficient to allege the enjoyment thereof as of right by the occupiers of the tenement in respect whereof the same is claimed for and during such of the periods mentioned in this Act as may be applicable to the case, and without claiming in the name or right of the owner of the fee, as is now usually done; and if the other party shall intend to rely on any proviso, exception, incapacity, disability, contract, agreement, or other matter herein-before mentioned, or on any cause or matter of fact or of law not inconsistent with the simple fact of enjoyment, the same shall be specially alleged and set forth in answer to the allegation of the party claiming, and shall not be received in evidence on any general traverse or denial of such allegation.
1

Notes

1 Short title "The Prescription Act 1832" given by Short Titles Act 1896 (c. 14); Act saved by Law of Property Act 1925 (c. 20), s. 12: amended by Commons Registration Act 1965 (c. 64), s. 16(1);

Words of enactment and certain other words repealed by Statute Law Revision (No. 2) Act 1888 (c. 57) and Statute Law Revision Act 1890 (c. 33); This Act is not necessarily in the form in which it has effect in Northern Ireland

Commencement

s. 5: December 1, 1832 (1832 c. 71 s. 10)

Extent

s. 5: England, Wales, Northern Ireland

☑ Law In Force

6. Presumption to be allowed in claims herein provided for.

In the several cases mentioned in and provided for by this Act, no presumption shall be allowed or made in favour or support of any claim, upon proof of the exercise or enjoyment of the right or matter claimed for any less period of time or number of years than for such period or number mentioned in this Act as may be applicable to the case and to the nature of the claim.
[1] [2]

Notes

1 Short title "The Prescription Act 1832" given by Short Titles Act 1896 (c. 14); Act saved by Law of Property Act 1925 (c. 20), s. 12: amended by Commons Registration Act 1965 (c. 64), s. 16(1); Words of enactment and certain other words repealed by Statute Law Revision (No. 2) Act 1888 (c. 57) and Statute Law Revision Act 1890 (c. 33); This Act is not necessarily in the form in which it has effect in Northern Ireland

2 S. 6 amended by the Rights of Light Act 1959 (c.5), s.1

Commencement

s. 6: December 1, 1832 (1832 c. 71 s. 10)

Extent

s. 6: England, Wales, Northern Ireland

☑ Law In Force

7. Proviso for infants, &c.

Provided also, that the time during which any person otherwise capable of resisting any claim to any of the matters before mentioned shall have been or shall be an infant, idiot, non compos mentis, feme covert, or tenant for life, or during which any action or suit shall have been pending, and which shall have been diligently prosecuted, until abated by the death of any party or parties thereto, shall be excluded in the computation of the periods herein-before mentioned, except only in cases where the right or claim is hereby declared to be absolute and indefeasible.
[1]

Notes

1 Short title "The Prescription Act 1832" given by Short Titles Act 1896 (c. 14); Act saved by Law of Property Act 1925 (c. 20), s. 12: amended by Commons Registration Act 1965 (c. 64), s. 16(1); Words of enactment and certain other words repealed by Statute Law Revision (No. 2) Act 1888 (c. 57) and Statute Law Revision Act 1890 (c. 33); This Act is not necessarily in the form in which it has effect in Northern Ireland

Commencement

s. 7: December 1, 1832 (1832 c. 71 s. 10)

Extent

s. 7 Proviso. 001: England, Wales, Northern Ireland

☑ Law In Force

8. What time to be excluded in computing the term of forty years appointed by this Act.

Provided always, that when any land or water upon, over, or from which any such way or other convenient watercourse or use of water shall have been or shall be enjoyed or derived hath been or shall be held under or by virtue of any term of life, or any term of years exceeding three years from the granting thereof, the time of the enjoyment of any such way or other matter as herein last before mentioned, during the continuance of such term, shall be excluded in the computation of the said period of forty years, in case the claim shall within three years next after the end or sooner determination of such term be resisted by any person entitled to any reversion expectant on the determination thereof.
[1]

Notes

1 Short title "The Prescription Act 1832" given by Short Titles Act 1896 (c. 14); Act saved by Law of Property Act 1925 (c. 20), s. 12: amended by Commons Registration Act 1965 (c. 64), s. 16(1); Words of enactment and certain other words repealed by Statute Law Revision (No. 2) Act 1888 (c. 57) and Statute Law Revision Act 1890 (c. 33); This Act is not necessarily in the form in which it has effect in Northern Ireland

Commencement

s. 8: December 1, 1832 (1832 c. 71 s. 10)

Extent

s. 8 Proviso. 002: England, Wales, Northern Ireland

☑ Law In Force

[8A.— Exclusion of time because of mediation in certain cross-border disputes.

(1) In this section—
  (a) "Mediation Directive" means Directive 2008/52/EC of the European Parliament and of the Council of 21 May 2008 on certain aspects of mediation in civil and commercial matters;
  (b) "mediation" has the meaning given by article 3(a) of the Mediation Directive;
  (c) "mediator" has the meaning given by article 3(b) of the Mediation Directive;
  (d) "relevant dispute" means a dispute to which article 8(1) of the Mediation Directive applies (certain cross-border disputes).

(2) Where a period is prescribed by this Act in relation to the subject of the whole or part of a relevant dispute, any time after the start of a mediation in relation to the relevant dispute is to be excluded in the computation of that period, but only if—
  (a) the time when the period must end by virtue of section 4 falls before the mediation ends or less than eight weeks after it ends, or
  (b) a further mediation in relation to the relevant dispute starts less than eight weeks after the previous mediation ends, and the time when the period must end by virtue of section 4 falls before the further mediation ends or less than eight weeks after it ends.

(3) Any time excluded under subsection (2) is also to be excluded in the computation of the second period of three years mentioned in section 8 (period within which claim is resisted).

(4) For the purposes of this section, a mediation starts on the date of the agreement to mediate that is entered into by the parties and the mediator.

(5) For the purposes of this section, a mediation ends on the date of the first of these to occur—
  (a) the parties reach an agreement in resolution of the relevant dispute;
  (b) a party completes the notification of the other parties that it has withdrawn from the mediation;
  (c) a party to whom a qualifying request is made fails to give a response reaching the other parties within 14 days of the request;
  (d) the parties, after being notified that the mediator's appointment has ended (by death, resignation or otherwise), fail to agree within 14 days to seek to appoint a replacement mediator;
  (e) the mediation otherwise comes to an end pursuant to the terms of the agreement to mediate.

(6) For the purpose of subsection (5), a qualifying request is a request by a party that another (A) confirm to all parties that A is continuing with the mediation.

(7) In the case of any relevant dispute, references in this section to a mediation are references to the mediation so far as it relates to that dispute, and references to a party are to be read accordingly.

][1]

Notes

1 Added by Cross-Border Mediation (EU Directive) Regulations 2011/1133 Pt 3 reg. 12 (May 20, 2011)

Extent

s. 8A(1)-(7): England, Wales, Northern Ireland

Law In Force

9. Limitation.

This Act shall not extend to Scotland [...][1]
2

Notes

1 Words repealed by Statute Law Revision Act 1874 (c. 35)

2 Short title "The Prescription Act 1832" given by Short Titles Act 1896 (c. 14); Act saved by Law of Property Act 1925 (c. 20), s. 12: amended by Commons Registration Act 1965 (c. 64), s. 16(1); Words of enactment and certain other words repealed by Statute Law Revision (No. 2) Act 1888 (c. 57) and Statute Law Revision Act 1890 (c. 33); This Act is not necessarily in the form in which it has effect in Northern Ireland

Commencement

s. 9: December 1, 1832 (1832 c. 71 s. 10)

Extent

s. 9: England, Wales, Northern Ireland

Repealed

10. [...][1]
2

Notes

1 Repealed by Statute Law Revision Act 1874 (c. 35)

2 Short title "The Prescription Act 1832" given by Short Titles Act 1896 (c. 14); Act saved by Law of Property Act 1925 (c. 20), s. 12: amended by Commons Registration Act 1965 (c. 64), s. 16(1); Words of enactment and certain other words repealed by Statute Law Revision (No. 2) Act 1888 (c. 57) and Statute Law Revision Act 1890 (c. 33); This Act is not necessarily in the form in which it has effect in Northern Ireland

R Repealed

11. [...][1]

[2]

Notes

1 Repealed by Statute Law Revision Act 1874 (c. 35)

2 Short title "The Prescription Act 1832" given by Short Titles Act 1896 (c. 14); Act saved by Law of Property Act 1925 (c. 20), s. 12: amended by Commons Registration Act 1965 (c. 64), s. 16(1); Words of enactment and certain other words repealed by Statute Law Revision (No. 2) Act 1888 (c. 57) and Statute Law Revision Act 1890 (c. 33); This Act is not necessarily in the form in which it has effect in Northern Ireland

APPENDIX 2—RIGHTS OF LIGHT ACT 1959

1959 (7 and 8 Eliz. 2 C. 56)

UK Statutes Crown Copyright. Reproduced by permission of the Controller of Her Majesty's Stationery Office.

Table of Contents

An Act to amend the law relating to rights of light, and for purposes connected therewith.

[16th July 1959]

1

Notes

[1] Words of enactment omitted under authority of Statute Law Revision Act 1948 (c. 62), s. 3

Extent

Preamble: England, Wales

Repealed

1.— […][1]

2

Notes

1 Repealed by Statute Law (Repeals) Act 1974 (c.22), s. 1, Sch. Pt. IV
2 Words of enactment omitted under authority of Statute Law Revision Act 1948 (c. 62), s. 3

Law In Force

2.— Registration of notice in lieu of obstruction of access of light.

(1) For the purpose of preventing the access and use of light from being taken to be enjoyed without interruption, any person who is an owner of land (in this and the next following section referred to as "the servient land") over which light passes to a dwelling-house, workshop or other building (in this and the next following section referred to as "the dominant building") may apply to the [Chief Land Registrar][1] for the registration of a notice under this section.

(2) An application for the registration of a notice under this section shall […][2] —

(a) identify the servient land and the dominant building in the prescribed manner, and

(b) state that the registration of a notice in pursuance of the application is intended to be equivalent to the obstruction of the access of light to the dominant building across the servient land which would be caused by the erection, in such position on the servient land as may be specified in the application, of an opaque structure of such dimensions (including, if the application so states, unlimited height) as may be so specified.

(3) Any such application shall be accompanied by [a copy of][3] one or other of the following certificates issued by the [Upper Tribunal][4], that is to say,—

(a) a certificate certifying that adequate notice of the proposed application has been given to all persons who, in the circumstances existing at the time when the certificate is issued, appear to the [Upper Tribunal][4] to be persons likely to be affected by the registration of a notice in pursuance of the application;

(b) a certificate certifying that, in the opinion of the [Upper Tribunal][4], the case is one of exceptional urgency, and that accordingly a notice should be registered forthwith as a temporary notice for such period as may be specified in the certificate.

(4) Where application is duly made to [the Chief Land Registrar][5] for the registration of a notice under this section, it shall be the duty of [[the Chief Land Registrar][7] to register the notice in the [...][8] local land charges register, and—][6]

[(a) any notice so registered under this section shall be a local land charge; but

(b) [section 5(2) and section 10 of the Local Land Charges Act 1975][9] shall not apply in relation thereto.][6]

(5) Provision [may be made by Tribunal Procedure Rules][10] with respect to the issue of certificates for the purposes of this section, and, subject to the approval of the Treasury, the fees chargeable in respect of those proceedings; and, without prejudice to the generality of subsection (6) of that section, any such rules made for the purposes of this section shall include provision—

(a) for requiring applicants for certificates under paragraph (a) of subsection (3) of this section to give such notices, whether by way of advertisement or otherwise, and to produce such documents and provide such information, as may be determined by or under the rules;

(b) for determining the period to be specified in a certificate issued under paragraph (b) of subsection (3) of this section; and

(c) in connection with any certificate issued under the said paragraph (b), for enabling a further certificate to be issued in accordance (subject to the necessary modifications) with paragraph (a) of subsection (3) of this section.

Notes

1 Words substituted by Infrastructure Act 2015 c. 7 Sch.5(3) para.28(2) (April 12, 2015: substitution has effect subject to transitional provisions specified in 2015 c.7 Sch.5 Pt 4)

2 Words repealed by Infrastructure Act 2015 c. 7 Sch.5(3) para.28(3) (April 12, 2015: repeal has effect subject to transitional provisions specified in 2015 c.7 Sch.5 Pt 4)

3 Words inserted by Infrastructure Act 2015 c. 7 Sch.5(3) para.28(4) (April 12, 2015: insertion has effect subject to transitional provisions specified in 2015 c.7 Sch.5 Pt 4)

4 Words substituted by Transfer of Tribunal Functions (Lands Tribunal and Miscellaneous Amendments) Order 2009/1307 Sch.1 para.35(a) (June 1, 2009)

5 Words substituted by Infrastructure Act 2015 c. 7 Sch.5(3) para.28(5)(a) (April 12, 2015: substitution has effect subject to transitional provisions specified in 2015 c.7 Sch.5 Pt 4)

6 Words substituted (with savings) by Local Land Charges Act 1975 (c.76) ss. 17(2), 19(2)–(4), Sch. 1

7 Words substituted by Infrastructure Act 2015 c. 7 Sch.5(3) para.28(5)(b) (April 12, 2015: substitution has effect subject to transitional provisions specified in 2015 c.7 Sch.5 Pt 4)

8 Word repealed by Infrastructure Act 2015 c. 7 Sch.5(3) para.28(5)(c) (April 12, 2015: repeal has effect subject to transitional provisions specified in 2015 c.7 Sch.5 Pt 4)

9 Words substituted by Infrastructure Act 2015 c. 7 Sch.5(3) para.28(5)(d) (April 12, 2015: substitution has effect subject to transitional provisions specified in 2015 c.7 Sch.5 Pt 4)

10 Words substituted by Transfer of Tribunal Functions (Lands Tribunal and Miscellaneous Amendments) Order 2009/1307 Sch.1 para.35(b) (June 1, 2009)

Commencement

s. 2: October 16, 1959 (1959 c. 56 s. 8(2))

Extent

s. 2(1)-(5)(c): England, Wales

☑ Law In Force

3.— Effect of registered notice and proceedings relating thereto.

(1) Where, in pursuance of an application made in accordance with the last preceding section, a notice is registered thereunder, then, for the purpose of determining whether any person is entitled (by virtue of the Prescription Act, 1832, or otherwise) to a right to the access of light to the dominant building across the servient land, the access of light to that building across that land shall be treated as obstructed to the same extent, and with the like consequences, as if an opaque structure, of the dimensions specified in the application,—

(a) had, on the date of registration of the notice, been erected in the position on the servient land specified in the application, and had been so erected by the person who made the application, and

(b) had remained in that position during the period for which the notice has effect and had been removed at the end of that period.

(2) For the purposes of this section a notice registered under the last preceding section shall be taken to have effect until either—

(a) the registration is cancelled, or

(b) the period of one year beginning with the date of registration of the notice expires, or

(c) in the case of a notice registered in pursuance of an application accompanied by a certificate issued under paragraph (b) of subsection (3) of the last preceding section, the period specified in the certificate expires without [a copy of][1] such a further certificate as is mentioned in paragraph (c) of subsection (5) of that section having before the end of that period been lodged with the [Chief Land Registrar][2].

and shall cease to have effect on the occurrence of any one of those events.

(3) Subject to the following provisions of this section, any person who, if such a structure as is mentioned in subsection (1) of this section had been erected as therein mentioned, would have had a right of action in any court in respect of that structure, on the grounds that he was entitled to a right to the access of light to the dominant building across the servient land, and that the said right was infringed by that structure, shall have the like right of action in

that court in respect of the registration of a notice under the last preceding section:

> Provided that an action shall not be begun by virtue of this subsection after the notice in question has ceased to have effect.

(4) Where, at any time during the period for which a notice registered under the last preceding section has effect, the circumstances are such that, if the access of light to the dominant building had been enjoyed continuously from a date one year earlier than the date on which the enjoyment thereof in fact began, a person would have had a right of action in any court by virtue of the last preceding subsection in respect of the registration of the notice, that person shall have the like right of action in that court by virtue of this subsection in respect of the registration of the notice.

(5) The remedies available to the plaintiff in an action brought by virtue of subsection (3) or subsection (4) of this section (apart from any order as to costs) shall be such declaration as the court may consider appropriate in the circumstances, and an order directing the registration of the notice to be cancelled or varied, as the court may determine.

(6) For the purposes of section four of the Prescription Act, 1832 (under which a period of enjoyment of any of the rights to which that Act applies is not to be treated as interrupted except by a matter submitted to or acquiesced in for one year after notice thereof)—

(a) as from the date of registration of a notice under the last preceding section, all persons interested in the dominant building or any part thereof shall be deemed to have notice of the registration thereof and of the person on whose application it was registered;

(b) until such time as an action is brought by virtue of subsection (3) or subsection (4) of this section in respect of the registration of a notice under the last preceding section, all persons interested in the dominant building or any part thereof shall be deemed to acquiesce in the obstruction which, in accordance with subsection (1) of this section, is to be treated as resulting from the registration of the notice;

(c) as from the date on which such an action is brought, no person shall be treated as submitting to or acquiescing in that obstruction:

> Provided that if, in any such action, the court decides against the claim of the plaintiff, the court may direct that the preceding provisions of this subsection shall apply in relation to the notice as if that action had not been brought.

Notes

[1] Words inserted by Infrastructure Act 2015 c. 7 Sch.5(3) para.29 a) (April 12, 2015: insertion has effect subject to transitional provisions specified in 2015 c.7 Sch.5 Pt 4)

[2] Words substituted by Infrastructure Act 2015 c. 7 Sch.5(3) para.29(b) (April 12, 2015: substitution has effect subject to transitional provisions specified in 2015 c.7 Sch.5 Pt 4)

Commencement

s. 3: October 16, 1959 (1959 c. 56 s. 8(2))

Extent

s. 3(1)-(6)(c) Proviso. 002: England, Wales

☑ Law In Force

4.— Application to Crown land.

(1) Subject to the next following subsection, this Act shall apply in relation to land in which there is a Crown or Duchy interest as it applies in relation to land in which there is no such interest.

(2) Section three of the Prescription Act, 1832, as modified by the preceding provisions of this Act, shall not by virtue of this section be construed as applying to any land to which (by reason that there is a Crown or Duchy interest therein) that section would not apply apart from this Act.

(3) In this section "Crown or Duchy interest" means an interest belonging to Her Majesty in right of the Crown or of the Duchy of Lancaster, or belonging to the Duchy of Cornwall, or belonging to a government department, or held in trust for Her Majesty for the purposes of a government department.

1

Notes

[1] Words of enactment omitted under authority of Statute Law Revision Act 1948 (c. 62), s. 3

Commencement

s. 4: October 16, 1959 (1959 c. 56 s. 8(2))

Extent

s. 4(1)-(3): England, Wales

☑ Law In Force

5.— Power to make rules.

(1) [...][1]

(2) Any rules made [under section 14 of the Local Land Charges Act 1975 for the purposes of section 2 of this Act][2] shall (without prejudice to the inclusion therein of other provisions as to cancelling or varying the registration

of notices or agreements) include provision for giving effect to any order of the court under subsection (5) of section three of this Act.

3

Notes

1 Repealed (with savings) by Local Land Charges Act 1975 (c.76), ss. 17(2), 19, Schs. 1, 2
2 Words substituted by Local Land Charges Act 1975 (c.76), ss. 17(2), 19(2)–(4), Sch. 1
3 Words of enactment omitted under authority of Statute Law Revision Act 1948 (c. 62), s. 3

Commencement

s. 5: October 16, 1959 (1959 c. 56 s. 8(2))

Extent

s. 5(1)-(2): England, Wales

R Repealed

6. [...][1]
2

Notes

1 Repealed by Northern Ireland Constitution Act 1973 (c.36), s. 41(1), Sch. 6 Pt. I
2 Words of enactment omitted under authority of Statute Law Revision Act 1948 (c. 62), s. 3

Law In Force

7.— Interpretation.

(1) In this Act, except in so far as the context otherwise requires, the following expressions have the meaning hereby assigned to them respectively, that is to say:—

"action" includes a counterclaim, and any reference to the plaintiff in an action shall be construed accordingly;

[...][1]

"owner", in relation to any land, means a person who is the estate owner in respect of the fee simple thereof, or is entitled to a tenancy thereof (within the meaning of the Landlord and Tenant Act, 1954) for a term of years certain of which, at the time in question, not less than seven years remain unexpired, or is a mortgagee in possession (within the meaning of the Law of Property Act, 1925) where the interest mortgaged is either the fee simple of the land or such a tenancy thereof;

["prescribed" means prescribed by rules under section 14 of the Local Land Charges Act 1975;][2]

(2) References in this Act to any enactment shall, except where the context otherwise requires, be construed as references to that enactment as amended by or under any other enactment.

Notes

1 Definition repealed by Infrastructure Act 2015 c. 7 Sch.5(3) para.30(b) (April 12, 2015: repeal has effect subject to transitional provisions specified in 2015 c.7 Sch.5 Pt 4)

2 Definition substituted by Infrastructure Act 2015 c. 7 Sch.5(3) para.30(a) (April 12, 2015: substitution has effect subject to transitional provisions specified in 2015 c.7 Sch.5 Pt 4)

Commencement

s. 7: October 16, 1959 (1959 c. 56 s. 8(2))

Extent

s. 7(1)–(2): England, Wales

☑ Law In Force

8.— Short title, commencement and extent.

(1) This Act may be cited as the Rights of Light Act, 1959.

(2) This Act, exceptsections one and six thereof, shall come into operation at the end of the period of three months beginning with the day on which it is passed.

(3) This Act shall not extend to Scotland.

(4) This Act, [...][1], shall not extend to Northern Ireland.

2

Notes

1 Words repealed by Northern Ireland Constitution Act 1973 (c.36), s. 41(1), Sch. 6 Pt. I

2 Words of enactment omitted under authority of Statute Law Revision Act 1948 (c. 62), s. 3

Commencement

s. 8: July 16, 1959

Extent

s. 8(1)-(4): England, Wales

GLOSSARY

This glossary is intended to provide a brief definition or description of legal and technical terms and expressions used in this book. Rights of light are of importance to landowners and developers and the lawyers and surveyors and others who advise them, so that, although some of the words and expressions defined will be familiar to those who practise in one discipline, they may nonetheless be of assistance to those who practise in other disciplines.

Abatement	Action taken to bring about the cessation of a nuisance otherwise than under an order of a court. The right of self-help is today very limited and is unlikely to be available in rights of light disputes.
Abandonment	A release or extinguishment of a right, including an easement of light, by the express agreement of the parties or by an implied agreement inferred from the conduct of the parties.
Aggravated damages	Damages awarded for mental distress and outrage which are a part of the result of the commission of a wrong by a defendant. Aggravated damages, which have been awarded for breach of an easement, should not be confused with exemplary damages.
Aperture	An opening in a building, such as a window or a skylight or a glass door, which permits the access of natural light into the building. Easements of light can only exist as the right to natural light through an aperture.
Book value damages	Damages assessed as the reduction in the value of the dominant building caused by the infringement of an easement of light appurtenant to that building.
BRE Guide	Paul Littlefair, *Site Layout and Planning for Daylight and Sunlight—A Guide to Good Practice*, 2nd edn (Watford, BRE Trust, 2011). The Guide gives advice to local authorities and others on daylighting matters including the likely effect of a new or extended building on the access of light to an existing building.

Charges register	That part of the register of a title to land which contains details of encumbrances adverse to the land such as easements.
CIE standard overcast sky	A completely overcast sky for which the ratio of its luminance at a particular angle of elevation above the horizontal to the luminance at the zenith (vertically overhead) is given by a particular formula. CIE means *Commission Internationale de l'Eclairage.*
Civil Procedure Rules (CPR)	Rules which govern the procedure to be followed in civil legal proceedings in the Court of Appeal, the High Court and the county court.
Clean hands	An equitable doctrine which means that the grant of a discretionary equitable remedy such as an injunction may be refused if the claimant has behaved in some way improperly in reference to the subject matter of the claim.
Common law damages	Damages awarded for a wrong which has been committed prior to the award. Common law damages are to be contrasted with equitable damages.
Common law prescription	The acquisition of an easement by prescription dependent on use and enjoyment from time immemorial (taken to be 1189).
Compensatory damages	Damages designed to compensate a claimant for his loss. In rights of light claims the normal forms of compensatory damages are either book value damages or voluntary release damages.
Constructive notice	The notice of some matter which a person would have had if he had conducted a reasonably careful investigation.
Corporeal interest	A proprietary interest in land which confers a right, either at present or in the future, to the possession of the land. Freehold and leasehold interests in land are the best examples. The interest is sometimes called a corporeal hereditament. A corporeal interest is to be compared with an incorporeal interest.
Covenant	A promise or obligation contained in a deed.
Covenantee	The person in whose favour a covenant is made.
Covenantor	A person who makes a covenant.
Declaration	A statement of the rights and obligations of the parties made by a court as a result of legal proceedings.

Definitive certificate	A certificate issued by the registrar of the Lands Chamber of the Upper Tribunal under the Rights of Light Act 1959 stating that sufficient notice has been given of a proposed light obstruction notice and enabling such a notice to be registered as a local land charge.
Derogation from grant	A principle of law which requires that a person who has granted an interest in land should not thereafter act so as to prevent or frustrate the enjoyment of that interest by the grantee. An obligation not to derogate from grant binds the successors in title of the grantor. Rights similar to an easement of light may arise from the operation of this principle.
Disclosure	A process (previously called discovery) which requires a party to legal proceedings to list and disclose documents in his control relevant to the proceedings whether the documents assist his case or otherwise. Certain documents are privileged and are immune from disclosure.
Disponee	The person to whom a disposition or transfer of an interest in land is made.
Doctrine of precedent	The principle that a statement of law made by a court as a part of and essential to its decision is binding on all lower courts (and sometimes (as with the Court of Appeal) on courts of co-ordinate status). Sometimes called the doctrine of stare decisis. The statement of law so made is termed the *ratio decidendi* of the decision. See also '*obiter dictum*' and '*per incuriam*'.
Dominant land	The land which has appurtenant to it the benefit of an easement. In the case of an easement of light the dominant land must necessarily be a building since an easement of light can exist only as appurtenant to a building. The dominant land is sometimes called the dominant tenement.
Easement	A proprietary interest appurtenant to one piece of land, the dominant land, which benefits that land and is exercisable over another piece of land, the servient land. An easement is an incorporeal interest since it does not give the right to possession of the servient land. A right of light is a species of easement.

Effective first zone (EFZ) loss	When an obstruction to light results in an area of a room having an insufficiency of natural light the area of the room is divided into four zones, the front zone, the first zone, the second zone, and the makeweight (MKWT) zone. The loss of sufficiently lit area in each zone is given a weighting and the EFZ loss is the total weighted floor area which has lost a sufficiency of light. The EFZ loss is used in the calculation of book value damages.
Enhanced damages	An expression sometimes used to describe an award of voluntary release damages which, in the absence of any better evidence, is calculated by multiplying the book value damages by a factor of 2 or 3. This process should be avoided if any better method of calculating the voluntary release damages can be found.
Equitable damages	Damages awarded in addition to or in place of an injunction. The damages may include compensation for loss which will be incurred by reason of future wrongs. Equitable damages are to be contrasted with common law damages.
Equitable easement	An easement which does not have the status of a legal easement, for example because the owner is not registered in the proprietorship register of the title when the easement has been created in favour of land with a registered title by an express grant or reservation made on or after 13 October 2003.
Ex parte	An application made by a party to a court (for example to obtain an interim injunction) without notice to the other party. This is acceptable only in cases of great urgency.
Exemplary damages	Damages over and above that required to compensate a claimant for his loss which are awarded in limited circumstances to mark the degree of unacceptability of the conduct of a defendant. Exemplary damages (sometimes called punitive damages) are unlikely to be relevant in rights of light cases.
Express easement	An easement created by an express provision, either a grant or a reservation, in a deed such as a transfer of land or a lease.
Foot candle	A unit of illuminance: 1 lumen per square foot. The more modern unit of illuminance is a lux.

Grumble line	A room may be divided into that part of it where the light from an aperture is adequate and that part of it where the light from that aperture is not adequate. It is often considered that if more than 50 per cent of the floorspace falls into the latter category the room as a whole is inadequately lit. The 50 per cent dividing line is sometimes called the grumble line.
Illuminance	The amount of light (usually measured in lumen) which falls on a given area. It is usually measured in foot candles (1 lumen per square foot), or, today, in lux (1 lumen per square metre). A level of illuminance of 1 foot candle or 10–11 lux at a point in a room at 850 mm above floor level is often considered a sufficient illumination to that point in the room.
Implied easement	An easement which arises by implication from the circumstances in which a deed is executed. For example, when a person sells a part of his land an easement may arise by implication in favour of the land granted and against the land retained.
Incorporeal interest	A proprietary interest in land which does not currently or in the future give a right to possession of the land. Easements, including easements of light, are a form of incorporeal interest. The interest is sometimes called an incorporeal hereditament. An incorporeal interest is to be compared with a corporeal interest.
Injunction	An order of the court which requires a person to carry out or refrain from carrying out some specified action or activity.
Injurious affection	An expression, derived from the Lands Clauses Consolidation Act 1845 or earlier, which means damage to land. The damage is often a reduction in the capital value of the land. Compensation for injurious affection is payable when an easement of light is overridden either by the exercise of statutory powers or by the operation of section 237 of the Town and Country Planning Act 1990. The compensation is assessed under section 10 of the Compulsory Purchase Act 1965.

Interim injunction	An injunction which has effect only until some further order of the court. It is to be compared with a perpetual injunction. An interim injunction is sometimes called an interlocutory injunction.
Judicial review	A procedure whereby the legality of the actions of an administrative body can be challenged in the High Court. It could for example be used to challenge the validity of a planning permission granted by a local planning authority without taking into consideration the effect of the development permitted on the access of light to neighbouring properties.
Laches	An equitable doctrine which states that delay in asserting a claim or commencing proceedings may result in the discretionary remedy of an injunction being refused.
Land charges	Certain interests or encumbrances over land, including easements, which are specified in the Land Charges Act 1972 and which need to be registered against the name of the owner of the land affected if that land does not have a registered title.
Licence	A right, often a right under a contract, to occupy or use the land of some other person which is not a proprietary right such as a lease or an easement.
Light obstruction notice	A notice of a notional obstruction to light to the dominant building erected on the servient land which may be registered as a local land charge by the servient owner under the Rights of Light Act 1959. Its purpose is to prevent the acquisition of easements of light by prescription.
Limitation of actions	Statutory provisions which limit the period after the accrual of a cause of action in which legal proceedings may be commenced. The limitation period for actions for damages for the infringement of a right of light is usually six years under section 2 of the Limitation Act 1980. There is no limitation period as such for equitable remedies such as an injunction but the grant of such remedies is subject to the equitable doctrine of laches.

Lord Cairns' Act	The Chancery Amendment Act 1858, which first conferred power on courts of equity to award damages in addition to or in place of specific relief such as an injunction. The power now depends on section 50 of the Senior Courts Act 1981 and is available in all Divisions of the High Court and in the county court. Damages awarded pursuant to this power are called equitable damages.
Lost modern grant	A form of prescription at common law which depends on at least twenty years of use and enjoyment but not necessarily use and enjoyment from time immemorial as is in theory required for common law prescription. A prescriptive easement of light may in principle be acquired by common law prescription or under the doctrine of lost modern grant but is now normally acquired under section 3 of the Prescription Act 1832.
Lumen	A unit of luminous flux. It is an amount of luminous energy per second.
Lux	A unit of illuminance: 1 lumen per square metre. This unit has today replaced the former unit of illuminance, the foot candle, which is 1 lumen per square foot.
Mandatory injunction	A form of injunction requiring that a person carries out some action. It is sometimes called a positive injunction.
Negative easement	An easement the enjoyment of which does not require positive action by its owner. A right of light is a negative easement.
Negative injunction	An injunction which requires a person to refrain from carrying out some specified action or activity. It is sometimes called a prohibitory injunction.
Notice	(1) Knowledge of some matter such as the existence of an easement (see also constructive notice). (2) A notice in the charges register of the registered title to land of some interest adverse to that land which protects that interest against a purchaser for value of the registered land.
No sky line	A line on the working plane of a room which divides the room into the part of it from which at a given height above floor level the sky is visible through an aperture or apertures and the part of it where the sky is not so visible.

Obiter dictum	A statement of law made by a court which is not essential to its decision. It is to be contrasted with the *ratio decidendi* of the decision. An obiter dictum is not binding on other courts in accordance with the doctrine of precedent but the ratio decidendi of a decision may be so binding.
Overriding interest	An interest which under the Land Registration Act 2002 binds a purchaser for value of the registered title in the servient land even though it is not protected by notice on the register of that title.
Parasitic damages	Where an easement of light enjoyed through certain windows in a building is infringed the damages for the infringement may include any loss caused to the access of light through other windows in the same building owned by the same person, or through other windows in another building owned by the same person, even though no easement exists in relation to those other windows. The additional element of damages to the windows which do not enjoy easements is called parasitic damages. Damages will, of course, only be payable in respect of the other windows if the reduction in light to those windows is such that, had those windows enjoyed an easement of light, the obstruction would be an actionable injury.
Per incuriam	A decision made by a court contrary to and in ignorance of some principle of law which binds the court such as a statutory provision or some previous decision which is binding in accordance with the doctrine of precedent.
Perpetual injunction	An injunction having perpetual or permanent effect. It is to be compared with an interim injunction.
Pleadings	Formal statements of the case of a party made in legal proceedings under Part 7 of the Civil Procedure Rules. Pleadings usually comprise a particulars of claim of the claimant and a defence of the defendant. There may be further pleadings and documents such as the clarification or particulars of pleadings.
Prescriptive easement	An easement which arises by long use and enjoyment, usually for a period of at least 20 years. It is to be contrasted with an easement which arises from the express provisions of a deed or by implication from the circumstances in which a deed is made.

Priority	A term, used in the Land Registration Act 2002, which indicates that one interest binds another. For example, a recently created equitable easement if protected by notice on the title of the servient land has priority over (ie binds) the title of a purchaser of the servient land, whereas if the easement is not protected by notice it loses its priority over (ie does not bind) the servient land when acquired by a purchaser.
Privileged documents	Documents which a party cannot be required to disclose or produce, for example without prejudice communications and communications between a client and his legal adviser.
Profit a prendre	A right to take some natural element or produce of the land of another person such as crops or minerals.
Prohibitory injunction	A form of injunction which requires that a party refrains from carrying on some action or activity. It is sometimes called a negative injunction.
Proprietary estoppel	A principle of law by which an owner of land encourages some other person to act in some way, such as by the expenditure of money, in the expectation that the other person may obtain some right or interest over the land of the owner. It is possible that an easement, including an easement of light, can arise by this means.
Proprietary right (or interest)	A right (or interest) over land which is in principle enforceable not only against the owner of the land who created the right or interest or who was the owner of the land when the right or interest over the land was created but also against all other persons who come to have interests in the land against which the right is exercisable. Such rights are sometimes called rights *in rem*. An easement is a proprietary right or interest.
Quia timet injunction	An injunction granted to prevent an injury which is threatened and is likely to occur in the near future.
Registration	(1) The obtaining of a registered title to an estate in land by registration at HM Land Registry. (2) The registration of a land charge.
Release	An expression used to signify the express or implied abandonment of a right, including an easement of light.

Restitutionary damages	Damages which are equivalent to the whole of the gain made by a defendant through his wrongful activities. Such damages are unlikely to be awarded in rights of light cases.
Restrictive covenant	A covenant which restricts the use of land and which may bind successors in title of the original covenantor.
Root of title	A transaction in land in the past, such as a sale or mortgage of the land, which indicates the title to the land. This concept is used in the conveyancing of unregistered land but is unnecessary if land has registered title.
Rule in *Wheeldon v Burrows*	A principle, derived from the decision of the Court of Appeal in *Wheeldon v Burrows* (1879) 12 Ch D 31, which results in the creation of an implied easement in certain circumstances where there is a transfer by the owner of a part of his land.
Servient land	The land which has the burden of an easement. It is sometimes called the servient tenement.
Sky factor	The percentage of the whole of the sky, regarded as a hemisphere and wholly unobstructed, which is visible through an aperture at any given point in a room which contains that aperture.
Statutory prescription	The acquisition of an easement by prescription under the Prescription Act 1832. In the case of an easement of light the prescription is under section 3 of the Act and is dependent on at least 20 years of the enjoyment of the access of light over the servient land without interruption.
Stokes v Cambridge principle	A principle of the valuation of land which operates when the owner of property A needs to acquire a right or the release of a right from the owner of property B in order that property A can be developed or used in a particular way. The parties will, in a negotiation for the acquisition or release of the right, divide between them the gain to be made from the development or use. The principle is relevant to the assessment of voluntary release damages in rights of light and other cases. The principle derives from the decision of the Lands Tribunal in *Stokes v Cambridge Corporation* (1961) 13 P & CR 77 and has been applied in many later cases involving the valuation of land.

Undertaking as to damages	An undertaking given by a person who obtains an interim injunction that he will pay such damages to the other party as the court may order if he does not succeed when the proceedings are finally determined.
Vertical sky component (VSC)	The ratio of the illuminance, at a point on a vertical plane such as the outside of a window, from a CIE standard overcast sky, to the illuminance received on a horizontal plane from the unobstructed hemisphere of the sky, such as from the flat roof of a building higher than any surrounding buildings.
Voluntary release damages	Damages for an infringement of an easement of light calculated as the amount which would be agreed in a hypothetical negotiation between the parties acting reasonably for the voluntary release of the easement.
Waldram diagrams	Diagrams of the floor area of a room which show the area of the room which in any given circumstances does and does not have a sufficiency of natural light through an aperture.
Working plane	The level, usually a horizontal level, above the floor of a room at which natural light is considered to be most important for ordinary activities in the room. The level is usually taken as 850 mm above the floor.
Without prejudice document or communication	A letter or other document or an oral communication made by a party in an attempt to settle a dispute and stated to be made without prejudice. Such a document or communication cannot normally be referred to in legal proceedings unless both parties agree.
0.2 per cent sky factor	The sky factor which is considered is the minimum needed to provide a sufficiency of natural light to the point in a room at which it is enjoyed.
50 per cent rule	A convention that if at least 50 per cent of the area of a room at the working plane is sufficiently lit in accordance with the 0.2 per cent sky factor test the room as a whole is sufficiently lit. Sometimes called the 50-50 rule.

INDEX